BEST ❤ LOVED
Cookies
& Bakeshop
Favorites

RDA ENTHUSIAST BRANDS, LLC
MILWAUKEE, WISCONSIN

Taste of Home. Reader's digest

A TASTE OF HOME/READER'S DIGEST BOOK

© 2014 RDA Enthusiast Brands, LLC
1610 N. 2nd St., Suite 102, Milwaukee WI 53212-3906.

EDITORIAL

Editor-in-Chief: CATHERINE CASSIDY

Creative Director: **HOWARD GREENBERG**

Editorial Operations Director: **KERRI BALLIET**

Managing Editor, Print & Digital Books: **MARK HAGEN**
Associate Creative Director: **EDWIN ROBLES JR.**
Editor: **JANET BRIGGS**
Associate Editor: **MOLLY JASINSKI**
Art Director: **MAGGIE CONNERS**
Layout Designers: **NANCY NOVAK, CATHERINE FLETCHER**
Editorial Production Manager: **DENA AHLERS**
Copy Chief: **DEB WARLAUMONT MULVEY**
Copy Editor: **MARY-LIZ SHAW**
Content Operations Manager: **COLLEEN KING**
Content Operations Assistant: **SHANNON STROUD**
Executive Assistant: **MARIE BRANNON**

Chief Food Editor: **KAREN BERNER**
Food Editors: **JAMES SCHEND; PEGGY WOODWARD, RD**
Associate Food Editor: **KRISTA LANPHIER**
Recipe Editors: **MARY KING; ANNIE RUNDLE; JENNI SHARP, RD; IRENE YEH**

Test Kitchen & Food Styling Manager: **SARAH THOMPSON**
Test Cooks: **NICHOLAS IVERSON (LEAD), MATTHEW HASS, LAUREN KNOELKE**
Food Stylists: **KATHRYN CONRAD (SENIOR), LEAH REKAU, SHANNON ROUM**
Prep Cooks: **MEGUMI GARCIA, MELISSA HANSEN, BETHANY VAN JACOBSON, SARA WIRTZ**

Photography Director: **STEPHANIE MARCHESE**
Photographers: **DAN ROBERTS, JIM WIELAND**
Photographer/Set Stylist: **GRACE NATOLI SHELDON**
Set Stylists: **STACEY GENAW, MELISSA HABERMAN, DEE DEE JACQ**
Editorial Business Manager: **KRISTY MARTIN**

BUSINESS

Vice President, Chief Sales Officer: **MARK S. JOSEPHSON**
Vice President, Business Development & Marketing: **ALAIN BEGUN**
General Manager, Taste of Home Cooking School: **ERIN PUARIEA**
Vice President, Digital Experience & E-Commerce: **JENNIFER SMITH**
Vice President, Marketing Operations: **DAVE FIEGEL**

THE READER'S DIGEST ASSOCIATION, INC.

President and Chief Executive Officer: **BONNIE KINTZER**

Vice President, Chief Operating Officer, North America: **HOWARD HALLIGAN**
Vice President, Enthusiast Brands, Books & Retail: **HAROLD CLARKE**
Vice President, North American Operations: **PHILIPPE CLOUTIER**
Vice President, Chief Marketing Officer: **LESLIE DOTY**
Vice President, North American Human Resources: **PHYLLIS E. GEBHARDT, SPHR**
Vice President, Consumer Marketing Planning: **JIM WOODS**

For other **TASTE OF HOME BOOKS** and products, visit us at **TASTEOFHOME.COM**.

For more **READER'S DIGEST** products and information, visit **RD.COM** (in the United States) or **RD.CA** (in Canada).

International Standard Book Number: **978-1-61765-368-1**
Library of Congress Control Number: **2014943155**

COVER PHOTOGRAPHY

Photographer: **GRACE NATOLI SHELDON**
Food Stylist: **SHANNON ROUM**
Set Stylists: **STACEY GENAW, MELISSA HABERMAN, DEE DEE JACQ**

PICTURED ON FRONT COVER:
Quick Chocolate Sandwich Cookies, page 178.

PICTURED ON BACK COVER (clockwise from top left): Lemon Tart with Almond Crust, page 366; Coffee-Klatch Kolaches, page 460; Watermelon Slice Cookies, page 97; Chocolate Hazelnut Torte, page 305.

PICTURED ON SPINE: Peanut Butter Cup Cookies, page 40.

PRINTED IN USA.
1 3 5 7 9 10 8 6 4 2

Table *of* Contents

10 *tips for* Baking Success

Are you ready to create gorgeous bakery-quality treats at home?

Follow these pointers to ensure baking success every time. Review the common baking terms, pan information and measurement guides on the following pages. Then grab an apron and get started!

1. Read—It's Fundamental

Read the entire recipe before you begin. If you are not familiar with a technique or term, refer to a cooking reference or search for information on the Internet. Visit *tasteofhome.com* for how-to videos, articles and tips on baking.

2. Check Out Ingredients

Gather all of the ingredients before you begin to make sure you have everything that is needed.

Assemble all of the ingredients for the recipe.

3. Prep Ingredients Before Mixing

Prepare all the ingredients. Let butter soften, separate eggs, chop nuts, etc.

Too firm—butter is too hard to cream.

Butter is softened just right.

Position oven rack before preheating the oven.

4. Get The Oven Ready

Position the oven rack so the baking pan will be in center of the oven, or position the oven rack as the recipe directs. Preheat the oven. For yeast breads, preheat the oven during the final rise time.

5. Select And Prep Pans

Use the type of pan and the size of pan stated in the recipe. Generally, pans are filled two-thirds to three-fourths full.

This pan is too full.

Use an 8-in. x 4-in. loaf pan filled two-thirds full, plus a muffin pan for extra batter; a larger 9-in. x 5-in. loaf pan; or several 5-3/4-in. x 3-in. loaf pans.

Grease and flour the pan if the recipe directs. For yeast breads, prepare pans before shaping the dough.

Grease the pan as the recipe directs with shortening or cooking spray.

6. Measure with Precision

Accurately measure the ingredients. Use a liquid measuring cup for wet ingredients, such as milk, honey, molasses, corn syrup, water, juice or oil. Before measuring sticky ingredients like molasses or corn syrup, coat the inside of the measuring tool with cooking spray. This will make cleanup easier.

Check level of liquid at your eye level.

Fill dry ingredients to the rim and sweep off excess with the flat edge of a metal spatula or knife.

Dry measuring cups allow ingredients to be measured right to the rim of the cup. They are used to measure dry and packable ingredients like flour, sugar, chocolate chips, nuts, shortening and sour cream.

Wet and dry ingredients should be filled to the rim of the spoon.

Measuring spoons are used to measure both liquid and dry ingredients. It's nice to have two sets when baking. Use one set for measuring the liquid ingredients and the other for dry.

7. Mix It Up

Follow the mixing directions as they are written. Altering the method may affect how the final baked good looks and/or tastes.

Cream until light and fluffy.

Fold lighter-weight ingredients into heavier ones with a rubber spatula.

Use a sturdy wooden spoon to stir chips, nuts and dried fruit into heavy batters.

8. Start the Timer

Most recipes give a range for the baking time. Set a kitchen timer for the low end of the time range immediately after the food has been placed in the oven.

Set the timer for the shortest time given in the recipe.

9. Check Doneness

Check for doneness at the shortest time given in the recipe using the stated doneness test. If the baked good does not test done, continue baking and check again.

The toothpick is clean; the cake is done.

The toothpick has crumbs on it; the cake needs more baking time.

10. Take Time To Cool

A wire rack is used for cooling baked goods because it allows air to circulate around the food, which prevents moist, soggy spots. Many cookies can be immediately removed from the baking pan to a wire rack.

Carefully transfer to wire rack to cool.

Cool most baked goods for 10 minutes before removing from the pan.

Other foods like cakes and quick breads need to rest for 10 minutes in their pans. The resting time helps prevent these items from crumbling when they are removed. Still other items—angel food cakes and chiffon cakes baked in tube pans—are cooled completely in their pans. Some baked goods are delicious warm, but others should cool completely for frosting or easy slicing.

Common Baking Terms

Bake—To cook in an oven surrounded by dry heat. When baking, it is important to preheat the oven before placing the food inside.

Beat—To rapidly mix with a spoon, fork, wire whisk or electric mixer.

Blend—To combine several ingredients with a spoon, electric mixer, blender or food processor.

Caramelize—To heat sugar in a skillet or saucepan over low heat until melted and golden brown in color.

Coats Spoon—To leave a thin, even, smooth film on the back of a spoon. This is one of the doneness tests for stirred custards.

Combine—To place several ingredients in a single bowl or container and thoroughly mix.

Cream—To beat softened butter, margarine or shortening alone or with sugar using a spoon or mixer until light and fluffy.

Cube—To cut foods into 1/2-inch to 1-inch square pieces.

Cut In—To break down and distribute cold butter, margarine or shortening into a flour mixture using a pastry blender or two knives.

Dash—A measurement less than 1/8 teaspoon that is used for herbs, spices or hot pepper sauce. This is not a precise measurement.

Dice—To cut foods into 1/8-inch to 1/4-inch cubes.

Dissolve—To stir a solid food with a liquid until none of the solid remains, such as yeast with warm water or gelatin in boiling water.

Dot—To break up small pieces of butter and distribute evenly over the top of pie filling or dough.

Drizzle—To slowly spoon or pour a thin stream of icing, melted butter or other liquid.

Flute—To make a "V" shape or scalloped edge on a pie crust with your thumb and fingers.

Fold—To combine light or delicate ingredients such as whipped cream or egg whites with other ingredients without beating. A rubber spatula is used to gently cut down through the ingredients, move across the bottom of the bowl and bring up part of the mixture.

Frost—To cover a cake, cupcake or cookie with a spreadable frosting.

Glaze—To coat the exterior of sweet or savory foods with a thin, glossy mixture.

Grease—To rub the inside of a baking dish or pan with shortening, butter or oil or to coat with cooking spray.

Grease and Flour—To rub a thin layer of shortening, butter or oil over the inside of a baking pan or dish and then dust with flour. The excess flour is shaken out of the pan. Cakes baked in round baking pans or fluted tube pans generally require that the pan be greased and floured.

Knead—To work dough by using a pressing and folding action to make it smooth and elastic.

Line—To cover a baking sheet with a piece of parchment paper, waxed paper or foil to prevent sticking.

Marble—To swirl light and dark batters for a cake, bar, pie or cheesecake. The batters should not be combined into one color; there should still be two distinctive batters after marbling.

Mince—To cut foods into very fine pieces no larger than 1/8 inch.

Mix—To stir or beat ingredients together with a spoon or a fork until well combined.

Moisten—To add enough liquid to dry ingredients while gently stirring to make a wet but not runny mixture. Often used in the preparation of muffins.

Pinch—A small amount (less than 1/8 teaspoon) of a seasoning or spice that is easily held between the thumb and index finger. This is not a precise measurement.

Pipe—To force a soft mixture, such as whipped cream, frosting or meringue, through a pastry bag and/or tip for a fancy shape or design.

Prick—To pierce food or pastry with the tines of a fork to prevent it from bursting or rising during baking.

Separate—To remove the egg white from the egg yolk.

Sift—To pass dry ingredients, such as confectioners' sugar or flour, through a fine-mesh strainer to remove lumps, add air and combine several dry ingredients.

Soft Peaks—The stage of beating egg whites or heavy whipping cream when the beater is lifted from the mixture and points of the peaks curl over.

Soften—To bring butter or cream cheese to a soft consistency by letting it stand at room temperature for a short time.

Stiff Peaks—The stage of beating egg whites or heavy whipping cream when the beater is lifted from the mixture and points of the peaks stand straight up.

Stir—To blend a combination of ingredients by hand using a spoon in a circular motion.

Whip—To beat rapidly by hand or with an electric mixer to add air and increase volume.

Choosing Bakeware

Baking pans are made of metal. Aluminum pans with dull finishes give the best overall results. Pans with dark finishes often cook and brown foods more quickly. If you use pans with dark finishes, you may need to adjust the baking time and cover tops of baked goods with foil to prevent overbrowning. Insulated pans and pans with shiny finishes generally take longer to bake and brown foods.

Baking dishes are made of ovenproof glass or ceramic. If you substitute a glass baking dish in a recipe calling for a metal pan, reduce the oven temperature by 25° to avoid overbaking.

To determine your bakeware's measurements, use a ruler to measure from one inside top edge to the opposite inside top edge. To measure height, place a ruler on the outside of the dish and measure from the bottom to a top edge. For volume, fill the pan or dish to the rim with measured water.

For best results, use the pan size called for in the recipe. However, the chart below offers some practical substitutions.

If you don't have this pan(s):	use this pan(s) instead:
One 9-in. x 5-in. loaf pan	Three 5¾-in. x 3-in. x 2-in. loaf pans
One 8-in. x 4-in. loaf pan	Two 5¾-in. x 3-in. x 2-in. loaf pans
One 9-in. round baking pan	One 8-in. square baking dish
Two 9-in. round baking pans	One 13-in. x 9-in. baking pan
One 10-in. fluted tube pan	One 10-in. tube pan or two 9-in. x 5-in. loaf pans
One 13-in. x 9-in. baking pan	Two 9-in. round baking pans or two 8-in. square baking dishes

Weight & Measurement Equivalents

Teaspoon and Tablespoon Measures

Dash or pinch	= less than ⅛ teaspoon
1½ teaspoons	= ½ tablespoon
3 teaspoons	= 1 tablespoon; ½ fluid ounce
4½ teaspoons	= 1½ tablespoons
2 tablespoons	= ⅛ cup; 1 fluid ounce
4 tablespoons	= ¼ cup; 2 fluid ounces
5⅓ tablespoons	= ⅓ cup; 5 tablespoons plus 1 teaspoon
8 tablespoons	= ½ cup; 4 fluid ounces
10⅔ tablespoons	= ⅔ cup; 10 tablespoons plus 2 teaspoons
12 tablespoons	= ¾ cup; 6 fluid ounces
16 tablespoons	= 1 cup; 8 fluid ounces; ½ pint

Cup Measures

⅛ cup	= 2 tablespoons; 1 fluid ounce
¼ cup	= 4 tablespoons; 2 fluid ounces
⅓ cup	= 5⅓ tablespoons
½ cup	= 8 tablespoons; 4 fluid ounces
⅔ cup	= 10⅔ tablespoons
¾ cup	= 12 tablespoons; 6 fluid ounces
⅞ cup	= ¾ cup plus 2 tablespoons
1 cup	= 16 tablespoons; 8 fluid ounces; ½ pint
2 cups	= 1 pint; 16 fluid ounces
4 cups	= 2 pints; 1 quart; 32 fluid ounces

Pints, Quarts, Gallons and Pounds

½ pint	= 1 cup; 8 fluid ounces
1 pint	= 2 cups; 16 fluid ounces
1 quart	= 4 cups; 32 fluid ounces
4 quarts	= 16 cups; 1 gallon
16 ounces	= 1 pound

Cookie Jar Favorites

Chocolate-Topped Surprise Cookies

I first tasted these cookies at a cookie swap at work a few years ago. Now I make them every Christmas for our family gathering. People who haven't had them are always delighted by the hidden treasure inside.

—**VERONICA STRANGE** GLOCESTER, RI

PREP: 45 MIN. + CHILLING • **BAKE:** 15 MIN. + COOLING
MAKES: 2 DOZEN

- 24 **maraschino cherries**
- ½ **cup butter, softened**
- ¾ **cup packed brown sugar**
- 1 **tablespoon maraschino cherry juice**
- 1 **teaspoon vanilla extract**
- 1½ **cups all-purpose flour**
- ⅛ **teaspoon salt**
- 1 **cup milk chocolate chips, divided**
- ½ **teaspoon shortening**

1. Pat the cherries with paper towels to remove excess moisture; set aside. In a large bowl, cream butter and brown sugar until light and fluffy. Beat in cherry juice and vanilla. Combine flour and salt; gradually add to creamed mixture and mix well. Cover and refrigerate for 1 hour or until dough is easy to handle.

2. Insert a chocolate chip into each maraschino cherry. Wrap a tablespoon of dough around each cherry. Place 1 in. apart on ungreased baking sheets.

3. Bake at 350° for 15-17 minutes or until set and edges are lightly browned. Remove to wire racks to cool.

4. In a microwave, melt remaining chips and shortening; stir until smooth. Dip tops of cookies in melted chocolate; allow excess to drip off. Place on wax paper; let stand until set. Store in an airtight container.

Soft Ginger Puffs

These spice cookies loaded with raisins and walnuts really do appeal to all generations—I found the recipe in a 1901 South Dakota cookbook! Sour cream adds a wonderful, unusual flair.

—**MARION LOWERY** MEDFORD, OR

PREP: 15 MIN. • **BAKE:** 10 MIN./BATCH • **MAKES:** 8 DOZEN

- ½ **cup butter, softened**
- ¾ **cup sugar**
- 3 **eggs**
- 1 **cup molasses**
- 1 **cup (8 ounces) sour cream**
- 3½ **cups all-purpose flour**
- 2 **teaspoons ground ginger**
- 1 **teaspoon baking soda**
- ½ **teaspoon each ground allspice, cinnamon and nutmeg**
- 1½ **cups raisins**
- 1½ **cups chopped walnuts**

1. In a large bowl, cream butter and sugar until light and fluffy. Add eggs, one at a time, beating well after each addition. Beat in molasses and sour cream. Combine the flour, ginger, baking soda, allspice, cinnamon and nutmeg; gradually add to the creamed mixture and mix well. Stir in raisins and walnuts.

2. Drop by tablespoonfuls 1 in. apart onto greased baking sheets. Bake at 375° for 10-12 minutes or until the edges begin to brown. Remove to wire racks to cool.

Scottish Shortbread

My mother, who is of Scottish heritage, passed this recipe along to me, as she did most of my favorite recipes. I entered Scottish Shortbread at our local fair and it won first place.

—**ROSE MABEE** SELKIRK, MB

PREP: 15 MIN. • **BAKE:** 20 MIN./BATCH • **MAKES:** ABOUT 4 DOZEN

- 2 **cups butter, softened**
- 1 **cup packed brown sugar**
- 4 **to 4½ cups all-purpose flour**

1. In a large bowl, cream butter and brown sugar until light and fluffy. Add 3¾ cups flour and mix well. Turn onto a floured surface. Knead for 5 minutes, adding enough remaining flour to form a soft dough.
2. Roll to ½-in. thickness. Cut into 3-in. x 1-in. strips. Place 1 in. apart on ungreased baking sheets. Prick with fork. Bake at 325° for 20-25 minutes or until cookies are lightly browned.

Tried 'n' True Peanut Butter Cookies

When I want to offer friends and family a reliable, tasty cookie, this is the recipe I turn to. Use either creamy or crunchy peanut butter for delicious results.

—**EMMA LEE GRANGER** LA PINE, OR

PREP: 20 MIN. • **BAKE:** 15 MIN./BATCH • **MAKES:** ABOUT 18 DOZEN

- 4 **cups butter-flavored shortening**
- 4 **cups peanut butter**
- 3 **cups sugar**
- 3 **cups packed brown sugar**
- 8 **eggs**
- 4 **teaspoons vanilla extract**
- 2 **teaspoons water**
- 9 **cups all-purpose flour**
- 4 **teaspoons baking soda**
- 4 **teaspoons salt**

1. In a several large bowls, cream the shortening, peanut butter and sugars until light and fluffy, about 4 minutes. Add eggs, one at a time, beating well after each addition. Beat in vanilla and water. Combine the flour, baking soda and salt; gradually add to creamed mixture and mix well.
2. Drop by heaping tablespoons 2 in. apart onto ungreased baking sheets. Flatten with a fork. Bake at 350° for 12-15 minutes or until golden brown. Remove cookies to wire racks to cool.
NOTE *Reduced-fat peanut butter is not recommended for this recipe.*

Bakeshop TIP

Making Shaped Cookies of the Same Size

Cookies bake more evenly if all the cookies on the baking sheet are the same size. To make 1½-inch balls of dough for cookies, use about 1 tablespoon of dough per cookie.

Toffee Almond Sandies

I knew after sampling these cookies from a friend that I had to add the recipe to my bulging files!

—**VICKI CROWLEY** MONTICELLO, IA

PREP: 15 MIN. • **BAKE:** 10 MIN./BATCH • **MAKES:** 9 DOZEN

- 1 **cup butter, softened**
- 1 **cup sugar**
- 1 **cup confectioners' sugar**
- 2 **eggs**
- 1 **cup canola oil**
- 1 **teaspoon almond extract**
- 4½ **cups all-purpose flour**
- 1 **teaspoon baking soda**
- 1 **teaspoon cream of tartar**
- 1 **teaspoon salt**
- 2 **cups sliced almonds**
- 1 **package (8 ounces) toffee bits**

1. Preheat oven to 350°. In a large bowl, cream butter and sugars until blended. Add eggs, one at a time, beating well after each addition. Gradually beat in oil and extract. Combine the flour, baking soda, cream of tartar and salt; gradually add to the creamed mixture and mix well. Stir in almonds and toffee bits.

2. Drop by teaspoonfuls 2 in. apart onto ungreased baking sheets. Bake 10-12 minutes or until golden brown. Remove to wire racks to cool.

Mom's Soft Raisin Cookies

With four sons in the service during World War II, my mother sent these favorite cookies as a taste from home to her boys in different parts of the world. These days, my grandchildren are enjoying them as we did, along with my stories of long ago.
—**PEARL COCHENOUR** WILLIAMSPORT, OH

PREP: 25 MIN. • **BAKE:** 15 MIN./BATCH • **MAKES:** 6 DOZEN

- 1 **cup water**
- 2 **cups raisins**
- 1 **cup shortening**
- 1¾ **cups sugar**
- 2 **eggs**
- 1 **teaspoon vanilla extract**
- 3½ **cups all-purpose flour**
- 1 **teaspoon baking powder**
- 1 **teaspoon baking soda**
- 1 **teaspoon salt**
- ½ **teaspoon ground cinnamon**
- ½ **teaspoon ground nutmeg**
- ½ **cup chopped walnuts**

1. Combine water and raisins in a small saucepan; bring to a boil. Cook for 3 minutes; remove from the heat and let cool (do not drain).
2. Preheat oven to 350°. In a large bowl, cream shortening and sugar until light and fluffy. Beat in eggs and vanilla. Combine flour, baking powder, baking soda, salt and spices; gradually add to creamed mixture and mix well. Stir in nuts and raisins.
3. Drop by teaspoonfuls 2 in. apart onto greased baking sheets. Bake 12-14 minutes or until golden brown. Remove to wire racks to cool.

Icebox Cookies

This cookie recipe from my grandmother was my grandfather's favorite. I keep the dough in the freezer because I love to make a fresh batch when company drops in.
—**CHRIS PAULSEN** GLENDALE, AZ

PREP: 20 MIN. + FREEZING • **BAKE:** 10 MIN.
MAKES: ABOUT 7 DOZEN

- ½ **cup butter, softened**
- 1 **cup packed brown sugar**
- 1 **egg, beaten**
- ½ **teaspoon vanilla extract**
- 2 **cups all-purpose flour**
- ½ **teaspoon baking soda**
- ½ **teaspoon cream of tartar**
- ½ **teaspoon salt**
- 1 **cup chopped walnuts, optional**

1. In a bowl, cream the butter and brown sugar. Add egg and vanilla; beat well. Combine dry ingredients; add to creamed mixture. Stir in nuts if desired.
2. On a lightly floured surface, shape the dough into three 10-in. x 1-in. rolls. Tightly wrap each roll in waxed paper. Freeze for at least 12 hours.
3. Cut into ⅜-in. slices and place on greased baking sheets. Bake at 350° for 6-8 minutes. Remove to a wire rack to cool.

Toffee Oat Cookies

A friend shared this delicious recipe with me. The crisp yet chewy cookies are bound to satisfy big and little kids alike.
—**JEAN DANDREA** BURKESVILLE, KY

PREP: 15 MIN. • **BAKE:** 10 MIN./BATCH • **MAKES:** ABOUT 4 DOZEN

- ¾ **cup butter, softened**
- 1 **cup packed brown sugar**
- ¾ **cup sugar**
- 2 **eggs**
- 3 **teaspoons vanilla extract**
- 2¼ **cups all-purpose flour**
- 2¼ **cups old-fashioned oats**
- 1 **teaspoon baking soda**
- 1 **teaspoon baking powder**
- ½ **teaspoon salt**
- 1 **package English toffee bits (10 ounces) or almond brickle chips (7½ ounces)**

1. In a large bowl, cream butter and sugars until light and fluffy. Add eggs, one at a time, beating well after each addition. Beat in vanilla. Combine the flour, oats, baking soda, baking powder and salt; gradually add to creamed mixture and mix well. Stir in toffee bits.
2. Drop by rounded tablespoonfuls 2 in. apart onto ungreased baking sheets. Bake at 375° for 10-12 minutes or until golden brown. Cool for 1 minute before removing from pans to wire racks to cool completely.

1. In a small bowl, cream the shortening, peanut butter and sugars until light and fluffy. Beat in milk and egg. Combine the flour, baking soda, baking powder and salt; gradually add to creamed mixture and mix well.
2. Shape dough into 1½-in. balls. Place 3½ in. apart on ungreased baking sheets. Flatten into 3-in. circles with a glass dipped in sugar.
3. Bake at 375° for 6-8 minutes or until golden brown. Cool for 2 minutes before removing to wire racks.
4. In a microwave, melt peanut butter chips; stir until smooth. Spread over half of each cookie; sprinkle with peanut brittle.
NOTE *Reduced-fat peanut butter is not recommended for this recipe.*

Mocha Crackle Cookies

These cakelike cookies are better than brownies. They have crackly tops and subtle coffee flavor.

—**LOUISE BEATTY** AMHERST, NY

PREP: 25 MIN. + CHILLING • **BAKE:** 15 MIN./BATCH
MAKES: ABOUT 5 DOZEN

- ½ **cup butter, cubed**
- 5 **ounces unsweetened chocolate, chopped**
- 1 **tablespoon instant coffee granules**
- 4 **eggs**
- ⅛ **teaspoon salt**
- 1 **cup sugar**
- 1 **cup packed brown sugar**
- 2 **cups plus 3 tablespoons all-purpose flour**
- 2 **teaspoons baking powder**
- ⅓ **cup confectioners' sugar**

1. In a microwave, heat the butter, chocolate and coffee until chocolate is melted; cool slightly. In a bowl, beat the eggs and salt; add sugar and brown sugar. Stir in chocolate mixture; mix well.
2. Combine flour and baking powder; gradually add to egg mixture to form a soft dough. Cover and refrigerate for 2 hours or until easy to handle.
3. Roll dough into ¾-in. balls. Roll in confectioners' sugar; place 2 in. apart on greased baking sheets. Bake at 350° for 12 minutes or until set. Remove to wire racks to cool.

Giant Peanut Brittle Cookies

Topped with leftover peanut brittle bits, these giant cookies take star billing on holiday trays. People can't seem to get enough of the jumbo treats.

—**CAROLYN HORNE** TIGARD, OR

START TO FINISH: 30 MIN. • **MAKES:** 1½ DOZEN

- ⅓ **cup butter-flavored shortening**
- ⅓ **cup creamy peanut butter**
- ⅓ **cup sugar**
- ⅓ **cup packed brown sugar**
- 2 **teaspoons 2% milk**
- 1 **egg**
- 1 **cup all-purpose flour**
- ½ **teaspoon baking soda**
- ¼ **teaspoon baking powder**
- ⅛ **teaspoon salt**
- ¾ **cup peanut butter chips**
- ⅔ **cup crushed peanut brittle**

Family-Favorite Oatmeal Cookies

My mother got this recipe in about 1910 when she was a housekeeper and cook for the local physician. The doctor's wife was an excellent cook and taught my mother of lot of her cooking techniques. The cookies soon became a favorite in our home and now are a favorite with my children's families.

—VIRGINIA BODNER SANDUSKY, OH

PREP: 20 MIN. • **BAKE:** 15 MIN. • **MAKES:** ABOUT 5 DOZEN

- 2 **cups packed brown sugar**
- 1 **cup shortening**
- 3 **eggs**
- 3 **cups all-purpose flour**
- 1 **teaspoon salt**
- 1 **teaspoon baking powder**
- 1 **teaspoon baking soda**
- 1 **teaspoon ground cinnamon**
- 1 **cup buttermilk**
- 2 **cups old-fashioned oats**
- 1 **cup raisins**
- 1 **cup chopped walnuts**

1. In a large bowl, cream sugar and shortening until light and fluffy. Add eggs, one at a time, beating well after each addition. Combine the flour, salt, baking powder, soda and cinnamon; add alternately to the creamed mixture with buttermilk. Fold in the oats, raisins and nuts.

2. Drop dough by heaping tablespoonfuls onto greased baking sheets. Bake at 350° for 12 minutes or until lightly browned. Remove to wire racks.

Vanilla Wafer Cookies

These cookies are chewy and irresistible and a wonderful way to round out a meal when you're on a budget.

—EDITH MACBEATH GAINES, PA

PREP: 20 MIN. • **BAKE:** 15 MIN./BATCH • **MAKES:** ABOUT 3½ DOZEN

- ½ **cup butter, softened**
- 1 **cup sugar**
- 1 **egg**
- 1 **tablespoon vanilla extract**
- 1⅓ **cups all-purpose flour**
- ¾ **teaspoon baking powder**
- ¼ **teaspoon salt**

1. In a large bowl, cream butter and sugar until light and fluffy. Beat in egg and vanilla. Combine dry ingredients; add to creamed mixture and mix well.

2. Drop by teaspoonfuls 2 in. apart onto ungreased baking sheets. Bake at 350° for 12-15 minutes or until edges are golden brown. Remove to wire racks to cool.

Low-Fat Oatmeal Raisin Cookies

These sweet, chewy cookies are low in fat, but I didn't tell my family that the first time I made them. The reaction when they found out? "No way!"

—**JULIE HAUSER** SHERIDAN, CA

PREP: 15 MIN. • **BAKE:** 10 MIN./BATCH • **MAKES:** 44 COOKIES

- 1 cup raisins
- ¼ cup water
- 3 egg whites
- 1 tablespoon molasses
- 1 cup sugar
- 1 cup packed brown sugar
- 1½ teaspoons vanilla extract
- 1 cup all-purpose flour
- ½ cup nonfat dry milk powder
- 1½ teaspoons baking powder
- 1½ teaspoons ground cinnamon
- 2½ cups quick-cooking oats

1. In a food processor, combine the raisins, water, egg whites and molasses. Cover and process for 10-15 seconds or until the raisins are finely chopped.

2. Transfer to a large bowl. Beat in sugars and vanilla. Combine the flour, milk powder, baking powder and cinnamon; gradually add to raisin mixture and mix well. Stir in oats.

3. Drop by tablespoonfuls 2 in. apart onto baking sheets coated with cooking spray.

4. Bake at 350° for 8-10 minutes or until edges are golden brown. Remove to wire racks to cool.

Championship Cookies

I got this recipe from a friend who baked at a conference center. Snickers candy bar pieces make them irresistible.

—**PATRICIA MILLER** NORTH FORK, CA

PREP: 15 MIN. • **BAKE:** 10 MIN./BATCH • **MAKES:** ABOUT 5 DOZEN

- ⅔ cup shortening
- 1¼ cups packed brown sugar
- 1 egg
- 1 teaspoon vanilla extract
- 1½ cups all-purpose flour
- 1 teaspoon baking powder
- 1 teaspoon baking soda
- ½ teaspoon ground cinnamon
- ¼ teaspoon salt
- 2 Snickers candy bars (2.07 ounces each), chopped
- ½ cup quick-cooking oats

1. In a bowl, cream shortening and brown sugar. Beat in egg and vanilla. Combine the flour, baking powder, baking soda, cinnamon and salt; gradually add to the creamed mixture. Stir in chopped candy bars and oats.

2. Drop by round tablespoonfuls 2 in. apart onto greased or parchment-lined baking sheets. Bake at 350° for 10-12 minutes or until cookies are lightly browned. Remove to wire racks to cool.

Mom's Molasses Cookies

The kitchen smells so good when Mom is baking these yummy cookies, which we like to make with sorghum. They're chewy and tender, with a sugary coating. It's hard to eat just one!

—**BRENDA BEACHY** BELVIDERE, TN

PREP: 15 MIN. + CHILLING • **BAKE:** 10 MIN./BATCH
MAKES: 5 DOZEN

- ¾ cup shortening
- 1¼ cups sugar, divided
- 1 egg
- ¼ cup molasses
- 2 tablespoons milk
- 1 teaspoon vanilla extract
- 2½ cups all-purpose flour
- 1½ teaspoons baking soda
- 1 teaspoon ground cinnamon
- ¾ teaspoon salt
- ¾ teaspoon ground nutmeg

1. In a large bowl, cream shortening and 1 cup sugar until light and fluffy. Beat in the egg, molasses, milk and vanilla. Combine the flour, baking soda, cinnamon, salt and nutmeg; gradually add to creamed mixture and mix well. Cover and refrigerate for 1 hour.

2. Roll into 1¼-in. balls; roll in remaining sugar. Place 2 in. apart on greased baking sheets.

3. Bake at 350° for 10-14 minutes or until tops crack and edges are slightly firm. Remove to wire racks to cool.

Soft Lemon-Ginger Cookies

Loaded with old-fashioned flavor, this yummy cookie is hard to beat. You'll love munching a few with coffee, tea or a glass of ice-cold milk.

—SHARON BRETZ HAVRE DE GRACE, MD

START TO FINISH: 30 MIN. • **MAKES:** 2 DOZEN

- ½ **cup butter, softened**
- 1 **cup packed brown sugar**
- 1 **egg**
- 3 **tablespoons sour cream**
- ½ **teaspoon lemon extract**
- ½ **teaspoon vanilla extract**
- 1¾ **cups all-purpose flour**
- 1 **teaspoon baking soda**
- 1 **teaspoon cream of tartar**
- 1 **teaspoon ground ginger**
- ¼ **teaspoon salt**

1. Preheat oven to 350°. In a large bowl, cream butter and brown sugar until light and fluffy. Beat in the egg, sour cream and extracts. Combine the flour, baking soda, cream of tartar, ginger and salt; gradually add to creamed mixture and mix well.

2. Drop by rounded teaspoonfuls 2 in. apart onto ungreased baking sheets. Bake 10-12 minutes or until lightly browned. Immediately remove to wire racks to cool.

Pudding Sugar Cookies

This recipe, which was passed on by a friend, has become a year-round favorite at our house. For fun, substitute other flavors of pudding.

—SHARON REED CATLIN, IL

PREP: 15 MIN. • **BAKE:** 15 MIN./BATCH • **MAKES:** 7 DOZEN

- 1 **cup butter, softened**
- 1 **cup canola oil**
- 1 **cup sugar**
- 1 **cup confectioners' sugar**
- 2 **eggs**
- 1 **teaspoon vanilla extract**
- 1 **package (3.4 ounces) instant lemon pudding mix or instant pudding mix of your choice**
- 4 **cups all-purpose flour**
- 1 **teaspoon cream of tartar**
- 1 **teaspoon baking soda**

1. In a large bowl, cream the butter, oil and sugars until light and fluffy. Beat in eggs, vanilla and dry pudding mix. Combine the flour, cream of tartar and baking soda; gradually add to creamed mixture and mix well.

2. Drop by tablespoonfuls 2 in. apart onto ungreased baking sheets. Flatten with a glass dipped in sugar.

3. Bake at 350° for 12-15 minutes or until lightly browned. Remove to wire racks.

Coconut Macaroons

I keep the ingredients for these easy-to-make cookies in my pantry. That way I can have a freshly made batch in minutes.

—NANCY TAFOYA FORT COLLINS, CO

START TO FINISH: 30 MIN. • **MAKES:** 1½ DOZEN

- 2½ **cups flaked coconut**
- ⅓ **cup all-purpose flour**
- ⅛ **teaspoon salt**
- ⅔ **cup sweetened condensed milk**
- 1 **teaspoon vanilla extract**

1. In a large bowl, combine the coconut, flour and salt. Add milk and vanilla; mix well (batter will be stiff).

2. Drop by tablespoonfuls 1 in. apart onto a greased baking sheet. Bake at 350° for 15-20 minutes or until golden brown. Remove to wire racks.

Oatmeal Animal Crackers

When I was a child, we kids helped Mom cut these crispy crackers into all sorts of shapes. They're not too sweet, but sweet enough that we always wanted more.

—**BOB DITTMAR** TROUT RUN, PA

PREP: 15 MIN. • **BAKE:** 10 MIN./BATCH • **MAKES:** ABOUT 4 DOZEN

- 2 **cups sugar**
- 2 **cups old-fashioned oats**
- 1 **teaspoon baking soda**
- ¼ **teaspoon salt**
- ½ **cup shortening**
- ½ **cup hot water**
- 1 **tablespoon vanilla extract**
- 2 **to 2½ cups all-purpose flour**

1. In a bowl, combine sugar, oats, baking soda and salt. Cut in shortening until crumbly. Add water and vanilla; stir until blended. Add enough flour to form a stiff dough.

2. On a lightly floured surface, roll dough to ⅛-in. thickness. Cut into rectangles or use cookie cutters dipped in flour. Using a floured spatula, transfer to greased baking sheets. Bake at 350° for 8-10 minutes or until lightly browned. Cool on wire racks.

Crisp Lemon Sugar Cookies

I have had this recipe for about 40 years, and in that time I've made a few changes. These cookies are my husband's favorite, so I bake them for him almost every week. One of my daughter's friends still remembers having these special treats when she stopped in on her way home from school.

—**DOLLIE AINLEY** DONIPHAN, MO

PREP: 15 MIN. • **BAKE:** 10 MIN./BATCH • **MAKES:** ABOUT 6½ DOZEN

- ½ **cup butter, softened**
- ½ **cup butter-flavored shortening**
- 1 **cup sugar**
- 1 **egg**
- 1 **tablespoon milk**
- 2 **teaspoons lemon extract**
- 1 **teaspoon vanilla extract**
- 2½ **cups all-purpose flour**
- ¾ **teaspoon salt**
- ½ **teaspoon baking soda**
  Additional sugar

1. In a large bowl, cream butter, shortening and sugar until light and fluffy. Beat in egg, milk and extracts. Combine the flour, salt and baking soda; gradually add to creamed mixture.

2. Shape into 1-in. balls or drop by rounded teaspoonfuls 2 in. apart onto ungreased baking sheets. Flatten with a glass dipped in sugar.

3. Bake at 400° for 9-11 minutes or until edges are lightly browned. Immediately remove to wire racks to cool.

Peanut Butter Chippers

The smell of peanut butter and chocolate always brings my cookie-hungry family running to the kitchen. The recipe is so quick and easy, I often stir up a batch while making dinner.

—**PAT DOERFLINGER** CENTERVIEW, MO

PREP: 10 MIN. • **BAKE:** 15 MIN./BATCH • **MAKES:** 3½ DOZEN

- 6 **tablespoons butter, softened**
- ¼ **cup peanut butter**
- ½ **cup sugar**
- ½ **cup packed brown sugar**
- 1 **egg**
- 1 **teaspoon vanilla extract**
- 1¼ **cups all-purpose flour**
- ½ **teaspoon baking soda**
- ¼ **teaspoon salt**
- 1 **cup milk chocolate chips**

1. In a small bowl, cream the butter, peanut butter and sugars until light and fluffy. Beat in egg and vanilla. Combine the flour, baking soda and salt; gradually add to creamed mixture and mix well. Stir in chocolate chips.

2. Drop by tablespoonfuls 2 in. apart onto ungreased baking sheets. Bake at 350° for 11-14 minutes or until golden brown. Remove to wire racks.

NOTE *Reduced-fat peanut butter is not recommended for this recipe.*

Cherry-Chocolate Chip Biscotti

A delicious "dunker," our biscotti is chock-full of dried cherries and chocolate chips. Wrapped in colored cellophane and curly ribbons, it makes a lovely homemade holiday or hostess gift.

—TASTE OF HOME TEST KITCHEN

PREP: 20 MIN. • **BAKE:** 25 MIN. + COOLING • **MAKES:** 2½ DOZEN

- ¾ cup sugar
- 1 tablespoon canola oil
- 2 eggs
- 2 egg whites
- 2 teaspoons vanilla extract
- ¼ teaspoon almond extract
- 2¾ cups all-purpose flour
- 1 teaspoon baking powder
- ¼ teaspoon baking soda
- ¼ teaspoon salt
- ⅔ cup dried cherries, chopped
- ½ cup miniature semisweet chocolate chips

1. In a large bowl, beat sugar and oil until blended; Beat in the eggs, egg whites, and extracts. Combine the flour, baking powder, baking soda and salt; gradually add to egg mixture and mix well. Stir in cherries and chocolate chips.

2. Divide dough in half. With lightly floured hands, shape each portion into a 12-in. x 3-in. rectangle; place logs on a baking sheet coated with cooking spray.

3. Bake at 350° for 15-20 minutes or until lightly browned. Carefully remove to wire racks; cool for 5 minutes.

4. Transfer to a cutting board; cut with a serrated knife into ¾-in. slices. Place cut side down on ungreased baking sheets. Bake for 5 minutes. Turn and bake 5-7 minutes longer or until firm. Remove to wire racks to cool. Store in an airtight container.

Cranberry Cashew Jumbles

I have baked these cookies for the Cranberry Festival Cooking Contest in nearby Warrens, where cranberry is "king."

—MARY WILHELM SPARTA, WI

PREP: 20 MIN. • **BAKE:** 10 MIN./BATCH • **MAKES:** 5 DOZEN

- ½ cup butter, softened
- 1 cup packed brown sugar
- ½ cup sour cream
- 1 egg
- 1 teaspoon vanilla extract
- 2 cups all-purpose flour
- ¾ teaspoon baking powder
- ¼ teaspoon baking soda
- ¼ teaspoon salt
- 1 package (5 ounces) dried cranberries
- 1 cup chopped cashews

GLAZE
- 1 cup confectioners' sugar
- 2 tablespoons orange juice

1. In a large bowl, cream butter and brown sugar until light and fluffy. Beat in the sour cream, egg and vanilla. Combine the flour, baking powder, baking soda and salt; gradually add to creamed mixture and mix well. Stir in cranberries and cashews.

2. Drop by tablespoonfuls 2 in. apart onto ungreased baking sheets. Bake 375° for 10-12 minutes or until lightly browned. Remove to wire racks to cool. Combine the glaze ingredients; drizzle over cookies.

Peanut Butter Candy Cookies

These great cookies don't last long—make a double batch!

—CAROL KITCHENS RIDGELAND, MS

PREP: 15 MIN. • **BAKE:** 10 MIN./BATCH • **MAKES:** 4 DOZEN

- ½ cup butter, softened
- ¾ cup sugar
- ⅔ cup packed brown sugar
- 2 egg whites
- 1¼ cups chunky peanut butter
- 1½ teaspoons vanilla extract
- 1 cup all-purpose flour
- ½ teaspoon baking soda
- ¼ teaspoon salt
- 5 Butterfinger candy bars (2.1 ounces each), chopped

1. In a large bowl, cream butter and sugars until light and fluffy. Beat in egg whites. Beat in peanut butter and vanilla. Combine the flour, baking soda and salt; gradually add to creamed mixture. Stir in candy bars.

2. Shape into 1½-in. balls and place 2 in. apart on greased baking sheets. Bake at 350° for 10-12 minutes or until golden brown. Remove to wire racks to cool.

Coconut Drop Cookies

Cathy Wilson says her mom—Winnie Nash—added nutritious ingredients to recipes whenever she could. Chock full of nuts and oats, these crispy-chewy cookies are the perfect example.

—CATHY WILSON ST. GEORGE, UT

PREP: 25 MIN. • **BAKE:** 15 MIN./BATCH • **MAKES:** 5½ DOZEN

- 1 cup shortening
- 1 cup sugar
- 1 cup packed brown sugar
- 2 eggs
- 1 teaspoon vanilla extract
- 2 cups all-purpose flour
- 2 cups old-fashioned oats
- 1 teaspoon baking powder
- 1 teaspoon baking soda
- ½ teaspoon salt
- 2 cups flaked coconut
- 1 cup chopped walnuts

1. In a large bowl, cream shortening and sugars until light and fluffy. Add eggs, one at a time, beating well after each addition. Beat in vanilla. Combine the flour, oats, baking powder, baking soda and salt; gradually add to creamed mixture and mix well. Stir in coconut and walnuts.

2. Drop by rounded tablespoonfuls 3 in. apart onto greased baking sheets. Flatten slightly.

3. Bake at 350° for 11-14 minutes or until golden brown. Cool for 2 minutes before removing to wire racks. Store in an airtight container.

Bakeshop **TIP**

Storing Cookies

Cookies should always be completely cooled, and icings should be completely dry before storing. Store crisp cookies separately from soft cookies, and strong-flavored cookies separately from delicate-flavored ones. If you like, place a sheet of waxed paper between each layer of cookies.

Crisp Graham Cookies

I was delighted to find the recipe for these fun cookies. The peanut butter makes them extra special.

—LORI DANIELS BEVERLY, WV

PREP: 25 MIN. • **BAKE:** 10 MIN./BATCH
MAKES: 7 DOZEN (2-INCH COOKIES)

- ½ **cup butter-flavored shortening**
- ½ **cup packed brown sugar**
- 1 **egg**
- 1½ **teaspoons vanilla extract**
- 1 **can (14 ounces) sweetened condensed milk**
- 3 **tablespoons creamy peanut butter**
- 1½ **cup all-purpose flour**
- 1 **cup graham cracker crumbs**
- 1 **teaspoon baking soda**
- 1 **teaspoon salt**
- ½ **cup chopped pecans**
- 1 **package (12.6 ounces) milk chocolate M&M's**

1. In a bowl, cream shortening and brown sugar; beat in egg. Add vanilla and milk. Blend in peanut butter. Combine dry ingredients; add to the creamed mixture. Stir in the M&M's and nuts.

2. Drop by teaspoonfuls 1 in. apart on ungreased baking sheets. Bake at 350° for 10-12 minutes or until golden brown. Cool on wire racks.

Pecan Sandies Cookies

Whenever Mother made these cookies, there never seemed to be enough! These melt-in-your-mouth treats are great with a cold glass of milk or a steaming mug of hot chocolate.
—**DEBBIE CARLSON** SAN DIEGO, CA

PREP: 20 MIN. • **BAKE:** 20 MIN./BATCH + COOLING
MAKES: ABOUT 5 DOZEN

- 2 **cups butter, softened**
- 1 **cup confectioners' sugar**
- 2 **tablespoons water**
- 4 **teaspoons vanilla extract**
- 4 **cups all-purpose flour**
- 2 **cups chopped pecans**
  Additional confectioners' sugar

1. In a large bowl, cream butter and sugar. Add water and vanilla; mix well. Gradually add flour; fold in pecans.
2. Roll dough into 1-in. balls. Place on ungreased baking sheets and flatten with fingers.
3. Bake at 300° for 20-25 minutes or until bottom edges are golden brown. Cool on a wire rack. When cool, dust with confectioners' sugar.

Golden Raisin Cookies

Now that my children are grown, I make these light butter cookies for the neighborhood kids.

—ISABEL PODESZWA LAKEWOOD, NJ

PREP: 25 MIN. • **BAKE:** 10 MIN./BATCH • **MAKES:** ABOUT 6 DOZEN

- 1 cup butter, softened
- 1½ cups sugar
- 1 tablespoon lemon juice
- 2 eggs
- 3½ cups all-purpose flour
- 1½ teaspoons cream of tartar
- 1½ teaspoons baking soda
- 1 package (15 ounces) golden raisins (2½ cups)

1. In a bowl, cream butter and sugar. Add lemon juice and eggs. Combine dry ingredients; gradually add to creamed mixture. Stir in raisins. Roll into 1-in. balls.

2. Place on greased baking sheets; flatten with a floured fork. Bake at 400° for 8-10 minutes or until cookies are lightly browned.

Cherry Kisses

Light, sweet meringues filled with dates, cherries and walnuts seem too good to be true. Is it any wonder these morsels disappear as fast as I can whip them up?

—JO ANN BLOMQUEST FREEPORT, IL

PREP: 10 MIN. + STANDING • **BAKE:** 20 MIN./BATCH
MAKES: 6 DOZEN

- 4 egg whites
- 1¼ cups sugar
- ⅓ cup chopped walnuts
- ⅓ cup chopped pitted dates
- ⅓ cup chopped candied cherries

1. Place egg whites in a large bowl; let stand at room temperature for 30 minutes. Beat on medium speed until soft peaks form. Gradually beat in sugar, 1 tablespoon at a time, on high until stiff glossy peaks form and the sugar is dissolved. Fold in the walnuts, dates and cherries.

2. Drop by teaspoonfuls 2 in. apart onto lightly greased baking sheets. Bake at 300° for 20-30 minutes or until firm to the touch. Cool for 1 minute before removing to a wire rack. Store in an airtight container.

Chunky Drop Cookies

The night before, I measure out the pretzels, peanuts, raisins and chocolate (I've even used a leftover hollow Easter bunny). Assembly goes quickly the next day.

—KELLY WARD-HARTMAN CAPE CORAL, FL

PREP: 15 MIN. • **BAKE:** 10 MIN./BATCH • **MAKES:** ABOUT 6½ DOZEN

- 1 cup butter, softened
- 1 cup packed brown sugar
- ½ cup sugar
- 2 eggs
- 3 teaspoons vanilla extract
- 2½ cups all-purpose flour
- ¾ teaspoon baking powder
- 2 cups halved pretzel sticks
- 1 cup coarsely chopped dry roasted peanuts
- 1 cup semisweet chocolate chunks
- 1 cup raisins

1. In a large bowl, cream butter and sugars until light and fluffy. Add eggs, one at a time, beating well after each addition. Beat in vanilla. Combine the flour and baking powder; gradually add to creamed mixture and mix well. Stir in the pretzels, peanuts, chocolate chunks and raisins.

2. Drop by heaping tablespoonfuls 2 in. apart onto ungreased baking sheets. Bake at 350° for 10-14 minutes or until edges are golden brown. Cool for 2 minutes before removing to wire racks.

Chock-Full of Chips

Banana Chocolate Chip Cookies

These soft cookies have a cakelike texture and lots of banana flavor that folks seem to love.

—**VICKI RAATZ** WATERLOO, WI

PREP: 20 MIN. • **BAKE:** 10 MIN./BATCH • **MAKES:** 3 DOZEN

- ⅓ cup butter, softened
- ½ cup sugar
- 1 egg
- ½ cup mashed ripe banana
- ½ teaspoon vanilla extract
- 1 cup all-purpose flour
- 1 teaspoon baking powder
- ¼ teaspoon salt
- ⅛ teaspoon baking soda
- 1 cup (6 ounces) semisweet chocolate chips

1. In a small bowl, cream butter and sugar until light and fluffy. Beat in the egg, banana and vanilla. Combine the flour, baking powder, salt and baking soda; gradually add to creamed mixture and mix well. Stir in chocolate chips.

2. Drop by tablespoonfuls 2 in. apart onto baking sheets coated with cooking spray. Bake at 350° for 9-11 minutes or until the edges are lightly browned. Remove to wire racks to cool.

Coconut Pecan Cookies

With chocolate chips and coconut in the batter and a yummy pecan-coconut frosting, these cookies will remind you of German chocolate cake. A drizzle of chocolate tops them off in a festive way.

—**DIANE SELICH** VASSAR, MI

PREP: 30 MIN. • **BAKE:** 10 MIN./BATCH + COOLING
MAKES: 6½ DOZEN

- 1 egg, lightly beaten
- 1 can (5 ounces) evaporated milk
- ⅔ cup sugar
- ¼ cup butter, cubed
- 1¼ cups flaked coconut
- ½ cup chopped pecans

COOKIE DOUGH

- 1 cup butter, softened
- ¾ cup sugar
- ¾ cup packed brown sugar
- 2 eggs
- 1 teaspoon vanilla extract
- 2¼ cups all-purpose flour
- 1 teaspoon baking soda
- 1 teaspoon salt
- 4 cups (24 ounces) semisweet chocolate chips, divided
- ¼ cup flaked coconut

1. For frosting, in a large saucepan, combine the egg, milk, sugar and butter. Cook and stir over medium-low heat for 10-12 minutes or until slightly thickened and mixture reaches 160° or is thick enough to coat the back of a metal spoon. Stir in coconut and pecans. Set aside.

2. In a large bowl, cream butter and sugars until light and fluffy. Beat in eggs and vanilla. Combine the flour, baking soda and salt; gradually add to creamed mixture and mix well. Stir in 2 cups chips and coconut.

3. Drop by tablespoonfuls 2 in. apart onto ungreased baking sheets. Bake at 350° for 8-10 minutes or until lightly browned. Cool for 10 minutes before removing to wire racks to cool completely.

4. In a microwave, melt the remaining chocolate chips; stir until smooth. Spread frosting over cooled cookies; drizzle with melted chocolate.

1. In a large bowl, beat the eggs and extracts. Beat in sugar. Combine the flour, pecans, cocoa and salt; gradually add to egg mixture and mix well. Stir in chocolate chips.

2. On a baking sheet coated with cooking spray, shape dough into a 14-in. x 3-in. rectangle. Bake at 350° for 20-25 minutes or until lightly browned. Cool for 5 minutes.

3. Transfer to a cutting board; cut with a serrated knife into 1-in. slices. Place cut side down on baking sheets coated with cooking spray. Bake for 15-20 minutes or until firm, turning once. Remove to wire racks to cool.

4. For icing, in a microwave, melt chocolate chips; stir until smooth. Stir in milk, confectioners' sugar and vanilla until smooth. Drizzle over cookies; let stand until set.

White Chocolate Chip Hazelnut Cookies

This is a cookie you will want to make again and again. It's very delicious...crispy on the outside and chewy on the inside.

—**DENISE DEJONG** PITTSBURGH, PA

PREP: 15 MIN. • **BAKE:** 10 MIN./BATCH • **MAKES:** 3 DOZEN

- 1¼ cups whole hazelnuts, toasted, divided
- 9 tablespoons butter, softened, divided
- ½ cup sugar
- ½ cup packed brown sugar
- 1 egg
- 1 teaspoon vanilla extract
- 1½ cups all-purpose flour
- ½ teaspoon baking soda
- ½ teaspoon salt
- 1 cup white baking chips

1. Coarsely chop ½ cup hazelnuts; set aside. Melt 2 tablespoons butter. In a food processor, combine the melted butter and remaining hazelnuts. Cover and process until the mixture forms a crumbly paste; set aside.

2. In a bowl, cream the remaining butter. Beat in sugars until light and fluffy. Beat in egg and vanilla. Beat in ground hazelnut mixture until blended. Combine the flour, baking soda and salt; add to batter and mix just until combined. Stir in chips and chopped hazelnuts.

3. Drop by rounded tablespoonfuls 2 in. apart onto greased baking sheets. Bake at 350° for 10-12 minutes or until lightly browned. Remove to wire racks to cool.

Double Chocolate Biscotti

Here's a more moist and tender version of biscotti. With a chocolaty taste and sweet drizzle on top, these irresistible cookies just beg for hot coffee to be served alongside.

—**TASTE OF HOME TEST KITCHEN**

PREP: 20 MIN. • **BAKE:** 35 MIN. + COOLING
MAKES: ABOUT 1 DOZEN

- 2 eggs
- 1 teaspoon vanilla extract
- ¼ teaspoon almond extract
- ½ cup sugar
- 1 cup all-purpose flour
- ½ cup finely chopped pecans
- ¼ cup baking cocoa
- ¼ teaspoon salt
- ½ cup miniature semisweet chocolate chips

ICING
- 1½ teaspoons miniature semisweet chocolate chips
- 3 teaspoons fat-free milk
- ½ cup confectioners' sugar
- ⅛ teaspoon vanilla extract

Chocolate Snowballs

This is my all-time favorite Christmas cookie recipe. The cookies remind me of the snowballs I'd pack as a child during winters here in Wisconsin.

—DEE DEREZINSKI WAUKESHA, WI

PREP: 20 MIN. • **BAKE:** 15 MIN. • **MAKES:** ABOUT 4 DOZEN

- ¾ **cup butter, softened**
- ½ **cup sugar**
- 1 **egg**
- 2 **teaspoons vanilla extract**
- 2 **cups all-purpose flour**
- ½ **teaspoon salt**
- 1 **cup chopped nuts**
- 1 **cup (6 ounces) chocolate chips**
  Confectioners' sugar

1. In a bowl, cream butter and sugar. Add egg and vanilla; mix well. Combine flour and salt; stir into creamed mixture. Fold in nuts and chips. Roll into 1-in. balls.
2. Place on ungreased baking sheets. Bake at 350° for 15-20 minutes. Cool cookies slightly before rolling in confectioners' sugar.

Chippy Peanut Butter Cookies

"Hey, these are good!" is what I always hear when I bake these cookies. The recipe is very simple, with directions that are easy to follow. Try it yourself and see what I mean!

—**IAN BADEER** HICKMAN, NE

PREP: 25 MIN. • **BAKE:** 15 MIN./BATCH • **MAKES:** ABOUT 4 DOZEN

- 1 cup butter, softened
- 1 cup creamy peanut butter
- 1 cup sugar
- 1 cup packed brown sugar
- 2 eggs
- 1 teaspoon vanilla extract
- 2¼ cups all-purpose flour
- 2 teaspoons baking soda
- ¼ teaspoon salt
- 1 package (11 ounces) peanut butter and milk chocolate chips

1. In a large bowl, cream the butter, peanut butter and sugars until light and fluffy. Beat in eggs and vanilla. Combine the flour, baking soda and salt; gradually add to creamed mixture and mix well. Stir in chips.
2. Drop by rounded tablespoonfuls onto ungreased baking sheets. Bake at 350° for 12-15 minutes or until golden brown. Cool for 2 minutes before removing to wire racks.
NOTE *This recipe was tested with Nestlé swirled milk chocolate and peanut butter chips. Reduced-fat or generic brands of peanut butter are not recommended for this recipe.*

Monster Chip Cookies

I share these treats with "monsters" who ring my doorbell on Halloween. I also give them as Christmas gifts.

—**JUDY MABREY** MYRTLE BEACH, SC

PREP: 20 MIN. + CHILLING • **BAKE:** 15 MIN./BATCH + COOLING
MAKES: ABOUT 3 DOZEN

- 1 cup shortening
- ½ cup butter, softened
- 1⅓ cups sugar
- 1 cup packed brown sugar
- 4 eggs
- 3 teaspoons vanilla extract
- 1 teaspoon lemon juice
- 3 cups all-purpose flour
- ½ cup quick-cooking oats
- 2 teaspoons baking soda
- 1½ teaspoons salt
- 1 teaspoon ground cinnamon
- 4 cups (24 ounces) semisweet chocolate chips
- 2 cups chopped nuts

1. In a large bowl, cream shortening, butter and sugars until light and fluffy. Add eggs, one at a time, beating well after each. Beat in vanilla and lemon juice. Combine the dry ingredients; add to creamed mixture and mix well. Stir in chips and nuts. Refrigerate 8 hours or overnight.
2. Drop by ¼ cupfuls 3 in. apart onto lightly greased baking sheet. Bake at 350° for 14-16 minutes or until lightly browned and center is set. Cool for 2 minutes before removing to wire racks.

Butterscotch Raisin Cookies

These chewy oatmeal cookies are loaded with goodies. Every so often, I add a half-cup of chopped pecans to a batch for something different.

—**VICTORIA HAHN** NORTHAMPTON, PA

PREP: 20 MIN. • **BAKE:** 10 MIN./BATCH • **MAKES:** 3½ DOZEN

- 1 cup butter, softened
- ¾ cup packed brown sugar
- ¼ cup sugar
- 2 eggs
- 3 cups quick-cooking oats
- 1½ cups all-purpose flour
- 1 package (3.4 ounces) instant butterscotch pudding mix
- 1 teaspoon baking soda
- 1 cup raisins
- ½ cup butterscotch chips

1. In a large bowl, cream butter and sugars until light and fluffy. Beat in eggs. Combine the oats, flour, dry pudding mix and baking soda; gradually add to creamed mixture and mix well. Stir in raisins and butterscotch chips (dough will be stiff).
2. Drop by tablespoonfuls 2 in. apart onto ungreased baking sheets. Bake at 375° for 9-11 minutes or until lightly browned. Remove to wire racks to cool.

Chocolate Chip Icebox Cookies

Putting chocolate chips in these refrigerator cookies makes them delicious. This treat is always welcome at my house.

—BETTY HOLZINGER WEST OLIVE, MI

PREP: 15 MIN. + CHILLING • **BAKE:** 10 MIN. • **MAKES:** 20 COOKIES

- 3 tablespoons butter, softened
- 2 tablespoons shortening
- ¼ cup sugar
- ¼ cup packed brown sugar
- 1 egg yolk
- ½ teaspoon vanilla extract
- ⅔ cup all-purpose flour
- ¼ teaspoon baking soda
- ¼ teaspoon salt
- ¼ cup miniature semisweet chocolate chips
- ¼ cup finely chopped pecans

1. In a small bowl, cream the butter, shortening and sugars. Beat in egg yolk and vanilla; mix well. Combine the flour, baking soda and salt; gradually add to creamed mixture and mix well. Stir in chips and pecans. Shape into a 9-in. roll; wrap in plastic wrap. Refrigerate overnight.

2. Unwrap and cut into ¼-in. slices. Place 2 in. apart on ungreased baking sheets. Bake at 375° for 8-10 minutes or until edges are golden brown. Cool for 2 minutes before removing to wire racks to cool completely.

White Chocolate Chip Maple Cookies

Since my husband farms, I try to have simple meals and snacks available, as I never know when he and his father will come in from the fields. These cookies have a distinct maple flavor and stay moist and soft.

—DEBRA HOGENSON BREWSTER, MN

PREP: 20 MIN. • **BAKE:** 10 MIN./BATCH • **MAKES:** ABOUT 7 DOZEN

- 1 cup shortening
- ½ cup butter, softened
- 2 cups packed brown sugar
- 2 eggs
- 1 teaspoon vanilla extract
- 1 teaspoon maple flavoring
- 3 cups all-purpose flour
- 2 teaspoons baking soda
- 2 cups white baking chips
- ½ cup chopped pecans

FROSTING
- ¼ cup butter, softened
- 4 cups confectioners' sugar
- 1 teaspoon maple flavoring
- 4 to 6 tablespoons 2% milk
- 3½ cups pecan halves

1. In a large bowl, cream the shortening, butter and brown sugar until light and fluffy. Beat in the eggs, vanilla and maple flavoring. Combine the flour and baking soda; gradually add to creamed mixture and mix well. Stir in chips and pecans.

2. Drop by rounded tablespoonfuls 2 in. apart onto ungreased baking sheets. Bake at 350° for 8-10 minutes or until golden brown. Cool for 2 minutes before removing to wire racks.

3. In a small bowl, cream butter and confectioners' sugar until light and fluffy. Beat in maple flavoring and enough of the milk to achieve spreading consistency. Frost cooled cookies. Top each with a pecan half.

Chunky Mocha Cookies

My home economics club has a cookie exchange every Christmas. These cookies flavored with a hint of coffee are always a big hit.

—**JANET SPARKS** SHIRLEY, IN

PREP: 20 MIN. • **BAKE:** 10 MIN./BATCH • **MAKES:** ABOUT 6 DOZEN

- 1 **cup butter-flavored shortening**
- ¾ **cup sugar**
- ½ **cup packed brown sugar**
- 2 **eggs**
- 2 **tablespoons milk**
- 1 **tablespoon instant coffee granules**
- 1 **teaspoon vanilla extract**
- 2⅓ **cups all-purpose flour**
- 2 **tablespoons baking cocoa**
- 1 **teaspoon baking soda**
- ½ **teaspoon salt**
- 1 **cup chopped pecans**
- 1 **cup (6 ounces) semisweet chocolate chips**
- ¾ **cup raisins**
- ¾ **cup flaked coconut**

1. In a large bowl, cream shortening and sugars until light and fluffy. Beat in eggs. Beat in the milk, coffee granules and vanilla. Combine the flour, cocoa, baking soda and salt; add to the creamed mixture and mix well. Fold in the pecans, chips, raisins and coconut.

2. Drop by rounded tablespoonfuls 2 in. apart onto ungreased baking sheets. Bake at 375° for 10-12 minutes or until golden brown.

Peanut Butter Maple Cookies

I bake these crispy yet chewy peanut butter cookies often. My grandchildren can't wait to dig into the cookie jar.

—LOIS BOWMAN SWANTON, MD

PREP: 20 MIN. • **BAKE:** 15 MIN./BATCH • **MAKES:** ABOUT 5 DOZEN

- 1 **cup butter, softened**
- ½ **cup peanut butter**
- 1 **cup sugar**
- 1 **cup packed brown sugar**
- 2 **eggs**
- 1 **tablespoon maple syrup**
- 2 **teaspoons vanilla extract**
- 2 **cups all-purpose flour**
- ¾ **cup quick-cooking oats**
- 1½ **teaspoons baking powder**
- 1 **teaspoon baking soda**
- 1 **teaspoon salt**
- 1 **package (10 ounces) peanut butter chips**

1. In a large bowl, cream the butter, peanut butter and sugars. Add the eggs, one at a time, beating well after each addition. Beat in syrup and vanilla. Combine the flour, oats, baking powder, baking soda and salt; add to the creamed mixture. Stir in peanut butter chips.

2. Drop by heaping tablespoonfuls 2 in. apart onto ungreased baking sheets. Bake at 325° for 15-18 minutes or until golden brown. Cool for 1 minute before removing to wire racks to cool completely.

NOTE *Reduced-fat peanut butter is not recommended for this recipe.*

Chips Galore Cookies

I've discovered how to make a cookie lover's dream come true! Loaded with pecans, walnuts and three types of chips, these crisp treats will be such a hit with your family that they might not make it to the bake sale or cookie jar.

—**SHAUNA STEPHENS** SAN DIEGO, CA

PREP: 10 MIN. + CHILLING • **BAKE:** 20 MIN./BATCH
MAKES: 9 DOZEN

- 1 **cup butter, softened**
- ¾ **cup sugar**
- ¾ **cup packed brown sugar**
- 2 **eggs**
- 1 **tablespoon almond extract**
- 2¼ **cups all-purpose flour**
- 1 **teaspoon baking soda**
- ½ **teaspoon salt**
- 1½ **cups each semisweet chocolate chips, milk chocolate chips and vanilla or white chips**
- 1½ **cups chopped pecans**
- 1½ **cups chopped walnuts**

1. In a large bowl, cream butter and sugars until light and fluffy. Add eggs, one at a time, beating well after each addition. Beat in extract. Combine the flour, baking soda and salt; gradually add to creamed mixture and mix well. Combine chips and nuts; stir into dough. Cover and refrigerate for 1 hour or until easy to handle.

2. Drop by tablespoonfuls 2 in. apart onto greased baking sheets. Bake at 325° for 18-20 minutes or until golden brown. Remove to wire racks to cool.

Raspberry Meringues

As rosy pink as Santa's cheeks, these merry meringue cookies are drizzled with dark chocolate and are almost too pretty to eat. Pecans add a nice crunch to these chewy treats. They lend a festive touch to my Christmas cookie tray.

—**IOLA EGLE** BELLA VISTA, AR

PREP: 20 MIN. • **BAKE:** 25 MIN./BATCH • **MAKES:** 7½ DOZEN

- 3 **egg whites**
- 3 **tablespoons plus 1 teaspoon raspberry gelatin powder**
- ¾ **cup sugar**
- 1 **teaspoon white vinegar**
- ⅛ **teaspoon salt**
- 2 **cups (12 ounces) semisweet chocolate chips**
- ½ **cup finely chopped pecans**

TOPPING
- ¼ **cup semisweet chocolate chips**
- 1 **teaspoon shortening**

1. Place egg whites in a large bowl; let stand at room temperature for 30 minutes.

2. Beat eggs whites until soft peaks form. Gradually add gelatin, beating until combined. Gradually add sugar, 1 tablespoon at a time, beating until stiff peaks form. Beat in vinegar and salt. Fold in chocolate chips and nuts.

3. Drop by rounded teaspoonfuls onto parchment-lined baking sheets. Bake at 250° for 20-25 minutes or until firm to the touch. Turn oven off; leave cookies in the oven with door ajar for about 1½ hours or until cool.

4. In a microwave, melt chocolate chips and shortening; stir until smooth. Drizzle over cookies.

1. In a large bowl, cream butter and sugars until light and fluffy. Add eggs, one at a time, beating well after each addition. Beat in vanilla. Combine the flour, baking soda, baking powder and salt; gradually add to the creamed mixture and mix well. Stir in the coconut and chips. Shape 3 tablespoonfuls of dough into a ball; repeat with remaining dough.

2. Place balls 3 in. apart on ungreased baking sheets. Bake at 350° for 12-18 minutes or until lightly browned. Remove to wire racks to cool.

3. If desired, in a microwave, melt candy coating; stir until smooth. Dip one end of cooled cookies in candy coating. Allow excess to drip off. Place on waxed paper; let stand until set.

Honey Maple Cookies

Honey and maple syrup make these chocolate chip cookies a little different. The maple flavor is light and subtle.

—**BARBARA KUDER** TRIBUNE, KS

PREP: 20 MIN. • **BAKE:** 10 MIN./BATCH • **MAKES:** 5 DOZEN

- 1 **cup shortening**
- ¾ **cup honey**
- ¾ **cup maple syrup**
- 2 **eggs**
- 1 **teaspoon vanilla extract**
- 2½ **cups all-purpose flour**
- 1 **teaspoon baking soda**
- 1 **teaspoon salt**
- 2 **cups (12 ounces) semisweet chocolate chips**
- 1 **cup chopped pecans**

1. In a large bowl, beat shortening until light and fluffy. Add honey and syrup, a little at a time, beating well after each addition. Add eggs, one at a time, beating well after each addition (mixture will appear curdled). Beat in vanilla. Combine the flour, baking soda and salt. Gradually add to honey mixture and mix just until moistened. Stir in the chocolate chips and pecans.

2. Drop by rounded tablespoonfuls onto greased baking sheets. Bake at 350° for 8-10 minutes or until golden brown. Remove to wire racks.

Jumbo Chocolate Chip Cookies

These gourmet cookies are my most-asked-for recipe. With coconut and chocolate chips, and dipped in white candy coating, they are truly a chocolate lover's delight.

—**JACKIE RUCKWARDT** COTTAGE GROVE, OR

PREP: 20 MIN. • **BAKE:** 15 MIN. • **MAKES:** ABOUT 2 DOZEN

- 1 **cup butter, softened**
- 1 **cup sugar**
- 1 **cup packed brown sugar**
- 2 **eggs**
- 2 **teaspoons vanilla extract**
- 2½ **cups all-purpose flour**
- 1 **teaspoon baking soda**
- 1 **teaspoon baking powder**
- 1 **teaspoon salt**
- 2⅔ **cups flaked coconut**
- 1 **cup (6 ounces) semisweet chocolate chips**
- ½ **cup milk chocolate chips**
- 5 **ounces white candy coating, coarsely chopped, optional**

Chocolate Chunk Cookies

It's such a pleasure to serve delicious cookies like these to neighbors and family. I love to bake cookies, and my four young daughters are eager to help with mixing, measuring and stirring!
—**ELAINE ANDERSON** NEW GALILEE, PA

PREP: 15 MIN. • **BAKE:** 20 MIN. • **MAKES:** 3 DOZEN

- 6 **ounces white baking chocolate, chopped, divided**
- 1 **cup butter, softened**
- ½ **cup sugar**
- ½ **cup packed brown sugar**
- 2 **eggs**
- 2 **teaspoons vanilla extract**
- 2½ **cups all-purpose flour**
- 1 **teaspoon baking soda**
- ¼ **teaspoon salt**
- 1 **package (11½ ounces) semisweet chocolate chunks or 2 cups semisweet chocolate chips**

1. In a microwave, melt 3 ounces of white chocolate at 70% power for 1 minute; stir. Microwave at additional 10- to 20-second intervals, stirring until smooth; cool.

2. In a large bowl, cream butter and sugars until light and fluffy. Add eggs, one at a time, beating well after each addition. Beat in melted chocolate and vanilla. Combine flour, baking soda and salt; gradually add to the creamed mixture and mix well. Stir in semisweet chocolate chunks.

3. Drop by tablespoonfuls onto ungreased baking sheets. Bake at 375° for 10-12 minutes or until golden brown. Cool for 1 minute before removing to wire racks.

4. In a microwave, melt remaining white chocolate at 70% power for 1 minute; stir. Microwave at additional 10- to 20-second intervals, stirring until smooth; drizzle over cookies. May be frozen for up to 3 months.

Cookie Pizza

Everyone seems to love the great-tasting combination of yummy chocolate and marshmallows on a homemade peanut butter cookie crust.

—DEBBIE JOHNSON JEFFERSON CITY, MO

START TO FINISH: 30 MIN. • **MAKES:** 10-12 SERVINGS

- ½ cup butter, softened
- ½ cup peanut butter
- ½ cup sugar
- ½ cup packed brown sugar
- 1 egg
- ½ teaspoon vanilla extract
- 1½ cups all-purpose flour
- 2 cups miniature marshmallows
- 1 cup (6 ounces) semisweet chocolate chips

1. In a bowl, cream butter, peanut butter and sugars. Beat in egg and vanilla. Stir in flour until blended.

2. Spread dough onto a greased 12-in. pizza pan. Bake at 375° for 12 minutes. Sprinkle with marshmallows and chips. Bake 5-6 minutes longer or until lightly browned.

Double Chocolate Chip Cookies

The cocoa in the batter gives these treats a double dose of chocolate. They disappear fast from my cookie jar.

—DIANE HIXON NICEVILLE, FL

PREP: 25 MIN. • **BAKE:** 10 MIN./BATCH • **MAKES:** 3-4 DOZEN

- 1 cup butter, softened
- 1 cup sugar
- ½ cup packed dark brown sugar
- 1 teaspoon vanilla extract
- 1 egg
- ⅓ cup baking cocoa
- 2 tablespoons milk
- 1¾ cups all-purpose flour
- ¼ teaspoon baking powder
- 1 cup chopped walnuts
- 1 cup (6 ounces) semisweet chocolate chips

1. In a large bowl, cream the butter, sugars and vanilla. Beat in egg. Add cocoa and milk. Combine flour and baking powder; fold into creamed mixture with walnuts and chocolate chips.

2. Roll teaspoonfuls of dough into balls; place 2 in. apart on ungreased baking sheets. Bake at 350° for 10-12 minutes. Cool for 5 minutes before removing to wire racks to cool.

Coconut Chocolate Chip Cookies

These are great for coconut lovers, since they contain both flaked coconut and a bit of extract. The cookies turn out crispy and chewy—a real winner.

—LAURA BANKARD MANCHESTER, MD

START TO FINISH: 25 MIN. • **MAKES:** ABOUT 1¼ DOZEN

- ½ cup butter, softened
- ¾ cup sugar
- 1 egg
- ½ teaspoon coconut extract
- 1 cup plus 2 tablespoons all-purpose flour
- ½ teaspoon baking soda
- ½ teaspoon salt
- 1 cup (6 ounces) semisweet chocolate chips
- ½ cup flaked coconut

1. In a large bowl, cream butter and sugar. Beat in egg and coconut extract. Combine the flour, baking soda and salt; add to the creamed mixture. Stir in chocolate chips and coconut.

2. Drop by rounded tablespoonfuls 2 in. apart onto ungreased baking sheets. Bake at 375° for 11-13 minutes or until golden brown. Remove to wire racks to cool.

Peanut Butter Cup Cookies

Here's a classic combination of chocolate and peanut butter. It's no wonder these are my family's favorite cookies.

—FAITH JENSEN MERIDIAN, ID

PREP: 20 MIN. • **BAKE:** 10 MIN./BATCH • **MAKES:** 7½ DOZEN

- 1 **cup butter, softened**
- ⅔ **cup peanut butter**
- 1 **cup sugar**
- 1 **cup packed brown sugar**
- 2 **eggs**
- 2 **teaspoons vanilla extract**
- 2¼ **cups all-purpose flour**
- 1 **teaspoon baking soda**
- ½ **teaspoon salt**
- 2 **cups (12 ounces) semisweet chocolate chips**
- 2 **cups chopped peanut butter cups (about six 1.6-ounce packages)**

1. In a large bowl, cream the butter, peanut butter and sugars until light and fluffy. Beat in eggs and vanilla. Combine the flour, baking soda and salt; gradually add to creamed mixture and mix well. Stir in chocolate chips and peanut butter cups.
2. Drop by rounded tablespoonfuls 2 in. apart onto ungreased baking sheets. Bake at 350° for 10-12 minutes or until edges are lightly browned. Cool for 2 minutes before removing to wire racks.
NOTE *Reduced-fat peanut butter is not recommended for this recipe.*

Special Chocolate Chip Cookies

Oats, white chips, a crunch candy bar and a strawberry drizzle pack each bite of this cookie with wonderful flavor!

—LINDA WHEELER SPARKS SEVERNA PARK, MD

PREP: 1 HOUR • **BAKE:** 15 MIN./BATCH + COOLING
MAKES: ABOUT 4½ DOZEN

- ½ **cup quick-cooking oats**
- 1 **Nestlé Crunch candy bar (1.4 ounces), broken into pieces**
- ¼ **cup chopped pecans**
- 1 **cup butter, softened**
- ¾ **cup packed brown sugar**
- ½ **cup sugar**
- 2 **eggs**
- 3 **teaspoons vanilla extract**
- 2 **cups all-purpose flour**
- 1 **teaspoon baking soda**
- ½ **teaspoon salt**
- 1 **cup semisweet chocolate chips**
- 1 **cup white baking chips**

ICING
- 2 **cups confectioners' sugar**
- 2 **tablespoons milk**
- 2 **teaspoons strawberry or raspberry extract**
- 1 **to 2 drops red food coloring, optional**

1. In a food processor, combine the oats, candy bar and pecans. Cover and process until finely chopped; set aside.
2. In a large bowl, cream butter and sugars until light and fluffy. Add eggs, one at a time, beating well after each addition. Beat in vanilla. Combine the flour, baking soda, salt and reserved oat mixture; gradually add to creamed mixture and mix well. Stir in chips.
3. Drop by tablespoonfuls 2 in. apart onto ungreased baking sheets. Bake at 350° for 11-13 minutes or until lightly browned. Cool for 2 minutes before removing to wire racks to cool completely.
4. Combine icing ingredients until smooth; drizzle over cookies. Let stand until set. Store in an airtight container.

Minty Meringue Drops

These pretty mint green drops are dotted with chocolate chips.
My kids don't consider it the Christmas season until I make them.
—**KAREN WISSING** VASHON, WA

PREP: 20 MIN. • **BAKE:** 30 MIN./BATCH • **MAKES:** ABOUT 2½ DOZEN

- 2 **egg whites**
- ¼ **teaspoon cream of tartar**
- ¾ **cup sugar**
- ⅛ **teaspoon vanilla extract**
- 2 **to 6 drops green food coloring, optional**
- 1 **package (10 ounces) mint chocolate chips**

1. Lightly grease baking sheets or line with parchment paper; set aside.

2. In a large bowl, beat egg whites until foamy. Add cream of tartar, beating until soft peaks form. Gradually beat in sugar, 1 tablespoon at a time, until stiff peaks form. Beat in vanilla and food coloring if desired. Fold in chocolate chips.

3. Drop by rounded tablespoonfuls 2 in. apart onto prepared baking sheets. Bake at 250° for 30-35 minutes or until dry to the touch. Remove to wire racks to cool. Store in an airtight container.

NOTE *If mint chocolate chips are not available, place 2 cups (12 ounces) semisweet chocolate chips and ¼ teaspoon peppermint extract in a plastic bag; seal and toss to coat. Allow chips to stand for 24-48 hours.*

White Chocolate Chip Cherry Cookies

Chopped maraschino cherries and white chips make a great color and flavor combination in these sweet treats.

—MARGARET WILSON SUN CITY, CA

PREP: 20 MIN. • **BAKE:** 10 MIN./BATCH • **MAKES:** 4½ DOZEN

- 1 **cup butter, softened**
- ¾ **cup sugar**
- ¾ **cup packed brown sugar**
- 2 **eggs**
- ¼ **teaspoon almond extract**
- 2¼ **cups all-purpose flour**
- 1 **teaspoon baking soda**
- ½ **teaspoon salt**
- 1 **package (10 to 12 ounces) white baking chips**
- 1 **jar (10 ounces) maraschino cherries, drained and chopped**

1. In a large bowl, cream butter and sugars. Add eggs, one at a time, beating well after each addition. Beat in extract. Combine flour, baking soda and salt; gradually add to the creamed mixture and mix well. Stir in chips and cherries.
2. Drop by rounded tablespoonfuls 2 in. apart onto ungreased baking sheets. Bake at 350° for 10-12 minutes or until lightly browned. Remove to wire racks to cool.

Chewy Peanut Butter Crisps

This flourless cookie is chewy inside and crisp outside. Try the recipe—you'll love it!

—LUCY GARRETT CEDARTOWN, GA

PREP: 10 MIN. • **BAKE:** 15 MIN./BATCH • **MAKES:** 3½ DOZEN

- 1 **cup peanut butter**
- 1 **cup sugar**
- ½ **cup evaporated milk**
- 4 **teaspoons cornstarch**
- ½ **cup semisweet chocolate chips**

1. In a large bowl, cream peanut butter and sugar until light and fluffy. Stir in milk and cornstarch until smooth. Fold in chocolate chips.
2. Drop by heaping teaspoonfuls 2 in. apart onto ungreased baking sheets. Bake at 350° for 12-15 minutes or until golden brown. Remove from pans to wire racks .

Five-Chip Cookies

With peanut butter, oats and five kinds of chips, these cookies make a hearty snack that appeals to everyone. I sometimes double the recipe to share with friends and neighbors.

—SHARON HEDSTROM MINNETONKA, MN

PREP: 20 MIN. • **BAKE:** 10 MIN./BATCH • **MAKES:** 4½ DOZEN

- 1 **cup butter, softened**
- 1 **cup peanut butter**
- 1 **cup sugar**
- ⅔ **cup packed brown sugar**
- 2 **eggs**
- 1 **teaspoon vanilla extract**
- 2 **cups all-purpose flour**
- 1 **cup old-fashioned oats**
- 2 **teaspoons baking soda**
- ½ **teaspoon salt**
- ⅔ **cup each milk chocolate chips, semisweet chocolate chips, peanut butter chips, white baking chips and butterscotch chips**

1. Preheat oven to 350°. In a large bowl, cream butter, peanut butter and sugars until light and fluffy. Add eggs, one at a time, beating well after each addition. Beat in vanilla. Combine flour, oats, baking soda and salt; gradually add to creamed mixture and mix well. Stir in chips.
2. Drop by rounded tablespoonfuls 2 in. apart onto ungreased baking sheets. Bake 10-12 minutes or until the cookies are lightly browned. Cool 1 minute before removing to wire racks.

NOTE *Reduced-fat peanut butter is not recommended for this recipe.*

1. In a microwave, melt 1 cup chocolate chips. Stir until smooth; set aside. In a small bowl, beat butter and sugar until crumbly, about 2 minutes. Add egg whites and vanilla; beat well. Stir in melted chocolate.

2. Combine the flour, baking powder and salt; gradually add to butter mixture alternately with water. Stir in remaining chocolate chips. Cover and refrigerate for 2 hours or until easy to handle.

3. Shape dough into 1-in. balls. Roll in confectioners' sugar. Place 2 in. apart on baking sheets coated with cooking spray. Bake at 350° for 10-12 minutes or until set. Remove to wire racks to cool.

Sour Cream Chocolate Cookies

These soft chocolaty cookies can be easily altered to make several different varieties—I've added everything from mints to macadamia nuts to them. My husband and I live on a farm with our young daughter and son. Baking for them is one of my favorite hobbies.

—TINA SAWCHUK ARDMORE, AB

START TO FINISH: 30 MIN. • **MAKES:** ABOUT 3 DOZEN

- ½ cup butter, softened
- ¾ cup sugar
- ½ cup packed brown sugar
- 1 egg
- ½ cup sour cream
- 1 teaspoon vanilla extract
- 1¾ cups all-purpose flour
- ½ cup baking cocoa
- 1 teaspoon baking powder
- ½ teaspoon baking soda
- ¼ teaspoon salt
- 1 cup (6 ounces) semisweet chocolate chips
- ½ cup vanilla or white chips

1. In a large bowl, cream butter and sugars until light and fluffy. Beat in egg, sour cream and vanilla. Combine dry ingredients; gradually add to the creamed mixture. Stir in the chips.

2. Drop by rounded tablespoonfuls 2 in. apart onto greased baking sheets. Bake at 350° for 12-15 minutes or until set. Cool for 2 minutes before removing to wire racks to cool completely.

Crinkle-Top Chocolate Cookies

When I baked these moist, fudgy cookies for the first time, my three preschool children loved them! I like them because they're lower in fat and easy to mix and bake.

—MARIA GROFF EPHRATA, PA

PREP: 15 MIN. + CHILLING • **BAKE:** 10 MIN./BATCH
MAKES: 3½ DOZEN

- 2 cups (12 ounces) semisweet chocolate chips, divided
- 2 tablespoons butter, softened
- 1 cup sugar
- 2 egg whites
- 1½ teaspoons vanilla extract
- 1½ cups all-purpose flour
- 1½ teaspoons baking powder
- ¼ teaspoon salt
- ¼ cup water
- ½ cup confectioners' sugar

Chocolate Chip Butter Cookies

At the downtown Chicago law firm where I work, we often bring in goodies for special occasions. When co-workers hear I've baked these melt-in-your-mouth cookies, they make a special trip to my floor to sample them. Best of all, these crisp, buttery treats can be made in no time.

—**JANIS GRUCA** MOKENA, IL

PREP: 20 MIN. • **BAKE:** 15 MIN./BATCH + COOLING
MAKES: ABOUT 4 DOZEN

- 1 **cup butter, cubed**
- ½ **teaspoon vanilla extract**
- 2 **cups all-purpose flour**
- 1 **cup confectioners' sugar**
- 1 **cup (6 ounces) miniature semisweet chocolate chips**
  Melted semisweet and/or white chocolate, optional

1. Melt butter in a microwave; stir in vanilla. Cool completely. In a large bowl, combine flour and the confectioners' sugar; stir in butter mixture and chocolate chips (mixture will be crumbly).

2. Shape into 1-in. balls. Place 2 in. apart on ungreased baking sheets; flatten slightly. Bake at 375° for 12 minutes or until edges begin to brown. Cool on wire racks. Dip or drizzle with chocolate if desired.

Cherry Chocolate Nut Cookies

Each Christmas, I make about 600 cookies to share with family and friends. The holidays wouldn't be the same without several batches of these colorful goodies.

—SYBIL NOBLE HAMBURG, AR

PREP: 30 MIN. • **BAKE:** 10 MIN./BATCH • **MAKES:** 5 DOZEN

- ½ **cup butter, softened**
- ½ **cup sugar**
- ½ **cup packed brown sugar**
- 1 **egg**
- ¼ **cup 2% milk**
- 1 **teaspoon vanilla extract**
- 2 **cups all-purpose flour**
- 1 **teaspoon baking powder**
- ½ **teaspoon salt**
- ¼ **teaspoon baking soda**
- 1 **cup (6 ounces) semisweet chocolate chips**
- ¾ **cup chopped maraschino cherries**
- ¾ **cup chopped pecans**

1. In a large bowl, cream butter and sugars until light and fluffy. Beat in the egg, milk and vanilla. Combine the flour, baking powder, salt and baking soda; gradually add to creamed mixture and mix well. Stir in the remaining ingredients.

2. Drop by tablespoonfuls 2 in. apart onto greased baking sheets. Bake at 375° for 10-12 minutes or until golden brown. Remove to wire racks to cool.

Potato Chip Cookies

Give this cookie a try the next time you're looking for a sweet and salty treat! They quickly bake to a crisp golden brown.

—MONNA LU BAUER LEXINGTON, KY

PREP: 15 MIN. • **BAKE:** 10 MIN./BATCH • **MAKES:** 4 DOZEN

- 1 **cup butter-flavored shortening**
- ¾ **cup sugar**
- ¾ **cup packed brown sugar**
- 2 **eggs**
- 2 **cups all-purpose flour**
- 1 **teaspoon baking soda**
- 2 **cups crushed potato chips**
- 1 **cup butterscotch chips**

1. Preheat oven to 375°. In a bowl, cream shortening and sugars until light and fluffy. Beat in eggs. In another bowl, whisk flour and baking soda; gradually beat into creamed mixture. Stir in potato chips and butterscotch chips.

2. Drop by tablespoonfuls 2 in. apart onto ungreased baking sheets. Bake 10-12 minutes or until golden brown. Cool on pans 1 minute. Remove to wire racks to cool.

Goblin Chewies

These light cookies are packed with fun ingredients that are perfect for Halloween.

—BERNICE MORRIS MARSHFIELD, MO

PREP: 30 MIN. • **BAKE:** 10 MIN. • **MAKES:** ABOUT 6 DOZEN

- 1 **cup shortening**
- 1 **cup packed brown sugar**
- 1 **cup sugar**
- 2 **eggs**
- 1 **teaspoon vanilla extract**
- 2 **cups all-purpose flour**
- 1 **teaspoon baking soda**
- ½ **teaspoon baking powder**
- ½ **teaspoon salt**
- 1½ **cups old-fashioned oats**
- 1 **cup crisp rice cereal**
- 1 **cup diced candy orange slices**
- 1 **cup (6 ounces) semisweet chocolate chips or raisins**
  Additional raisins or chocolate chips and candy orange slices

1. In a bowl, cream shortening and sugars. Add eggs and vanilla; mix well. Combine the flour, baking soda, baking powder and salt; add to creamed mixture. Stir in oats, cereal, orange slices and chips or raisins.

2. Drop by tablespoonfuls 2 in. apart onto greased baking sheets. Flatten slightly with a fork. Decorate with raisin or chocolate chip eyes and orange slice mouths. Bake at 350° for 10-14 minutes. Cool on wire racks.

Bakeshop TIP

Mixing It Up

Drop cookie dough is usually so thick that it can be dropped from a spoon and requires no shaping. If the mixer begins to strain while you are mixing the dough, use a wooden spoon to stir the last of the flour or all of the chips, nuts and dried fruit.

Iced Pumpkin Cookies

My 2-year-old son, Joshua, especially likes testing—or should I say consuming?— these chunky cookies!

—**JOHNA NILSON** VISTA, CA

PREP: 45 MIN. • **BAKE:** 15 MIN./BATCH + COOLING
MAKES: 3 DOZEN

- 1 **cup butter, softened**
- ½ **cup sugar**
- ½ **cup packed brown sugar**
- 1 **egg**
- 1 **cup canned pumpkin**
- 1 **cup all-purpose flour**
- 1 **cup whole wheat flour**
- 1½ **teaspoons ground cinnamon**
- 1 **teaspoon baking powder**
- 1 **teaspoon ground ginger**
- ½ **teaspoon salt**
- ½ **teaspoon baking soda**
- ½ **teaspoon ground nutmeg**
- ¼ **teaspoon ground cloves**
- 1 **cup granola without raisins**
- 1 **cup chopped walnuts**
- 1 **cup white baking chips**
- 1 **cup dried cranberries**

ICING
- ¼ **cup butter, softened**
- 2 **cups confectioners' sugar**
- 3 **tablespoons 2% milk**

1. In a large bowl, cream butter and sugars until light and fluffy. Beat in egg and pumpkin. Combine the flours, cinnamon, baking powder, ginger, salt, baking soda, nutmeg and cloves; gradually add to creamed mixture and mix well. Stir in the granola, walnuts, chips and cranberries.

2. Drop by tablespoonfuls 2 in. apart onto greased baking sheets. Bake at 350° for 15-18 minutes or until lightly browned. Remove to wire racks to cool.

3. In a small bowl, combine icing ingredients until smooth. Spread over cooled cookies. Store in the refrigerator.

Chocolate Chip Oatmeal Cookies

Crazy about chocolate chips? This chewy cookie has plenty, not to mention lots of heart-healthy oatmeal. Everyone will come back for another, so this big batch is perfect.

—**DIANE NETH** MENNO, SD

PREP: 20 MIN. • **BAKE:** 10 MIN./BATCH • **MAKES:** ABOUT 7 DOZEN

- 1 **cup butter, softened**
- ¾ **cup sugar**
- ¾ **cup packed brown sugar**
- 2 **eggs**
- 1 **teaspoon vanilla extract**
- 3 **cups quick-cooking oats**
- 1½ **cups all-purpose flour**
- 1 **package (3.4 ounces) instant vanilla pudding mix**
- 1 **teaspoon baking soda**
- 1 **teaspoon salt**
- 2 **cups (12 ounces) semisweet chocolate chips**
- 1 **cup chopped nuts**

1. In a large bowl, cream butter and sugars until light and fluffy. Beat in eggs and vanilla. Combine the oats, flour, dry pudding mix, baking soda and salt; gradually add to creamed mixture and mix well. Stir in chips and nuts.

2. Drop by rounded teaspoonfuls 2 in. apart onto ungreased baking sheets. Bake at 375° for 10-12 minutes or until lightly browned. Remove to wire racks.

Chocolate Malted Cookies

Like good old-fashioned malted milk? Here's the next best thing! With malted milk powder, chocolate syrup plus chocolate chips and chunks, these are the yummiest cookies I've ever tasted. I have six kids, so I've made a lot of them over the years.

—TERI RASEY CADILLAC, MI

START TO FINISH: 30 MIN. • **MAKES:** ABOUT 1½ DOZEN

- 1 cup butter-flavored shortening
- 1¼ cups packed brown sugar
- ½ cup malted milk powder
- 2 tablespoons chocolate syrup
- 1 tablespoon vanilla extract
- 1 egg
- 2 cups all-purpose flour
- 1 teaspoon baking soda
- ½ teaspoon salt
- 1½ cups semisweet chocolate chunks
- 1 cup milk chocolate chips

1. In a large bowl, beat the shortening, brown sugar, malted milk powder, chocolate syrup and vanilla for 2 minutes. Add egg.

2. Combine the flour, baking soda and salt; gradually add to shortening mixture, mixing well after each addition. Stir in chocolate chunks and chips.

3. Shape into 2-in. balls; place 3 in. apart on ungreased baking sheets. Bake at 375° for 12-14 minutes or until golden brown. Cool for 2 minutes before removing to a wire rack.

Crisp 'n' Chewy Cookies

Knowing I'm a cookie lover, my mother-in-law sent me this recipe years ago. Many folks have told me these are the best cookies they've ever tasted. I think it's the Butterfinger candy bars that make them so special.

—KRISTEN SNYDER SUGAR LAND, TX

PREP: 15 MIN. • **BAKE:** 10 MIN./BATCH • **MAKES:** 7 DOZEN

- 1¼ cups butter-flavored shortening
- ¾ cup sugar
- ¾ cup packed brown sugar
- 1 egg
- 3 tablespoons maple syrup
- 1 teaspoon vanilla extract
- 3 cups quick-cooking oats
- 1¾ cups all-purpose flour
- 1 teaspoon baking soda
- 1 teaspoon salt
- ¾ cup semisweet chocolate chips
- 2 Butterfinger candy bars (2.1 ounces each), chopped

1. In a large bowl, cream shortening and sugars until light and fluffy. Beat in the egg, syrup and vanilla. Combine the oats, flour, baking soda and salt; gradually add to creamed mixture and mix well. Stir in chips and candy bars.

2. Roll dough into 1-in. balls. Place 2 in. apart on ungreased baking sheets. Bake at 375° for 7-9 minutes or until golden brown. Remove to wire racks to cool.

Macadamia Chip Cookies

If you like cookies with a crunch, you'll love these golden treats. Crushed peanut brittle adds a kick to the white chips and brown sugar that flavor the dough. It's hard to believe something this easy to make tastes so terrific.

—DOROTHY KOLLMEYER DUPO, IL

PREP: 20 MIN. • **BAKE:** 10 MIN./BATCH • **MAKES:** 5½ DOZEN

- 1 cup butter, softened
- ¾ cup packed brown sugar
- ¼ cup sugar
- 2 eggs
- 1 teaspoon vanilla extract
- 2¼ cups all-purpose flour
- 1 package (3.4 ounces) instant vanilla pudding mix
- 1 teaspoon baking soda

- ¼ teaspoon salt
- 1 package (10 to 12 ounces) white baking chips
- 2 jars (3¾ ounces each) macadamia nuts, chopped
- ½ cup finely crushed peanut brittle

1. In a large bowl, cream butter and sugars until light and fluffy. Add eggs, one at a time, beating well after each addition. Beat in vanilla. Combine the flour, dry pudding mix, baking soda and salt; gradually add to creamed mixture and mix well. Stir in the chips, nuts and peanut brittle.

2. Drop by rounded tablespoonfuls 2 in. apart onto greased baking sheets. Bake at 375° for 10-12 minutes or until golden brown. Remove to wire racks to cool.

Bakeshop **TIP**

Breaking Up Candy Bars

To quickly break up the Butterfinger candy bars, place them in a resealable plastic bag and pound with a meat mallet. Or, break into quarters, place in a mini food processor and pulse until broken into pieces. The pieces should be a little bigger than the chocolate chips.

Easy Drop Cookies

Chocolate Macadamia Macaroons

This perfect macaroon has dark chocolate, chewy coconut and macadamia nuts. It is dipped in chocolate, which puts it over the top—sinful and delicious!

—DARLENE BRENDEN SALEM, OR

PREP: 20 MIN. • **BAKE:** 15 MIN. + COOLING • **MAKES:** 1½ DOZEN

- 2 cups flaked coconut
- ½ cup finely chopped macadamia nuts
- ⅓ cup sugar
- 3 tablespoons baking cocoa
- 2 tablespoons all-purpose flour
  Pinch salt
- 2 egg whites, lightly beaten
- 1 tablespoon light corn syrup
- 1 teaspoon vanilla extract
- 4 ounces semisweet chocolate, melted

1. Preheat oven to 325°. In a large bowl, mix the first six ingredients. Stir in the egg whites, corn syrup and vanilla until blended.

2. Drop dough by rounded tablespoonfuls 2 in. apart onto greased baking sheets. Bake 15-20 minutes or until set and dry to the touch. Cool on pans 5 minutes. Remove to wire racks to cool completely.

3. Dip bottom of each cookie in melted chocolate, allowing excess to drip off. Place on waxed paper; let stand until set.

White Chocolate Pumpkin Dreams

If you like pumpkin pie, you'll love these delicious pumpkin cookies dotted with white chocolate chips and chopped pecans. Drizzled with a brown sugar icing, they're irresistible.

—JEAN KLECKNER SEATTLE, WA

PREP: 25 MIN. + COOLING • **BAKE:** 15 MIN./BATCH + COOLING
MAKES: ABOUT 4½ DOZEN

- 1 cup butter, softened
- ½ cup sugar
- ½ cup packed brown sugar
- 1 egg
- 2 teaspoons vanilla extract
- 1 cup canned pumpkin
- 2 cups all-purpose flour
- 3½ teaspoons pumpkin pie spice
- 1 teaspoon baking powder
- 1 teaspoon baking soda
- ¼ teaspoon salt
- 1 package (10 to 12 ounces) white baking chips
- 1 cup chopped pecans

PENUCHE FROSTING
- ½ cup packed brown sugar
- 3 tablespoons butter
- ¼ cup milk
- 1½ to 2 cups confectioners' sugar

1. In a large bowl, cream butter and sugars until light and fluffy. Beat in the egg, vanilla and pumpkin. Combine dry ingredients; gradually add to the creamed mixture and mix well. Stir in chips and pecans.

2. Drop dough by rounded teaspoonfuls 2 in. apart onto ungreased baking sheets. Bake at 350° for 12-14 minutes or until firm. Remove to wire racks to cool.

3. For frosting, combine the brown sugar and butter in a small saucepan. Bring to a boil; cook over medium heat for 1 minute or until slightly thickened. Cool for 10 minutes. Add milk; beat until smooth. Beat in enough confectioners' sugar to reach the desired consistency. Spread over the cooled cookies.

Rhubarb-Filled Cookies

I won a blue ribbon at our local fair for these tender cookies. They're so pretty with the filling peeking through the dough. When not just any cookie will do, try making these and watch the smiles appear.

—PAULINE BONDY GRAND FORKS, ND

PREP: 25 MIN. • **BAKE:** 10 MIN./BATCH • **MAKES:** ABOUT 4½ DOZEN

- 1 **cup butter, softened**
- 1 **cup sugar**
- 1 **cup packed brown sugar**
- 4 **eggs**
- 4½ **cups all-purpose flour**
- 1 **teaspoon baking soda**
- 1 **teaspoon salt**

FILLING
- 3½ **cups chopped fresh or frozen rhubarb, thawed**
- 1½ **cups sugar**
- 6 **tablespoons water, divided**
- ¼ **cup cornstarch**
- 1 **teaspoon vanilla extract**

1. In a bowl, cream butter and sugars until light and fluffy. Add eggs, one at a time, beating well after each addition. Combine the flour, baking soda and salt; gradually add to creamed mixture and mix well (dough will be sticky).

2. For filling, combine rhubarb, sugar and 2 tablespoons water in a large saucepan. Bring to a boil. Reduce heat; simmer, uncovered, for 10 minutes or until thickened, stirring frequently. Combine cornstarch and remaining water until smooth; stir into rhubarb mixture. Bring to a boil; cook and stir for 2 minutes or until thickened. Remove from the heat; stir in vanilla.

3. Drop the dough by tablespoonfuls 2 in. apart onto ungreased baking sheets. Using the end of a wooden spoon handle, make an indentation in the center of each cookie; fill with a rounded teaspoon of the filling. Top with ½ teaspoon of dough, allowing some filling to show. Bake at 375° for 8-10 minutes or until lightly browned.

NOTE *If using frozen rhubarb, measure rhubarb while still frozen, then thaw completely. Drain in a colander, but do not press liquid out.*

Almond Sugar Cookies

We made these crisp cookies often when I worked in the lunchroom at our daughters' grade school. The almond flavor makes them so good.

—LINDA HOLT WICHITA FALLS, TX

PREP: 15 MIN. • **BAKE:** 10 MIN./BATCH • **MAKES:** 5 DOZEN

- 2 **cups butter-flavored shortening**
- 1 **cup sugar**
- 1 **cup packed brown sugar**
- 2 **eggs**
- 1 **teaspoon vanilla extract**
- 1 **teaspoon almond extract**
- 4 **cups all-purpose flour**
- 2 **teaspoons baking soda**
- 2 **teaspoons cream of tartar**
   Additional sugar or colored sugar

1. In a large bowl, cream the shortening and sugars until light and fluffy. Add eggs, one at a time, beating well after each addition. Beat in extracts. Combine the flour, baking soda and cream of tartar; gradually add to creamed mixture and mix well.

2. Drop by tablespoonfuls 2 in. apart onto ungreased baking sheets. Flatten with a glass dipped in sugar. Bake at 350° for 10-12 minutes or until lightly browned. Remove to wire racks to cool.

Pumpkin Cookie Pops

Cookie pops are a great way to get in the spirit of Halloween. They're fun, but not too spooky.

—**TASTE OF HOME TEST KITCHEN**

PREP: 1 HOUR • **BAKE:** 15 MIN./BATCH + COOLING
MAKES: 2½ DOZEN

- ½ cup butter, softened
- ¾ cup packed brown sugar
- ½ cup sugar
- 1 egg
- 1 teaspoon vanilla extract
- 1 cup canned pumpkin
- 2½ cups all-purpose flour
- 1 teaspoon baking powder
- 1 teaspoon baking soda
- 1 teaspoon ground cinnamon
- 30 Popsicle sticks
- ⅓ cup green gumdrops, quartered lengthwise

ICING

- 4 cups confectioners' sugar
- ¼ cup water
  Orange, black, purple, green and red paste or gel food coloring

1. In a large bowl, cream butter and sugars until light and fluffy. Beat in egg and vanilla. Beat in pumpkin. Mix flour, baking powder, baking soda and cinnamon; gradually add to creamed mixture and mix well (dough will be soft).

2. Drop by rounded tablespoonfuls 2 in. apart onto greased or parchment paper-lined baking sheets. Insert Popsicle sticks into dough. Insert a gumdrop piece into the top of each for the pumpkin stem.

3. Bake at 350° for 14-16 minutes or until set and lightly browned around the edges. Remove to wire racks to cool.

4. For icing, in a large bowl, combine confectioners' sugar and water until smooth. Remove ½ cup to another bowl; cover and set aside. Stir orange food coloring into remaining icing. Spread or pipe over cookies. Let stand for 30 minutes or until icing is set and dry.

5. Tint reserved icing with colors of your choice; use colored icing to create jack-o'-lantern faces.

Frosted Ginger Cookies

My husband and I live in a small rural community in western New York. I work all day in an office, and I enjoy baking in the evening to relax. The wonderful aroma of these soft delicious cookies in our oven makes our house a home.

—JEANNE MATTESON SOUTH DAYTON, NY

PREP: 20 MIN. • **BAKE:** 15 MIN./BATCH • **MAKES:** ABOUT 6 DOZEN

- 1½ cups butter, softened
- 1 cup sugar
- 1 cup packed brown sugar
- 2 eggs
- ½ cup molasses
- 2 teaspoon vanilla extract
- 4½ cups all-purpose flour
- 1 tablespoon ground ginger
- 2 teaspoons baking soda
- 2 teaspoons ground cinnamon
- ½ teaspoon salt
- ½ teaspoon ground cloves

FROSTING
- ⅓ cup packed brown sugar
- ¼ cup milk
- 2 tablespoons butter
- 2 cups confectioners' sugar
- ½ teaspoon vanilla extract
  Pinch salt

1. In a large bowl, cream butter and sugars. Add the eggs, one at a time, beating well after each addition. Stir in molasses and vanilla; mix well. Combine dry ingredients; gradually add to creamed mixture.

2. Drop by tablespoonfuls 2 in. apart onto ungreased baking sheets. Bake at 325° for 12-15 minutes or until cookies spring back when touched lightly (do not overbake). Remove to wire racks.

3. For frosting, in a large saucepan, bring the brown sugar, milk and butter to a boil; cook and stir for 1 minute. Remove from the heat (mixture will look curdled at first). Cool for 3 minutes. Add confectioners' sugar, vanilla and salt; mix well. Frost warm cookies.

Almond Sandies

Buttery, rich and delicious, these are my husband's favorite cookies—and very popular wherever I take them.

—JOYCE PIERCE CALEDONIA, MI

PREP: 20 MIN. • **BAKE:** 25 MIN./BATCH • **MAKES:** 4 DOZEN

- 1 cup butter, softened
- 1 cup sugar
- 1 teaspoon almond extract
- 1¾ cups all-purpose flour
- ½ teaspoon baking soda
- ¼ teaspoon baking powder
- ¼ teaspoon salt
- ½ cup slivered almonds

1. In a bowl, cream butter and sugar. Add extract; mix well.

2. Combine the flour, baking soda, baking powder and salt; gradually add to creamed mixture. Fold in almonds.

3. Drop by rounded teaspoonfuls onto ungreased baking sheets. Bake at 300° for 22-24 minutes or until edges are lightly browned. Cool for 1-2 minutes before removing to wire racks.

Butter Wafers

These crisp drop cookies are great for folks who don't like their treats too sweet.

—EVELYN STARR RAYMOND, WA

PREP: 20 MIN. • **BAKE:** 15 MIN. • **MAKES:** ABOUT 2½ DOZEN

- 1 cup butter, softened
- ⅓ cup confectioners' sugar
- 1 cup all-purpose flour
- ⅔ cup cornstarch
  Colored sugar, optional

1. In a large bowl, cream butter and confectioners' sugar until light and fluffy. Combine flour and cornstarch; add to creamed mixture and mix well.

2. Drop by rounded tablespoonfuls 3 in. apart onto ungreased baking sheets (cookies will spread). Sprinkle with colored sugar if desired.

3. Bake at 325° for 12-15 minutes or until edges are lightly browned and tops are set. Cool for 2 minutes before carefully removing to wire racks.

Peanut Butter Oatmeal Cookies

My cookies are soft and chewy with the old-fashioned goodness of oatmeal and peanut butter. I like to take them to work and on camping trips since they travel very well.

—ROLLIN BARKEIM TREMPEALEAU, WI

PREP: 20 MIN. • **BAKE:** 10 MIN./BATCH • **MAKES:** 5 DOZEN

- 3 egg whites
- 1 cup packed brown sugar
- 1 cup reduced-fat peanut butter
- ½ cup unsweetened applesauce
- ¼ cup honey
- 2 teaspoons vanilla extract
- 3 cups quick-cooking oats
- 1 cup all-purpose flour
- 1 cup nonfat dry milk powder
- 2 teaspoons baking soda

1. In a large bowl, beat egg whites and brown sugar until frothy. Beat in peanut butter, applesauce, honey and vanilla. Combine the oats, flour, milk powder and baking soda; gradually add to peanut butter mixture.

2. Drop by tablespoonfuls 2 in. apart onto baking sheets coated with cooking spray. Bake at 350° for 8-10 minutes or until golden brown. Remove to wire racks to cool.

Frosted Cashew Drops

If your family likes cashews, they will love these caramel-flavored cookies. I think they make a nice nutty addition to any holiday cookie platter, but they always disappear quickly no matter what time of year I serve them.

—LOIS MCGRADY HILLSVILLE, VA

PREP: 15 MIN. • **BAKE:** 10 MIN./BATCH + COOLING
MAKES: ABOUT 4 DOZEN

- ½ cup butter, softened
- 1 cup packed brown sugar
- ½ cup sour cream
- 1 egg
- 1 teaspoon vanilla extract
- 1¾ cups all-purpose flour
- 1 teaspoon baking powder
- ½ teaspoon baking soda
- ¼ teaspoon salt
- 1 cup salted cashews, chopped and toasted

FROSTING
- ¼ cup butter, cubed
- 2 cups confectioners' sugar
- 2 to 3 tablespoons milk

1. In a large bowl, cream butter and brown sugar until fluffy; beat in the sour cream, egg and vanilla. Combine the flour, baking powder, baking soda and salt; gradually add to creamed mixture and mix well. Stir in the cashews.

2. Drop by rounded tablespoonfuls onto greased baking sheets. Bake at 375° for 8-10 minutes or until lightly browned. Remove to wire racks to cool.

3. For frosting, in a heavy saucepan, cook butter over medium heat for 7-9 minutes or until golden brown. Whisk in the confectioners' sugar and enough milk to achieve a smooth consistency. Spread over cooled cookies.

Vanilla-Glazed Apple Cookies

This delicious fruit-and-nut cookie recipe from my mother has been a favorite for many years.

—**SHARON CRIDER** JUNCTION CITY, KS

PREP: 25 MIN. • **BAKE:** 10 MIN./BATCH • **MAKES:** ABOUT 4 DOZEN

- ½ cup shortening
- 1⅓ cups packed brown sugar
- 1 egg
- ¼ cup 2% milk
- 2 cups all-purpose flour
- 1 teaspoon baking soda
- 1 teaspoon ground nutmeg
- 1 teaspoon ground cinnamon
- ½ teaspoon ground cloves
- 1 cup chopped walnuts
- 1 cup finely diced peeled apple
- 1 cup raisins

VANILLA GLAZE
- 1½ cups confectioners' sugar
- 1 tablespoon butter, melted
- ½ teaspoon vanilla extract
- ⅛ teaspoon salt
- 2 to 4 teaspoons 2% milk

1. Preheat oven to 400°, In a large bowl, cream shortening and brown sugar until light and fluffy. Beat in egg and milk. Combine the flour, baking soda, nutmeg, cinnamon and cloves; gradually add to the creamed mixture and mix well. Stir in walnuts, apple and raisins.

2. Drop by rounded tablespoonfuls 2 in. apart onto ungreased baking sheets. Bake 8-10 minutes or until edges begin to brown. Remove to wire racks.

3. In a small bowl, combine the confectioners' sugar, butter, vanilla, salt and enough milk to achieve drizzling consistency. Drizzle over warm cookies.

Sugar 'n' Spice Cookies

These sweet and tart cookies are a treat. They're even more delicious with the homemade lemon frosting spread on top.

—DOTTIE LAPIERRE WOBURN, MA

PREP: 20 MIN. • **BAKE:** 10 MIN./BATCH + COOLING
MAKES: ABOUT 4½ DOZEN

- ¾ **cup shortening**
- 1 **cup sugar**
- 1 **egg**
- ¼ **cup molasses**
- 2 **cups all-purpose flour**
- 1½ **teaspoons ground ginger**
- 1 **teaspoon baking soda**
- 1 **teaspoon ground cinnamon**
- ¾ **teaspoon ground cloves**
- ½ **teaspoon salt**

LEMON FROSTING
- 2 **cups confectioners' sugar**
- 3 **tablespoons butter, softened**
- 1 **teaspoon grated lemon peel**
- 3 **to 4 tablespoons lemon juice**

1. In a large bowl, cream shortening and sugar until light and fluffy. Beat in egg and molasses. Combine the dry ingredients; gradually add to the creamed mixture and mix well.

2. Drop by rounded teaspoonfuls onto greased baking sheets. Bake at 350° for 8-10 minutes. Remove to wire racks; cool.

3. For frosting, cream the confectioners' sugar, butter and peel in a large bowl. Gradually add lemon juice, beating until frosting achieves desired spreading consistency. Frost cookies.

Root Beer Cookies

Since it's too difficult to take root beer floats on a picnic, take these cookies instead! I've found the flavor is even better the next day. The hard part is convincing my family to wait that long before sampling them.

—VIOLETTE BAWDEN WEST VALLEY CITY, UT

PREP: 20 MIN. • **BAKE:** 10 MIN./BATCH • **MAKES:** ABOUT 6 DOZEN

- 1 cup butter, softened
- 2 cups packed brown sugar
- 2 eggs
- 1 cup buttermilk
- ¾ teaspoon root beer concentrate
- 4 cups all-purpose flour
- 1 teaspoon baking soda
- 1 teaspoon salt
- 1½ cups chopped pecans

FROSTING

- 3½ cups confectioners' sugar
- ¾ cup butter, softened
- 3 tablespoons water
- 1¼ teaspoons root beer concentrate or extract

1. In a large bowl, cream butter and brown sugar. Add eggs, one at a time, beating well after each addition. Beat in buttermilk and root beer concentrate. Combine the flour, baking soda and salt; gradually add to creamed mixture. Stir in pecans.

2. Drop by tablespoonfuls 3 in. apart onto ungreased baking sheets. Bake at 375° for 10-12 minutes or until lightly browned. Remove to wire racks to cool. In a small bowl, combine frosting ingredients; beat until smooth. Frost cooled cookies.

NOTE *This recipe was tested with McCormick root beer concentrate.*

Cherry Chocolate Chip Cookies

We run a cherry orchard, so I'm always dreaming up new cherry recipes. This recipe is one of my family's favorites.

—PAMELA ALEXANDER PROSSER, WA

PREP: 15 MIN. • **BAKE:** 15 MIN./BATCH • **MAKES:** ABOUT 3½ DOZEN

- 1 cup dried cherries, chopped
- ⅓ cup hot water
- 6 tablespoons shortening
- 6 tablespoons butter, softened
- 1½ cups packed brown sugar
- ½ cup sugar
- 2 eggs
- 3 teaspoons grated orange peel
- 1½ teaspoons vanilla extract
- 3 cups quick-cooking oats
- 1¾ cups all-purpose flour
- ¾ teaspoon baking soda
- ¾ teaspoon ground cinnamon
- ½ teaspoon salt
- 1 cup (6 ounces) semisweet chocolate chips

1. In a small bowl, soak cherries in hot water for at least 10 minutes.

2. Meanwhile, in a large bowl, cream the shortening, butter and sugars until light and fluffy. Beat in the eggs, orange peel and vanilla. Combine the oats, flour, baking soda, cinnamon and salt; gradually add to creamed mixture and mix well. Stir in the chocolate chips and cherries with liquid.

3. Drop by rounded tablespoonfuls 2 in. apart onto ungreased baking sheets. Bake at 350° for 12-14 minutes or until edges are lightly browned. Cool for 1 minute before removing from pans to wire racks.

1 egg white
  Sugar
½ cup sliced almonds

1. In a large bowl, cream the shortening, cream cheese and sugar until light and fluffy. Beat in the egg yolk, lemon peel and extract. Combine the flour, oats and salt; gradually add to creamed mixture and mix well.

2. Drop by heaping teaspoonfuls 2 in. apart onto greased baking sheets. Beat egg and egg white; brush over dough. Sprinkle with sugar; top with almonds.

3. Bake at 350° for 10-12 minutes or until edges are lightly browned. Remove to wire racks.

Peanut Butter Crunch Cookies

The next time you're craving peanut butter cookies, try this variation studded with oats and Grape-Nuts. I think it's even better than regular peanut butter cookies, which I like a lot.

—KATHIE AND JOHN HORST WESTFIELD, NY

PREP: 15 MIN. • **BAKE:** 10 MIN./BATCH • **MAKES:** 2½ DOZEN

¼ cup butter, softened
¼ cup creamy peanut butter
¼ cup sugar
¼ cup packed brown sugar
1 egg
¼ teaspoon vanilla extract
½ cup all-purpose flour
¼ cup quick-cooking oats
¼ teaspoon baking soda
⅛ teaspoon salt
¼ cup Grape-Nuts

1. In a large bowl, cream the butter, peanut butter and sugars until light and fluffy. Beat in egg and vanilla. Combine the flour, oats, baking soda and salt; gradually add to creamed mixture and mix well. Stir in Grape-Nuts.

2. Drop by rounded teaspoonfuls 3 in. apart onto ungreased baking sheets. Flatten slightly with a fork dipped in flour. Bake at 350° for 9-12 minutes or until lightly browned. Cool for 5 minutes before removing from pans to wire racks.

NOTE *Reduced-fat peanut butter is not recommended for this recipe.*

Lemon Oatmeal Cookies

My grandmother always made these cookies for us at Christmas, and now I have inherited that task. With rich cream cheese in the dough and a sugary almond topping, they never last very long at my house!

—MICHELLE NABER TONAWANDA, NY

PREP: 20 MIN. • **BAKE:** 10 MIN./BATCH • **MAKES:** 4½ DOZEN

1 cup butter-flavored shortening
1 package (3 ounces) cream cheese, softened
1¼ cups sugar
1 egg yolk
2 teaspoons grated lemon peel
1 teaspoon lemon extract
1⅓ cups all-purpose flour
1⅓ cups quick-cooking oats
½ teaspoon salt
TOPPING
1 egg

Lemon Poppy Seed Cookies

These soft cookies are a comforting, old-fashioned variety everyone will enjoy. Try them with tea or coffee as an afternoon pick-me-up.

—PAT WOOLLEY JACKSON CENTER, OH

PREP: 20 MIN. • **BAKE:** 15 MIN./BATCH + COOLING
MAKES: 3½ DOZEN

- ½ cup poppy seed filling
- 2 teaspoons lemon juice
- 1 cup butter, softened
- 1½ cups sugar
- 3 egg yolks
- 1 tablespoon grated lemon peel
- 2 teaspoons lemon extract
- 1 teaspoon vanilla extract
- 3½ cups all-purpose flour
- 2 teaspoons baking powder
- 1¼ teaspoons baking soda
- ¾ cup buttermilk

FROSTING
- 3 cups confectioners' sugar
- 2 tablespoons butter, softened
- ¼ cup 2% milk
- 2 teaspoons lemon extract
- 1 teaspoon grated lemon peel
  Poppy seeds, optional

1. In a small bowl, combine the poppy seed filling and lemon juice; set aside. In a large bowl, cream butter and sugar until light and fluffy. Beat in the egg yolks, lemon peel and extracts. Combine the flour, baking powder and baking soda; gradually add to creamed mixture alternately with buttermilk, beating well after each addition.

2. Drop by tablespoonfuls onto greased baking sheets. Using the end of a wooden spoon handle, make an indentation about ½ in. deep in the center of each. Fill with about ½ teaspoon of poppy seed filling. Top with a teaspoonful of dough.

3. Bake at 350° for 14-16 minutes or until edges are golden brown. Remove to wire racks to cool.

4. For frosting, in a large bowl, beat the confectioners' sugar, butter, milk, extract and lemon peel until blended. Spread over cookies. Sprinkle with poppy seeds if desired.

Rosemary Honey Cookies

You'll be delighted with this unusual cookie's wonderful flavor.

—AUDREY THIBODEAU GILBERT, AZ

PREP: 20 MIN. • **BAKE:** 15 MIN./BATCH • **MAKES:** ABOUT 4 DOZEN

- ½ cup shortening
- ¼ cup butter, softened
- ¾ cup sugar
- 1 egg
- ¼ cup honey
- 1 tablespoon lemon juice
- 2 cups all-purpose flour
- 2 teaspoons dried rosemary, crushed
- 1 teaspoon baking soda
- ½ teaspoon salt
- ½ teaspoon ground cinnamon
- ¼ teaspoon ground nutmeg

1. In a bowl, cream shortening, butter and sugar. Beat in egg, honey and lemon juice. Combine dry ingredients; add to creamed mixture.

2. Drop by teaspoonfuls 2 in. apart onto greased baking sheets. Bake at 325° for 12-14 minutes or until cookies are lightly browned.

Cranberry Oat Yummies

I like to think these oatmeal treats are better for you than the standard chocolate chip cookie. Our three sons just can't get enough of them. And they have no idea I've modified the recipe to make it healthier.

—CAROL BIRKEMEIER NASHVILLE, IN

START TO FINISH: 30 MIN. • **MAKES:** 3 DOZEN

- ½ cup butter, melted
- ½ cup sugar
- 1 cup packed brown sugar
- 1 egg
- ¼ cup egg substitute
- 2 tablespoons corn syrup
- 1½ teaspoons vanilla extract
- 3 cups quick-cooking oats
- 1 cup all-purpose flour
- 1 teaspoon baking soda
- 1 teaspoon ground cinnamon
- ½ teaspoon baking powder

- ½ teaspoon salt
- ⅛ teaspoon ground nutmeg
- 1 cup dried cranberries

1. In a large bowl, beat butter and sugars. Add egg, egg substitute, corn syrup and vanilla; mix well. Combine the oats, flour, baking soda, cinnamon, baking powder, salt and nutmeg; gradually add to egg mixture and mix well. Stir in cranberries.

2. Drop dough by heaping tablespoonfuls 2 in. apart onto ungreased baking sheets. Bake at 375° for 8-10 minutes or until golden brown. Cool for 2 minutes before removing from pans to wire racks.

Whole Wheat Cookies

These soft, old-fashioned cookies are quite flavorful. With the goodness of wheat germ, they make a wholesome snack.

—BERTIE CARTER TAHLEQUAH, OK

PREP: 10 MIN. + CHILLING • **BAKE:** 10 MIN./BATCH
MAKES: ABOUT 4 DOZEN

- ½ cup butter, softened
- ½ cup peanut butter
- ½ cup honey
- 1 egg
- 1 teaspoon vanilla extract
- 1 cup whole wheat flour
- ½ cup nonfat dry milk powder
- ½ cup toasted wheat germ
- 1 teaspoon baking soda

1. In a large bowl, cream the butter, peanut butter and honey. Beat in egg and vanilla. Combine dry ingredients; gradually add to creamed mixture and mix well. Cover and refrigerate for 30 minutes.

2. Drop by teaspoonfuls 2 in. apart onto ungreased baking sheets. Flatten with a fork dipped in sugar.

3. Bake at 350° for 8-10 minutes or until golden brown. Cool for 1 minute before removing to wire racks to cool completely.

NOTE *Reduced-fat peanut butter is not recommended for this recipe.*

Frosted Brown Sugar Cookies

These cakelike cookies are sweet and buttery. I enjoy them with a glass of cold milk or a cup of hot coffee.

—**LORETTA PATTERSON** MENTOR, OH

PREP: 20 MIN. • **BAKE:** 10 MIN. + COOLING
MAKES: ABOUT 2 DOZEN

½ cup butter, softened
1 cup packed brown sugar
1 egg
½ cup sour cream
1¾ cups all-purpose flour
½ teaspoon baking soda
¼ teaspoon salt
BROWN SUGAR FROSTING
¼ cup butter
½ cup packed brown sugar
2 tablespoons milk
1 cup confectioners' sugar

1. In a small bowl, cream butter and brown sugar. Beat in egg and sour cream; mix well. Combine flour, baking soda and salt; gradually add to creamed mixture and mix well.
2. Drop by tablespoonfuls 2 in. apart onto greased baking sheets. Bake at 375° for 9-11 minutes or until golden brown. Remove to wire racks to cool.
3. For frosting, in a small saucepan, melt the butter over low heat; add brown sugar. Cook and stir for 2 minutes. Gradually add the milk. Bring to a boil, stirring constantly. Remove from the heat. Stir in confectioners' sugar. Cool for 20-30 minutes. Frost cooled cookies.

White Chocolate Macaroons

The chocolate and coconut combination in my macaroons make them a very rich treat that everyone seems to love.

—**JOYLYN TRICKEL** HELENDALE, CA

PREP: 45 MIN. • **BAKE:** 25 MIN./BATCH + CHILLING
MAKES: 5 DOZEN

5 egg whites
½ teaspoon vanilla extract
1⅓ cups sugar
5¼ cups flaked coconut, toasted, divided
¾ cup ground almonds
6 ounces white baking chocolate, coarsely chopped

1. Place egg whites in a large bowl; let stand at room temperature for 30 minutes. Add vanilla; beat on medium speed until soft peaks form. Gradually beat in sugar, about 2 tablespoons at a time, on high until stiff glossy peaks form and sugar is dissolved. Gradually fold in 4 cups coconut and nuts, about ½ cup at a time.
2. Drop by rounded tablespoonfuls 2 in. apart onto parchment-lined baking sheets. Bake at 275° for 25 minutes or until firm to the touch. Remove to wire racks to cool completely.
3. In a microwave-safe bowl, melt chocolate; stir until smooth. Spoon ¼ teaspoon white chocolate on each cookie; sprinkle each with 1 teaspoon coconut. Place on waxed paper-lined baking sheets. Refrigerate for 1 hour or until chocolate is set. Store in an airtight container.

Brazil Nut Cookies

Brazil nuts may be an unusual ingredient for a cookie recipe, but the flavor is absolutely outstanding. My mother's recipe for these rich cookies goes back more than 70 years.

—CHARLOTTE MAINS CUYAHOGA FALLS, OH

PREP: 15 MIN. • **BAKE:** 10 MIN./BATCH • **MAKES:** ABOUT 4½ DOZEN

- 1 **cup butter, softened**
- 1 **cup sugar**
- 2 **eggs**
- 1½ **teaspoons vanilla extract**
- 2¼ **cups all-purpose flour**
- ½ **teaspoon baking soda**
- ¼ **teaspoon salt**
- 2 **cups chopped Brazil nuts**
- ½ **cup flaked coconut**

1. In a large bowl, cream butter and sugar until light and fluffy. Add eggs, one at a time, beating well after each addition. Beat in vanilla. Combine the flour, baking soda and salt; gradually add to creamed mixture and mix well. Stir in nuts and coconut.

2. Drop the dough by tablespoonfuls 3 in. apart onto ungreased baking sheets. Bake at 350° for 10-12 minutes or until bottom of cookies are lightly browned. Remove to wire racks.

Apricot Cream Cheese Drops

This treasured recipe is from a favorite aunt. Her soft, rich cookies have yummy apricot flavor, but you could substitute strawberry, pineapple or raspberry preserves if you prefer.

—MELINDA LEONOWITZ BIRDSBORO, PA

PREP: 20 MIN. • **BAKE:** 10 MIN./BATCH + COOLING
MAKES: 3 DOZEN

- ½ **cup butter, softened**
- 1 **package (3 ounces) cream cheese, softened**
- ½ **cup apricot preserves**
- ¼ **cup packed brown sugar**
- 1 **tablespoon 2% milk**
- 1¼ **cups all-purpose flour**
- 1½ **teaspoons baking powder**
- 1½ **teaspoons ground cinnamon**
- ¼ **teaspoon salt**

FROSTING

- 1 **cup confectioners' sugar**
- ¼ **cup apricot preserves**
- 1 **tablespoon butter, softened**
- 1 **to 2 teaspoons milk**
  Ground nuts or flaked coconut

1. In a large bowl, beat the butter, cream cheese, apricot preserves, brown sugar and milk until blended. Combine the flour, baking powder, cinnamon and salt; gradually add to cream cheese mixture and mix well.

2. Drop by teaspoonfuls onto ungreased baking sheets. Bake at 350° for 8-10 minutes or until lightly browned. Remove to wire racks to cool.

3. For frosting, in a small bowl, combine the confectioners' sugar, apricot preserves, butter and enough milk to achieve desired consistency. Spread over cooled cookies. Sprinkle with nuts or coconut.

Chocolate Peanut Butter Drops

This soft and chewy low-carb cookie recipe calls for canola oil instead of butter to reduce the saturated fat.

—TASTE OF HOME TEST KITCHEN

PREP: 15 MIN. • **BAKE:** 10 MIN./BATCH + COOLING
MAKES: 4 DOZEN

- 1 **cup chunky peanut butter**
- ¼ **cup canola oil**
- ¾ **cup packed brown sugar**
- ½ **cup sugar**
- 2 **eggs**
- 1 **tablespoon vanilla extract**
- 1 **cup all-purpose flour**
- ⅓ **cup baking cocoa**
- 1 **teaspoon baking soda**
- ½ **teaspoon salt**
- ½ **cup miniature chocolate chips**

1. In a large bowl, beat the peanut butter, oil and sugars until blended. Beat in eggs and vanilla. Combine the flour, cocoa, baking soda and salt; gradually add to peanut butter mixture just until blended (dough will be sticky). Stir in chocolate chips.

2. Drop by rounded teaspoonfuls 2 in. apart on ungreased baking sheets. Flatten slightly with a glass.

3. Bake at 350° for 8-10 minutes or until set and tops are cracked. Cool for 2 minutes before removing to wire racks.

Jelly-Topped Sugar Cookies

On busy days, I appreciate this easy drop sugar cookie recipe. Top each with your favorite flavor of jam or jelly.

—JUNE QUINN KALAMAZOO, MI

PREP: 15 MIN. • **BAKE:** 10 MIN./BATCH + COOLING
MAKES: ABOUT 3½ DOZEN

- ¾ cup sugar
- ¾ cup canola oil
- 2 eggs
- 2 teaspoons vanilla extract
- 1 teaspoon lemon extract
- 1 teaspoon grated lemon peel
- 2 cups all-purpose flour
- 2 teaspoons baking powder
- ½ teaspoon salt
- ½ cup jam or jelly

1. In a large bowl, beat sugar and oil until blended. Beat in eggs, extracts and lemon peel. Mix flour, baking powder, and salt; gradually add to sugar mixture and mix well.

2. Drop by rounded tablespoonfuls 2 in. apart onto ungreased baking sheets. Coat bottom of a glass with cooking spray, then dip in sugar. Flatten cookies with prepared glass, redipping in sugar as needed.

3. Place ¼ teaspoon jelly in the center of each cookie. Bake at 400° for 8-10 minutes or until set. Remove to wire racks to cool.

Pecan Grahams

Years ago, I was eager to enter a recipe contest I'd read about. I went to my pantry and threw together these nutty cookies. Although they didn't win, they've been a hit with my family and friends ever since!

—JUNE RUSSELL GREEN COVE SPRINGS, FL

PREP: 15 MIN. • **BAKE:** 10 MIN./BATCH + COOLING
MAKES: ABOUT 4½ DOZEN

- ½ cup shortening
- ½ cup sugar
- ½ cup packed brown sugar
- 1 egg
- 1 cup all-purpose flour
- ½ teaspoon baking powder
- ½ teaspoon baking soda
- ¼ teaspoon salt
- 1 cup graham cracker crumbs
- 1 cup ground pecans
- 54 to 60 pecan halves

1. In a bowl, cream shortening and sugars. Add egg and mix well. Combine flour, baking powder, baking soda and salt; add to the creamed mixture. Stir in cracker crumbs and ground pecans; mix well.

2. Drop by rounded teaspoonfuls 2 in. apart onto ungreased baking sheets. Place a pecan half in the center of each cookie; press down lightly.

3. Bake at 350° for 9-11 minutes or until lightly browned. Cool for 2 minutes before removing to wire racks.

Chewy Maple Cookies

My husband, Bob, and I have a small sugaring operation with his father. I put some of our syrup to use in these cookies.

—REBA LEGRAND JERICHO, VT

PREP: 20 MIN. • **BAKE:** 15 MIN./BATCH + COOLING
MAKES: 3 DOZEN

½ **cup shortening**
1 **cup packed brown sugar**
1 **egg**
½ **cup maple syrup**
½ **teaspoon vanilla extract or maple flavoring**

1½ **cups all-purpose flour**
2 **teaspoons baking powder**
½ **teaspoon salt**
1 **cup flaked coconut**

1. In a bowl, cream shortening and brown sugar until fluffy. Beat in the egg, syrup and vanilla until well mixed. Combine flour, baking powder and salt; add to the creamed mixture. Stir in coconut.
2. Drop by tablespoonfuls 2 in. apart onto greased baking sheets. Bake at 375° for 12-15 minutes or until edges are lightly browned.

Mom's Buttermilk Cookies

The recipe for these comforting "cookie pillows" originated with my mother. The tender treats are jazzed up with thick frosting and a sprinkling of chopped walnuts.

—JANE DARLING SIMI VALLEY, CA

PREP: 15 MIN. • **BAKE:** 10 MIN./BATCH + COOLING
MAKES: 3 DOZEN

- ½ **cup butter, softened**
- 1 **cup sugar**
- 1 **egg**
- 1 **teaspoon vanilla extract**
- 2½ **cups all-purpose flour**
- ½ **teaspoon baking soda**
- ½ **teaspoon salt**
- ½ **cup buttermilk**

FROSTING
- 3 **tablespoons butter, softened**
- 3½ **cups confectioners' sugar**
- ¼ **cup whole milk**
- 1 **teaspoon vanilla extract**
- ½ **cup finely chopped walnuts, optional**

1. In a large bowl, cream butter and sugar until light and fluffy. Beat in egg and vanilla. Combine the flour, baking soda and salt; add to the creamed mixture alternately with buttermilk, beating well after each addition.

2. Drop by rounded tablespoonfuls 2 in. apart onto greased baking sheets. Bake at 375° for 10-12 minutes or until edges are lightly browned. Remove to wire racks .

3. For frosting, combine butter, confectioners' sugar, milk and vanilla in a bowl; beat until smooth. Frost the cookies; sprinkle with chopped walnuts if desired.

Cherry Oatmeal Cookies

Although this recipe calls for cherry chips, I also like to make these old-fashioned treats with raspberry chips. The cookies stack nicely for packing.

—BETTY HUDDLESTON LIBERTY, IN

PREP: 25 MIN. • **BAKE:** 15 MIN./BATCH • **MAKES:** ABOUT 4 DOZEN

- 1 cup butter, softened
- 1 cup packed brown sugar
- ½ cup sugar
- 2 eggs
- 1 teaspoon vanilla extract
- 3 cups old-fashioned oats
- 1½ cups all-purpose flour
- 1 teaspoon baking soda
- 1 teaspoon ground cinnamon
- ½ teaspoon salt
- 1 package (10 ounces) cherry chips
- ½ cup chopped walnuts

1. In a large bowl, cream butter and sugars until light and fluffy. Beat in eggs and vanilla. Combine the oats, flour, baking soda, cinnamon and salt; gradually add to creamed mixture and mix well. Stir in chips and walnuts.

2. Drop by tablespoonfuls 3 in. apart onto ungreased baking sheets. Bake at 350° for 11-13 minutes or until lightly browned. Cool for 2 minutes before removing to wire racks.

Toasted Coconut Cookies

Coconut, walnuts and oats make my cookies a satisfying snack no matter what time of day. They're a hit with everyone who tries them.

—CINDY COLLEY OTHELLO, WA

PREP: 15 MIN. • **BAKE:** 10 MIN./BATCH • **MAKES:** ABOUT 5 DOZEN

- ½ cup butter, softened
- ½ cup shortening
- ¾ cup sugar
- ¾ cup packed brown sugar
- 2 eggs
- 2 teaspoons vanilla extract
- 2 cups all-purpose flour
- 1 teaspoon baking powder
- 1 teaspoon baking soda
- ¾ teaspoon salt
- 1½ cups quick-cooking oats
- 1½ cups flaked coconut, toasted
- ¾ cup chopped walnuts, toasted

1. In a bowl, cream butter, shortening and sugars until fluffy. Add eggs and vanilla; beat well. Combine flour, baking powder, baking soda and salt; gradually add to creamed mixture. Fold in oats, coconut and nuts.

2. Drop by tablespoonfuls onto greased baking sheets. Bake at 375° for 10-11 minutes or until golden brown. Cool 2-3 minutes before removing to a wire rack.

Chocolate Meringues

Here are cookies that are great for fancy occasions but easy enough to make as a snack. My grandma was an avid baker, known in her neighborhood as the "cookie lady." With 18 nieces and nephews, I'm carrying on her tradition.

—NANCY GRACE SAN DIEGO, CA

START TO FINISH: 30 MIN. • **MAKES:** ABOUT 2½ DOZEN

- 2 egg whites
- ¼ teaspoon cream of tartar
- ⅛ teaspoon salt
- ½ cup sugar
- ½ teaspoon white vinegar
- ½ teaspoon vanilla or almond extract
- 1 cup (6 ounces) semisweet chocolate chips
- ½ cup flaked coconut
- ¼ cup chopped almonds

1. In a large bowl, beat the egg whites, cream of tartar and salt until soft peaks form. Add sugar, 1 tablespoon at a time, beating until stiff peaks form, about 5 minutes. Beat in vinegar and vanilla.

2. Meanwhile, in a microwave, melt chocolate chips; stir until smooth. Fold into egg white mixture; fold in coconut and almonds.

3. Drop by tablespoonfuls 2 in. apart onto lightly greased baking sheets. Bake at 350° for 10-11 minutes or until firm. Remove to wire racks to cool. Store in an airtight container.

Crunchy Macaroons

These chewy little cookies have wonderful coconut and almond flavor. And with only five ingredients, they're easy to whip up.

—TASTE OF HOME TEST KITCHEN

PREP: 15 MIN. • **BAKE:** 20 MIN. • **MAKES:** 2 DOZEN

- 1½ cups crisp rice cereal
- 1¼ cups flaked coconut
- 2 egg whites
- 3 tablespoons sugar
- ⅛ teaspoon almond extract

1. In a small bowl, combine all ingredients. With damp fingers, shape into 1½-in. mounds on parchment paper-lined baking sheets.
2. Bake at 300° for 20-25 minutes or just until edges turn brown. Remove to wire racks to cool.

Fudgy No-Bake Cookies

This recipe can be changed to suit your sweet tooth. Try adding almond or mint extract.

—BETH BROWN NAPLES, FL

START TO FINISH: 15 MIN. • **MAKES:** 1 DOZEN

- 1 cup sugar
- 2 tablespoons baking cocoa
- ¼ cup butter, cubed
- ¼ cup milk
- 1 cup quick-cooking oats
- ¼ cup flaked coconut
- 2 tablespoons peanut butter
- ½ teaspoon vanilla extract

1. In a large saucepan, combine sugar and cocoa; add butter and milk. Cook and stir over medium heat until mixture comes to a boil; boil for 1 minute. Remove from the heat; stir in oats, coconut, peanut butter and vanilla.
2. Let stand until the mixture mounds when dropped by tablespoonfuls onto waxed paper. Cool until set.

Apple Peanut Butter Cookies

My spiced peanut butter cookies are great for fall gatherings. They're crisp on the outside and soft inside.

—MARJORIE BENSON NEW CASTLE, PA

PREP: 20 MIN. • **BAKE:** 10 MIN./BATCH • **MAKES:** ABOUT 2½ DOZEN

- ½ cup shortening
- ½ cup chunky peanut butter
- ½ cup sugar
- ½ cup packed brown sugar
- 1 egg
- ½ teaspoon vanilla extract
- 1½ cups all-purpose flour
- ½ teaspoon baking soda
- ½ teaspoon salt
- ½ teaspoon ground cinnamon
- ½ cup grated peeled apple

1. In a large bowl, cream the shortening, peanut butter and sugars until light and fluffy. Beat in egg and vanilla. Combine the dry ingredients; gradually add to creamed mixture and mix well. Stir in apple.
2. Drop by rounded tablespoonfuls 2 in. apart onto greased baking sheets. Bake at 375° for 10-12 minutes or until golden brown. Cool for 5 minutes before removing to wire racks.
NOTE *Reduced-fat peanut butter is not recommended for this recipe.*

Cute Pig Cookies

I created this recipe for a party my friend had for National Pig Day, which is March 1. The little piggies were a hit there, and they were popular at my son's school parties, too.

—BECKY BALDWIN ANNVILLE, PA

PREP: 35 MIN. • **BAKE:** 10 MIN./BATCH + COOLING
MAKES: 6 DOZEN

- 1 **cup butter, softened**
- 1½ **cups sugar**
- 2 **eggs**
- 1 **cup (8 ounces) sour cream**
- 1 **teaspoon vanilla extract**
- 3 **cups all-purpose flour**
- 1 **teaspoon baking powder**
- ½ **teaspoon salt**

FROSTING/DECORATING

- 4 **cups confectioners' sugar**
- ½ **cup butter, melted**
- 6 **tablespoons milk**
- 2 **teaspoons vanilla extract**
- 3 **to 4 drops red food coloring**
  Pink sugar wafer cookies
- 36 **large marshmallows, halved**
  Butterscotch chips and miniature semisweet chocolate chips

1. In a large bowl, cream butter and sugar until light and fluffy. Beat in the eggs, sour cream and vanilla. Combine the dry ingredients; gradually add to creamed mixture and mix well.

2. Drop by tablespoonfuls onto ungreased baking sheets. Bake at 375° for 10-12 minutes or until the edges are lightly browned. Remove from the pans to wire racks to cool completely.

3. For frosting, in a large bowl, combine the confectioners' sugar, butter, milk, vanilla and food coloring. Frost cookies.

4. Cut sugar wafers into triangles; place two on each cookie for ears. With a toothpick, poke two holes in each marshmallow half for nostrils; press butterscotch chips into holes. Place noses on cookies; add chocolate chip eyes.

Apple Butter Cookies

My mother used to bake these mouthwatering cookies for an after-school treat. Though it's been many years since I first had them, I still savor the aroma that fills the house as these cookies bake. They stay moist and fresh for a long time. You also can store the dough in the refrigerator for a few days so you can bake as you need them.

—DOROTHY HAWKINS SPRINGHILL, FL

PREP: 20 MIN. + CHILLING • **BAKE:** 15 MIN.
MAKES: ABOUT 2½ DOZEN

- ¼ cup butter, softened
- 1 cup packed brown sugar
- 1 egg
- ½ cup quick-cooking oats
- ½ cup apple butter
- 1 cup all-purpose flour
- ½ teaspoon baking soda
- ½ teaspoon baking powder
- ½ teaspoon salt
- 2 tablespoons milk
- ½ cup chopped nuts
- ½ cup raisins

1. In a small bowl, cream butter and sugar. Beat in egg, oats and apple butter. Combine dry ingredients; gradually add to creamed mixture along with the milk; beat until blended. Stir in nuts and raisins. Cover and refrigerate until easy to handle.

2. Drop by teaspoonfuls onto lightly greased baking sheets. Bake at 350° for 15 minutes or until set. Remove to wire racks.

Chocolate Mint Dreams

Since chocolate-mint is my favorite flavor combination, I find these dainty shortbread-like treats hard to resist. But I manage to save some for guests because they make my cookie trays look so elegant.

—ANNE REVERS OMAHA, NE

PREP: 30 MIN. • **BAKE:** 10 MIN./BATCH + COOLING
MAKES: 4 DOZEN

- ¾ cup butter, softened
- ½ cup confectioners' sugar
- 2 ounces unsweetened chocolate, melted and cooled
- ¼ teaspoon peppermint extract
- 1½ cups all-purpose flour
- 1 cup miniature semisweet chocolate chips

ICING
- 2 tablespoons butter, softened
- 1 cup confectioners' sugar
- ¼ teaspoon peppermint extract
- 1 to 2 drops green food coloring
- 1 to 2 tablespoons milk

DRIZZLE
- ½ cup semisweet chocolate chips
- ½ teaspoon shortening

1. In a large bowl, cream butter and confectioners' sugar until light and fluffy. Beat in the chocolate and extract. Gradually add flour and mix well. Stir in chocolate chips. (Dough will be soft.)

2. Drop dough by tablespoonfuls 2 in. apart on ungreased baking sheets. Bake at 375° for 6-8 minutes or until cookies are firm. Cool for 2 minutes before removing to wire racks to cool completely.

3. Meanwhile, combine the butter, confectioners' sugar, extract, food coloring and enough milk to achieve desired consistency; spread over cooled cookies. Let set. In a microwave, melt chocolate chips and shortening; stir until smooth. Drizzle over cookies.

Cranberry Oat Cookies

You'll delight everyone with these goodies. My tasty cookies are crunchy on the outside, chewy on the inside, and dotted with dried cranberries.

—HEATHER BREEN CHICAGO, IL

PREP: 15 MIN. • **BAKE:** 10 MIN./BATCH • **MAKES:** 2½ DOZEN

- ½ cup plus 2 tablespoons packed brown sugar
- ¼ cup sugar
- ⅓ cup canola oil
- 1 egg
- 1 tablespoon fat-free milk
- ¾ teaspoon vanilla extract
- 1¼ cups quick-cooking oats
- ¾ cup plus 2 tablespoons all-purpose flour
- ½ teaspoon baking soda
- ½ teaspoon salt
- ½ cup dried cranberries

1. In a large bowl, combine sugars and oil until blended. Beat in egg, milk and vanilla. Combine the oats, flour, baking soda and salt; gradually add to sugar mixture and mix well. Stir in cranberries.
2. Drop by tablespoonfuls onto baking sheets coated with cooking spray. Bake at 375° for 10-12 minutes or until lightly browned. Remove to wire racks.

Fudge-Topped Orange Cookies

Cookies and fudge are two classic sweets around the holidays, so I decided to combine them. The chocolate marshmallow topping works well on a variety of cookies.

—LISA EVANS RILEYVILLE, VA

PREP: 15 MIN. • **BAKE:** 20 MIN. + COOLING • **MAKES:** 2 DOZEN

- ¾ cup butter, softened
- 1 cup sugar
- 1 egg
- 2 egg yolks
- 2 teaspoons grated orange peel
- 1½ teaspoons orange extract
- 2 cups all-purpose flour
- 1 teaspoon ground ginger
- ½ teaspoon baking soda

TOPPING
- 1 jar (7 ounces) marshmallow creme
- ¾ cup sugar
- ⅓ cup evaporated milk
- 2 tablespoons butter
- ⅛ teaspoon salt
- 1 cup (6 ounces) semisweet chocolate chips
- ½ teaspoon vanilla extract

1. In a large bowl, cream butter and sugar until light and fluffy. Beat in the egg, egg yolks, orange peel and extract. Combine the flour, ginger and baking soda; gradually add to creamed mixture and mix well.
2. Drop by rounded tablespoonfuls 2 in. apart onto ungreased baking sheets. Bake at 300° for 20-22 minutes or until golden brown. Remove to wire racks to cool.
3. In a large saucepan, combine the marshmallow creme, sugar, milk, butter and salt. Bring to a rolling boil over medium heat; boil for 5 minutes, stirring constantly. Remove from the heat. Add chocolate chips and vanilla; stir until chips are melted. Spread over tops of cookies.

Cheery Cherry Cookies

With a tall glass of ice-cold milk, a couple of my cherry cookies will really hit the spot for dessert or as a snack. The coconut and bits of cherry provide a fun look and texture.

—**JUDY CLARK** ELKHART, IN

PREP: 10 MIN. • **BAKE:** 10 MIN./BATCH • **MAKES:** 4 DOZEN

- 1 **cup packed brown sugar**
- ¾ **cup butter, softened**
- 1 **egg**
- 2 **tablespoons 2% milk**
- 1 **teaspoon vanilla extract**
- 2 **cups all-purpose flour**
- ½ **teaspoon salt**
- ½ **teaspoon baking soda**
- ½ **cup maraschino cherries, well drained and chopped**
- ½ **cup flaked coconut**
- ½ **cup chopped pecans**

1. In a large bowl, cream brown sugar and butter until light and fluffy. Beat in the egg, milk and vanilla. In another bowl, combine the flour, salt and baking soda; gradually beat into creamed mixture. Stir in the cherries, coconut and pecans.

2. Drop by teaspoonfuls onto ungreased baking sheets. Bake at 375° for 10-12 minutes or until golden brown. Remove from pans to wire racks to cool.

Butter Meltaways

Add variety to this recipe by substituting lemon flavoring for the vanilla, plus a teaspoon of lemon peel.

—SUE CALL BEECH GROVE, IN

PREP: 15 MIN. • **BAKE:** 15 MIN./BATCH + COOLING
MAKES: ABOUT 4 DOZEN

- ½ cup butter, softened
- ½ cup canola oil
- ½ cup sugar
- ½ cup confectioners' sugar
- 1 egg
- ½ teaspoon vanilla extract
- 2¼ cups all-purpose flour
- ½ teaspoon baking soda
- ½ teaspoon cream of tartar
- Additional sugar

1. In a bowl, cream butter, oil and sugars. Add egg and vanilla. Combine flour, baking soda and cream of tartar; gradually add to the creamed mixture. Chill for several hours or overnight.

2. Preheat oven to 350°. Drop by rounded teaspoonfuls 2 in. apart onto ungreased baking sheets. Flatten with a fork dipped in flour; sprinkle with sugar. Bake 13-15 minutes or until lightly browned. Cool on wire racks.

Chewy Chocolate Chip Cookies

Everyone who has tried these cookies says they're the best they've ever eaten. I'm sure the addition of pudding mix makes all the difference.

—IONA HAMILTON ROCKY FORD, CO

PREP: 15 MIN. • **BAKE:** 10 MIN./BATCH • **MAKES:** 9½ DOZEN

- 1 cup butter, softened
- ¾ cup packed brown sugar
- ¼ cup sugar
- 2 eggs
- 1 package (3.4 ounces) instant vanilla pudding mix
- 1 teaspoon vanilla extract
- 2¼ cups all-purpose flour
- 1 teaspoon baking soda
- 2 cups (12 ounces) semisweet chocolate chips
- 1 cup finely chopped walnuts

1. In a large bowl, cream butter and sugar, until light and fluffy. Add the eggs, one at a time, beating well after each addition. Beat in pudding mix and vanilla. Combine the flour and baking soda; gradually add to creamed mixture and mix well. Stir in chocolate chips and walnuts (dough will be stiff).

2. Drop dough by rounded teaspoonfuls 2 in. apart onto ungreased baking sheets. Bake at 350° for 8-10 minutes or until lightly browned. Remove to wire racks to cool.

Macadamia Almond Delights

A few years ago, I decided to liven up my basic chocolate chip cookie recipe by adding macadamia nuts, white chocolate chips and almond paste. Since the scrumptious results got such raves from my 26 grandchildren, we've designated this version a keeper.

—ETHEL MARSHALL SALEM, OR

PREP: 15 MIN. • **BAKE:** 15 MIN./BATCH • **MAKES:** 4 DOZEN

- ⅔ cup butter, softened
- ⅔ cup shortening
- 1 cup sugar
- 1 cup packed brown sugar
- 2 eggs
- 2 teaspoons vanilla extract
- 1 cup almond paste
- 3 cups plus 3 tablespoons all-purpose flour
- 1 teaspoon baking soda
- 1 teaspoon salt
- 1½ cups macadamia nuts, chopped
- 1 package (10 to 12 ounces) white baking chips

1. In a large bowl, cream the butter, shortening and sugars until light and fluffy. Add eggs, one at a time, beating well after each addition. Beat in vanilla and almond paste. Combine the flour, baking soda and salt; gradually add to the creamed mixture and mix well. Stir in nuts and chips.

2. Drop by heaping tablespoonfuls 2 in. apart onto ungreased baking sheets. Bake at 350° for 12-15 minutes or until lightly browned. Remove to wire racks to cool.

1. In a large bowl, cream shortening and sugars until light and fluffy. Beat in eggs and vanilla. Combine the oats, flour, baking soda and salt; gradually add to creamed mixture and mix well. Stir in walnuts and raisins.

2. Drop by tablespoonfuls 2 in. apart onto ungreased baking sheets. Bake at 375° for 10-12 minutes or until golden brown. Remove to wire racks to cool.

Rhubarb Cranberry Cookies

I like the sudden hit of sweetness when you bite into the white chocolate. It really complements the tart flavor from the rhubarb and cranberries.

—**ELAINE SCOTT** LAFAYETTE, IN

PREP: 30 MIN. • **BAKE:** 10 MIN./BATCH + COOLING
MAKES: ABOUT 5½ DOZEN

- 1 cup butter, softened
- 1 cup packed brown sugar
- ½ cup sugar
- 2 eggs
- 1 teaspoon vanilla extract
- 1½ cups all-purpose flour
- 1 teaspoon baking soda
- ½ teaspoon salt
- ½ teaspoon ground cinnamon
- 2½ cups old-fashioned oats
- 1½ cups diced frozen rhubarb
- 1 cup white baking chips
- 1 cup dried cranberries
- 4 ounces white baking chocolate, chopped

1. In a large bowl, cream the butter and sugars until light and fluffy. Beat in eggs and vanilla. Combine the flour, baking soda, salt and cinnamon; gradually add to creamed mixture and mix well. Stir in the oats, rhubarb, chips and cranberries.

2. Drop by tablespoonfuls 2 in. apart onto parchment paper-lined baking sheets. Bake at 350° for 10-12 minutes or until set. Remove to wire racks to cool.

3. In a microwave, melt the white chocolate; stir until smooth. Drizzle over the cookies; let stand until set. Store in an airtight container.

Oatmeal Raisin Cookies

A friend gave me this recipe many years ago, and it's since become a family favorite.

—**GERALDINE LARKIN** SAN ANTONIO, TX

PREP: 20 MIN. • **BAKE:** 10 MIN./BATCH + COOLING
MAKES: 5 DOZEN

- 1 cup shortening
- 1 cup sugar
- 1 cup packed brown sugar
- 2 eggs
- 1 teaspoon vanilla extract
- 3 cups old-fashioned oats
- 1½ cups all-purpose flour
- 1 teaspoon baking soda
- 1 teaspoon salt
- ½ cup chopped walnuts
- ½ cup golden raisins

Double Chocolate Cookies

When I make these yummy treats with my young grandson, Ben, I use an extra-big mixing bowl to prevent the flour and other ingredients from flying all over. He seems to enjoy making the cookies almost as much as eating them.

—CHANTAL CORNWALL PRINCE RUPERT, BC

PREP: 15 MIN. • **BAKE:** 10 MIN./BATCH • **MAKES:** ABOUT 9 DOZEN

- 1¼ **cups butter, softened**
- 2 **cups sugar**
- 2 **eggs**
- 2 **teaspoons vanilla extract**
- 2 **cups all-purpose flour**
- ¾ **cup baking cocoa**
- 1 **teaspoon baking soda**
- ½ **teaspoon salt**
- 2 **cups (12 ounces) semisweet chocolate chips**

1. In a large bowl, cream butter and sugar until light and fluffy. Beat in eggs and vanilla. Combine the flour, cocoa, baking soda and salt; gradually add to creamed mixture and mix well. Stir in chocolate chips.

2. Drop by rounded teaspoonfuls 2 in. apart onto greased baking sheets. Bake at 350° for 8-10 minutes or until the cookies are set. Cool for 2 minutes before removing from pans to wire racks.

Giant Cherry Oatmeal Cookies

These colossal cookies bake up golden around the edges and moist and chewy in the center. I serve them with a glass of milk, and my grandchildren polish them off in no time.

—IRENE MCDADE CUMBERLAND, RI

PREP: 15 MIN. • **BAKE:** 10 MIN./BATCH + COOLING
MAKES: 1 DOZEN

- ½ cup shortening
- ½ cup butter, softened
- ¾ cup packed brown sugar
- ½ cup sugar
- 2 eggs
- 1 teaspoon vanilla extract
- 2½ cups old-fashioned oats
- 1⅓ cups all-purpose flour
- 2 teaspoons apple pie spice
- ½ teaspoon baking powder
- ¼ teaspoon baking soda
- ¼ teaspoon salt
- 1½ cups dried cherries, chopped
- ½ to 1 teaspoon grated orange peel

1. In a large bowl, cream shortening, butter and sugars. Beat in the eggs and vanilla. Combine the oats, flour, apple pie spice, baking powder, baking soda and salt; gradually add to creamed mixture. Stir in cherries and orange peel.
2. Drop by ⅓ cupfuls onto an ungreased baking sheet. Press to form a 4-in. circle. Bake at 375° for 9-12 minutes or until golden brown. Let stand for 1 minute before removing to wire racks to cool.

No-Bake Fudgy Oat Cookies

I got this recipe from my mother-in-law back in 1949. My grown daughter asked me to share it with her so she could make the cookies for Christmas.

—**ELIZABETH HUNTER** PROSPERITY, SC

START TO FINISH: 15 MIN. • **MAKES:** ABOUT 3 DOZEN

- 2¼ cups quick-cooking oats
- 1 cup flaked coconut
- ½ cup 2% milk
- ¼ cup butter, cubed
- 2 cups sugar
- ½ cup baking cocoa
- 1 teaspoon vanilla extract

1. In a large bowl, combine oats and coconut; set aside. In a large saucepan, combine milk and butter. Stir in sugar and cocoa. Bring to a boil. Add the oat mixture; cook for 1 minute, stirring constantly. Remove from the heat; stir in the vanilla.
2. Drop by rounded tablespoonfuls 1 in. apart onto waxed paper. Let stand until set.

Peach Oat Cookies

I modified a recipe to create soft and chewy cookies that are better for you. There's not too much sugar in them, but lots of oats and fruit.

—**RACHEL GREENAWALT KELLER** ROANOKE, VA

PREP: 20 MIN. • **BAKE:** 10 MIN./BATCH + COOLING
MAKES: 5 DOZEN

- ⅓ cup butter, softened
- ½ cup sugar
- ½ cup packed brown sugar
- 2 eggs
- 1½ teaspoons vanilla extract
- ½ cup each all-purpose flour, whole wheat flour and oat flour
- 2 teaspoons baking powder
- 1 teaspoon salt
- 2½ cups quick-cooking oats
- ½ cup oat bran
- 1½ cups drained canned sliced peaches in extra-light syrup, chopped
- 1 cup raisins

1. In a large bowl, cream butter and sugars until light and fluffy. Add eggs, one at a time, beating well after each addition. Beat in vanilla. Combine the flours, baking powder and salt; gradually add to creamed mixture and mix well. Stir in oats and oat bran just until combined. Stir in peaches and raisins.
2. Drop by rounded tablespoonfuls onto baking sheets coated with cooking spray. Bake at 350° for 9-13 minutes or until the edges are lightly browned. Remove to a wire rack to cool.
NOTE *As a substitute for 1 cup oat flour, process 1¼ cups quick-cooking or old-fashioned oats until finely ground.*

Maple Raisin Oatmeal Cookies

My five children love maple and brown sugar oatmeal, so I decided to add those ingredients to my oatmeal cookies. The first time I made them, they vanished before I knew it!

—**KAREN NIENABER** ERSKINE, MN

PREP: 15 MIN. • **BAKE:** 10 MIN./BATCH + COOLING
MAKES: 6 DOZEN

- 1 cup butter, softened
- 1 cup packed brown sugar
- ½ cup sugar
- 2 eggs
- 1 teaspoon maple flavoring
- 1½ cups all-purpose flour
- 1 teaspoon baking soda
- 1 teaspoon ground cinnamon
- ½ teaspoon salt
- 3 cups quick-cooking oats
- 1 cup raisins

1. In a bowl, cream the butter and sugars. Add eggs, one at a time, beating well after each addition. Beat in maple flavoring. Combine flour, baking soda, cinnamon and salt; gradually add to creamed mixture. Stir in oats and raisins.
2. Drop by rounded teaspoonfuls 2 in. apart onto ungreased baking sheets. Bake at 350° for 10-12 minutes or until golden brown. Remove to wire racks to cool.

Molasses Raisin Cookies

These old-fashioned, mildly sweet cookies are dotted with walnuts and raisins. We like them soft right from the oven. When they crisp up later, they are perfect for dunking.

—**DENISE AND GEORGE HYMEL** GRAMERCY, LA

PREP: 15 MIN. • **BAKE:** 10 MIN./BATCH • **MAKES:** ABOUT 3½ DOZEN

- ¾ cup shortening
- 1 cup packed brown sugar
- ¼ cup molasses
- 2 eggs
- 2¼ cups all-purpose flour
- 1 teaspoon baking soda
- 1 teaspoon ground ginger
- 1 teaspoon ground cinnamon
- ½ teaspoon salt
- ½ teaspoon ground cloves
- ½ cup raisins
- ½ cup chopped walnuts

1. In a large bowl, cream shortening and brown sugar. Beat in molasses. Add eggs, one at a time, beating well after each addition. Combine the flour, baking soda, ginger, cinnamon, salt and cloves; gradually add to creamed mixture. Stir in raisins and nuts.

2. Drop by rounded tablespoonfuls 2 in. apart onto greased baking sheets. Bake at 375° for 8-10 minutes or until the edges are lightly browned. Remove to wire racks to cool.

Cranberry Chip Cookies

I received these delightful cookies for Christmas a few years ago. I was watching my diet, but I couldn't stay away from them! The tart cranberries blend beautifully with the sweet chocolate and white baking chips.

—**JO ANN MCCARTHY** CANTON, MA

PREP: 10 MIN. • **BAKE:** 10 MIN./BATCH • **MAKES:** 6 DOZEN

- ½ cup butter, softened
- ½ cup shortening
- ¾ cup sugar
- ¾ cup packed brown sugar
- 2 eggs
- 1 teaspoon vanilla extract
- 2¼ cups all-purpose flour
- 1 teaspoon baking soda
- ½ teaspoon salt
- 1 cup semisweet chocolate chips
- 1 cup white baking chips
- 1 cup dried cranberries
- 1 cup chopped pecans

1. Preheat oven to 375°. In a large bowl, cream butter, shortening and sugars until light and fluffy. Add eggs, one at a time, beating well after each addition. Beat in vanilla. Combine the flour, baking soda and salt; gradually add to the creamed mixture and mix well. Stir in the chips, cranberries and pecans.

2. Drop the dough by tablespoonfuls 2 in. apart onto ungreased baking sheets. Bake 9-11 minutes or until golden brown. Cool 2 minutes before removing to wire racks to cool completely.

Bakeshop **TIP**

Creaming Butter

To cream butter, it should be soft enough that a table knife will glide through it. The easiest way to soften butter is to let it stand at room temperature. When warming in the microwave, take care not to melt the butter. Melted butter will not cream properly and will adversely affect baking.

Ginger Drop Cookies

My mother shared the recipe for these soft spice cookies.

—**BETHEL WALTERS** WILLOW RIVER, MN

PREP: 15 MIN. + CHILLING • **BAKE:** 10 MIN./BATCH
MAKES: ABOUT 5½ DOZEN

- 1 **cup shortening**
- 1 **cup packed brown sugar**
- 1 **cup molasses**
- 2 **eggs**
- 4 **cups all-purpose flour**
- 2 **teaspoons baking soda**
- 2 **teaspoons ground cinnamon**
- 2 **teaspoons ground ginger**
- 1 **teaspoon salt**
- ½ **cup water**

1. In a large bowl, cream shortening and brown sugar until light and fluffy. Beat in molasses and eggs. Combine the dry ingredients; add to the creamed mixture alternately with water. Refrigerate for at least 8 hours.

2. Drop dough by tablespoonfuls 2 in. apart onto greased baking sheets. Bake at 350° for 10-12 minutes or until lightly browned. Remove to wire racks to cool.

Chocolate Maple Cookies

My aunt made these one year for Christmas, and my husband devoured them. Since he liked them so much, I asked for the recipe and have made them often since.
—**SHEREE GILPIN** LEHIGHTON, PA

PREP: 15 MIN. • **BAKE:** 10 MIN./BATCH + COOLING
MAKES: 4 DOZEN

- 1¼ **cups shortening**
- 1½ **cups packed brown sugar**
- 5 **eggs**
- 1 **teaspoon vanilla extract**
- ½ **teaspoon maple flavoring**
- 2½ **cups all-purpose flour**
- ¾ **teaspoon baking soda**
- ½ **teaspoon salt**

FROSTING
- 2 **ounces semisweet chocolate**
- 1 **tablespoon butter**
- 1½ **cups confectioners' sugar**
- ¼ **cup milk**

1. In a large bowl, cream shortening and brown sugar until light and fluffy. Add eggs, one at a time, beating well after each addition. Beat in vanilla and maple flavoring. Combine the flour, baking soda and salt; gradually add to the creamed mixture and mix well.

2. Drop by teaspoonfuls 2 in. apart onto greased baking sheets. Bake at 350° for 8-10 minutes or until edges begin to brown. Remove to wire racks to cool.

3. For frosting, in a microwave, melt chocolate and butter; stir until smooth. Stir in confectioners' sugar and milk until smooth. Spread over cooled cookies.

Frosted Orange Cookies

I remember my dad making a big batch of these tender citrus cookies when I was growing up.
—**TAMMIE YOUNG** MATTOON, IL

PREP: 30 MIN. • **BAKE:** 10 MIN./BATCH + COOLING
MAKES: ABOUT 4 DOZEN

- 2 **medium navel oranges**
- ½ **cup butter-flavored shortening**
- 1 **cup sugar**
- ½ **cup milk**
- 2 **cups all-purpose flour**
- 1 **teaspoon baking powder**
- ½ **teaspoon baking soda**
- ½ **teaspoon salt**
- 2½ **cups confectioners' sugar**
- 1 **tablespoon butter, melted**

1. With a sharp knife, score each orange into quarters; remove peel. Use knife to remove white pith from peel and fruit; discard. Quarter oranges and place in a blender. Add peel; cover and process until smooth (mixture should measure ¾ cup).

2. In a large bowl, cream shortening and sugar until light and fluffy. Beat in milk and 6 tablespoons orange mixture. Combine the flour, baking powder, baking soda and salt; gradually add to creamed mixture until blended.

3. Drop dough by rounded teaspoonfuls 2 in. apart onto greased baking sheets. Bake at 350° for 10-13 minutes or until set and edges are lightly browned. Remove to wire racks to cool.

4. For frosting, in a small bowl, combine confectioners' sugar, butter and enough of the remaining orange mixture to achieve spreading consistency. Frost cookies.

Chocolate Waffle Cookies

I've had this recipe for years. It's economical to make, yet results in a delicious cookie.

—PAT OVIATT ZIMMERMAN, MN

START TO FINISH: 15 MIN. • **MAKES:** ABOUT 1½ DOZEN

- ¼ cup butter, softened
- 6 tablespoons sugar
- 1 egg
- ½ teaspoon vanilla extract
- 1 ounce unsweetened chocolate, melted
- ½ cup all-purpose flour
  Confectioners' sugar

1. In a large bowl, cream butter and sugar until light and fluffy. Beat in egg and vanilla. Beat in chocolate. Gradually add flour and mix well.

2. Drop by rounded teaspoonfuls 1 in. apart onto a preheated waffle iron. Bake for 1 minute. Remove to wire racks to cool. Dust with confectioners' sugar.

Prune-Pecan Cookies

Tuck some extra nutrition into these crisp, lightly sweet cookies by adding pureed dried plums.

—LUCILLE DENT GALESBURG, MI

PREP: 10 MIN. • **BAKE:** 15 MIN./BATCH • **MAKES:** 2 DOZEN

- 1 egg
- 7 pitted dried plums
- ½ cup sugar
- 1 cup all-purpose flour
- ½ teaspoon baking soda
  Pinch salt
- 24 pecan halves

1. In a blender, puree eggs and plums until finely chopped. Pour into a bowl. Add sugar. Combine the flour, baking soda and salt; add to plum mixture and mix well.

2. Drop by rounded teaspoonfuls onto greased baking sheets. Top each with a pecan half. Bake at 350° for 13-15 minutes or until golden brown. Remove to wire racks.

Chewy Ginger Drop Cookies

This recipe originated with my grandmother and my mom. I, too, baked them for my family, then my daughters made them. Now my granddaughters are making them—a true legacy I'm happy to share.

—LOIS FURCRON COUDERSPORT, PA

PREP: 10 MIN. • **BAKE:** 15 MIN./BATCH • **MAKES:** ABOUT 2½ DOZEN

- ½ cup shortening
- ½ cup sugar
- 2 cups all-purpose flour
- ½ teaspoon baking soda
- ½ teaspoon ground ginger
- ¼ teaspoon salt
- ½ cup molasses
- ¼ cup water
  Additional sugar

1. In a bowl, cream shortening and sugar. Combine flour, baking soda, ginger and salt. Combine molasses and water. Add dry ingredients to the creamed mixture alternately with molasses mixture.

2. Drop by rounded teaspoonfuls 2 in. apart onto greased baking sheets. Sprinkle with sugar. Bake at 350° for 13-15 minutes or until edges are set. Remove to wire racks.

Honey Lemon Cookies

Grated lemon peel in the batter and sprinkled over the icing of these soft cakelike cookies gives them a tart, fresh citrus flavor you'll enjoy.

—BETTY THOMPSON LA PORTE, TX

PREP: 15 MIN. • **BAKE:** 10 MIN./BATCH • **MAKES:** ABOUT 3 DOZEN

- 7 **tablespoons butter, softened**
- ½ **cup sugar**
- 1 **egg**
- 1¾ **cups all-purpose flour**
- 1 **teaspoon baking powder**
- ½ **teaspoon salt**
- ⅓ **cup honey**
- ¼ **cup plain yogurt**
- 2 **teaspoons grated lemon peel**
- ½ **teaspoon lemon extract**

ICING
- 1 **cup confectioners' sugar**
- 2 **tablespoons lemon juice**
- 2 **teaspoons grated lemon peel**

1. In a small bowl, cream butter and sugar until light and fluffy. Beat in egg. Combine the flour, baking powder and salt. Combine honey, yogurt, lemon peel and lemon extract. Add dry ingredients to creamed mixture alternately with honey mixture, mixing well after each addition.

2. Drop by tablespoonfuls 2 in. apart onto greased baking sheets. Bake at 350° for 10-12 minutes or until golden brown. Remove to wire racks.

3. In a small bowl, combine the confectioners' sugar and lemon juice until smooth. Brush over the warm cookies; sprinkle with lemon peel.

Timeless Slice & Bake

Icebox Honey Cookies

My Grandma Wruble always had a batch of these cookies in the cookie jar and another roll in the refrigerator ready to slice and bake. Their honey and lemon flavor is delicious!
—**KRISTI GLEASON** FLOWER MOUND, TX

PREP: 20 MIN. + CHILLING • **BAKE:** 15 MIN./BATCH
MAKES: 8 DOZEN

- 1½ cups shortening
- 2 cups packed brown sugar
- 2 eggs
- ½ cup honey
- 1 teaspoon lemon extract
- 4½ cups all-purpose flour
- 2 teaspoons baking soda
- 2 teaspoons baking powder
- 1 teaspoon salt
- 1 teaspoon ground cinnamon

1. In a large bowl, cream shortening and brown sugar until light and fluffy. Add eggs, one at a time, beating well after each addition. Beat in honey and extract. Combine remaining ingredients; gradually add to creamed mixture and mix well.
2. Shape into two 12-in. rolls; wrap each in plastic wrap. Refrigerate 2 hours or until firm.
3. Preheat oven to 325°. Unwrap and cut into ¼-in. slices. Place 1 in. apart on ungreased baking sheets. Bake 12-14 minutes or until cookies are golden brown. Remove to wire racks to cool.

Cream Cheese-Filled Cookies

My aunt baked these cookies as part of my wedding day dinner. Everyone was impressed with their eye-catching appeal.
—**RUTH GLICK** NEW HOLLAND, PA

PREP: 20 MIN. + CHILLING • **BAKE:** 10 MIN./BATCH + COOLING
MAKES: ABOUT 2½ DOZEN

- ⅓ cup butter, softened
- ⅓ cup shortening
- ¾ cup sugar
- 1 egg
- 1 teaspoon vanilla extract
- 1¾ cups all-purpose flour
- 1 teaspoon baking powder
- ½ teaspoon salt

FILLING
- 2 packages (3 ounces each) cream cheese, softened
- 1½ cups confectioners' sugar
- 2 tablespoons all-purpose flour
- 1 teaspoon vanilla extract
- 1 drop yellow food coloring, optional

TOPPING
- ¾ cup semisweet chocolate chips
- 3 tablespoons butter

1. In a large bowl, cream butter, shortening and sugar until light and fluffy. Beat in egg. Beat in vanilla. Combine flour, baking powder and salt; gradually add to creamed mixture and mix well. Shape into two 12-in. rolls; wrap each in plastic wrap. Refrigerate for 4 hours or overnight.
2. Unwrap and cut into 1-in. slices. Place 1 in. apart on greased baking sheet. Bake at 375° for 10-12 minutes or until lightly browned. Immediately make an indentation in the center of each cookie using the end of a wooden spoon handle. Remove to wire racks to cool.
3. In a small bowl, combine the filling ingredients. Place 2 teaspoonfuls in the center of each cookie. Let stand until set. In a microwave, melt chocolate chips and butter; stir until smooth. Drizzle over cookies. Store the cookies in the refrigerator.

Pinwheels and Checkerboards

My mom used to make these every Christmas, and I still love them. They are so colorful and you can get two kinds of cookies from one dough! They're perfect for including in gift boxes.

—JILL HEATWOLE PITTSVILLE, MD

PREP: 30 MIN. + CHILLING • **BAKE:** 10 MIN./BATCH
MAKES: 6 DOZEN PINWHEEL AND 4 DOZEN CHECKERBOARD COOKIES

1¼ cups butter, softened
1 cup packed brown sugar
½ cup sugar
2 eggs
¼ teaspoon vanilla extract
4 cups all-purpose flour
1 teaspoon baking powder
1 teaspoon salt
¼ teaspoon baking soda
    Red and green gel food coloring
1 ounce unsweetened chocolate, melted and cooled

1. In a large bowl, cream butter and sugars until light and fluffy. Beat in eggs and vanilla. Combine the flour, baking powder, salt and baking soda; gradually add to creamed mixture and mix well.

2. Divide dough into fourths. Tint one portion red and one portion green. Stir chocolate into another portion. Wrap chocolate and plain portions in plastic wrap; chill for 1 hour or until easy to handle.

3. For pinwheel cookies, divide red and green portions in half. Roll out each portion between waxed paper into a 9-in. x 6-in. rectangle. Refrigerate for 30 minutes.

4. Remove waxed paper. Place one green rectangle over a red rectangle. Roll up tightly jelly-roll style, starting with a long side; wrap in plastic wrap. Repeat. Chill for 2 hours or until firm.

5. For checkerboard cookies, divide plain and chocolate portions in half. Roll out each portion between waxed paper into a 6-in. x 4-in. rectangle. Cut each rectangle lengthwise into eight ½-in. strips.

6. Stack the strips in groups of four, alternating plain and chocolate strips and forming eight separate stacks. Form a four-stack block by alternating chocolate-topped and plain-topped stacks. Repeat. Press together gently. Wrap in plastic. Chill for at least 2 hours.

7. Unwrap and cut pinwheel and checkerboard dough into ¼-in. slices. Place 1 in. apart on ungreased baking sheets. Bake at 375° for 9-11 minutes or until set. Remove to wire racks to cool.

Bakeshop **TIP**

Slicing Refrigerator Cookie Dough

To make the dough easier to slice, use nuts and fruits that are finely chopped. If the nuts and fruit are too large, the cookie dough may break apart when sliced. Use a thin, sharp knife to slice through the dough. After each slice, rotate the dough to avoid having one side that's flat.

Coconut Chocolate Slices

These crispy cookies with a chewy coconut center travel really well. When I sent care boxes to our son in the Army, they always arrived unbroken.

—**CHERI BOOTH** GERING, NE

PREP: 30 MIN. + CHILLING • **BAKE:** 10 MIN./BATCH
MAKES: ABOUT 4 DOZEN

- 1 **package (3 ounces) cream cheese, softened**
- ⅓ **cup sugar**
- 1 **teaspoon vanilla extract**
- 1 **cup flaked coconut**
- ½ **cup finely chopped nuts**

COOKIE DOUGH

- 6 **tablespoons butter, softened**
- 1 **cup confectioners' sugar**
- 1 **egg**
- 2 **ounces semisweet chocolate, melted and cooled**
- 1 **teaspoon vanilla extract**
- 1½ **cups all-purpose flour**
- ½ **teaspoon baking soda**
- ½ **teaspoon salt**

1. In a small bowl, beat the cream cheese, sugar and vanilla until smooth. Stir in coconut and nuts. Refrigerate until easy to handle.

2. Meanwhile, in a large bowl, cream the butter and confectioners' sugar until light and fluffy. Beat in the egg, chocolate and vanilla. Combine the flour, baking soda and salt; gradually add to creamed mixture and mix well. Refrigerate for 30 minutes or until easy to handle.

3. Roll dough between waxed paper into a 14-in. x 4½-in. rectangle. Remove top piece of waxed paper. Shape coconut filling into a 14-in. roll; place on dough, 1 in. from a long side. Roll dough around filling and seal edges. Wrap in plastic wrap. Refrigerate for 2-3 hours or overnight.

4. Unwrap and cut into ¼-in. slices. Place 2 in. apart on greased baking sheets. Bake at 350° for 8-10 minutes or until set. Cool for 1 minute before removing to wire racks.

Watermelon Slice Cookies

When I made these butter cookies for an event, a neighbor thought they were so attractive, she froze one to show friends.
—**SUE ANN BENHAM** VALPARAISO, IN

PREP: 25 MIN. + CHILLING • **BAKE:** 10 MIN./BATCH
MAKES: ABOUT 3 DOZEN

¾ **cup butter, softened**
¾ **cup sugar**
1 **egg**
½ **teaspoon almond extract**
2 **cups all-purpose flour**
¼ **teaspoon baking powder**
⅛ **teaspoon salt**
  Red and green gel food coloring
⅓ **cup miniature semisweet chocolate chips or raisins, chopped**
1 **teaspoon sesame seeds, optional**

1. In a large bowl, cream butter and sugar until light and fluffy. Beat in egg and extract. In another bowl, whisk flour, baking powder and salt; gradually beat into creamed mixture. Reserve 1 cup dough.
2. Tint remaining dough red; shape into a 3½-in.-long roll. Wrap in plastic wrap. Tint ⅓ cup of reserved dough green; wrap in plastic wrap. Wrap remaining plain dough. Refrigerate 2 hours or until firm.
3. On a lightly floured surface, roll plain dough into an 8½x3½-in. rectangle. Unwrap red dough and place on a short end of the plain dough; roll up.
4. Roll green dough into a 10x3½-in. rectangle. Place red and plain roll on a short end of the green dough; roll up. Wrap in plastic wrap; refrigerate overnight.
5. Preheat oven to 350°. Unwrap and cut dough into ³⁄₁₆-in. slices (just less than ¼ in.). Place 2 in. apart on ungreased baking sheets. If desired, lightly press chocolate chips into red dough to resemble watermelon seeds.
6. Bake 9-11 minutes or until firm. Immediately cut cookies in half. Remove to wire racks to cool.

Sesame Coconut Cookies

Even folks who normally pass up coconut treats can't resist these crisp butter cookies. They make a nice accompaniment to a hot cup of coffee or tea.
—**ROBERTA MYERS** ELWOOD, IN

PREP: 20 MIN. + CHILLING • **BAKE:** 25 MIN./BATCH
MAKES: 10 DOZEN

2 **cups butter, softened**
1½ **cups sugar**
1 **teaspoon vanilla extract**
3 **cups all-purpose flour**
½ **teaspoon salt**
2 **cups flaked coconut**
1 **cup sesame seeds**
½ **cup finely chopped almonds**

1. In a large bowl, cream butter and sugar. Beat in vanilla. Combine flour and salt; gradually add to creamed mixture. Stir in the coconut, sesame seeds and almonds.
2. Shape into three 10-in. rolls; wrap each in plastic wrap. Refrigerate for 1-2 hours or until firm.
3. Unwrap dough and cut into ¼-in. slices. Place 1 in. apart on ungreased baking sheets. Bake at 300° for 25-30 minutes or until lightly browned. Cool for 2 minutes before removing to wire racks.

Bakeshop TIP

Keeping it Shapely

To keep a nice round shape for refrigerated cookie cough, place each wrapped roll in a tall glass and place the glass on its side in the refrigerator. The rounded glass will prevent the bottom of the roll from flattening out. A carboard tube from a roll of paper towels or wrapping paper will also work. Cut the tube lengthwise in half if it is too narrow.

Candy Corn Cookies

Get a head start on these buttery cookies by shaping and chilling the homemade dough ahead of time. When you're ready, just slice and bake.

—TASTE OF HOME TEST KITCHEN

PREP: 20 MIN. + CHILLING • **BAKE:** 10 MIN./BATCH
MAKES: ABOUT 5 DOZEN

- 1½ **cups butter, softened**
- 1½ **cups sugar**
- ½ **teaspoon vanilla extract**
- 3 **cups all-purpose flour**
- 1 **teaspoon baking soda**
- ½ **teaspoon salt**
  Yellow and orange paste food coloring

1. In a large bowl, cream butter and sugar until light and fluffy. Beat in vanilla. Combine flour, baking soda and salt; gradually add to creamed mixture and mix well.
2. Divide dough in half. Tint one portion yellow. Divide remaining dough into two-thirds and one-third portions.

Color the larger portion orange; leave smaller portion white.
3. Shape each portion of dough into two 8-in. logs. Flatten top and push sides in at a slight angle. Place orange logs on yellow logs; push the sides in at a slight angle. Top with white logs; form a rounded top. Wrap in plastic wrap. Chill for 4 hours or until firm.
4. Unwrap and cut into ¼-in. slices. Place 2 in. apart on ungreased baking sheets. Bake at 350° for 10-12 minutes or until set. Remove to wire racks to cool.

Butterscotch Cookies

This time-tested recipe has been in my family for years. It's also delicious with miniature chocolate chips or coconut in place of the toffee bits.

—BEVERLY DUNCAN LAKEVILLE, OH

PREP: 20 MIN. + CHILLING • **BAKE:** 10 MIN./BATCH
MAKES: ABOUT 1½ DOZEN

- 2 **tablespoons butter, softened**
- 2 **tablespoons shortening**
- 1 **cup packed brown sugar**
- 1 **egg**
- 1 **teaspoon vanilla extract**
- 1½ **cups all-purpose flour**
- ¾ **teaspoon baking soda**
- ¾ **teaspoon cream of tartar**
- ¼ **teaspoon salt**
- ¼ **cup English toffee bits or almond brickle chips**
- ¼ **cup finely chopped pecans**

1. In a large bowl, cream butter, shortening and brown sugar until light and fluffy. Beat in the egg and vanilla. Combine flour, baking soda, cream of tartar and salt; gradually add to creamed mixture and mix well. Stir in toffee bits and pecans. Shape into a 10-in. roll; wrap in plastic wrap. Refrigerate 4 hours or until firm.
2. Preheat oven to 375°. Unwrap dough and cut into ½-in. slices. Place 2 in. apart on baking sheets coated with cooking spray. Bake 9-11 minutes or until lightly browned. Cool 1-2 minutes before removing from pans to wire racks.

Cherry Cranberry Pinwheels

The combination of cranberries, cherries, orange zest and cinnamon makes these festive cookies as fragrant as they are flavorful.

—DEB PERRY BLUFFTON, IN

PREP: 1 HOUR + CHILLING • **BAKE:** 10 MIN./BATCH
MAKES: 4½ TO 5 DOZEN

- 1½ cups dried cranberries
- 1 jar (10 ounces) cherry spreadable fruit
- ¼ cup water
- ½ teaspoon ground cinnamon

DOUGH

- ¼ cup butter, softened
- 1¼ cups sugar
- 3 egg whites
- 3 tablespoons canola oil
- 2 tablespoons fat-free milk
- 2 teaspoons vanilla extract
- 1½ teaspoons grated orange peel
- 3⅓ cups all-purpose flour
- ¾ teaspoon baking powder
- ½ teaspoon ground cinnamon
- ⅛ teaspoon baking soda

1. For filling, combine the first four ingredients in a small saucepan. Cook and stir over medium heat for 8 minutes or until liquid is absorbed and cranberries are softened. Remove from the heat; cool slightly. Transfer to a blender; cover and process until smooth. Transfer to a bowl; cover and refrigerate until chilled.

2. For dough, in a large bowl, beat butter and sugar for 2 minutes or until crumbly. Beat in the egg whites, oil, milk, vanilla and orange peel. Combine the flour, baking powder, cinnamon and baking soda; gradually add to sugar mixture and mix well.

3. Divide dough in half. On a floured surface, roll one portion of dough into a 14-in. x 9-in. rectangle. Spread with half of the filling. Roll up jelly-roll style, starting with a long side. Repeat with remaining dough and filling. Wrap each roll in plastic wrap; refrigerate for at least 4 hours.

4. Unwrap dough; cut into ½-in. slices. Place 2 in. apart on baking sheets coated with cooking spray. Bake at 375° for 10-12 minutes or until bottoms are lightly browned (do not overbake). Remove to wire racks to cool.

Jeweled Coconut Crisps

When I anticipate a busy day during the holiday season, I make this cookie dough the night before. The next day, I just take it out of the refrigerator, then slice and bake.

—EILEEN MILACEK WAUKOMIS, OK

PREP: 15 MIN. + CHILLING • **BAKE:** 10 MIN./BATCH
MAKES: ABOUT 5 DOZEN

- 1 **cup butter, softened**
- 1 **cup sugar**
- 2 **tablespoons milk**
- 1½ **teaspoons vanilla extract**
- 2½ **cups all-purpose flour**
- ¾ **cup finely chopped red and green candied cherries**
- ¾ **cup finely chopped pecans**
- 1 **cup flaked coconut**

1. In a large bowl, cream butter and sugar until light and fluffy. Beat in milk and vanilla. Gradually add flour and mix well. Stir in cherries and pecans.

2. Shape into two 8-in. logs. Sprinkle the coconut over waxed paper; place each log on waxed paper and roll in coconut. Wrap in plastic wrap. Refrigerate for 4 hours or until firm.

3. Unwrap dough and cut into ¼-in. slices. Place 2 in. apart on ungreased baking sheets. Bake at 375° for 10-12 minutes or until edges are lightly browned. Remove to wire racks to cool.

Crisp Pecan Rounds

I adapted an old recipe to produce these lightly sweet cookies. They have a wonderful cinnamon and nutmeg flavor that makes them a favorite at our house for the holidays.

—DENISE DEJONG PITTSBURGH, PA

PREP: 20 MIN. + CHILLING • **BAKE:** 20 MIN./BATCH
MAKES: ABOUT 3½ DOZEN

1½ cups all-purpose flour
¼ cup packed brown sugar
2 tablespoons sugar
½ teaspoon salt
¼ teaspoon ground cinnamon
¼ teaspoon ground nutmeg
⅔ cup cold butter
2 tablespoons maple syrup
½ cup chopped pecans
GLAZE
1 egg yolk
1 teaspoon water
TOPPING
1½ teaspoons sugar
½ teaspoon ground cinnamon

1. In a large bowl, combine the first six ingredients. Cut in butter until mixture resembles coarse crumbs. Stir in the syrup. Add pecans. Shape into a 12-in. roll; wrap in plastic wrap. Refrigerate for 4 hours or until firm.
2. Unwrap and cut into ¼-in. slices. Place 1 in. apart on ungreased baking sheets.
3. For glaze, beat egg yolk and water. For topping, combine sugar and cinnamon. Brush glaze over cookies and sprinkle with cinnamon-sugar.
4. Bake at 325° for 20-25 minutes or until golden brown. Remove to wire racks to cool.

Delicate Mint Thins

When I was newly married, I needed something to impress my relatives at a reunion. I served these subtle mint flavored cookies.

—KRISTINE MCDANIEL KETTERING, OH

PREP: 20 MIN. + CHILLING • **BAKE:** 20 MIN. + COOLING
MAKES: ABOUT 4½ DOZEN

½ cup butter, softened
½ cup sugar
1 egg yolk
½ teaspoon vanilla extract
1½ cups all-purpose flour
1½ teaspoons baking powder
⅛ teaspoon salt
3 tablespoons 2% milk
1 cup fresh mint, finely chopped
1⅔ cups semisweet chocolate chips
1 tablespoon shortening

1. In a large bowl, cream butter and sugar until light and fluffy. Beat in egg yolk and vanilla. Combine the flour, baking powder and salt; add to the creamed mixture alternately with milk, beating well after each addition. Stir in the mint. Shape into two 8-in. rolls; wrap each in plastic wrap. Refrigerate for 2 hours or until firm.
2. Unwrap and cut into ¼-in. slices. Place 1 in. apart on greased baking sheets. Bake at 350° for 8-12 minutes or until edges are golden. Remove to wire racks to cool.
3. In a microwave, melt chocolate chips and shortening; stir until smooth. Dip each cookie halfway; allow excess to drip off. Place on waxed paper; let stand until set.

Date Swirl Cookies

My granddaughter nicknamed my mother "Cookie Grandma" because she made wonderful cookies. Mom made these crisp and chewy cookies every Christmas.

—DONNA GRACE CLANCY, MT

PREP: 30 MIN. + CHILLING • **BAKE:** 10 MIN./BATCH
MAKES: 4 DOZEN

FILLING
- 2 cups chopped dates
- 1 cup water
- 1 cup sugar
- 1 cup chopped nuts
- 2 teaspoons lemon juice

DOUGH
- 1 cup butter, softened
- 1 cup packed brown sugar
- 1 cup sugar
- 3 eggs
- 1 teaspoon lemon extract
- 4 cups all-purpose flour
- 1 teaspoon salt
- ¾ teaspoon baking soda

1. In a saucepan, combine filling ingredients. Cook over medium-low heat, stirring constantly, until mixture becomes stiff, about 15-20 minutes. Chill.
2. For dough, cream butter and sugars in a bowl. Add eggs, one at a time, beating well after each addition. Add extract. Combine flour, salt and baking soda; gradually add to creamed mixture and mix well. Chill for at least 1 hour.
3. On a lightly floured surface, roll out half of the dough to a 12-in. x 9-in. rectangle, about ¼ in. thick. Spread with half of the filling. Roll up, starting with the long end. Repeat with remaining dough and filling. Wrap with plastic wrap; chill overnight.
4. Cut rolls into ¼-in. slices. Place 2 in. apart on greased baking sheets. Bake at 375° for 8-10 minutes or until lightly browned. Cool on wire racks.

Rolled Oat Cookies

I like to keep some of this dough in the freezer at all times since it's so handy to slice, bake and serve at a moment's notice. These cookies are super with a cup of coffee—in fact, we occasionally grab a few for breakfast when we're in a hurry.

—KATHI PETERS CHILLIWACK, BC

PREP: 15 MIN. + CHILLING • **BAKE:** 15 MIN./BATCH
MAKES: 3½ DOZEN

- 1 cup butter, softened
- 1 cup packed brown sugar
- ¼ cup water
- 1 teaspoon vanilla extract
- 3 cups quick-cooking oats
- 1¼ cups all-purpose flour
- 1 teaspoon salt
- ¼ teaspoon baking soda

1. In a large bowl, cream butter and sugar until light and fluffy. Beat in water and vanilla. Combine dry ingredients; add to creamed mixture and mix well. Chill for 30 minutes.
2. Shape into two 1½ in. rolls; wrap tightly in waxed paper. Chill for 2 hours or until firm.
3. Cut into ½-in. slices and place 2 in. apart on greased baking sheets. Bake at 375° for 12 minutes or until lightly browned. Remove to wire racks to cool.

COOKIES & BAKESHOP *favorites*

Two-Tone Butter Cookies

During the hectic holiday season, you'll appreciate the ease of these irresistible butter cookies. It's great to pull the two-tone dough from the freezer and bake a festive batch in no time.
—**KATHY KITTELL** LENEXA, KS

PREP: 20 MIN. + CHILLING • **BAKE:** 10 MIN./BATCH
MAKES: ABOUT 5 DOZEN

- 1 **cup butter, softened**
- 1 **cup confectioners' sugar**
- 1 **teaspoon vanilla extract**
- 2 **cups all-purpose flour**
  Red and green liquid food coloring
  Red colored sugar, optional

1. In a large bowl, cream butter and confectioners' sugar until light and fluffy. Beat in vanilla. Gradually add flour and mix well. Divide dough in half; with food coloring, tint half red and half green. Shape each portion into a rough log, then place logs on sheets of parchment paper.
2. Roll dough in paper into an even, smooth 8-in. log, using a ruler to compact log and to squeeze out air as you go. Wrap in plastic wrap and refrigerate for at least 30 minutes or until slightly firm.
3. Cut each log in half lengthwise. Press red and green halves together. Tightly wrap each roll in plastic wrap; freeze for 30 minutes or until firm.
4. Cut into ¼-in. slices; place 2 in. apart on ungreased baking sheets. Sprinkle with the colored sugar if desired. Bake at 350° for 8-10 minutes or until set. Remove the cookies to wire racks to cool.

Honey Spice Cookies

With four children, I bake a lot of cookies. These nicely seasoned sweets are a favorite with my family.

—**JOAN GERBER** BLUFFTON, IN

PREP: 20 MIN. + CHILLING • **BAKE:** 10 MIN./BATCH
MAKES: 12½ DOZEN

- 2 **cups honey**
- 2 **cups sugar**
- 3 **eggs**
- 7½ **cups all-purpose flour**
- 3 **teaspoons baking soda**
- 3 **teaspoons ground cinnamon**
- 1 **teaspoon salt**
- 1 **teaspoon ground allspice**
- 1 **teaspoon ground cloves**
- 2 **cups confectioners' sugar**
- 3 **tablespoon fat-free milk**

1. In a large bowl, beat honey and sugar. Add eggs, one at a time, beating well after each addition. Combine the flour, baking soda, cinnamon, salt, allspice and cloves; gradually add to honey mixture and mix well.
2. Shape dough into five 10-in. rolls; wrap in plastic wrap. Refrigerate for 2 hour or until firm.
3. Unwrap the dough and cut into ¼-in. slices. Place the slices 2 in. apart on baking sheets coated with cooking spray. Combine the confectioners' sugar and milk; lightly brush over cookies.
4. Bake at 350° for 8-10 minutes or until lightly browned. Remove from pans to wire racks to cool.

Butterscotch Pecan Slices

I love the rich, buttery flavor these crisp cookies get from pecans and brown sugar. Once the dough is in the refrigerator, I can have freshly baked cookies in just minutes.

—**ESTHER THYS** BELLE PLAINE, IA

PREP: 15 MIN. • **BAKE:** 10 MIN. • **MAKES:** 4 DOZEN

- 6 **tablespoons butter, softened**
- ⅔ **cup packed brown sugar**
- 1 **egg**
- ½ **teaspoon vanilla extract**
- 1¼ **cups all-purpose flour**
- ½ **teaspoon baking powder**
- ¼ **teaspoon salt**
- ¾ **cup finely chopped pecans, divided**

1. In a large bowl, cream the butter and brown sugar until light and fluffy. Beat in egg and vanilla. Combine flour, baking powder and salt; gradually add to the creamed mixture and mix well. Stir in ½ cup pecans. Shape into two 7-in. rolls; wrap each in plastic wrap. Refrigerate for 2 hours or until firm.
2. Unwrap and cut into ¼-in. slices. Place 2 in. apart on ungreased baking sheets. Sprinkle with remaining nuts; press gently. Bake at 350° for 10-12 minutes or until edges begin to brown. Remove to wire racks to cool.

Chewy Almond Cookies

My children and grandchildren often request these old-fashioned cookies. The unbaked cookie dough, can be frozen for up to a year. When you are ready to bake, let it stand at room temperature for 15-30 minutes. Then just slice and bake.

—**BETTY SPETH** VINCENNES, IN

PREP: 15 MIN. + CHILLING • **BAKE:** 10 MIN./BATCH
MAKES: 4½ DOZEN

    3 **tablespoons butter**
    1 **cup packed brown sugar**
    1 **egg**
    ¼ **teaspoon vanilla extract**
    ¼ **teaspoon almond extract**
  1½ **cups all-purpose flour**
    ¼ **teaspoon baking soda**
    ¼ **teaspoon ground cinnamon**
    ½ **cup sliced almonds**

1. In a large bowl, beat butter and brown sugar until crumbly. Beat in egg and extracts. Combine the flour, baking soda and cinnamon; gradually add to the butter mixture and mix well. Shape into two 6-in. rolls; wrap each in plastic wrap. Refrigerate overnight.

2. Unwrap; cut into ¼-in. slices. Place 2 in. apart on greased baking sheets. Sprinkle with almonds.
3. Bake at 350° for 7-10 minutes or until lightly browned. Cool for 2-3 minutes before removing to wire racks.

Lemon Meltaways

These melt-in-your-mouth goodies get zing from lemon in both the cookie and the frosting.

—**MARY HOUCHIN** LEBANON, IL

PREP: 15 MIN. + CHILLING • **BAKE:** 10 MIN. + COOLING
MAKES: ABOUT 5 DOZEN

    ¾ **cup butter, softened**
    ⅓ **cup confectioners' sugar**
    1 **teaspoon lemon juice**
  1¼ **cups all-purpose flour**
    ½ **cup cornstarch**
FROSTING
    ¼ **cup butter, softened**
    ¾ **cup confectioners' sugar**
    1 **teaspoon lemon juice**
    1 **teaspoon grated lemon peel**
    1 **to 3 drops yellow food coloring, optional**

1. In a large bowl, cream butter and confectioners' sugar until light and fluffy; beat in lemon juice. Combine flour and cornstarch; gradually add to the creamed mixture and mix well. Shape into two 8-in. rolls; wrap each roll in plastic wrap. Refrigerate for 2 hours or until firm.
2. Unwrap and cut into ¼-inch slices. Place 2 in. apart on ungreased baking sheets. Bake at 350° for 8-12 minutes or until the cookies are firm to the touch. Remove to wire racks to cool completely.
3. For frosting, in a small bowl, beat the butter and confectioners' sugar until smooth. Stir in the lemon juice, lemon peel and food coloring. Frost cooled cookies.

Peppermint Candy Cookies

These buttery mint treats practically melt on your tongue. The bright food coloring gives them a festive look for holiday parties.

—GLORIA MCKENZIE PANAMA CITY, FL

PREP: 25 MIN. • **BAKE:** 10 MIN./BATCH • **MAKES:** ABOUT 4 DOZEN

- 1¼ **cups butter, softened**
- ¾ **cup confectioners' sugar**
- 2½ **cups all-purpose flour**
- ½ **teaspoon salt**
- ½ **teaspoon peppermint extract**
  Green and red paste or gel food coloring

1. In a large bowl, cream butter and sugar until light and fluffy. Add the flour, salt and extract and mix well. Divide dough into fourths. Tint one portion green and one red; leave the remaining portions plain.

2. Divide each portion into thirds; shape each into a 6-in. log. Flatten into triangular logs, bending the top of one point slightly (to give finished cookies a pinwheel effect). Assemble one large roll by alternating three green and three plain logs. Wrap in plastic wrap. Repeat with red and remaining plain dough. Chill for 4 hours or until firm.

3. Unwrap dough and cut into ¼-in. slices. Place 2 in. apart on ungreased baking sheets. Bake at 375° for 8-10 minutes or until edges are golden brown. Cool for 1 minute before removing to wire racks.

4. Cut 6-in.-square pieces of cellophane or plastic wrap to wrap each cookie; twist ends securely or tie with a ribbon.

Peanut Chocolate Whirls

The tantalizing combination of chocolate and peanut butter is irresistible in these tender swirl cookies.

—JOANNE WOLOSCHUK YORKTON, SK

PREP: 20 MIN. + CHILLING • **BAKE:** 10 MIN./BATCH
MAKES: ABOUT 3 DOZEN

- ½ cup shortening
- ½ cup creamy peanut butter
- 1 cup sugar
- 1 egg
- 2 tablespoons milk
- 1 teaspoon vanilla extract
- 1¼ cups all-purpose flour
- ½ teaspoon baking soda
- ½ teaspoon salt
- 1 cup (6 ounces) semisweet chocolate chips

1. In a large bowl, cream the shortening, peanut butter and sugar until light and fluffy. Beat in the egg, milk and vanilla. Combine the flour, baking soda and salt; gradually add to creamed mixture and mix well.

2. Cover and refrigerate for 1 hour or until easy to handle. Turn onto a lightly floured surface; roll into a 16-in. x 12-in. rectangle.

3. In a microwave, melt chocolate chips; stir until smooth. Cool slightly. Spread over dough to within ½ in. of edges. Tightly roll up jelly-roll style, starting with a short side. Wrap in plastic wrap. Refrigerate for up to 30 minutes.

4. Unwrap and cut into ¼-in. slices with a serrated knife. Place 1 in. apart on ungreased baking sheets. Bake at 350° for 8-10 minutes or until lightly browned. Remove to wire racks to cool.

Chocolate Coconut Neapolitans

My yummy striped cookies with a chocolaty twist are easy and fun to make, but they do need some time in the freezer.

—LENA MARIE BROWNELL ROCKLAND, MA

PREP: 30 MIN. + FREEZING • **BAKE:** 15 MIN./BATCH + COOLING
MAKES: 5½ DOZEN

- 1 cup butter, softened
- 1½ cups sugar
- 1 egg
- 1 teaspoon vanilla extract
- 2½ cups all-purpose flour
- 1½ teaspoons baking powder
- ½ teaspoon salt
- 1 teaspoon almond extract
- 4 drops red food coloring
- ½ cup flaked coconut, finely chopped
- 4½ teaspoons chocolate syrup
- ½ cup semisweet chocolate chips
- 1½ teaspoons shortening

1. Line a 9-in. x 5-in. loaf pan with waxed paper; set aside. In a large bowl, cream butter and sugar until light and fluffy. Beat in egg and vanilla. Combine the flour, baking powder and salt; gradually add to creamed mixture and mix well.

2. Divide dough into thirds. Add almond extract and red food coloring to one portion; spread evenly into prepared pan. Add coconut to second portion; spread evenly over first layer. Add chocolate syrup to third portion; spread over second layer. Cover with foil; freeze for 4 hours or overnight.

3. Unwrap loaf and cut in half lengthwise. Cut each portion widthwise into ¼-in. slices. Place 2 in. apart on ungreased baking sheets. Bake at 350° for 12-14 minutes or until edges are lightly browned. Remove the cookies to wire racks to cool.

4. In a microwave, melt chocolate chips and shortening; stir until smooth. Dip one end of each cookie into chocolate; allow excess to drip off. Place on waxed paper; let stand until set.

Chocolate Peppermint Pinwheels

My cookie-loving family is never satisfied with just one batch of these minty pinwheels. I automatically double the recipe each time I bake them!

—ELLEN JOHNSON HAMPTON, VA

PREP: 15 MIN. + CHILLING • **BAKE:** 10 MIN./BATCH
MAKES: 4 DOZEN

- 1 cup shortening
- 1½ cups sugar
- 2 eggs
- 2 tablespoons milk
- 2 teaspoons peppermint extract
- 2½ cups all-purpose flour
- ½ teaspoon salt
- ½ teaspoon baking powder
- 2 ounces unsweetened chocolate, melted

1. In a large bowl, cream shortening and sugar until light and fluffy. Beat in the eggs, milk and extract. Combine the flour, salt and baking powder; gradually add to creamed mixture and mix well. Divide dough in half. Add chocolate to one portion and mix well.

2. Roll each portion between waxed paper into a 16-in. x 7-in. rectangle, about ¼ in. thick. Remove top sheet of waxed paper; place plain dough over chocolate dough. Roll up jelly-roll style, starting with a long side. Wrap in plastic wrap; refrigerate for 2 hours or until firm.

3. Unwrap dough and cut into ¼-in. slices. Place 2 in. apart on greased baking sheets. Bake at 375° for 8-10 minutes or until lightly browned. Remove to wire racks to cool.

Lemon Pecan Slices

These attractive morsels are my daughter's favorite. The lemon glaze pairs well with the delicate nut-topped cookie.

—MELISSA BRANNING FONTANA, WI

PREP: 20 MIN. + CHILLING • **BAKE:** 10 MIN./BATCH
MAKES: ABOUT 7 DOZEN

- 1 cup butter, softened
- ¾ cup packed brown sugar
- ½ cup sugar
- 2 eggs
- 1½ teaspoons vanilla extract
- 1 tablespoon grated lemon peel
- 3 cups all-purpose flour
- 1½ teaspoons baking powder
- ¾ teaspoon salt

TOPPING
- ¾ cup finely chopped pecans
- ¼ cup sugar

LEMON GLAZE
- 1¼ cups confectioners' sugar
- 5 teaspoons lemon juice
- 1 drop yellow food coloring, optional

1. In a bowl, cream the butter and sugars. Separate one egg; refrigerate egg white. Add the egg yolk, second egg, vanilla and lemon peel to creamed mixture; mix well. Combine the flour, baking powder and salt; gradually beat into creamed mixture. Shape into three 7-in. rolls; wrap each in plastic wrap. Refrigerate for 2 hours or until firm.

2. Unwrap logs. Lightly beat reserved egg white. Combine pecans and sugar. Brush each log with egg white, then roll in pecan mixture, pressing firmly into dough.

3. Cut into ¼-in. slices. Place 2 in. apart on ungreased baking sheets. Bake at 400° for 6-7 minutes or until very lightly browned. Remove to wire racks to cool. Combine glaze ingredients; drizzle over cookies.

Ginger Thins

I pair my cookies with a scoop of lemon sherbet. The lemon and ginger complement each other nicely.

—ELEANOR SENSKE ROCK ISLAND, IL

PREP: 15 MIN. + FREEZING • **BAKE:** 10 MIN./BATCH
MAKES: 3½ DOZEN

- 6 **tablespoons butter, softened**
- ½ **cup plus 2 tablespoons sugar, divided**
- 2 **tablespoons molasses**
- 1 **tablespoon cold strong brewed coffee**
- 1¼ **cups all-purpose flour**
- ¾ **teaspoon ground ginger**
- ½ **teaspoon baking soda**
- ½ **teaspoon ground cinnamon**
- ¼ **teaspoon ground cloves**
- ⅛ **teaspoon salt**

1. In a large bowl, cream butter and ½ cup sugar until light and fluffy; set remaining sugar aside. Beat in molasses and coffee to creamed mixture. Combine the remaining ingredients; add to creamed mixture until well combined (dough will be soft).

2. Cover and freeze for 15 minutes. Shape dough into a 7-in. roll; flatten to 1-in. thickness. Wrap in plastic wrap. Freeze for 8 hours or overnight.

3. Unwrap dough and cut into ⅛-in. slices; place 2 in. apart on parchment paper-lined baking sheets. Sprinkle with reserved sugar. Bake at 350° for 8-10 minutes or until firm. Remove from pans to wire racks to cool.

Pastelitos De Boda

In Mexico, these rich cookies are called little wedding cakes and are usually served with hot chocolate. Having moved from the Midwest to a location that's closer to Mexico, I've enjoyed trying authentic recipes. These treats are a sharp departure from the Iowa favorites I grew up with!

—TERRI LINS SAN DIEGO, CA

PREP: 20 MIN. + CHILLING • **BAKE:** 15 MIN./BATCH
MAKES: ABOUT 3 DOZEN

- ¾ **cup butter, softened**
- ½ **cup confectioners' sugar**
- 2 **teaspoons vanilla extract**
- 2 **cups sifted all-purpose flour**
- ¼ **teaspoon salt**
- 1 **cup finely chopped walnuts**
- ¼ **cup heavy whipping cream**
  Additional confectioners' sugar

1. In a large bowl, cream butter and sugar until light and fluffy; add vanilla. Combine flour, salt and nuts; gradually add to the creamed mixture and mix well. Add the cream; knead lightly.

2. Shape into a roll 2½ in. in diameter. Wrap in plastic wrap. Refrigerate several hours or overnight.

3. Preheat oven to 375°. Unwrap and cut into ¼-in. slices. Place 2 in. apart on ungreased baking sheets. Bake 15 minutes or until delicately browned around edges. Remove to wire rack. While warm, roll in additional confectioners' sugar.

Three-Nut Cherry Slices

These impressive cookies are ideal for situations when you want a treat that really stands out—but is easy on the baker! Using three types of nuts takes slice-and-bake cookies to another level, and the candied cherries add sweetness and color.

—SUE MEGONIGLE GREENDALE, WI

PREP: 40 MIN. + CHILLING • **BAKE:** 10 MIN./BATCH
MAKES: 7 DOZEN

- 1½ **cups butter, softened**
- 1 **cup packed brown sugar**
- ¼ **cup 2% milk**
- 1 **teaspoon vanilla extract**
- 3½ **cups all-purpose flour**
- 1 **teaspoon ground cinnamon**
- ½ **teaspoon baking soda**
- ½ **teaspoon salt**
- ½ **pound red candied cherries, chopped**
- ¼ **cup each chopped walnuts, Brazil nuts and hazelnuts**

1. In a large bowl, cream butter and brown sugar until light and fluffy; beat in the milk and vanilla. Combine the flour, cinnamon, baking soda and salt; gradually add to the creamed mixture and mix well. Stir in the cherries and nuts.
2. Shape into three 10-in. rolls; wrap each in plastic wrap. Refrigerate for 4 hours or overnight.
3. Unwrap and cut into ¼-in. slices. Place 2 in. apart on ungreased baking sheets. Bake at 350° for 10-12 minutes or until golden brown. Remove to wire racks to cool.

Raspberry Nut Pinwheels

A number of years ago, I won first prize in a recipe contest with these yummy swirl cookies. The raspberry and walnut flavor really comes through in each bite, and they are so much fun to make!

—PAT HABIGER SPEARVILLE, KS

PREP: 20 MIN. + CHILLING • **BAKE:** 10 MIN./BATCH
MAKES: ABOUT 3½ DOZEN

- ½ **cup butter, softened**
- 1 **cup sugar**
- 1 **egg**
- 1 **teaspoon vanilla extract**
- 2 **cups all-purpose flour**
- 1 **teaspoon baking powder**
- ¼ **cup seedless raspberry jam**
- ¾ **cup finely chopped walnuts**

1. In a large bowl, cream butter and sugar until light and fluffy. Beat in egg and vanilla. Combine flour and baking powder; gradually add to creamed mixture and mix well.
2. Roll out dough between waxed paper into a 12-in. square. Remove top piece of waxed paper. Spread dough with jam and sprinkle with nuts. Roll up tightly jelly-roll style; wrap in plastic wrap. Chill for 2 hours or until firm.
3. Unwrap dough and cut into ¼-in. slices. Place 2 in. apart on ungreased baking sheets. Bake at 375° for 9-12 minutes or until edges are lightly browned. Remove to wire racks to cool.

Double Delights

These treats are perfect for folks who like both chocolate and vanilla cookies because it gives them the best of both worlds.

—RUTH ANN STELFOX RAYMOND, AB

PREP: 30 MIN. + CHILLING • **BAKE:** 10 MIN./BATCH
MAKES: ABOUT 15 DOZEN

CHOCOLATE DOUGH

- 1 cup butter, softened
- 1½ cups sugar
- 2 eggs
- 2 teaspoons vanilla extract
- 2 cups all-purpose flour
- ⅔ cup baking cocoa
- ¾ teaspoon baking soda
- ½ teaspoon salt
- 1 cup coarsely chopped pecans
- 5 ounces white baking chocolate, chopped

VANILLA DOUGH

- 1 cup butter, softened
- 1½ cups sugar
- 2 eggs
- 2 teaspoons vanilla extract
- 2¾ cups all-purpose flour
- 2 teaspoons cream of tartar
- 1 teaspoon baking soda
- ½ teaspoon salt
- 1 cup coarsely chopped pecans
- 4 ounces German sweet chocolate, chopped

1. For chocolate dough, in a large bowl, cream butter and sugar until light and fluffy. Beat in the eggs and vanilla. Combine the flour, cocoa, baking soda and salt; gradually add to creamed mixture and mix well. Stir in pecans and white chocolate.

2. For vanilla dough, in another large bowl, cream butter and sugar until light and fluffy. Beat in eggs and vanilla. Combine the flour, cream of tartar, baking soda and salt; gradually add to creamed mixture and mix well. Stir in pecans and German chocolate. Cover and refrigerate both doughs for 2 hours.

3. Divide both doughs in half. Shape each portion into a 12-in. roll; wrap in plastic wrap. Refrigerate for 3 hours or until firm.

4. Unwrap and cut each roll in half lengthwise. Place a chocolate half and vanilla half together, pressing to form a log; wrap in plastic wrap. Refrigerate for 1 hour or until the dough holds together when cut.

5. Using a serrated knife, cut into ¼-in. slices. Place 2 in. apart on greased baking sheets. Bake at 350° for 8-10 minutes or until set. Remove to wire racks to cool.

Cherry Icebox Cookies

Maraschino cherries add colorful flecks to these cookies. When I was a home economics teacher, I often supplied treats for school functions, and these delectable treats were always very popular.

—PATTY COURTNEY JONESBORO, TX

PREP: 20 MIN. + CHILLING • **BAKE:** 10 MIN./BATCH
MAKES: 16 DOZEN

- 1 cup butter, softened
- 1 cup sugar
- ¼ cup packed brown sugar
- 1 egg
- ¼ cup maraschino cherry juice
- 4½ teaspoons lemon juice
- 1 teaspoon vanilla extract
- 3¼ cups all-purpose flour
- ½ teaspoon baking soda
- ½ teaspoon ground cinnamon
- ¼ teaspoon cream of tartar
- ½ cup chopped walnuts
- ½ cup chopped maraschino cherries

1. In a large bowl, cream butter and sugars until light and fluffy. Beat in the egg, cherry and lemon juices and vanilla. Combine dry ingredients; gradually add to the creamed mixture and mix well. Stir in nuts and cherries.

2. Shape into four 12-in. rolls; wrap each in plastic wrap. Refrigerate for 4 hours or until firm.

3. Unwrap and cut into ¼-in. slices. Place 2 in. apart on ungreased baking sheets. Bake at 375° for 8-10 minutes or until the edges begin to brown. Remove the cookies to wire racks to cool.

Ribbon Icebox Cookies

Three ribbons of flavor—cherry, chocolate and poppy seed—combine into one tender, Neapolitan-style cookie. My mom made these when we were kids. They are so good.

—**KARLYNE MOREAU** YAKIMA, WA

PREP: 25 MIN. + CHILLING • **BAKE:** 10 MIN. • **MAKES:** 20 COOKIES

- ½ **cup shortening**
- ⅔ **cup sugar**
- 2 **tablespoons beaten egg**
- ½ **teaspoon vanilla extract**
- 1¼ **cups all-purpose flour**
- ¾ **teaspoon baking powder**
- ¼ **teaspoon salt**
- 2 **tablespoons red candied cherries, chopped**
- ½ **ounce unsweetened chocolate, melted**
- 2 **teaspoons poppy seeds**

1. Line a 5-in. x 3-in. x 2-in. loaf pan with waxed paper; set aside. In a small bowl, cream shortening and sugar until light and fluffy. Beat in egg and vanilla. Combine the flour, baking powder and salt; gradually add to creamed mixture and mix well.

2. Divide dough into thirds. Add cherries to one portion; spread evenly into prepared pan. Add melted chocolate to second portion; spread evenly over first layer. Add poppy seeds to third portion; spread over second layer. Cover with waxed paper; refrigerate overnight.

3. Unwrap and cut into ¼-in. slices. Place 1 in. apart on ungreased baking sheets. Bake at 375° for 8-9 minutes or until lightly browned. Cool for 1 minute before removing to wire racks.

Peppermint Cookies

Some years ago, I whipped up these minty morsels as a way to use leftover candy canes. My daughter has enthusiastically anticipated the cookies for Christmas ever since!

—MRS. ROBERT NELSON DES MOINES, IA

PREP: 20 MIN. + CHILLING • **BAKE:** 10 MIN./BATCH
MAKES: ABOUT 6 DOZEN

- 1 **cup shortening**
- ½ **cup sugar**
- ½ **cup packed brown sugar**
- 2 **eggs**
- 1½ **teaspoons vanilla extract**
- 2¾ **cups all-purpose flour**
- 1 **teaspoon salt**
- ½ **teaspoon baking soda**
- ½ **cup crushed peppermint candies**

1. In a bowl, cream shortening and sugars. until light and fluffy. Add the eggs, one at a time, beating well after each addition. Beat in vanilla. Combine the dry ingredients; gradually add to the creamed mixture. Stir in crushed candies. Shape into a 15-in. roll; wrap in plastic wrap. Refrigerate for 4 hours or until firm.

2. Unwrap and cut into ⅛-in. slices. Place 2 in. apart on ungreased baking sheets. Bake at 375° for 6-8 minutes or until edges begin to brown. Remove to wire racks to cool.

Raspberry Swirls

My mother-in-law shared the recipe for these old-fashioned cookies with me. Swirls of raspberry jam give them a yummy twist, and they look so festive on a Christmas buffet.

—MARCIA HOSTETTER CANTON, NY

PREP: 25 MIN. + CHILLING • **BAKE:** 10 MIN./BATCH
MAKES: 8 DOZEN

- 1 **cup butter, softened**
- 2 **cups sugar**
- 2 **eggs**
- 1 **teaspoon vanilla extract**
- ½ **teaspoon lemon extract**
- 3¾ **cups all-purpose flour**
- 2 **teaspoons baking powder**
- 1 **teaspoon salt**
- 1 **jar (12 ounces) seedless raspberry jam**
- 1 **cup flaked coconut**
- ½ **cup chopped pecans**

1. In a large bowl, cream butter and sugar until light and fluffy. Beat in the eggs and extracts. Combine the flour, baking powder and salt; add to creamed mixture and mix well. Cover and refrigerate for at least 2 hours.

2. Divide dough in half. On a lightly floured surface, roll each half into a 12-in. x 9-in. rectangle. Combine the jam, coconut and pecans; spread over rectangles. Carefully roll up, starting with the long end, into a tight jelly roll. Wrap in plastic wrap. Refrigerate overnight or freeze for 2-3 hours.

3. Cut into ¼-in. slices; place on greased baking sheets. Bake at 375° for 10-12 minutes or until lightly browned. Cool cookies on wire racks.

Browned-Butter Sandwich Spritz

A heavenly sweet maple filling makes these scrumptious spritz cookies a little different. You can count on them to come out buttery and tender. They're almost too pretty to eat.

—DEIRDRE COX KANSAS CITY, MO

PREP: 50 MIN. + CHILLING • **BAKE:** 10 MIN./BATCH + COOLING
MAKES: ABOUT 3 DOZEN

- 1 **cup plus 2 tablespoons butter, cubed**
- 1¼ **cups confectioners' sugar, divided**
- 1 **egg**
- 1 **egg yolk**
- 2 **teaspoons vanilla extract**
- 2¼ **cups all-purpose flour**
- ½ **teaspoon salt**
- ½ **cup maple syrup**

1. In a heavy saucepan, cook and stir butter over medium heat for 8-10 minutes or until golden brown. Transfer to a small bowl; refrigerate until firm, about 1 hour.
2. Set aside 2 tablespoons browned butter for filling. In a large bowl, beat ½ cup confectioners' sugar and remaining browned butter until smooth. Beat in the egg, yolk and vanilla. Combine flour and salt; gradually add to creamed mixture and mix well.
3. Using a cookie press fitted with the disk of your choice, press dough 2 in. apart onto parchment paper-lined baking sheets. Bake at 375° for 8-9 minutes or until set (do not brown). Remove to wire racks to cool.
4. In a small heavy saucepan, bring syrup to a boil. Cool slightly. Whisk in remaining confectioners' sugar until smooth. Beat reserved browned butter until light and fluffy. Beat in syrup mixture until smooth.
5. Spread 1 teaspoon filling over the bottom of half of the cookies. Top with remaining cookies.

Angel Wings

I knew this cookie was a winner when my sister sampled one. She was so impressed, she asked me to bake her wedding cake!

—R. LANE TENAFLY, NJ

PREP: 30 MIN. + CHILLING • **BAKE:** 20 MIN.
MAKES: ABOUT 3 DOZEN

- 1 **cup cold butter, cubed**
- 1½ **cups all-purpose flour**
- ½ **cup sour cream**
- 10 **tablespoons sugar, divided**
- 3 **teaspoons ground cinnamon, divided**
  Colored sugar, optional

1. In a large bowl, cut butter into flour until the mixture resembles coarse crumbs. Stir in the sour cream. Turn onto a lightly floured surface; knead 6-8 times or until mixture holds together. Shape into four balls; flatten slightly. Wrap in plastic wrap; refrigerate for 4 hours or overnight.
2. Unwrap one ball. Sprinkle 2 tablespoons sugar on waxed paper; coat all sides of ball with sugar. Roll into a 12-in. x 5-in. rectangle between two sheets of waxed paper. Remove top sheet of waxed paper. Sprinkle dough with ¾ teaspoon cinnamon. Lightly mark a line down the center of the dough, making two 6-in. x 5-in. rectangles.
3. Starting with a short side, roll up jelly-roll style to the center mark; peel waxed paper away while rolling. Repeat with other short side. Wrap in plastic wrap; freeze for 30 minutes. Repeat three times.
4. Place the remaining sugar or place colored sugar if desired on waxed paper. Unwrap one roll. Cut into ½-in. slices; dip each side into sugar. Place 2 in. apart on ungreased baking sheets.
5. Bake at 375° for 12 minutes or until golden brown. Turn cookies; bake 5-8 minutes longer. Remove to wire racks to cool.

Chocolate Puddles

The variations on this original recipe are almost endless. For double chocolate puddles, use semisweet chocolate chips for the white baking chips. Or make peanut butter puddles by substituting peanut butter chips and peanuts for the white chips and mixed nuts.

—**KATHIE GRIFFIN** ANTELOPE, CA

PREP: 25 MIN. + CHILLING • **BAKE:** 10 MIN./BATCH
MAKES: ABOUT 5 DOZEN

- 1 **cup butter, softened**
- 1 **cup sugar**
- 1 **cup packed brown sugar**
- 2 **eggs**
- 2 **teaspoons vanilla extract**
- 3 **cups all-purpose flour**
- ¾ **cup baking cocoa**
- 1 **teaspoon baking soda**

FILLING
- 1 **cup white baking chips**
- ½ **cup plus 2 tablespoons sweetened condensed milk**
- ¾ **cup finely chopped mixed nuts**

1. In a large bowl, cream butter and sugars until light and fluffy. Add the eggs, one at a time, beating well after each addition. Beat in vanilla. Combine the flour, cocoa and baking soda; gradually add to the creamed mixture and mix well. Cover and refrigerate for 2 hours or until dough is stiff.

2. Meanwhile, for filling, heat chips and milk in a heavy saucepan over low heat until chips are melted, stirring constantly. Stir in nuts. Cover and refrigerate for 1 hour or until easy to handle.

3. Roll cookie dough into 1¼-in. balls. Place 2 in. apart on lightly greased baking sheets. Using the end of a wooden spoon handle, make an indentation in the center; smooth any cracks.

4. Roll filling into ½-in. balls; gently push one into each cookie. Bake at 375° for 8-10 minutes or until cookies are set. Remove to wire racks to cool.

Peanut Crescents

I've been making these festive crescents for more than 30 years. They freeze well and look pretty served on Christmas dishes.
—**KAY BRANTLEY** SHAVER LAKE, CA

PREP: 25 MIN. + CHILLING • **BAKE:** 15 MIN./BATCH + COOLING
MAKES: ABOUT 3 DOZEN

- 1 **cup butter, softened**
- ⅓ **cup sugar**
- 1 **tablespoon water**
- 1 **teaspoon vanilla extract**
- 2 **cups all-purpose flour**
- ½ **cup finely chopped salted peanuts**
  Confectioners' sugar

1. In a small bowl, cream the butter and sugar until light and fluffy. Beat in water and vanilla. Gradually add flour and mix well. Stir in peanuts. Cover and refrigerate for 1 hour or until easy to handle.

2. Shape rounded tablespoonfuls of dough into 2½-in. crescents. Place 2 in. apart on ungreased baking sheets. Bake at 350° for 15-18 minutes or until set (do not brown).

3. Roll warm cookies in confectioners' sugar; cool completely on wire racks. Roll cooled cookies again in confectioners' sugar.

Honey-Peanut Butter Cookies

It's not unusual for my husband to request these cookies by name. You'll love 'em.

—LUCILE PROCTOR PANGUITCH, UT

PREP: 15 MIN. • **BAKE:** 10 MIN./BATCH • **MAKES:** 5 DOZEN

- ½ **cup shortening**
- 1 **cup creamy peanut butter**
- 1 **cup honey**
- 2 **eggs, lightly beaten**
- 3 **cups all-purpose flour**
- 1 **cup sugar**

- 1½ **teaspoons baking soda**
- 1 **teaspoon baking powder**
- ½ **teaspoon salt**

1. Preheat oven to 350°. In a bowl, mix shortening, peanut butter and honey. Add eggs; mix well. Combine flour, sugar, baking soda, baking powder and salt; add to peanut butter mixture and mix well.

2. Roll into 1- to 1½-in. balls and place on ungreased baking sheets. Flatten with a fork dipped in flour. Bake 8-10 minutes or until set. Remove to wire racks to cool.

Smiling Sugar Cookies

These cute cookie pops are a big hit at bake sales. I sell them for $1 each and watch them disappear! The bright and cheery faces always catch kids' attention.

—BRENDA BAWDON ALPENA, SD

PREP: 30 MIN. • **BAKE:** 10 MIN. + STANDING
MAKES: ABOUT 2 DOZEN

- ½ cup butter, softened
- ½ cup sugar
- ½ cup packed brown sugar
- 1 egg
- ⅓ cup 2% milk
- 2 teaspoons vanilla extract
- 3 cups all-purpose flour
- 2 teaspoons cream of tartar
- 1 teaspoon baking soda
- ½ teaspoon salt
  About 24 Popsicle sticks
- 1 cup vanilla frosting
  Red, blue and green paste food coloring
  Assorted small candies

1. In a large bowl, cream the butter and sugars until light and fluffy. Beat in the egg, milk and vanilla. Combine the flour, cream of tartar, baking soda and salt; gradually add to creamed mixture and mix well. Roll dough into 1½-in. balls; insert a Popsicle stick in the center of each.
2. Place 2 in. apart on lightly greased baking sheets; flatten slightly. Bake at 375° for 8-10 minutes or until lightly browned. Remove to wire racks to cool.
3. Divide frosting among three bowls; tint as desired. Place each color of frosting in a resealable plastic bag; cut a small hole in a corner of bag. Pipe hair and mouths onto cookies; use a dab of frosting to attach small candies for eyes. Let dry for at least 30 minutes.

Coffee Bonbons

When I first sampled this unique cookie, I decided it was the best I'd ever tasted! The coffee flavor and chocolate icing make it a delightful treat at buffets and church socials.

—LEITZEL MALZAHN FOX POINT, WI

PREP: 20 MIN. + CHILLING • **BAKE:** 20 MIN./BATCH
MAKES: 5 DOZEN

- 1 cup butter, softened
- ¾ cup confectioners' sugar
- ½ teaspoon vanilla extract
- 1 tablespoon instant coffee granules
- 1¾ cups all-purpose flour

CHOCOLATE GLAZE
- 1 tablespoon butter
- ½ ounce unsweetened chocolate
- 1 cup confectioners' sugar
- 2 tablespoons milk

1. In a bowl, cream butter and sugar until light and fluffy. Add vanilla. Combine coffee and flour; stir into creamed mixture and mix well. Refrigerate until easy to handle. Shape into ¾-in. balls and place on ungreased baking sheets. Bake at 350° for 18-20 minutes.
2. Meanwhile, for glaze, melt butter and chocolate together. Add melted mixture to sugar along with milk; beat until smooth. Frost cookies while still warm.

Apricot Cheese Crescents

I traditionally bake these for Christmas. A cross between sweet breads and cookies, they're such elegant treats that I have been asked to make them for weddings. They're so versatile—and, as you can see, they're also beautiful.

—RUTH GILHOUSEN KNOXDALE, PA

PREP: 1 HOUR + CHILLING • **BAKE:** 15 MIN./BATCH
MAKES: 4½ DOZEN

- 2 **cups all-purpose flour**
- ½ **teaspoon salt**
- 1 **cup cold butter**
- 1 **cup (8 ounces) 4% cottage cheese**

FILLING

- 1 **package (6 ounces) dried apricots**
- ½ **cup water**
- ½ **cup sugar**

TOPPING

- ¾ **cup finely chopped almonds**
- ½ **cup sugar**
- 1 **egg white, lightly beaten**

1. In a large bowl, combine flour and salt; cut in butter until crumbly. Add cottage cheese; mix well. Shape into 1-in. balls. Cover the dough and refrigerate several hours or overnight.

2. For the filling, combine apricots and water in a saucepan. Cover and simmer for 20 minutes. Cool for 10 minutes.

3. Pour into a blender; cover and process on high speed until smooth. Transfer to a bowl; stir in sugar. Cover and refrigerate.

4. For topping, combine almonds and sugar; set aside. On a floured surface, roll the balls into 2½-in. circles. Spoon about 1 teaspoon of filling onto each. Fold dough over filling and pinch edges to seal.

5. Place on greased baking sheets. Brush tops with egg white; sprinkle with almond mixture. Bake at 375° for 12-15 minutes or until lightly browned.

Cardamom Cookies

Cardamom, almond extract and walnuts enhance the flavor of these buttery, melt-in-your-mouth cookies.

—MARY STEINER WEST BEND, WI

PREP: 20 MIN. • **BAKE:** 15 MIN./BATCH • **MAKES:** 6 DOZEN

- 2 **cups butter, softened**
- 2½ **cups confectioners' sugar, divided**
- 1½ **teaspoons almond extract**
- 3¾ **cups all-purpose flour**
- 1 **teaspoon ground cardamom**
- ⅛ **teaspoon salt**
- 1 **cup finely chopped walnuts**

1. In a large bowl, cream the butter and 1½ cups confectioners' sugar until smooth. Beat in extract. Combine flour, cardamom and salt; gradually add to the creamed mixture. Stir in walnuts.

2. Roll into 1-in. balls. Place 2 in. apart on ungreased baking sheets. Bake at 350° for 15-17 minutes or until edges are golden.

3. Roll warm cookies in the remaining confectioners' sugar. Cool on wire racks.

Fudge-Filled Dessert Strips

This family favorite was handed down to me by my mother. Everyone who tastes the flaky chocolate-filled strips asks for the recipe. They're delicious!

—KIMBERLY SANTORO PALM CITY, FL

PREP: 40 MIN. • **BAKE:** 30 MIN./BATCH + COOLING
MAKES: 3 DOZEN

- 1 cup butter, softened
- 1 package (8 ounces) cream cheese, softened
- 2 cups all-purpose flour
- 2 cups (12 ounces) semisweet chocolate chips
- 1 can (14 ounces) sweetened condensed milk
- 2 cups chopped walnuts
  Confectioners' sugar, optional

1. In a large bowl, cream butter and cream cheese until light and fluffy. Gradually add flour and mix well.

2. Turn onto lightly floured surface; knead until smooth, about 3 minutes. Divide dough into fourths; cover and refrigerate for 1-2 hours or until easy to handle.

3. In a microwave-safe bowl, melt chocolate chips and milk; stir until smooth. Stir in walnuts. Cool to room temperature.

4. Roll out each portion of dough onto an ungreased baking sheet into an 11-in. x 6½-in. rectangle. Spread ¾ cup chocolate filling down the center of each rectangle. Fold long sides to the center; press to seal all edges. Turn over so the seam sides are down.

5. Bake at 350° for 27-32 minutes or until lightly browned. Remove to wire racks to cool. Cut into ½-in. slices. Dust with confectioners' sugar if desired.

Braided Sweetheart Cookies

Grandma Lilly Person has been making these tender cookies for 48 years. When our daughter, Naomi, married Philip Shellenberg, Grandma made them in heart shapes for the wedding. The guests gobbled them up in a heartbeat!

—RHONDA BERSTAD MELFORT, SK

PREP: 25 MIN. + CHILLING • **BAKE:** 10 MIN. • **MAKES:** 2 DOZEN

1	**cup butter, softened**
1½	**cups confectioners' sugar**
1	**egg**
½	**teaspoon vanilla extract**
2½	**cups all-purpose flour**
½	**teaspoon baking powder**
½	**teaspoon salt**
6	**to 8 drops red food coloring**

1. In a large bowl, cream butter and sugar until light and fluffy. Beat in egg and vanilla. Combine the flour, baking powder and salt; gradually add to creamed mixture and mix well.

2. Divide dough in half; tint one portion pink, leaving the remaining portion white. Wrap each portion in plastic wrap; refrigerate for 4 hours or overnight.

3. For each cookie, shape a 1-in. ball of each color into an 8-in. rope. Place a pink and white rope side-by-side; press together gently and twist. Place 2 in. apart on ungreased baking sheets; shape into a heart and pinch ends to seal.

4. Bake at 350° for 8-11 minutes or until edges are lightly browned. Cool on wire racks.

Mocha Cookie Pretzels

Looking for a little something special to bake up for the holidays? Try these elegant mocha-frosted cookies. They're great with coffee and make an eye-catching addition to any cookie platter.
—TASTE OF HOME TEST KITCHEN

PREP: 1½ HOURS + CHILLING • **BAKE:** 10 MIN./BATCH
MAKES: 4 DOZEN

- ½ **cup butter, softened**
- ½ **cup sugar**
- 1 **egg**
- 2 **ounces white baking chocolate, melted and cooled**
- 1 **teaspoon vanilla extract**
- 2 **cups cake flour**
- ¼ **teaspoon salt**

GLAZE

- 1 **cup (6 ounces) semisweet chocolate chips**
- 1 **teaspoon shortening**
- 1 **teaspoon light corn syrup**
- 1 **cup confectioners' sugar**
- 3 **to 5 tablespoons hot brewed coffee**
- 2 **ounces white baking chocolate, chopped**
  Green colored sugar, optional

1. In a large bowl, cream butter and sugar until light and fluffy. Beat in egg. Beat in melted chocolate and vanilla. Combine flour and salt; gradually add to the creamed mixture and mix well. Cover and refrigerate for 1 hour or until dough is easy to handle.

2. Divide the dough into fourths; divide each portion into 12 pieces. Shape each piece into a 6 in. rope; twist into a pretzel shape. Place 1 in. apart onto lightly greased baking sheets.

3. Bake at 400° for 7-9 minutes or until set. Remove to wire racks to cool.

4. For glaze, in a microwave, melt the semisweet chips, shortening and corn syrup; stir until smooth. Stir in confectioners' sugar and enough coffee to achieve a glaze consistency. Dip cookies in glaze; allow excess to drip off. Place on waxed paper until set.

5. In a microwave, melt white chocolate over 30% power; stir until smooth. Drizzle over cookies. Decorate with green sprinkles if desired; let stand until set.

Scandinavian Pecan Cookies

We enjoyed these rich, buttery cookies at a bed-and-breakfast in Galena, Illinois, and the hostess was kind enough to share her simple recipe. The pretty nut-topped treats are so special you could give a home-baked batch as a gift.
—LAURIE KNOKE DEKALB, IL

START TO FINISH: 30 MIN. • **MAKES:** 5 DOZEN

- 1 **cup butter, softened**
- ¾ **cup packed brown sugar**
- 1 **egg, separated**
- 2 **cups all-purpose flour**
- ½ **cup finely chopped pecans**

1. In a large bowl, cream butter and brown sugar until light and fluffy. Beat in the egg yolk. Gradually add flour until blended.

2. Shape into 1-in. balls. In a small bowl, beat egg white. Dip balls in egg white, then roll in pecans. Place 2 in. apart on ungreased baking sheets; flatten slightly. Bake at 375° for 8-12 minutes or until the edges are lightly browned. Remove to wire racks to cool.

Raspberry Almond Strips

A cup of tea is the perfect complement to these scrumptious cookie strips dressed up with raspberry filling. The chopped almonds make them an extra-special treat.

—TASTE OF HOME TEST KITCHEN

START TO FINISH: 30 MIN. • **MAKES:** 16 COOKIES

- ½ **tube refrigerated sugar cookie dough, softened**
- ⅓ **cup all-purpose flour**
- ¼ **cup finely chopped almonds**
- 3 **tablespoons raspberry cake and pastry filling**

OPTIONAL ICING

- ¼ **cup confectioners' sugar**
- 1½ **teaspoons 2% milk**
- ⅛ **teaspoon almond extract**

1. Preheat oven to 350°. In a small bowl, beat cookie dough, flour and almonds until blended. Roll into a 13½x2-in. rectangle on an ungreased baking sheet.

2. Using a wooden spoon handle, make a ¼-in.-deep indentation lengthwise down center of rectangle. Bake 5 minutes.

3. Spoon raspberry filling into indentation. Bake 8-10 minutes longer or until cookie is golden brown. Cool on pan 2 minutes.

4. Remove from pan to a cutting board; cut crosswise into 16 slices. Transfer to a wire rack to cool. If desired, in a small bowl, mix remaining ingredients until smooth; drizzle over warm cookies.

Walnut Horn Cookies

At our house, it wouldn't be Christmas without these Pennsylvania Dutch cookies known locally as "kiffels."

—SHARON ALLEN ALLENTOWN, PA

PREP: 35 MIN. + CHILLING • **BAKE:** 20 MIN./BATCH
MAKES: ABOUT 8 DOZEN

- 1 **pound butter, softened**
- 2 **packages (one 8 ounces, one 3 ounces) cream cheese, softened**
- 4 **egg yolks**
- 4¼ **cups all-purpose flour**

FILLING

- 4 **cups ground walnuts (about 1 pound)**
- 5¾ **cups confectioners' sugar, divided**
- 4 **egg whites**
- ½ **teaspoon vanilla extract**
- ½ **teaspoon almond extract**

1. In a large bowl, combine butter, cream cheese, egg yolks and flour; beat until smooth. Shape into 1-in. balls; place in a container with waxed paper separating each layer. Cover and refrigerate overnight.

2. For filling, combine walnuts and 3¾ cups sugar (the mixture will be dry). In a small bowl, beat egg whites until soft peaks form; fold into nut mixture. Add extracts and a few drops of water if necessary until filling reaches a spreading consistency.

3. Place remaining sugar in a bowl; roll cream cheese balls in sugar until completely covered. Place a few balls at a time between two sheets of waxed paper.

4. Roll balls into 2½-in. circles. Gently spread about 2 teaspoons of filling over each. Roll up; place seam side down on ungreased baking sheets. Curve the ends slightly. Bake at 350° for 20 minutes or until lightly browned. Cool on wire racks.

Caramel-Filled Chocolate Cookies

These cookies have a tasty caramel center. With pecans and a white chocolate drizzle on top, they're almost too pretty to eat!

—**DEB WALSH** CABERY, IL

PREP: 25 MIN. • **BAKE:** 10 MIN./BATCH
MAKES: ABOUT 5 DOZEN

- 1 **cup butter, softened**
- 1 **cup plus 1 tablespoon sugar, divided**
- 1 **cup packed brown sugar**
- 2 **eggs**
- 1 **teaspoon vanilla extract**
- 2½ **cups all-purpose flour**
- ¾ **cup baking cocoa**
- 1 **teaspoon baking soda**
- 1¼ **cups chopped pecans, divided**
- 1 **package (13 ounces) Rolo candies**
- 4 **ounces white baking chocolate, chopped**

1. In a large bowl, cream butter, 1 cup sugar and brown sugar until light and fluffy. Add the eggs, one at a time, beating well after each addition. Beat in vanilla. Combine the flour, cocoa and baking soda; gradually add to the creamed mixture, beating just until combined. Stir in ½ cup pecans.

2. Shape a tablespoonful of dough around each candy, forming a ball. In a small bowl, combine the remaining sugar and pecans; dip half of each cookie into mixture. Place nut side up 2 in. apart on greased baking sheets.

3. Bake at 375° for 7-10 minutes or until tops are slightly cracked. Cool for 3 minutes before removing to wire racks to cool completely.

4. In a microwave, melt white chocolate at 70% power for 1 minute; stir. Microwave at additional 10- to 20-second intervals, stirring until smooth. Drizzle over cookies.

Peppermint Snowballs

These snowball cookies have a surprise peppermint filling. One bite and you'll know these are special.

—JUDITH SCHOLOVICH WAUKESHA, WI

PREP: 30 MIN. • **BAKE:** 15 MIN./BATCH • **MAKES:** ABOUT 4 DOZEN

- 1 cup butter, softened
- ½ cup confectioners' sugar
- 1 teaspoon vanilla extract
- 2½ cups all-purpose flour

FILLING
- 2 tablespoons cream cheese, softened
- 1 tablespoon milk
- ½ cup confectioners' sugar
- 2 tablespoons finely crushed peppermint candy or candy canes
- 1 drop red food coloring

TOPPING
- ¼ cup confectioners' sugar
- 6 tablespoons finely crushed peppermint candy or candy canes

1. In a bowl, cream butter and sugar; add vanilla. Stir in flour; knead until mixed well. Reserve ½ cup of dough; shape remaining dough into 1-in. balls.

2. For filling, combine cream cheese and milk in a small bowl. Stir in sugar, candy and food coloring; mix well. Make a deep well in the center of each ball; fill with ¼ teaspoon filling. Use reserved dough to cover filling. Reshape if necessary into smooth balls.

3. Place on ungreased baking sheets. Bake at 350° for 12-14 minutes. Combine topping ingredients; roll cookies in mixture while still warm. Cool on wire racks.

Almond Kiss Cookies

These cookies are unbelievable! They're easy to make, look elegant and are absolutely delicious. Almond, raspberry and chocolate make a delectable combination.

—KATHY ALDRICH WEBSTER, NY

PREP: 30 MIN. + CHILLING • **BAKE:** 10 MIN./BATCH + COOLING
MAKES: 40 COOKIES

- ½ cup butter, softened
- ½ cup sugar
- ½ cup packed brown sugar
- 1 egg
- 1 teaspoon almond extract
- 2 cups all-purpose flour
- 1 teaspoon baking soda
- ¼ teaspoon salt
  Additional sugar
- 40 milk chocolate kisses with almonds

GLAZE
- 1 cup confectioners' sugar
- 1 tablespoon milk
- 4 teaspoons raspberry jam
- ¼ teaspoon almond extract

1. In a bowl, cream the butter and sugars. Beat in egg and extract. Combine the flour, baking soda and salt; gradually add to creamed mixture. Cover and chill for 1 hour or until easy to handle.

2. Roll into 1-in. balls, then roll in additional sugar. Place 2 in. apart on ungreased baking sheets. Bake at 325° for 13-15 minutes or until golden brown. Immediately press a chocolate kiss into the center of each cookie. Cool on wire racks. Combine glaze ingredients; drizzle over cookies.

Meringue Bunnies

These cute cookies are a great addition to the table when entertaining at Easter. Encourage the kids to lend a hand and help decorate the bunnies.

—TASTE OF HOME TEST KITCHEN

PREP: 30 MIN. • **BAKE:** 1½ HOURS + COOLING • **MAKES:** 1 DOZEN

- 2 **egg whites**
- ⅛ **teaspoon cream of tartar**
- ½ **cup sugar**
- ¼ **cup pink candy coating disks**
- 36 **heart-shaped red decorating sprinkles**

1. Place egg whites in a small bowl; let stand at room temperature 30 minutes.

2. Preheat oven to 225°. Add cream of tartar to egg whites; beat on medium speed until foamy. Gradually add sugar, 1 tablespoon at a time, beating on high after each addition until sugar is dissolved. Continue beating until stiff glossy peaks form.

3. Cut a small hole in the tip of a pastry bag or in a corner of a food-safe plastic bag. Transfer meringue to bag. Pipe 4¾-in. bunny shapes onto parchment paper-lined baking sheets. Bake 1½ hours or until firm. Remove to wire racks to cool completely.

4. In a microwave, melt candy coating; stir until smooth. Place in another pastry or plastic bag; cut a small hole in the tip of the bag. Pipe ears, whiskers and mouths on bunnies with melted candy coating. Attach hearts for eyes and nose.

Apricot Coconut Treasures

These elegant filled cookies are some of my favorites for holiday time. Try them for a bridal shower, spring brunch or ladies' luncheon, too.

—HELEN KEBER OSHKOSH, WI

PREP: 45 MIN. • **BAKE:** 20 MIN./BATCH • **MAKES:** 2½ DOZEN

- 1 **cup butter, softened**
- 1 **cup (8 ounces) sour cream**
- 2 **cups all-purpose flour**
- ½ **teaspoon salt**
- ½ **cup flaked coconut**
- ½ **cup apricot preserves**
- ¼ **cup chopped walnuts**

1. In a large bowl, cream butter and sour cream until light and fluffy. Combine flour and salt; gradually add to the creamed mixture and mix well. Divide dough into fourths; wrap in plastic wrap. Refrigerate for 4 hours or until easy to handle.

2. In a small bowl, combine the coconut, preserves and walnuts; set aside. On a lightly floured surface, roll out each portion of dough to ⅛-in. thickness.

3. Cut into 2½-in. squares; spread each with a rounded teaspoonful of coconut mixture. Carefully fold one corner over filling. Moisten opposite corner with water and fold over first corner; seal.

4. Place 1½ in. apart on ungreased baking sheets. Bake at 350° for 18-20 minutes or until lightly browned. Remove to wire racks to cool.

Bakeshop TIP

Shaped Cookie Know-How

Shaped cookie dough is easier to handle if it is first chilled in the refrigerator. The heat from your hands can soften the butter in the dough, making it harder to shape, so work quickly. Dust hands lightly with flour to prevent dough from sticking while shaping it.

Cinnamon Oatmeal Cookies

My family loves these big old-fashioned cookies. They're crisp, yet still chewy in the center, and the cinnamon makes them a little different from typical oatmeal cookies.

—**ANNA BRYDL** TOBIAS, NE

PREP: 15 MIN. • **BAKE:** 10 MIN./BATCH • **MAKES:** 4 DOZEN

- 1 **cup butter, softened**
- 1 **cup sugar**
- 1 **cup packed brown sugar**
- 2 **eggs**
- 1 **teaspoon vanilla extract**
- 1½ **cups all-purpose flour**
- 1 **teaspoon baking soda**
- 1 **teaspoon ground cinnamon**
- ½ **teaspoon baking powder**
- ½ **teaspoon salt**
- 3 **cups quick-cooking oats**

1. In a large bowl, cream butter and sugars until light and fluffy. Beat in eggs and vanilla. Combine the flour, baking soda, cinnamon, baking powder and salt; gradually add to creamed mixture and mix well. Stir in oats.

2. Shape into 1½-in. balls. Place 2 in. apart on ungreased baking sheets. Bake at 350° for 10-12 minutes or until golden brown. Cool for 1 minute before removing cookies to wire racks.

No-Bake Cookie Balls

These quick bites are great when you're short on time or don't want to turn on the oven. I make them a day or two ahead to let the flavors blend.

—CARMELETTA DAILEY WINFIELD, TX

PREP: 25 MIN. • **MAKES:** 5 DOZEN

- 1 cup (6 ounces) semisweet chocolate chips
- 3 cups confectioners' sugar
- 1¾ cups crushed vanilla wafers (about 55 wafers)
- 1 cup chopped walnuts, toasted
- ⅓ cup orange juice
- 3 tablespoons light corn syrup
  Additional confectioners' sugar

1. In a large microwave-safe bowl, melt chocolate chips; stir until smooth. Stir in the confectioners' sugar, vanilla wafers, walnuts, orange juice and corn syrup.

2. Shape into 1-in. balls; roll in additional confectioners' sugar. Store in an airtight container.

Mexican Wedding Cakes

It's a Mexican tradition to serve these tender, shortbread-like cookies at weddings, but we also enjoy them around the holidays. You can shape the dough into 2-inch crescents or 1-inch balls before baking.

—SARITA JOHNSTON SAN ANTONIO, TX

PREP: 15 MIN. • **BAKE:** 15MIN./BATCH • **MAKES:** ABOUT 6 DOZEN

- 2 cups butter, softened
- 1 cup confectioners' sugar
- 4 cups all-purpose flour
- 1 teaspoon vanilla extract
- 1 cup finely chopped pecans
  Additional confectioners' sugar

1. In a large bowl, cream butter and sugar until light and fluffy. Beat in vanilla. Gradually add flour and mix well. Stir in pecans.

2. Shape tablespoonfuls into 2-in. crescents. Place 2 in. apart on ungreased baking sheets.

3. Bake at 350° for 12-15 minutes or until cookies are lightly browned. Roll warm cookies in confectioners' sugar; cool on wire racks.

Butter Pecan Cookies

My crisp shortbread-like cookies are wonderful with a cup of coffee. They're delicious and so easy to make.

—SHARON CRIDER JUNCTION CITY, KS

START TO FINISH: 30 MIN. • **MAKES:** ABOUT 2 DOZEN

- ¾ cup butter, softened
- 1 package (3.4 ounces) instant butterscotch pudding mix
- 1¼ cups all-purpose flour
- ½ cup chopped pecans

1. In a small bowl, beat butter and pudding mix until smooth. Gradually beat in flour. Fold in pecans. Roll into 1½-in. balls.

2. Place 2 in. apart on greased baking sheets; flatten to ½ in. with the bottom of a glass coated with cooking spray.

3. Bake at 375° for 10-13 minutes or until light golden brown. Remove from pans to wire racks.

Brownie Biscotti

Daintily drizzled with white chocolate, these pretty biscotti are loaded with chocolate chips and crunchy almonds. They look gorgeous in a holiday gift basket with a hot chocolate and tea assortment.
—**AMBER SUMNER** CONGRESS, AZ

PREP: 20 MIN. • **BAKE:** 50 MIN. + COOLING • **MAKES:** 3 DOZEN

- ½ cup butter, melted
- 3 eggs
- 2 teaspoons vanilla extract
- 2½ cups all-purpose flour
- 1⅓ cups sugar
- ¾ cup baking cocoa
- 2 teaspoons baking powder
- ½ teaspoon baking soda
- 1 cup unblanched almonds, toasted and coarsely chopped
- ½ cup miniature semisweet chocolate chips

DRIZZLE
- ½ cup white baking chips
- 1½ teaspoons shortening

1. In a large bowl, combine the butter, eggs and vanilla until well blended. Combine the flour, sugar, cocoa, baking powder and baking soda; gradually add to butter mixture just until combined (dough will be crumbly).

2. Turn dough onto a lightly floured surface; knead in almonds and chocolate chips. Divide dough in half. On an ungreased baking sheet, shape each portion into a 12-in. x 3-in. log, leaving 3 in. between the logs.

3. Bake at 325° for 30-35 minutes or until set and tops are cracked. Cool for 15 minutes. Carefully transfer to a cutting board; cut the log diagonally with a serrated knife into ½-in. slices.

4. Place cut side down on ungreased baking sheets. Bake for 20-25 minutes or until firm and dry. Remove to wire racks to cool.

5. For drizzle, in a microwave, melt white chips and shortening at 70% power for 1 minute; stir. Microwave at additional 10- to 20-second intervals, stirring until smooth. Drizzle over biscotti.

Cinnamon Almond Crescents

I set out these cookies as we open our gifts on Christmas Eve. Before long, the plate is empty and I'm being asked to refill it!
—**JENNIFER BRANUM** O'FALLON, IL

PREP: 15D MIN. • **BAKE:** 10 MIN./BATCH
MAKES: ABOUT 3½ DOZEN

- 1 cup butter, softened
- ⅓ cup sugar
- ½ teaspoon vanilla extract
- 1⅔ cups all-purpose flour
- ½ cup finely ground blanched almonds

TOPPING
- ½ cup sugar
- ½ teaspoon ground cinnamon

1. In a large bowl, cream butter and sugar until light and fluffy. Beat in vanilla. Combine flour and almonds; gradually add to creamed mixture and mix well.

2. Roll into 1-in. balls; shape into crescents. Place 2 in. apart on lightly greased baking sheets. Bake at 350° for 10-12 minutes or until set (do not brown).

3. In a small bowl, combine sugar and cinnamon. Roll warm cookies in cinnamon-sugar; cool on wire racks.

Dipped Spice Cookies

A hint of orange and a sprinkling of spices lend old-fashioned goodness to these delightful treats. The logs are dipped in melted chocolate and sprinkled with nuts for a special look.

—TASTE OF HOME TEST KITCHEN

PREP: 25 MIN. • **BAKE:** 10 MIN./BATCH + STANDING
MAKES: ABOUT 3½ DOZEN

- ½ **tube refrigerated sugar cookie dough, softened**
- ½ **cup all-purpose flour**
- ¼ **cup packed brown sugar**
- 1 **tablespoon orange juice**
- ¾ **teaspoon ground cinnamon**
- ½ **teaspoon ground ginger**
- ½ **teaspoon grated orange peel**

- ½ **cup semisweet chocolate chips**
- 4 **teaspoons shortening**
- ¼ **cup finely chopped walnuts**

1. In a large bowl, beat the cookie dough, flour, brown sugar, orange juice, cinnamon, ginger and orange peel until combined. Shape teaspoonfuls of dough into 2-in. logs. Place 2 in. apart on ungreased baking sheets.

2. Bake at 350° for 8-10 minutes or until edges are golden brown. Remove to wire racks to cool.

3. In a microwave-safe bowl, melt chocolate chips and shortening; stir until smooth. Dip one end of each cookie into melted chocolate, allowing excess to drip off; sprinkle with walnuts. Place on waxed paper; let stand until set.

Frosted Peanut Butter Cookies

This is our go-to chocolate frosting recipe for topping peanut butter, sugar or chocolate chip cookies. The chocolate dries with a glossy sheen that will make your cookies shine.

—TASTE OF HOME TEST KITCHEN

START TO FINISH: 30 MIN. • **MAKES:** ABOUT 2 DOZEN

- 1 **package (17½ ounces) peanut butter cookie mix**
- 2 **cups confectioners' sugar**
- ¼ **cup baking cocoa**
- ¼ **cup hot water**
- 1 **teaspoon vanilla extract**
  Sliced almonds or pecan halves

1. In a large bowl, prepare cookie dough according to package directions. Shape into 1-in. balls. Place 2 in. apart on ungreased baking sheets.

2. Bake at 375° for 8-10 minutes or until edges are golden brown. Cool for 1 minute before removing to wire racks.

3. For frosting, in a large bowl, combine the confectioners' sugar, cocoa, water and vanilla. Spread over cookies; top with nuts.

Caramel Tassies

Buttery cookie cups with a smooth caramel filling make a nice addition to a Christmas dessert tray. These are treats my family looks forward to every year.

—**JANE BRICKER** SCOTTDALE, PA

PREP: 1 HOUR • **BAKE:** 15 MIN./BATCH + COOLING
MAKES: 4 DOZEN

- 1 cup butter, softened
- 2 packages (3 ounces each) cream cheese, softened
- 2 cups all-purpose flour

FILLING
- 1 package (14 ounces) caramels
- ¼ cup plus 3 tablespoons evaporated milk

FROSTING
- 2 tablespoons shortening
- 2 tablespoons butter, softened
- 1 cup confectioners' sugar
- 1 tablespoon evaporated milk

1. In a large bowl, cream butter and cream cheese until light and fluffy. Gradually add flour and mix well. Cover and refrigerate for 1 hour or until easy to handle.

2. Roll dough into 1-in. balls; press onto the bottom and up the sides of ungreased miniature muffin cups. Prick bottoms with a fork. Bake at 375° for 15-17 minutes or until golden brown. Cool for 5 minutes before removing from pans to wire racks.

3. In a large heavy saucepan over low heat, melt caramels with milk. Remove from the heat; cool slightly. Transfer to a heavy-duty resealable plastic bag; cut a small hole in a corner of the bag. Pipe filling into pastry cups. Cool to room temperature.

4. For frosting, in a small bowl, beat shortening and butter until smooth. Gradually beat in confectioners' sugar and milk until fluffy. Pipe onto filling. Store in the refrigerator.

Buttery Almond Cookies

My husband absolutely loves these cookies. They have an old-fashioned flavor that goes well with a cup of tea. And I love how simple they are to put together.

—**ELAINE ANDERSON** NEW GALILEE, PA

PREP: 20 MIN. • **BAKE:** 15 MIN./BATCH + COOLING
MAKES: ABOUT 4 DOZEN

- 1 cup butter, softened
- 1 cup confectioners' sugar, divided
- 1 teaspoon vanilla extract
- 2 cups all-purpose flour
- ¾ cup chopped almonds

1. In a small bowl, cream butter and ½ cup confectioners' sugar until light and fluffy. Beat in vanilla. Gradually add flour and mix well. Stir in almonds. Shape into 1-in. balls.

2. Place 2 in. apart on ungreased baking sheets. Bake at 350° for 13-16 minutes or until bottoms are golden brown and cookies are set. Cool for 1-2 minutes before removing to wire racks to cool completely. Roll in remaining confectioners' sugar.

Beary Cute Cookies

You don't have to be a kid to enjoy the cheery cookie cubs I served at my teddy bear picnic! I like to make fun foods but don't care to spend a whole lot of time fussing. So the idea of using candy for the bears' features was right up my alley.
—**SUSAN SCHULLER** BRAINERD, MN

PREP: 25 MIN. • **BAKE:** 10 MIN./BATCH • **MAKES:** 2½ DOZEN

- ¾ cup shortening
- ½ cup sugar
- ½ cup packed brown sugar
- 1 egg
- 1 teaspoon vanilla extract
- 2 cups all-purpose flour
- 1 teaspoon salt
- ½ teaspoon baking soda
    Additional sugar
- 30 miniature milk chocolate kisses
- 60 M&M's miniature baking bits

1. In a large bowl, cream shortening and sugars until light and fluffy. Beat in egg and vanilla. Combine the flour, salt and baking soda; gradually add to creamed mixture and mix well (dough will be crumbly).
2. Set aside about ½ cup of dough for ears. Shape remaining dough into 1-in. balls; roll in additional sugar. Place 3 in. apart on ungreased baking sheets. Flatten to about ½-in. thickness. Roll reserved dough into ½-in.

balls; roll in sugar. Place two smaller balls about 1 in. apart touching each flattened ball (do not flatten smaller balls).
3. Bake at 375° for 10-12 minutes or until set and edges are lightly browned. Remove from oven; immediately press one kiss and two baking bits into each cookie for nose and eyes. Cool for 5 minutes before removing from pans to wire racks to cool completely.

Chocolate-Dipped Coconut Snowballs

If you like the taste of coconut and chocolate, you can't help but love these fancy and festive-looking cookies.
—**EMILY BARRETT** WYOMING, PA

PREP: 20 MIN. • **BAKE:** 10 MIN./BATCH + CHILLING
MAKES: ABOUT 5½ DOZEN

- ⅓ cup butter, softened
- ⅔ cup packed brown sugar
- 1 egg
- ½ teaspoon vanilla extract
- 1⅓ cups all-purpose flour
- ¼ teaspoon baking powder
- ¼ teaspoon baking soda
- ¼ teaspoon salt
- 4 ounces German sweet chocolate, finely chopped
- ½ cup flaked coconut
- ½ cup finely chopped pecans, toasted
TOPPING
- 12 ounces semisweet chocolate, chopped
- 4 teaspoons shortening
- 2½ cups flaked coconut, toasted

1. In a large bowl, cream butter and brown sugar until light and fluffy. Beat in egg and vanilla. Combine the flour, baking powder, baking soda and salt; gradually add to creamed mixture and mix well. Stir in the German sweet chocolate, coconut and pecans.
2. Roll into ¾-in. balls. Place 2 in. apart on ungreased baking sheets. Bake at 350° for 10-12 minutes or until edges are browned. Remove to wire racks to cool.
3. In a microwave, melt semisweet chocolate and shortening; stir until smooth. Dip tops of cookies into chocolate mixture; allow excess to drip off. Place on waxed paper-lined baking sheets; sprinkle with toasted coconut. Chill for 1 hour or until firm.

Eggnog Thumbprints

My cute cookie bites always generate recipe requests. They make special holiday gifts and freeze well, too.

—MARY ANN LUDWIG EDWARDSVILLE, IL

PREP: 30 MIN. + CHILLING • **BAKE:** 10 MIN./BATCH + COOLING
MAKES: 4 DOZEN

- ⅔ **cup butter, softened**
- ½ **cup sugar**
- 2 **eggs, separated**
- 1 **teaspoon vanilla extract**
- 1½ **cups all-purpose flour**
- ¼ **teaspoon salt**
- ⅛ **teaspoon ground nutmeg**
- 1 **cup finely chopped walnuts**

FILLING
- ¼ **cup butter, softened**
- 1 **cup confectioners' sugar**
- ¼ **teaspoon rum extract**
- 1 **to 2 teaspoons 2% milk**
- 1 **to 2 drops yellow food coloring, optional**

1. In a large bowl, cream butter and sugar until light and fluffy. Beat in egg yolks and vanilla. Gradually stir in the flour, salt and nutmeg and mix well. Cover and refrigerate for 1 hour or until firm.

2. In a small bowl, whisk egg whites until foamy. Shape dough into 1-in. balls; dip in egg whites, then roll in walnuts. Place 2 in. apart on baking sheets coated with cooking spray.

3. Using a wooden spoon handle, make a ½-in. indentation in the center of each ball. Bake at 350° for 10-12 minutes or until center is set. Carefully remove from pans to wire racks to cool.

4. For filling, combine butter, confectioners' sugar, extract and enough milk to achieve a spreading consistency. Tint with food coloring if desired. Pipe about ½ teaspoon into each cookie.

Butterscotch Snickerdoodles

This recipe is a combination of the traditional snickerdoodle recipe and my mother's best spritz recipe. Everyone comments on the unique combination of ingredients.

—NANCY RADENBAUGH WHITE LAKE, MI

PREP: 20 MIN. • **BAKE:** 15 MIN./BATCH • **MAKES:** 8 DOZEN

- 1 **cup butter, softened**
- ⅓ **cup canola oil**
- 1¼ **cups sugar**
- ⅓ **cup confectioners' sugar**
- 2 **eggs**
- 3 **tablespoons plain yogurt**
- 1½ **teaspoons almond extract**
- ⅛ **teaspoon lemon extract**
- 3½ **cups all-purpose flour**
- 1 **cup whole wheat flour**
- 1 **teaspoon cream of tartar**
- 1 **teaspoon baking soda**
- ½ **teaspoon salt**
- 1 **cup butterscotch chips**
- ½ **cup chopped almonds**
  Additional sugar

1. In a large bowl, beat the butter, oil and sugars until blended. Add eggs, one at a time, beating well after each addition. Beat in yogurt and extracts. Combine flours, cream of tartar, baking soda and salt; gradually add to the butter mixture and mix well. Stir in butterscotch chips and almonds.

2. Roll into 1-in. balls, then in sugar. Place 2 in. apart on ungreased baking sheets. Flatten with a fork dipped in sugar. Bake at 350° for 12-15 minutes or until lightly browned. Remove to wire racks to cool.

Bakeshop TIP

Shaping Cookie Dough into Balls

Use about 2 teaspoons of dough for a 1-inch ball. Roll between the palms of your hands. If the dough is sticky, chill it. You can also spray your hands with cooking spray to help prevent dough from sticking.

Butter Cookies

These cookies are favorites of my nephews, who love the creamy frosting.

—RUTH GRIGGS SOUTH HILL, VA

PREP: 25 MIN. • **BAKE:** 10 MIN./BATCH • **MAKES:** ABOUT 6½ DOZEN

- 1 **cup butter, softened**
- ¾ **cup sugar**
- 1 **egg**
- ½ **teaspoon vanilla extract**
- 2½ **cups all-purpose flour**
- 1 **teaspoon baking powder**
- ¼ **teaspoon salt**

FROSTING
- ½ **cup butter, softened**
- 4 **cups confectioners' sugar**
- 1 **teaspoon vanilla extract**
- 3 **to 4 tablespoons 2% milk**
  Red food coloring, optional

1. In a large bowl, cream butter and sugar until light and fluffy. Beat in egg and vanilla. Combine the flour, baking powder and salt; add to creamed mixture and mix well.

2. Place the dough in a cookie press fitted with a heart plate; form cookies on ungreased baking sheets. Bake at 375° for 6-8 minutes or until set but not brown. Cool on wire racks.

3. Beat butter, sugar and vanilla until smooth. Blend in enough milk until desired spreading consistency is reached. Add food coloring to a portion or all of the frosting if desired. Frost cookies.

Chocolate Gingersnaps

When my daughter, Jennifer, was 15 years old, she created this recipe as a way to combine two of her favorite flavors. The cookies are great with a glass of milk.

—PAULA ZSIRAY LOGAN, UT

PREP: 45 MIN. + CHILLING • **BAKE:** 10 MIN./BATCH
MAKES: 3 DOZEN

- ½ cup butter, softened
- ½ cup packed dark brown sugar
- ¼ cup molasses
- 1 tablespoon water
- 2 teaspoons minced fresh gingerroot
- 1½ cups all-purpose flour
- 1 tablespoon baking cocoa
- 1¼ teaspoons ground ginger
- 1 teaspoon baking soda
- 1 teaspoon ground cinnamon
- ¼ teaspoon ground nutmeg
- ¼ teaspoon ground cloves
- 7 ounces semisweet chocolate, finely chopped
- ¼ cup sugar

1. In a large bowl, cream butter and brown sugar until light and fluffy. Beat in the molasses, water and gingerroot. Combine the flour, cocoa, ginger, baking soda, cinnamon, nutmeg and cloves; gradually add to creamed mixture and mix well. Stir in chocolate. Cover and refrigerate the dough for 2 hours or until easy to handle.

2. Shape dough into 1-in. balls; roll in sugar. Place 2 in. apart on greased baking sheets.

3. Bake at 350° for 10-12 minutes or until tops begin to crack. Cool for 2 minutes before removing to wire racks.

Thumbprint Cookies

Looking for a lighter alternative to traditional Christmas cookies? Try these pretty jam-filled thumbprints. The melt-in-your-mouth treats have a buttery taste and get a nice crunch from pecans.
—TASTE OF HOME TEST KITCHEN

START TO FINISH: 30 MIN. • **MAKES:** 2½ DOZEN

- 6 tablespoons butter, softened
- ½ cup sugar
- 1 egg
- 2 tablespoons canola oil
- 1 teaspoon vanilla extract
- ¼ teaspoon butter flavoring or almond extract
- 1½ cups all-purpose flour
- ¼ cup cornstarch
- 1 teaspoon baking powder
- ¼ teaspoon salt
- 1 egg white
- ⅓ cup chopped pecans
- 7½ teaspoons assorted jams

1. In a large bowl, cream butter and sugar until light and fluffy. Beat in egg. Beat in the oil, vanilla and butter flavoring. Combine the flour, cornstarch, baking powder and salt; gradually stir into creamed mixture and mix well.

2. Roll into 1-in. balls. In a bowl, lightly beat egg white. Dip each ball halfway into egg white, then into pecans.

3. Place nut side up 2 in. apart on baking sheets coated with cooking spray. Using the end of a wooden spoon handle, make an indentation in the center of each.

4. Bake at 350° for 8-10 minutes or until the edges are lightly browned. Remove to wire racks. Fill each cookie with ¼ teaspoon jam; cool.

Frosted Snowmen

These cookies were created when I used regular sugar instead of the confectioners' sugar as my recipes specified. I didn't notice the error until I tasted one and thought it was even better than the original! I took a batch of these frosty fellows to my son's class and everyone loved them.

—LEAH GALLINGTON CORONA, CA

PREP: 25 MIN. • **BAKE:** 10 MIN./BATCH + COOLING
MAKES: 6 DOZEN

1½ cups butter, softened
2¼ cups sugar
1 egg
3 teaspoons vanilla extract
3¾ cups all-purpose flour
½ teaspoon baking powder
72 pretzel sticks
1 can (16 ounces) vanilla frosting
Blue and red decorating icing

1. In a bowl, cream butter and sugar. Gradually beat in the egg and vanilla. Combine flour and baking powder; add to the creamed mixture. Shape dough into 1-in., ⅝-in. and ¼-in. balls.

2. For each snowman, place one of each size ball ¼ in. apart on ungreased baking sheets; place snowmen 2 in. apart. Break pretzel sticks in half; press into sides of middle ball.

3. Bake at 375° for 10-12 minutes or until bottoms are lightly browned. Cool 1 minute before removing to wire racks. Frost cooled cookies. Decorate with blue icing for eyes, mouth and buttons, and red for nose and scarf.

Boo-rrific Kisses

We turned meringue cookies into whimsical kisses perfect for Halloween. With just 15 calories, each little treat can be enjoyed guilt-free!

—TASTE OF HOME TEST KITCHEN

PREP: 20 MIN. • **BAKE:** 40 MIN. + STANDING • **MAKES:** 2½ DOZEN

- 2 **egg whites**
- ½ **teaspoon vanilla extract**
- ¼ **teaspoon almond extract**
- ⅛ **teaspoon cider vinegar**
- ½ **cup sugar**
  Orange food coloring, optional
- 1½ **teaspoons miniature semisweet chocolate chips**

1. Place egg whites in a small bowl; let stand at room temperature for 30 minutes. Add extracts and vinegar; beat on medium speed until soft peaks form. Gradually beat in sugar, 1 tablespoon at a time, on high until stiff glossy peaks form and sugar is dissolved, about 6 minutes. Beat in food coloring if desired.

2. Cut a small hole in the corner of a pastry or plastic bag; insert a #10 round pastry tip. Fill bag with egg white mixture. Pipe 1½-in.-diameter ghosts onto parchment paper-lined baking sheets. Add two chips on each for eyes.

3. Bake at 250° for 40-45 minutes or until set and dry. Turn the oven off; leave cookies in oven for 1 hour. Carefully remove from parchment paper. Store in an airtight container.

Special Chocolate Treats

I'm proud to serve these lovely cookies to guests. They freeze well.

—WALTER MAX WABASHA, MN

PREP: 35 MIN. + CHILLING • **BAKE:** 15 MIN./BATCH + COOLING
MAKES: ABOUT 3½ DOZEN

- ¾ **cup butter, softened**
- ¾ **cup packed brown sugar**
- 1½ **teaspoons vanilla extract**
- ½ **teaspoon salt**
- 1¾ **cups all-purpose flour**

FILLING/GLAZE
- 1 **cup (6 ounces) semisweet chocolate chips**
- 1 **tablespoon shortening**
- ⅔ **cup finely chopped pecans**

- ½ **cup sweetened condensed milk**
- 1 **teaspoon vanilla extract**
- ⅛ **teaspoon salt**
- 1 **tablespoon light corn syrup**
- 1 **teaspoon water**

1. In a large bowl, cream butter and sugar until light and fluffy. Beat in vanilla and salt. Gradually add flour and mix well. Cover and refrigerate.

2. For filling, melt chocolate chips and shortening in a microwave-safe bowl; stir until smooth. Set aside ¼ cup for glaze. To remaining chocolate, stir in the pecans, milk, vanilla and salt. Cover and refrigerate until cool, about 15 minutes.

3. Place a 16-in. x 12-in. piece of foil in a greased baking sheet; lightly sprinkle with flour. Divide dough in half; place one portion on foil. Roll into a 14-in. x 5-in. rectangle. Spread half of the filling lengthwise on half of the dough to within ½ in. of edges. Using foil, fold dough over filling; seal edges. Repeat with remaining dough and filling. Bake at 350° for 15-20 minutes or until golden brown. Cool on a wire rack for 10 minutes.

4. For glaze, warm reserved chocolate; stir in corn syrup and water. Spread over cookies. Cool completely. Cut widthwise into ¾-in. strips.

Pecan Cheddar Crisps

These crispy snacks are super as a party appetizer, They're also nice to nibble on anytime.

—OZELA HAYNES MAGNOLIA, AR

PREP: 20 MIN. • **BAKE:** 15 MIN. • **MAKES:** ABOUT 2 DOZEN

- ½ **cup butter, softened**
- ½ **cup finely shredded cheddar cheese**
- 1 **cup all-purpose flour**
- ¼ **teaspoon paprika**
- ¼ **teaspoon salt**
- ½ **cup pecan halves**

1. In a bowl, cream the butter and cheese. Combine flour, paprika and salt; add to creamed mixture.

2. Shape dough into 1-in. balls. Place 2 in. apart on ungreased baking sheets. Top each with a pecan; press down to flatten. Bake at 350° for 15-20 minutes or until golden brown. Remove to wire rack to cool.

Chocolate Mint Crisps

If you like chocolate and mint, you can't help but love these delicious crispy cookies with their creamy icing. We always make them for the holidays and guests can never seem to eat just one!
—**KAREN ANN BLAND** GOVE, KS

PREP: 20 MIN. + CHILLING • **BAKE:** 15 MIN./BATCH + STANDING
MAKES: 6½ DOZEN

- 1½ **cups packed brown sugar**
- ¾ **cup butter, cubed**
- 2 **tablespoons plus 1½ teaspoons water**
- 2 **cups (12 ounces) semisweet chocolate chips**
- 2 **eggs**
- 2½ **cups all-purpose flour**
- 1¼ **teaspoons baking soda**
- ½ **teaspoon salt**
- 3 **packages (4.67 ounces each) mint Andes candies**

1. In a heavy saucepan, combine the brown sugar, butter and water. Cook and stir over low heat until butter is melted and mixture is smooth. Remove from the heat; stir in chocolate chips until melted.

2. Transfer to a bowl. Let stand for 10 minutes. With mixer on high speed, add eggs one at a time, beating well after each addition. Combine the flour, baking soda and salt; add to chocolate mixture, beating on low until blended. Cover and refrigerate for 8 hours or overnight.

3. Roll dough into 1-in. balls. Place 3 in. apart on lightly greased baking sheets. Bake at 350° for 11-13 minutes or until edges are set and tops are puffed and cracked (cookies will become crisp after cooling).

4. Immediately top each cookie with a mint. Let stand for 1-2 minutes; spread over cookie. Remove to wire racks; let stand until chocolate is set and cookies are cooled.

Tassies

These tiny tarts make a pretty addition to any cookie tray, but they're also a wonderful dessert by themselves. If you don't have miniature tart pans, use miniature muffin pans instead.
—**JOY CORIE** RUSTON, LA

PREP: 25 MIN. + CHILLING • **BAKE:** 20 MIN. • **MAKES:** 24 TARTS

PASTRY
- 1 **package (3 ounces) cream cheese, softened**
- ½ **cup butter, softened**
- 1 **cup all-purpose flour**

FILLING
- ¾ **cup packed brown sugar**
- 1 **tablespoon butter, softened**
- 1 **egg**
- 1 **teaspoon vanilla extract**
  Dash salt
- ⅔ **cup finely chopped pecans, divided**
  Maraschino cherries, halved, optional

1. For pastry, blend cream cheese and butter until smooth; stir in flour. Cover and refrigerate for about 1 hour.

2. Shape into twenty-four 1-in. balls. Place in ungreased miniature muffin tins or small cookie tarts; press the dough against bottom and sides to form shell. Set aside.

3. In a bowl, beat brown sugar, butter and egg until combined. Add the vanilla, salt and half the pecans; spoon into pastry. Top with remaining pecans.

4. Bake at 375° for 20 minutes, or until filling is set and pastry is light golden brown. Cool and remove from pans. Top each with a maraschino cherry half if desired.

Raspberry Treasures

Light and flaky, these delicate fruit-filled cookies have the look of petite and elegant pastries. We like them with a spot of raspberry or apricot filling and a cup of Christmas tea.

—**TASTE OF HOME TEST KITCHEN**

PREP: 50 MIN. • **BAKE:** 15 MIN. • **MAKES:** 2 DOZEN

- ½ **cup butter, softened**
- 1 **package (3 ounces) cream cheese, softened**
- 1 **teaspoon vanilla extract**
- 1 **cup all-purpose flour**
- ⅛ **teaspoon salt**
- ½ **cup raspberry cake and pastry filling**
- 1 **egg**
- 1 **teaspoon water**

1. In a large bowl, cream butter and cream cheese until light and fluffy. Beat in vanilla. Combine flour and salt; add to the creamed mixture and mix well. Divide dough in half; wrap each in plastic wrap. Refrigerate for 1 hour or until dough is easy to handle.

2. On a lightly floured surface, roll out dough to ⅛ in. thickness. Cut with a lightly floured 3-in. round cookie cutter. Place 1 teaspoon raspberry filling in the center of each. Bring three edges together over filling, overlapping slightly (a small amount of filling will show); pinch edges gently. In a small bowl, beat the egg and water; brush over the dough.

3. Place 1 in. apart on ungreased baking sheets. Bake at 375° for 10-12 minutes or until golden brown. Cool for 1 minute before removing to wire racks.

NOTE *This recipe was tested with Solo brand cake and pastry filling. Look for it in the baking aisle.*

Frosted Cocoa Cookies

Almond flavor in the chocolate frosting accents these soft cookies nicely. When I set a plate of them out, my husband and two sons gobble them up quickly!

—**DIANE MORAN** RHAME, ND

PREP: 15 MIN. • **BAKE:** 15 MIN./BATCH + COOLING
MAKES: 3½ DOZEN

- 1 **cup shortening**
- 2 **cups sugar**
- 4 **eggs**
- 2 **teaspoons vanilla extract**
- 3½ **cups all-purpose flour**
- 1 **cup baking cocoa**
- 2 **teaspoons baking soda**
- 1 **teaspoon salt**

FROSTING
- ⅓ **cup butter, softened**
- 3 **cups confectioners' sugar**
- ⅓ **cup baking cocoa**
- ¼ **teaspoon almond extract**
- 3 **to 4 tablespoons milk**

1. In a large bowl, cream shortening and sugar until light and fluffy. Add eggs, one at a time, beating well after each addition. Beat in vanilla. Combine the flour, cocoa, baking soda and salt; gradually add to the creamed mixture and mix well.

2. Roll into 1½-in. balls. Place 2 in. apart on ungreased baking sheets. Bake at 350° for 13-16 minutes or until set. Remove to wire racks to cool.

3. For frosting, in a small bowl, combine the butter, confectioners' sugar, cocoa and extract. Add enough milk to achieve desired consistency. Drizzle over cookies.

Jeweled Coconut Drops

Red raspberry preserves add a festive flair to these tender coconut cookies. Perfect for potlucks and cookie exchanges, these shaped cookies never last long when I make them for my husband and two sons.

—ELLEN MARIE BYLER MUNFORDVILLE, KY

PREP: 20 MIN. + CHILLING • **BAKE:** 10 MIN.
MAKES: ABOUT 3½ DOZEN

- ⅓ cup butter, softened
- 1 package (3 ounces) cream cheese, softened
- ¾ cup sugar
- 1 egg yolk
- 2 teaspoons orange juice
- 1 teaspoon almond extract
- 1¼ cups all-purpose flour
- 1½ teaspoons baking powder
- ¼ teaspoon salt
- 3¾ cups flaked coconut, divided
- 1 cup seedless raspberry preserves, warmed

1. In a large bowl, cream the butter, cream cheese and sugar until light and fluffy. Beat in egg yolk, orange juice and almond extract. Combine the flour, baking powder and salt; gradually add to creamed mixture and mix well. Stir in 3 cups of coconut. Refrigerate for 30 minutes or until easy to handle.

2. Shape dough into 2-in. balls; roll in remaining coconut. Place 2 in. apart on ungreased baking sheets. Using the end of a wooden spoon handle, make an indentation in the center of each ball.

3. Bake at 350° for 8-10 minutes or until cookies are lightly browned. Remove to wire racks to cool. Fill each cookie with preserves.

Chocolate-Dipped Peanut Logs

A cookie exchange introduced me to these fancy peanut butter treats. They're eye-catching for the holidays and bake sales.

—PATRICIA GRALL HORTONVILLE, WI

PREP: 30 MIN. • **BAKE:** 10 MIN./BATCH + STANDING
MAKES: ABOUT 8½ DOZEN

- 1 cup creamy peanut butter
- ½ cup butter, softened
- ½ cup shortening
- 1 cup sugar
- 1 cup packed brown sugar
- 2 eggs
- 2½ cups all-purpose flour
- 1½ teaspoons baking soda
- 1 teaspoon baking powder
- ¼ teaspoon salt
- 8 ounces dark chocolate candy coating, coarsely chopped
- ⅔ cup ground salted peanuts

1. In a large bowl, cream peanut butter, butter, shortening and sugars until light and fluffy. Add eggs, one at a time, beating well after each addition. Combine dry ingredients; gradually add to the creamed mixture and mix well.

2. Shape into 2-in. logs. Place 2 in. apart on ungreased baking sheets. Bake at 350° for 8-10 minutes or until lightly browned. Remove to wire racks to cool.

3. In a microwave, melt candy coating; stir until smooth. Dip one end of each cookie into coating; allow excess to drip of. Dip into peanuts. Place on waxed paper to set.

NOTE *Reduced-fat peanut butter is not recommended for this recipe.*

Cookie Cutter Delights

Chocolate Heart Cookies

For a dramatic presentation, I dust dessert plates with cocoa powder and drizzle on a bit of melted raspberry fruit spread. I place a couple of these melt-in-your-mouth cookies in the center, along with some fresh rasberries, lemon zest and a sprig of mint.

—TERRYANN MOORE VINELAND, NJ

PREP: 30 MIN. • **BAKE:** 10 MIN. + COOLING
MAKES: ABOUT 2 DOZEN

- 1 **cup butter, softened**
- ½ **cup sugar**
- 1 **teaspoon vanilla extract**
- 2 **cups all-purpose flour**
- ¼ **cup baking cocoa**
- 1 **cup white baking chips**
- 2 **tablespoons shortening, divided**
- ½ **cup semisweet chocolate chips**

1. In a small bowl, cream butter and sugar until light and fluffy. Beat in vanilla. Combine the flour and cocoa; gradually add to creamed mixture and mix well.
2. On a lightly floured surface, roll out dough to ¼-in. thickness. Cut with a 3-in. heart-shaped cookie cutter. Place 2 in. apart on ungreased baking sheets.
3. Bake at 375° for 8-10 minutes or until firm. Remove to wire racks to cool.
4. In a microwave, melt white chips and 1 tablespoon shortening at 70% power for 1 minute; stir. Microwave at additional 10- to 20-second intervals, stirring until smooth.
5. Dip both sides of cookies into melted mixture; allow excess to drip off. Place on waxed paper; let stand until set.
6. In a microwave, melt the chocolate chips and remaining shortening; stir until smooth. Drizzle over the cookies. Place on wire racks to dry.

Old-Fashioned Cutout Cookies

These cookies are so crisp and buttery, it's hard to eat just one. I make them for special holidays, but they're welcome anytime.

—ELIZABETH TURNER LULA, GA

START TO FINISH: 25 MIN. • **MAKES:** ABOUT 1½ DOZEN

- ¼ **cup butter, softened**
- ¾ **cup sugar**
- 1 **egg**
- 1 **teaspoon whole milk**
- ½ **teaspoon vanilla extract**
- 1½ **cups self-rising flour**
  Additional sugar

1. In a small bowl, cream butter and sugar until light and fluffy. Beat in the egg, milk and vanilla. Gradually add flour and mix well.
2. On a lightly floured surface, roll out dough to ⅛-in. thickness. Cut with 3-in. cookie cutters dipped in flour. Sprinkle with additional sugar.
3. Place 1 in. apart on greased baking sheets. Reroll scraps if desired. Bake at 375° for 7-8 minutes or until edges are lightly browned. Remove to wire racks to cool.
NOTE *As a substitute for 1½ cups self-rising flour, place 2¼ teaspoons baking powder and ¾ teaspoon salt in a measuring cup. Add all-purpose flour to measure 1 cup. Combine with an additional ½ cup all-purpose flour.*

Smooth Sailing Sugar Cookies

With a fresh breeze, my longtime-favorite sugar cookie recipe set sail for a new course. I cut out sailboats and frisky fish, frosting them brightly for a nautical gathering. My guests ate their limit!

—MARTHA CONAWAY PATASKALA, OH

PREP: 30 MIN. + CHILLING • **BAKE:** 5 MIN./BATCH + COOLING
MAKES: ABOUT 4 DOZEN

- 1 **cup butter, softened**
- ¾ **cup sugar**
- 1 **egg**
- 2 **tablespoons milk**
- 1½ **teaspoons vanilla extract**
- 3 **cups all-purpose flour**
- 1 **teaspoon baking powder**
- ½ **teaspoon salt**

FROSTING

- 1 **cup confectioners' sugar**
- ½ **teaspoon vanilla or almond extract**
- ¼ **teaspoon salt**
- 1 **to 2 tablespoons milk**
  Food coloring, optional

1. In a large bowl, cream butter and sugar until smooth. Beat in the egg, milk and vanilla. Combine flour, baking powder and salt; gradually add to the creamed mixture. Cover and refrigerate for 1 hour or until easy to handle.
2. On a lightly floured surface, roll out dough to ⅛-in. thickness. Cut with cookie cutters of your choice. Place 2 in. apart on greased baking sheets. Bake at 375° for 5-8 minutes or until lightly browned. Remove to wire racks to cool.
3. In a small bowl, combine the confectioners' sugar, extract, salt and enough milk to achieve spreading consistency. Add food coloring if desired. Frost cookies; decorate as desired.

Dutch Spice Cookies

My sister gave me the recipe for these cookies, which have become a holiday tradition at our house. My kids tear into the spicy, crisp cookies right out of the oven. I prefer them when they've cooled—but it's risky waiting. I might not get any!

—MARY PETERSON CHARLESTOWN, RI

PREP: 20 MIN. + CHILLING • **BAKE:** 10 MIN./BATCH
MAKES: 40 COOKIES

- ¾ **cup butter, softened**
- 1 **cup packed brown sugar**
- 2¼ **cups all-purpose flour**
- 2 **teaspoons ground cinnamon**
- ½ **teaspoon ground mace**
- ½ **teaspoon crushed aniseed**
- ¼ **teaspoon each ground ginger, nutmeg and cloves**
- ¼ **teaspoon baking powder**
- ⅛ **teaspoon salt**
- 3 **tablespoons 2% milk**
- 1 **cup finely chopped slivered almonds**

1. In a large bowl, cream butter and brown sugar until light and fluffy. Combine the flour, spices, baking powder and salt; gradually add to creamed mixture and mix well. Stir in milk and almonds.
2. Roll dough into a 16-in. x 10-in. rectangle between two sheets of waxed paper. Cut into 2-in. squares. Cover with waxed paper and refrigerate for 30 minutes.
3. Place squares 1 in. apart on ungreased baking sheets. Bake 375° for 8-10 minutes or until firm. Remove to wire racks to cool.

Sand Dollar Cookies

When the military relocated our family, my children had never lived near the beach before. I came up with this special treat with a beach theme—it made our move more fun!

—**MICHELLE DUNCAN** CALLAWAY, FL

PREP: 15 MIN. + CHILLING • **BAKE:** 15 MIN. • **MAKES:** 9 COOKIES

- ¾ **cup butter, softened**
- ⅓ **cup confectioners' sugar**
- 4½ **teaspoons sugar**
- 2 **teaspoons almond extract**
- 1⅓ **cups all-purpose flour**
- ¼ **teaspoon salt**
- 1 **egg, lightly beaten**
  Slivered almonds and cinnamon-sugar

1. In a large bowl, cream the butter and sugars until light and fluffy. Beat in extract. Combine the flour and salt; gradually add to the creamed mixture and mix well. Cover and refrigerate for 1 hour or until easy to handle.

2. Roll dough between waxed paper to ⅛-in. thickness. Cut with a 3½-in. round cookie cutter dipped in flour. Using a floured spatula, place 1 in. apart on ungreased baking sheets. Brush with egg. Decorate with almonds and sprinkle with cinnamon-sugar.

3. Bake at 325° for 12-16 minutes or until edges begin to brown. Cool for 2 minutes before removing to wire racks.

Lime Hazelnut Zingers

The tangy lime and mellow hazelnut flavors are a unique combination that sets these apart from other cutout cookies. After baking and cooling them, you can keep the cookies in the freezer until decorating...or bake, frost and eat the same day. They won't last long!

—**KAREN MORRELL** CANBY, OR

PREP: 25 MIN. + CHILLING • **BAKE:** 10 MIN. + COOLING
MAKES: 4 DOZEN

- 1 **cup butter, softened**
- ½ **cup sugar**
- ¼ **cup lime juice**
- 2 **teaspoons grated lime peel**
- 1 **teaspoon vanilla extract**
- 2¼ **cups all-purpose flour**
- ¾ **cup finely chopped hazelnuts**

FROSTING

- 1 **package (3 ounces) cream cheese, softened**
- ¾ **cup confectioners' sugar**
- 2 **teaspoons lime juice**
- ½ **teaspoon vanilla extract**
- 1 **to 2 drops green food coloring, optional**

1. In a large bowl, cream butter and sugar. Add the lime juice, peel and vanilla. Gradually add the flour. Stir in hazelnuts. Cover and refrigerate for 1 hour or until easy to handle.

2. On a lightly floured surface, roll out dough to ¼-in. thickness. Cut with a 2-in. cookie cutter dipped in flour. Place 1 in. apart on ungreased baking sheets.

3. Bake at 350° for 10-12 minutes or until the edges are lightly browned. Remove to wire racks to cool.

4. In a small bowl, combine the frosting ingredients; beat until smooth. Transfer to a resealable plastic bag. Cut a small hole in a corner of the bag; drizzle frosting over cookies. Store in the refrigerator in an airtight container.

Ladybug Cookies

The spotlight shines on these confections every time I serve them. The sugar cookies themselves are yummy, but they're even better when I decorate them.

—**SHARON KOTSOVOS** COOS BAY, OR

PREP: 45 MIN. + CHILLING • **BAKE:** 10 MIN./BATCH
MAKES: ABOUT 5 DOZEN

- 1 **cup butter, softened**
- 1 **cup canola oil**
- 1 **cup sugar**
- 1 **cup confectioners' sugar**
- 4 **eggs**
- 1 **teaspoon vanilla extract**
- 4¾ **cups all-purpose flour**
- 1 **teaspoon cream of tartar**
- 1 **teaspoon baking soda**
  Red and black liquid food coloring
- 1 **cup (6 ounces) semisweet chocolate chips**
- ½ **cup white baking chips**
- 1 **cup miniature semisweet chocolate chips**

1. In a large bowl, beat butter, oil and sugars until blended. Add two eggs, one at a time, beating well after each addition. Beat in vanilla. Combine the flour, cream of tartar and baking soda; gradually add to creamed mixture and mix well. Cover and refrigerate for 2 hours or until easy to handle.

2. On a floured surface, roll out dough to ¼-in. thickness. Cut with a 3-in. round cookie cuter dipped in flour. Place 1 in. apart on lightly greased baking sheets.

3. In a small bowl, beat remaining eggs. Add red food coloring; mix well. Brush over cutouts.

4. Bake at 375° for 8 minutes. With a small new paintbrush and black food coloring, paint two lines, forming wings.

5. Arrange four chocolate chips in a half circle on the top third of each cookie. Randomly place 16 chocolate chips on the lower part of the cookie for spots. Return to the oven for 1 minute or until chips are melted. Spread the four chips to form the head.

6. For eyes, position two white chips, pointed side down, over melted chocolate. Return to the oven for 1 minute or until slightly melted. Place one miniature chocolate chip in the center of each white chip. Remove the cookies to wire racks to cool completely.

Pear Crescent Cookies

I first made these cream cheese cookies, traditionally called rugalach, for my son-in-law, and we all loved them.

—**CAROLYN HAYES** MARION, IL

PREP: 20 MIN. + CHILLING • **BAKE:** 20 MIN./BATCH
MAKES: 4 DOZEN

- 1 **cup butter, softened**
- 1 **package (8 ounces) cream cheese, softened**
- 2 **cups all-purpose flour**
- ⅛ **teaspoon salt**
- ¼ **cup packed brown sugar**
- 2 **teaspoons ground cinnamon**
- ½ **cup diced peeled pears**
- ½ **cup finely chopped walnuts**
- ¾ **cup confectioners' sugar**
- 2 **tablespoons milk**

1. In a bowl, cream butter and cream cheese until light and fluffy. Mix flour and salt; gradually add to creamed mixture and mix well. Cover and chill 2 hours or until easy to handle. Combine brown sugar and cinnamon; set aside.
2. Divide dough into fourths. On a floured surface; roll out each portion into a 12-in. circle. Cut into 12 wedges. Place about ¼ teaspoon cinnamon-sugar at the wide end of each wedge. Top with ½ teaspoon each pears and walnuts.
3. Roll up, beginning at wide end. Place pointed side down

2 in. apart on ungreased baking sheets; curve ends to form a crescent.
4. Bake at 375° for 16-19 minutes or until lightly browned. Immediately remove to wire racks. Combine the confectioners' sugar and milk; drizzle over cooled cookies.

Frosted Spice Cookies

This recipe has been handed down through many generations of my husband's family. His grandmother always had these in her cookie jar when he visited her.

—**DEBBIE HURLBERT** HOWARD, OH

PREP: 25 MIN. + CHILLING • **BAKE:** 15 MIN./BATCH + COOLING
MAKES: 5-6 DOZEN

- 1 **cup butter, softened**
- 1 **cup sugar**
- 1 **egg**
- 1 **cup molasses**
- 1 **cup buttermilk**
- 6 **cups all-purpose flour**
- 1 **tablespoon baking powder**
- 1 **teaspoon baking soda**
- 1 **teaspoon ground cinnamon**
- 1 **teaspoon ground ginger**
- ½ **teaspoon salt**
- 1 **cup chopped walnuts**
- 1 **cup golden raisins**
- 1 **cup chopped dates**

FROSTING
- 3¾ **cups confectioners' sugar**
- ⅓ **cup orange juice**
- 2 **tablespoons butter, melted**

1. In a large bowl, cream butter and sugar until light and fluffy. Beat in egg: Beat in molasses and buttermilk. Combine the flour, baking powder, baking soda, cinnamon, ginger and salt; gradually add to creamed mixture and mix well. Stir in the walnuts, raisins and dates. Chill for 2 hours or until easy to handle.
2. On a floured surface, roll out dough to ¼-in. thickness. Cut with a 2½-in. round cookie cutter.
3. Place on greased baking sheets. Bake at 350° for 12-15 minutes. Cool completely.
4. For frosting, beat all ingredients in a small bowl until smooth. Spread over cooled cookies; let stand until set.

Shamrock Cookies

A handy cookie cutter shapes these sensational sweets. With a hint of mint flavor, they're especially yummy.

—EDNA HOFFMAN HEBRON, IN

PREP: 25 MIN. + CHILLING • **BAKE:** 10 MIN./BATCH
MAKES: 3 DOZEN

- 1 cup shortening
- 1 cup confectioners' sugar
- 1 egg
- 1 teaspoon peppermint extract
- 2½ cups all-purpose flour
- 1 teaspoon salt

Green paste food coloring
Green colored sugar, optional

1. In a large bowl, cream shortening and confectioners' sugar until light and fluffy. Beat in the egg and extract. Gradually add flour and salt. Tint with food coloring. Cover and refrigerate for 1 hour or until easy to handle.

2. On a lightly floured surface, roll out dough to ¼-in. thickness. Cut with a lightly floured 2-in. shamrock cookie cutter. Place 1 in. apart on ungreased baking sheets. Sprinkle with colored sugar if desired.

3. Bake at 375° for 10-12 minutes or until edges are lightly browned. Cool for 1 minute before removing to wire racks.

Coffee Shortbread

Remember this recipe next time you need a treat to bring to a brunch or plan to host a few friends for coffee. It's the perfect way to satisfy a morning sweet tooth while enjoying a hot cup of joe.

—DIXIE TERRY GOREVILLE, IL

PREP: 15 MIN. **• BAKE:** 20 MIN./BATCH + COOLING
MAKES: ABOUT 5 DOZEN

- 1 **cup butter, softened**
- ½ **cup packed brown sugar**
- ¼ **cup sugar**
- 2 **tablespoons instant coffee granules**
- 2 **cups all-purpose flour**
- ¼ **teaspoon salt**
- ½ **cup white baking chips, melted**
- ½ **cup semisweet chocolate chips, melted**

1. In a large bowl, cream the butter, sugars and coffee granules until light and fluffy. Combine flour and salt; gradually add to creamed mixture.
2. On a lightly floured surface, roll dough to ¼-in. thickness. Cut with floured 2-in. to 3-in. cookie cutters. Place 2 in. apart on ungreased baking sheets.
3. Bake at 300° for 20-22 minutes or until set. Remove to wire racks to cool. Drizzle with melted chips.

Cherry Shortbread Hearts

This recipe for heart-shaped cookies is one of the tastiest I've tried. Folks always ooh and aah over the buttery taste combined with chocolate. They make great Valentine's Day gifts wrapped up in cellophane and ribbon.

—ELAINE ANDERSON NEW GALILEE, PA

PREP: 20 MIN. • **BAKE:** 20 MIN. + COOLING
MAKES: ABOUT 1½ DOZEN

- 1¼ cups all-purpose flour
- 3 tablespoons sugar
- ½ cup cold butter, cubed
- ½ cup maraschino cherries, patted dry and finely chopped
- 1 tablespoon cold water
- ¼ teaspoon almond extract
- 1 cup (6 ounces) semisweet chocolate chips
- 1 tablespoon shortening

1. In a large bowl, combine flour and sugar; cut in butter until crumbly. Stir in the cherries, water and extract until dough forms a ball.

2. On a lightly floured surface, roll dough to ¼-in. thickness. Cut with a floured 2½-in. heart-shaped cookie cutter. Place 1 in. apart on ungreased baking sheets.

3. Bake at 325° for 20-25 minutes or until edges are lightly browned. Remove to wire racks to cool.

4. In a microwave, melt chocolate chips and shortening; stir until smooth. Dip half of each cookie into chocolate; allow excess to drip off. Place on waxed paper until set.

Sour Cream Cutout Cookies

My soft cookies make a comforting evening snack. They have a delicious, delicate flavor and cakelike texture.

—MARLENE JACKSON KINGSBURG, CA

PREP: 25 MIN. + CHILLING • **BAKE:** 10 MIN./BATCH + COOLING
MAKES: ABOUT 3½ DOZEN

- 1 cup butter, softened
- 1½ cups sugar
- 3 eggs
- 1 cup (8 ounces) sour cream
- 2 teaspoons vanilla extract
- 3½ cups all-purpose flour
- 2 teaspoons baking powder
- 1 teaspoon baking soda

FROSTING
- ⅓ cup butter, softened
- 2 cups confectioners' sugar
- 1½ teaspoons vanilla extract
- ¼ teaspoon salt
- 2 to 3 tablespoons milk

1. In a large bowl, cream butter and sugar until light and fluffy. Beat in eggs. Add sour cream and vanilla; mix well. In another bowl, whisk flour, baking powder and baking soda; gradually beat into creamed mixture. Divide dough in half. Shape each into a disk; wrap in plastic wrap. Refrigerate 2 hours or until firm enough to roll.

2. Preheat oven to 350°. On a well-floured surface, roll each portion of dough to ¼-in. thickness. Cut with a floured 3-in. cookie cutter. Place 2 in. apart on greased baking sheets.

3. Bake 10-12 minutes or until tops spring back when lightly touched. Remove from pans to wire racks to cool completely.

4. For frosting, in a bowl, beat butter, confectioners' sugar, vanilla, salt and enough milk to reach desired consistency. Spread over cookies.

Apple Cutout Sugar Cookies

Not only are these pretty cookies fun to serve, they bake up delicate and flaky, and they taste wonderful.

—**MARLYS BENNING** ACKLEY, IA

PREP: 20 MIN. + CHILLING • **BAKE:** 10 MIN./BATCH + COOLING
MAKES: 4 DOZEN

- 1 **cup butter, softened**
- 1½ **cups confectioners' sugar**
- 1 **egg**
- 1½ **teaspoons vanilla extract**
- 2¼ **cups all-purpose flour**
- 1 **teaspoon baking soda**
- 1 **teaspoon cream of tartar**

FROSTING

- 2 **cups confectioners' sugar**
- ¼ **cup light corn syrup**
- 2 **tablespoons water**
  Red and green food coloring

1. In a large bowl, cream butter and sugar. Beat in egg and vanilla. Combine dry ingredients; gradually add to the creamed mixture, beating well after each addition. Chill dough for 2-3 hours or until easy to handle.

2. Roll out on a lightly floured surface to ¼-in. thickness. Cut with a floured apple-shaped cookie cutter. Place on greased baking sheets. Bake at 375° for 7-8 minutes or until lightly browned. Cool on wire racks.

3. For frosting, combine sugar, corn syrup and water in a small bowl. Transfer three fourths of the frosting into another bowl; add red food coloring for apples. Add green food coloring to remaining frosting for stems. Frost cookies. Let stand until set.

Finnish Pinwheels

When my sister was hosting an exchange student from Finland, she served my pinwheel cookies to her guest. The young lady instantly recognized what they were. I felt good knowing they're still being made in our ancestors' country.

—**ILONA BARRON** ONTONAGON, MI

PREP: 1 HOUR • **BAKE:** 15 MIN./BATCH • **MAKES:** ABOUT 7 DOZEN

FILLING

- ½ **pound pitted dried plums, chopped**
- ½ **pound pitted dates, chopped**
- 1 **cup water**
- 2 **tablespoons sugar**
- 1 **tablespoon butter**

PASTRY

- 3 **cups all-purpose flour**
- 1 **cup sugar**
- 2 **teaspoons baking powder**
- ½ **teaspoon salt**
- 1 **cup cold butter**
- 1 **egg, beaten**
- 3 **tablespoons heavy whipping cream**
- 1 **teaspoon vanilla extract**

1. In a saucepan, combine dried plums, dates, water and sugar. Cook over low heat, stirring constantly, until thickened. Remove from the heat and stir in butter. Cool.

2. Meanwhile, in a bowl, sift together flour, sugar, baking powder and salt. Cut in butter as for a pie pastry. Blend in egg, cream and vanilla. Form into two balls.

3. Place one ball at a time on a floured surface and roll to ⅛-in. thickness. Cut into 2-in. squares. Place on ungreased baking sheets. Make 1-in. slits in corners. Place ½ teaspoon filling in the center of each square. Bring every other corner up into center to form a pinwheel and press lightly. Bake at 325° for 12 minutes or until the points are light golden brown. Remove to wire racks.

Brown Sugar Cutouts

I bake so many cookies for the holidays that I have one recipe box just for cookies alone! Of all of them, these simple cutouts are among my husband's favorites.

—NORMA MUELLER WAUWATOSA, WI

PREP: 35 MIN. + CHILLING • **BAKE:** 10 MIN./BATCH + COOLING
MAKES: ABOUT 6 DOZEN

- 1 **cup butter, softened**
- 2 **cups packed brown sugar**
- 3 **eggs**
- 2 **teaspoons grated lemon peel**
- 3 **cups all-purpose flour**
- 1 **teaspoon baking soda**
- 1 **teaspoon ground ginger**
FROSTING
- 1½ **cups confectioners' sugar**
- ½ **teaspoon vanilla extract**
- 2 **to 3 tablespoons half-and-half cream**
  Green food coloring, optional

1. In a large bowl, cream butter and brown sugar until light and fluffy. Beat in eggs and lemon peel. Combine the flour, baking soda and ginger; gradually add to creamed mixture and mix well. Divide dough in half. Shape each into a ball, then flatten into a disk. Wrap in plastic wrap and refrigerate for 2 hours or until easy to handle.

2. On a lightly floured surface, roll one portion of dough to ⅛-in. thickness. Cut with floured 2-in. cookie cutters. Place 2 in. apart on ungreased baking sheets. Repeat.

3. Bake at 350° for 8-10 minutes or until golden brown. Remove to wire racks to cool.

4. For frosting, in a small bowl, combine the confectioners' sugar, vanilla and enough cream to achieve spreading consistency. Add food coloring if desired to some or all of the frosting. Decorate cookies.

Surprise Sugar Stars

I make dozens of these buttery cutout cookies at holiday time. The basic sugar cookie recipe is my mother's. I came up with the sweet surprise inside.

—**JOYCE BERRY** SANDPOINT, ID

PREP: 30 MIN. + CHILLING • **BAKE:** 15 MIN./BATCH + COOLING
MAKES: 4 DOZEN

- 1 **cup butter, softened**
- 1¼ **cups sugar**
- 2 **eggs**
- 1 **teaspoon vanilla extract**
- 4 **cups all-purpose flour**
- 2 **teaspoons baking powder**
- 2 **teaspoons ground nutmeg**
- 1 **teaspoon baking soda**
- ½ **teaspoon salt**
- ⅔ **cup buttermilk**
- 1 **can (21 ounces) cherry pie filling**

ICING
- 2 **cups confectioners' sugar**
- ½ **teaspoon almond extract**
- 2 **to 3 tablespoons whole milk**
  Colored sugar, optional

1. In a large bowl, cream butter and sugar until light and fluffy. Add the eggs, one at a time, beating well after each addition. Stir in vanilla. Combine the dry ingredients; add to the creamed mixture alternately with buttermilk, beating well after each addition. Refrigerate for 2-3 hours or until easy to handle.

2. On a floured surface, roll out dough to ¼-in. thickness. Cut with 2-in star cookie cutter or the cutter of your choice. Place half of the stars on ungreased baking sheets. Spoon 1½ teaspoonfuls of pie filling into the centers of each. Top with remaining stars. Pinch edges to seal; cut a small slit in top of each cookie.

3. Bake at 350° for 12-15 minutes or until lightly browned. Cool on wire racks.

4. For icing, in a small bowl, combine confectioners' sugar, extract and enough milk to achieve desired consistency. Spread over cookies. Sprinkle with colored sugar if desired.

Anise Butter Cookies

Here in New Mexico, these cookies are known as *biscochitos*, which means "small biscuits." There are many variations of the recipe, which has been passed down through the generations. The cookies are enjoyed during the Christmas holidays and at wedding receptions and other special celebrations. They're good by themselves or dunked in milk or coffee.

—**MARI LYNN VAN GINKLE** SANDIA PARK, NM

PREP: 30 MIN. • **BAKE:** 15 MIN./BATCH • **MAKES:** 5 DOZEN

- 2 **cups butter, softened**
- 1¾ **cups sugar, divided**
- 2 **eggs**
- ¼ **cup thawed orange juice concentrate**
- 4 **teaspoons aniseed, crushed**
- 6 **cups all-purpose flour**
- 3 **teaspoons baking powder**
- ½ **teaspoon salt**
- 1 **teaspoon ground cinnamon**

1. In a large bowl, cream the butter and 1½ cups sugar until light and fluffy. Add eggs, one at a time, beating well after each addition. Beat in orange juice concentrate and aniseed. Combine the flour, baking powder and salt; gradually add to creamed mixture and mix well.

2. On a lightly floured surface, roll out dough to ¼-in. thickness. Cut with a floured 2½-in. round cookie cutter. Place 1 in. apart on ungreased baking sheets.

3. Combine the cinnamon and remaining sugar; sprinkle over cookies. Bake at 350° for 12-15 minutes or until golden brown. Remove to wire racks.

Frosted Valentine Cookies

Sharing delicious sweets has long been the way to show affection. Why not demonstrate your love this Valentine's Day by making a batch of these buttery cookies?

—**MARCY CELLA** L'ANSE, MI

PREP: 25 MIN. • **BAKE:** 15 MIN./BATCH • **MAKES:** 3½ DOZEN

- 2 **cups butter, softened**
- 1 **cup confectioners' sugar**
- 4 **cups all-purpose flour**
- 2 **cups quick-cooking oats**
- 2 **teaspoons vanilla extract**
- ½ **teaspoon almond extract**
- ½ **teaspoon salt**
- ½ **pound dark or milk chocolate candy coating, melted**
    Confectioners' sugar icing, optional

1. In a bowl, cream butter and sugar until light and fluffy. Add the flour, oats, extracts and salt; mix well.

2. Roll out dough to ¼-in thickness. Cut with a 3-in. heart-shaped cookie cutter; place on ungreased baking sheets. Bake at 350° for 12-15 minutes. Spread warm cookies with candy coating; cool. Decorate with icing if desired.

Old-Fashioned Raisin Cookies

My mother has been making these morsels for many years, much to the delight of all in our family. The fruit-filled sugar cookies will please any sweet tooth. They disappear quickly!

—**DARLENE BRENDEN** SALEM, OR

PREP: 30 MIN. + CHILLING • **BAKE:** 10 MIN./BATCH
MAKES: ABOUT 4 DOZEN

- ½ **cup sugar**
- 1½ **teaspoons cornstarch**
- ¼ **teaspoon ground cinnamon**
- 1 **cup chopped dates**
- ½ **cup raisins**
- ½ **cup water**
DOUGH
- 1 **cup butter, softened**
- 2 **cups sugar**
- 3 **eggs**
- 1 **teaspoon vanilla extract**
- 4 **cups all-purpose flour**
- ½ **teaspoon salt**

1. In a small saucepan, combine the first six ingredients. Cook and stir over medium heat until thickened and bubbly. Cool.

2. In a large bowl, cream butter and sugar until light and fluffy. Add eggs, one at a time, beating well after each addition. Beat in vanilla. Combine flour and salt; gradually add to the creamed mixture and mix well. Cover and refrigerate for 2-3 hours or until easy to handle.

3. On a lightly floured surface, roll half of the dough to ⅛-in. thickness. Cut with a 2-in. round cookie cutter. Place 1 in. apart on ungreased baking sheets. Place 1 teaspoon of raisin filling in the center of each cookie.

4. Roll out the remaining dough. Cut with a 2-in. cookie cutter. With a 1-in. round cookie cutter, cut a hole in the center of each; place over filling. With a fork, press the edges to seal.

5. Bake at 400° for 10-12 minutes or until edges begin to brown. Remove to wire racks to cool.

Strawberry Wedding Bell Cookies

To ring in a joyous occasion like a bridal shower or wedding, I'm often asked to make these festive cookies. You can use different flavors of jam to suit your tastes.

—LAURIE MESSER BONIFAY, FL

PREP: 30 MIN. + CHILLING • **BAKE:** 10 MIN./BATCH
MAKES: ABOUT 5 DOZEN

- 1 cup butter, softened
- 1 package (3 ounces) cream cheese, softened
- ¼ cup sugar
- 1 teaspoon vanilla extract
- 2 cups all-purpose flour
- ¼ teaspoon salt
- ½ cup strawberry jam
  Confectioners' sugar

1. In a large bowl, cream butter, cream cheese and sugar until light and fluffy. Beat in vanilla. Combine flour and salt; gradually add to the creamed mixture and mix well. Divide dough into fourths. Cover and refrigerate for 2 hours or until easy to handle.

2. On a lightly floured surface, roll out each piece of dough to ⅛-in. thickness. Cut with floured 2-in. round cookie cutters. Place 1 in. apart on ungreased baking sheets. Spoon ¼ teaspoon jam in the center and spread to within ¼ in. of edge.

3. Shape into a bell by folding edges of dough to meet over filling. Bake at 375° for 8-10 minutes or until lightly browned. Remove to wire racks to cool. Dust with the confectioners' sugar.

Anise Cutout Cookies

Mother prepared these soft cookies for holidays and special-occasion meals. My seven siblings and I gobbled them up as fast as she made them. I still can't resist the cinnamon-sugar coating.
—**JERRI MOROR** RIO RANCHO, NM

PREP: 20 MIN. • **BAKE:** 15 MIN./BATCH • **MAKES:** ABOUT 5 DOZEN

- 2 **cups shortening**
- 1 **cup sugar**
- 2 **eggs**
- 2 **teaspoons aniseed**
- 6 **cups all-purpose flour**
- 1 **tablespoon baking powder**
- 1 **teaspoon salt**
- ¼ **cup apple juice**
- ½ **cup sugar**
- 1 **teaspoon ground cinnamon**

1. In a bowl, cream shortening and sugar until light and fluffy; add eggs and aniseed. Combine flour, baking powder and salt; add to the creamed mixture. Add apple juice and mix well.

2. On a floured surface, knead until well blended, about 4-5 minutes. Roll dough to ½-in. thickness; cut into 2-in. shapes. Place on greased baking sheets.

3. Bake at 375° for 12-16 minutes or until lightly browned. Combine sugar and cinnamon; roll cookies in the mixture while still warm. Cool on wire racks.

Bakeshop TIP

Cutting Out Cutouts

After the dough is rolled out, position the shapes from the cookie cutters as close together as possible to avoid having too many scraps. Save all the scraps and chill them in the refrigerator. Reroll all the scraps just once. Overhandling will make the cookies tough.

Cottage Cheese Cookies

These delicate, puffy turnover cookies flecked with raspberry and almonds are delightful with afternoon tea.
—**LINDA HOBBS** ALBION, NY

PREP: 25 MIN. + CHILLING • **BAKE:** 15 MIN./BATCH
MAKES: 4 DOZEN

- 2 **cups sifted all-purpose flour**
- 1 **cup cold butter**
- 1 **cup (8 ounces) plus 2 tablespoons cream-style cottage cheese**
  Raspberry jam
- **GLAZE**
- 1 **cup confectioners' sugar**
- ⅛ **teaspoon almond extract**
  Milk

1. Place flour in a medium bowl; cut in butter as for pie crust. Blend in cottage cheese until mixture forms a ball (can use a food processor). Chill 1 hour.

2. On a floured surface, roll dough to ⅛-in. thickness. Cut with a 3-in. round cutter. Place a level ¼ teaspoon of jam in center of reach cookie. Moisten edges and fold in half; seal tightly with a fork. Place on lightly greased baking sheets; prick tops with fork.

3. Bake at 400° for 15 minutes or until lightly browned. Cool on wire racks. For glaze, combine the sugar, extract and enough milk to make thin spreading consistency; drizzle over cooled cookies.

Crisp Sugar Cookies

This recipe is great for kids because it has two manageable time blocks—mixing and chilling the dough, then cutting out and baking the cookies.

—JOSIAH HILDENBRAND SAN LEANDRO, CA

PREP: 20 MIN. + CHILLING • **BAKE:** 10 MIN./BATCH
MAKES: ABOUT 4 DOZEN

- ¾ cup shortening
- 1 cup sugar
- 2 eggs
- ½ teaspoon lemon extract
- 2½ cups all-purpose flour
- 1 teaspoon baking powder
- 1 teaspoon salt
  Colored sugar

1. In a large bowl, cream shortening and sugar until light and fluffy. Beat in eggs and extract. Combine the flour, baking powder and salt; gradually add to creamed mixture and mix well. Cover and refrigerate for at least 2 hours or until easy to handle.

2. On a floured surface, roll dough to ⅛-in. thickness. Cut with 2½-in. cookie cutters. Place on greased baking sheets. Sprinkle with colored sugar.

3. Bake at 400° for 7-9 minutes or until lightly browned. Remove to wire racks to cool.

Almond-Butter Cookie Bouquet

I make these cookie pops often during the year. In the spring, I cut them into flower shapes and insert the pops into a block of foam fitted into a basket or bowl. You can cover the foam with tissue paper or cellophane. Add a bow if you like. They make a great centerpiece or hostess gift. The cookies look pretty, and they taste good, too.

—KRISSY FOSSMEYER HUNTLEY, IL

PREP: 2 HOURS + CHILLING • **BAKE:** 10 MIN./BATCH + COOLING
MAKES: ABOUT 2½ DOZEN

- 1¼ cups butter, softened
- 1¾ cups confectioners' sugar
- 2 ounces almond paste
- 1 egg
- ¼ cup 2% milk
- 1 teaspoon vanilla extract
- 4 cups all-purpose flour
- ½ teaspoon salt
  Wooden skewers or lollipop sticks

ICING
- 1 cup confectioners' sugar
- 4 teaspoons evaporated milk
  Food coloring of your choice

1. In a large bowl, cream butter and confectioners' sugar until light and fluffy; add almond paste. Beat in the egg, milk and vanilla. Combine flour and salt; gradually add to creamed mixture and mix well. Cover and refrigerate for 1 hour.

2. On a lightly floured surface, roll out dough to ¼-in. thickness. Cut out with floured 3-in. cookie cutters. Place 1 in. apart on ungreased baking sheets. Insert skewers or sticks. Bake at 375° for 7-8 minutes or until firm. Let stand for 2 minutes before removing to wire racks to cool.

3. In a bowl, whisk confectioners' sugar and milk. Divide into small bowls; tint with food coloring. Gently spread icing over cooled cookies. Decorate with other colors of icing if desired.

Little Piggy Sugar Cookies

Have some fun with your dessert and whip up a platter of these pig-shaped cookies. The dough can be mixed in a flash and is easy to roll and cut.

—WILMA BRAND PROCTORVILLE, OH

PREP: 15 MIN. + CHILLING • **BAKE:** 20 MIN./BATCH + COOLING
MAKES: ABOUT 4 DOZEN

- ¾ **cup butter, softened**
- 1 **cup sugar**
- 2 **eggs**
- 2 **tablespoons milk**
- ½ **teaspoon almond extract**
- 3¼ **cups all-purpose flour**
- 2 **teaspoons baking powder**
     Tinted frosting

1. In a large bowl, cream the butter and sugar until light and fluffy. Beat in the eggs, milk and extract. Combine the flour and baking powder; gradually add to creamed mixture and mix well. Cover and refrigerate for 2-3 hours or until easy to handle.

2. On a lightly floured surface, roll out the dough to ⅛-in. thickness. Cut out with a floured 3-in. pig-shaped cookie cutter. Place 1 in. apart on ungreased baking sheets.

3. Bake at 375° for 7-9 minutes or until edges begin to brown. Remove to wire racks to cool. Outline cutouts with tinted frosting.

Creamy Frosted Butter Cutouts

With their soft tender insides, these cookies quickly disappear from the cookie jar. Vanilla pudding mix gives the frosting a velvety texture and fabulous flavor.

—STEPHANIE MCKINNON WEST VALLEY CITY, UT

PREP: 30 MIN. + CHILLING • **BAKE:** 40 MIN. • **MAKES:** 5½ DOZEN

- ½ **cup butter, softened**
- 1 **cup sugar**
- 1 **egg**
- ½ **cup sour cream**
- 1 **teaspoon vanilla extract**
- 3½ **cups all-purpose flour**
- 1 **teaspoon baking soda**
- ½ **teaspoon salt**

FROSTING

- ¼ **cup cold milk**
- 3 **tablespoons instant vanilla pudding mix**
- ¼ **cup butter, softened**
- 2½ **cups confectioners' sugar**
- 1 **teaspoon vanilla extract**
  Food coloring, optional

1. In a large bowl, cream the butter and sugar. Beat in egg, sour cream and vanilla. Combine flour, baking soda and salt; gradually add to creamed mixture. Cover and chill for 1 hour or until easy to handle.

2. On a work surface that has been sprinkled heavily with confectioners' sugar, roll out dough to ⅛-in. thickness. Cut with a 2½-in. cookie cutters. Place 1 in. apart on greased baking sheets. Bake at 375° for 8-10 minutes or until lightly browned. Immediately remove to wire racks to cool.

3. For frosting, combine milk and pudding mix until smooth; set aside. In a large bowl, cream butter. Beat in pudding mixture. Gradually add confectioners' sugar, vanilla and food coloring if desired; beat on high speed until light and fluffy. Frost cookies.

Cherry-Filled Cookies

Luscious cherry filling peeking out of these rounds only hints at how scrumptious they are. Using a doughnut cutter to shape each cookie top really speeds up the process.

—MRS. DELBERT BENTON GUTHRIE CENTER, IA

PREP: 25 MIN. + CHILLING • **BAKE:** 10 MIN./BATCH
MAKES: ABOUT 3 DOZEN

- ½ **cup shortening**
- 1 **cup packed brown sugar**
- ½ **cup sugar**
- 2 **eggs**
- ¼ **cup buttermilk**
- 1 **teaspoon vanilla extract**
- 3½ **cups all-purpose flour**
- ½ **teaspoon salt**
- ½ **teaspoon baking soda**
- 1 **can (21 ounces) cherry pie filling**

1. In a bowl, cream shortening and sugars. Add eggs, buttermilk and vanilla; mix well. Combine flour, salt and baking soda; gradually add to creamed mixture and mix well. Cover and chill for 1 hour or until firm.

2. Divide dough in half. On a floured surface, roll each portion to ⅛-in. thickness. Cut with a 2¾-in. round cutter. Place half of the circles 2 in. apart on greased baking sheets; top each with a heaping teaspoon of pie filling. Cut holes in the center of remaining circles with a 1-in. round cutter; place over filled circles. Seal edges.

3. Bake at 375° for 10 minutes or until golden brown. Cool on wire racks.

Chocolate Skeleton Cookies

Put these cute treats out for your next ghost and goblin party and watch them vanish!

—LISA RUPPLE KEENESBURG, CO

PREP: 45 MIN. + CHILLING • **BAKE:** 10 MIN./BATCH + COOLING
MAKES: 3 DOZEN

- 1 **cup butter, softened**
- 1 **cup sugar**
- ½ **cup packed brown sugar**
- 1 **egg**
- 1 **teaspoon vanilla extract**
- 2¾ **cups all-purpose flour**
- ½ **cup baking cocoa**
- 1 **teaspoon baking soda**
- 1½ **cups confectioners' sugar**
- 2 **tablespoons 2% milk**

1. In a large bowl, cream butter and sugars until light and fluffy. Beat in egg and vanilla. Combine the flour, cocoa and baking soda; gradually add to creamed mixture and mix well. Cover and refrigerate the dough for 1-2 hours or until easy to handle.

2. On a lightly floured surface, roll out dough to ⅛-in. thickness. Cut with a floured 3-in. gingerbread boy cookie cutter. Place on greased baking sheets.

3. Bake at 375° for 7-8 minutes or until set. Cool the cookies for 1 minute before removing from pans to wire racks to cool completely.

4. For icing, in a small bowl, combine confectioners' sugar and milk until smooth. Fill a resealable pastic bag with icing; cut a small hole in the corner of bag. Pipe skeleton bones on cookies.

Zebra Butter Cookies

For a party with a jungle or animal theme, these striped cookies are a lot of fun. I started with a horse cookie cutter and got exotic, turning them into zebras!

—SHANNON WADE KANSAS CITY, KS

PREP: 20 MIN. + CHILLING • **BAKE:** 10 MIN./BATCH
MAKES: 1½ DOZEN

 1¼ cups butter, softened
 1 cup sugar
 ⅔ cup confectioners' sugar
 1 egg
 1 teaspoon vanilla extract
 3 cups all-purpose flour
 ¼ teaspoon salt
 ¼ cup baking cocoa

1. In a large bowl, cream butter and sugars until light and fluffy. Beat in egg and vanilla. Combine flour and salt; gradually add to the creamed mixture and mix well.
2. Divide dough in half. Add cocoa to one half and mix well. Roll each half between waxed paper into a 9-in. square. Cut both squares into three 3-in. strips. Cut the strips in half lengthwise to make six 4½-in. x 3-in. rectangles.
3. Place one cream-colored rectangle on a large piece of plastic wrap; top with a chocolate rectangle. Repeat layers twice. Wrap in plastic wrap and refrigerate for 2 hours. Unwrap and cut widthwise into eighteen ¼-in. slices.
4. Cut each slice with a foured horse-shaped cookie cutter . Place 1 in. apart on ungreased baking sheets. Bake at 375° for 8-10 minutes or until edges are lightly golden. Let stand for 2 minutes before removing to wire racks to cool.

Cream Cheese Cutouts

Decorating cookies always puts me in a happy mood. Cookies from this recipe don't rise a lot or lose their shape.

—JULIE DAWSON GALENA, OH

PREP: 15 MIN. + CHILLING • **BAKE:** 10 MIN./BATCH + COOLING
MAKES: ABOUT 7 DOZEN

 1 cup butter, softened
 1 package (3 ounces) cream cheese, softened
 1 cup sugar
 ¼ teaspoon salt
 1 egg
 1 teaspoon vanilla extract
 2½ cups all-purpose flour
FROSTING
 3 cups confectioners' sugar
 ⅓ cup butter, softened
 1½ teaspoons vanilla extract
 2 to 3 tablespoons 2% milk
  Food coloring, optional
  Assorted sprinkles or candies

1. In a large bowl, cream butter, cream cheese, sugar and salt until light and fluffy. Beat in egg and vanilla. Gradually beat in flour. Refrigerate, covered, 1-2 hours or until firm enough to roll.
2. Preheat oven to 375°. On a lightly floured surface, roll dough to ⅛-in. thickness. Cut with floured cookie cutters. Place 1 in. apart on ungreased baking sheets.
3. Bake 7-8 minutes or until edges are lightly browned. Cool 1 minute. Remove to wire racks to cool completely.
4. In a small bowl, beat the confectioners' sugar, butter, vanilla and enough milk to reach desired consistency. If desired, add food coloring. Decorate cookies with frosting and sprinkles.

Sandwich Cookies

Peanut Butter Ice Cream Sandwiches

Store-bought ice cream treats can't hold a candle to homemade ones. This frozen dessert is fantastic.

—**TERESA GAETZKE** NORTH FREEDOM, WI

PREP: 45 MIN. • **BAKE:** 10 MIN. + FREEZING • **MAKES:** 16 SERVINGS

- ½ cup shortening
- ½ cup creamy peanut butter
- ¾ cup sugar, divided
- ½ cup packed brown sugar
- 1 egg
- ½ teaspoon vanilla extract
- 1½ cups all-purpose flour
- 1 teaspoon baking soda
- ½ teaspoon salt
- 12 ounces dark chocolate candy coating, chopped
- 1 quart vanilla ice cream, softened

1. In a large bowl, cream the shortening, peanut butter, ½ cup sugar and brown sugar until light and fluffy. Beat in egg and vanilla. Combine the flour, baking soda and salt; gradually add to creamed mixture and mix well.

2. Roll into 1-in. balls; roll in remaining sugar. Place 1 in. apart on ungreased baking sheets. Flatten with a fork, forming a crisscross pattern.

3. Bake at 350° for 9-11 minutes or until set (do not overbake). Remove to wire racks to cool completely.

4. In a microwave, melt candy coating; stir until smooth. Spread a heaping teaspoonful on the bottom of each cookie; place chocolate side up on waxed paper until set.

5. To make sandwiches, place ¼ cup ice cream on the bottom of half of the cookies; top with remaining cookies. Wrap in plastic wrap; freeze.

Berry-Almond Sandwich Cookies

Almond shortbread cookies cradle a delightful berry filling for this Christmas cookie favorite. They're unbeatable!

—**HELGA SCHLAPE** FLORHAM PARK, NJ

PREP: 30 MIN. • **BAKE:** 10 MIN./BATCH + COOLING
MAKES: 3 DOZEN

- 1½ cups butter, softened
- 1 cup sugar
- 1 teaspoon vanilla extract
- 2¾ cups all-purpose flour
- ½ teaspoon salt
- 2 cups ground almonds
- ¾ cup raspberry filling
  Edible glitter or confectioners' sugar

1. In a large bowl, cream butter and sugar until light and fluffy. Beat in vanilla. Combine the flour and salt; gradually add to creamed mixture and mix well. Stir in almonds.

2. On a heavily floured surface, roll out dough to ⅛-in. thickness. With floured 2½-in. cookie cutters, cut into desired shapes.

3. Place 1 in. apart on ungreased baking sheets. Bake at 325° for 10-12 minutes or until edges begin to brown. Remove to wire racks to cool.

4. Spread 1 teaspoon raspberry filling on the bottoms of half of the cookies; top with remaining cookies. Sprinkle with edible glitter or confectioners' sugar. Store in an airtight container.

NOTE *Edible glitter is available from Wilton Industries at* wilton.com.

Quick Chocolate Sandwich Cookies

These cookies freeze well, so it's easy to keep some on hand for last-minute munching. In summer, I often make them larger to use for ice cream sandwiches.

—MARY REMPEL ALTONA, MB

PREP: 15 MIN. • **BAKE:** 10 MIN./BATCH + COOLING
MAKES: ABOUT 6 DOZEN

- 2 **packages devil's food cake mix (regular size)**
- 1 **cup canola oil**
- 4 **eggs**

FILLING
- 1 **package (8 ounces) cream cheese, softened**
- ¼ **cup butter, softened**
- 2½ **cups confectioners' sugar**
- 1 **teaspoon vanilla extract**

1. In a large bowl, combine the cake mixes, oil and eggs until well blended. Roll into 1-in. balls. Place 2 in. apart on ungreased baking sheets. Do not flatten.
2. Bake at 350° for 8-10 minutes or until set. Cool for 5 minutes before removing to wire racks (cookies will flatten as they cool).

3. In a small bowl, beat cream cheese and butter until fluffy. Beat in sugar and vanilla until smooth. Spread or pipe filling on the bottom of half of the cookies; top with remaining cookies. Store in the refrigerator.

Cutout Pumpkin Sandwich Cookies

Apricot preserves peek out of these buttery, tender sugar cookies. Make them throughout the year with a variety of cookie cutter shapes.

—SCHELBY THOMPSON CAMDEN WYOMING, DE

PREP: 40 MIN. + CHILLING • **BAKE:** 10 MIN./BATCH + COOLING
MAKES: 2 DOZEN

- 1 **cup butter, softened**
- 1¼ **cups sugar, divided**
- 2 **eggs, separated**
- 2½ **cups all-purpose flour**
- ¼ **teaspoon salt**
  Confectioners' sugar
- ½ **cup ground almonds**
- ¾ **cup apricot preserves**

1. In a large bowl, cream butter and ¾ cup sugar until light and fluffy. Add egg yolks, one at a time, beating well after each addition. Combine flour and salt; gradually add to creamed mixture and mix well. Shape dough into a ball; chill for 1 hour or until firm.
2. On a surface dusted with confectioners' sugar, roll dough to ⅛-in. thickness; cut with a 3-in. pumpkin-shaped cookie cutter. Cut a 1½-in. pumpkin from the center of half the cookies and remove (set aside small pumpkin cutouts to bake separately).
3. Place on greased baking sheets. Beat egg whites until frothy. Combine almonds and remaining sugar. Brush each cookie with egg whites; sprinkle with almond mixture. Bake at 350° for 6-8 minutes or until lightly browned. Remove immediately to wire racks to cool completely.
4. Spread 1½ teaspoons of apricot preserves on the bottoms of the solid cookies; place cookies with cutout centers, almond side up, over filling.

Filled Chocolate Spritz

I like to use a cookie disk with an open center so the creamy mint filling peeks through. A chocolate drizzle on top is a flavorful finishing touch.

—MARILYN BLANKSCHIEN CLINTONVILLE, WI

PREP: 15 MIN. + CHILLING • **BAKE:** 10 MIN./BATCH + COOLING
MAKES: ABOUT 2 DOZEN

- ¾ **cup semisweet chocolate chips**
- ¼ **cup butter, cubed**
- ½ **cup packed brown sugar**
- 2 **eggs, lightly beaten**
- 1 **teaspoon vanilla extract**
- 1½ **cups all-purpose flour**
- ⅛ **teaspoon baking soda**

PEPPERMINT FILLING
- ¼ **cup butter, softened**
- ¾ **cup confectioners' sugar**
- 1 **tablespoon milk**
- ½ **teaspoon peppermint extract**
- 3 **to 4 drops green food coloring**

GLAZE
- ⅔ **cup milk chocolate chips**
- 1 **teaspoon shortening**

1. In a large microwave-safe bowl, melt chocolate chips; stir until smooth. Stir in the butter, brown sugar, eggs and vanilla. Add flour and baking soda and mix well. Cover and refrigerate for 30 minutes or until easy to handle.

2. Using a cookie press fitted with the disk of your choice, press dough 2 in. apart onto ungreased baking sheets. Bake at 375° for 6-8 minutes or until set. Remove to wire racks to cool.

3. In a small bowl, combine filling ingredients; stir until smooth. Spread on the bottoms of half of the cookies; top with the remaining cookies.

4. In a microwave, melt milk chocolate chips and shortening; stir until smooth. Drizzle over cookies. Let stand until set.

Dipped Sandwich Cookies

With a lemon filling and chocolate coating, these buttery sandwich cookies are often requested at my house.

—JANE DELAHOYDE POUGHKEEPSIE, NY

PREP: 25 MIN. • **BAKE:** 10 MIN. + COOLING
MAKES: 2 DOZEN

- 1 cup butter, softened
- ½ cup sugar
- 1 egg yolk
- 1 teaspoon vanilla extract
- 2 cups all-purpose flour

LEMON FILLING
- ½ cup butter, softened
- 2 cups confectioners' sugar
- 2 tablespoons lemon juice

DIPPING CHOCOLATE
- 4 ounces semisweet chocolate, chopped
- 2 tablespoons butter
- ½ cup finely chopped nuts

1. In a large bowl, cream butter and sugar until light and fluffy. Beat in egg yolk and vanilla. Gradually add flour and mix well.

2. Shape into 1-in. balls. Place 2 in. apart on ungreased baking sheets. With a glass dipped in sugar, flatten into 2-in. circles. Bake at 350° for 10-12 minutes or until firm. Remove to wire racks to cool.

3. Combine filling ingredients. Spread on the bottom of half of the cookies; top with remaining cookies.

4. In a microwave, melt chocolate and butter; stir until smooth. Dip each cookie halfway in chocolate; allow excess to drip off. Dip in nuts. Place on waxed paper; let stand until set.

Chocolaty Double Crunchers

I first tried these fun crispy cookies at a family picnic when I was a child. Packed with oats, cornflakes and coconut, they quickly became a regular treat at our house.

—CHERYL JOHNSON UPPER MARLBORO, MD

PREP: 20 MIN. • **BAKE:** 10 MIN./BATCH + COOLING
MAKES: 2 DOZEN

- ½ cup butter, softened
- ½ cup sugar
- ½ cup packed brown sugar
- 1 egg
- ½ teaspoon vanilla extract
- 1 cup all-purpose flour
- ½ teaspoon baking soda
- ¼ teaspoon salt
- 1 cup quick-cooking oats
- 1 cup crushed cornflakes
- ½ cup flaked coconut

FILLING
- 2 packages (3 ounces each) cream cheese, softened
- 1½ cups confectioners' sugar
- 2 cups (12 ounces) semisweet chocolate chips, melted

1. In a large bowl, cream butter and sugars until light and fluffy. Beat in egg and vanilla. Combine the flour, baking soda and salt; gradually add to creamed mixture and mix well. Stir in the oats, cornflakes and coconut.

2. Shape into 1-in. balls and place 2 in. apart on greased baking sheets. Flatten with a glass dipped lightly in flour. Bake at 350° for 8-10 minutes or until lightly browned. Remove to wire racks to cool.

3. For filling, beat cream cheese and sugar until smooth. Beat in chocolate. Spread about 1 tablespoon on half of the cookies and top each with another cookie. Store in the refrigerator.

S'more Sandwich Cookies

Capture the taste of campfire s'mores in your kitchen. With graham cracker crumbs added to the dough, these are just as good as the real thing! Softening the marshmallow centers in the microwave makes the cookies simple to assemble.

—**ABBY METZGER** LARCHWOOD, IA

PREP: 25 MIN. • **BAKE:** 10 MIN. + COOLING
MAKES: ABOUT 2 DOZEN

- ¾ **cup butter, softened**
- ½ **cup sugar**
- ½ **cup packed brown sugar**
- 1 **egg**
- 2 **tablespoons milk**
- 1 **teaspoon vanilla extract**
- 1¼ **cups all-purpose flour**
- 1¼ **cups graham cracker crumbs (about 20 squares)**
- ½ **teaspoon baking soda**
- ¼ **teaspoon salt**
- ⅛ **teaspoon ground cinnamon**
- 2 **cups (12 ounces) semisweet chocolate chips**
- 24 **to 28 large marshmallows**

1. In a large bowl, cream butter and sugars until light and fluffy. Beat in the egg, milk and vanilla. Combine the flour, graham cracker crumbs, baking soda, salt and cinnamon; gradually add to creamed mixture and mix well. Stir in chocolate chips.

2. Drop by tablespoonfuls 2 in. apart onto ungreased baking sheets. Bake at 375° for 8-10 minutes or until golden brown. Remove to wire racks to cool.

3. Place four of the cookies bottom side up on a microwave-safe plate; top each with a marshmallow. Microwave, uncovered, on high for 10-15 seconds or until marshmallows begin to puff (do not overcook). Top each with another cookie. Repeat.

NOTE *This recipe was tested in a 1,100-watt microwave.*

Lemon-Cream Sandwich Cookies

A light lemon filling sandwiched between flaky butter cookies makes these a perfect accompaniment to hot tea or coffee.

—**CAROL STEINER** ARROWWOOD, AB

PREP: 30 MIN. + CHILLING • **BAKE:** 10 MIN. + COOLING
MAKES: 2 DOZEN

- ¾ **cup butter, softened**
- ½ **cup confectioners' sugar**
- 2 **teaspoons lemon extract**
- 1½ **cups all-purpose flour**
- ¼ **cup cornstarch**

LEMON FILLING

- ¼ **cup butter, softened**
- 1½ **cups confectioners' sugar**
- 2 **tablespoons lemon juice**
- 2 **teaspoons grated lemon peel**

1. In a bowl, cream butter and confectioners' sugar. Beat in extract. Combine flour and cornstarch; beat into creamed mixture. Divide into two balls; wrap in plastic wrap and refrigerate for 1 hour.

2. On a lightly floured surface, roll each portion of dough to ⅛-in. thickness. Cut into 2-in. rounds. Place on ungreased baking sheets. Bake at 350° for 10-12 minutes or until edges are lightly browned. Remove to wire racks to cool.

3. For filling, in a small bowl, cream butter and confectioners' sugar. Beat in lemon juice and peel. Spread over the bottoms of half of the cookies; top with remaining cookies.

NOTE *This recipe does not use eggs.*

Evergreen Sandwich Cookies

A fluffy vanilla filling makes these cookies a big holiday favorite at our house. My family also likes the rich shortbread flavor.

—**EVELYN MOLL** TULSA, OK

PREP: 30 MIN. + CHILLING • **BAKE:** 10 MIN./BATCH + COOLING
MAKES: ABOUT 2 DOZEN

- 1 **cup butter, softened**
- 2 **cups all-purpose flour**
- ⅓ **cup milk**
- ¼ **teaspoon salt**

FILLING
- ¼ **cup shortening**
- ¼ **cup butter, softened**
- 2 **cups confectioners' sugar**
- 4½ **teaspoons milk**
- ½ **teaspoon vanilla extract**
  Green paste food coloring

GLAZE
- 1⅓ **cups confectioners' sugar**
- 4 **teaspoons milk**
  Green paste food coloring
  Green colored sugar

1. In a large bowl, combine the butter, flour, milk and salt. Cover and refrigerate for 1½ hours or until easy to handle.
2. Divide dough into thirds. On a floured surface, roll out each portion to ⅛-in. thickness. Cut with a floured 3¾-in. Christmas tree cookie cutter. Place on ungreased baking sheets. Prick each with a fork several times. Bake at 375° for 8-11 minutes or until set. Cool completely on wire racks.
3. For filling, in a small bowl, cream the shortening, butter and confectioners' sugar until light and fluffy. Beat in milk and vanilla until smooth. Tint with food coloring. Spread about a tablespoon filling on the bottoms of half of the cookies; top with remaining cookies.
4. For glaze, combine confectioners' sugar and milk until smooth; set aside ¼ cup. Stir food coloring into remaining glaze; spread a thin layer over the top of each sandwich. If desired, sprinkle tops of half of the cookies with colored sugar. Let stand until set. Pipe garland onto half of the cookies with reserved glaze. Let stand until set.

Oatmeal Sandwich Cookies

My fun treats put a sweet, fluffy filling between two chewy oatmeal cookies. They're perfect for snacks and tucking in lunch boxes. At bake sales, they sell instantly.

—JAN WOODALL INDIANAPOLIS, IN

PREP: 25 MIN. • **BAKE:** 10 MIN./BATCH + COOLING
MAKES: ABOUT 4½ DOZEN

- 1½ cups shortening
- 2⅔ cups packed brown sugar
- 4 eggs
- 2 teaspoons vanilla extract
- 2¼ cups all-purpose flour
- 2 teaspoons ground cinnamon
- 1½ teaspoons baking soda
- 1 teaspoon salt
- ½ teaspoon ground nutmeg
- 4 cups old-fashioned oats

FILLING
- ¾ cup shortening
- 3 cups confectioners' sugar
- 1 jar (7 ounces) marshmallow creme
- 1 to 3 tablespoons 2% milk

1. In a large bowl, cream shortening and brown sugar until light and fluffy. Beat in eggs and vanilla. Combine the flour, cinnamon, baking soda, salt and nutmeg; gradually add to creamed mixture and mix well. Stir in oats.

2. Drop by rounded teaspoonfuls 2 in. apart onto lightly greased baking sheets. Bake at 350° for 10-12 minutes or until golden brown. Remove to wire racks to cool.

3. For filling, in a small bowl, cream the shortening, sugar and marshmallow creme. Add enough milk to achieve spreading consistency. Spread filling on the bottom of half of the cookies; top with remaining cookies.

Lacy Oat Sandwich Wafers

These cookies appear on my table for various special occasions. I'm often asked for the recipe, so I always have copies on hand.

—RUTH LEE TROY, ON

PREP: 25 MIN. • **BAKE:** 10 MIN./BATCH + COOLING
MAKES: ABOUT 3½ DOZEN

- ⅔ **cup butter**
- 2 **cups quick-cooking oats**
- 1 **cup sugar**
- ⅔ **cup all-purpose flour**
- ¼ **cup milk**
- ¼ **cup corn syrup**
- 2 **cups semisweet chocolate, milk chocolate or white baking chips, melted**

1. Line a baking sheet with parchment paper or foil; set aside. In a saucepan, melt butter over low heat. Remove from the heat. Stir in the oats, sugar, flour, milk and corn syrup; mix well.

2. Drop by teaspoonfuls 2 in. apart onto prepared baking sheets. Bake at 375° for 8-10 minutes or until golden brown. Cool completely; peel cookies off paper or foil. Spread melted chocolate on the bottom of half of the cookies; top with remaining cookies.

Old-Fashioned Whoopie Pies

Who can resist soft chocolate sandwich cookies filled with a layer of fluffy white frosting? Mom has made these for years. They never lasted very long with me and my two brothers around, though.

—MARIA COSTELLO MONROE, NC

PREP: 35 MIN. + CHILLING • **BAKE:** 10 MIN./BATCH + COOLING
MAKES: 2 DOZEN

- ½ **cup baking cocoa**
- ½ **cup hot water**
- ½ **cup shortening**
- 1½ **cups sugar**
- 2 **eggs**
- 1 **teaspoon vanilla extract**
- 2⅔ **cups all-purpose flour**
- 1 **teaspoon baking powder**
- 1 **teaspoon baking soda**
- ¼ **teaspoon salt**
- ½ **cup buttermilk**

FILLING

- 3 **tablespoons all-purpose flour**
  Dash salt
- 1 **cup 2% milk**
- ¾ **cup shortening**
- 1½ **cups confectioners' sugar**
- 2 **teaspoons vanilla extract**

1. In a small bowl, combine the cocoa and water. Cool for 5 minutes. In a large bowl, cream shortening and sugar until light and fluffy. Beat in the eggs, vanilla and cocoa mixture. Combine dry ingredients; gradually add to creamed mixture alternately with buttermilk, beating well after each addition

2. Drop by rounded tablespoonfuls 2 in. apart onto greased baking sheets. Flatten slightly with a spoon. Bake at 350° for 10-12 minutes or until firm to the touch. Remove to wire racks to cool.

3. In a small saucepan, combine flour and salt. Gradually whisk in milk until smooth; cook and stir over medium-high heat until thick, 5-7 minutes. Remove from heat. Cover and refrigerate until completely cool.

4. In a small bowl, cream the shortening, sugar and vanilla until light and fluffy. Add milk mixture; beat for 7 minutes or until fluffy. Spread filling on half of the cookies; top with remaining cookies. Store in the refrigerator.

Hamburger Cookies

My husband loves peppermint patties, and our son is crazy for vanilla wafers. So I put the two together to make a cool cookie that looks just like a burger.

—**JULIE WELLINGTON** YOUNGSTOWN, OH

START TO FINISH: 30 MIN. • **MAKES:** 20 COOKIES

- ½ cup vanilla frosting
  Red and yellow paste or gel food coloring
- 40 vanilla wafers
- 20 peppermint patties
- 1 teaspoon corn syrup
- 1 teaspoon sesame seeds

Place ¼ cup frosting in each of two small bowls. Tint one red and the other yellow. Spread yellow frosting on the bottoms of 20 vanilla wafers; top with a peppermint patty. Spread with red frosting. Brush tops of the remaining vanilla wafers with corn syrup; sprinkle with sesame seeds. Place over red frosting.

Strawberry Sandwich Cookies

These sandwich cookies are absolutely yummy. Try them!

—**BARBARA SESSOYEFF** REDWOOD VALLEY, CA

PREP: 25 MIN. + CHILLING • **BAKE:** 10 MIN. + COOLING
MAKES: 1½ DOZEN

- 1 cup blanched almonds
- ¾ cup butter, softened
- 1 cup confectioners' sugar, divided
- 1 egg
- ½ teaspoon almond extract
- 1½ cups all-purpose flour
- ⅛ teaspoon salt
- 1 tablespoon lemon juice
- 3 tablespoons strawberry jam

1. In a food processor, process almonds until ground; set aside. In a large bowl, cream butter and ½ cup sugar until light and fluffy. Beat in egg and extract. Combine flour and salt; gradually add to creamed mixture and mix well. Stir in the ground almonds.

2. Divide dough in half; cover and refrigerate for 2 hours or until easy to handle.

3. On a lightly floured surface, roll out each portion of dough into a 12-in. x 9-in. rectangle. Cut lengthwise into three strips; cut each strip widthwise into six pieces. With a ¾-in. round cutter, cut out a circle in the center of half of the pieces (discard circles).

4. Place 1 in. apart on ungreased baking sheets. Bake at 375° for 8-10 minutes or until golden brown. Remove to wire racks to cool completely.

5. For glaze, combine lemon juice and remaining sugar; thinly spread over whole cookies. Top with cutout cookies; fill center with ½ teaspoon jam.

Bakeshop **TIP**

Removing Cookies From a Baking Sheet

If cookies crumble when you remove them from a baking sheet, let them cool for 1 to 2 minutes first. However, if they cool too long, they can become hard and can break when lifted. If this happens, return the baking sheet to the oven to warm the cookies slightly so they'll release more easily.

Date-Filled Sandwich Cookies

Of all the cookies I've baked over the years, these remain one of my all-time favorites. The dough is very easy to work with.
—**DEBBIE RODE** OXBOW, SK

PREP: 30 MIN. + CHILLING • **BAKE:** 10 MIN./BATCH + COOLING
MAKES: 3 DOZEN

- 1 **cup butter, softened**
- 2 **cups packed brown sugar**
- 2 **eggs**
- 2 **teaspoons vanilla extract**
- 3½ **cups all-purpose flour**
- 1 **teaspoon baking powder**
- 1 **teaspoon baking soda**

FILLING
- 2 **cups chopped dates**
- ¾ **cup sugar**
- ¾ **cup water**

1. In a large bowl, cream butter and brown sugar until light and fluffy. Add eggs, one at a time, beating well after each addition. Beat in vanilla. Combine the flour, baking powder and baking soda; gradually add to creamed mixture and mix well. Refrigerate for 1 hour or until easy to handle.

2. On a lightly floured surface, roll out dough to ⅛-in. thickness. Cut with a floured 2½-in. cookie cutter. Place 1 in. apart on greased baking sheets. Bake at 350° for 10-12 minutes or until edges are lightly browned. Remove to wire racks to cool.

3. In a small saucepan, combine filling ingredients. Cook over medium heat for 3 minutes or until thickened and bubbly. Cool to room temperature. Spread on the bottoms of half of the cookies; top with remaining cookies.

Star Sandwich Cookies

These dazzling sandwich cookies will be the star of your holiday dessert tray. A rich mixture of white chocolate and cream cheese forms the sweet yet simple filling.

—TASTE OF HOME TEST KITCHEN

PREP: 30 MIN. • **BAKE:** 10 MIN. + COOLING
MAKES: ABOUT 1 DOZEN

- ½ **tube refrigerated sugar cookie dough, softened**
- ⅓ **cup all-purpose flour**
   Red sugars, nonpareils or sprinkles
- 1 **ounce white baking chocolate**
- 2 **tablespoons cream cheese, softened**
- 1 **tablespoon butter, softened**
- 4 **drops red food coloring**
- ½ **cup confectioners' sugar**

1. In a small bowl, beat cookie dough and flour until combined. Roll out on a lightly floured surface to ⅛-in. thickness. Cut with a floured 2¾-in. star cookie cutter. Place 2 in. apart on ungreased baking sheets.

2. Decorate half of the cookies with sugars and nonpareils. Bake at 350° for 7-9 minutes or until edges are golden brown. Remove to wire racks to cool.

3. In a microwave, melt white chocolate; stir until smooth. Cool. In a small bowl, beat the cream cheese, butter and food coloring until fluffy. Gradually beat in confectioners' sugar and melted chocolate until smooth. Spread over the tops of plain cookies; top with decorated cookies. Store in the refrigerator.

Fruit-Filled Spritz Cookies

From the first time I baked these cookies, they've been a divine success. Old-fashioned and attractive, they make a perfect holiday pastry.

—INGEBORG KEITH NEWARK, DE

PREP: 30 MIN. • **BAKE:** 15 MIN./BATCH • **MAKES:** ABOUT 7½ DOZEN

- 1½ **cups chopped dates**
- 1 **cup water**
- ½ **cup sugar**
- 2 **teaspoons orange juice**
- 2 **teaspoons grated orange peel**
- 1 **cup maraschino cherries, chopped**
- ½ **cup flaked coconut**
- ½ **cup ground nuts**

DOUGH

- 1 **cup butter, softened**
- 1 **cup sugar**
- ½ **cup packed brown sugar**
- 3 **eggs**
- ½ **teaspoon almond extract**
- ½ **teaspoon vanilla extract**
- 4 **cups all-purpose flour**
- ½ **teaspoon baking soda**
- ½ **teaspoon salt**
   Confectioners' sugar, optional

1. In a small saucepan, combine the first five ingredients; bring to a boil, stirring constantly. Reduce heat; cook and stir for 8 minutes or until thickened. Cool completely. Stir in the cherries, coconut and nuts; set aside.

2. In a large bowl, cream butter and sugars until light and fluffy. Beat in eggs and extracts. Combine the flour, baking soda and salt; gradually add to the creamed mixture and mix well.

3. Using a cookie press fitted with a bar disk, press a 12-in.-long strip of dough onto an ungreased baking sheet. Spread fruit filling over dough. Press another strip over filling. Cut into 1-in. pieces (there is no need to separate the pieces). Repeat with remaining dough and filling.

4. Bake at 375° for 12-15 minutes or until edges are golden. Recut into pieces if necessary. Remove to wire racks to cool. Dust with confectioners' sugar if desired.

Lemon Curd Cookies

I've made these cookies for years. It's a pleasure to give them out to family and friends.

—CAROLE VOGEL ALLISON PARK, PA

PREP: 30 MIN. + CHILLING • **BAKE:** 10 MIN. + COOLING
MAKES: 1½ DOZEN

>   1 cup butter, softened
>   ¾ cup sugar
>   1 egg
>   1 teaspoon lemon extract
>   1 teaspoon vanilla extract
>   2½ cups all-purpose flour
>   ½ teaspoon baking soda
>   ½ teaspoon salt
>   1 cup ground pecans, toasted
> **FILLING**
>   1½ cups sugar
>   2 tablespoons cornstarch
>   ⅛ teaspoon salt
>   ½ cup lemon juice
>   4 egg yolks, lightly beaten
>   6 tablespoons butter, cubed
>   2 teaspoons grated lemon peel
>   Confectioners' sugar

1. In a large bowl, cream butter and sugar until light and fluffy. Beat in egg and extracts. Combine the flour, baking soda and salt; gradually add to creamed mixture and mix well. Stir in pecans.

2. Divide dough in half; shape into logs. Wrap each in plastic wrap. Refrigerate for 1-2 hours or until firm.

3. On a floured surface, roll each portion to ⅛-in. thickness. Cut with a floured 3-in. fluted round cookie cutter. With a floured ½-in. round cookie cutter, cut out the centers of half of the cookies. (Reroll small cutouts if desired.)

4. Place solid and cutout cookies 1 in. apart on ungreased baking sheets. Bake at 350° for 10-12 minutes or until lightly browned. Remove to wire racks to cool.

5. In a small saucepan, combine the sugar, cornstarch and salt. Stir in lemon juice until smooth. Cook and stir until slightly thickened and bubbly, about 2 minutes. Stir a small amount into egg yolks. Return all to the pan; bring to a gentle boil; stirring constantly. Cook and stir 2 minutes longer until mixture reaches 160° and coats the back of a metal spoon.

6. Remove from the heat; stir in butter and lemon peel. Pour into a bowl; cover surface with plastic wrap. Chill for 2-3 hours (mixture will be thick).

7. Spread 1 tablespoon filling on bottoms of the solid cookies; place cookies with cutout centers over filling, pressing down lightly. Sprinkle with confectioners' sugar. Store in the refrigerator.

Sweet Sandwich Cookies

My caramel cookie is a past winner of our family's holiday bake-off. The tender brown sugar cookie melts together with the rich browned butter frosting for a yummy flavor combination.

—**PAT SCHAR** ZELIENOPLE, PA

PREP: 30 MIN. • **BAKE:** 10 MIN. + COOLING
MAKES: ABOUT 1½ DOZEN

- 1 cup butter, softened
- ¾ cup packed brown sugar
- 1 egg yolk
- 2 cups all-purpose flour
- ¼ teaspoon salt

BROWNED BUTTER FILLING
- 2 tablespoons butter
- 1¼ cups confectioners' sugar
- ½ teaspoon vanilla extract
- 4 to 5 teaspoons 2% milk

1. In a large bowl, cream butter and brown sugar until light and fluffy. Beat in egg yolk. Combine flour and salt; gradually add to creamed mixture and mix well. Cover and refrigerate for 20 minutes.

2. Shape into 1-in. balls. Place 1½ in. apart on ungreased baking sheets. Flatten with a fork, forming a crisscross pattern.

3. Bake at 325° for 8-10 minutes or until golden brown. Remove to wire racks to cool.

4. For filling, heat butter in a saucepan over medium heat until golden brown. Remove from the heat; stir in the confectioners' sugar, vanilla and enough milk to achieve spreading consistency. Spread on the bottoms of half of the cookies; top with remaining cookies.

Lemon Tea Cookies

These sandwich cookies taste rich and buttery and have a lovely lemon filling. The recipe has been in our family since the 1950s, when my mother got it from a French friend in her club. Mom always made these cookies at Christmas.

—**PHYLLIS DIETZ** WESTLAND, MI

PREP: 25 MIN. + CHILLING • **BAKE:** 10 MIN./BATCH + COOLING
MAKES: ABOUT 4½ DOZEN

- ¾ cup butter, softened
- ½ cup sugar
- 1 egg yolk
- ½ teaspoon vanilla extract
- 2 cups all-purpose flour
- ¼ cup finely chopped walnuts

FILLING
- 3 tablespoons butter, softened
- 4½ teaspoons lemon juice
- ¾ teaspoon grated orange peel
- 1½ cups confectioners' sugar
- 2 drops yellow food coloring, optional

1. In a large bowl, cream butter and sugar until light and fluffy. Beat in the egg yolk and vanilla. Gradually add flour and mix well.

2. Shape into two 14-in. rolls; reshape each roll into a 14-in. x 1⅛-in. x 1⅛-in. block. Wrap each in plastic wrap. Refrigerate overnight.

3. Unwrap and cut into ¼-in. slices. Place 2 in. apart on ungreased baking sheets. Sprinkle half of the cookies with nuts, gently pressing into dough.

4. Bake at 400° for 8-10 minutes or until golden brown around the edges. Remove to wire racks to cool.

5. In a small bowl, cream the butter, lemon juice and orange peel until fluffy. Gradually add confectioners' sugar until smooth. Tint yellow if desired. Spread about 1 teaspoon on bottoms of the plain cookies; place nut topped cookies over filling.

Cherry-Filled Heart Cookies

Bake a batch of these crisp, flaky cookies to show you care. They take a little effort, but the smiles of delight make it worthwhile.

—**AUDREY GROE** LAKE MILLS, IA

PREP: 50 MIN. + CHILLING • **BAKE:** 10 MIN./BATCH
MAKES: ABOUT 4½ DOZEN FILLED COOKIES

- ½ cup butter, softened
- ½ cup shortening
- 1 cup sugar
- 1 egg
- ½ cup milk
- 1 teaspoon vanilla extract
- 3½ cups all-purpose flour
- 2 teaspoons baking powder
- 1 teaspoon baking soda
- ½ teaspoon salt

FILLING
- ½ cup sugar
- 4½ teaspoons cornstarch
- ½ cup orange juice
- ¼ cup red maraschino cherry juice
- 12 red maraschino cherries, chopped
- 1 tablespoon butter
  Additional sugar

1. In a bowl, cream the butter and shortening; gradually add sugar. Add egg, milk and vanilla. Combine the dry ingredients; gradually add to creamed mixture. Mix well. Cover and refrigerate for at least 2 hours.

2. Meanwhile, for filling, combine sugar and cornstarch in small saucepan. Add juices, cherries and butter. Bring to a boil; boil and stir for 1 minute. Chill.

3. Roll out dough on a lightly floured surface to ⅛-in. thickness; cut with a 2½-in. heart-shaped cookie cutter dipped in flour.

4. Place half of the cookies on greased baking sheets; spoon ½ teaspoon filling in the center of each. Use a 1½-in.heart-shaped cutter to cut small hearts out of the other half of the cookies. (Bake small heart cutouts separately.) Place the remaining hearts over filled cookies; press edges together gently. Fill centers with additional filling if needed. Sprinkle with sugar.

5. Bake at 375° for 8-10 minutes or until lightly browned. Cool on wire racks.

Chocolate Mint Cookies

My dad sandwiches mint patties between two tender chocolate cookies to create these chewy treats. The blend of chocolate and mint is a big hit at our house. Best of all, the cookies are easy and fun to make.

—**CHRISTINA BURBAGE** SPARTANBURG, SC

PREP: 15 MIN. • **BAKE:** 10 MIN./BATCH
MAKES: 32 SANDWICH COOKIES

- 1¼ cups butter, softened
- 2 cups sugar
- 2 eggs
- 2 teaspoons vanilla extract
- 2 cups all-purpose flour
- ¾ cup baking cocoa
- 1 teaspoon baking soda
- ½ teaspoon salt
- 32 round thin chocolate-covered mint patties

1. In a bowl, cream butter and sugar. Add eggs, one at a time, beating well after each addition. Beat in vanilla. Combine the flour, cocoa, baking soda and salt; gradually add to the creamed mixture, beating until well combine.

2. Drop by tablespoonfuls 2 in. apart onto ungreased baking sheets. Bake at 350° for 8-9 minutes or until puffy and tops are cracked. Invert half of the cookies onto wire racks. Immediately place a mint patty on each, then top with the remaining cookies. Press cookies lightly to seal. Cool completely.

Unbeatable Brownies

Peanut Butter Brownie Bars

A brownie mix base makes this a no-fuss treat that will appeal to adults and children alike. Creamy peanut butter, crunchy nuts and crisp cereal make the bars fun to bite into.

—RADELLE KNAPPENBERGER OVIEDO, FL

PREP: 20 MIN. • **BAKE:** 25 MIN. + CHILLING • **MAKES:** 3 DOZEN

- 1 package fudge brownie mix (13-inch x 9-inch pan size)
- 12 peanut butter cups, chopped
- ½ cup salted peanuts, chopped
- 2 cups (12 ounces) semisweet chocolate chips
- 1¼ cups creamy peanut butter
- 1 tablespoon butter
- 1½ cups crisp rice cereal
- 1 teaspoon vanilla extract
- ⅛ teaspoon salt

1. Prepare the brownie batter according to the package directions. Spread into a greased 13x9-in. baking pan. Bake at 350° for 20-25 minutes or until a toothpick inserted near the center comes out with moist crumbs.

2. Sprinkle with peanut butter cups and peanuts. Bake 4-6 minutes longer or until chocolate is melted. Cool on a wire rack.

3. Meanwhile, in a microwave-safe bowl, melt chocolate chips, peanut butter and butter; stir until smooth. Stir in the cereal, vanilla and salt. Carefully spread over brownies. Cover and refrigerate for at least 2 hours before cutting.

Raspberry Truffle Brownies

Each rich, fudgelike brownie is bursting with fresh raspberries and topped with a dreamy bittersweet ganache. It's true perfection for chocolate lovers!

—AGNES WARD STRATFORD, ON

PREP: 30 MIN. • **BAKE:** 25 MIN. + CHILLING • **MAKES:** 1 DOZEN

- 6 ounces bittersweet chocolate, chopped
- ½ cup butter, cubed
- 2 eggs
- 1 cup sugar
- 1 teaspoon vanilla extract
- 1 cup all-purpose flour
- ¼ teaspoon baking soda
- ¼ teaspoon salt
- 1 cup fresh raspberries

FROSTING
- 6 ounces bittersweet chocolate, chopped
- ¾ cup heavy whipping cream
- 2 tablespoons seedless raspberry jam
- 1 teaspoon vanilla extract
- 12 fresh raspberries

1. In a microwave, melt chocolate and butter; stir until smooth. In a large bowl, beat the eggs, sugar and vanilla. Stir in chocolate mixture. Combine the flour, baking soda and salt; gradually add to chocolate mixture just until combined. Gently fold in raspberries.

2. Spread into a greased 9-in.-square baking pan. Bake at 350° for 25-30 minutes or until a toothpick inserted near the center comes out clean (do not overbake). Cool on a wire rack.

3. For frosting, in a microwave-safe bowl, combine the chocolate, cream and jam. Microwave at 50% power for 2-3 minutes or until smooth, stirring twice. Transfer to a small bowl; stir in vanilla. Place in a bowl of ice water; stir for 3-5 minutes. With a hand mixer, beat on medium speed until soft peaks form.

4. Cut a small hole in a corner of a heavy-duty resealable plastic bag; insert #825 star tip. Fill with ½ cup frosting. Spread remaining frosting over brownies. Cut into 12 bars. Pipe a chocolate rosette in the center of each brownie; top with a raspberry. Cover and refrigerate for 30 minutes or until frosting is set. Refrigerate leftovers.

NOTE *This recipe was tested in a 1,100-watt microwave.*

Walnut Oat Brownies

Oatmeal and wheat germ are healthy additions to these fudgy brownies. If the recipe sounds too nutritious to also be delicious, don't worry. These brownies really taste great.

—MARILYN YATES ROANOKE, VA

PREP: 15 MIN. • **BAKE:** 25 MIN. + COOLING • **MAKES:** 1 DOZEN

- 6 ounces semisweet chocolate
- ¼ cup butter
- ½ cup egg substitute
- ¼ cup packed brown sugar
- 2 tablespoons sugar
- 1 teaspoon vanilla extract
- ⅓ cup quick-cooking oats
- ⅓ cup nonfat dry milk powder
- ¼ cup toasted wheat germ
- ½ teaspoon baking powder
- ¼ teaspoon salt
- ¼ cup chopped walnuts
  Confectioners' sugar, optional

1. In a microwave, melt chocolate and butter; stir until smooth. Cool slightly. In a large bowl, beat egg substitute and sugars. Stir in vanilla and chocolate mixture. Combine the dry ingredients; gradually add to chocolate mixture. Stir in walnuts.

2. Pour into an 8-in.-square baking dish coated with cooking spray. Bake at 350° for 25-30 minutes or until a toothpick inserted near the center comes out clean. Cool on a wire rack. Dust with confectioners' sugar if desired. Cut into bars.

Frosted Fudge Brownies

A neighbor brought over a pan of these rich brownies along with the recipe when I came home from the hospital with our baby daughter years ago. I've made them ever since for many family occasions, potlucks and parties at work.

—SUE SODERLUND ELGIN, IL

PREP: 10 MIN. + COOLING • **BAKE:** 25 MIN. + COOLING
MAKES: 2 DOZEN

- 1 cup plus 3 tablespoons butter, cubed
- ¾ cup baking cocoa
- 4 eggs
- 2 cups sugar
- 1½ cups all-purpose flour
- 1 teaspoon baking powder
- 1 teaspoon salt
- 1 teaspoon vanilla extract

FROSTING

- 6 tablespoons butter, softened
- 2⅔ cups confectioners' sugar
- ½ cup baking cocoa
- 1 teaspoon vanilla extract
- ¼ to ⅓ cup milk

1. In a saucepan, melt butter. Remove from the heat. Stir in cocoa; cool. In a large bowl, beat eggs and sugar until blended. Combine flour, baking powder and salt; gradually add to egg mixture. Stir in vanilla and the cooled chocolate mixture until well blended.

2. Spread into a greased 13-in. x 9-in. baking pan. Bake at 350° for 25-28 minutes or until a toothpick inserted near the center comes out clean (do not overbake). Cool on a wire rack.

3. For frosting, in a large bowl, cream the butter and confectioners' sugar until light and fluffy. Beat in cocoa and vanilla. Add enough of the milk until the frosting achieves spreading consistency. Spread over the brownies. Cut into bars.

Zucchini Brownies

A fast peanut butter and chocolate frosting tops these moist brownies that are a sweet way to use up your garden s zucchini. We really like the cakelike texture of these brownies.

—ALLYSON WILKINS AMHERST, NH

PREP: 20 MIN. • **BAKE:** 35 MIN. + COOLING
MAKES: ABOUT 1½ DOZEN

- 1 **cup butter, softened**
- 1½ **cups sugar**
- 2 **eggs**
- ½ **cup plain yogurt**
- 1 **teaspoon vanilla extract**
- 2½ **cups all-purpose flour**
- ¼ **cup baking cocoa**
- 1 **teaspoon baking soda**
- ½ **teaspoon salt**
- 2 **cups shredded zucchini**

FROSTING
- ⅔ **cup semisweet chocolate chips**
- ½ **cup creamy peanut butter**

1. In a large bowl, cream butter and sugar until light and fluffy. Add eggs, one at a time, beating well after each addition. Beat in yogurt and vanilla. Combine the flour, cocoa, baking soda and salt; gradually add to creamed mixture. Stir in zucchini.

2. Pour into a greased 13-in. x 9-in. baking pan. Bake at 350° for 35-40 minutes or until a toothpick inserted near the center comes out clean.

3. For frosting, in a small saucepan, combine chocolate chips and peanut butter. Cook and stir over low heat until smooth. Spread over warm brownies. Cool on a wire rack. Cut into bars.

Cream Cheese Brownies

A friend from church shared this recipe with me. Cream cheese makes it a moist and chewy bar that's finger-lickin' good!

—CAROLYN REED NORTH ROBINSON, OH

PREP: 20 MIN. • **BAKE:** 35 MIN. + COOLING • **MAKES:** 2½ DOZEN

- 2 packages (8 ounces each) cream cheese, softened
- 2 cups sugar, divided
- 3 tablespoons milk
- 1 cup butter, softened
- ⅔ cup instant hot cocoa mix
- 4 eggs
- 2 teaspoons vanilla extract
- 1½ cups all-purpose flour
- 1 cup chopped nuts

1. In a small bowl, beat the cream cheese, ½ cup sugar and milk until fluffy; set aside. In a large bowl, cream the butter, cocoa mix and remaining sugar until light and fluffy. Beat in eggs and vanilla. Stir in flour and nuts and mix well.

2. Pour half into a greased 13-in. x 9-in. baking pan. Spread with the cream cheese mixture. Top with remaining batter. Cut through batter with a knife to swirl the cream cheese.

3. Bake at 350° for 35-40 minutes or until a toothpick inserted near the center comes out clean. Cool on a wire rack. Cut into bars.

Really Rocky Road Brownies

This recipe is from a family reunion cookbook that I put together. "Rocky road" refers to any kind of dessert featuring nuts, marshmallows and chocolate.

—BRENDA WOOD EGBERT, ON

PREP: 20 MIN. • **BAKE:** 25 MIN. + COOLING • **MAKES:** 4 DOZEN

- 8 ounces unsweetened chocolate, chopped
- 1½ cups butter
- 6 eggs
- 3 cups sugar
- 1 tablespoon vanilla extract
- 1½ cups all-purpose flour
- 1 cup chopped walnuts, optional

TOPPING

- 2 cups miniature marshmallows
- 1 ounce unsweetened chocolate, melted

1. In a microwave-safe bowl, melt butter and chocolate; stir until smooth. Cool slightly. In a large bowl, beat eggs and sugar. Stir in vanilla and chocolate mixture. Combine flour and salt; gradually add flour to chocolate mixture. Stir in nuts if desired.

2. Pour into two greased and floured 9-in.- square baking pans. Bake at 350° for 25-30 minutes or until a toothpick inserted near the center comes out with moist crumbs (do not overbake).

3. For topping, sprinkle each pan with 1 cup of the marshmallows. Broil until marshmallows are golden brown, about 30-60 seconds. Drizzle with melted chocolate. Cool on a wire rack. Refrigerate for several hours before cutting.

Chocolate-Covered Cherry Brownies

Prefer sweet to salty? I top these chewy brownies with mini marshmallows, maraschino cherries and a chocolate drizzle.

—SUSAN MYERS DUBLIN, OH

PREP: 20 MIN. • **BAKE:** 30 MIN. + COOLING • **MAKES:** 2 DOZEN

- 2 cups sugar
- 1 cup butter, melted
- 4 eggs
- 1 cup all-purpose flour
- 1 cup baking cocoa
- 2 teaspoons baking powder
- ½ teaspoon salt
- 2 cups miniature marshmallows
- 1 jar (10 ounces) maraschino cherries, chopped and well drained
- ½ cup semisweet chocolate chips
- 1 to 2 tablespoons heavy whipping cream

1. In a large bowl, cream sugar and butter until light and fluffy. Beat in eggs. Combine the flour, cocoa, baking powder and salt; gradually add to creamed mixture.

2. Pour into a greased 13-in. x 9-in. baking pan. Bake at 350° for 28 minutes. Sprinkle with marshmallows. Bake 1-2 minutes longer or until marshmallows are soft but not browned. Sprinkle with cherries. Cool on a wire rack.

3. In a microwave, melt chocolate chips and cream; stir until smooth. Drizzle over brownies. Let stand until chocolate is set.

Blond Toffee Brownies

Whenever a co-worker brought these brownies to company bake sales, they sold in minutes. After getting the recipe from her, I was happy to discover how quickly they could be put together. I was even more excited when my family said the thin, chewy bars were the best they'd ever tasted.

—MARY WILLIAMS LANCASTER, CA

PREP: 15 MIN. • **BAKE:** 35 MIN. • **MAKES:** 1½ DOZEN

- ½ **cup butter, softened**
- 1 **cup sugar**
- ½ **cup packed brown sugar**
- 2 **eggs**
- 1 **teaspoon vanilla extract**
- 1½ **cups all-purpose flour**
- 2 **teaspoons baking powder**
- ¼ **teaspoon salt**
- 1 **cup English toffee bits or almond brickle chips**

1. In a large bowl, cream butter and sugars. Add eggs, one at a time, beating well after each addition. Beat in vanilla.

Combine the flour, baking powder and salt; gradually add to creamed mixture. Stir in toffee bits.

2. Spread batter into a greased 13-in. x 9-in. baking pan. Bake at 350° for 35-40 minutes or until a toothpick inserted near the center comes out clean. Cool on a wire rack. Cut into bars.

Treasured Brownies

This terrific treat is included in a book of good-but-easy recipes my sister put together as a wedding present for me. They turn out perfectly every time.

—MARIANNE WOLFE WESTLOCK, AB

PREP: 20 MIN. • **BAKE:** 25 MIN. + COOLING • **MAKES:** 1½ DOZEN

- 1 **cup butter, melted and cooled**
- 3 **eggs**
- 1½ **teaspoons vanilla extract**
- 1 **cup all-purpose flour**
- 1 **cup sugar**
- 1 **cup packed brown sugar**
- ¾ **cup baking cocoa**
- 1½ **teaspoons baking powder**
- 1 **cup chopped nuts**

ICING
- ½ **cup butter, softened**
- 1¼ **cups confectioners' sugar**
- ⅔ **cup baking cocoa**
- 2 **tablespoons milk**
- 2 **tablespoons hot brewed coffee**
- 1 **teaspoon vanilla extract**

1. In a large bowl, beat the butter, eggs and vanilla. Combine the dry ingredients; gradually add to butter mixture. Stir in nuts (do not overmix).

2. Spread into a greased 13-in. x 9-in. baking pan. Bake at 350° for 25-30 minutes or until a toothpick inserted near the center comes out clean. Cool on a wire rack.

3. In a small bowl, beat the icing ingredients until smooth. Spread over cooled brownies. Cut into bars.

Meringue Coconut Brownies

Looking for an ooey-gooey brownie that's delicious and different? This luscious recipe combines a shortbread-like crust and a brown sugar meringue with chocolate, coconut and nuts. Put a few on the side for yourself— they go fast.

—**DIANE BRIDGE** CLYMER, PA

PREP: 30 MIN. • **BAKE:** 30 MIN. + COOLING • **MAKES:** 3 DOZEN

- ¾ **cup butter, softened**
- 1½ **cups packed brown sugar, divided**
- ½ **cup sugar**
- 3 **eggs, separated**
- 1 **teaspoon vanilla extract**
- 2 **cups all-purpose flour**
- 1 **teaspoon baking powder**
- ¼ **teaspoon baking soda**
- ¼ **teaspoon salt**
- 2 **cups (12 ounces) semisweet chocolate chips**
- 1 **cup flaked coconut**
- ¾ **cup chopped walnuts**

1. Preheat oven to 350°. In a large bowl, cream the butter, ½ cup brown sugar and sugar until light and fluffy. Beat in egg yolks and vanilla. Combine the flour, baking powder, baking soda and salt; gradually add to creamed mixture just until blended (batter will be thick). Spread into a greased 13x9-in. baking pan. Sprinkle with the chocolate chips, coconut and walnuts.

2. In another large bowl, beat egg whites until soft peaks form. Gradually beat in the remaining brown sugar, 1 tablespoon at a time. Beat until stiff peaks form. Spread over the top.

3. Bake 30-35 minutes or until a toothpick inserted near the center comes out clean (do not overbake). Cool on a wire rack. Cut into bars. Store in the refrigerator.

Peanut Butter Blondies

The kids I baby-sit for love these moist, chewy bars. They're loaded with peanut butter flavor, with a yummy chocolate frosting and a sprinkling of peanut butter chips.

—KARLA JOHNSON TYLER, MN

PREP: 30 MIN. • **BAKE:** 35 MIN. + COOLING • **MAKES:** 2 DOZEN

- ¾ cup creamy peanut butter
- ⅔ cup butter, softened
- 1 cup packed brown sugar
- ½ cup sugar
- 2 eggs
- 1 teaspoon vanilla extract
- 1¾ cups all-purpose flour
- 1 teaspoon baking powder
- ⅓ cup milk
- 1 cup peanut butter chips

FROSTING
- ¼ cup butter, softened
- ¼ cup baking cocoa
- 2 tablespoons milk
- 1 tablespoon light corn syrup
- 1 teaspoon vanilla extract
- 1½ cups confectioners' sugar
- ⅓ cup peanut butter chips

1. In a large bowl, cream the peanut butter, butter and sugars until light and fluffy. Beat in eggs and vanilla. Combine the flour and baking powder; add to creamed mixture alternately with milk, beating well after each addition. Stir in chips.

2. Spread into a greased 13-in. x 9-in. baking pan. Bake at 325° for 35-40 minutes or until a toothpick inserted near the center comes out clean (do not overbake). Cool on a wire rack.

3. For frosting, in a small bowl, combine the butter, cocoa, milk, corn syrup and vanilla. Gradually add confectioners' sugar; beat until smooth. Frost brownies. Sprinkle with chips. Cut into bars.

Simply Fudgy Brownies

I don't know where I got this recipe, but I've had it for more than 30 years—it's written on an old yellow piece of paper. Adding chocolate chips was my idea. When my children were in school, I found out they were selling these brownies to their friends!

—MARJORIE HOYT CENTER CONWAY, NH

PREP: 10 MIN. • **BAKE:** 30 MIN. + COOLING • **MAKES:** 16 BROWNIES

- ½ **cup canola oil**
- ¼ **cup baking cocoa**
- 1 **cup sugar**
- 2 **eggs**
- 1 **teaspoon vanilla extract**
- ¾ **cup all-purpose flour**
- ⅛ **teaspoon salt**
- ½ **cup chopped walnuts**
- ½ **cup milk chocolate chips**

1. In a small bowl, combine oil and cocoa until smooth; set aside. In a large bowl, beat sugar and eggs. Stir in vanilla and cocoa mixture. Combine flour and salt; gradually add to chocolate mixture just until moistened. Stir in walnuts.
2. Pour into a greased 8-in.-square baking pan; sprinkle with chocolate chips. Bake at 325° for 30 minutes or until a toothpick inserted near the center comes out clean (do not overbake). Cool on a wire rack.

Bakeshop TIP

Keeping Brownies

Cool brownies completely before storing. Most brownies can be stored in an airtight container at room temperature. For brownies baked in a square pan, simply slide the entire pan into a resealable plastic bag. Brownies that contain a pudding layer, cream cheese or other perishable ingredients should be stored in the refrigerator.

Banana Nut Brownies

My recipe comes from my Grandma Schlientz. Anytime there are ripe bananas around our house, it's time to make these brownies! People are always surprised to learn that there are bananas in them.

—CHRISTINE MOL GRAND RAPIDS, MI

PREP: 10 MIN. • **BAKE:** 40 MIN. + COOLING • **MAKES:** 16 SERVINGS

- ½ **cup butter, melted, cooled**
- 1 **cup sugar**
- 3 **tablespoons baking cocoa**
- 2 **eggs, lightly beaten**
- 1 **tablespoon milk**
- 1 **teaspoon vanilla extract**
- ½ **cup all-purpose flour**
- 1 **teaspoon baking powder**
- ¼ **teaspoon salt**
- 1 **cup mashed ripe bananas (2½ to 3 medium)**
- ½ **cup chopped walnuts**
   Confectioners' sugar, optional

1. In a bowl, combine butter, sugar and cocoa. Stir in eggs, milk and vanilla. Blend in flour, baking powder and salt. Stir in bananas and nuts.
2. Pour the batter into a greased 9-in.-square baking pan. Bake at 350° for 40-45 minutes or until brownies test done. Cool on a wire rack. Just before serving, dust with confectioners' sugar if desired.

Brownies in a Cone

Brownie-filled ice cream cones are a fun addition to any summer get-together. They appeal to the child in all of us.

—**MITZI SENTIFF** ANNAPOLIS, MD

PREP: 10 MIN. • **BAKE:** 25 MIN. + COOLING • **MAKES:** 17 SERVINGS

- 1 **package fudge brownie mix (13-inch x 9-inch pan size)**
- 17 **ice cream cake cones (about 3 inches tall)**
- 1 **cup (6 ounces) semisweet chocolate chips**
- 1 **tablespoon shortening**
  Colored sprinkles

1. Prepare brownie batter according to the package directions, using 3 eggs. Place ice cream cones in muffin cups; spoon about 3 tablespoons batter into each cone.
2. Bake at 350° for 25-30 minutes or until a toothpick comes out clean and the tops are dry (do not overbake). Cool completely.
3. In a microwave, melt chocolate chips and shortening; stir until smooth. Dip tops of brownies in melted chocolate; allow excess to drip off. Decorate with sprinkles.

Great Pumpkin Brownie

Our kids beg for a one of these big brownies every year. I just bake brownie batter in a pizza pan, spread with orange-tinted frosting and let the kids design a pumpkin stem and jack-o'-lantern face using candy.

—**DARLA WESTER** MERIDEN, IA

PREP: 25 MIN. • **BAKE:** 20 MIN. + COOLING • **MAKES:** 16 SERVINGS

- 1 **package fudge brownie mix (13-inch x 9-inch pan size)**
- 1 **can (16 ounces) vanilla frosting**
  Orange paste food coloring
- 9 **green milk chocolate M&M's**
- 57 **dark brown milk chocolate M&M's**

1. Preheat oven to 350°. Prepare brownie batter according to package directions for fudge-like brownies. Spread on a greased 12-in. pizza pan to within 1 in. of edges.
2. Bake 20-25 minutes or until a toothpick inserted in center comes out clean. Cool in pan on a wire rack.
3. Tint frosting orange; frost brownie. For stem, arrange green M&M's in a square pattern at top of pumpkin. For each eye, arrange 10 brown M&M's in a triangle. For nose, arrange six brown M&M's in a triangle. Arrange remaining M&M's for a mouth.

Blond Brownie Nut Squares

Pecans give these rich bars a subtle, satisfying crunch.

—**EDIE FARM** FARMINGTON, NM

START TO FINISH: 30 MIN. • **MAKES:** 16 SQUARES

- ¼ **cup butter, melted**
- 1 **cup packed brown sugar**
- 1 **egg**
- 1 **teaspoon vanilla extract**
- ¾ **cup all-purpose flour**
- 1 **teaspoon baking powder**
- ¼ **teaspoon salt**
- ½ **cup finely chopped pecans**

1. In a bowl, beat the butter, sugar, egg and vanilla. Combine the flour, baking powder and salt; gradually add to sugar mixture and mix well. Fold in nuts.
2. Spread in a greased 8-in.-square baking dish. Bake at 350° for 15-20 minutes or until a toothpick comes out clean. Cool on a wire rack. Cut into squares.

Orange Cream Cheese Brownies

I doubt you'll even want to try another brownie recipe after eating these delicious treats.

—CAROL GILLESPIE CHAMBERSBURG, PA

PREP: 20 MIN. • **BAKE:** 30 MIN. + COOLING • **MAKES:** 16 BROWNIES

- 1 package fudge brownie mix (13-inch x 9-inch pan size)
- ½ cup white baking chips

FILLING

- 1 package (3 ounces) cream cheese, softened
- 2 tablespoons butter, softened
- ¼ cup sugar
- 1 egg
- 1 tablespoon all-purpose flour
- ½ teaspoon orange extract

FROSTING

- 1 ounce unsweetened chocolate
- 1 ounce semisweet chocolate
- 2 tablespoons butter
- 1 cup confectioners' sugar
- 2 to 3 tablespoons milk

1. Prepare brownies according to package directions for cakelike brownies; fold in white chips. Spread half of the batter in a greased 13-in. x 9-in. baking pan.

2. In a small bowl, beat the cream cheese, butter and sugar until smooth. Beat in egg, flour and orange extract.

3. Carefully spread cream cheese mixture over batter. Drop remaining brownie batter by tablespoonfuls over cream cheese layer. Cut through batter with a knife to swirl.

4. Bake at 350° for 30-35 minutes or until a toothpick inserted near the center comes out almost clean. Cool on a wire rack.

5. For frosting, in a microwave-safe bowl, melt chocolate and butter; stir until smooth. Cool slightly; stir in the confectioners' sugar and enough milk to achieve spreading consistency. Frost brownies.

Chunky Peanut Butter Brownies

A friend of mine gave me the recipe for these layered brownies, but I added my own touch—chunky peanut butter. Every time I take it to a group gathering, someone requests the recipe. It's a real crowd-pleaser!

—**JUDY SIMS** WEATHERFORD, TX

PREP: 30 MIN. • **BAKE:** 20 MIN. + CHILLING • **MAKES:** 4 DOZEN

- 1½ cups butter, divided
- ¾ cup baking cocoa, divided
- 4 eggs
- 2 cups sugar
- 1 teaspoon vanilla extract
- 1½ cups all-purpose flour
- ½ teaspoon salt
- 1 jar (18 ounces) chunky peanut butter
- ⅓ cup 2% milk
- 10 large marshmallows
- 2 cups confectioners' sugar

1. In a small saucepan, melt 1 cup butter; stir in ½ cup cocoa until smooth. Remove from the heat. In a large bowl, beat the eggs, sugar and vanilla until blended. Combine flour and salt; gradually add to egg mixture. Beat in cocoa mixture.

2. Transfer to a greased 15-in. x 10-in. x 1-in. baking pan. Bake at 350° for 18-22 minutes or until toothpick inserted near the center comes out clean. Cool for 3-4 minutes on a wire rack.

3. Meanwhile, in a microwave, melt the peanut butter, uncovered, at 50% power for 2 minutes, stirring once. Stir until peanut butter is blended. Spread peanut butter over warm brownies. Refrigerate for 45 minutes or until peanut butter is set.

4. In a heavy saucepan, combine the milk, remaining cocoa, marshmallows and remaining butter. Cook and stir over medium heat until butter and marshmallows are melted and mixture is smooth. Remove from the heat. Gradually stir in confectioners' sugar until smooth. Spread over the peanut butter layer. Refrigerate for at least 30 minutes. Cut into squares.

NOTE *This recipe was tested in a 1,100-watt microwave.*

Chippy Blond Brownies

If you love chocolate and butterscotch, you won't be able to resist these chewy brownies. I often include the recipe inside a baking dish as a wedding present. Everyone enjoys these delectable treats.

—**ANNA ALLEN** OWINGS MILLS, MD

PREP: 15 MIN. • **BAKE:** 25 MIN. • **MAKES:** 2 DOZEN

- 6 tablespoons butter, softened
- 1 cup packed brown sugar
- 2 eggs
- 1 teaspoon vanilla extract
- 1¼ cups all-purpose flour
- 1 teaspoon baking powder
- ½ teaspoon salt
- 1 cup (6 ounces) semisweet chocolate chips
- ½ cup chopped pecans

1. In a large bowl, cream butter and brown sugar until light and fluffy. Add the eggs, one at a time, beating well after each addition. Beat in vanilla. Combine the flour, baking powder and salt; gradually add to creamed mixture. Stir in the chocolate chips and pecans.

2. Spread into a greased 11-in. x 7-in. baking pan. Bake at 350° for 25-30 minutes or until a toothpick inserted near the center comes out clean. Cool on a wire rack.

Chocolate Macaroon Brownies

The brownie base makes this recipe a bit different from other macaroon bars, and it also gives you a time-saving option. If you don't have time to make the brownie base in the recipe, just use a boxed mix and then top it with the filling and frosting.

—EMILY ENGEL QUILL LAKE, SK

PREP: 20 MIN. • **BAKE:** 30 MIN. • **MAKES:** ABOUT 2 DOZEN

BROWNIE BASE
- 1½ cups sugar
- ⅔ cup canola oil
- 4 eggs, lightly beaten
- 1 teaspoon vanilla extract
- 1⅓ cups all-purpose flour
- ⅔ cup baking cocoa
- 1 teaspoon baking powder
- ½ teaspoon salt

COCONUT FILLING
- 1 can (14 ounces) sweetened condensed milk
- 3 cups flaked coconut
- 1 teaspoon vanilla extract

BUTTER FROSTING
- 2 cups confectioners' sugar
- ½ cup baking cocoa
- ½ cup butter, softened
- 1 teaspoon vanilla extract
- 1 to 2 tablespoons 2% milk, divided

1. In a large bowl, combine sugar and oil until blended. Beat in eggs and vanilla. Combine dry ingredients; gradually add to mixture. Pour into a greased 13-in. x 9-in. baking pan.

2. In a small bowl, combine the filling ingredients. Spoon over brownie mixture. Bake at 350° for 30-35 minutes or until a toothpick inserted near the center comes out clean. Cool on a wire rack.

3. Meanwhile, for frosting, in a small bowl, beat the sugar, cocoa, butter, vanilla and enough milk to achieve desired spreading consistency. Spread over filling.

Apricot Angel Brownies

With white chocolate and apricots, these brownies are just right for folks who prefer fruit desserts over chocolate creations.

—TAMARA SELLMAN BARRINGTON, IL

PREP: 25 MIN. • **BAKE:** 25 MIN. + COOLING
MAKES: ABOUT 2 DOZEN

- 4 ounces white baking chocolate, chopped
- ⅓ cup butter
- ½ cup packed brown sugar
- 2 eggs, beaten
- ¼ teaspoon vanilla extract
- ¾ cup all-purpose flour
- ½ teaspoon baking powder
- ¼ teaspoon salt
- 1 cup finely chopped dried apricots
- ¼ cup sliced almonds
- ¼ cup flaked coconut

1. In a saucepan, melt chocolate and butter over low heat, stirring constantly. Remove from the heat; stir in brown sugar, eggs and vanilla until blended. Set aside. In a bowl, combine the flour, baking powder and salt. Stir in the chocolate mixture. Combine apricots, almonds and coconuts; stir half into the batter.

2. Pour into a greased 9-in.-square baking pan. Sprinkle remaining apricot mixture on top. Bake at 350° for 25 minutes or until golden brown. Cool on a wire rack. Cut into bars.

Blond Butterscotch Brownies

Toffee and chocolate dot the golden brown batter of these delightful brownies. I do a lot of cooking for the police officers I work with, and they always line up for these treats.
—**JENNIFER ANN SOPKO** BATTLE CREEK, MI

PREP: 15 MIN. • **BAKE:** 20 MIN. + COOLING • **MAKES:** 2 DOZEN

- 2 **cups all-purpose flour**
- 2 **cups packed brown sugar**
- 2 **teaspoons baking powder**
- ¼ **teaspoon salt**
- ½ **cup butter, melted and cooled**
- 2 **eggs**
- 1 **teaspoon vanilla extract**
- 1 **cup semisweet chocolate chunks**
- 4 **Heath candy bars (1.4 ounces each), coarsely chopped**

1. In a large bowl, combine the flour, brown sugar, baking powder and salt. In another bowl, beat the butter, eggs and vanilla until smooth. Stir into dry ingredients just until combined (batter will be thick).

2. Spread into a 13-in. x 9-in. baking pan coated with cooking spray. Sprinkle with chocolate chunks and chopped candy bars; press gently into batter.

3. Bake at 350° for 20-25 minutes or until a toothpick inserted near the center comes out clean. Cool on a wire rack. Cut into bars.

Marble Brownies

I like trying new recipes, and the cream cheese topping in these delights made them a fast favorite in my house.

—DIANA COPPERNOLL LINDEN, NC

PREP: 20 MIN. • **COOK:** 15 MIN. • **MAKES:** 1 DOZEN

- 5 tablespoons butter
- 2 ounces unsweetened chocolate
- ⅔ cup sugar
- 2 eggs
- 1 teaspoon vanilla extract
- ⅔ cup all-purpose flour
- ½ teaspoon baking powder

CHEESECAKE LAYER
- 1 package (8 ounces) cream cheese, softened
- ½ cup sugar
- 1 egg
- 1 teaspoon vanilla extract
- 1 cup (6 ounces) semisweet chocolate chips

1. In a large microwave-safe bowl, combine the butter and chocolate. Cover bowl and microwave on high for 30-60 seconds; stir until smooth. Beat in sugar, eggs and vanilla. Combine flour and baking powder; gradually add to chocolate mixture until blended. Spread into a greased microwave-safe 8-in.-square dish; set aside.
2. In a large microwave-safe bowl, beat cream cheese until fluffy. Beat in the sugar, egg and vanilla until smooth. Spoon over brownie batter; cut through batter with a knife to swirl. Sprinkle with chocolate chips.
3. Cook, uncovered, at 70% power for 8-10 minutes or until a toothpick comes out clean. Cook on high for 1 minute longer. Remove to a wire rack to cool completely. Store in the refrigerator.
NOTE *This recipe was tested in a 1,100-watt microwave.*

Orange Brownies

Chocolate and orange go together deliciously in these moist and fudgy brownies. Pecans add crunch, and orange peel sprinkled on the frosting lends the finishing touch.

—ROSELLA PETERS GULL LAKE, SK

PREP: 25 MIN. • **BAKE:** 30 MIN. + COOLING • **MAKES:** 16 SERVINGS

- ½ cup butter
- ¼ cup baking cocoa
- 2 eggs
- 1 cup sugar
- ¾ cup all-purpose flour
- ½ cup chopped pecans
- 2 tablespoons orange juice concentrate
- 1 tablespoon grated orange peel
- ⅛ teaspoon salt

FROSTING
- 1½ cups confectioners' sugar
- 3 tablespoons butter, softened
- 2 tablespoons orange juice concentrate
- 1 tablespoon grated orange peel, optional

1. In a small saucepan, melt butter. Stir in cocoa until smooth. In a large bowl, beat eggs until frothy. Without stirring, add sugar, flour, pecans, orange juice concentrate, peel and salt. Pour cocoa mixture over the top; mix well. Transfer to a greased 8-in.-square baking pan.
2. Bake at 350° for 28-32 minutes or until edges begin to pull away from sides of the pan. Cool completely on a wire rack.
3. For frosting, combine confectioners' sugar, butter and orange juice concentrate. Spread over the brownies. Cut into bars; garnish with orange peel if desired.

Chocolate Peanut Butter Brownies

My husband and I have two sons, and I sent these brownies to them regularly when they were in college. They told me they used to hide a few from their roommates just so they could make sure there'd be some left!

—**PATSY BURGIN** LEBANON, IN

PREP: 30 MIN. • **BAKE:** 25 MIN. + CHILLING
MAKES: ABOUT 5 DOZEN

- 2 **ounces unsweetened chocolate**
- ½ **cup butter, cubed**
- 2 **eggs**
- 1 **cup sugar**
- ½ **cup all-purpose flour**

FILLING
- 1½ **cups confectioners' sugar**
- ½ **cup creamy peanut butter**
- ¼ **cup butter, softened**
- 2 **to 3 tablespoons half-and-half cream or milk**

GLAZE
- 1 **ounce unsweetened chocolate**
- 1 **tablespoon butter**

1. In a small saucepan, melt chocolate and butter over low heat; set aside. In a bowl, beat eggs and sugar until light and pale colored. Add flour and melted chocolate; stir well. Pour into a greased 9-in.-square baking pan. Bake at 350° for 25 minutes or until the brownies test done. Cool.
2. For filling, beat confectioners' sugar, peanut butter and butter in a bowl. Stir in cream until mixture reaches desired spreading consistency. Spread over cooled brownies; cover and chill until firm.
3. For glaze, melt chocolate and butter in a saucepan, stirring until smooth. Drizzle over the filling. Chill before cutting. Store in the refrigerator.

Fudge-Filled Brownie Bars

I always have the ingredients to put together these soft, chewy bars. They have been a hit at many potlucks.

—**NOLA BURSKI** LAKEVILLE, MN

PREP: 10 MIN. • **BAKE:** 30 MIN. + COOLING • **MAKES:** 4 DOZEN

- 1½ **cups all-purpose flour**
- ¾ **cup packed brown sugar**
- ¾ **cup butter, softened**
- 1 **egg yolk**
- ¾ **teaspoon vanilla extract**

FILLING
- 1 **package fudge brownie mix (13-inch x 9-inch pan size)**
- 1 **egg**
- ⅓ **cup water**
- ⅓ **cup canola oil**

TOPPING
- 1 **package (11½ ounces) milk chocolate chips, melted**
- ¾ **cup chopped walnuts, toasted**

1. In a large bowl, combine the first five ingredients. Press onto the bottom of a greased 15-in. x 10-in. x 1-in. baking pan. Bake at 350° for 15-18 minutes or until golden brown.
2. Meanwhile, in a large bowl, combine filling ingredients. Spread over hot crust. Bake for 15 minutes or until set. Cool on a wire rack for 30 minutes.
3. Spread melted chocolate over filling; sprinkle with walnuts. Cool completely. Cut into bars.

Caramel Fudge Brownies

My brownies are so rich and yummy, you'd never guess they're actually lighter than most. The caramel is a nice surprise most folks enjoy.

—PRISCILLA RENFROW WILSON, NC

PREP: 15 MIN. • **BAKE:** 30 MIN. • **MAKES:** 9 SERVINGS

- 4 **ounces unsweetened chocolate, chopped**
- 3 **egg whites, lightly beaten**
- 1 **cup sugar**
- 2 **jars (2½ ounces each) prune baby food**
- 1 **teaspoon vanilla extract**
- ½ **cup all-purpose flour**
- ½ **teaspoon salt**
- ¼ **cup chopped walnuts**

- 6 **tablespoons fat-free caramel ice cream topping**
- 9 **tablespoons reduced fat-whipped topping**

1. In a microwave, melt chocolate; stir until smooth. Cool slightly. In a large bowl, beat eggs whites and sugar. Stir in the prunes, vanilla and chocolate mixture. Combine the flour and salt; gradually add to the chocolate mixture just until moistened.

2. Pour the batter into an 8-in.-square baking pan coated with cooking spray. Sprinkle with walnuts. Bake at 350° for 30-32 minutes or until the top springs back when lightly touched.

3. Cool on a wire rack. Cut into squares; drizzle with caramel topping and dollop with whipped topping.

Brownies from Heaven

There's always a flurry of activity around the snack bar in my kitchen, especially when I set out a plate of these brownies. Topped with fluffy chocolaty frosting, they live up to their name.

—LINDA HARDIN-ELDRIDGE LAKE ALFRED, FL

PREP: 15 MIN. • **BAKE:** 25 MIN. + COOLING • **MAKES:** 2 DOZEN

- 1 **cup butter, softened**
- 2 **cups sugar**
- 2 **eggs**
- 1 **teaspoon vanilla extract**
- 2 **cups all-purpose flour**
- ½ **cup baking cocoa**
- 1 **cup chopped walnuts**

FROSTING
- ½ **cup butter, softened**
- 3½ **cups confectioners' sugar**
- ⅓ **cup baking cocoa**
- ¼ **cup milk**
- 1 **teaspoon vanilla extract**

1. In a large bowl, cream butter and sugar until light and fluffy. Add eggs, one at a time, beating well after each addition. Beat in vanilla. Combine flour and cocoa; add to creamed mixture just until combined. Stir in walnuts.

2. Spread into an ungreased 13-in. x 9-in. baking pan. Bake at 350° for 23-28 minutes or until a toothpick inserted near the center comes out clean. Cool on a wire rack.

3. For frosting, in a small bowl, beat butter until fluffy. Beat in the confectioners' sugar, cocoa, milk and vanilla until smooth. Spread over brownies. Cut into bars.

Swiss Chocolate Brownies

I make these for big occasions. Everyone thinks that they're quite delicious.

—**GLORIA STANGE** CLARESHOLM, AB

PREP: 25 MIN. • **BAKE:** 20 MIN. + COOLING
MAKES: ABOUT 3 DOZEN

- 1 cup water
- ½ cup butter
- 1½ ounces unsweetened chocolate
- 2 cups all-purpose flour
- 2 cups sugar
- 1 teaspoon baking soda
- ½ teaspoon salt
- 2 eggs, lightly beaten
- ½ cup sour cream
- ½ teaspoon vanilla extract
- 1 cup chopped walnuts

ICING
- ½ cup butter
- 1½ ounces unsweetened chocolate
- 3 cups confectioners' sugar, divided
- 5 tablespoons milk
- 1 teaspoon vanilla extract

1. In a saucepan, bring water, butter and chocolate to a boil. Boil for 1 minute. Remove from the heat; cool. In a bowl, combine flour, sugar, baking soda and salt. Add chocolate mixture and mix. Add eggs, sour cream and vanilla; mix. Fold in walnuts.

2. Pour into a greased 15-in. x 10-in. x 1-in. baking pan. Bake at 350° for 20-25 minutes or until brownies test done. Cool for 10 minutes.

3. For icing, melt butter and chocolate. Mix in 1½ cups confectioners' sugar. Add milk, vanilla and remaining sugar; beat until smooth. Spread over warm brownies.

Fudgy Walnut Brownies

We have great cooks in our clan, so adding to our collection of family recipes is a tradition. This is one of my additons.

—**DIANE TRUVER** VALENCIA, PA

PREP: 20 MIN. • **BAKE:** 40 MIN. + COOLING • **MAKES:** 1½ DOZEN

- ¾ cup butter, cubed
- 4 ounces unsweetened chocolate, chopped
- 4 eggs
- 2 cups sugar
- 1 teaspoon vanilla extract
- 1 cup all-purpose flour

WALNUT CRUNCH TOPPING
- ¾ cup packed brown sugar
- ¼ cup butter, cubed
- 2 eggs, lightly beaten
- 2 tablespoons all-purpose flour
- 1 teaspoon vanilla extract
- 4 cups chopped walnuts

1. In a microwave, melt the butter and chocolate; stir until smooth. Cool slightly. In a large bowl, beat eggs and sugar; stir in vanilla and chocolate mixture. Stir in the flour until well blended. Pour into a greased 13-in. x 9-in. baking pan; set aside.

2. For topping, in a small saucepan, combine brown sugar and butter. Cook and stir over low heat until butter is melted. Stir in the eggs, flour and vanilla until well blended. Stir in nuts.

3. Spread evenly over brownie batter. Bake at 350° for 40-45 minutes or until a toothpick inserted near the center comes out with moist crumbs (do not overbake). Cool completely on a wire rack.

Almond Truffle Brownies

This wonderful recipe is one I had to have Mom share with me after she baked them. These fudgy almond delights are made in several steps, but the extra effort is well worth it!

—LYNN SNOW TAYLORS, SC

PREP: 15 MIN. • **BAKE:** 25 MIN. + CHILLING • **MAKES:** 1½ DOZEN

- 1 **package fudge brownie mix (13-inch x 9-inch pan size)**
- ½ **cup water**
- ½ **cup canola oil**
- 1 **egg**
- ¾ **cup chopped almonds**
- 1 **teaspoon almond extract**

FILLING
- 1 **cup (6 ounces) semisweet chocolate chips**
- 1 **package (8 ounces) cream cheese, softened**
- ¼ **cup confectioners' sugar**
- 2 **tablespoons milk**
- ½ **teaspoon almond extract**

TOPPING
- ½ **cup semisweet chocolate chips**
- ¼ **cup heavy whipping cream**
- ½ **cup sliced almonds, toasted**

1. In a large bowl, combine the first six ingredients. Pour into a greased 13-in. x 9-in. baking pan. Bake at 350° for 23-25 minutes or until a toothpick inserted near the center comes out clean (do not overbake). Cool on a wire rack.

2. In a microwave, melt chocolate chips; stir until smooth. In a large bowl, beat cream cheese and confectioners' sugar until smooth. Beat in the milk, extract and melted chips. Spread over brownies. Refrigerate for 1 hour or until firm.

3. For topping, in a small saucepan, melt chips and cream over low heat, stirring occasionally. Spread over filling. Sprinkle with almonds. Refrigerate at least 1 hour longer before cutting.

Double Chocolate Orange Brownies

We love chocolate and orange together, so my husband suggested I create a brownie featuring both. I'm always asked to bake them for family gatherings.

—ELINOR TOWNSEND NORTH GRAFTON, MA

PREP: 15 MIN. • **BAKE:** 30 MIN. + COOLING • **MAKES:** 2 DOZEN

- ¾ **cup butter, cubed**
- 4 **ounces unsweetened chocolate, chopped**
- 3 **eggs**
- 2 **cups sugar**
- 1 **teaspoon orange extract**
- 1 **cup all-purpose flour**
- 1 **cup (6 ounces) semisweet chocolate chips**
  Confectioners' sugar

1. In a microwave, melt butter and chocolate; stir until smooth. Cool slightly. In a large bowl, beat eggs and sugar. Stir in chocolate mixture. Beat in extract. Gradually add flour to chocolate mixture.

2. Pour into a greased 13-in. x 9-in. baking dish. Sprinkle with chocolate chips. Bake at 350° for 30-35 minutes or until a toothpick inserted near the center comes out clean (do not overbake).

3. Cool completely on a wire rack. Cut into squares. Just before serving, sprinkle with confectioners' sugar.

Triple-Tier Brownies

With a creamy frosting and crunchy topping, these rich three-layer brownie bars are a decadent treat. People having them for the first time always ask for the recipe.

—ANNMARIE SAVAGE SKOWHEGAN, ME

PREP: 15 MIN. • **BAKE:** 30 MIN. + CHILLING
MAKES: ABOUT 5 DOZEN

- 1 **package fudge brownie mix (13-inch x 9-inch pan size)**
- 1 **package (11½ ounces) milk chocolate chips**
- 1 **cup peanut butter**
- 3 **cups crisp rice cereal**
- 1 **can (16 ounces) cream cheese frosting**
- 1 **cup salted peanuts, chopped**

1. Prepare and bake brownie mix according to package directions, using a greased 13-in. x 9-in. baking pan. Cool on a wire rack.
2. In a large saucepan, combine chocolate chips and peanut butter. Cook over low heat for 4-5 minutes or until blended, stirring occasionally. Stir in cereal; set aside.
3. Spread frosting over brownies. Sprinkle with peanuts. Spread with peanut butter mixture. Chill for 30 minutes or until set before cutting. Store in the refrigerator.

Malted Milk Ball Brownies

You don't have to be a kid to love these delicious brownies! Malted milk balls in the batter and sprinkled on top make them special.

—**MITZI SENTIFF** ANNAPOLIS, MD

PREP: 15 MIN. • **BAKE:** 30 MIN. + COOLING • **MAKES:** 2 DOZEN

- 1 package fudge brownie mix (13-inch x 9-inch pan size)
- 1⅓ cups chopped malted milk balls, divided
- 1 cup (6 ounces) semisweet chocolate chips
- 2 tablespoons butter
- 2 tablespoons milk
- ¼ teaspoon vanilla extract

1. Prepare brownie batter according to the package directions; stir in 1 cup malted milk balls. Spread into a greased 13-in. x 9-in. baking pan.

2. Bake at 350° for 28-30 minutes or until a toothpick inserted 2 in. from an edge comes out with moist crumbs. Cool completely on a wire rack.

3. In a microwave, melt chocolate chips and butter; stir until smooth. Cool slightly. Stir in the milk and vanilla. Spread over brownies. Sprinkle with the remaining malted milk balls. Refrigerate for 10-15 minutes or until set. Cut into bars.

Irish Mint Brownies

I wanted something special to take to a church potluck, so I invented these layered treats. The brownies are topped with a mint-flavored mousse and bittersweet chocolate icing.

—**LORI RISDAL** SIOUX CITY, IA

PREP: 45 MIN. • **BAKE:** 30 MIN. + CHILLING • **MAKES:** 2½ DOZEN

- 1 cup butter, cubed
- 4 ounces bittersweet chocolate, chopped
- 4 eggs
- 2 cups sugar
- 2 teaspoons vanilla extract
- 1½ cups all-purpose flour
- 1 cup (6 ounces) dark chocolate chips or semisweet chocolate chips
- ½ cup chopped walnuts

FILLING

- 4 ounces white baking chocolate, chopped
- ¼ cup refrigerated Irish creme nondairy creamer
- 1 cup heavy whipping cream
- 15 mint Andes candies, chopped

ICING

- 12 ounces bittersweet chocolate, chopped
- 1 cup heavy whipping cream
- 2 tablespoons butter
  Mint Andes candies, halved, optional

1. In a microwave, melt butter and bittersweet chocolate; stir until smooth. Cool slightly. In a large bowl, beat eggs, sugar and vanilla. Stir in chocolate mixture. Gradually add flour until blended. Stir in chips and walnuts.

2. Spread into a greased 13-in. x 9-in. baking pan. Bake at 350° for 30-35 minutes or until a toothpick inserted near the center comes out clean (do not overbake). Cool on a wire rack.

3. In a microwave, melt white chocolate with creamer; stir until smooth. Transfer to a small bowl. Refrigerate for 30-40 minutes or until chilled.

4. In another small bowl, beat cream until soft peaks form; fold into white chocolate mixture. Beat on medium speed until stiff peaks form, about 4 minutes. Fold in chopped candies. Spread over brownies. Cover and refrigerate.

5. In a small saucepan, combine bittersweet chocolate and cream. Cook and stir over low heat until chocolate is melted and smooth; remove from the heat. Stir in butter until melted. Cool to room temperature. Carefully spread over filling. Cover and refrigerate for 1 hour or until icing is set. Cut into bars. Garnish with additional candies if desired. Store in the refrigerator.

Coffee 'n' Cream Brownies

A friend gave me the recipe for these rich, cakelike brownies topped with a creamy coffee-enhanced filling and chocolate glaze. I like to garnish each square with a chocolate-covered coffee bean.

—**MICHELLE TIEMSTRA** LACOMBE, AB

PREP: 35 MIN. • **BAKE:** 25 MIN. + STANDING • **MAKES:** 16 SERVINGS

- ½ cup butter, cubed
- 3 ounces unsweetened chocolate, chopped
- 2 eggs
- 1 cup sugar
- 1 teaspoon vanilla extract
- ⅔ cup all-purpose flour
- ¼ teaspoon baking soda

FILLING
- 1 tablespoon heavy whipping cream
- 1 teaspoon instant coffee granules
- 2 tablespoons butter, softened
- 1 cup confectioners' sugar

GLAZE
- 1 cup (6 ounces) semisweet chocolate chips
- ⅓ cup heavy whipping cream

1. In a microwave, melt butter and chocolate; stir until smooth. Cool slightly. In a small bowl, beat the eggs, sugar and vanilla; stir in chocolate mixture. Combine flour and baking soda; stir into chocolate mixture.

2. Spread into a greased 8-in.-square baking pan. Bake at 350° for 25-30 minutes or until a toothpick inserted near the center comes out clean (do not overbake). Cool on a wire rack.

3. For filling, combine cream and coffee granules in a small bowl; stir until coffee is dissolved. In another bowl, cream butter and confectioners' sugar until light and fluffy; beat in coffee mixture. Spread over brownies.

4. In a small saucepan, combine chips and cream. Cook and stir over low heat until chips are melted. Cool slightly. Carefully spread over filling. Let stand for 30 minutes or until glaze is set. Cut into squares. Store in the refrigerator.

Granola Blondies

You won't be able to pass up these treats. I often welcome guests into our home with them.

—**JANET FARLEY** SNELLVILLE, GA

PREP: 15 MIN. • **BAKE:** 25 MIN. • **MAKES:** 1 DOZEN

- 1 egg
- 1 egg white
- 1¼ cups packed brown sugar
- ¼ cup canola oil
- 1 cup all-purpose flour
- 1 teaspoon baking powder
- ½ teaspoon salt
- 2 cups reduced-fat granola with raisins
- 1 cup dried cranberries or cherries

1. In a large bowl, beat the egg, egg white, brown sugar and oil until blended. Combine the flour, baking powder and salt; gradually stir into sugar mixture just until blended. Stir in granola and cranberries (batter will be thick).

2. Spread into a 9-in.-square baking pan coated with cooking spray. Bake at 350° for 25-30 minutes or until golden brown and set. Cool on a wire rack. Cut into bars.

Cinnamon Brownies

No frosting is needed on top of these chewy, fudgelike brownies. This nice, basic bar has a burst of cinnamon in every bite.

—**CHRISTOPHER WOLF** BELVIDERE, IL

PREP: 15 MIN. • **BAKE:** 20 MIN. • **MAKES:** 2 DOZEN

- ¾ cup butter, melted
- 1⅔ cups sugar
- 2 tablespoons strong brewed coffee
- 2 eggs
- 2 teaspoons vanilla extract
- 1⅓ cups all-purpose flour
- ¾ cup baking cocoa
- 1 tablespoon ground cinnamon
- ½ teaspoon baking powder
- ¼ teaspoon salt
- 1 cup chopped walnuts
  Confectioners' sugar

1. In a large bowl, beat the butter, sugar and coffee until smooth. Beat in eggs and vanilla. Combine the flour, cocoa, cinnamon, baking powder and salt; gradually add to the sugar mixture. Stir in walnuts.

2. Spread into a greased 13-in. x 9-in. baking pan. Bake at 350° for 18-22 minutes or until a toothpick inserted near the center comes out clean (do not overbake). Cool on a wire rack. Dust with confectioners' sugar.

Delectable Bars

Apricot Date Squares

Memories of my mom's fruity date bars inspired me to create this wonderful treat. I've had great results replacing the apricot jam with orange marmalade, too.

—SHANNON KOENE BLACKSBURG, VA

PREP: 45 MIN. • **BAKE:** 20 MIN. + COOLING • **MAKES:** 3 DOZEN

- 1 cup water
- 1 cup sugar
- 1 cup chopped dates
- ½ cup 100% apricot spreadable fruit or jam
- 1¾ cups old-fashioned oats
- 1½ cups all-purpose flour
- 1 cup flaked coconut
- 1 cup packed brown sugar
- 1 teaspoon ground cinnamon
- ¼ teaspoon salt
- ¾ cup cold butter, cubed

1. In a small saucepan, combine the water, sugar and dates. Bring to a boil. Reduce heat; simmer, uncovered, for 30-35 minutes or until mixture is reduced to 1⅓ cups and is slightly thickened, stirring occasionally.

2. Remove from the heat. Stir in spreadable fruit until blended; set aside. In a food processor, combine the oats, flour, coconut, brown sugar, cinnamon and salt. Add the butter; cover and process until the mixture resembles coarse crumbs.

3. Press 3 cups crumb mixture into a 13-in. x 9-in. baking dish coated with cooking spray. Spread date mixture to within ½ in. of edges. Sprinkle with remaining crumb mixture; press down gently.

4. Bake at 350° for 20-25 minutes or until edges are lightly browned. Cool on a wire rack. Cut into squares.

Ginger Cranberry Bars

These beautiful bars were among the winners of a cranberry festival bake-off. They're tangy, crunchy and subtly sweet.

—LYNN NEWMAN GAINESVILLE, FL

PREP: 15 MIN. • **BAKE:** 40 MIN. + COOLING • **MAKES:** 2 DOZEN

- 1 cup butter, softened
- ½ cup sugar
- 2 teaspoons almond extract, divided
- 2 cups all-purpose flour
- 2 cans (16 ounces each) whole-berry cranberry sauce
- 2 tablespoons chopped crystallized ginger
- 3 egg whites
- ½ cup confectioners' sugar
- ½ cup sliced almonds

1. In a large bowl, cream butter and sugar until light and fluffy. Stir in 1½ teaspoons almond extract. Beat in flour until crumbly.

2. Press into a greased 13-in. x 9-in. baking dish. Bake at 350° for 25-28 minutes or until golden brown.

3. Meanwhile, in a small saucepan, heat the cranberry sauce and ginger. In a small bowl, beat the egg whites on medium speed until soft peaks form. Gradually beat in the confectioners' sugar, 1 tablespoon at a time, and remaining extract on high until stiff glossy peaks form. Spread the cranberry mixture over crust. Spread the meringue over cranberry layer; sprinkle with almonds.

4. Increase heat to 400°. Bake for 14-15 minutes or until lightly browned. Cool completely before cutting. Store in the refrigerator.

Lemon Crumb Bars

I'm always looking for a great new cookie or bar to try, but I often return to this tried-and-true recipe.
—**ANNA MILLER** QUAKER CITY, OH

PREP: 15 MIN. • **BAKE:** 40 MIN. + COOLING • **MAKES:** 2 DOZEN

- 1 package lemon cake mix (regular size)
- ½ cup cold butter, cubed
- 1 egg
- 2 cups crushed saltines (about 60 crackers)
- 3 egg yolks
- 1 can (14 ounces) sweetened condensed milk
- ½ cup lemon juice

1. In a large bowl, beat the cake mix, butter and egg until crumbly. Stir in cracker crumbs; set aside 2 cups for topping.
2. Press remaining mixture into a 13-in. x 9-in. baking dish coated with cooking spray. Bake at 350° for 18-20 minutes or until edges are lightly browned.
3. In a small bowl, beat the egg yolks, milk and lemon juice. Pour over crust; sprinkle with reserved topping. Bake 20-25 minutes longer or until edges are lightly browned. Cool on a wire rack. Cut into bars. Store in the refrigerator.

Apple Walnut Squares

If you need a homespun snack that can be assembled in a hurry, try these nutty bars. They are loaded with chopped apples.
—**JENNIFER DZUBINSKI** SAN ANTONIO, TX

PREP: 15 MIN. • **BAKE:** 35 MIN. • **MAKES:** 16 SERVINGS

- ½ cup butter, softened
- 1 cup sugar
- 1 egg
- 1 cup all-purpose flour
- ½ teaspoon baking powder
- ½ teaspoon baking soda
- ½ teaspoon ground cinnamon
- 1 medium tart apple, peeled and chopped
- ¾ cup chopped walnuts

1. In a large bowl, cream butter and sugar until light and fluffy. Beat in egg. Combine the flour, baking powder, baking soda and cinnamon; gradually add to the creamed mixture, just until combined. Stir in apple and walnuts.
2. Pour into a greased 8-in.-square baking dish. Bake at 350° for 35-40 minutes or until a toothpick inserted near the center comes out clean. Cool on a wire rack.

Apricot Bars

This recipe is down-home baking at its best. The bars have won blue ribbons at county fairs and cookie contests in several states! They're easy to make, and perfect for potluck suppers, bake sales, lunch boxes or just plain snacking.
—**JILL MORITZ** IRVINE, CA

PREP: 15 MIN. • **BAKE:** 30 MIN. + COOLING • **MAKES:** 3 DOZEN

- ¾ cup butter, softened
- 1 cup sugar
- 1 egg
- ½ teaspoon vanilla extract
- 2 cups all-purpose flour
- ¼ teaspoon baking powder
- 1⅓ cups flaked coconut
- ½ cup chopped walnuts
- 1 jar (10 to 12 ounces) apricot preserves

1. In a large bowl, cream butter and sugar until light and fluffy. Add egg and vanilla; mix well. Combine flour and baking powder. Gradually add to creamed mixture. Fold in coconut and walnuts.
2. Press two-thirds of dough into a greased 13-in. x 9-in. baking pan. Spread with preserves; crumble remaining dough over preserves. Bake at 350° for 30-35 minutes or until golden brown. Cool in pan on wire rack. Cut into bars.

Almond Coconut Bars

These goodies are perfect to take to a potluck supper. I think they taste like Almond Joy candy bars.

—DOLORES SKROUT SUMMERHILL, PA

PREP: 15 MIN. • **BAKE:** 20 MIN. + CHILLING • **MAKES:** 2 DOZEN

- 1½ cups graham cracker crumbs
- ½ cup butter, melted
- 1 can (14 ounces) sweetened condensed milk
- 1 package (7 ounces) flaked coconut
- 2 cups (12 ounces) semisweet chocolate chips
- ½ cup peanut butter
- 24 blanched almonds

1. In a small bowl, combine the graham cracker crumbs and butter. Press into an ungreased 13-in. x 9-in. baking pan. Combine milk and coconut; carefully spread over crust. Bake at 350° for 18-20 minutes or until lightly browned.

2. In a microwave, combine the chocolate chips and peanut butter; stir until smooth. Microwave 30-60 seconds longer or until chips are melted; stir until smooth.

3. Spread over warm bars. Garnish with almonds. Refrigerate for 1 hour before cutting.

Oaty Cereal Treats

Peanut butter, Cheerios and M&M's put a sweet spin on crispy bars. Whether I take them to picnics or bake sales, I'm always asked for the recipe. Great for on-the-go snacks, too.

—PENNY REIFENRATH WYNOT, NE

START TO FINISH: 20 MIN. • **MAKES:** 15 SERVINGS

- 3 tablespoons butter
- 1 package (10½ ounces) miniature marshmallows
- ½ cup peanut butter
- 5 cups Cheerios
- 1 cup milk chocolate M&M's

Place butter and marshmallows in a large microwave-safe bowl. Microwave, uncovered, on high for 1-2 minutes or until melted. Stir in peanut butter until blended. Add the cereal and M&M's. Spoon into a greased 13-in. x 9-in. pan; press down gently. Cool slightly before cutting.

NOTE *Reduced-fat or generic brands of peanut butter are not recommended for this recipe. This recipe was tested in a 1,100-watt microwave.*

Rhubarb Custard Bars

Once I tried these rich, gooey bars, I just had to have the recipe so I could make them for my family and friends. The shortbread-like crust and rhubarb and custard layers inspire people to find rhubarb they can use to fix a batch for themselves.

—**SHARI ROACH** SOUTH MILWAUKEE, WI

PREP: 25 MIN. + CHILLING • **BAKE:** 50 MIN. + CHILLING
MAKES: 3 DOZEN

- 2 **cups all-purpose flour**
- ¼ **cup sugar**
- 1 **cup cold butter**

FILLING

- 2 **cups sugar**
- 7 **tablespoons all-purpose flour**
- 1 **cup heavy whipping cream**
- 3 **eggs, beaten**
- 5 **cups finely chopped fresh or frozen rhubarb, thawed and drained**

TOPPING

- 2 **packages (3 ounces each) cream cheese, softened**
- ½ **cup sugar**
- ½ **teaspoon vanilla extract**
- 1 **cup heavy whipping cream, whipped**

1. In a bowl, combine flour and sugar; cut in butter until the mixture resembles coarse crumbs. Press into a greased 13-in. x 9-in. baking pan. Bake at 350° for 10 minutes.
2. Meanwhile, for filling, combine sugar and flour in a bowl. Whisk in cream and eggs. Stir in the rhubarb. Pour over crust. Bake at 350° for 40-45 minutes or until custard is set. Cool.
3. For topping, beat cream cheese, sugar and vanilla until smooth; fold in whipped cream. Spread over top. Cover and chill. Cut into bars. Store in the refrigerator.

Lemon-Glazed Pecan Slices

A tart lemon icing pairs well with rich bars that resemble pecan pie. Everyone loves them when I take them to work or potlucks.

—**JOAN HALLFORD** NORTH RICHLAND HILLS, TX

PREP: 10 MIN. • **BAKE:** 40 MIN. + COOLING • **MAKES:** 4 DOZEN

- ½ **cup cold butter, cubed**
- 1 **cup plus 2 tablespoons all-purpose flour, divided**
- 2 **eggs**
- 1½ **cups packed brown sugar**
- 1 **teaspoon vanilla extract**
- ½ **teaspoon baking powder**
- ½ **teaspoon salt**
- 1 **cup chopped pecans**
- ½ **cup flaked coconut**
- 1½ **cups confectioners' sugar**
- 2 **tablespoons lemon juice**

1. In a small bowl, cut butter into 1 cup flour until crumbly. Press into a greased 13-in. x 9-in. baking pan. Bake at 350° for 12 minutes.
2. Meanwhile, in a small bowl, beat the eggs, brown sugar and vanilla until blended. Combine the baking powder, salt and remaining flour; gradually add to egg mixture. Stir in pecans and coconut. Spread over warm crust. Bake for 25 minutes or until set. Cool on a wire rack.
3. For glaze, combine the confectioners' sugar and lemon juice; spread over bars. Let set before cutting.

Cranberry Nut Bars

My husband's aunt sent us these bars one Christmas. The fresh cranberry flavor was such a nice change from the usual cookies. I had to have the recipe, and she was gracious enough to provide it.

—**KAREN JAROCKI** MONTE VISTA, CO

PREP: 10 MIN. • **BAKE:** 20 MIN. + COOLING • **MAKES:** 3 DOZEN

- ½ **cup butter, softened**
- ¾ **cup sugar**
- ¾ **cup packed brown sugar**
- 2 **eggs**
- 1 **teaspoon vanilla extract**
- 1½ **cups all-purpose flour**
- 1 **teaspoon baking powder**
- ½ **teaspoon salt**
- 1 **cup chopped fresh or frozen cranberries**
- ½ **cup chopped walnuts**

1. In a large bowl, cream butter and sugars until light and fluffy. Add the eggs, one at a time, beating well after each addition. Beat in vanilla. Combine the flour, baking powder and salt; gradually add to creamed mixture and mix well. Stir in cranberries and walnuts.
2. Spread into a greased 13-in. x 9-in. baking pan. Bake at 350° for 20-25 minutes or until golden brown. Cool on a wire rack. Cut into bars.

Walnut Bars

Walnuts grow everywhere in California! I grew up on a "walnut acre" and love them. When I use walnuts, I always think back to my family and harvesttime. The lemon glaze adds just the right touch to this sensational treat.

—**CHANTE JONES** ALTURAS, CA

PREP: 15 MIN. • **BAKE:** 45 MIN. + COOLING • **MAKES:** 2½ DOZEN

½ cup butter, softened
¼ cup sugar
1 egg
½ teaspoon vanilla extract
1¼ cups all-purpose flour
½ teaspoon salt

FILLING
2 eggs
1½ cups packed brown sugar
2 tablespoons all-purpose flour
1 teaspoon vanilla extract
½ teaspoon salt
½ teaspoon baking powder
1½ cups chopped walnuts

LEMON GLAZE
1½ cups confectioners' sugar
2 to 3 tablespoons lemon juice

1. In a small bowl, cream butter and sugar until light and fluffy. Beat in the egg and vanilla. Combine flour and salt; gradually add to creamed mixture and mix well.
2. Press dough onto the bottom of a greased 13-in. x 9-in. baking pan. Bake at 350° for 20 minutes or until edges are lightly browned.
3. For filling, in a small bowl, combine the eggs, brown sugar, flour, vanilla, salt and baking powder. Stir in walnuts. Spread over crust.
4. Bake for 25 minutes or until filling is golden brown. Cool on a wire rack.
5. Combine confectioners' sugar and enough lemon juice to achieve desired consistency; spread over filling. Let the bars stand until set before cutting.

Chewy Pecan Bars

A friend from Texas gave me this recipe years ago. Because it's so easy to make, I've relied on it quite often.

—**JEANNE GERLACH** FRISCO, CO

PREP: 10 MIN. • **BAKE:** 30 MIN. + COOLING • **MAKES:** 3 DOZEN

¼ cup butter, melted
4 eggs
2 cups packed brown sugar
2 teaspoons vanilla extract
⅔ cup all-purpose flour
¼ teaspoon baking soda
¼ teaspoon salt
2 cups chopped pecans
Confectioners' sugar

1. Spread butter evenly in an ungreased 13-in. x 9-in. baking pan. In a large bowl, beat eggs, brown sugar and vanilla until blended. Combine flour, baking soda and salt; gradually add to the egg mixture until well blended. Stir in the pecans.
2. Spread into prepared pan. Bake at 350° for 30-35 minutes or until browned. Dust with confectioners' sugar. Cool on a wire rack. Cut into bars.

Cranberry Shortbread Bars

Here's a lovely confection that combines cranberries, coconut and white chocolate! Colorful and tasty, the bars and a glass of milk make the perfect treat after an afternoon of raking leaves.
—TASTE OF HOME TEST KITCHEN

PREP: 20 MIN. • **BAKE:** 30 MIN. + COOLING • **MAKES:** 2 DOZEN

- 1 **cup butter, softened**
- ½ **cup confectioners' sugar**
- 1 **egg**
- 1½ **cups all-purpose flour**
- ½ **cup flaked coconut**
- ⅛ **teaspoon salt**
- ½ **cup sugar**
- ½ **cup packed brown sugar**
- 3 **tablespoons cornstarch**
- 1 **package (12 ounces) fresh or frozen cranberries**
- 1 **cup unsweetened apple juice**
- 1 **cup chopped walnuts**
- 2 **ounces white baking chocolate, melted**

1. In a large bowl, cream butter and confectioners' sugar until light and fluffy. Beat in the egg. Combine the flour, coconut and salt; gradually add to creamed mixture and mix well. Set aside 1 cup for topping. Spread remaining mixture into a greased 13-in. x 9-in. baking dish. Bake at 425° for 10 minutes.

2. Meanwhile, in a small saucepan, combine the sugars and cornstarch. Stir in cranberries and apple juice. Bring to a boil. Reduce heat; cook and stir for 5 minutes or until thickened. Remove from the heat; stir in walnuts.

3. Spread over crust. Sprinkle with reserved crumb mixture. Bake for 20-25 minutes or until golden brown and bubbly. Cool on a wire rack. Drizzle with the white chocolate. Cut into bars.

Cherry Coconut Bars

I came across these bars while stationed at a Michigan Air Force base in 1964 and have been making them ever since. My children don't think an event is special unless these bars are part of it.

—MARGUERITE EMERY ORLAND, CA

PREP: 15 MIN. • **BAKE:** 30 MIN. + COOLING
MAKES: 3 DOZEN

- 1 **cup all-purpose flour**
- 3 **tablespoons confectioners' sugar**
- ½ **cup cold butter, cubed**

FILLING

- 2 **eggs**
- 1 **cup sugar**
- 1 **teaspoon vanilla extract**
- ¼ **cup all-purpose flour**
- ½ **teaspoon baking powder**
- ¼ **teaspoon salt**
- ¾ **cup chopped walnuts**
- ½ **cup quartered maraschino cherries**
- ½ **cup flaked coconut**

1. In a small bowl, combine flour and confectioners' sugar; cut in butter until crumbly. Press into a lightly greased 13-in. x 9-in. baking pan. Bake at 350° for 10-12 minutes or until lightly browned. Cool on wire rack.

2. For filling, in a small bowl, combine the eggs, sugar and vanilla. Combine flour, baking powder and salt; add to the egg mixture and mix well. Stir in walnuts, cherries and coconut. Spread over crust. Bake for 20-25 minutes or until firm. Cool on a wire rack. Cut into bars.

Springtime Strawberry Bars

Warmer weather calls for a lighter dessert like these fruity bars. The recipe makes a big batch, so it's perfect for company.

—MARNA HEITZ FARLEY, IA

PREP: 20 MIN. • **BAKE:** 25 MIN. + COOLING
MAKES: ABOUT 3 DOZEN

- 1 **cup butter, softened**
- 1½ **cups sugar**
- 2 **eggs**
- 1 **teaspoon grated lemon peel**
- 3¼ **cups all-purpose flour**
- ¾ **cup slivered almonds, chopped**
- 1 **teaspoon baking powder**
- ½ **teaspoon salt**
- 1 **jar (12 ounces) strawberry preserves**

1. In a large bowl, cream butter and sugar until light and fluffy. Add eggs, one at a time, beating well after each addition. Beat in lemon peel. Combine 3 cups flour, almonds, baking powder and salt; gradually add to creamed mixture until mixture resembles coarse crumbs (do not over mix).
2. Set aside 1 cup of dough. Press the remaining dough into a greased 15-in. x 10-in. x 1-in. baking pan. Spread preserves to within ¼ in. of edges. Combine the reserved dough with the remaining flour; sprinkle over preserves.
3. Bake at 350° for 25-30 minutes or until lightly browned. Cool on wire rack. Cut into bars.

Hungarian Strawberry Pastry Bars

This Hungarian pastry has always been a family favorite. The dough is rich and soft , and the layers of nuts and jam make a delicious filling.

—RONALD ROTH THREE RIVERS, MI

PREP: 45 MIN. + CHILLING • **BAKE:** 25 MIN. + COOLING
MAKES: 2 DOZEN

- 5 **cups all-purpose flour**
- 1 **cup plus 3 tablespoons sugar, divided**
- 4 **teaspoons baking powder**
- 2 **teaspoons baking soda**
- ⅛ **teaspoon salt**
- 1¼ **cups shortening**
- 4 **egg yolks**
- ½ **cup sour cream**

- ¼ **cup water**
- 1 **teaspoon vanilla extract**
- 2½ **cups chopped walnuts, divided**
- 1 **jar (18 ounces) seedless strawberry jam**

1. In a large bowl, combine the flour, 1 cup sugar, baking powder, baking soda and salt. Cut in shortening until mixture resembles coarse crumbs. In a bowl, whisk the egg yolks, sour cream, water and vanilla; gradually add to crumb mixture, tossing with a fork until dough forms a ball. Divide into thirds. Chill for 30 minutes.
2. Between two large sheets of waxed paper, roll out one portion of dough into a 15-in. x 10-in. rectangle. Transfer to an ungreased 15-in. x 10-in. x 1-in. baking pan. Sprinkle with 1¼ cups walnuts and 2 tablespoons sugar. Roll out another portion of dough into a 15-in. x 10-in. rectangle; place over walnuts. Spread with jam; sprinkle with remaining walnuts and sugar.
3. Roll out remaining pastry; cut into strips. Arrange in a crisscross pattern over filling. Trim and seal edges. Bake at 350° for 25-30 minutes or until golden brown. Cool on a wire rack. Cut into bars.

Rhubarb Oat Bars

My soft rhubarb bars provide just the right amount of tartness and sweetness. They are simply unbeatable!

—**RENETTE CRESSEY** FORT MILL, SC

PREP: 20 MIN. • **BAKE:** 25 MIN. + COOLING • **MAKES:** 16 BARS

- 1½ cups chopped fresh or frozen rhubarb
- 1 cup packed brown sugar, divided
- 4 tablespoons water, divided
- 1 teaspoon lemon juice
- 4 teaspoons cornstarch
- 1 cup old-fashioned oats
- ¾ cup all-purpose flour
- ½ cup flaked coconut
- ½ teaspoon salt
- ⅓ cup butter, melted

1. In a large saucepan, combine the rhubarb, ½ cup brown sugar, 3 tablespoons water and lemon juice. Bring to a boil. Reduce heat to medium; cook and stir for 4-5 minutes or until rhubarb is tender.

2. Combine the cornstarch and remaining water until smooth; gradually stir into rhubarb mixture. Bring to a boil; cook and stir for 2 minutes or until thickened. Remove from the heat; set aside.

3. In a large bowl, combine the oats, flour, coconut, salt and remaining brown sugar. Stir in butter until mixture is crumbly.

4. Press half of the mixture into a greased 8-in.-square baking dish. Spread with rhubarb mixture. Sprinkle with remaining oat mixture and press down lightly.

5. Bake at 350° for 25-30 minutes or until golden brown. Cool on a wire rack. Cut into squares.

NOTE *If using frozen rhubarb, measure rhubarb while still frozen, then thaw completely. Drain in a colander, but do not press liquid out.*

Bakeshop TIP

Cut Like a Pro

For a bakeshop appearance, remove bars without soft fillings and toppings from pan before cutting. Trim sides and then cut into rectangles, squares or diamonds. The trimmings can be crumbled and used as a topping for ice cream or pudding.

Crunchy Peanut Bars

You'll need only a handful of ingredients to fix these no-bake bars packed with peanut flavor. The recipe makes a small batch, so it's perfect when you don't want lots of leftovers.

—**NOLA BURSKI** LAKEVILLE, MN

PREP: 20 MIN. + CHILLING • **MAKES:** 8 BARS

- ¼ cup light corn syrup
- 2 tablespoons brown sugar
- 1 tablespoon sugar
- ¼ cup creamy peanut butter
- 1½ cups cornflakes
- ¼ cup Spanish peanuts
- ½ cup milk chocolate chips, melted

1. In a large saucepan over medium heat, bring corn syrup and sugars to a boil. Remove from the heat; stir in peanut butter. Fold in cornflakes and peanuts.

2. Gently press into a 9-in. x 5-in. loaf pan coated with cooking spray. Spread melted chocolate evenly over top. Cover and refrigerate for 1 hour or until firm. Cut into bars.

Raspberry Patch Crumb Bars

To give these fresh, fruity bars even more crunch, add a sprinkling of nuts to the yummy crumb topping. The pastry bottom is a sweet complement to the juicy raspberries. Everyone will want to indulge.

—**LEANNA THORNE** LAKEWOOD, CO

PREP: 30 MIN. • **BAKE:** 35 MIN. + COOLING • **MAKES:** 3 DOZEN

  3 **cups all-purpose flour**
1½ **cups sugar, divided**
  1 **teaspoon baking powder**
  ¼ **teaspoon salt**
  ¼ **teaspoon ground cinnamon**
  1 **cup shortening**
  2 **eggs, lightly beaten**
  1 **teaspoon almond extract**
  1 **tablespoon cornstarch**
  4 **cups fresh or frozen raspberries**

1. In a large bowl, combine the flour, 1 cup sugar, baking powder, salt and cinnamon. Cut in the shortening until mixture resembles coarse crumbs. Stir in eggs and extract. Press two-thirds of the mixture into a greased 13-in. x 9-in. baking dish.

2. In a large bowl, combine cornstarch and remaining sugar; add berries and gently toss. Spoon over crust. Sprinkle with remaining crumb mixture.

3. Bake at 375° for 35-45 minutes or until bubbly and golden brown. Cool on a wire rack. Cut into bars. Store in the refrigerator.

NOTE *If using frozen raspberries, do not thaw before tossing with cornstarch mixture.*

Ginger-Cream Bars

I rediscovered this old-time recipe recently and found it's everyone's favorite. Even 4-year-olds have asked for these frosted bars as nursery school treats.

—CAROL NAGELKIRK HOLLAND, MI

PREP: 20 MIN. • **BAKE:** 20 MIN. • **MAKES:** 5-6 DOZEN

- 1 cup sugar
- 1 cup butter, softened
- 2 cups all-purpose flour
- 1 teaspoon salt
- 2 teaspoons baking soda
- 1 tablespoon ground cinnamon
- 1 tablespoon ground cloves
- 1 tablespoon ground ginger
- 2 eggs
- ½ cup molasses
- 1 cup hot coffee

FROSTING

- ½ cup butter, softened
- 1 package (3 ounces) cream cheese, softened
- 2 cups confectioners' sugar
- 2 teaspoons vanilla extract
- Chopped nuts, optional

1. In a medium bowl, cream sugar and butter. Sift together flour, salt, soda and spices; add to creamed mixture. Add eggs, one at a time, beating well after each addition, and molasses. Blend in coffee. Spread in a 15-in. x 10-in. x 1-in. baking pan.

2. Bake at 350° for 20-25 minutes. Cool. For frosting, cream butter and cream cheese; add sugar and vanilla. Spread over bars. Top with nuts if desired.

White Chip Cranberry Blondies

Using applesauce instead of oil keeps the batter moist without sacrificing the taste.

—TASTE OF HOME TEST KITCHEN

PREP: 15 MIN. • **BAKE:** 15 MIN. + COOLING • **MAKES:** 20 BARS

- 2 eggs
- ¼ cup canola oil
- ¼ cup unsweetened applesauce
- 1½ teaspoons vanilla extract
- 1⅓ cups all-purpose flour
- ⅔ cup packed brown sugar
- 1 teaspoon baking powder
- ½ teaspoon salt
- 1 cup dried cranberries, divided
- ½ cup white baking chips
- ½ cup chopped pecans

1. In a large bowl, beat the eggs, oil, applesauce and vanilla. Combine the flour, brown sugar, baking powder and salt; stir into egg mixture until blended. Stir in ½ cup cranberries (batter will be thick).

2. Spread into a 13-in. x 9-in. baking pan coated with cooking spray. Top with chips, pecans and remaining cranberries; gently press toppings down.

3. Bake at 350° for 15-20 minutes or until a toothpick inserted near the center comes out clean. Cool on a wire rack. Cut into bars.

Frosted Banana Bars

I make these bars whenever I have ripe bananas on hand, then store them in the freezer to frost later and share at a potluck. With creamy frosting and big banana flavor, this treat is a real crowd-pleaser.

—**DEBBIE KNIGHT** MARION, IA

PREP: 15 MIN. • **BAKE:** 20 MIN. + COOLING • **MAKES:** 3-4 DOZEN

- ½ cup butter, softened
- 1½ cups sugar
- 2 eggs
- 1 cup (8 ounces) sour cream
- 1 teaspoon vanilla extract
- 2 cups all-purpose flour
- 1 teaspoon baking soda
- ¼ teaspoon salt
- 2 medium ripe bananas, mashed (about 1 cup)

FROSTING
- 1 package (8 ounces) cream cheese, softened
- ½ cup butter, softened
- 2 teaspoons vanilla extract
- 3¾ to 4 cups confectioners' sugar

1. In a large bowl, cream butter and sugar until light and fluffy. Add the eggs, sour cream and vanilla. Combine the flour, baking soda and salt; gradually add to the creamed mixture. Stir in bananas.

2. Spread into a greased 15-in. x 10-in. x 1-in. baking pan. Bake at 350° for 20-25 minutes or until a toothpick inserted near the center comes out clean (do not overbake). Cool.

3. For frosting, in a large bowl, beat the cream cheese, butter and vanilla until fluffy. Gradually beat in enough confectioners' sugar to achieve desired consistency. Frost bars. Store in the refrigerator.

Coconut Pecan Bars

With their rich butterscotch flavor, these tasty bars have always been welcomed with open arms by my family. Since they're simple to make, kids can have fun pitching in.

—**SUSAN HAMILTON** FULTON, MO

PREP: 10 MIN. • **BAKE:** 20 MIN. + COOLING • **MAKES:** 4 DOZEN

- 1 cup butter, softened
- 2 cups packed brown sugar
- 2 eggs
- 2 teaspoons vanilla extract
- 2 cups all-purpose flour
- 1 teaspoon salt
- 1 teaspoon baking powder
- 1½ cups flaked coconut
- 1 cup chopped pecans
   Confectioners' sugar

1. In a large bowl, cream butter and brown sugar until light and fluffy. Add eggs, one at a time, beating well after each addition. Beat in vanilla. Combine the flour, salt and baking powder; gradually add to the creamed mixture and mix well. Stir in coconut and pecans (batter will be thick).

2. Spread into a greased 15-in. x 10-in. x 1-in. baking pan. Bake at 350° for 20-25 minutes or until a toothpick inserted near the center comes out clean. Cool on a wire rack. Dust with confectioners' sugar. Cut into bars.

White Chocolate Cranberry Granola Bars

I created these chewy granola bars while searching for a healthful, portable snack for my family. I often get recipe requests when I bring them to our kids' athletic events and school bake sales.

—JANIS LOOMIS MADISON, VA

PREP: 10 MIN. • **BAKE:** 20 MIN. + COOLING • **MAKES:** 2 DOZEN

- ¼ cup sugar
- ¼ cup honey
- ¼ cup maple syrup
- 2 tablespoons reduced-fat peanut butter
- 1 egg white
- 1 tablespoon fat-free evaporated milk
- 1 teaspoon vanilla extract
- 1 cup whole wheat flour
- ½ teaspoon baking soda
- ½ teaspoon ground cinnamon
- ¼ teaspoon ground allspice
- 2 cups old-fashioned oats
- 1½ cups crisp rice cereal
- ⅓ cup white baking chips
- ¼ cup dried cranberries
- ¼ cup chopped walnuts

1. In a large bowl, combine the first seven ingredients. Combine the flour, baking soda, cinnamon and allspice; stir into sugar mixture. Stir in the oats, cereal, chips, cranberries and walnuts.
2. Press into a 13-in. x 9-in. baking pan coated with cooking spray. Bake at 350° for 18-20 minutes or until golden brown. Cool on a wire rack. Cut into bars. Store in an airtight container.

Caramel-Cashew Cake Bars

My rich bars are a hit with everyone who tries them. The cakelike crust pairs beautifully with the chewy caramel and salty cashew topping. Delicious!

—MARLENE COLLINS DETROIT LAKES, MN

PREP: 15 MIN. • **BAKE:** 20 MIN. + COOLING • **MAKES:** 16 BARS

- ¾ cup all-purpose flour
- ½ cup sugar
- ½ cup packed brown sugar
- ½ teaspoon baking powder
- ¼ teaspoon salt
- 2 eggs
- ½ cup salted cashews, chopped

CASHEW TOPPING
- ½ cup salted cashews, chopped
- ¼ cup packed brown sugar
- 2 tablespoons butter, melted
- 4½ teaspoons heavy whipping cream

1. In a large bowl, combine flour, sugars, baking powder and salt. Beat in the eggs just until combined. Fold in the cashews. Spread into a greased 8-in.-square baking dish.

2. Bake at 350° for 20-25 minutes or until top springs back when lightly touched.

3. In a small bowl, combine topping ingredients. Spread over cake. Broil for 1-2 minutes or until bubbly and lightly browned. Cut into bars while warm. Cool on a wire rack.

Fudgy Macaroon Bars

Sweet tooths make a beeline for my dessert tray whenever these rich squares show up. They're so attractive on a platter! Fudge and coconut make them delectable.

—BEVERLY ZDURNE EAST LANSING, MI

PREP: 25 MIN. • **BAKE:** 35 MIN. + COOLING • **MAKES:** 3 DOZEN

- 4 ounces unsweetened chocolate
- 1 cup butter
- 2 cups sugar
- 1 cup all-purpose flour
- ¼ teaspoon salt
- 1 teaspoon vanilla extract
- 3 eggs, lightly beaten

FILLING
- 3 cups flaked coconut
- 1 can (14 ounces) sweetened condensed milk
- 1 teaspoon vanilla extract
- ½ teaspoon almond extract

TOPPING
- 1 cup (6 ounces) semisweet chocolate chips
- ½ cup chopped walnuts

1. In a microwave, melt chocolate and butter; stir until smooth. Cool slightly. Stir in sugar, flour, salt, vanilla and eggs. Spread half of the batter into a greased 13-in. x 9-in. baking pan.

2. In a large bowl, combine the filling ingredients. Spoon over chocolate layer. Carefully spread remaining chocolate mixture over filling.

3. Bake at 350° for 35-40 minutes or until the sides pull away from the pan. Immediately sprinkle with chocolate chips. Allow chips to soften for a few minutes, then spread over bars. Sprinkle with walnuts. Cool completely before cutting.

Halloween Pumpkin Bars

My family just loves the warm pumpkin fragrance that wafts all through our kitchen on cool afternoons when I make these bars. Jack-o'-lantern faces add to the festive fall flavor.

—KARLA JOHNSON EAST HELENA, MT

PREP: 30 MIN. • **BAKE:** 20 MIN. + COOLING • **MAKES:** 35 BARS

 1½ cups pumpkin pie filling
 2 cups sugar
 1 cup canola oil
 4 eggs
 1 teaspoon vanilla extract
 2 cups all-purpose flour
 2 teaspoons baking powder
 1 teaspoon baking soda
 ½ teaspoon salt
 1 cup chopped pecans
 1 can (16 ounces) cream cheese frosting
   Yellow and red food coloring
 70 pieces candy corn
 ½ cup milk chocolate chips

1. In a large bowl, beat the pumpkin, sugar, oil, eggs and vanilla. Combine the flour, baking powder, baking soda and salt; gradually add to pumpkin mixture and mix well. Stir in the pecans.

2. Pour the batter into a greased 15-in. x 10-in. x 1-in. baking pan. Bake at 350° for 20-25 minutes or until a toothpick inserted near the center comes out clean. Cool on a wire rack.

3. Tint frosting orange with yellow and red food coloring. Frost bars; cut into 35 squares. For eyes, place two pieces of candy corn on each bar.

4. In a microwave, melt chocolate chips; stir until smooth. Transfer to a heavy-duty resealable plastic bag; cut a small hole in a corner of the bag. Pipe dots on candy corn for pupils; decorate faces as desired.

Spicy Butter Thins

I spotted this recipe in a newspaper when teaching in California more than 20 years ago. Even today, my son says these are his all-time favorite treat.

—ELSIE VINCE PEORIA, AZ

PREP: 15 MIN. • **BAKE:** 25 MIN. + COOLING
MAKES: ABOUT 3 DOZEN

 ¾ cup all-purpose flour
 ¼ cup sugar
 1 teaspoon ground cinnamon
 1 teaspoon instant coffee granules
 ½ teaspoon ground ginger
 ½ cup butter, cubed
 1 cup butterscotch chips, divided
 1 egg
 ½ cup chopped salted peanuts

1. In a large bowl, combine the first five ingredients; set aside. In a heavy saucepan over low heat, melt butter and ⅔ cup butterscotch chips. Remove from the heat. Stir in the dry ingredients and egg until well blended.

2. Spread into an ungreased 15-in. x 10-in. x 1-in. baking pan. Sprinkle with peanuts and remaining chips. Bake at 300° for 25-30 minutes or until lightly browned.

3. Immediately cut into bars and remove from pan. Cool on wire racks. Store in an airtight container.

Glazed Lebkuchen

Honey and spices give great flavor to these cakelike bars topped with a thin sugar glaze. Their festive look makes them especially popular around the holidays.

—TASTE OF HOME TEST KITCHEN

PREP: 15 MIN. • **BAKE:** 20 MIN. • **MAKES:** ABOUT 2 DOZEN

- ¾ cup honey
- ½ cup sugar
- ¼ cup packed brown sugar
- 2 eggs
- 2½ cups all-purpose flour
- 1¼ teaspoons ground cinnamon
- 1 teaspoon baking soda
- ¼ teaspoon ground cloves
- ⅛ teaspoon ground allspice
- ¾ cup chopped slivered almonds
- ½ cup finely chopped citron
- ½ cup finely chopped candied lemon peel

FROSTING
- 1 cup confectioners' sugar
- 3 tablespoons hot milk or water
- ¼ teaspoon vanilla extract
  Candied cherries and additional citron

1. In a small saucepan, bring honey to a boil. Remove from the heat; cool to room temperature. Meanwhile in a large bowl, beat honey and sugars until smooth. Add eggs, one at a time, beating well after each addition. Combine the flour, cinnamon, baking soda, cloves and allspice; gradually add to honey mixture. Stir in the nuts, citron and lemon peel (mixture will be thick).

2. Press into a greased 15-in. x 10-in. x 1-in. baking pan. Bake at 350° for 20-28 minutes or until top springs back when lightly touched.

3. Meanwhile, in a small bowl, combine the confectioners' sugar, milk and vanilla. Spread over bars while warm. Immediately cut into bars. Decorate with cherries and citron. Cool in pan on a wire rack.

Bakeshop TIP

Bar Math

8-in.-square pan =	16 (2-in.) squares or 64 (1-in.) squares
9-in.-square pan =	54 (1½-in. x 1-in.) bars or 81 (1-in.) squares
13-in. x 9-in. pan =	78 (1½-in. x 1-in.) bars

Pecan Pie Bars

I love to cook for big crowds and do most of the cooking for our church functions. People seem to enjoy these scrumptious bars even more than pecan pie.

—CLARA HONEYAGER NORTH PRAIRIE, WI

PREP: 20 MIN. • **BAKE:** 45 MIN. • **MAKES:** 6-8 DOZEN

- 6 **cups all-purpose flour**
- 1½ **cups sugar**
- 1 **teaspoon salt**
- 2 **cups cold butter, cubed**

FILLING

- 8 **eggs**
- 3 **cups sugar**
- 3 **cups corn syrup**
- ½ **cup butter, melted**
- 3 **teaspoons vanilla extract**
- 5 **cups chopped pecans**

1. In a large bowl, combine the flour, sugar and salt. Cut in butter until crumbly. Press onto the bottom and up the sides of two greased 15-in. x 10-in. x 1-in. baking pans. Bake at 350° for 18-22 minutes or until crust edges are beginning to brown and bottom is set.

2. For filling, combine the eggs, sugar, corn syrup, butter and vanilla in a large bowl. Stir in pecans. Pour over crust.

3. Bake 25-30 minutes longer or until edges are firm and center is almost set. Cool on wire racks. Cut into bars. Refrigerate until serving.

Pear Bar Cookies

When you're in the mood for something a little bit different, bake these spiced goodies featuring mellow pears and tender coconut. The small batch will disappear before you know it.

—**CORA DUNLOP** BOSTON BAR, BC

PREP: 20 MIN. • **BAKE:** 45 MIN. + COOLING • **MAKES:** 16 BARS

- 1¼ cups all-purpose flour
- ½ cup sugar
- ½ cup cold butter, cubed

FILLING

- 2 eggs
- ½ cup packed brown sugar
- ½ teaspoon vanilla extract
- ⅓ cup all-purpose flour
- ¼ teaspoon baking powder
- ¼ teaspoon salt
- ¼ teaspoon ground ginger
- 2 medium pears, peeled and diced
- ½ cup flaked coconut

1. In a small bowl, combine the flour and sugar. Cut in butter until mixture resembles coarse crumbs. Press into a greased 9-in.-square baking pan. Bake at 350° for 25-28 minutes or until golden brown.

2. In a small bowl, beat the eggs, brown sugar and vanilla. Combine the flour, baking powder, salt and ginger; stir into egg mixture just until moistened. Gently stir in the pears and coconut.

3. Spread over warm crust. Bake 20-23 minutes longer or until golden brown. Cool on a wire rack. Cut into bars.

Simple Raspberry Almond Bars

A pan of these thick bars looks pretty at any gathering. Almond extract is a nice complement to the buttery crust.

—**ANN MIDKIFF** JACKSON, MI

PREP: 15 MIN. • **BAKE:** 40 MIN. + COOLING • **MAKES:** ABOUT 3 DOZEN

- 2 cups butter, softened
- 2 cups sugar
- 2 eggs
- 1 teaspoon almond extract
- 5 cups all-purpose flour
- 1 teaspoon baking powder
- 1 jar (12 ounces) raspberry jam

1. In a large bowl, cream butter and sugar until light and fluffy. Add eggs, one at a time, beating well after each addition. Beat in extract. Combine flour and baking powder; gradually add to the creamed mixture and mix well.

2. Press into a greased 13-in. x 9-in. baking pan. With a moistened finger, make diagonal indentations every 2 in. in both directions, about ⅓ in. deep.

3. Fill indentations with jam. Bake at 350° for 40 minutes or until lightly browned. Cool on a wire rack. Cut into bars.

Caramel Cereal Treats

I've received a lot of praise for these bars. Even my husband's friends at work request them!

—**LAURIE LINGENFELTER** NEVADA, IA

PREP: 20 MIN. + STANDING • **MAKES:** 3½ DOZEN

- 8 cups Sugar Smacks cereal
- 1¾ cups dry roasted peanuts
- 1 package (14 ounces) caramels
- ½ cup sweetened condensed milk
- 1 tablespoon butter
- ½ cup milk chocolate chips

1. In a large bowl, combine cereal and peanuts; set aside. In a large microwave-safe bowl, combine caramels, milk and butter. Microwave, uncovered, on high for 1-2 minutes or until caramels are melted, stirring every 30 seconds.

2. Pour over cereal mixture; stir to coat. With greased hands, pat mixture into a greased 15-in. x 10-in. x 1-in. pan.

3. In a microwave, melt chips stir until smooth. Cool slightly. Drizzle chocolate over caramels. Let stand until set. Cut into bars.

NOTE *This recipe was tested in a 1,100-watt microwave.*

Banana Nut Bars

My sister gave me this recipe, which is always in demand with family, friends and co-workers. It's amazing how fast these tempting bars vanish when I serve them! The cream cheese frosting is heavenly.

—SUSAN HUCKABY SMITHS, AL

PREP: 15 MIN. • **BAKE:** 20 MIN. • **MAKES:** 3 DOZEN

- 1 cup butter, cubed
- ½ cup water
- 1½ cups sugar
- ½ cup packed brown sugar
- 1 cup mashed ripe bananas (about 2 medium)
- ½ cup buttermilk
- 2 eggs
- 1 teaspoon vanilla extract
- 2 cups all-purpose flour
- 1 teaspoon baking soda
- ½ cup chopped pecans or walnuts

FROSTING

- 1 package (8 ounces) cream cheese, softened
- ½ cup butter, softened
- 1 teaspoon vanilla extract
- 3½ cups confectioners' sugar

1. In a small saucepan, bring butter and water to a boil. Remove from the heat; set aside. In a large bowl, beat the sugars, bananas, buttermilk, eggs and vanilla until blended.

Combine flour and baking soda; gradually add to sugar mixture. Beat in butter mixture until blended. Stir in nuts.

2. Pour into a greased 15-in. x 10-in. x 1-in. baking pan. Bake at 350° for 18-22 minutes or until a toothpick inserted near the center comes out clean. Cool on a wire rack.

3. For frosting, in a large bowl, beat cream cheese and butter until light and fluffy. Beat in vanilla. Gradually add confectioners' sugar until smooth. Spread over bars. Store in the refrigerator.

Mock Apple Pie Squares

No one ever guesses these sweet "apple" slices are made with zucchini. In fact, there isn't a bit of apple in them. I love that it's not only yummy, but makes a big batch using budget-friendly ingredients.

—LYNN HAMILTON NAPERVILLE, IL

PREP: 30 MIN. • **BAKE:** 25 MIN. + COOLING
MAKES: ABOUT 2½ DOZEN

- 4 cups all-purpose flour
- 2 cups sugar
- ½ teaspoon salt
- 1½ cups cold butter, cubed

FILLING

- 8 cups sliced peeled zucchini
- ⅔ cup lemon juice
- 1 cup sugar
- 1 teaspoon ground cinnamon
- ¼ teaspoon ground nutmeg
- ½ cup chopped walnuts
- ½ cup golden raisins

1. In a large bowl, combine the flour, sugar and salt. Cut in butter until mixture resembles coarse crumbs. Press half of the crumb mixture into a greased 15-in. x 10-in. x 1-in. baking pan. Bake at 375° for 10-12 minutes or until lightly browned. Set remaining crumb mixture aside.

2. Meanwhile, in a large saucepan, bring zucchini and lemon juice to a boil. Reduce heat; cover and simmer for 5-6 minutes or until tender. Drain. Stir in the sugar, cinnamon, nutmeg and ½ cup reserved crumb mixture. Cook and stir for 2-3 minutes. Stir in walnuts and raisins.

3. Spread filling evenly over crust. Sprinkle with remaining crumb mixture. Bake for 25-30 minutes or until golden brown. Cool on a wire rack. Cut into squares.

Raspberry Walnut Shortbread

A sweet raspberry filling is sandwiched between a crispy crust and a crunchy brown sugar topping in these satisfying bars.

—**PAT HABIGER** SPEARVILLE, KS

PREP: 15 MIN. • **BAKE:** 20 MIN. + COOLING • **MAKES:** 16 SERVINGS

- 1¼ **cups plus 2 tablespoons all-purpose flour, divided**
- ½ **cup sugar**
- ½ **cup cold butter**
- ½ **cup raspberry jam**
- 2 **eggs**
- ½ **cup packed brown sugar**
- 1 **teaspoon vanilla extract**
- ⅛ **teaspoon baking soda**
- 1 **cup finely chopped walnuts**

1. In a bowl, combine 1¼ cups flour and sugar; cut in butter until crumbly. Press into a greased 9-in.-square baking pan. Bake at 350° for 20-25 minutes or until edges are lightly browned. Place on a wire rack. Spread jam over hot crust.

2. In a bowl, beat eggs, brown sugar and vanilla. Combine baking soda and remaining flour; stir into the egg mixture just until combined. Fold in walnuts. Spoon over jam; spread evenly. Bake for 17-20 minutes or until golden brown and set. Cool completely on a wire rack.

Grandma's Chocolate Chip Bars

My grandmother made these delicious bars with a unique meringue topping for every holiday and birthday gathering. She's now gone, but her wonderful recipe lives on.

—**SANDY HARTIG** NEW BERLIN, WI

PREP: 15 MIN. • **BAKE:** 40 MIN. + COOLING • **MAKES:** 2 DOZEN

- 1 cup shortening
- ½ cup sugar
- ½ cup packed brown sugar
- 3 egg yolks
- 1 tablespoon water
- 1 teaspoon vanilla extract
- 2 cups all-purpose flour
- 1 teaspoon baking powder
- ½ teaspoon salt
- ¼ teaspoon baking soda
- 1 cup semisweet chocolate chips

TOPPING

- 3 egg whites
- 1 teaspoon vanilla extract
- ⅛ teaspoon salt
- 1 cup packed brown sugar
- ¼ cup chopped walnuts

1. In a large bowl, cream the shortening and sugars until light and fluffy. Beat in the egg yolks, water and vanilla. Combine the flour, baking powder, salt and baking soda; gradually add to creamed mixture and mix well. Stir in chocolate chips.

2. Spread into a greased 13-in. x 9-in. baking pan. Bake at 350° for 15 minutes or until top is dry.

3. Meanwhile, in a large bowl, beat egg whites, vanilla and salt on medium speed until soft peaks form. Gradually beat in brown sugar, 1 tablespoon at a time, on high until stiff peaks form.

4. Spread over warm crust to within 1 in. of edges. Sprinkle with walnuts. Bake for 25 minutes or until a toothpick inserted near the center comes out clean. Cool on a wire rack. Cut into bars.

Fudge-Topped Shortbread

This combination of buttery shortbread and sweet chocolate is wonderful. Whenever I make it, there are nothing but crumbs left. Be sure to cut these into small squares—they're rich.

—**VALARIE WHEELER** DEWITT, MI

PREP: 15 MIN. + CHILLING • **BAKE:** 20 MIN. • **MAKES:** 4 DOZEN

- 1 cup butter, softened
- ½ cup confectioners' sugar
- ¼ teaspoon salt
- 1¼ cups all-purpose flour
- 1 can (14 ounces) sweetened condensed milk
- 2 cups (12 ounces) semisweet chocolate chips
- ½ teaspoon almond extract
- ⅓ cup sliced almonds, toasted

1. In a bowl, cream butter, sugar and salt until fluffy. Gradually beat in flour. Spread into a greased 13-in. x 9-in. baking pan. Bake at 350° for 16-20 minutes or until lightly browned.

2. In a microwave-safe bowl, combine condensed milk and chocolate chips. Microwave, uncovered, on high for 30-60 seconds or until chips are melted; stir until smooth. Stir in extract. Spread over the shortbread. Sprinkle with almonds and press down. Refrigerate until firm. Cut into squares.

NOTE *This recipe was tested in a 1,100-watt microwave.*

Crimson Crumble Bars

Baking is my favorite pastime. These refreshing cranberry bars have a sweet-tart taste and a pleasant crumble topping. They're great as a snack or anytime treat.

—PAULA ERIKSEN PALM HARBOR, FL

PREP: 20 MIN. + COOLING • **BAKE:** 25 MIN. • **MAKES:** 2 DOZEN

- 1 cup sugar
- 2 teaspoons cornstarch
- 2 cups fresh or frozen cranberries
- 1 can (8 ounces) unsweetened crushed pineapple, undrained
- 1 cup all-purpose flour
- ⅔ cup old-fashioned oats
- ⅔ cup packed brown sugar
- ¼ teaspoon salt
- ½ cup cold butter, cubed
- ½ cup chopped pecans

1. In a large saucepan, combine the sugar, cornstarch, cranberries and pineapple; bring to a boil, stirring often. Reduce heat; cover and simmer for 10-15 minutes or until the berries pop. Remove from the heat.

2. In a large bowl, combine the flour, oats, brown sugar and salt. Cut in butter until mixture resembles coarse crumbs. Stir in pecans. Set aside 1½ cups for topping.

3. Press remaining crumb mixture onto the bottom of a 13-in. x 9-in. baking pan coated with cooking spray. Bake at 350° for 8-10 minutes or until firm; cool for 10 minutes.

4. Pour fruit filling over crust. Sprinkle with reserved crumb mixture. Bake for 25-30 minutes longer or until golden brown. Cool on a wire rack.

Spice Bars

These bars smell so good while they are baking—the spicy aroma brings everyone to the kitchen in a hurry!

—BROOKE PIKE DURHAM, NC

PREP: 20 MIN. • **BAKE:** 20 MIN. + COOLING • **MAKES:** 1 DOZEN

- 6 tablespoons buttermilk
- ⅓ cup packed brown sugar
- ¼ cup molasses
- 3 tablespoons butter, melted
- 1 egg
- 1 teaspoon vanilla extract
- 1¼ cups all-purpose flour
- 1¼ teaspoons Chinese five-spice powder
- ¾ teaspoon ground cinnamon, divided
- ½ teaspoon baking powder
- ¼ teaspoon baking soda
- ¼ teaspoon salt
- ⅓ cup raisins
- 1 tablespoon confectioners' sugar

1. In a large bowl, beat the buttermilk, brown sugar, molasses, butter, egg and vanilla until smooth. Combine the flour, ½ teaspoon cinnamon, Chinese five-spice, baking powder, baking soda and salt; gradually add to buttermilk mixture and beat until blended. Stir in raisins.

2. Pour into a 9-in.-square baking pan coated with cooking spray. Bake at 350° for 18-20 minutes or until a toothpick inserted near the center comes out clean. Cool on a wire rack. Combine confectioners' sugar and remaining cinnamon; sprinkle over bars.

Glazed Peanut Butter Bars

Memories of lunchtime at school and my aunt's kitchen come to mind when I bite into these sweet, chewy bars. My husband is also a big fan of these peanut butter and chocolate treats.

—JANIS LUEDTKE WESTMINSTER, CO

PREP: 15 MIN. • **BAKE:** 20 MIN. + COOLING • **MAKES:** 4 DOZEN

¾ cup butter, softened
¾ cup creamy peanut butter
¾ cup sugar
¾ cup packed brown sugar
2 eggs
2 teaspoons water
1½ teaspoons vanilla extract
1½ cups all-purpose flour
1½ cups quick-cooking oats
¾ teaspoon baking soda
½ teaspoon salt
GLAZE
1¼ cups milk chocolate chips
½ cup butterscotch chips
½ cup creamy peanut butter

1. In a large bowl, cream butter, peanut butter and sugars until light and fluffy, about 4 minutes. Beat in the eggs, water and vanilla. Combine the flour, oats, baking soda and salt; gradually add to creamed mixture and mix well.

2. Spread into a greased 15-in. x 10-in. x 1-in. baking pan. Bake at 325° for 18-22 minutes or until lightly browned.

3. For glaze, in a microwave, melt chips and peanut butter; stir until smooth. Pour over warm bars; spread evenly. Cool completely on a wire rack before cutting.

Blueberry Squares

I've made these easy berry squares for many, many years and they never fail to bring raves from people of all ages. I'm always being asked for the recipe! When things get really busy, I like the convenience of being able to make this fuss-free treat a day ahead of time.

—**BARBARA ROBBINS** CHANDLER, AZ

PREP: 25 MIN. • **BAKE:** 10 MIN. + CHILLING • **MAKES:** 9 SERVINGS

- 1 cup crushed vanilla wafers (about 30 wafers)
- 2 tablespoons butter, melted
- ¾ cup sugar
- ¼ cup cornstarch
- ¼ cup cold water
- 3 cups fresh blueberries, divided
- 3 tablespoons lemon juice
- 1 teaspoon grated lemon peel
- 1 cup heavy whipping cream
- 2 tablespoons confectioners' sugar
- 1½ cups miniature marshmallows

1. Preheat oven to 350°. In a small bowl, combine the wafers and butter. Press into a greased 8-in.-square baking dish. Bake 8-10 minutes or until lightly browned. Cool on a wire rack.

2. In a small saucepan, combine sugar and cornstarch. Gradually whisk in water until smooth. Stir in 1½ cups blueberries. Bring to a boil; cook and stir for 1-2 minutes or until thickened. Stir in the lemon juice, peel and remaining blueberries. Cool completely.

3. In a small bowl, beat cream until it begins to thicken. Add confectioners' sugar; beat until soft peaks form. Fold in marshmallows. Spread over crust. Top with blueberry mixture. Cover and refrigerate until set, about 45 minutes.

Spiced Pumpkin Bars

These bars are moist, with bold pumpkin and spice flavors. When I want to lower the cholesterol, I use egg whites in place of the eggs.

—**RICHARD CASE** JOHNSTOWN, PA

START TO FINISH: 30 MIN. • **MAKES:** 2½ DOZEN

- 2 cups all-purpose flour
- 1½ cups sugar
- 1 tablespoon baking powder
- 2 teaspoons ground cinnamon
- 1 teaspoon baking soda
- ½ teaspoon salt
- ½ teaspoon ground ginger
- ¼ teaspoon ground nutmeg
- ¼ teaspoon ground cloves
- 4 eggs
- 1 can (15 ounces) solid-pack pumpkin
- 1 cup unsweetened applesauce
  Confectioners' sugar, optional

1. In a large bowl, combine the dry ingredients. In a small bowl, combine the eggs, pumpkin and applesauce. Stir into the dry ingredients.

2. Spread into a greased 15-in. x 10-in. x 1-in. baking pan. Bake at 350° for 20-25 minutes or until lightly browned (do not overbake). Cool on a wire rack before cutting. Dust with confectioners' sugar if desired.

Pineapple Almond Bars

My yummy bar cookies are filled with oats and almonds, which are a crunchy complement to the sweet pineapple filling.

—**JANICE SMITH** CYNTHIANA, KY

PREP: 10 MIN. • **BAKE:** 25 MIN. • **MAKES:** 1 DOZEN

- ¾ cup all-purpose flour
- ¾ cup quick-cooking oats
- ⅓ cup packed brown sugar
- 5 tablespoons reduced-fat butter
- ½ teaspoon almond extract
- 3 tablespoons sliced almonds
- 1 cup pineapple preserves

1. In a food processor, combine the flour, oats and brown sugar; cover and process until blended. Add butter and extract; cover and pulse until crumbly. Remove ½ cup crumb mixture to a bowl; stir in sliced almonds.

2. Press remaining crumb mixture into a 9-in.-square baking pan coated with cooking spray. Spread preserves over crust. Sprinkle with the reserved crumb mixture. Bake at 350° for 25-30 minutes or until golden. Cool on a wire rack.

No-Bake Sunflower Bars

My sweet peanut butter treats get plenty of cruch from a generous supply of sunflower kernels and crisp rice cereal.

—**BRENDA LEWING** MANY, LA

START TO FINISH: 30 MIN. • **MAKES:** 3 DOZEN

- 3 **cups sunflower kernels**
- 2 **cups flaked coconut**
- 1 **cup crisp rice cereal**
- 1 **cup packed brown sugar**
- 1 **cup light corn syrup**
- 1 **cup peanut butter**

1. In a large bowl, combine the sunflower kernels, coconut and rice cereal. In a saucepan, combine brown sugar and syrup. Bring to a boil; boil and stir for 2 minute.

2. Remove from the heat; stir in peanut butter until well blended. Pour over sunflower mixture; stir until coated. Press into a greased 13-in. x 9-in. pan. Cool; cut into bars.

Graham Coconut Treats

To satisfy a sweet tooth, try these deliciously different bars. A variety of flavors and textures assures that they never last long.

—**RENEE SCHWEBACH** DUMONT, MN

PREP: 20 MIN. + CHILLING • **MAKES:** 3 DOZEN

- 3 **eggs, lightly beaten**
- 1½ **cups sugar**
- 1 **cup butter, cubed**
- 4 **cups miniature marshmallows**
- 3 **cups graham cracker crumbs (about 48 squares)**
- ¾ **cup flaked coconut**
- ¾ **cup chopped pecans**
- 1½ **teaspoon vanilla extract**

1. In a double boiler, combine the eggs, sugar and butter. Cook and stir over boiling water until mixture thickness and reaches 160°. Remove from the heat; cool. Add the remaining ingredients.

2. Spoon into a greased 13-in. x 9-in. dish. Cover and refrigerate for at least 2 hours. Cut into squares.

Frosted Creams

These tasty bars have wonderful flavor from the molasses and spices. They taste like an old-fashioned treat.

—**VIVIAN CLARK** MILWAUKEE, WI

PREP: 20 MIN. • **BAKE:** 15 MIN. • **MAKES:** 3 DOZEN

- ¼ **cup shortening**
- ¼ **cup sugar**
- ½ **cup molasses**
- 1 **egg**
- 2 **cups all-purpose flour**
- 1 **teaspoon baking soda**
- 1 **to 2 teaspoons ground ginger**
- 1 **teaspoon ground cinnamon**
- ½ **teaspoon salt**
- ¾ **cup water**

GLAZE
- 1½ **cups confectioners' sugar**
- ¼ **teaspoon vanilla extract**
- 2 **tablespoons plus 1½ teaspoons 2% milk**

1. In a large bowl, cream shortening and sugar until light and fluffy. Beat in molasses and egg. Combine the flour, baking soda, ginger, cinnamon and salt; gradually add to the creamed mixture alternately with water mixing well after each addition.

2. Pour into a greased 13-in. x 9-in. baking pan. Bake at 400° for 13-15 minutes or until a toothpick inserted near the center comes out clean. Cool completely on a wire rack.

3. In a small bowl, combine confectioners' sugar, vanilla and enough milk to achieve desired consistency. Spread over cooled bars.

Chocolate Peanut Squares

I received this recipe from a friend at our local fire hall's annual quilting bee, where ladies bring in treats to serve at break time. It was a big hit with our family.

—MARIE MARTIN LITITZ, PA

PREP: 15 MIN. + CHILLING • **MAKES:** 2 DOZEN

- 1 **cup butter, divided**
- 6 **ounces semisweet chocolate, divided**
- 1½ **cups graham cracker crumbs**
- ½ **cup unsalted dry roasted peanuts, chopped**
- 2 **packages (8 ounces each) cream cheese, softened**
- 1 **cup sugar**
- 1 **teaspoon vanilla extract**

1. In a small microwave-safe bowl, melt ¾ cup butter and two ounces of chocolate; stir until smooth. Stir in cracker crumbs and peanuts.

2. Press into a greased 13-in. x 9-in. pan. Cover and refrigerate for 30 minutes or until set.

3. In a small bowl, beat the cream cheese, sugar and vanilla until fluffy. Spread over chocolate layer.

4. Melt the remaining butter and chocolate; stir until smooth. Carefully spread over cream cheese layer. Cover and refrigerate until set. Cut into squares.

Raspberry Walnut Bars

Many of my treasured recipes have come from a group of moms I used to meet with for tea and coffee when our children were small. I adapted this recipe from a friend who made it with strawberry jam. I use raspberry jam and fresh berries from my big raspberry patch.

—**MARILYN FORSELL** HYDESVILLE, CA

PREP: 10 MIN. • **BAKE:** 35 MIN. + COOLING • **MAKES:** 16 BARS

- 1 **cup butter, softened**
- 1 **cup sugar**
- 2 **egg yolks**
- 2 **cups all-purpose flour**
- 1 **cup finely chopped walnuts**
- ½ **cup seedless raspberry jam**

1. In a large bowl, cream butter and sugar until light and fluffy. Beat in egg yolks. Gradually add flour and mix well. Stir in walnuts.

2. Pat half of the mixture into a greased 8-in.-square baking pan. Spread with jam. Crumble remaining crust mixture over jam. Bake at 350° for 35-40 minutes or until lightly browned. Cool on a wire rack.

Toffee Crunch Grahams

Only four ingredients are needed for toffee bars loaded with crunchy almonds. My sister gave me the recipe years ago, and it's still a family favorite.

—**CAROL ANN HORNE** PERTH, ON

PREP: 15 MIN. • **BAKE:** 10 MIN. + COOLING • **MAKES:** 4 DOZEN

- 12 **whole graham crackers**
- 1½ **cups butter, cubed**
- 1 **cup packed brown sugar**
- 2 **cups sliced almonds**

1. Line a 15-in. x 10-in. x 1-in. baking pan with heavy-duty foil. Place graham crackers in pan. In a saucepan, combine butter and brown sugar bring to a boil, stirring constantly. Carefully pour over graham crackers. Sprinkle with almonds.

2. Bake at 400° for 6-8 minutes or until bubbly. Cool in pan for 4 minutes. Cut each cracker into four sections; transfer to wire racks to cool completely.

Frosted Raspberry Bars

While visiting a friend, I tried one of these tempting treats that her daughter made. After one bite, I knew I had to have the recipe. These cakelike bars with a fruity filling are perfect for any potluck or party.

—ESTHER HORST AUGUSTA, WI

PREP: 25 MIN. + CHILLING • **BAKE:** 30 MIN. + COOLING
MAKES: ABOUT 2 DOZEN

- 1 cup butter, softened
- ¼ cup sugar
- 3 cups all-purpose flour
- 3 teaspoons baking powder
- 1 teaspoon salt
- 2 eggs
- ½ cup milk
- 1 teaspoon vanilla extract
- 1 can (21 ounces) raspberry pie filling

FROSTING
- 1 tablespoon butter, softened
- 1 tablespoon shortening
- 1 ounce cream cheese, softened
- 2 tablespoons marshmallow creme
- ½ cup plus 1 tablespoon confectioners' sugar
- 1 tablespoon milk

1. In a large bowl, cream butter and sugar until light and fluffy. Combine the flour, baking powder and salt. Combine the eggs, milk and vanilla.

2. Add dry ingredients to the creamed mixture alternately with egg mixture, beating well after each addition. Divide dough in half; chill for 2 hours or until firm.

3. Roll out one portion of dough into a 15-in. x 10-in. rectangle; carefully transfer to a greased 15-in. x 10-in. x 1-in. baking pan. Spread with raspberry filling.

4. Roll out the remaining dough to ¼-in. thickness. Cut into ½-in.-wide strips; make a lattice crust over the filling. Bake at 350° for 30 minutes or until golden brown. Cool on a wire rack.

5. In a small bowl, beat the butter, shortening, cream cheese and marshmallow creme until smooth. Gradually add the confectioners' sugar and milk until smooth. Drizzle over bars. Chill until set. Cut into bars.

Salty Peanut Squares

If you like corn chips, you'll love the sweet and salty blend in these bars. They make great take-along treats for picnics or tailgate parties. They are so easy to whip up, the kids may just want to make their own batch!

—WANDA BORGEN MINOT, ND

PREP: 15 MIN. + COOLING • **MAKES:** 2 DOZEN

- 1 package (10 ounces) corn chips, lightly crushed, divided
- 1 cup unsalted peanuts, divided
- 1 cup light corn syrup
- 1 cup sugar
- 1 cup peanut butter
- ½ cup milk chocolate chips, melted

1. Place half of the corn chips and peanuts in a greased 13-in. x 9-in. pan; set aside. In a large saucepan, bring the corn syrup and sugar to a boil. Stir in peanut butter until blended. Drizzle half over corn chip mixture in pan.

2. Add remaining corn chips and peanuts to remaining syrup; stir until combined. Spoon over mixture in pan; press down lightly. Drizzle with melted chocolate. Cool before cutting.

Pistachio Apricot Bars

Mom tops a pistachio crust with apricot preserves and more chopped nuts to make these buttery bars.

—**WEDA MOSELLIE** PHILLIPSBURG, NJ

PREP: 15 MIN. • **BAKE:** 25 MIN. + COOLING • **MAKES:** 2½ DOZEN

- 1 cup butter, softened
- 1 cup sugar
- 1 egg
- 1 teaspoon vanilla extract
- 2½ cups all-purpose flour
- ½ cup chopped pistachios
- 1 jar (18 ounces) apricot preserves
  Additional chopped pistachios, optional

1. In a small bowl, cream butter and sugar until light and fluffy. Beat in the egg and vanilla. Gradually add flour to creamed mixture and mix well. Stir in pistachios. Press into a greased 13-in. x 9-in. baking dish. Spread with preserves.
2. Bake at 350° for 25-30 minutes or until edges begin to brown. Cool on a wire rack. Cut into bars. Garnish with additional pistachios if desired.

Fruit 'n' Nut Bars

Here's a healthy treat that grandchildren are sure to enjoy. For convenient snacking, wrap the bars individually in plastic wrap.

—**MRS. JOHN NAGEL** DEERBROOK, WI

PREP: 15 MIN. • **BAKE:** 25 MIN. + COOLING •**MAKES:** 18 BARS

- 1¼ cups chopped almonds
- 1 jar (2 ounces) sesame seeds
- 4 cups quick-cooking oats
- 1 cup dark seedless raisins
- 1 cup light corn syrup
- ⅔ cup canola oil
- ½ cup sunflower kernels
- ½ cup toasted wheat germ
- ½ cup nonfat dry milk powder
- 2 teaspoons ground cinnamon
- 1 teaspoon vanilla extract
- ½ teaspoon salt

1. In a large bowl, combine all ingredients; mix well. Press mixture firmly and evenly into a greased 15-in. x 10-in. x 1-in. baking pan.
2. Bake at 350° for 25 minutes or until golden brown. Cool in pan on wire rack at least 2 hours. Store in refrigerator.

Black-Bottom Banana Bars

These bars stay moist, and their rich banana and chocolate flavor is even better the second day. My mother-in-law gave me the recipe, and it's a big favorite with my husband and two sons.

—**RENEE WRIGHT** FERRYVILLE, WI

PREP: 20 MIN. • **BAKE:** 25 MIN. • **MAKES:** 2½ TO 3 DOZEN

- ½ cup butter, softened
- 1 cup sugar
- 1 egg
- 1 teaspoon vanilla extract
- 1½ cups mashed ripe bananas (about 3 medium)
- 1½ cups all-purpose flour
- 1 teaspoon baking powder
- 1 teaspoon baking soda
- ½ teaspoon salt
- ¼ cup baking cocoa

1. In a large bowl, cream butter and sugar until light and fluffy. Beat in egg and vanilla. Stir in the bananas. Combine the flour, baking powder, baking soda and salt; add to creamed mixture and mix well.
2. Divide batter in half. Add cocoa to half; spread into a greased 13-in. x 9-in. baking pan. Spoon remaining batter on top and swirl with a knife.
3. Bake at 350° for 25 minutes or until a toothpick inserted near center comes out clean. Cool on a wire rack.

Butterscotch Peanut Bars

With lots of peanuts and butterscotch flavor plus a rich, buttery crust, these easy-to-make bars are so good.

—MARGERY RICHMOND FORT COLLINS, CO

PREP: 15 MIN. • **BAKE:** 20 MIN. + COOLING • **MAKES:** 4 DOZEN

- ½ **cup butter, softened**
- ¾ **cup packed brown sugar**
- 1½ **cups all-purpose flour**
- ½ **teaspoon salt**
- 3 **cups salted peanuts**

TOPPING

- 1 **package (10 to 11 ounces) butterscotch chips**
- ½ **cup light corn syrup**
- 2 **tablespoons butter**
- 1 **tablespoon water**

1. Line a 15-in. x 10-in. x 1-in. baking pan with aluminum foil. Coat the foil with cooking spray; set aside.

2. In a small bowl, cream butter and brown sugar until light and fluffy. Combine flour and salt; gradually add to creamed mixture and mix well.

3. Press into prepared pan. Bake at 350° for 6 minutes. Sprinkle with peanuts.

4. In a large saucepan, combine topping ingredients. Cook and stir over medium heat until chips and butter are melted. Spread over hot crust. Bake for 12-15 minutes longer or until topping is bubbly. Cool on a wire rack. Cut into bars.

Bakeshop TIP

Perfectly Sized Bars

For uniform bars or squares, use a ruler and make cut marks with the point of a sharp knife. Lay the ruler on top of the bars between the guide marks and use the edge as a cutting guide. If you're cutting the bars in the pan, remove a corner piece first. Then the rest will be easier to remove.

Oatmeal Raisin Bars

These tender bars have a delicious raisin filling between a golden oat crust and topping. The old-fashioned treats are perfect for potlucks.

—**RITA CHRISTIANSON** GLENBURN, ND

PREP: 20 MIN. • **BAKE:** 25 MIN. • **MAKES:** ABOUT 3 DOZEN

- 1 cup sugar
- 2 tablespoons plus 1½ teaspoons cornstarch
- 1 teaspoon ground cinnamon
- 1½ cups (12 ounces) sour cream
- 3 eggs, lightly beaten
- 2 cups raisins

CRUMB MIXTURE

- 1¾ cups all-purpose flour
- 1¾ cups quick-cooking oats
- 1 cup packed brown sugar
- 1 teaspoon baking soda
- ½ teaspoon salt
- 1 cup cold butter, cubed

1. In a large saucepan, combine the sugar, cornstarch and cinnamon. Stir in sour cream until smooth. Cook and stir over medium-high heat until thickened and bubbly. Reduce heat; cook and stir 2 minutes longer. Remove from the heat. Stir a small amount of hot filling into eggs; return all to pan, stirring constantly. Bring to a gentle boil; cook and stir 2 minutes longer. Remove from the heat. Gently stir in raisins. Cool to room temperature without stirring.

2. Meanwhile, in a large bowl, combine the flour, oats, brown sugar, baking soda and salt. Cut in butter until crumbly.

3. Firmly press 3½ cups of crumb mixture into a greased 13-in. x 9-in. baking pan. Spread with raisin filling. Sprinkle with remaining crumb mixture.

4. Bake at 350° for 25-30 minutes or until golden brown. Cool on a wire rack. Cut into bars. Refrigerate leftovers.

Macadamia-Coconut Lime Bars

The shortbread-nut crust and tangyy filling make my bars a satisfying dessert or afternoon snack.

—**KATIE ROSE** PEWAUKEE, WI

PREP: 15 MIN. • **BAKE:** 40 MIN. + COOLING • **MAKES:** 6 SERVINGS

- ½ cup all-purpose flour
- 3 tablespoons confectioners' sugar
- 2 tablespoons macadamia nuts, toasted
- ¼ teaspoon grated lime peel
- 3 tablespoons cold butter, cubed

FILLING

- 1 egg
- ½ cup sugar
- 3 tablespoons flaked coconut, chopped
- 2 tablespoons lime juice
- 1 tablespoon all-purpose flour
- ¼ teaspoon grated lime peel
- ⅛ teaspoon baking powder
  Confectioners' sugar

1. In a food processor, combine flour, confectioners' sugar, nuts and lime peel; cover and process until nuts are finely chopped. Add butter; pulse just until mixture is crumbly.

2. Press into an 8-in. x 4-in. loaf pan coated with cooking spray. Bake at 350° for 20-22 minutes or until golden brown.

3. In a small bowl, whisk the egg, sugar, coconut, lime juice, flour, lime peel and baking powder until blended. Pour over hot crust. Bake 20-22 minutes longer or until light golden brown. Cool on a wire rack. Dust with confectioners' sugar. Cut into bars.

Christmas Classics

Lemon Ginger Cutouts

I bake these cutouts for Christmas, then decorate them in the colors of the season. If I run out of time before the holidays, I simply skip the frosting step and sprinkle the colored sugar directly on the cookies before they go in the oven.

—VICTORIA SAMPSON HENDERSONVILLE, NC

PREP: 1½ HOURS + CHILLING • **BAKE:** 10 MIN./BATCH + COOLING
MAKES: ABOUT 8 DOZEN

- 1 **cup butter, softened**
- ⅔ **cup packed brown sugar**
- ⅔ **cup light corn syrup**
- ⅓ **cup honey**
- 1 **teaspoon grated lemon peel**
- 4½ **cups all-purpose flour**
- 1 **teaspoon salt**
- 1 **teaspoon baking soda**
- 1 **teaspoon ground cinnamon**
- ¾ **teaspoon ground ginger**
FROSTING
- 1½ **cups confectioners' sugar**
- 1 **to 2 tablespoons water**
  Colored sugar, optional

1. In a large bowl, cream butter and brown sugar until light and fluffy. Gradually add corn syrup, honey and lemon peel. Combine the flour, salt, baking soda, cinnamon and ginger; gradually add to creamed mixture and mix well. Cover and refrigerate for 2 hours or until easy to handle.

2. Divide dough into fourths. On a lightly floured surface, roll one portion to ⅛-in. thickness. Cut into desired shapes with floured 2-in. cookie cutters. Place 2 in. apart on greased baking sheets. Bake at 350° for 8-10 minutes or until light golden brown. Remove to wire racks to cool. Repeat with remaining dough.

3. For frosting, in a small bowl, combine confectioners' sugar and enough water to achieve desired consistency. Spread over cookies. Sprinkle with colored sugar if desired.

Finnish Christmas Cookies

A friend bakes these cookies at Christmas. They're popular at cookie exchanges, but her husband urges her not to trade any of them!

—JUDITH OUTLAW PORTLAND, OR

PREP: 20 MIN. + CHILLING • **BAKE:** 10 MIN.
MAKES: ABOUT 6 DOZEN

- 2 **cups butter, softened**
- 1 **cup sugar**
- 4 **cups all-purpose flour**
- 1 **egg, lightly beaten**
- ⅔ **cup finely chopped almonds**
  Colored sugar, optional

1. In a large bowl, cream butter and sugar until light and fluffy. Gradually beat in flour and mix well. Cover and refrigerate for 1 hour.

2. Roll out onto a well-floured surface to ¼-in. thickness. Brush lightly with egg. Sprinkle with almonds and sugar if desired. Using a fluted pastry cutter or knife, cut into 2-in. x 1-in. strips. Place 1 in. apart on ungreased baking sheets.

3. Bake at 350° for 10-12 minutes or until lightly browned. Cool on wire racks.

three-fourths up the sides of iron (do not let batter run over top of iron). Immediately place in hot oil; loosen rosette with fork and remove iron.

3. Fry rosettes 1-2 minutes on each side or until golden brown. Remove to paper towel-lined wire racks. Repeat with remaining batter.

4. For icing, combine the confectioners' sugar, vanilla and enough water to achieve a dipping consistency. Dip edges of rosettes into icing; let dry on wire racks.

Gingersnaps

My friends and neighbors look for these old-time cookies on the goody trays that I give out every year. They're great for dunking in milk and they bring back the spicy flavor of Christmases past.

—ELIZABETH FLATT KELSO, WA

PREP: 20 MIN. • **BAKE:** 10 MIN. + CHILLING • **MAKES:** 2 DOZEN

- ⅓ cup shortening
- ½ cup sugar
- 1 egg
- 2 tablespoons molasses
- 1 cup all-purpose flour
- 1 teaspoon baking soda
- ½ teaspoon each ground cinnamon, cloves and ginger
- ⅛ teaspoon salt
  Additional sugar

1. In a large bowl, cream the shortening and sugar until light and fluffy. Beat in egg and molasses. Combine the flour, baking soda, cinnamon, cloves, ginger and salt; gradually add to creamed mixture and mix well. Cover and refrigerate for at least 4 hours.

2. Shape tablespoonfuls of dough into balls. Roll in additional sugar. Place 2 in. apart on lightly greased baking sheets. Flatten slightly with a glass.

3. Bake at 350° for 8-10 minutes or until edges are lightly browned and tops are set and starting to crack. Cool for 2 minutes before removing to wire racks.

NOTE *Cookie dough may be frozen. Freeze balls of dough on waxed paper-lined baking sheets until firm. Remove from the pan and place in resealable freezer bags for up to 3 months. To bake, place frozen balls of dough 2 in. apart on lightly greased baking sheets.. Bake until edges are lightly browned and tops are set and starting to crack.*

Rosettes

Dipping the edges of these traditional favorites in icing defines their lacy pattern.

—IOLA EGLE BELLA VISTA, AR

PREP: 20 MIN. • **COOK:** 30 MIN. • **MAKES:** ABOUT 5 DOZEN

- 2 eggs
- 2 teaspoons sugar
- 1 cup 2% milk
- 3 teaspoons vanilla extract
- 1 cup all-purpose flour
- ¼ teaspoon salt
  Oil for deep-fat frying

ICING

- 2 cups confectioners' sugar
- 1 teaspoon vanilla extract
- 1 to 3 tablespoons water

1. In a small bowl, beat eggs and sugar; stir in milk and vanilla. Combine flour and salt; gradually add to batter until smooth.

2. Heat 2½ in. of oil to 375° in a deep-fat fryer or electric skillet. Place rosette iron in hot oil, then dip in batter,

Frosted Ginger Creams

I have many recipes featuring ginger, but these soft cookies are real gems. The hint of lemon in the cream cheese frosting is a nice addition.

—SHIRLEY CLARK COLUMBIA, MO

PREP: 20 MIN. • **BAKE:** 10 MIN./BATCH + COOLING
MAKES: ABOUT 4 DOZEN

- ¼ **cup shortening**
- ½ **cup sugar**
- 1 **egg**
- ⅓ **cup molasses**
- 2 **cups all-purpose flour**
- 1 **teaspoon ground ginger**
- ½ **teaspoon baking soda**
- ½ **teaspoon salt**
- ½ **teaspoon ground cinnamon**
- ½ **teaspoon ground cloves**
- ⅓ **cup water**

FROSTING
- 1½ **ounces cream cheese, softened**
- 3 **tablespoons butter, softened**
- 1 **cup plus 3 tablespoons confectioners' sugar**
- ½ **teaspoon vanilla extract**
- 1 **to 2 teaspoons lemon juice**

1. In a large bowl cream shortening and sugar. Beat in egg and molasses. Combine the flour, ginger, baking soda, salt, cinnamon and cloves; gradually add to creamed mixture alternately with water (dough will be soft).

2. Drop by heaping teaspoonfuls 2 in. apart onto greased baking sheets. Bake at 400° for 7-8 minutes or until tops are cracked. Remove to wire racks to cool.

3. In a small bowl, beat the cream cheese, butter and confectioners' sugar until light and fluffy. Beat in vanilla and enough lemon juice to achieve spreading consistency. Frost cookies. Store in the refrigerator.

Gumdrop Cookies

Children really get a kick out of these cookies dotted with chewy gumdrops. I use red and green ones for Christmas, black and orange for Halloween, and pastel colors for Easter.

—**CAROLYN STROMBERG** WEVER, IA

PREP: 20 MIN. • **BAKE:** 15 MIN. + COOLING • **MAKES:** 3½ DOZEN

- ¾ cup shortening
- 1 cup sugar, divided
- ½ teaspoon almond extract
- 1¾ cups all-purpose flour
- ½ teaspoon baking soda
- ¼ teaspoon salt
- 1 cup chopped fruit-flavored or spiced gumdrops
- 2 egg whites

1. In a large bowl, cream shortening and ¾ cup sugar until light and fluffy. Beat in extract. Combine the flour, baking soda and salt; gradually add to creamed mixture and mix well. Stir in gumdrops.
2. In a small bowl, beat egg whites until soft peaks form. Gradually add remaining sugar, beating until stiff peaks form. Fold into dough.
3. Drop the dough by heaping teaspoonfuls 2 in. apart onto ungreased baking sheets. Bake at 350° for 12-15 minutes or until golden brown. Cool for 1 minute before removing from pans to wire racks to cool completely.

Slice 'n' Bake Fruitcake Cookies

A cross between classic fruitcake and butter cookies, these treats are perfect for Christmas. Each one is loaded with raisins and candied cherries.

—**MARLENE ROBINSON** SEXSMITH, AB

PREP: 20 MIN. + CHILLING • **BAKE:** 15 MIN./BATCH
MAKES: 5 DOZEN

- 1 cup butter, softened
- 1 cup confectioners' sugar
- ½ cup sugar
- 1 egg
- 2 teaspoons vanilla extract
- 2¼ cups all-purpose flour
- ½ teaspoon baking soda
- ½ cup raisins
- ½ cup each red and green candied cherries, chopped

1. In a large bowl, cream butter and sugars until light and fluffy. Beat in egg and vanilla. Combine flour and baking soda; gradually add to creamed mixture and mix well. Fold in raisins and cherries.
2. Shape dough into two 2-in.-thick logs; wrap each in plastic wrap. Refrigerate for 2 hours or until firm.
3. Cut logs into ¼-in. slices. Place 2 in. apart on ungreased baking sheets. Bake at 350° for 12-15 minutes or until lightly browned. Remove to wire racks to cool.

Peppermint Brownies

My grandmother encouraged me to enter these mint brownies at the county fair some years ago—and they earned top honors! They're a great chewy treat to serve during the holidays.

—**MARCY GREENBLATT** REDDING, CA

PREP: 15 MIN. • **BAKE:** 35 MIN. • **MAKES:** 2 DOZEN

- ¾ cup canola oil
- 2 cups sugar
- 2 teaspoons vanilla extract
- 4 eggs
- 1⅓ cups all-purpose flour
- 1 cup baking cocoa
- 1 teaspoon baking powder
- 1 teaspoon salt
- ¾ cup crushed peppermint candy, divided

GLAZE
- 1 cup (6 ounces) semisweet chocolate chips
- 1 tablespoon shortening

1. Line a 13-in. x 9-in. baking pan with foil; grease foil and set aside. In a large bowl, beat oil and sugar until blended. Beat in vanilla. Add eggs, one at a time, beating well after each addition. Combine flour, cocoa, baking powder and salt; gradually add to oil mixture. Set aside 2 tablespoons peppermint candy for garnish; stir in remaining candy. Spread into prepared pan.
2. Bake at 350° for 35-40 minutes or until a toothpick inserted in center comes out clean. Cool on a wire rack.
3. For glaze, in a microwave, melt chocolate chips and shortening; stir until smooth. Spread over brownies; sprinkle with reserved candy.

Two-Tone Christmas Cookies

I dreamed up this recipe using two of my favorite flavors, pistachio and raspberry. These cookies are tasty and really stand out on a cookie platter. They're perfect for formal or informal gatherings, and everybody likes them.

—MARIE CAPOBIANCO PORTSMOUTH, RI

PREP: 25 MIN. + CHILLING • **BAKE:** 10 MIN./BATCH + COOLING
MAKES: 6½ DOZEN

- 1 **cup butter, softened**
- 1½ **cups sugar**
- 2 **egg yolks**
- 2 **teaspoons vanilla extract**
- 1 **teaspoon almond extract**
- 3½ **cups all-purpose flour**
- 1 **teaspoon salt**
- 1 **teaspoon baking powder**
- ½ **teaspoon baking soda**
- 9 **drops green food coloring**
- 1 **tablespoon 2% milk**
- ⅓ **cup finely chopped pistachios**
- 9 **drops red food coloring**
- 3 **tablespoons seedless raspberry preserves**
- 2 **cups (12 ounces) semisweet chocolate chips, melted**
    Additional chopped pistachios, optional

1. In a large bowl, cream butter and sugar until light and fluffy. Beat in egg yolks and extracts. Combine the flour, salt, baking powder and baking soda; gradually add to creamed mixture and mix well. Divide dough in half. Stir green food coloring, milk and nuts into one portion; mix well. Add red food coloring and jam to the other half.

2. Between two pieces of waxed paper, shape each portion into an 8-in. x 6-in. rectangle. Cut in half lengthwise. Place one green rectangle on a piece of plastic wrap. Top with one pink rectangle; press together lightly. Repeat, forming a second stack. Wrap each in plastic wrap and refrigerate overnight.

3. Remove one stack from the refrigerator at a time. Unwrap dough; cut in half lengthwise. Return one portion to the refrigerator. Cut the remaining portion into ⅛-in. slices. Place 1 in. apart on ungreased baking sheets. Bake at 375° for 7-9 minutes or until set. Remove to wire racks to cool. Repeat with the remaining dough.

4. Drizzle cooled cookies with melted chocolate. Sprinkle with additional pistachios if desired.

Cream Cheese Delights

These cute cherry-topped cookies are as light as air and so easy to make. They're perfect for holiday entertaining or to serve anytime.

—AGNES GOLIAN GARFIELD HEIGHTS, OH

START TO FINISH: 25 MIN. • **MAKES:** 2 DOZEN

- ½ **cup butter-flavored shortening**
- 1 **package (3 ounces) cream cheese, softened**
- ½ **cup sugar**
- 1 **egg yolk**
- 1 **teaspoon vanilla extract**
- 1 **cup all-purpose flour**
- 1 **teaspoon salt**
    Halved maraschino cherries or candied cherries

1. In a small bowl, cream the shortening, cream cheese and sugar until light and fluffy. Beat in egg yolk and vanilla. Combine flour and salt; gradually add to the creamed mixture and mix well.

2. Drop by teaspoonfuls 2 in. apart onto greased baking sheets. Top each with a cherry half. Bake at 350° for 12-15 minutes or until lightly browned. Cool for 1 minute before removing to wire racks.

Candied Orange Date Bars

A good friend gave me the recipe for these yummy, rich date bars. Chopped candied orange slices really make them special. I dip my kitchen shears in hot water to make cutting the orange slices a little easier.

—EUNICE STOEN DECORAH, IA

PREP: 20 MIN. • **BAKE:** 30 MIN. + COOLING
MAKES: ABOUT 3 DOZEN

- 1 package (7 ounces) orange candy slices
- ½ cup sugar
- 2 tablespoons plus 1¾ cups all-purpose flour, divided
- ½ cup water
- ½ pound chopped dates
- 1 cup butter, softened
- 1 cup packed brown sugar
- 2 eggs
- 1 teaspoon baking soda
- ½ teaspoon salt
- ½ cup chopped walnuts
  Confectioners' sugar

1. Cut orange slices horizontally in half, then into ¼-in. pieces; set aside. In a saucepan, combine the sugar and 2 tablespoons flour. Stir in water until smooth. Add dates. Bring to a boil; cook and stir for 2 minutes or until thickened. Remove from the heat; cool.

2. In a large bowl, cream butter and brown sugar until light and fluffy. Add eggs, one at a time, beating well after each addition. Combine baking soda, salt and remaining flour; add to creamed mixture and mix well. Stir in walnuts.

3. Spread half of the batter into a greased 13-in. x 9-in. baking pan. Spread date mixture over batter; sprinkle with reserved orange pieces. Spread remaining batter over top.

4. Bake at 350° for 30-35 minutes or until a toothpick inserted near the center comes out clean. Cool on a wire rack. Dust with confectioners' sugar.

Holiday Snickerdoodles

It simply wouldn't be Christmas without these melt-in-your-mouth cookies! They have a lovely eggnog flavor and look great with their crunchy tops. The aroma while they bake is just as delectable as their taste.

—**DARLENE BRENDEN** SALEM, OR

PREP: 20 MIN. • **BAKE:** 15 MIN. • **MAKES:** 6½ DOZEN

- ½ cup butter, softened
- ½ cup shortening
- 1¾ cups sugar, divided
- 2 eggs
- ¼ to ½ teaspoon rum extract
- 2¾ cups all-purpose flour
- 2 teaspoons cream of tartar
- 1 teaspoon baking soda
- ¼ teaspoon salt
- 2 teaspoons ground nutmeg

1. In a large bowl, cream butter, shortening and 1½ cups sugar until light and fluffy. Beat in the eggs and extract. Combine the flour, cream of tartar, baking soda and salt; gradually add to creamed mixture and mix well.

2. In a shallow bowl, combine the nutmeg and remaining sugar. Roll dough into 1-in. balls; roll in sugar mixture. Place 2 in. apart on ungreased baking sheets.

3. Bake at 400° for 10-12 minutes or until lightly browned. Remove to wire racks to cool.

Italian Christmas Cookies

A single batch of these mouthwatering cookies is never enough. I usually make one to give away and two more to keep. Adding ricotta cheese to the batter makes the morsels extra moist.

—DORIS MARSHALL STRASBURG, PA

PREP: 25 MIN. • **BAKE:** 10 MIN./BATCH + COOLING
MAKES: 8½ DOZEN

- 1 **cup butter, softened**
- 2 **cups sugar**
- 3 **eggs**
- 1 **carton (15 ounces) ricotta cheese**
- 2 **teaspoons vanilla extract**
- 4 **cups all-purpose flour**
- 1 **teaspoon salt**
- 1 **teaspoon baking soda**

FROSTING

- ¼ **cup butter, softened**
- 3 **to 4 cups confectioners' sugar**
- ½ **teaspoon vanilla extract**
- 3 **to 4 tablespoons milk**
   Colored sprinkles

1. In a bowl, cream butter and sugar. Add the eggs, one at a time, beating well after each addition. Beat in ricotta and vanilla. Combine flour, salt and baking soda; gradually add to the creamed mixture.

2. Drop by rounded teaspoonfuls 2 in. apart onto greased baking sheets. Bake at 350° for 10-12 minutes or until lightly browned. Remove to wire racks to cool.

3. In a bowl, cream butter, sugar and vanilla. Add enough milk until frosting reaches spreading consistency. Frost cooled cookies and immediately decorate with sprinkles. Store in the refrigerator.

Peppermint Pinwheels

Put a colorful spin on your holidays with these bright swirls! This recipe makes rich-tasting cookies with a minty flavor that pleasantly surprises people.

—MARCIA HOSTETTER CANTON, NY

PREP: 15 MIN. + CHILLING • **BAKE:** 15 MIN./BATCH
MAKES: ABOUT 4 DOZEN

- ¾ **cup butter, softened**
- ¾ **cup sugar**
- 1 **egg yolk**
- 1 **teaspoon vanilla extract**
- 2 **cups all-purpose flour**
- ½ **teaspoon baking powder**
- ½ **teaspoon salt**
- ½ **teaspoon peppermint extract**
- ¼ **teaspoon red liquid food coloring**

1. In a large bowl, cream butter and sugar. Beat in egg yolk and vanilla. Combine the flour, baking powder and salt; gradually add to the creamed mixture and mix well. Divide the dough in half; add the extract and red food coloring to one portion.

2. On a work surface, roll out each portion of the dough between waxed paper into a 16-in. x 10-in. rectangle. Remove the waxed paper. Place the red rectangle over plain rectangle; roll up tightly jelly-roll style, starting with a long side. Wrap in plastic wrap. Refrigerate overnight or until firm.

3. Unwrap the dough and cut into ¼-in. slices. Place 2 in. apart on lightly greased baking sheets. Bake at 350° for 12-14 minutes or until set. Cool for 2 minutes; remove to wire racks to cool completely.

Pumpkin Pecan Tassies

These delicious mini tarts are lovely for Christmas or to serve at a tea. They're worth the extra time it takes to make them.

—PAT HABIGER SPEARVILLE, KS

PREP: 20 MIN. • **BAKE:** 35 MIN. + COOLING • **MAKES:** 2 DOZEN

- ½ cup butter, softened
- 1 package (3 ounces) cream cheese, softened
- 1 cup all-purpose flour

FILLING

- ¾ cup packed brown sugar, divided
- ¼ cup canned pumpkin
- 4 teaspoons plus 1 tablespoon butter, melted, divided
- 1 egg yolk
- 1 tablespoon half-and-half cream
- 1 teaspoon vanilla extract
- ¼ teaspoon rum extract
- ⅛ teaspoon ground cinnamon
- ⅛ teaspoon ground nutmeg
- ½ cup chopped pecans

1. In a bowl, cream butter and cream cheese. Beat in flour. Shape into 24 balls. With floured fingers, press onto the bottom and up the sides of greased miniature muffin cups.

2. Bake at 325° for 8-10 minutes or until edges are lightly browned.

3. Meanwhile, in a bowl, mix ½ cup brown sugar, pumpkin, 4 teaspoons butter, egg yolk, cream, extracts, and spices. Spoon into warm cups. Mix pecans and remaining brown sugar and butter; sprinkle over filling.

4. Bake 23-27 minutes longer or until set and edges are golden brown. Cool for 10 minutes before removing from pans to wire racks.

Chocolate Reindeer

These cute reindeer really fly off the plate when my brother's around. They're his favorite!

—LISA RUPPLE KEENESBURG, CO

PREP: 30 MIN. + CHILLING • **BAKE:** 10 MIN./BATCH
MAKES: ABOUT 3½ DOZEN

- 1 cup butter, softened
- 1 cup sugar
- ½ cup packed brown sugar
- 1 egg
- 1 teaspoon vanilla extract
- 2¼ cups all-purpose flour
- ½ cup baking cocoa
- 1 teaspoon baking soda
- 44 red-hot candies

ICING (OPTIONAL)

- 1½ cups confectioners' sugar
- 2 to 3 tablespoons milk
  - Coarse sugar
  - Brown decorating icing

1. In a large bowl, cream butter and sugars until fluffy. Beat in egg and vanilla. Combine the flour, cocoa and baking soda; add to creamed mixture and mix well. Cover and refrigerate for at least 2 hours or until easy to handle.

2. On a lightly floured surface, roll the dough to ⅛-in. thickness. Cut with a reindeer-shaped cookie cutter. Place on greased baking sheets.

3. Bake at 375° for 8-9 minutes. Immediately press a red-hot onto each nose. Cool for 2-3 minutes; remove from pans to wire racks.

4. If desired, combine confectioners' sugar and milk until smooth. Fill a heavy-duty resealable plastic bag with icing; cut a small hole in the corner of bag. Pipe around edges of cookies and add a dot for the eye. Sprinke with coarse sugar and add a dot of brown icing for pupil.

Peppermint Biscotti

Dipped in melted chocolate and rolled in crushed peppermint candy, this flavorful biscotti is a showstopper. It's one of the many sweets I make for Christmas.

—PAULA MARCHESI LENHARTSVILLE, PA

PREP: 1 HOUR • **BAKE:** 15 MIN./BATCH + COOLING
MAKES: ABOUT 3½ DOZEN

- ¾ **cup butter, softened**
- ¾ **cup sugar**
- 3 **eggs**
- 2 **teaspoons peppermint extract**
- 3¼ **cups all-purpose flour**
- 1 **teaspoon baking powder**
- ¼ **teaspoon salt**
- 1 **cup crushed peppermint candies**

FROSTING

- 2 **cups (12 ounces) semisweet chocolate chips**
- 2 **tablespoons shortening**
- ½ **cup crushed peppermint candies**

1. In a large bowl, cream butter and sugar. Add eggs, one at a time, beating well after each addition. Beat in extract. Combine the flour, baking powder and salt; stir in peppermint candy. Gradually add to creamed mixture, beating until blended (dough will be stiff).

2. Divide dough in half. On an ungreased baking sheet, shape each portion into a 12-in. x 2½-in. rectangle. Bake at 350° for 25-30 minutes or until golden brown. Carefully remove to wire racks; cool for 15 minutes. Transfer to a cutting board; cut diagonally with a sharp knife into ½-in. slices. Place cut side down on ungreased baking sheets. Bake for 12-15 minutes or until firm. Remove to wire racks to cool.

3. In a microwave-safe bowl, melt chocolate chips and shortening; stir until smooth. Drizzle over biscotti; sprinkle with candy. Place on waxed paper until set. Store in an airtight container.

Mincemeat Cookies

Shh! Don't reveal the secret ingredient in this tender, chewy, old-time cookie until after they take a taste. These will win over even those who think they don't like mincemeat.

—**LUCIE FITZGERALD** SPRING HILL, FL

PREP: 20 MIN. + CHILLING • **BAKE:** 10 MIN./BATCH
MAKES: 4 DOZEN

- ½ **cup butter, softened**
- 1 **cup sugar, divided**
- 1 **egg**
- 1 **teaspoon vanilla extract**
- 1¾ **cups all-purpose flour**
- 1½ **teaspoons baking powder**
- ¼ **teaspoon salt**
- 1 **package (9 ounces) condensed mincemeat, cut into small pieces**
- 1 **egg white, lightly beaten**

1. In a bowl, cream butter and ¾ cup sugar until light and fluffy. Beat in egg and vanilla. Combine the flour, baking powder and salt; gradually add to creamed mixture and mix well. Stir in mincemeat. Cover and refrigerate for 2 hours.
2. Roll dough into 1-in. balls; dip into egg white and remaining sugar. Place sugar side up 2 in. apart on greased baking sheets. Bake at 375° for 10-12 minutes or until set. Remove to wire racks.

Caramel Heavenlies

My mom made these treats for cookie exchanges when I was little, letting me sprinkle on the almonds and coconut. They're so easy to fix, making them perfect when you're crunched for time during the holidays.

—**DAWN BURNS** LAKE ST. LOUIS, MO

PREP: 20 MIN. • **BAKE:** 15 MIN. + COOLING
MAKES: ABOUT 6 DOZEN

- 12 **whole graham crackers**
- 2 **cups miniature marshmallows**
- ¾ **cup butter, cubed**
- ¾ **cup packed brown sugar**
- 1 **teaspoon ground cinnamon**
- 1 **teaspoon vanilla extract**
- 1 **cup sliced almonds**
- 1 **cup flaked coconut**

1. Preheat oven to 350°. Line a 15x10x1-in. baking pan with foil, letting foil extend over sides by 1 in.; lightly coat foil with cooking spray. Arrange graham crackers in prepared pan; sprinkle with marshmallows.
2. In a small saucepan, combine butter, brown sugar and cinnamon; cook and stir over medium heat until the butter is melted and sugar is dissolved. Remove from heat; stir in the vanilla.
3. Spoon butter mixture over marshmallows. Sprinkle with almonds and coconut. Bake 14-16 minutes or until browned. Cool completely in pan on a wire rack.
4. Using foil, lift cookies out of pan. Cut into triangles; discard foil.

Christmas Sugar Cookies

Sour cream keeps my favorite sugar cookies extra tender. I dress them up with a drizzle of tinted white chocolate or dip them in white chocolate, then sprinkle with crushed candy canes.
—**LISA MACLEAN** WINSLOW, AZ

PREP: 20 MIN. + CHILLING • **BAKE:** 10 MIN./BATCH
MAKES: ABOUT 8 DOZEN

- 1 **cup butter, softened**
- 2 **cups confectioners' sugar**
- 1 **egg**
- ¼ **cup sour cream**
- ¼ **cup honey**
- 2 **teaspoons vanilla extract**
- 3½ **cups all-purpose flour**
- 1 **teaspoon baking soda**
- 1 **teaspoon cream of tartar**
- ½ **teaspoon ground mace**
- ⅛ **teaspoon salt**
  White candy coating
  Green paste food coloring

1. In a large bowl, cream butter and sugar until light and fluffy. Beat in egg. Beat in the sour cream, honey and vanilla. Combine the dry ingredients; gradually add to creamed mixture and mix well. Cover and chill for 2 hours or until easy to handle.
2. On a lightly floured surface, roll out dough to ⅛-in. thickness. Cut with a floured 3-in. cookie cutters. Place 1 in. apart on ungreased baking sheets.
3. Bake at 325° for 8-10 minutes or until lightly browned. Remove to wire racks to cool.
4. In a microwave-safe bowl, melt white coating; stir until smooth. Stir in food coloring; drizzle over cookies.

Eggnog Logs

A lady at church gave me this old-fashioned recipe. I always include these logs with holiday food gifts for family and friends.
—**KIM JORDAN** DUNSMUIR, CA

PREP: 30 MIN. + CHILLING • **BAKE:** 15 MIN./BATCH + COOLING
MAKES: 4½ DOZEN

- 1 **cup butter, softened**
- ¾ **cup sugar**
- 1¼ **teaspoons ground nutmeg**
- 1 **egg**
- 2 **teaspoons vanilla extract**
- ½ **to 1 teaspoon rum extract**
- 3 **cups all-purpose flour**

FROSTING
- ¼ **cup butter, softened**
- 3 **cups confectioners' sugar**
- 1 **teaspoon vanilla extract**
- ½ **to 1 teaspoon rum extract**
- 2 **tablespoons half-and-half cream**
  Ground nutmeg

1. In a bowl, cream butter and sugar. Add the nutmeg, egg and extracts; mix thoroughly. Stir in flour. If necessary, chill dough for easier handling.
2. On a lightly floured surface, shape dough into ½-in.-diameter rolls; cut each into 3-in.-long pieces. Place 2 in. apart on ungreased baking sheets. Bake at 350° for 15 minutes or until lightly browned. Cool on wire racks.
3. For frosting, beat butter until light and fluffy. Add 2 cups confectioners' sugar and extracts; mix well. Beat in cream and remaining confectioners' sugar. Frost cookies. With tines of a small fork, make lines down the frosting to simulate bark. Sprinkle with nutmeg.

Poinsettia Cookies

To make these, I adapted a traditional cherry blossom cookie recipe by leaving out the lemon zest and adding almond extract, plus food coloring and sprinkles to create a more festive look.
—**GLORIA WARD** MESA, AZ

PREP: 20 MIN. + CHILLING • **BAKE:** 10 MIN./BATCH
MAKES: ABOUT 3 DOZEN

- ½ **cup butter, softened**
- ½ **cup sugar**
- 1 **egg**
- 1 **tablespoon milk**
- ½ **teaspoon almond extract**
- ½ **teaspoon cherry or vanilla extract**
- 5 **to 10 drops red food coloring, optional**
- 1¾ **cups all-purpose flour**
- 1 **teaspoon baking powder**
- ¼ **teaspoon salt**
- ½ **cup candied cherry halves**
  Pink or red sprinkles, optional

1. In a large bowl, cream butter and sugar until light and fluffy. Beat in the egg, milk, extracts and food coloring if desired. Combine the flour, baking powder and salt; gradually add to creamed mixture and mix well. Cover and refrigerate for 30 minutes or until easy to handle.

2. Roll dough into 1¼-in. balls. Place 2 in. apart on parchment paper-lined baking sheets. With floured kitchen scissors, snip the top of each ball in half, cutting three-fourths of the way through. Cut each half into thirds; carefully spread the wedges apart, forming flower petals.

3. Place a cherry half in the center of each; top with sprinkles if desired. Bake at 350° for 10-12 minutes or until set. Cool for 1-2 minutes before removing from pans to wire racks.

Cranberry Swirl Biscotti

A friend known for her excellent cookies shared this recipe with me, and I'm thankful she did. The mix of cranberries and cherry preserves is so refreshing.

—**LISA KILCUP** GIG HARBOR, WA

PREP: 20 MIN. • **BAKE:** 40 MIN. + COOLING
MAKES: ABOUT 2½ DOZEN

- ⅔ cup dried cranberries
- ½ cup cherry preserves
- ½ teaspoon ground cinnamon
- ½ cup butter, softened
- ⅔ cup sugar
- 2 eggs
- 1 teaspoon vanilla extract
- 2¼ cups all-purpose flour
- ¾ teaspoon baking powder
- ¼ teaspoon salt

GLAZE
- ¾ cup confectioners' sugar
- 1 tablespoon 2% milk
- 2 teaspoons butter, melted
- 1 teaspoon almond extract

1. Preheat oven to 325°. Place cranberries, preserves and cinnamon in a food processor; process until smooth.
2. In a large bowl, cream butter and sugar until light and fluffy. Beat in eggs and vanilla. In another bowl, whisk flour, baking powder and salt; gradually beat into the creamed mixture.
3. Divide dough in half. On a lightly floured surface, roll each portion of dough into a 12x8-in. rectangle. Spread each with half of the cranberry mixture; roll up jelly-roll style, starting with a short side.
4. Place rolls 4 in. apart on a lightly greased baking sheet, seam side down. Bake 25-30 minutes or until biscotti are lightly browned.
5. Carefully transfer the rolls to a cutting board; cool 5 minutes. Using a serrated knife, cut crosswise into ½-in. slices. Place slices upright on lightly greased baking sheets.
6. Bake 15-20 minutes longer or until centers are firm and dry. Remove from pans to wire racks.
7. In a small bowl, mix glaze ingredients. Drizzle glaze over warm cookies; cool completely. Store cookies in an airtight container.

Nutmeg Sugar Crisps

My grandma gave me her recipe for these classic sugar cookies with the unexpected taste of nutmeg. They are light, crunchy and so delicious. These treats are always a part of our family's Christmas celebration.

—**KRISTI THORPE** PORTLAND, OR

START TO FINISH: 25 MIN. • **MAKES:** ABOUT 6 DOZEN

- 1 cup butter, softened
- ¾ cup sugar
- ½ cup confectioners' sugar
- 1 egg
- 1 teaspoon vanilla extract
- 2½ cups all-purpose flour
- ½ teaspoon baking soda
- ½ teaspoon cream of tartar
- ¼ to ½ teaspoon ground nutmeg
- ⅛ teaspoon salt

1. In a bowl, cream butter and sugars. Beat in egg and vanilla; mix well. Combine the flour, baking soda, cream of tartar, nutmeg and salt; add to the creamed mixture and mix well. Refrigerate for 1 hour.
2. Shape into ¾-in. balls; place 2 in. apart on greased baking sheets. Flatten with a glass dipped in sugar. Bake at 350° for 10-12 minutes or until lightly browned. Cool on wire racks.

Frosted Gingerbread Nut Cookies

I received the recipe for these soft ginger cookies from a dear friend, who has since passed away. A comforting classic like this always satisfies my sweet tooth.

—KARYN ROGERS HEMET, CA

PREP: 15 MIN. • **BAKE:** 10 MIN. + COOLING • **MAKES:** 5 DOZEN

- ½ **cup butter, softened**
- ⅔ **cup sugar**
- 1 **egg**
- ½ **cup molasses**
- 2¾ **cups all-purpose flour**
- 1 **teaspoon baking soda**
- 1 **teaspoon ground cinnamon**
- 1 **teaspoon ground ginger**
- ½ **teaspoon salt**
- ¼ **teaspoon ground cloves**
- ½ **cup buttermilk**
- ½ **cup chopped walnuts**

FROSTING

- 1½ **cups confectioners' sugar**
- 4½ **teaspoons butter, softened**
- ½ **teaspoon vanilla extract**
- 2 **to 3 tablespoons half-and-half cream**
  Walnuts halves, optional

1. In a large bowl, cream butter and sugar until light and fluffy. Beat in egg and molasses. Combine the flour, baking soda, cinnamon, ginger, salt and cloves; add to creamed mixture alternately with buttermilk, beating well after each addition. Stir in chopped walnuts.

2. Drop by tablespoonfuls 2 in. apart onto greased baking sheets. Bake at 350° for 10-12 minutes or until edges are firm. Remove to wire racks to cool.

3. For frosting, in a small bowl, combine the confectioners' sugar, butter, vanilla and enough cream to achieve desired consistency. Frost cooled cookies. Top each with a walnut half if desired.

Raspberry Ribbons

I make these attractive, buttery cookies to serve at our remote guest lodge, and all the girls in the kitchen are addicted to them!

—PATSY WOLFENDEN GOLDEN, BC

PREP: 20 MIN. • **BAKE:** 20 MIN. + COOLING
MAKES: ABOUT 5 DOZEN

- 1 **cup butter, softened**
- ½ **cup sugar**
- 1 **egg**
- 1 **teaspoon vanilla extract**
- 2¼ **cups all-purpose flour**
- ½ **teaspoon baking powder**
- ¼ **teaspoon salt**
- ½ **cup raspberry jam**

GLAZE

- 1 **cup confectioners' sugar**
- 2 **tablespoons evaporated milk**
- ½ **teaspoon vanilla extract**

1. In a large bowl, cream butter and sugar until light and fluffy. Beat in egg and vanilla. Combine the flour, baking powder and salt; gradually add to creamed mixture and mix well.

2. Divide dough into four portions; shape each into a 10-in. x 2½-in. log. Place 4 in. apart on greased or foil-lined baking sheets. Make a ½-in. depression down the center of each log. Bake at 350° for 10 minutes.

3. Fill depressions with jam. Bake 10-15 minutes longer or until lightly browned. Cool for 2 minutes. Remove to a cutting board; cut into ¾-in. slices. Place on wire racks.

4. In a small bowl, combine glaze ingredients. Drizzle over warm cookies. Cool completely.

Surprise Package Cookies

Each of these buttery cookies has a chocolate mint candy inside. They're my absolute favorite and I always include them on our Christmas cookie trays.

—LORRAINE MEYER BEND, OR

PREP: 25 MIN. + CHILLING • **BAKE:** 10 MIN./BATCH
MAKES: 3½ DOZEN

- 1 **cup butter, softened**
- 1 **cup sugar**
- ½ **cup packed brown sugar**
- 2 **eggs**
- 1 **teaspoon vanilla extract**
- 3 **cups all-purpose flour**
- 1 **teaspoon baking powder**
- ½ **teaspoon salt**
- 65 **mint Andes candies**

1. In a bowl, cream butter and sugars. Add eggs, one at a time, beating well after each addition. Beat in vanilla. Combine the flour, baking powder and salt; gradually add to creamed mixture. Cover and refrigerate for 2 hours or until easy to handle.

2. With floured hands, shape a tablespoonful of dough around 42 candies, forming rectangular cookies. Place 2 in. apart on greased baking sheets.

3. Bake at 375° for 10-12 minutes or until edges are golden brown. Remove to wire racks to cool. In a microwave, melt the remaining candies; drizzle over cookies.

Painted Holiday Delights

These soft sandwich cookies are eye-catching, thanks to the holiday designs you paint on with food coloring. Orange juice in the dough and strawberry preserves in the filling add a light fruity flavor. I make them for special occasions.

—JUDY DEGENSTEIN OTTAWA, KS

PREP: 45 MIN. + CHILLING • **BAKE:** 10 MIN.
MAKES: ABOUT 2 DOZEN

- 2 **cups all-purpose flour**
- ½ **cup sugar**
- ½ **cup confectioners' sugar**
- 2 **teaspoons ground cinnamon**
- ¾ **teaspoon baking powder**
- ¼ **teaspoon salt**
- ½ **cup cold butter**
- 1 **egg**
- ¼ **cup orange juice**

FILLING

- 1 **package (8 ounces) cream cheese, softened**
- 3 **tablespoons confectioners' sugar**
- 3 **tablespoons strawberry preserves**

GLAZE

- 1 **cup confectioners' sugar**
- ¼ **teaspoon vanilla extract**
- 1 **to 2 tablespoons milk**
  Assorted food coloring

1. In a bowl, combine the first six ingredients. Cut in butter until mixture resembles coarse crumbs. Combine egg and orange juice; stir into crumb mixture just until moistened. Shape into a ball; cover and chill for 1-2 hours or until easy to handle.

2. On a floured surface, roll out dough to ⅛-in. thickness. Cut with a 2-in. round cookie cutter. Place 1 in. apart on ungreased baking sheets. Bake at 375° for 8-10 minutes or until lightly browned. Remove to wire racks to cool.

3. Combine filling ingredients; spread on the bottom of half of the cookies. Top with remaining cookies.

4. For glaze, combine sugar, vanilla and enough milk to achieve desired consistency. Spread over tops of cookies; dry. Using a small new paintbrush and food coloring, paint holiday designs on cookie tops. Store in the refrigerator.

Sour Cream Sugar Cookies

As a city kid, I was always eager to visit my grandparents on their Oklahoma farmstead. That's where I acquired my taste for country food, like these tender cookies with buttery icing.

—BOBBIE HANKS TULSA, OK

PREP: 25 MIN. + CHILLING • **BAKE:** 10 MIN./BATCH
MAKES: ABOUT 9 DOZEN

- 1 cup butter, softened
- 2 cups sugar
- 3 eggs
- 6 cups all-purpose flour
- 2 teaspoons baking soda
- ½ teaspoon salt
- 1 cup (8 ounces) sour cream

FROSTING
- ½ cup butter, softened
- 4 cups confectioners' sugar
- 3 tablespoons milk
  Food coloring, optional

1. In a large bowl, cream butter and sugar until light and fluffy. Add eggs, one at a time, beating well after each addition. Combine dry ingredients; add to the creamed mixture alternately with sour cream, beating well after each addition (dough will be sticky). Cover and refrigerate for 2 hours or until easy to handle.

2. On a floured surface, roll out dough to ¼-in. thickness. Cut into desired shapes with floured cookie cutters.

3. Place 1 in. apart on greased baking sheets. Bake at 375° for 8-12 minutes or until lightly browned. Cool for 1-2 minutes before removing to wire racks.

4. For frosting, in a large bowl, beat butter, confectioners' sugar and milk until smooth. Add food coloring if desired. Frost cookies..

Caramel Cranberry Bars

My mom created this wonderful dessert after tasting something similar. The sweet bars boast a tangy cranberry flavor.

—DEBBIE KERSH SPRINGTOWN, TX

PREP: 30 MIN. • **BAKE:** 30 MIN. + COOLING • **MAKES:** 2 DOZEN

- 1 package (12 ounces) fresh or frozen cranberries, thawed
- 1 package (8 ounces) chopped dates
- ¾ cup chopped pecans
- 2 tablespoons plus ½ cup sugar, divided
- 2⅓ cups all-purpose flour, divided
- 2 cups old-fashioned oats
- ½ cup packed brown sugar
- ½ teaspoon baking soda
- 1 cup butter, melted
- ¾ cup caramel ice cream topping

1. In a small bowl, combine the cranberries, dates, pecans and 2 tablespoons sugar; set aside.

2. In a large bowl, combine 2 cups flour, oats, brown sugar, baking soda and remaining sugar. Stir in the butter; set aside 1 cup for topping. Press remaining crumb mixture into a greased 13-in. x 9-in. baking dish. Bake at 350° for 15 minutes.

3. Meanwhile, place the remaining flour in a small bowl. Stir in caramel topping until smooth; set aside. Sprinkle cranberry mixture over crust; drizzle with caramel mixture. Sprinkle with reserved crumb mixture.

4. Bake for 30-35 minutes or until bars are golden brown and bubbly. Cool in pan on a wire rack. Cut into bars. Store in the refrigerator.

Greek Holiday Cookies

These golden twists are a traditional treat in Greece, where they are made for celebrations.

—NICOLE MOSKOU NEW YORK, NY

PREP: 30 MIN. + CHILLING • **BAKE:** 10 MIN./BATCH
MAKES: ABOUT 6½ DOZEN

- 1½ **cups butter, softened**
- 1¼ **cups sugar**
- 4 **eggs**
- 2 **tablespoons orange juice**
- 3 **teaspoons vanilla extract**
- 5¼ **cups all-purpose flour**
- 1½ **teaspoons baking powder**
- ¾ **teaspoon baking soda**

1. In a large bowl, cream butter and sugar. Add 2 eggs; beat well. Beat in orange juice and vanilla. Combine the flour, baking powder and baking soda; gradually add to creamed mixture. Cover the dough and refrigerate for 1 hour or until easy to handle.

2. Roll dough into 1¼-in. balls. Shape each into a 6-in. rope; fold in half and twist twice. Place 2 in. apart on ungreased baking sheets.

3. In a small bowl, beat the remaining eggs; brush over dough. Bake at 350° for 7-12 minutes or until edges are golden brown. Remove to wire racks.

Molasses Cutouts

Making these soft, rich, chewy cookies has been a family tradition since my children were small. At Christmastime, I shape the dough into gingerbread men.

—SUE BARTLETT BERLIN, WI

PREP: 25 MIN. + CHILLING • **BAKE:** 10 MIN./BATCH
MAKES: ABOUT 3 DOZEN

- 1 **cup butter, softened**
- 1 **cup sugar**
- 2 **eggs**
- 1 **cup molasses**
- ½ **cup cold water**
- 5½ **cups all-purpose flour**
- 4 **teaspoons baking soda**
- 1 **teaspoon salt**
- 1 **teaspoon ground cinnamon**
- 1 **teaspoon ground ginger**

FROSTING

- 4 **cups confectioners' sugar**
- ¼ **cup butter, softened**
- 1 **teaspoon ground ginger**
- ½ **teaspoon salt**
- ½ **teaspoon ground cinnamon**
- 3 **to 4 tablespoons boiling water**
  M&M's minis and red shoestring licorice

1. In a large bowl, cream butter and sugar until light and fluffy. Add eggs, one at a time, beating well after each addition. Beat in molasses and water. Combine the flour, baking soda, salt, cinnamon and ginger; gradually add to creamed mixture and mix well. Cover and refrigerate for 4 hours or until easy to handle.

2. On a lightly floured surface, roll out dough to ⅛-in. thickness. Cut with a floured 5-in. gingerbread man cutter. Place 1 in. apart on ungreased baking sheets.

3. Bake at 375° for 6-8 minutes or until edges are golden brown. Remove to wire racks to cool.

4. For frosting, in a large bowl, combine the confectioners' sugar, butter, ginger, salt, cinnamon and enough water to achieve spreading consistency. Frost and decorate cookies with candies as desired.

Holly Wreaths

I've never come across another spritz cookie like this, with cream cheese as an ingredient. It helps keep these wreaths moist a long time, and adds a delicious flavor.

—DEE LEIN LONGMONT, CO

PREP: 20 MIN. • **BAKE:** 10 MIN./BATCH + COOLING
MAKES: ABOUT 3 DOZEN

- 1 **cup butter, softened**
- 1 **package (3 ounces) cream cheese, softened**
- ½ **cup sugar**
- 1 **teaspoon vanilla extract**
- 2 **cups all-purpose flour**

Green cherries, cut into thin slices
Red-hot candies
Frosting and decorator gel

1. In a bowl, cream butter and cream cheese. Add sugar; blend well. Stir in vanilla. Gradually beat in flour.
2. Using a cookie press fitted with star tip, form dough into 2½-in. wreaths on ungreased baking sheets. Bake at 375° for 10-12 minutes or until set but not brown. Cool on wire racks. Decorate wreaths with green cherry "leaves" and red-hot candy "berries" attached with a drop of frosting. Add bows with decorator gel.

Meringue Kisses

There's a nice chocolate surprise inside these frothy kisses. They're my husband's top choice each Christmas.

—**TAMI HENKE** LOCKPORT, IL

PREP: 15 MIN. • **BAKE:** 30 MIN./BATCH + COOLING
MAKES: 44 COOKIES

- 3 **egg whites**
- ¼ **teaspoon cream of tartar**
  Pinch salt
- 1 **cup sugar**
- 1 **teaspoon vanilla extract**
  Red and green food coloring, optional
- 44 **milk chocolate kisses**

1. Place egg whites in a small bowl; let stand at room temperature for 30 minutes. Beat egg whites until foamy. Sprinkle with cream of tartar and salt; beat until soft peaks form. Gradually add sugar and vanilla, beating until stiff peaks form, about 5-8 minutes. If desired, divide batter in half and fold in red and green food coloring.

2. Drop by rounded tablespoonfuls 1½-in. apart onto lightly greased baking sheets. Press a chocolate kiss into the center of each cookie and cover it with meringue using a knife.

3. Bake at 275° for 30-35 minutes or until firm to the touch. Immediately remove to a wire rack to cool. Store in an airtight container.

Christmas Sandwich Cremes

These melt-in-your-mouth sandwich cookies have scrumptious filling. I helped my sister make these in high school when she needed a project for her home economics class. The teacher gave her an A+!

—**JANICE POECHMAN** WALKERTON, ON

PREP: 40 MIN. + CHILLING • **BAKE:** 10 MIN./BATCH + COOLING
MAKES: 4 DOZEN

- 1 **cup butter, softened**
- ⅓ **cup heavy whipping cream**
- 2 **cups all-purpose flour**
  Sugar

FILLING

- ½ **cup butter, softened**
- 1½ **cups confectioners' sugar**
- 2 **teaspoons vanilla extract**
  Food coloring

1. In a bowl, combine the butter, cream and flour. Cover and refrigerate for 2 hours or until dough is easy to handle.

2. Divide into thirds; let one portion stand at room temperature for 15 minutes (keep remaining dough refrigerated until ready to roll out). Preheat oven to 375°. On a floured surface, roll out dough to ⅛-in. thickness. Cut with a 1½-in. round cookie cutter. Place cutouts in a shallow dish filled with sugar; turn to coat. Place on ungreased baking sheets. Prick with a fork several times. Bake 7-9 minutes or until set. Cool on wire racks.

3. For filling, in a small bowl, cream butter and sugar until light and fluffy. Add vanilla. Tint with food coloring. Spread about 1 teaspoon filling over half of the cookies; top with remaining cookies.

Swirled Mint Cookies

No one will believe that these rich, tender cookies are "light," but they are! With their colorful swirls, each minty, sugary bite is unique.

—**LOIS HILL** THOMASVILLE, NC

PREP: 40 MIN. + CHILLING • **BAKE:** 10 MIN./BATCH
MAKES: 4 DOZEN

- ½ **cup butter, softened**
- ½ **cup reduced-fat butter, softened**
- ¾ **cup plus 1 tablespoon sugar, divided**
- 1 **egg**
- 1 **teaspoon vanilla extract**
- ½ **teaspoon peppermint extract**
- 2 **cups all-purpose flour**
- ½ **teaspoon baking powder**
- ¼ **teaspoon salt**
- 10 **to 20 drops red food coloring**
- 10 **to 20 drops green food coloring**

1. In a large bowl, cream butters and ¾ cup sugar until light and fluffy. Beat in egg and extracts. Combine the flour, baking powder and salt; gradually add to creamed mixture and mix well.

2. Divide dough into thirds. Stir red food coloring into one portion of the dough; stir green food coloring into another portion. Leave remaining dough plain. Cover and refrigerate for at least 1 hour.

3. Divide each portion of dough into four equal pieces. Roll each piece into a 12-in. rope. Place a red, a green and a plain rope next to each other. Cut through all three ropes at 1-in. intervals, forming sets of three differently colored doughs. Repeat.

4. Roll each set of doughs into a ball; place balls 3 in. apart on ungreased baking sheets. Flatten to ⅛-in. thickness with a glass dipped in remaining sugar. Bake at 375° for 8-10 minutes or until cookie bottoms are lightly browned. Remove to wire racks to cool.

NOTE *This recipe was tested with Land O'Lakes light stick butter.*

Pfeffernuesse

These mild spice cookies, perfect for dunking, come from an old family recipe.

—**BETTY HAWKSHAW** ALEXANDRIA, VA

PREP: 20 MIN. + CHILLING • **BAKE:** 15 MIN./BATCH
MAKES: 8 DOZEN

- 1 **cup butter, softened**
- 1 **cup sugar**
- 2 **eggs**
- ½ **cup light corn syrup**
- ½ **cup molasses**
- ⅓ **cup water**
- 6⅔ **cups all-purpose flour**
- ¼ **cup crushed aniseed**
- 1 **teaspoon baking soda**
- 1 **teaspoon ground cinnamon**
- ½ **teaspoon ground nutmeg**
- ¼ **teaspoon ground cloves**
- ¼ **teaspoon ground allspice**
   Confectioners' sugar

1. In a bowl, cream butter and sugar. Add eggs, one at a time, beating well after each addition. In a bowl, combine corn syrup, molasses and water; set aside. Combine the flour, aniseed, baking soda and spices; add to creamed mixture alternately with molasses mixture. Cover and refrigerate overnight.

2. Roll into 1-in. balls. Place 2 in. apart on greased baking sheets. Bake at 400° for 11 minutes or until golden brown. Roll warm cookies in the confectioners' sugar. Cool on wire racks.

Chocolate Shortbread

My chocolate-flavored shortbread only requires a few ingredients that are always in my pantry. Most people love both chocolate and shortbread, so it's a winning combination.

—KATHERINE BOTH ROCKY MOUNTAIN HOUSE, AB

PREP: 15 MIN. + CHILLING • **BAKE:** 20 MIN./BATCH
MAKES: ABOUT 4 DOZEN

- **1 cup butter, softened**
- **1½ cups all-purpose flour**
- **⅔ cup confectioners' sugar**
- **⅓ cup baking cocoa**
  Dash salt

1. In a large bowl, beat butter until light and fluffy. Combine the remaining ingredients; gradually beat into the butter. Chill for 1 hour.
2. Drop by rounded teaspoonfuls 2 in. apart on greased baking sheets. Bake at 300° for 20 minutes or until set. Remove to wire racks.

Cherry Macaroons

I received this recipe along with all the ingredients at my bridal shower. It was a fantastic gift. Now my husband and kids can't get enough of them!

—**SHERMA TALBOT** SALT LAKE CITY, UT

PREP: 20 MIN. • **BAKE:** 10 MIN. + COOLING
MAKES: ABOUT 6 DOZEN

- 1⅓ cups shortening
- 1½ cups sugar
- 2 eggs
- 1 teaspoon almond extract
- 3½ cups all-purpose flour
- 2 teaspoons baking powder
- 2 teaspoons baking soda
- 1 teaspoon salt
- 1½ cups flaked coconut
- 1 cup maraschino cherries, chopped

1. In a large bowl, cream shortening and sugar until light and fluffy. Add eggs and extract; mix well. Combine the flour, baking powder, baking soda and salt; gradually add to creamed mixture. Stir in the coconut and cherries (dough will be very stiff).

2. Drop by rounded teaspoonfuls 2 in. apart onto greased baking sheets. Bake at 375° for 10-12 minutes or until lightly browned. Cool on wire racks.

Candy Cane Cookies

Guests will have a merry time munching these mild mint cookies. The crunchy candy canes are easy to form once you color the dough—just roll into ropes and twist together.

—**TASTE OF HOME TEST KITCHEN**

PREP: 40 MIN. + CHILLING • **BAKE:** 15 MIN./BATCH
MAKES: ABOUT 6 DOZEN

- ½ cup butter, softened
- ½ cup shortening
- 1 cup sugar
- ¼ cup confectioners' sugar
- ½ cup milk
- 1 egg
- 1 teaspoon peppermint extract
- 1 teaspoon vanilla extract
- 3½ cups all-purpose flour

- ¼ teaspoon salt
  Green and red food coloring

1. In a bowl, cream butter, shortening and sugars. Beat in milk, egg and extracts. Gradually add flour and salt. Set aside half of the dough. Divide remaining dough in half; add green food coloring to one portion and red food coloring to the other. Wrap dough separately in plastic wrap. Refrigerate for 1 hour or until easy to handle.

2. Roll ½ teaspoonfuls of each color of dough into 3-in. ropes. Place each green rope next to a white rope; press together gently and twist. Repeat with red ropes and remaining white ropes. Place 2 in. apart on ungreased baking sheets. Curve one end, forming a cane. Bake at 350° for 11-13 minutes or until set. Cool for 2 minutes; carefully remove to wire racks.

Fennel Tea Cookies

My tender cookies have a lovely fennel flavor and add a touch of elegance to any holiday cookie tray. Rolled in confectioners' sugar, they look like snowballs!

—**SUSAN BECK** NAPA, CA

PREP: 20 MIN. • **BAKE:** 15 MIN. • **MAKES:** 3 DOZEN

- 1 tablespoon fennel seed, crushed
- 2 tablespoons boiling water
- ¾ cup butter, softened
- ⅔ cup packed brown sugar
- 1 egg
- 2 cups all-purpose flour
- ½ teaspoon baking soda
  Confectioners' sugar

1. In a small bowl, soak fennel seed in boiling water; set aside. In a large bowl, cream butter and brown sugar until light and fluffy. Beat in egg. Drain fennel seed. Combine the flour, baking soda and fennel seed; gradually add to creamed mixture and mix well.

2. Roll into 1-in. balls; place 2 in. apart on ungreased baking sheets. Bake at 350° for 10-12 minutes or until lightly browned. Roll warm cookies in confectioners' sugar. Cool on wire racks.

Big Batch Bonanza

Nutty Chocolate Batons

Enjoy the great taste of a buttery cookie with a touch of chocolate and the crunch of nuts.

—ANGELA LEINENBACH MECHANICSVILLE, VA

PREP: 45 MIN. + CHILLING • **BAKE:** 10 MIN./BATCH + COOLING
MAKES: 8 DOZEN

- ¾ cup butter, softened
- ⅓ cup sugar
- ⅓ cup almond paste
- 1 egg yolk
- 1⅔ cups all-purpose flour
- 1 cup (6 ounces) semisweet chocolate chips
- ½ cup pistachios, finely chopped and toasted

1. In a bowl, cream butter, sugar and almond paste until light and fluffy. Beat in egg yolk. Gradually add flour and mix well. Shape into a ball, then flatten into a disk. Wrap in plastic wrap and chill for 2 hours or until easy to handle.
2. Divide dough into eight equal portions; divide each portion in half. On a lightly floured surface, roll each half into a 12-in. rope; cut each rope into 2-in. lengths. Place 2 in. apart on greased baking sheets. Bake at 350° for 6-8 minutes or until edges are lightly browned. Remove to wire racks to cool completely.
3. In a microwave, melt chocolate chips; stir until smooth. Dip ends of each cookie in chocolate, then in pistachios. Let stand on waxed paper until set. Store in an airtight container.

Cookies For a Crowd

I'm a cook at a 4-H camp. Our campers go wild over these crisp cookies with excellent peanut flavor.

—MARY GREEN MISHICOT, WI

PREP: 20 MIN. • **BAKE:** 10 MIN./BATCH • **MAKES:** ABOUT 20 DOZEN

- 4 cups shortening
- 4 cups peanut butter
- 4 cups packed brown sugar
- 4 cups sugar
- 8 eggs
- 4 teaspoons vanilla extract
- 10 cups all-purpose flour
- 4 teaspoons baking soda
- 4 teapoons salt
- 1 cup chopped salted peanuts, optional

1. In a large bowl, cream the shortening, peanut butter and sugars until light and fluffy. Beat in eggs one at a time; beating well after each addition. Beat in vanilla. Combine the flour, baking soda and salt; add to creamed mixture and mix well. Stir in peanuts if desired.
2. Drop dough by rounded teaspoonfuls 2 in. apart onto ungreased baking sheets. Flatten with a fork if desired. Bake at 350° for 10-12 minutes or until set. Remove to wire racks to cool.

Itty Bitty Peppernuts

Before Christmas, my grandmother would bake peppernuts and store them until the big day. When we came home from school, the whole house would smell like anise.

—MARILYN KUTZLI CLINTON, IA

PREP: 40 MIN. + CHILLING • **BAKE:** 10 MIN./BATCH
MAKES: 30 DOZEN

- 3 eggs
- 2 cups sugar
- 2¾ cups all-purpose flour
- 1 teaspoon anise extract or crushed aniseed

1. In a large bowl, beat eggs and sugar at medium speed for 15 minutes. Reduce speed and slowly add flour and anise. Mix well. On a lightly floured surface, shape dough into ropes about ½ in. in diameter. Chill for 1 hour.
2. Cut ropes into ½-in. pieces. Place on greased baking sheets. Bake at 350° for 6-8 minutes or until set. Carefully remove to wire racks. Cookies will harden upon standing.
3. When cool, store in airtight containers; they are best if allowed to age before serving.

Mint Morsels

Is it a cookie or a candy? No matter which answer folks choose, they find these yummy. The recipe makes so much that you can whip up lots of gifts at once.

—**ADINA SKILBRED** PRAIRIE DU SAC, WI

PREP: 30 MIN. + CHILLING • **BAKE:** 10 MIN. + COOLING
MAKES: ABOUT 10 DOZEN

- ⅓ cup shortening
- ⅓ cup butter, softened
- ¾ cup sugar
- 1 egg
- 1 tablespoon 2% milk
- 1 teaspoon vanilla extract
- 1¾ cups all-purpose flour
- ⅓ cup baking cocoa
- 1½ teaspoons baking powder
- ¼ teaspoon salt
- ⅛ teaspoon ground cinnamon

PEPPERMINT LAYER
- 4 cups confectioners' sugar
- 6 tablespoons light corn syrup
- 6 tablespoons butter, melted
- 2 to 3 teaspoons peppermint extract

CHOCOLATE COATING
- 2 packages (11½ ounces each) milk chocolate chips
- ¼ cup shortening

1. In a large bowl, cream the shortening, butter and sugar until light and fluffy. Beat in the egg, milk and vanilla. Combine the flour, cocoa, baking powder, salt and cinnamon; gradually add to the creamed mixture. Cover and refrigerate for 8 hours or overnight.

2. On a lightly floured surface, roll the dough to ⅛-in. thickness. Cut with a lightly floured 1½-in. round cookie cutter; place on ungreased baking sheets.

3. Bake at 375° for 6-8 minutes or until set. Cool for 2 minutes; remove to wire racks to cool completely.

4. In a large bowl, combine all the peppermint layer ingredients. Knead for 1 minute or until smooth. Shape into 120 balls, ½ in. each. Place a ball on each cookie and flatten to cover cookie. Place on waxed paper-lined baking sheets; refrigerate for 30 minutes.

5. In a microwave, melt chips and shortening; stir until smooth. Spread about 1 teaspoonful over each cookie. Chill until firm.

Pecan Crescents

This recipe came from a church cookbook; I altered a few ingredients. Everyone who tries these crescents likes the nutty flavor and texture.

—**KATHY HENSON** ALICE, TX

PREP: 30 MIN. • **BAKE:** 20 MIN./BATCH • **MAKES:** 9 DOZEN

- 1 cup butter, softened
- ¾ cup sugar
- 1½ teaspoons almond extract
- 2½ cups all-purpose flour
- 1 cup ground pecans
- 1 cup confectioners' sugar

1. In a large bowl, cream butter and sugar until light and fluffy. Beat in extract. Gradually add flour and mix well. Stir in pecans.

2. Shape teaspoonfuls of dough into crescents. Place 2 in. apart on ungreased baking sheets.

3. Bake at 300° for 18-20 minutes or until firm. Roll warm cookies in confectioners' sugar. Cool on wire racks.

Cherry Christmas Slices

Brilliant red and green candied cherries add extra sparkle to these delicious holiday cookies. What I like best is that the dough is easy to mix up ahead of time. In fact, I've often made the dough in November and kept it in the freezer until I needed it in December!

—KATIE KOZIOLEK HARTLAND, MN

PREP: 20 MIN. + CHILLING • **BAKE:** 10 MIN./BATCH
MAKES: ABOUT 11 DOZEN

- 1 **cup butter, softened**
- 1 **cup confectioners' sugar**
- 1 **egg**
- 1 **teaspoon vanilla extract**
- 2¼ **cups all-purpose flour**
- 2 **cups red and green candied cherries, halved**
- 1 **cup pecan halves**

1. In a bowl, cream the butter and sugar. Add the egg and vanilla; beat until fluffy. Add flour; mix well. Stir in cherries and pecans. Chill for 1 hour.

2. Shape dough into three 10-in. rolls; wrap in plastic wrap and place in a freezer bag. Freeze up to 2 months.

3. To bake, cut frozen rolls into ⅛-in. slices. Place on ungreased baking sheets. Bake at 325° for 10-12 minutes or until edges are golden brown. Cool on wire racks.

tasteofhome.com

Salted Peanut Cookies

Instead of walnuts or pecans, this chocolate chip cookie recipe calls for salted peanuts. Whenever I bake these, friends and family are eager to sample them.

—**CHARLEEN BLOCK** HUTCHINSON, MN

PREP: 25 MIN. • **BAKE:** 10 MIN./BATCH • **MAKES:** 10 DOZEN

- 1½ cups shortening
- 1 cup sugar
- 1 cup packed brown sugar
- 3 eggs
- 1 teaspoon vanilla extract
- 3¾ cups all-purpose flour
- 2 teaspoons baking soda
- 1 teaspoon salt
- 1½ cups semisweet chocolate chips
- 1½ cups salted peanuts

1. In a large bowl, cream shortening and sugars until light fluffy. Add eggs, one at a time, beating well after each addition. Beat in vanilla. Combine the flour, baking soda and salt; gradually add to creamed mixture and mix well. Stir in chocolate chips and peanuts.
2. Drop by tablespoonfuls 2 in. apart onto greased baking sheets. Bake at 350° for 10-12 minutes or until lightly browned. Remove to wire racks.

Shortbread Meltaways

You'll need just five everyday ingredients to stir up a batch of these bite-size cookies. Although they won't break your grocery budget, they're rich and melt-in-your-mouth good.

—**RUTH WHITTAKER** WAYNE, PA

PREP: 20 MIN. • **BAKE:** 15 MIN./BATCH • **MAKES:** 7 DOZEN

- 1 cup butter, softened
- ½ cup confectioners' sugar
- 1 teaspoon vanilla extract
- 1 cup all-purpose flour
- ⅔ cup cornstarch

1. In a small bowl, cream butter and confectioners' sugar until light and fluffy. Beat in vanilla. Combine the flour and cornstarch; gradually add to creamed mixture and mix well.
2. Drop by ½ teaspoonfuls onto ungreased baking sheets. Bake at 350° for 11-13 minutes or until bottoms are lightly browned. Cool for 5 minutes before removing from pans to wire racks.

Whole Wheat Toffee Sandies

Crisp and loaded with goodies, these are my husband's favorite cookies. I used to bake them in large batches when our four sons still lived at home. Now I whip them up for our grandchildren.

—**ALICE KAHNK** KENNARD, NE

PREP: 35 MIN. • **BAKE:** 15 MIN./BATCH • **MAKES:** ABOUT 12 DOZEN

- 1 cup butter, softened
- 1 cup sugar
- 1 cup confectioners' sugar
- 1 cup canola oil
- 2 eggs
- 1 teaspoon almond extract
- 3½ cups all-purpose flour
- 1 cup whole wheat flour
- 1 teaspoon baking soda
- 1 teaspoon cream of tartar
- 1 teaspoon salt
- 2 cups chopped almonds
- 1 package (8 ounces) milk chocolate English toffee bits
  Additional sugar

1. In a large bowl, cream butter and sugars until light and fluffy. Beat in oil, eggs and extract. Combine flours, baking soda, cream of tartar and salt; gradually add to creamed mixture and mix well. Stir in almonds and toffee bits.
2. Shape into 1-in. balls; roll in sugar. Place on ungreased baking sheets and flatten with a fork. Bake at 350° for 12-14 minutes or until lightly browned.

Lemon Butter Cookies

My tender cutout cookies have a slight lemon flavor that makes them stand out from the rest. They're very easy to roll out compared to other sugar cookies I've worked with. I know you'll enjoy them as much as we do.

—JUDY MCCREIGHT SPRINGFIELD, IL

PREP: 20 MIN. + CHILLING • **BAKE:** 10 MIN./BATCH
MAKES: ABOUT 13 DOZEN

- 1   **cup butter, softened**
- 2   **cups sugar**
- 2   **eggs, lightly beaten**
- ¼   **cup milk**
- 2   **teaspoons lemon extract**
- 4½ **cups all-purpose flour**
- 2   **teaspoons baking powder**
- ½   **teaspoon salt**
- ¼   **teaspoon baking soda**
     Colored sugar, optional

1. In a large bowl, cream butter and sugar until light and fluffy. Beat in the eggs, milk and extract. Combine dry ingredients; gradually add to creamed mixture and mix well. Cover and chill for 2 hours.
2. Roll out on a lightly floured surface to ⅛-in. thickness. Cut with a 2-in. cookie cutter dipped in flour. Place 2 in. apart on ungreased baking sheets. Sprinkle with colored sugar if desired.
3. Bake at 350° for 8-9 minutes or until the edges just begin to brown. Remove to wire racks to cool.

Bushel of Cookies

This recipe turns out what seems like a bushelful of cookies—that's probably how it got its name. But the cookies disappear fast, even with a crowd. Raisins and pecans comes through in every bite, and the butterscotch chips add a distinctive taste.

—MARTHA SCHWARTZ JACKSON, OH

PREP: 35 MIN. + CHILLING • **BAKE:** 15 MIN./BATCH
MAKES: 24 DOZEN

- 2   **pounds raisins**
- 1   **pound pecans**
- 5   **cups butter, softened**
- 11 **cups sugar**
- 12 **eggs**
- 1   **cup maple syrup**
- 1   **quart milk**
- ¼   **cup vanilla extract**
- 12 **cups quick-cooking oats**
- 21 **cups all-purpose flour**
- ¼   **cup baking powder**
- ¼   **cup baking soda**
- 2   **teaspoons salt**
- 2   **packages (11 ounces each) butterscotch chips**

1. Grind or finely chop raisins and pecans; set aside. In a large bowl, cream butter and sugar. Add eggs, a few at a time, mixing well after each. Add syrup, milk and vanilla; mix well. Stir in oats, raisins and pecans. Combine flour, baking powder, baking soda and salt; stir into oat mixture. Fold in chips. Cover and chill for 2 hours.
2. Drop by rounded tablespoonfuls 2 in. apart onto greased baking sheets. Bake at 350° for 15 minutes. Remove to wire racks to cool.

Bakeshop TIP

Finely Chopping Nuts

A food processor takes just seconds to finely chop nuts and just a few more to turn them into nut butter. To avoid that problem, try these tricks. Combine 1 or 2 tablespoons of flour (from the amount called for in the recipe) with the nuts. Then process with short bursts of chopping. If the nuts on top are still too large, stir them up and continue processing.

Back-to-School Cookies

Pull this recipe from your files the next time you need to send the kids off with a sweet treat to share with classmates. These peanut butter cookies are great for bake sales, too.

—**FRANCES PIERCE** WADDINGTON, NY

PREP: 30 MIN. • **BAKE:** 10 MIN./BATCH • **MAKES:** 6½ DOZEN

- 1 cup butter-flavored shortening
- 1 cup creamy peanut butter
- 2 cups packed brown sugar
- 4 egg whites
- 1 teaspoon vanilla extract
- 2 cups all-purpose flour
- 1 teaspoon baking soda
- ½ teaspoon baking powder
- 2 cups crisp rice cereal
- 1½ cups chopped nuts
- 1 cup flaked coconut
- 1 cup quick-cooking oats

1. In a large bowl, cream the shortening, peanut butter and brown sugar until light and fluffy. Beat in egg whites and vanilla. Combine the flour, baking soda and baking powder; gradually add to creamed mixture and mix well. Stir in the cereal, nuts, coconut and oats.

2. Drop by rounded tablespoonfuls 2 in. apart onto ungreased baking sheets. Flatten with a fork, forming a crisscross pattern. Bake at 375° for 7-8 minutes. Remove to wire racks.

NOTE *Reduced-fat peanut butter is not recommended for this recipe.*

Chewy Surprise Cookies

With four daughters, plus grandchildren and great-grandkids, I've baked lots of cookies. This recipe is one of my favorites.

—LAVON TIMKEN CIMMARON, KS

PREP: 25 MIN. + CHILLING • **BAKE:** 10 MIN./BATCH
MAKES: ABOUT 8 DOZEN

- 1½ **cups butter-flavored shortening**
- 1½ **cups peanut butter**
- 2 **cups sugar, divided**
- 1½ **cups packed brown sugar**
- 4 **eggs**
- 3¾ **cups all-purpose flour**
- 2 **teaspoons baking soda**
- 1½ **teaspoons baking powder**
- ¾ **teaspoon salt**
- 1 **package (10 ounces) Milk Duds**

1. In a large bowl, cream the shortening, peanut butter, 1½ cups sugar and brown sugar until light and fluffy. Add eggs, one at a time, beating well after each addition. Combine dry ingredients; gradually add to the creamed mixture and mix well. Chill for at least 1 hour.

2. Shape 4 teaspoons of dough around each Milk Dud so it is completely covered. Roll balls in remaining sugar.

3. Place 2 in. apart on ungreased baking sheets. Bake at 350° for 10-12 minutes or until set. Cool for 5 minutes before removing to wire racks.

NOTE *Reduced-fat peanut butter is not recommended for this recipe.*

Orange Slice Cookies

Soft candy orange slices are a refreshing addition to these crispy white chip cookies. To quickly cut the orange candy, use scissors, rinsing the blades with cold water occasionally to reduce sticking.

—BRITT STRAIN IDAHO FALLS, ID

START TO FINISH: 30 MIN. • **MAKES:** ABOUT 10 DOZEN

- 1 **cup orange candy slices**
- 1½ **cups sugar, divided**
- 1 **cup butter, softened**
- 1 **cup shortening**
- 1½ **cups packed brown sugar**
- 2 **eggs**
- 2 **teaspoons vanilla extract**
- 4 **cups all-purpose flour**
- 2 **teaspoons baking soda**
- 1 **teaspoon salt**
- 1 **package (10 to 12 ounces) white baking chips**
- 1 **cup chopped pecans**

1. Cut each orange slice into eight pieces. Roll in ¼ cup sugar; set aside. In a bowl, cream the butter, shortening, brown sugar and remaining sugar. Add eggs, one at a time, beating well after each addition. Beat in vanilla. Combine the flour, baking soda and salt; gradually add to creamed mixture. Stir in chips, pecans and orange slice pieces.
2. Roll into 1-in. balls. Place 2 in. apart on ungreased baking sheets. Bake at 375° for 10-12 minutes or until golden brown. Remove to wire racks to cool.

Italian Holiday Cookies

Many of our holiday traditions center around the foods my mother made while I was growing up. These cookies, which we called *strufoli*, bring back wonderful memories.

—SUE SEYMOUR VALATIE, NY

PREP: 20 MIN. • **COOK:** 15 MIN. + COOLING
MAKES: ABOUT 15 DOZEN

- 1 **tablespoon sugar**
- 1 **teaspoon grated lemon peel**
- 1 **teaspoon vanilla extract**
- ½ **teaspoon salt**
- 4 **eggs**
- 2½ **cups all-purpose flour**

Oil for deep-fat frying
1 **cup honey**
Candy sprinkles

1. In a bowl, combine sugar, lemon peel, vanilla and salt. Add eggs and 2 cups flour; mix well. Turn onto a floured surface and knead in remaining flour (dough will be soft). With a floured knife or scissors, cut into 20 pieces.
2. With hands, roll each piece into pencil shapes. Cut "pencils" into ½-in. pieces.
3. In an electric skillet or deep-fat fryer, heat oil to 350°. Fry pieces, a few at a time, for 2 minutes per side or until golden brown. Drain on paper towels.
4. Place in a large bowl. Heat honey to boiling; pour over cookies and mix well. With a slotted spoon, spoon onto a serving platter and slowly mound into a tree shape if desired. Decorate with candy sprinkles. Cool completely.

gradually add to chocolate mixture and mix well. Stir in the walnuts and remaining chocolate chips.

2. Drop by rounded teaspoonfuls 2 in. apart onto ungreased baking sheets. Bake at 350° for 10-11 minutes or until edges are set. Remove to wire racks to cool.

Pumpkin Spice Cookies

These soft cookies are almost like little pieces of cake. With chopped pecans sprinkled over a confectioners' sugar frosting, they're a pretty addition to a dessert table.

—**BEV MARTIN** HARDIN, MT

PREP: 20 MIN. • **BAKE:** 10 MIN./BATCH + COOLING
MAKES: 7 DOZEN

- 1 package (8 ounces) cream cheese, softened
- 1½ cups packed brown sugar
- ½ cup sugar
- 2 eggs
- 1 cup canned pumpkin
- 1 teaspoon vanilla extract
- 3½ cups all-purpose flour
- 1 to 1½ teaspoons pumpkin pie spice
- 1 teaspoon baking soda
- 1 teaspoon salt
- ½ teaspoon baking powder

FROSTING
- 2 cups confectioners' sugar
- ¼ cup butter, melted
- 1 teaspoon vanilla extract
- 2 to 3 tablespoons boiling water
- 2 cups chopped pecans

1. In a large bowl, beat the cream cheese and sugars until smooth. Add the eggs, one at a time, beating well after each addition. Beat in the pumpkin and vanilla. Combine the dry ingredients; gradually add to pumpkin mixture and mix well.

2. Drop by rounded teaspoonfuls 2 in. apart onto ungreased baking sheets. Bake at 350° for 10-12 minutes or until golden brown. Remove to wire racks to cool.

3. For frosting, in a small bowl, combine the confectioners' sugar, butter, vanilla and enough water to achieve frosting consistency. Frost cookies; sprinkle with pecans.

Mocha Fudge Cookies

These rich, soft cookies are convenient to make ahead. The dough and cookies freeze well.

—**BERNIECE WALLACE** VAN METER, IA

PREP: 30 MIN. • **BAKE:** 10 MIN./BATCH • **MAKES:** 18½ DOZEN

- 4 cups (24 ounces) semisweet chocolate chips, divided
- 2 cups butter
- 3 cups sugar
- 3 cups packed brown sugar
- 1 cup baking cocoa
- 1 tablespoon instant coffee granules
- 8 eggs, lightly beaten
- 3 tablespoons vanilla extract
- 8 cups all-purpose flour
- 2 teaspoons baking powder
- 1 teaspoon salt
- 1½ cups chopped walnuts

1. In a large microwave-safe bowl, melt 2 cups of chocolate chips and butter; stir until smooth. Combine the sugars, cocoa and coffee; add to chocolate mixture. Stir in eggs and vanilla. Combine the flour, baking powder and salt;

Papa's Sugar Cookies

My grandchildren love these sugar cookies. They're crisp and melt in your mouth. Their subtle macadamia nut, cinnamon and orange flavors go perfectly together.

—LEE DOVERSPIKE NORTH RIDGEVILLE, OH

PREP: 20 MIN. + CHILLING • **BAKE:** 10 MIN./BATCH • **MAKES:** 8 DOZEN

- 1 **cup butter, softened**
- 1 **cup canola oil**
- 1 **cup sugar**
- 1 **cup confectioners' sugar**
- 2 **eggs**
- 2 **tablespoons butter flavoring**
- 1 **tablespoon grated orange peel**
- 1 **tablespoon vanilla extract**
- 5½ **cups all-purpose flour**
- ¼ **cup ground macadamia nuts**
- 1½ **teaspoons baking soda**
- 1 **teaspoon salt**
- 1 **teaspoon cream of tartar**
- 1 **teaspoon ground cinnamon**
  Additional granulated sugar

1. In a large bowl, beat the butter, oil and sugars until well blended. Add eggs, one at a time, beating well after each addition. Beat in the butter flavoring, orange peel and vanilla.

2. Combine the flour, nuts, baking soda, salt, cream of tartar and cinnamon; gradually add to butter mixture and mix well. Cover and refrigerate for 1 hour or until easy to handle.

3. Roll into 1-in. balls, then roll in additional sugar. Place 2 in. apart on ungreased baking sheets. Flatten with a glass dipped in additional sugar.

4. Bake at 350° for 10-12 minutes or until edges begin to brown. Remove to wire racks.

Jumbo Raisin Cookies

When I was growing up, my mother made these soft and spicy raisin cookies once a month. Since the recipe makes a huge batch, she always froze some to snack on later.

—**BECKY MELANDER** CLINTON TOWNSHIP, MI

PREP: 25 MIN. • **BAKE:** 15 MIN./BATCH • **MAKES:** 13 DOZEN

- 2 **cups water**
- 4 **cups raisins**
- 1 **cup butter, softened**
- 1 **cup shortening**
- 4 **cups sugar**
- 6 **eggs**
- 2 **teaspoons vanilla extract**
- 8 **cups all-purpose flour**
- 4 **teaspoons baking soda**
- 4 **teaspoons baking powder**
- 4 **teaspoons salt**
- 1 **tablespoon ground cinnamon**
- 1 **teaspoon ground nutmeg**
- ½ **teaspoon ground allspice**
- 2 **cups (12 ounces) semisweet chocolate chips**

1. In a saucepan, combine the water and raisins. Bring to a boil. Remove from the heat; cool to room temperature (do not drain).

2. In a large bowl, cream butter, shortening and sugar. Add eggs, one at a time, beating well after each addition. Beat in vanilla. Combine the dry ingredients; gradually add to the creamed mixture. Stir in chocolate chips and raisins with any liquid.

3. Drop by heaping tablespoonfuls 2 in. apart onto greased baking sheets. Bake at 350° for 12-15 minutes or until golden brown. Remove to wire racks to cool.

Cocoa Chocolate Chip Cookies

Crisp outside but chewy inside, these sweet sensations will disappear in a hurry. My kids always have friends over, so I like to keep snacks on hand for them. They love these cookies.

—**MARY DUDEK** ALLIANCE, OH

PREP: 30 MIN. • **BAKE:** 10 MIN./BATCH • **MAKES:** ABOUT 8½ DOZEN

- ⅔ **cup butter, softened**
- ½ **cup canola oil**
- 1 **cup sugar**
- 1 **cup packed brown sugar**
- 2 **eggs**
- 1 **package (3.9 ounces) instant chocolate pudding mix**
- 3 **tablespoons water**
- 3 **cups all-purpose flour**
- 1 **teaspoon baking soda**
- 1 **teaspoon salt**
- 1 **package (12 ounces) miniature semisweet chocolate chips**

1. In a large bowl, cream the butter, oil and sugars until light and fluffy. Beat in eggs. Beat in pudding mix and water. Combine the flour, baking soda and salt; gradually add to the chocolate mixture and mix well (dough will be stiff). Stir in the chocolate chips.

2. Roll into 1-in. balls. Place 2 in. apart on ungreased baking sheets. Bake at 350° for 9-11 minutes or until set and edges are firm. Cool for 2 minutes before removing to wire racks.

Cakes & Cupcakes

Chocolate Cherry Cupcakes

Inside each of these little cakes is a fruity surprise! At kids' parties, adult soirees or anything in between, guests will adore them.

—BERTILLE COOPER CALIFORNIA, MD

PREP: 15 MIN. • **BAKE:** 20 MIN. • **MAKES:** 2 DOZEN

- 1 package (18¼ ounces) chocolate cake mix
- 1⅓ cups water
- ½ cup canola oil
- 3 eggs
- 1 can (21 ounces) cherry pie filling
- 1 can (16 ounces) vanilla frosting
   Chocolate curls, optional

1. In a large bowl, combine the cake mix, water, oil and eggs; beat on low speed for 30 seconds. Beat on medium for 2 minutes.

2. Spoon batter by ¼ cupfuls into paper-lined muffin cups. Spoon a rounded teaspoon of pie filling onto the center of each cupcake. Set remaining pie filling aside.

3. Bake at 350° for 20-25 minutes or until a toothpick inserted near the center comes out clean. Remove from pans to wire racks to cool completely.

4. Frost cupcakes; top each with one cherry from pie filling. Refrigerate remaining pie filling for another use. Garnish with chocolate curls if desired.

Chocolate Hazelnut Torte

Most cake recipes feed a crowd. So we came up with this elegant little cake that serves six. That's plenty for two, with enough leftovers to sneak bites and midnight snacks for a few days after!

—TASTE OF HOME TEST KITCHEN

PREP: 30 MIN. + CHILLING • **BAKE:** 25 MIN. + COOLING
MAKES: 6 SERVINGS

- ⅓ cup butter, softened
- 1 cup packed brown sugar
- 1 egg
- 1 teaspoon vanilla extract
- 1 cup all-purpose flour
- ¼ cup baking cocoa
- 1 teaspoon baking soda
- ⅛ teaspoon salt
- ½ cup sour cream
- ½ cup brewed coffee, room temperature

FROSTING

- 7 ounces semisweet chocolate, chopped
- 1 cup heavy whipping cream
- 2 tablespoons sugar
- ⅓ cup Nutella
   Chocolate curls and hazelnuts, optional

1. In a small bowl, cream butter and brown sugar until light and fluffy. Beat in egg and vanilla. Combine the flour, cocoa, baking soda and salt; gradually beat into creamed mixture alternately with sour cream and coffee.

2. Pour into two greased and floured 6-in. round baking pans. Bake at 350° for 25-30 minutes or until a knife inserted near the center comes out clean. Cool for 10 minutes before removing from pans to wire racks to cool completely.

3. For frosting, in a small saucepan, melt chocolate with cream and sugar over low heat; stir until smooth. Remove from the heat; whisk in Nutella. Transfer to a small bowl; cover and refrigerate until frosting reaches spreading consistency, stirring occasionally.

4. Spread the frosting between layers and over top and sides of cake. Garnish with chocolate curls and hazelnuts if desired.

Lemon-Lime Poppy Seed Cake

There's plenty of lemon-lime flavor in this tender cake to please any citrus lover. Plus, it's a breeze to make.

—**VICTORIA HAHN** NORTHAMPTON, PA

PREP: 20 MIN. • **BAKE:** 40 MIN. + COOLING • **MAKES:** 12 SERVINGS

- 1 **package (18¼ ounces) yellow cake mix**
- 1 **package (3.4 ounces) instant vanilla pudding mix**
- ¼ **cup poppy seeds**
- 4 **eggs**
- ½ **cup water**
- ½ **cup canola oil**
- ¼ **cup lemon juice**
- ¼ **cup lime juice**

GLAZE

- 1¾ **cups confectioners' sugar**
- 2 **tablespoons lemon juice**
- 2 **tablespoons lime juice**

1. In a large bowl, combine first eight ingredients. Beat on low speed for 30 seconds; beat on medium for 2 minutes. Pour into a greased and floured 10-in. fluted tube pan.

2. Bake at 350° for 40-45 minutes or until a toothpick inserted near the of the cake center comes out clean. Cool for 10 minutes before removing from pan to a wire rack to cool completely.

3. In a small bowl, combine the glaze ingredients until smooth; drizzle over cake.

Low-Fat Carrot Cake

Loaded with spice and carrot flavor, this moist and luscious cake is guaranteed to impress.

—**REBECCA BAIRD** SALT LAKE CITY, UT

PREP: 30 MIN. • **BAKE:** 30 MIN. + COOLING • **MAKES:** 16 SERVINGS

- 2 **cups packed brown sugar**
- ½ **cup buttermilk**
- 2 **egg whites**
- 1 **egg**
- 2 **tablespoons canola oil**
- 1 **teaspoon vanilla extract**
- 2½ **cups cake flour**
- 1 **teaspoon baking soda**
- 1 **teaspoon ground cinnamon**
- ½ **teaspoon ground allspice**
- ¼ **teaspoon ground nutmeg**
- ¼ **teaspoon ground cloves**
- ⅛ **teaspoon salt**
- 3 **cups grated carrots**
- 1 **can (8 ounces) unsweetened crushed pineapple, drained**
- 2 **ounces reduced-fat cream cheese**
- 1 **cup confectioners' sugar**
- ½ **teaspoon lemon juice**
- ⅛ **teaspoon vanilla extract**

1. In a large bowl, beat the brown sugar, buttermilk, egg whites, egg, oil and vanilla until well blended. Combine the flour, baking soda, spices and salt; gradually beat into sugar mixture until blended. Fold in carrots and pineapple. Pour into a 13-in. x 9-in. baking dish coated with cooking spray.

2. Bake at 350° for 30-35 minutes or until a toothpick inserted near the center comes out clean. Cool completely on a wire rack.

3. In a small bowl, beat cream cheese until fluffy. Add the confectioners' sugar, lemon juice and vanilla; beat until smooth. Drizzle over cake.

Caramel Cashew Cake Pops

Nothing beats the pairing of buttery caramel and rich cashews; add it to a chocolaty cake pop and you have one little treat that is so irresistible.

—**TASTE OF HOME TEST KITCHEN**

PREP: 1½ HOURS + CHILLING • **MAKES:** 4 DOZEN

- 1 **package (18¼ ounces) chocolate cake mix**
- ¾ **cup canned dulce de leche**
- 48 **lollipop sticks**
- 2½ **pounds milk chocolate candy coating, coarsely chopped**
  Chopped cashews

1. Prepare and bake cake mix according to package directions, using a greased 13-in. x 9-in. baking pan. Cool completely on a wire rack.

2. Crumble cake into a large bowl. Add dulce de leche and mix well. Shape into 1-in. balls. Place on baking sheets; insert sticks. Freeze for at least 2 hours or refrigerate for at least 3 hours or until cake balls are firm.

3. In a microwave, melt the candy coating. Dip each cake ball in coating; allow excess to drip off. Coat with the cashews. Insert cake pops into a foam block to stand. Let stand until set.

Raspberry Fudge Torte

People are surprised to hear this impressive torte starts with a simple cake mix—they're sure I bought it at a bakery.

—JULIE HEIN YORK, PA

PREP: 30 MIN. + CHILLING • **BAKE:** 25 MIN. + COOLING
MAKES: 12 SERVINGS

- 1 **package (18¼ ounces) devil's food cake mix**
- 1 **cup (8 ounces) sour cream**
- ¾ **cup water**
- 3 **eggs**
- ⅓ **cup canola oil**
- 1 **teaspoon vanilla extract**
- 1 **cup miniature semisweet chocolate chips**

GANACHE
- 1 **cup (6 ounces) semisweet chocolate chips**
- ½ **cup heavy whipping cream**
- 1 **tablespoon butter**

RASPBERRY CREAM
- 1 **package (10 ounces) frozen sweetened raspberries, thawed**
- 3 **tablespoons sugar**
- 4 **teaspoons cornstarch**
- ½ **cup heavy whipping cream, whipped**

1. In a large bowl, combine cake mix, sour cream, water, eggs, oil and vanilla; beat on low speed for 30 seconds. Beat on medium for 2 minutes. Fold in miniature chips.
2. Pour into three greased and floured 9-in. round baking pans. Bake at 350° for 25-30 minutes or until a toothpick inserted near the center of the cake comes out clean. Cool for 10 minutes before removing from pans to wire racks to cool completely.
3. For ganache, place the chocolate chips in a small bowl. In a small saucepan, bring cream just to a boil. Pour over the chocolate; whisk until smooth. Whisk in butter. Chill until the mixture reaches spreading consistency, stirring occasionally.
4. For raspberry cream, mash and strain the raspberries, reserving juice; discard the seeds. In a small saucepan, combine the sugar and cornstarch; stir in raspberry juice. Bring to a boil, cook and stir over low heat for 1-2 minutes or until thickened. Place in a bowl; chill for 30 minutes. Fold in whipped cream.
5. Place one cake layer on a serving plate; spread with half of the ganache. Top with second cake layer and the raspberry cream. Top with remaining cake layer; spread with remaining ganache. Store in the refrigerator.

Sweet Potato Pound Cake

Since we are originally from Texas, we naturally love sweet potatoes. But this rich and buttery pound cake deserves to be a tradition in any home, whether you're from the South, East, North or West.

—DIANE MANNIX HELMVILLE, MT

PREP: 25 MIN. • **BAKE:** 50 MIN. + COOLING • **MAKES:** 12 SERVINGS

- 1 **cup butter, softened**
- 2 **cups sugar**
- 4 **eggs**
- 1 **teaspoon vanilla extract**
- 3 **cups all-purpose flour**
- 2 **teaspoons baking powder**
- 1 **teaspoon ground cinnamon**
- ½ **teaspoon baking soda**
- ¼ **teaspoon salt**
- ¼ **teaspoon ground nutmeg**
- 2 **cups cold mashed sweet potatoes**

GLAZE
- 1 **cup confectioners' sugar**
- 1 **teaspoon grated orange peel**
- 3 **to 5 teaspoons orange juice**

1. In a large bowl, cream butter and sugar until light and fluffy. Add eggs, one at a time, beating well after each addition. Beat in vanilla.
2. Combine the flour, baking powder, cinnamon, baking soda, salt and nutmeg; beat into the creamed mixture alternately with the sweet potatoes. Beat just until combined (batter will be stiff).
3. Pour into a greased and floured 10-in. fluted tube pan. Bake at 350° for 50-60 minutes or until a toothpick inserted near the center comes out clean.
4. Cool for 10 minutes before removing from pan to a wire rack to cool completely.
5. For glaze, in a small bowl, combine the confectioners' sugar, orange peel and enough orange juice to achieve desired consistency. Drizzle over cake.

Heavenly Chocolate-Fudge Cake Balls

My special treat is similar to the popular cake pops—but without the stick! They're guaranteed to calm any chocolate craving and jazz up holiday goodie trays all at the same time. Best of all, their pretty appearance doesn't give away their simple prep.

—LYNN DAVIS MORENO VALLEY, CA

PREP: 1¾ HOURS + STANDING • **BAKE:** 30 MIN. + COOLING
MAKES: 95 CAKE BALLS

- 1 **package (18¼ ounces) devil's food cake mix**
- 2 **tablespoons hot water**
- 1 **teaspoon instant coffee granules**
- 1 **cup chocolate fudge frosting**
- ⅓ **cup baking cocoa**
- ¼ **cup chocolate syrup**
- 1⅓ **cups miniature semisweet chocolate chips**
- 2 **pounds white candy coating, chopped**
    Optional toppings: milk chocolate English toffee bits, toasted flaked coconut and crushed candy canes

1. Prepare and bake cake according to package directions. Cool completely. Crumble cake into a large bowl.
2. In a small bowl, combine hot water and coffee granules; stir until dissolved. Add the frosting, cocoa and chocolate syrup; stir until combined. Add to cake; beat on low speed until blended. Stir in chocolate chips. Shape into 1-in. balls.
3. In a microwave, melt candy coating; stir until smooth. Dip balls in coating mixture; allow excess to drip off. Place on waxed paper; sprinkle with toppings of your choice. Let stand until set. Store in airtight containers.

Pistachio Cake

Mom is well-known for her holiday cookies, candies and cakes. This delicious dessert starts conveniently with a cake mix and instant pudding. You're sure to get requests for second helpings when you serve it.

—BECKY BRUNETTE MINNEAPOLIS, MN

PREP: 15 MIN. • **BAKE:** 45 MIN. + CHILLING
MAKES: 12-15 SERVINGS

- 1 **package (18¼ ounces) white cake mix**
- 1 **package (3.4 ounces) instant pistachio pudding mix**
- 1 **cup lemon-lime soda**
- 1 **cup canola oil**
- 3 **eggs**
- 1 **cup chopped walnuts**

FROSTING
- 1½ **cups cold milk**
- 1 **package (3.4 ounces) instant pistachio pudding mix**
- 1 **carton (8 ounces) frozen whipped topping, thawed**
- ½ **cup pistachios, toasted**

1. In a large bowl, combine first five ingredients; beat on low speed for 30 seconds. Beat on medium for 2 minutes; stir in walnuts.
2. Pour into a greased 13-in. x 9-in. baking pan. Bake at 350° for 45-50 minutes or until a toothpick inserted near the center comes out clean. Cool on a wire rack.
3. For frosting, in a large bowl, beat milk and pudding mix on low speed for 2 minutes. Fold in whipped topping. Spread over cake. Sprinkle with pistachios. Refrigerate for at least 1 hour before cutting.

Amaretto Dream Cupcakes

Treat yourself to these indulgent little cupcakes laced with the irresistible flavor of amaretto and slivered almonds.

—**ANETTE STEVENS, OLDS, AB**

PREP: 20 MIN. • **BAKE:** 15 MIN. + COOLING • **MAKES:** 2 DOZEN

- ¾ **cup butter, softened**
- 1½ **cups packed brown sugar**
- 2   **eggs**
- 2   **cups all-purpose flour**
- 1½ **teaspoons baking powder**
- ½ **teaspoon baking soda**
- ¼ **teaspoon salt**
- ½ **cup buttermilk**
- ¼ **cup amaretto**
- ⅓ **cup slivered almonds**
     Amaretto Butter Frosting (recipe at right)

1. In a large bowl, cream the butter and brown sugar until light and fluffy. Add the eggs, one at a time, beating well after each.

2. Combine the flour, baking powder, baking soda and salt. Add to the creamed mixture alternately with buttermilk and amaretto, beating well after each addition. Stir in the almonds.

3. Fill paper-lined muffins cups two-thirds full. Bake at 375° for 14-16 minutes or until a toothpick comes out clean. Cool for 5 minutes before removing from pans to wire racks to cool completely. Frost cupcakes.

Amaretto Butter Frosting

Put the crowning touch on amaretto cupcakes with this rich and buttery topper.

—**ANETTE STEVENS, OLDS, AB**

START TO FINISH: 15 MIN. • **MAKES:** 2¼ CUPS

- 3   **cups confectioners' sugar**
- ¼   **cup butter, melted**
- 3 to 4 **tablespoons heavy whipping cream**
- 2 to 3 **tablespoons amaretto**

In a small bowl, beat confectioners' sugar and butter. Add 3 tablespoons cream and 2 tablespoons amaretto; beat until smooth. Add remaining cream and amaretto if needed to achieve spreading consistency.

Pound Cake

I'm happy to share a third-generation family recipe with you. This cake is rich and buttery with a lovely golden brown crust. Seasonal fresh fruit is perfect with this one.

—**MARGIE DALTON** CHICAGO, IL

PREP: 20 MIN. • **BAKE:** 1 HOUR + COOLING
MAKES: 2 CAKES (12 SERVINGS EACH)

- 2 **cups butter, softened**
- 4 **cups confectioners' sugar**
- 6 **eggs**
- 1 **teaspoon almond extract**
- 3 **cups all-purpose flour**
- ½ **teaspoon salt**
  Fresh raspberries and whipped cream, optional

1. In a large bowl, cream butter and confectioners' sugar until light and fluffy, about 5 minutes. Add eggs, one at a time, beating well after each addition. Beat in extract. Combine flour and salt; gradually add to creamed mixture. Beat just until combined.

2. Transfer to two greased 8-in. x 4-in. loaf pans. Bake at 325° for 60-70 minutes or until a toothpick inserted near the center comes out clean. Cool for 10 minutes before removing from pans to wire racks. Serve with raspberries and whipped cream if desired.

Chocolate Angel Cake

When I first got married, I could barely boil water. My dear mother-in-law taught me how to make the lightest angel food cakes ever. This chocolate version is an easy yet impressive treat. For many years, it was our son's birthday cake.

—JOYCE SHIFFLER COLORADO SPRINGS, CO

PREP: 25 MIN. • **BAKE:** 35 MIN. + COOLING • **MAKES:** 16 SERVINGS

- 1½ cups egg whites (about 10)
- 1½ cups confectioners' sugar
- 1 cup cake flour
- ¼ cup baking cocoa
- 1½ teaspoons cream of tartar
- ½ teaspoon salt
- 1 cup sugar

FROSTING
- 1½ cups heavy whipping cream
- ½ cup sugar
- ¼ cup baking cocoa
- ½ teaspoon salt
- ½ teaspoon vanilla extract
  Chocolate leaves, optional

1. Place egg whites in a large bowl; let stand at room temperature for 30 minutes. Sift together confectioners' sugar, flour and cocoa three times; set aside.

2. Add cream of tartar and salt to egg whites; beat on medium speed until soft peaks form. Gradually add sugar, about 2 tablespoons at a time, beating on high until stiff glossy peaks form and sugar is dissolved. Gradually fold in flour mixture, about ½ cup at a time.

3. Spoon into an ungreased 10-in. tube pan. Cut through batter with a knife to remove air pockets. Bake on the lowest oven rack at 375° for 35-40 minutes or until lightly browned and entire top appears dry. Immediately invert pan; cool completely, about 1 hour. Run a knife around side and center tube of pan. Remove cake to a serving plate.

4. In a large bowl, combine first five frosting ingredients; cover and chill for 1 hour. Beat until stiff peaks form.

5. Spread over the top and sides of cake. Store in the refrigerator. Garnish with chocolate leaves if desired.

Bakeshop HOW-TO

Beating Meringue to Stiff Peaks

In a large bowl, beat egg whites, cream of tartar, vanilla and salt on medium speed until egg whites begin to increase in volume and soft peaks form. To test for soft peaks, lift the beaters from the whites; the peaks should curl down. Gradually add sugar on high speed as you beat meringue to stiff peaks. Whites should stand straight up and cling to the beaters as shown. Avoid overbeating.

Tiramisu Toffee Torte

Tiramisu is Italian for "pick-me-up," and this treat truly lives up to its name. It's worth every bit of effort to see my husband's eyes light up when I put a piece of this delicious torte in front of him.
—DONNA GONDA NORTH CANTON, OH

PREP: 25 MIN. • **BAKE:** 25 MIN. + CHILLING • **MAKES:** 12 SERVINGS

- 1 **package (18¼ ounces) white cake mix**
- 1 **cup strong brewed coffee, room temperature**
- 4 **egg whites**
- 4 **Heath candy bars (1.4 ounces each), chopped**

FROSTING
- 4 **ounces cream cheese, softened**
- ⅔ **cup sugar**
- ⅓ **cup chocolate syrup**
- 2 **teaspoons vanilla extract**
- 2 **cups heavy whipping cream**
- 6 **tablespoons strong brewed coffee, room temperature**
- 1 **Heath candy bar (1.4 ounces), chopped**

1. Line two greased 9-in. round baking pans with waxed paper and grease the paper; set aside. In a large bowl, combine the cake mix, coffee and egg whites; beat on low speed for 30 seconds. Beat on medium for 2 minutes. Fold in chopped candy bars.

2. Pour into prepared pans. Bake at 350° for 25-30 minutes or until a toothpick inserted near the center comes out clean. Cool for 10 minutes before removing to wire racks to cool.

3. For frosting, in a large bowl, beat cream cheese and sugar until smooth. Beat in chocolate syrup and vanilla. Add the whipping cream. Beat on high speed until light and fluffy, about 5 minutes.

4. Cut each cake horizontally into two layers. Place bottom layer on a serving plate; drizzle with 2 tablespoons coffee. Spread with ¾ cup frosting. Repeat layers twice. Top with the remaining cake layer; frost cake with remaining frosting. Refrigerate overnight. Garnish with chopped candy bar.

Raspberry Truffle Cake Pops

Rich chocolate with a hint of raspberry liqueur...it doesn't get more enticing than this!
—TASTE OF HOME TEST KITCHEN

PREP: 1½ HOURS + CHILLING • **MAKES:** 4 DOZEN

- 1 **package (18¼ ounces) white cake mix**
- ½ **cup canned vanilla frosting**
- ⅓ **cup seedless raspberry jam, melted**
- 2 **to 3 tablespoons raspberry liqueur**
  Red food coloring, optional
- 48 **lollipop sticks**
- 2½ **pounds dark chocolate candy coating, chopped**
  Pink candy coating, chopped
  Pink sprinkles and decorative sugar, optional

1. Prepare and bake cake mix according to the package directions, using a greased 13-in. x 9-in. baking pan. Cool completely on a wire rack.

2. Crumble cake into a large bowl. Add the frosting, jam, liqueur and food coloring if desired; mix well. Shape into 1-in. balls. Place on baking sheets; insert sticks. Freeze for at least 2 hours or refrigerate for at least 3 hours or until cake pops are firm.

3. In a microwave, melt dark candy coating. Dip each cake pop in coating; allow excess to drip off. Insert cake pops into a foam block to stand. Melt pink candy coating; drizzle over cake pops. Decorate some cake pops with sprinkles and sugar if desired. Let stand until set.

Orange-Lemon Cake

Family and friends will love this moist cake's refreshing citrus taste and its pretty presentation.

—ANN ROBINSON BLOOMINGTON, IN

PREP: 15 MIN. • **BAKE:** 35 MIN. + COOLING • **MAKES:** 12 SERVINGS

- **1 package (18¼ ounces) lemon cake mix**
- **1 package (3 ounces) orange gelatin**
- **⅔ cup water**
- **⅔ cup canola oil**
- **4 eggs**

ICING

- **1 cup confectioners' sugar**
- **3 to 4 teaspoons orange juice**

1. In a large bowl, combine the cake mix, gelatin, water, oil and eggs; beat on low speed for 30 seconds. Beat on medium for 2 minutes. Pour into a greased and floured 10-in. fluted tube pan.

2. Bake at 350° for 35-40 minutes or until a toothpick inserted near the center of the cake comes out clean. Cool for 10 minutes before removing from pan to a wire rack to cool completely.

3. Combine confectioners' sugar and enough orange juice to achieve desired consistency. Drizzle over cake.

Cherry Vanilla Cake Pops

Pop goes the party! No worries about who's cutting the cake; just serve and pop.

—TASTE OF HOME TEST KITCHEN

PREP: 1½ HOURS + CHILLING • **MAKES:** 4 DOZEN

- 1 **package (18¼ ounces) white cake mix**
- 1 **cup cream cheese frosting**
- 2 **to 3 tablespoons maraschino cherry juice**
- 48 **lollipop sticks**
- 48 **maraschino cherries, stems removed, drained**
- 2½ **pounds white candy coating, chopped**
  Red pearl sugar

1. Prepare and bake cake mix according to the package directions, using a greased 13-in. x 9-in. baking pan. Cool completely on a wire rack.

2. Crumble cake into a large bowl. Add frosting and cherry juice; mix well. Shape mixture by tablespoonfuls around cherries. Place on baking sheets; insert sticks. Freeze for at least 2 hours or refrigerate for at least 3 hours or until cake balls are firm.

3. In a microwave, melt the candy coating; stir until smooth. Dip each cake pop in coating; allow excess to drip off. Sprinkle with red pearl sugar. Insert cake pops into a foam block to let stand until set.

Strawberry Poke Cake

Strawberry shortcake takes on a wonderful new twist with this super-simple recipe. Strawberry gelatin and strawberries liven up each pretty slice of this lovely layered cake that's made from a handy boxed mix.

—MARY JO GRIGGS WEST BEND, WI

PREP: 25 MIN. • **BAKE:** 25 MIN. + CHILLING • **MAKES:** 12 SERVINGS

- 1 **package (18¼ ounces) white cake mix**
- 1¼ **cups water**
- 2 **eggs**
- ¼ **cup canola oil**
- 2 **packages (10 ounces each) frozen sweetened sliced strawberries, thawed**
- 2 **packages (3 ounces each) strawberry gelatin**
- 1 **carton (12 ounces) frozen whipped topping, thawed, divided**
  Fresh strawberries, optional

1. In a large bowl, beat the cake mix, water, eggs and oil on low speed for 30 seconds. Beat on medium for 2 minutes.

2. Pour batter into two greased and floured 9-in. round baking pans. Bake at 350° for 25-35 minutes or until a toothpick inserted near the center of the cake comes out clean. Cool for 10 minutes; remove from pans to wire racks to cool completely.

3. Using a serrated knife, level tops of cakes if necessary. Return layers, top side up, to two clean 9-in. round baking pans. Pierce cakes with a meat fork or wooden skewer at ½-in. intervals.

4. Drain juice from strawberries into a 2-cup measuring cup; refrigerate berries. Add water to juice to measure 2 cups; pour into a small saucepan. Bring to a boil; stir in gelatin until dissolved. Chill for 30 minutes. Gently spoon over each cake layer. Chill for 2-3 hours.

5. Dip bottom of one pan in warm water for 10 seconds. Invert cake onto a serving platter. Top with reserved strawberries and 1 cup whipped topping. Place second cake layer over topping.

6. Frost cake with remaining whipped topping. Chill for at least 1 hour. Serve with fresh berries if desired. Refrigerate leftovers.

Chocolate Mint Layer Cake

With its rich chocolate icing and minty whipped cream filling, this cake is the perfect finale to a special meal.

—**JEAN PORTWINE** RECLUSE, WY

PREP: 35 MIN. • **BAKE:** 25 MIN. + CHILLING • **MAKES:** 12 SERVINGS

- ½ cup butter, softened
- 1¾ cups sugar
- 3 eggs
- 4 ounces unsweetened chocolate, melted and cooled
- 1 teaspoon vanilla extract
- 1¾ cups all-purpose flour
- ¾ teaspoon baking soda
- ½ teaspoon salt
- ¾ cup 2% milk
- ½ cup water

FILLING
- 1 cup heavy whipping cream
- 3 tablespoons confectioners' sugar
- ⅛ teaspoon peppermint extract
- 3 to 4 drops green food coloring, optional

ICING
- 1 cup (6 ounces) semisweet chocolate chips
- ¼ cup butter, cubed
- ⅓ cup evaporated milk
- 1 teaspoon vanilla extract
- 1½ cups confectioners' sugar

1. Line two greased 9-in. round baking pans with waxed paper. Grease and flour the paper; set aside.

2. In a large bowl, cream the butter and sugar until light and fluffy. Add eggs, one at a time, beating well after each addition. Beat in chocolate and vanilla. Combine the flour, baking soda and salt; add to creamed mixture alternately with milk and water, beating well after each addition.

3. Pour into prepared pans. Bake at 350° for 24-28 minutes or until a toothpick inserted near the center comes out clean. Cool for 10 minutes before removing from pans to wire racks.

4. For filling, in a small bowl, beat the cream until it begins to thicken. Add confectioners' sugar and extract; beat until stiff peaks form. Beat in food coloring if desired. Place one cake layer on a serving plate; spread with filling. Top with second layer.

5. For icing, in a microwave-safe bowl, melt the chips and butter; stir until smooth. Cool slightly. Beat in evaporated milk and vanilla. Gradually beat in the confectioners' sugar until smooth. Frost and decoratethe cake. Chill for 2 hours before slicing.

Brownie Cupcakes

I grew up in my parents' bakery, which might explain why I don't like frosting! These cupcakes are just my style. They come out shiny on top and are great without frosting.

—**CINDY LANG** HAYS, KS

PREP: 15 MIN. • **BAKE:** 20 MIN. + COOLING • **MAKES:** 4 SERVINGS

- ¼ cup semisweet chocolate chips
- ¼ cup butter, cubed
- 1 egg
- ¼ cup sugar
- ¼ teaspoon vanilla extract
- ¼ cup all-purpose flour
- ¼ cup chopped pecans

1. In a microwave, melt chocolate chips and butter; stir until smooth. Cool slightly. In a small bowl, beat egg and sugar. Stir in vanilla and chocolate mixture. Gradually add flour; fold in pecans.

2. Fill paper-lined muffin cups two-thirds full. Bake at 325° for 20-25 minutes or until tops begin to crack. Cool for 10 minutes before removing from pan to a wire rack.

Applesauce Spice Cupcakes

I began making these moist cupcakes in grade school and I still bake them today!

—EDNA HOFFMAN HEBRON, IN

PREP: 15 MIN. • **BAKE:** 25 MIN. + COOLING • **MAKES:** 1 DOZEN

- ⅓ **cup butter, softened**
- ¾ **cup sugar**
- 2 **eggs**
- 1 **teaspoon vanilla extract**
- 1⅓ **cups all-purpose flour**
- 1 **teaspoon baking powder**
- ½ **teaspoon baking soda**
- ½ **teaspoon salt**
- 1 **teaspoon ground cinnamon**
- ½ **teaspoon ground nutmeg**
- ⅛ **teaspoon ground cloves**
- ¾ **cup applesauce**
  Cream cheese frosting

1. In a large bowl, cream butter and sugar until light and fluffy. Add eggs, one at a time, beating well after each addition. Beat in vanilla. Combine the dry ingredients; add to creamed mixture alternately with applesauce.

2. Fill greased or paper-lined muffin cups two-thirds full. Bake at 350° for 25 minutes or until a toothpick inserted near the center comes out clean. Cool for 10 minutes before removing to a wire rack to cool completely. Frost the cupcakes.

Lemon Chiffon Cake

This moist, airy cake was my dad's favorite. Mom revamped the original recipe to include lemons. I'm not much of a baker, so I don't make it very often. But when I do, my family is thrilled!

—**TRISHA KAMMERS** CLARKSTON, WA

PREP: 25 MIN. • **BAKE:** 50 MIN. + COOLING • **MAKES:** 16 SERVINGS

- 7 eggs, separated
- 2 cups all-purpose flour
- 1½ cups sugar
- 3 teaspoons baking powder
- 1 teaspoon salt
- ¾ cup water
- ½ cup canola oil
- 4 teaspoons grated lemon peel
- 2 teaspoons vanilla extract
- ½ teaspoon cream of tartar

LEMON FROSTING

- ⅓ cup butter, softened
- 3 cups confectioners' sugar
- ¼ cup lemon juice
- 4½ teaspoons grated lemon peel
  Dash salt

1. Place egg whites in a large bowl; let stand at room temperature for 30 minutes.

2. In a large bowl, combine the flour, sugar, baking powder and salt. In another bowl, whisk the egg yolks, water, oil, lemon peel and vanilla; add to dry ingredients and beat until well blended. Add cream of tartar to egg whites; beat on medium speed until stiff peaks form. Fold into batter.

3. Gently spoon into an ungreased 10-in. tube pan. Cut through batter with a knife to remove air pockets. Bake on the lowest oven rack at 325° for 50-55 minutes or until cake springs back when lightly touched. Immediately invert pan; cool completely, about 1 hour.

4. Run a knife around side and center tube of pan. Remove cake to a serving plate. In a small bowl, combine frosting ingredients; beat until smooth. Spread over top of cake, allowing frosting to drape down the sides.

Chocolate Cupcakes

This classic recipe is simply amazing! Try sitting down with a glass of cold milk and see if you can eat just one!

—**MARLENE MARTIN** COUNTRY HARBOUR MINES, NS

PREP: 20 MIN. • **BAKE:** 15 MIN. + COOLING • **MAKES:** 16 CUPCAKES

- ½ cup butter, softened
- 1 cup sugar
- 1 egg
- 1 teaspoon vanilla extract
- 1½ cups all-purpose flour
- ½ cup baking cocoa
- 1 teaspoon baking soda
- ¼ teaspoon salt
- ½ cup water
- ½ cup buttermilk
  Frosting of your choice

1. In a small bowl, cream butter and sugar until light and fluffy. Beat in egg and vanilla. Combine the flour, cocoa, baking soda and salt; gradually add to creamed mixture alternately with water and buttermilk, beating well after each addition.

2. Fill paper-lined muffin cups two-thirds full. Bake at 375° for 12-15 minutes or until a toothpick inserted near the center comes out clean. Cool for 10 minutes before removing from pans to wire racks to cool completely. Frost the cupcakes.

Cream-Filled Pumpkin Cupcakes

Here's a deliciously different use for pumpkin. Bursting with flavor and plenty of eye-catching appeal, these sweet and spicy filled cupcakes are bound to dazzle your family.

—ALI JOHNSON PETERSBURG, PA

PREP: 35 MIN. • **BAKE:** 20 MIN. + COOLING
MAKES: ABOUT 1½ DOZEN

- 2 **cups sugar**
- ¾ **cup canola oil**
- 1 **can (15 ounces) solid-pack pumpkin**
- 4 **eggs**
- 2 **cups all-purpose flour**
- 2 **teaspoons baking soda**
- 1 **teaspoon salt**
- 1 **teaspoon baking powder**
- 1 **teaspoon ground cinnamon**

FILLING

- 1 **tablespoon cornstarch**
- 1 **cup milk**
- ½ **cup shortening**
- ¼ **cup butter, softened**
- 2 **cups confectioners' sugar**
- ½ **teaspoon vanilla extract, optional**
  Whole cloves, optional

1. In a large bowl, beat the sugar, oil, pumpkin and eggs until well blended. Combine the flour, baking soda, salt, baking powder and cinnamon; gradually beat into pumpkin mixture until well blended.

2. Fill paper-lined muffin cups two-thirds full. Bake at 350° for 18-22 minutes or until a toothpick inserted near the center comes out clean. Cool for 10 minutes before removing from pans to wire racks to cool completely.

3. For filling, combine cornstarch and milk in a small saucepan until smooth. Bring to a boil, stirring constantly. Remove from the heat; cool to room temperature.

4. In a large bowl, cream the shortening, butter and confectioners' sugar until light and fluffy. Beat in vanilla if desired. Gradually add the cornstarch mixture, beating until smooth.

5. Using a sharp knife, cut a 1-in. circle 1 in. deep in the top of each cupcake. Carefully remove tops and set aside. Spoon or pipe filling into the cupcakes. Replace tops. If desired, add a clove "pumpkin stem" to each top.

Pineapple Upside-Down Cake

Try this traditional dessert, which has been updated with packaged items for convenience. It has the same fabulous flavor as any from-scratch version.

—KAREN ANN BLAND GOVE, KS

PREP: 10 MIN. • **BAKE:** 45 MIN. • **MAKES:** 12-15 SERVINGS

- ¼ **cup butter, melted**
- 1 **can (20 ounces) sliced pineapple**
- 10 **pecan halves**
- 1 **jar (12 ounces) apricot preserves**
- 1 **package (18¼ ounces) yellow cake mix**

1. Pour butter into a well-greased 13-in. x 9-in. baking dish. Drain pineapple, reserving ¼ cup juice. Arrange pineapple slices in prepared pan; place a pecan half in the center of each slice. Combine the apricot preserves and reserved pineapple juice; spoon over pineapple slices.

2. Prepare cake batter according to package directions; pour over pineapple.

3. Bake at 350° for 45-50 minutes or until a toothpick inserted near the center comes out clean. Immediately invert onto a large serving platter. Cool slightly; serve warm.

Cherry Pound Cake

Nothing beats this rich, classic pound cake, with the pretty surprise of bright red cherries tucked inside and dotting the creamy icing. This one's perfect for the holidays.

—EVVA FOLTZ HANES CLEMMONS, NC

PREP: 25 MIN. • **BAKE:** 1¼ HOURS + COOLING • **MAKES:** 12 SERVINGS

- 1 jar (10 ounces) maraschino cherries, divided
- 1 cup butter, softened
- ½ cup shortening
- 3 cups sugar
- 6 eggs
- 1 teaspoon vanilla extract
- ¾ cup 2% milk
- 3¾ cups all-purpose flour

FROSTING
- 1 package (3 ounces) cream cheese, softened
- ¼ cup butter, softened
- 3¾ cups confectioners' sugar
- ½ teaspoon vanilla extract
- ½ cup flaked coconut
- ¼ cup chopped walnuts
  Additional coconut, optional

1. Drain and chop cherries, reserving juice; set aside.
2. In a large bowl, cream the butter, shortening and sugar until light and fluffy. Add eggs, one at a time, beating well after each addition. Beat in vanilla. Combine milk and ¼ cup reserved cherry juice; add to creamed mixture alternately with flour, beating well after each addition. Fold in ½ cup cherries.
3. Transfer to a greased and floured 10-in. tube pan. Bake at 325° for 1¼ to 1½ hours or until a toothpick inserted near the center comes out clean. Cool for 10 minutes; remove from pan to a wire rack to cool completely.
4. In a large bowl, beat cream cheese and butter until fluffy. Add the confectioners' sugar, vanilla and enough reserved cherry juice to achieve spreading consistency. Fold in coconut and remaining chopped cherries. Frost the cake. Sprinkle with the walnuts and additional coconut if desired.

Black Forest Cake

When my daughter went to Germany on a backpacking trip, she said the streets were lined with pastry shops. Here's an easy take on one of the country's most popular desserts.

—PATRICIA RUTHERFORD WINCHESTER, IL

PREP: 10 MIN. • **BAKE:** 25 MIN. + CHILLING • **MAKES:** 6-8 SERVINGS

1 **package (9 ounces) chocolate cake mix**
½ **cup water**
1 **egg**
1 **package (3 ounces) cream cheese, softened**
2 **tablespoons sugar**
1 **carton (8 ounces) frozen whipped topping, thawed**
1 **can (21 ounces) cherry pie filling**

1. In a small bowl, beat the cake mix, water and egg on medium speed for 3-4 minutes. Pour into a greased 9-in. springform pan; place pan on a baking sheet.
2. Bake at 350° for 23-25 minutes or until cake springs back when lightly touched. Cool on a wire rack.
3. In a small bowl, beat cream cheese and sugar until fluffy; fold in whipped topping. Spread pie filling over cake; top with cream cheese mixture. Cover and refrigerate for 4 hours. Remove sides of pan.

Heavenly Surprise Mini Cupcakes

My grandmother was an accomplished baker, and this was one of the many special desserts she enjoyed making. It's fun to bite into these dense chocolate goodies and discover an extra-delicious treat inside.

—JORUN MEIERDING MANKATO, MN

PREP: 35 MIN. • **BAKE:** 15 MIN./BATCH + COOLING
MAKES: 6 DOZEN

FILLING

- 1 package (8 ounces) cream cheese, softened
- ⅓ cup sugar
- 1 egg
- ⅛ teaspoon salt
- 1 cup flaked coconut
- 1 cup finely chopped walnuts
- 1 cup (6 ounces) miniature semisweet chocolate chips

BATTER

- 2 cups sugar
- 1½ cups water
- ¾ cup canola oil
- 2 eggs
- 2 teaspoons vanilla extract
- 1 teaspoon white vinegar
- 3 cups all-purpose flour
- ½ cup baking cocoa
- 1 teaspoon baking soda
- 1 teaspoon salt

FROSTING

- ½ cup heavy whipping cream
- 1⅓ cups semisweet chocolate chips

1. For filling, in a small bowl, beat cream cheese and sugar until light and fluffy. Add egg and salt; mix well. Stir in the coconut, walnuts and chocolate chips. Set aside.

2. For batter, in a large bowl, beat the sugar, water, oil, eggs, vanilla and vinegar until well blended. Combine the flour, cocoa, baking soda and salt; gradually beat into oil mixture until blended.

3. Fill paper-lined miniature muffin cups one-third full with the batter. Drop filling by teaspoonfuls into the center of each. Top with additional batter, filling cups three-fourths full.

4. Bake at 350° for 12-15 minutes or until a toothpick inserted in the cake portion of a cupcake comes out clean. Cool for 10 minutes before removing from pans to wire racks to cool completely.

5. For frosting, in a small saucepan, melt chocolate with cream over low heat; stir until blended. Remove from the heat. Cool to room temperature. Frost cupcakes. Refrigerate leftovers.

NOTE *Cupcakes may also be baked in 30 paper-lined muffin cups for 20-25 minutes.*

Bakeshop **TIP**

Cupcake Baking Success

To allow good air circulation while baking cupcakes, leave at least 1 inch of space between the pans and between the sides of the oven. If using two oven racks, stagger the pans so that they are not direcly over one another. Switch pan positions and rotate them 180° halfway through baking. Cool in the pans for 10 minutes before removing and cooling completely on wire racks.

Cherry Cheese Torte

You can't help but impress people when you set out this lovely torte. It makes any occasion feel a bit more special. No one will guess how straightforward it really was!

—**LISA RADELET** BOULDER, CO

PREP: 20 MIN. + CHILLING • **MAKES:** 12 SERVINGS

- 2 **packages (3 ounces each) ladyfingers**
- 1 **package (8 ounces) cream cheese, softened**
- 1 **cup plus 1 teaspoon sugar, divided**
- 2 **teaspoons vanilla extract, divided**
- 2 **teaspoons lemon juice**
- 1 **teaspoon grated lemon peel**
- 2 **cups heavy whipping cream**
- 1 **can (21 ounces) cherry or blueberry pie filling**

1. Place a layer of ladyfingers on the bottom and around the sides of an ungreased 9-in. springform pan. In a large bowl, beat the cream cheese, 1 cup sugar and 1 teaspoon vanilla until smooth. Beat in lemon juice and peel.

2. In a small bowl, beat the cream until it begins to thicken. Add the remaining sugar and vanilla; beat until stiff peaks form. Fold into the cream cheese mixture. Spread half over crust.

3. Arrange remaining ladyfingers in a spoke pattern over top. Evenly spread with the remaining cream cheese mixture. Top with pie filling. Refrigerate overnight.

Jelly Gem Cupcakes

My mother taught me this simple way to fill cupcakes with fruit jelly. Take these tender treats to your next get-together and watch faces light up after just one bite.

—**EDITH HOLLIDAY** FLUSHING, MI

PREP: 20 MIN. • **BAKE:** 15 MIN. + COOLING • **MAKES:** 3 DOZEN

- 1 **cup shortening**
- 2 **cups sugar**
- 2 **eggs**
- 2 **teaspoons vanilla extract**
- 3½ **cups all-purpose flour**
- 5 **teaspoons baking powder**
- 1 **teaspoon salt**
- 1½ **cups 2% milk**
- ¾ **cup strawberry or grape jelly**
  Frosting of your choice
  Colored sprinkles, optional

1. In a large bowl, cream shortening and sugar until light and fluffy. Add eggs, one at a time, beating well after each addition. Beat in vanilla. Combine the flour, baking powder and salt; add to creamed mixture alternately with milk, beating well after each addition.

2. Fill 36 paper-lined muffin cups half full. Drop jelly by teaspoonfuls into the center of each.

3. Bake at 375° for 15-20 minutes or until a toothpick inserted in cupcake comes out clean. Cool for 10 minutes; remove from pans to wire racks to cool completely. Frost cupcakes; decorate with sprinkles if desired.

Cherry Cordial Cake Balls

Brandy and coffee add mild flavor to these scrumptious cherry cake balls.

—SUSAN WESTERFIELD ALBUQUERQUE, NM

PREP: 1 HOUR • **BAKE:** 35 MIN. + STANDING • **MAKES:** 6 DOZEN

- 1 **package (18¼ ounces) fudge marble cake mix**
- 1¼ **cups plus 3 tablespoons strong brewed coffee, divided**
- ¼ **cup canola oil**
- 3 **eggs**
- 1 **jar (10 ounces) maraschino cherries without stems, well drained**
- ⅓ **cup brandy**
- ¼ **cup cherry preserves**
- 1 **cup canned chocolate frosting**
- 4 **pounds milk chocolate candy coating, chopped**
- 2 **tablespoons shortening**

1. In a large bowl, combine the cake mix, 1¼ cups coffee, oil and eggs; beat on low speed for 30 seconds. Beat on medium for 2 minutes.

2. Pour batter into a greased and floured 13-in. x 9-in. baking pan. Bake at 350° for 30-35 minutes or until a toothpick inserted near the center comes out clean. Cool completely. Place cherries in a food processor; cover and process until coarsely chopped. Transfer to a small bowl; stir in brandy, preserves and remaining coffee. Crumble cake into a large bowl. Add frosting and cherry mixture; beat well. Shape into 1-in. balls.

3. In a microwave, melt candy coating and shortening; stir until smooth. Dip balls in chocolate mixture; allow excess to drip off. Place on waxed paper; let stand until set. Store in an airtight container overnight before serving.

Hummingbird Cake

This impressive cake is my dad's favorite, so I always make it for his birthday. It also makes a great Easter dessert and is lovely with a summer meal.

—NANCY ZIMMERMAN CAPE MAY COURT HOUSE, NJ

PREP: 40 MIN. • **BAKE:** 25 MIN. + COOLING • **MAKES:** 12 SERVINGS

- 2 **cups mashed ripe bananas**
- 1½ **cups canola oil**
- 3 **eggs**
- 1 **can (8 ounces) unsweetened crushed pineapple, undrained**
- 1½ **teaspoons vanilla extract**
- 3 **cups all-purpose flour**
- 2 **cups sugar**
- 1 **teaspoon salt**
- 1 **teaspoon baking soda**
- 1 **teaspoon ground cinnamon**
- 1 **cup chopped walnuts**

PINEAPPLE FROSTING
- ¼ **cup shortening**
- 2 **tablespoons butter, softened**
- 1 **teaspoon grated lemon peel**
- ¼ **teaspoon salt**
- 6 **cups confectioners' sugar**
- ½ **cup unsweetened pineapple juice**
- 2 **teaspoons half-and-half cream**
  Chopped walnuts, optional

1. In a large bowl, beat the bananas, oil, eggs, pineapple and vanilla until well blended. Combine the flour, sugar, salt, baking soda and cinnamon; gradually beat into banana mixture until blended. Stir in walnuts.

2. Pour batter into three greased and floured 9-in. round baking pans. Bake at 350° for 25-30 minutes or until a toothpick inserted near the center comes out clean. Cool for 10 minutes before removing from pans to wire racks to cool completely.

3. For frosting, in a large bowl, beat the shortening, butter, lemon peel and salt until fluffy. Add confectioners' sugar alternately with pineapple juice. Beat in cream. Spread between layers and over top and sides of cake. Sprinkle with walnuts if desired.

Bakeshop HOW-TO

Easily Finishing a Cake

Peaks: Press the flat side of a tablespoon or teaspoon into the frosting and pull straight up, forming a peak. Repeat over top and sides of cake.

Zigzags: Run the tines of a table fork through the frosting in a wavy motion.

Waves: Use the back of a tablespoon or teaspoon to make a small twisting motion in one direction. Then move the spoon over a little and make another twist in the opposite direction. Repeat until entire cake is covered.

Chocolate Cream Cheese Cupcakes

I got the recipe for these filled cupcakes from a dear friend many years ago. I have made them many times for my family and for church functions. They're irresistible.

—VIVIAN MORRIS CLEBURNE, TX

PREP: 30 MIN. • **BAKE:** 25 MIN. + COOLING • **MAKES:** 20 CUPCAKES

- 1 package (8 ounces) cream cheese, softened
- 1½ cups sugar, divided
- 1 egg
- 1 teaspoon salt, divided
- 1 cup (6 ounces) semisweet chocolate chips
- 1½ cups all-purpose flour
- ¼ cup baking cocoa
- 1 teaspoon baking soda
- 1 cup water
- ⅓ cup canola oil
- 1 tablespoon white vinegar

FROSTING
- 3¾ cups confectioners' sugar
- 3 tablespoons baking cocoa
- ½ cup butter, melted
- 6 tablespoons milk
- 1 teaspoon vanilla extract
- ⅓ cup chopped pecans

1. For filling, in a small mixing bowl, beat cream cheese and ½ cup sugar until smooth. Beat in egg and ½ teaspoon salt until combined. Fold in chocolate chips; set aside.

2. In a bowl, combine the flour, cocoa, baking soda, and remaining sugar and salt. In another bowl, whisk water, oil and vinegar; stir into dry ingredients just until moistened.

3. Fill paper-lined muffin cups half full with batter. Drop filling by heaping tablespoonfuls into the center of each. Bake at 350° for 24-26 minutes or until a toothpick inserted in cake comes out clean. Cool for 10 minutes; remove from pans to wire racks to cool completely.

4. For frosting, in a large bowl, combine confectioners' sugar, cocoa, butter, milk and vanilla; beat until blended. Frost the cupcakes; sprinkle with the pecans. Store in the refrigerator.

Coconut-Rum Cake Pops

Plan your own tropical escape with these surprisingly light-tasting pops. Angel food cake is a nice change of pace.

—TASTE OF HOME TEST KITCHEN

PREP: 1½ HOURS + CHILLING • **MAKES:** 4 DOZEN

- 1 package (16 ounces) angel food cake mix
- ¾ cup canned vanilla frosting
- 1 cup flaked coconut
- 1 teaspoon coconut extract
- ½ teaspoon rum extract
- 48 lollipop sticks
- 2½ pounds white candy coating, chopped
  - Lightly toasted flaked coconut

1. Prepare and bake cake mix according to the package directions. Cool completely on a wire rack.

2. Crumble cake into a large bowl. In a small bowl, combine the frosting, coconut and extracts; stir into cake until blended. Shape into 1-in. balls. Place on baking sheets; insert sticks. Freeze at least 2 hours or refrigerate at least 3 hours or until cake balls are firm.

3. In a microwave, melt candy coating; stir until smooth. Dip each cake pop in coating; allow excess to drip off. Roll in toasted coconut. Insert cake pops into a foam block to stand. Let stand until set.

Cinnamon Mocha Cupcakes

Like to end a meal with a little something sweet? These chocolaty cupcakes will do the trick. They don't make a huge batch, so you can share a few and enjoy the rest yourself!

—EDNA HOFFMAN HEBRON, IN

PREP: 15 MIN. • **BAKE:** 20 MIN. + COOLING • **MAKES:** 8 CUPCAKES

- ¼ cup butter, softened
- ⅔ cup sugar
- 1 egg
- ½ teaspoon vanilla extract
- ¾ cup plus 2 tablespoons all-purpose flour
- ¼ cup baking cocoa
- ½ teaspoon baking soda
- ½ teaspoon salt
- ¼ teaspoon baking powder
- ¼ teaspoon ground cinnamon
- ¼ cup strong brewed coffee, room temperature
- 3 tablespoons buttermilk
- 1 cup chocolate frosting
- ¾ teaspoon instant coffee granules
- 1 teaspoon hot water

1. In a small bowl, cream the butter and sugar until light and fluffy. Beat in egg and vanilla. Combine the flour, cocoa, baking soda, salt, baking powder and cinnamon; add to the creamed mixture alternately with the coffee and buttermilk, beating well after each addition.

2. Fill paper-lined muffin cups half full with batter. Bake at 350° for 18-20 minutes or until a toothpick comes out clean. Cool for 5 minutes before removing from pan to a wire rack to cool completely.

3. Place the frosting in a bowl. Dissolve coffee granules in hot water; stir into frosting until smooth. Frost cupcakes.

Sachertorte

Guests will be surprised to hear this dessert starts with a basic cake mix. Each bite features the delightful flavors of chocolate, almonds and apricots.

—TASTE OF HOME TEST KITCHEN

PREP: 30 MIN. • **BAKE:** 25 MIN. + CHILLING • **MAKES:** 16 SERVINGS

- ½ cup chopped dried apricots
- ½ cup amaretto
- 1 package (18¼ ounces) devil's food cake mix
- ¾ cup water
- ⅓ cup canola oil
- 3 eggs

APRICOT FILLING

- ⅔ cup apricot preserves
- 1 tablespoon amaretto

FROSTING

- ½ cup butter, softened
- 4½ cups confectioners' sugar
- ¾ cup baking cocoa
- ⅓ cup boiling water
- 1 tablespoon amaretto
- 1 cup sliced almonds, toasted

1. In a small bowl, combine apricots and amaretto; let stand for 15 minutes. In a large bowl, combine the cake mix, water, oil, eggs and apricot mixture. Beat on low speed for 30 seconds; beat on medium for 2 minutes.

2. Pour the batter into two greased and floured 9-in. round baking pans. Bake at 350° for 25-30 minutes or until a toothpick inserted near the center comes out clean. Cool for 10 minutes before removing from pans to wire racks to cool completely.

3. For filling, in a small saucepan, heat apricot preserves and amaretto on low until preserves are melted, stirring occasionally; set aside.

4. For frosting, in a large bowl, cream the butter, confectioners' sugar and cocoa until light and fluffy. Add water and amaretto. Beat on low speed until combined. Beat on medium for 1 minute or until frosting achieves spreading consistency.

5. Cut each cake horizontally into two layers. Place a bottom layer on a serving plate; spread with half of the filling. Top with another cake layer; spread with ⅔ cup frosting. Top with third layer and remaining filling. Top with remaining cake layer.

6. Frost top and sides of cake with remaining frosting. Gently press almonds into the sides. Refrigerate for several hours before slicing.

Cream Cheese Sheet Cake

This tender, buttery sheet cake with a thin layer of fudge frosting is perfect for a crowd. It's always popular at potlucks and parties. It's not uncommon to see folks going back for second and even third slices.

—GAYE MANN ROCKY MOUNT, NC

PREP: 20 MIN. + COOLING • **BAKE:** 30 MIN. + COOLING
MAKES: 24-30 SERVINGS

- 1 cup plus 2 tablespoons butter, softened
- 2 packages (3 ounces each) cream cheese, softened
- 2¼ cups sugar
- 6 eggs
- ¾ teaspoon vanilla extract
- 2¼ cups cake flour

FROSTING

- 1 cup sugar
- ⅓ cup evaporated milk
- ½ cup butter, cubed
- ½ cup semisweet chocolate chips

1. In a large bowl, cream the butter, cream cheese and sugar until light and fluffy. Add eggs, one at a time, beating well after each addition. Beat in vanilla. Add flour until well blended.

2. Pour into a greased 15-in. x 10-in. x 1-in. baking pan. Bake at 325° for 30-35 minutes or until a toothpick inserted near the center comes out clean. Cool completely on a wire rack.

3. For frosting, in a small saucepan, combine the sugar and milk; bring to a boil over medium heat. Cover and cook for 3 minutes (do not stir). Stir in the butter and chocolate chips until melted. Cool slightly. Stir the frosting; spread over top of cake.

Mini Blueberry Bundt Cakes

These pretty little blueberry cakes are topped with a yummy lemon-flavored glaze. The recipe makes three tiny cakes so you might want to bake up a couple of batches if you plan to serve more people.

—CATHY ISAAK RIVERS, MB

PREP: 20 MIN. • **BAKE:** 25 MIN. + COOLING • **MAKES:** 3 SERVINGS

¼ **cup butter, softened**
½ **cup sugar**
1 **egg**
¼ **cup 2% milk**
½ **teaspoon vanilla extract**
1 **cup all-purpose flour**
1 **teaspoon baking powder**
¼ **teaspoon salt**
1½ **cups fresh or frozen blueberries**

LEMON ICING
½ **cup confectioners' sugar**
1½ **teaspoons 2% milk**
1 **teaspoon lemon juice**
   Additional blueberries, optional

1. In a small bowl, cream butter and sugar. Beat in the egg, milk and vanilla. Combine the flour, baking powder and salt; beat into creamed mixture. Fold in blueberries.

2. Pour into three 4-in. fluted tube pans coated with cooking spray. Bake at 350° for 25-30 minutes or until a toothpick inserted near the center comes out clean. Cool for 10 minutes before removing from pans to wire racks to cool completely.

3. For icing, in a small bowl, combine the confectioners' sugar, milk and lemon juice; drizzle over cakes. Garnish with additional berries if desired.

NOTE *If using frozen blueberries, use without thawing to avoid discoloring the batter.*

Caramel Apple Cupcakes

Bring these extra-special cupcakes to your next bake sale and watch how quickly they disappear! Kids will go for the fun appearance and tasty toppings, while adults will appreciate the moist spiced cake underneath.

—DIANE HALFERTY CORPUS CHRISTI, TX

PREP: 25 MIN. • **BAKE:** 20 MIN. + COOLING • **MAKES:** 1 DOZEN

1 **package (18¼ ounces) spice cake mix or 1 package (18 ounces) carrot cake mix**
2 **cups chopped peeled tart apples**
20 **caramels**
3 **tablespoons 2% milk**
1 **cup finely chopped pecans, toasted**
12 **Popsicle sticks**

1. Prepare cake batter according to package directions; fold in apples.

2. Fill 12 greased or paper-lined jumbo muffin cups three-fourths full. Bake at 350° for 20 minutes or until a toothpick inserted near the center comes out clean. Cool for 10 minutes before removing from pans to wire racks to cool completely.

3. In a small saucepan, cook the caramels and milk over low heat until smooth. Spread over the cupcakes. Sprinkle with the pecans. Insert a wooden stick into the center of each cupcake.

Chai Cupcakes

You'll get a double dose of the the spicy blend that's frequently used to flavor tea in these tender single-size cakes. Both the cupcake and frosting use the sweet blend of spices.

—TASTE OF HOME TEST KITCHEN

PREP: 25 MIN. • **BAKE:** 25 MIN. + COOLING • **MAKES:** 1 DOZEN

- ½ teaspoon each ground ginger, cinnamon, cardamom and cloves
- ⅛ teaspoon pepper
- ½ cup butter, softened
- 1 cup sugar
- 1 egg
- ½ teaspoon vanilla extract
- 1½ cups cake flour
- 1½ teaspoons baking powder
- ¼ teaspoon salt
- ⅔ cup 2% milk

FROSTING
- 6 tablespoons butter, softened
- 3 cups confectioners' sugar
- ¾ teaspoon vanilla extract
- 3 to 4 tablespoons 2% milk
  Ground cinnamon

1. In a small bowl, combine the ginger, cinnamon, cardamom, cloves and pepper; set aside.

2. In a large bowl, cream butter and sugar until light and fluffy. Beat in egg and vanilla. Combine the flour, baking powder, salt and 1½ teaspoons spice mixture. Gradually add to creamed mixture alternately with milk, beating well after each addition.

3. Fill paper-lined muffin cups two-thirds full. Bake at 350° for 24-28 minutes or until a toothpick inserted near the center comes out clean. Cool for 10 minutes before removing from pans to wire racks to cool completely.

4. In a large bowl, beat butter until fluffy; beat in the confectioners' sugar, vanilla and remaining spice mixture until smooth. Add enough milk to reach desired consistency. Pipe frosting over cupcakes; sprinkle with cinnamon.

Pumpkin Spice Layer Cake

No one will guess this stunning dessert with yummy cinnamon frosting started with a mix. It's a perfect treat year-round.
—**LINDA MURRAY** ALLENSTOWN, NH

PREP: 25 MIN. • **BAKE:** 25 MIN. + COOLING • **MAKES:** 10-12 SERVINGS

- 1 **package (18¼ ounces) yellow cake mix**
- 3 **eggs**
- 1 **cup water**
- 1 **cup canned pumpkin**
- 1¾ **teaspoons ground cinnamon, divided**
- ¼ **teaspoon ground ginger**
- ¼ **teaspoon ground nutmeg**
- 2½ **cups vanilla frosting**
- 1¼ **cups chopped walnuts**

1. In a large bowl, combine the cake mix, eggs, water, pumpkin, 1 teaspoon cinnamon, ginger and nutmeg; beat on low speed for 30 seconds. Beat on medium for 2 minutes.

2. Pour into two well-greased and floured 9-in. round baking pans. Bake at 375° for 25-30 minutes or until a toothpick inserted near the center comes out clean. Cool for 10 minutes before removing from pans to wire racks to cool completely.

3. Combine frosting and remaining cinnamon; spread between layers and over top and sides of cake. Press walnuts lightly into frosting on sides of cake.

Orange Grove Cake

A few years ago, I won Best in Show at the Western Idaho State Fair for this citrusy cake with its luscious filling and creamy frosting. It's bursting with orange flavor.

—AMANDA BOWYER CALDWELL, ID

PREP: 55 MIN. + CHILLING • **BAKE:** 20 MIN. + COOLING
MAKES: 16 SERVINGS

- 1 **cup butter, softened**
- 1¾ **cups sugar**
- 4 **eggs**
- ⅓ **cup orange juice**
- 2 **teaspoons grated orange peel**
- 3 **cups cake flour**
- 2½ **teaspoons baking powder**
- ½ **teaspoon salt**
- ⅔ **cup 2% milk**

FILLING

- ½ **cup sugar**
- 1 **tablespoon plus 2 teaspoons cornstarch**
- ⅔ **cup orange juice**
- 2 **tablespoons water**
- 3 **egg yolks, beaten**
- 2 **tablespoons lemon juice**
- 1 **teaspoon grated orange peel**
- ⅛ **teaspoon salt**

SYRUP

- ½ **cup sugar**
- ⅓ **cup water**
- ¼ **cup orange juice**
- 1 **teaspoon orange extract**

FROSTING

- 1 **cup butter, softened**
- 4 **cups confectioners' sugar**
- 3 **tablespoons heavy whipping cream**
- 1 **teaspoon grated orange peel**
- 1 **teaspoon orange extract**
- ¼ **teaspoon salt**

1. In a large bowl, cream butter and sugar until light and fluffy. Add eggs, one at a time, beating well after each addition. Beat in orange juice and peel. Combine the flour, baking powder and salt; add to the creamed mixture alternately with milk, beating well after each addition.

2. Transfer to two greased and floured 9-in. round baking pans. Bake at 350° for 20-25 minutes or until a toothpick inserted near the center ot the cake comes out clean. Cool for 10 minutes before removing from pans to wire racks to cool completely.

3. For filling, in a small saucepan, combine sugar and cornstarch. Stir in orange juice and water until smooth. Bring to a boil; cook and stir for 1 minute or until thickened. Remove from the heat.

4. Stir a small amount of hot mixture into egg yolks; return all to the pan, stirring constantly. Bring to a gentle boil; cook and stir 1 minute longer. Remove from the heat; gently stir in the lemon juice, orange peel and salt. Cool to room temperature without stirring. Refrigerate for 1 hour.

5. For syrup, in a small saucepan, bring the sugar, water and orange juice to a boil. Reduce heat; simmer, uncovered, for 10 minutes or until reduced to about ½ cup. Remove from the heat; stir in extract. Cool.

6. For frosting, in a large bowl, beat butter until light and fluffy. Add the remaining ingredients; beat until smooth

7. Cut each cake horizontally into two layers. Place bottom layer on a serving plate; brush with 2 tablespoons syrup and spread with ⅓ cup filling. Repeat layers twice. Top with remaining cake layer; brush with remaining syrup. Frost top and sides of cake.

Hawaiian Sunset Cake

This three-layer orange cake is lovely enough to share—though you may not want to!—yet it's so simple to fix that you'll find yourself making it all the time. A boxed mix keeps it convenient while the pineapple-coconut filling makes it feel extra special.

—KARA DE LA VEGA SANTA ROSA, CA

PREP: 20 MIN. + CHILLING • **BAKE:** 25 MIN. + COOLING
MAKES: 16 SERVINGS

- 1 **package (18¼ ounces) white or orange cake mix**
- 1½ **cups milk**
- 1 **package (3.4 ounces) instant vanilla pudding mix**
- 1 **package (3 ounces) orange gelatin**
- 4 **eggs**
- ½ **cup canola oil**

FILLING

- 1 **can (20 ounces) crushed pineapple, drained**
- 2 **cups sugar**
- 1 **package (10 ounces) flaked coconut**
- 1 **cup (8 ounces) sour cream**
- 1 **carton (8 ounces) frozen whipped topping, thawed**
  Toasted coconut, optional

1. In a large bowl, combine first six ingredients; beat on low speed for 30 seconds. Beat on medium for 2 minutes.
2. Pour into three greased and floured 9-in. round baking pans. Bake at 350° for 25-30 minutes or until a toothpick inserted near the center of the cake comes out clean. Cool for 10 minutes before removing from pans to wire racks to cool completely.
3. In a large bowl, combine the pineapple, sugar, coconut and sour cream. Set aside 1 cup for frosting. Place one cake on a serving plate; top with a third of the remaining pineapple mixture. Repeat layers twice.
4. Fold whipped topping into the reserved pineapple mixture. Spread over top and sides of cake. Sprinkle with toasted coconut if desired. Refrigerate until serving.

Cannoli Cupcakes

These jumbo cupcakes feature a fluffy cannoli-like filling. White chocolate curls on top are the crowning touch.

—TASTE OF HOME TEST KITCHEN

PREP: 50 MIN. • **BAKE:** 25 MIN. + COOLING • **MAKES:** 8 CUPCAKES

- 1 **package (18¼ ounces) white cake mix**
- ¾ **cup heavy whipping cream, divided**
- 1 **cup ricotta cheese**
- 1 **cup confectioners' sugar**
- ½ **cup Mascarpone cheese**
- ¼ **teaspoon almond extract**
- ½ **cup chopped pistachios**
- 4 **ounces white baking chocolate, chopped**
  White chocolate curls

1. Prepare cake mix batter according to the package directions. Fill paper-lined jumbo muffin cups three-fourths full. Bake according to package directions for 24-28 minutes or until a toothpick inserted near the center comes out clean. Cool for 10 minutes before removing from pans to wire racks to cool completely.
2. In a small bowl, beat ½ cup cream until stiff peaks form; set aside. In a large bowl, combine the ricotta cheese, confectioners' sugar, Mascarpone cheese and extract until smooth. Fold in pistachios and the whipped cream.
3. Cut the top off of each cupcake. Spread or pipe cupcakes with cheese mixture; replace tops. In a small saucepan, melt white baking chocolate with remaining cream over low heat; stir until smooth. Remove from the heat. Cool to room temperature. Spoon over cupcakes; sprinkle with chocolate curls. Refrigerate leftovers.

Blueberry Angel Cupcakes

Like angel food cake, these yummy cupcakes don't last long at my house. They're so light and airy that they melt in your mouth.

—KATHY KITTELL LENEXA, KS

PREP: 25 MIN. • **BAKE:** 15 MIN. + COOLING • **MAKES:** 2½ DOZEN

- **11 egg whites**
- **1 cup plus 2 tablespoons cake flour**
- **1½ cups sugar, divided**
- **1¼ teaspoons cream of tartar**
- **1 teaspoon vanilla extract**
- **½ teaspoon salt**
- **1½ cups fresh or frozen blueberries**
- **1 teaspoon grated lemon peel**

GLAZE
- **1 cup confectioners' sugar**
- **3 tablespoons lemon juice**

1. Place egg whites in a large bowl; let stand at room temperature for 30 minutes. Sift together flour and ½ cup sugar three times; set aside.

2. Add cream of tartar, vanilla and salt to egg whites; beat on medium speed until soft peaks form. Gradually add remaining sugar, about 2 tablespoons at a time, beating on high until stiff glossy peaks form and sugar is dissolved. Gradually fold in flour mixture, about ½ cup at a time. Fold in blueberries and lemon peel.

3. Fill paper-lined muffin cups three-fourths full. Bake at 375° for 14-17 minutes or until cupcakes spring back when lightly touched. Immediately remove from pans to wire racks to cool completely.

4. In a small bowl, whisk the confectioners' sugar and lemon juice until smooth. Brush over the cupcakes. Let stand until set.

NOTE *If using frozen blueberries, use without thawing to avoid discoloring the batter.*

Boston Cream Pie

This classic dessert can be made for a crowd without much fuss. It's pretty, tasty and always popular at picnics and potlucks.

—**CLARA HONEYAGER** NORTH PRAIRIE, WI

PREP: 20 MIN. + CHILLING • **BAKE:** 25 MIN. + COOLING
MAKES: 24 SERVINGS

- 1 package (18¼ ounces) yellow cake mix
- 2¾ cups cold milk
- 1 package (5.1 ounces) instant vanilla pudding mix
- 1 jar (16 ounces) hot fudge ice cream topping, warmed
- 24 maraschino cherries with stems, optional

1. Prepare and bake cake according to package directions, using a greased 13-in. x 9-in. baking pan. Cool completely on a wire rack.

2. Meanwhile, in a large bowl, beat milk and pudding mix on low for 2-3 minutes. Cover and chill for at least 30 minutes. Cut cake into 24 pieces; split each piece horizontally. Place about 1 heaping tablespoon of pudding between layers. Spread each with 1 tablespoon fudge topping and garnish with a cherry if desired.

Poppy Seed Chiffon Cake

This attractive cake never fails to please. It's a great choice for that special birthday celebration.

—**MARILYN BECK** MEDICINE HAT, AB

PREP: 70 MIN. + STANDING • **BAKE:** 50 MIN. + COOLING
MAKES: 16 SERVINGS

- ½ cup poppy seeds
- 1 cup water
- 8 eggs
- 2 cups all-purpose flour
- 1½ cups sugar
- 3 teaspoons baking powder
- 1 teaspoon salt
- ¼ teaspoon baking soda
- ½ cup canola oil
- 2 teaspoons vanilla extract
- ½ teaspoon cream of tartar

GLAZE
- 1 cup confectioners' sugar
- ¼ cup milk
- 2 tablespoons butter, melted
- ¼ teaspoon vanilla extract
  Edible flowers, optional

1. In a small bowl, soak the poppy seeds in water for 1 hour. Separate eggs; let stand at room temperature for 30 minutes.

2. In a large bowl, combine the flour, sugar, baking powder, salt and baking soda. In another bowl, whisk the egg yolks, oil, vanilla and poppy seed mixture. Add to dry ingredients; beat until well blended. In another large bowl, beat the egg whites and cream of tartar until stiff peaks form. Fold into the batter.

3. Pour into an ungreased 10-in. tube pan. Cut through batter with a knife to remove air pockets. Bake at 325° for 50-55 minutes or until cake springs back when lightly touched. Immediately invert pan; cool completely, about 1 hour. Run a knife around side and center tube of pan. Remove cake to a serving plate.

4. In a small bowl, combine glaze ingredients. Pour over cake; garnish with flowers if desired.

NOTE *Verify that flowers are edible and have not been treated with chemicals.*

Pies & Tarts

Chocolate Berry Tarts

I sometimes use a ready-made graham tart shells if I'm short on time. Either way, this rich berry dessert is an elegant treat.
—**LOUISE GILBERT** QUESNEL, BC

PREP: 20 MIN. + CHILLING • **MAKES:** 2 SERVINGS

- 5 tablespoons butter, divided
- 1 cup chocolate graham cracker crumbs (about 5 whole crackers)
- 2 teaspoons sugar
- 3 tablespoons heavy whipping cream
- ⅛ teaspoon ground cinnamon
- ⅔ cup semisweet chocolate chips
- ⅓ cup fresh blackberries
- ⅓ cup fresh raspberries
  Confectioners' sugar

1. In a small microwave-safe bowl, melt 4 tablespoons butter; stir in cracker crumbs and sugar. Press onto the bottom and up the sides of two 4-in. fluted tart pans with removable bottoms. Freeze for 1 hour or until firm.
2. In a small saucepan, combine the cream, cinnamon and remaining butter. Bring to a boil over medium heat, stirring constantly. Remove from the heat; stir in chocolate chips until melted. Pour into crusts. Refrigerate until firm, about 1 hour.
3. Just before serving, arrange berries over filling; sprinkle with confectioners' sugar.

Apple Pie in a Goblet

This dish is not only easy but very elegant. I obtained the recipe from a church cooking class and now make it often. You can serve it in bowls, but I always get more oohs and aahs when I put it in pretty goblets.
—**RENEE ZIMMER** GIG HARBOR, WA

PREP: 10 MIN. • **COOK:** 25 MIN. • **MAKES:** 4 SERVINGS

- 3 large tart apples, peeled and chopped
- ¼ cup sugar
- ¼ cup water
- ¾ teaspoon ground cinnamon
- ¼ teaspoon ground nutmeg
- 12 shortbread cookies, crushed
- 2 cups vanilla ice cream
  Whipped cream

1. In a large saucepan, combine the apples, sugar, water, cinnamon and nutmeg. Bring to a boil. Reduce heat; cover and simmer for 10 minutes or until apples are tender. Uncover; cook 9-11 minutes longer or until most of the liquid has evaporated. Remove from the heat.
2. In each of four goblets or parfait glasses, layer 1 tablespoon cookie crumbs, the ice cream and the apple mixture. Top with remaining cookie crumbs and whipped cream. Serve immediately.

Key Lime Mousse Cups

Light and lovely, these little key lime phyllo tarts are so refreshing served as an after-dinner treat—and they take just minutes to whip up!

—SUZANNE PAULEY RENTON, WA

START TO FINISH: 20 MIN. • **MAKES:** 2½ DOZEN

- **4** ounces cream cheese, softened
- **⅔** cup sweetened condensed milk
- **¼** cup key lime juice
- **½** cup heavy whipping cream, whipped
- **2** packages (1.9 ounces each) frozen miniature phyllo tart shells
  Fresh raspberries and lime wedges, optional

1. In a large bowl, beat the cream cheese, milk and juice until smooth; fold in whipped cream.

2. Spoon or pipe into tart shells. Garnish with raspberries and lime wedges if desired. Serve immediately.

Lemon Meringue Pie

My father loves lemon meringue pie and always wants one for his birthday. I rely on this recipe, which won first place at our county fair. It has a flaky crust, refreshing lemon filling and soft meringue with pretty golden peaks.

—**SUSAN JONES** BRADFORD, OH

PREP: 30 MIN. • **BAKE:** 30 MIN. + CHILLING • **MAKES:** 6-8 SERVINGS

- 1½ cups all-purpose flour
- ½ teaspoon salt
- ½ cup shortening
- ¼ cup cold water

FILLING
- 1½ cups sugar
- ¼ cup cornstarch
- 3 tablespoons all-purpose flour
- ¼ teaspoon salt
- 1½ cups water
- 3 egg yolks, lightly beaten
- 2 tablespoons butter
- ⅓ cup lemon juice
- 1 teaspoon grated lemon peel
- 1 teaspoon lemon extract

MERINGUE
- 3 egg whites
- ¼ teaspoon cream of tartar
- 6 tablespoons sugar

1. In a small bowl, combine flour and salt; cut in the shortening until crumbly. Gradually add water, tossing with a fork until dough forms a ball. Roll out pastry to fit a 9-in. pie plate. Transfer pastry to pie plate. Trim pastry to ½ in. beyond edge of pie plate; flute edges.

2. Line with a double thickness of heavy-duty foil. Bake at 450° for 8 minutes or until lightly browned. Remove foil; cool on a wire rack.

3. For filling, in a small saucepan, combine the sugar, cornstarch, flour and salt. Gradually stir in water until smooth. Cook and stir over medium-high heat until thickened and bubbly. Reduce heat; cook and stir 2 minutes longer. Remove from the heat. Stir a small amount of mixture into egg yolks; return all to the pan, stirring constantly. Bring to a gentle boil; cook and stir for 2 minutes. Remove from the heat. Gently stir in the butter, lemon juice, peel and extract until butter is melted. Pour hot filling into crust.

4. In a small bowl, beat egg whites and cream of tartar on medium speed until soft peaks form. Gradually beat in sugar, 1 tablespoon at a time, on high until stiff glossy peaks form and sugar is dissolved. Spread evenly over hot filling, sealing edges to crust.

5. Bake at 350° for 12-15 minutes or until the meringue is golden brown. Cool on a wire rack for 1 hour. Refrigerate for at least 3 hours before serving. Store leftovers in the refrigerator.

Bakeshop HOW-TO

Topping a Pie with Meringue

Spread meringue over hot filling to minimize "weeping" (the watery layer between the meringue and pie filling). Use a small spatula or butter knife to create attractive peaks. Seal meringue to the pie's edges to keep it from shrinking in the oven. Cool the pie away from drafts, then chill well before serving.

Cranberry Custard Meringue Pie

I love to serve this pie when my family is here. My grandchildren call it the red-colored pie with the fluff topping.
—**LEE BREMSON** KANSAS CITY, MO

PREP: 35 MIN. • **BAKE:** 15 MIN. + CHILLING
MAKES: 8 SERVINGS

- 3 **eggs, separated**
  Pastry for single-crust pie (9 inches)
- 1¾ **cups fresh or frozen cranberries**
- 1 **tablespoon grated orange peel**
- 1¼ **cups plus 6 tablespoons sugar, divided**
- 1 **cup water**
  Dash salt
  Dash ground cinnamon
- 4 **teaspoons plus ¼ cup cornstarch, divided**
- ¼ **cup orange juice**
- 2 **cups 2% milk, divided**
- 1 **tablespoon butter**
- 1 **teaspoon vanilla extract**
- ¼ **teaspoon cream of tartar**

1. Place egg whites in a small bowl; let stand at room temperature for 30 minutes.
2. Meanwhile, line a 9-in. pie plate with pastry; trim and flute edges. Line pastry shell with a double thickness of heavy-duty foil. Bake at 450° for 8 minutes. Remove foil; bake 5 minutes longer. Cool on a wire rack.
3. In a small saucepan, combine the cranberries, orange peel, ½ cup sugar, water, salt and cinnamon. Cook over medium heat until berries pop, about 15 minutes. Combine 4 teaspoons cornstarch and orange juice until smooth; stir into the cranberry mixture. Bring to a boil; cook and stir for 1-2 minutes or until thickened. Remove from the heat; set aside.
4. In another small saucepan, heat ¾ cup sugar and 1¾ cups milk until bubbles form around sides of pan. In a small bowl, combine the remaining cornstarch and milk. Whisk in egg yolks until blended. Add a small amount of hot milk mixture; return all to the pan, whisking constantly.
5. Whisk vigorously over medium heat as mixture begins to thicken (mixture will become very thick). Bring to a boil; whisk 2 minutes longer. Remove from the heat; whisk in butter and vanilla. Transfer custard to crust; spread evenly with reserved cranberry mixture.
6. Add cream of tartar to egg whites; beat on medium speed until soft peaks form. Gradually beat in remaining sugar, 1 tablespoon at a time, on high until stiff glossy peaks form and sugar is dissolved. Spread meringue over hot filling, sealing edges to crust.
7. Bake at 350° for 12-15 minutes or until meringue is golden brown. Cool on a wire rack for 1 hour. Refrigerate overnight.

Fresh Blueberry Pie

I've been making this dessert for decades. It represents our state well because Michigan is the leader in blueberry production. Nothing says summer like a piece of fresh blueberry pie!
—**LINDA KERNAN** MASON, MI

PREP: 15 MIN. + COOLING • **MAKES:** 6-8 SERVINGS

- ¾ **cup sugar**
- 3 **tablespoons cornstarch**
- ⅛ **teaspoon salt**
- ¼ **cup cold water**
- 5 **cups fresh blueberries, divided**
- 1 **tablespoon butter**
- 1 **tablespoon lemon juice**
  1 pastry shell (9 inches), baked

1. In a large saucepan, combine sugar, cornstarch, salt and water over medium heat until smooth. Add 3 cups blueberries. Bring to a boil; cook and stir for 2 minutes or until thickened and bubbly.
2. Remove from the heat. Add butter, lemon juice and remaining berries; stir until butter is melted. Cool.
3. Pour pie filling into prepared pastry shell. Refrigerate until serving.

Cranberry Pear Crisp Pie

Filled with a bubbling combination of cranberries and pears, this oat- and cinnamon-topped pie is a wonderful change of pace from the traditional.

—PRISCILLA GILBERT INDIAN HARBOUR BEACH, FL

PREP: 25 MIN. • **BAKE:** 55 MIN. + COOLING • **MAKES:** 8 SERVINGS

- 5 **cups sliced peeled fresh pears**
- 1 **tablespoon lemon juice**
- 1 **teaspoon vanilla extract**
- 1⅔ **cups fresh or frozen cranberries**
- ½ **cup packed brown sugar**
- ⅓ **cup all-purpose flour**
  Pastry for single-crust pie (9 inches)

TOPPING
- ¼ **cup all-purpose flour**
- ¼ **cup quick-cooking oats**
- 3 **tablespoons packed brown sugar**
- ¾ **teaspoon ground cinnamon**
- 2 **tablespoons cold butter**

1. Place the pears in a large bowl; sprinkle with lemon juice and vanilla. Add cranberries. Combine the brown sugar and flour; sprinkle over fruit and gently toss to coat.
2. Roll out pastry to fit a 9-in. pie plate. Transfer pastry to pie plate. Trim pastry to ½ in. beyond edge of plate; flute edges. Add filling.
3. In a small bowl, combine the flour, oats, brown sugar and cinnamon. Cut in the butter until crumbly. Sprinkle over filling.
4. Cover edges of pastry loosely with foil. Bake at 375° for 30 minutes. Remove foil; bake 25-30 minutes longer or until filling is bubbly. Cool on a wire rack.

Cran-Orange Pie in a Jar

These individual pudding pies in a jar are simply irresistible! Be prepared for compliments when you serve these.

—TASTE OF HOME TEST KITCHEN

PREP: 20 MIN. + CHILLING • **MAKES:** 4 SERVINGS

- 1 **cup graham cracker crumbs**
- 2 **tablespoons butter, melted**
- 2 **cups cold milk**
- 1 **package (3.3 ounces) instant white chocolate pudding mix**
- ½ **teaspoon grated orange peel**
- ½ **cup whole-berry cranberry sauce**

1. In a small bowl, combine cracker crumbs and butter. Press into the bottoms of four half-pint canning jars.

2. In another bowl, whisk milk and pudding mix for 2 minutes. Stir in orange peel. Let stand for 2 minutes or until soft-set. Spoon over crusts. Top with cranberry sauce. Cover and refrigerate for at least 1 hour.

Macaroon Cherry Pie

In summer, I use homegrown cherries in this amazing pie with a crunchy coconut topping. But canned tart cherries yield a dessert that's almost as delicious. I always bake this pie around Presidents' Day or Valentine's Day, but it's popular with my family the whole year through.

—LORI DANIELS BEVERLY, WV

PREP: 25 MIN. • **BAKE:** 40 MIN. + CHILLING • **MAKES:** 6-8 SERVINGS

   Pastry for single-crust pie (9 inches)
- 3 **cans (14½ ounces each) pitted tart cherries**
- 1 **cup sugar**
- ⅓ **cup cornstarch**
- ½ **teaspoon ground cinnamon**
- ¼ **teaspoon red food coloring, optional**

TOPPING
- 1 **egg, lightly beaten**
- 2 **tablespoons milk**
- 1 **tablespoon butter**
- ¼ **teaspoon almond extract**
- ¼ **cup sugar**
- ⅛ **teaspoon salt**
- 1 **cup flaked coconut**
- ½ **cup sliced almonds**

1. Line a 9-in. deep-dish pie plate with pastry. Trim to ½-in. beyond edge of plate; flute edges. Bake at 400° for 6 minutes; set aside.

2. Drain the cherries, reserving 1 cup juice. Set cherries aside. In a large saucepan, combine sugar and cornstarch; gradually stir in the cherry juice until blended. Bring to a boil over medium heat; cook and stir for 2 minutes or until thickened.

3. Remove from the heat; stir in cinnamon and food coloring if desired. Gently fold in cherries. Pour into crust. Cover edges loosely with foil. Bake at 400° for 20 minutes.

4. Meanwhile, in a large bowl, combine the first six topping ingredients. Stir in coconut and almonds.

5. Remove foil from pie; spoon topping over pie. Bake at 350° for 20 minutes or until topping is lightly browned. Cool on a wire rack for 1 hour. Chill for 4 hours or overnight before cutting.

Strawberry Tart

Looking for the perfect ending to any summertime meal? Here's a creamy swift-to-fix tart that boasts a surprise chocolate layer just next to the crust. You could also make individual tartlets instead of one big one.

—**DAWN TRINGALI** HAMILTON SQUARE, NJ

PREP: 30 MIN. + CHILLING • **YIELD:** 6-8 SERVINGS

- 1 **sheet refrigerated pie pastry**
- 3 **ounces German sweet chocolate, melted**
- 2 **packages (8 ounces each) cream cheese, softened**
- 3 **tablespoons heavy whipping cream**
- 2 **teaspoons vanilla extract**
- 1¾ **cups confectioners' sugar**
- 2½ **cups sliced fresh strawberries**
- ¼ **cup red currant jelly**

1. Press pastry onto the bottom and up the sides of an ungreased 9-in. fluted tart pan with a removable bottom. Place on a baking sheet. Bake at 450° for 10-12 minutes or until golden brown. Cool on a wire rack.

2. Spread melted chocolate over bottom of crust. Refrigerate for 5-10 minutes or until almost set. Meanwhile, in a large bowl, beat the cream cheese, cream and vanilla until smooth. Gradually beat in confectioners' sugar. Spread filling over chocolate layer.

3. Arrange strawberries over filling; brush with jelly. Refrigerate for at least 2 hours. Remove sides of pan before serving.

Easy Pumpkin Pie

Pumpkin pie does not have to be difficult to make. This recipe has wonderful flavor and is sure to be a hit at your holiday meal.

—**MARTY RUMMEL** TROUT LAKE, WA

PREP: 10 MIN. • **BAKE:** 50 MIN. + COOLING • **MAKES:** 8 SERVINGS

- 3 **eggs**
- 1 **cup canned pumpkin**
- 1 **cup evaporated milk**
- ½ **cup sugar**
- ¼ **cup maple syrup**
- 1 **teaspoon ground cinnamon**
- ½ **teaspoon salt**
- ½ **teaspoon ground nutmeg**
- ½ **teaspoon maple flavoring**
- ½ **teaspoon vanilla extract**
- 1 **frozen pie shell (9 inches)**
   Additional pie pastry, optional
   Whipped cream, optional

1. In a large bowl, beat the first 10 ingredients until smooth; pour into pastry shell. Cover the edges loosely with foil.

2. Bake at 400° for 10 minutes. Reduce heat to 350°; bake 40-45 minutes longer or until a knife inserted near the center comes out clean. Remove foil. Cool on a wire rack.

3. If decorative cutouts are desired, roll additional pastry to ⅛-in. thickness; cut out with 1-in. to 1½-in. leaf-shaped cookie cutters. With a sharp knife, score leaf veins on the cutouts.

4. Place on an ungreased baking sheet. Bake at 400° for 6-8 minutes or until golden brown. Remove to a wire rack to cool. Arrange around edge of pie. Garnish with whipped cream if desired.

Bumbleberry Pie

This pie recipe makes one of the flakiest crusts ever and is sure to impress! The filling is delicious with the different berries, tart apple and rhubarb.

—SUZANNE ALBERTS ONALASKA, WI

PREP: 20 MIN. + CHILLING • **BAKE:** 1 HOUR + COOLING
MAKES: 6-8 SERVINGS

1½ cups all-purpose flour
1 teaspoon salt
1 teaspoon sugar
1 cup cold butter
¼ cup cold water
FILLING
1 medium tart apple, peeled and diced
1 cup diced fresh or frozen rhubarb, thawed
1 cup fresh or frozen raspberries, thawed and drained
1 cup fresh or frozen blueberries, thawed and drained
1 cup sliced fresh or frozen strawberries, thawed and drained
1 cup sugar
½ cup all-purpose flour
1 tablespoon lemon juice

1. In a small bowl, combine the flour, salt and sugar. Cut in butter until mixture ensembles coarse crumbs. Gradually add water, tossing with a fork until a ball forms. Cover and refrigerate for 1 hour.
2. On a lightly floured surface, roll out half of the dough to fit a 9-in. pie plate. Transfer pastry to pie plate. Trim pastry to ½ in. beyond edge of plate.
3. In a large bowl, combine the filling ingredients; pour into crust. Roll out the remaining pastry; make a lattice crust. Seal and flute edges. Cover edges loosely with foil.
4. Bake at 400° for 20 minutes. Reduce heat to 350°; remove foil. Bake 40-45 minutes longer or until crust is golden brown and filling is bubbly. Cool on a wire rack.

Berry Shortbread Pizza

This beautiful berry-topped pizza tastes as good as it looks! It's impossible to resist the pecan shortbread crust, rich cheesecake-like layer, glossy berry topping and sprinkling of luscious fresh fruit. It's an ideal summertime dessert or take-along treat for a brunch buffet.

—MARIA SCHUSTER WOLF POINT, MT

PREP: 30 MIN. • **BAKE:** 10 MIN. + CHILLING
MAKES: 10-12 SERVINGS

- 1 **cup all-purpose flour**
- ¼ **cup confectioners' sugar**
- ½ **cup cold butter, cubed**
- ½ **cup chopped pecans**
- 1 **package (8 ounces) cream cheese, softened**
- 1 **egg**
- ⅓ **cup sugar**

TOPPING

- 1¾ **cups frozen mixed berries, thawed**
- ½ **cup sugar**
- 2 **tablespoons cornstarch**
- ¼ **cup water**
- 2½ **cups fresh strawberries, sliced**
- 2 **cups fresh blackberries**
- 2 **cups fresh raspberries**
- 1 **cup fresh blueberries**

1. In a bowl, combine flour and confectioners' sugar. Cut in butter until crumbly. Stir in pecans. Press into an ungreased 12-in. pizza pan.

2. Bake at 350° for 12-14 minutes or until crust is set and edges are lightly browned.

3. Meanwhile, in a bowl, beat cream cheese, egg and sugar until smooth. Spread over crust. Bake 8-10 minutes longer or until set. Cool to room temperature.

4. For topping, process mixed berries and sugar in a food processor until blended. In a small saucepan, combine cornstarch and water until smooth. Stir in mixed berry mixture until blended. Bring to a boil; cook and stir for 2 minutes or until thickened. Set mixture aside to cool, stirring frequently.

5. Spread berry mixture over the cream cheese layer. Arrange fresh berries on top. Refrigerate for at least 2 hours before slicing.

Mini Apple Tarts

These cute tarts have a golden crust brimming with a sweet-tart apple and cherry filling. They look and taste delicious!

—TASTE OF HOME TEST KITCHEN

PREP: 20 MIN. • **BAKE:** 20 MIN. + COOLING • **MAKES:** 4 SERVINGS

- **Pastry for single-crust pie (9 inches)**
- 1 **cup apple pie filling**
- 2 **tablespoons dried cherries**
- 1 **teaspoon finely chopped crystallized ginger**
- ¼ **teaspoon ground cinnamon**
- 1 **egg white**
- 1 **tablespoon water**
- 1 **teaspoon coarse sugar**

1. Divide pastry in half. On a lightly floured surface, roll each half into a 9-in. circle. Transfer to a parchment paper-lined baking sheet.

2. In a small bowl, combine the pie filling, cherries, ginger and cinnamon. Spoon over each pastry to within 2 in. of edges. Fold up edges of pastry over filling, leaving center uncovered. Beat egg white and water; brush over folded pastry. Sprinkle with sugar.

3. Bake at 400° for 20-25 minutes or until crusts are lightly browned. Using parchment paper, slide tarts onto a wire rack to cool.

Cherry Tarts

At our house, we celebrate George Washington's birthday with these tasty little cherry pies.

—**VERNA BURKHOLDER** DORCHESTER, WI

PREP: 30 MIN. + CHILLING • **BAKE:** 10 MIN. + COOLING
MAKES: 8 SERVINGS

- 1½ cups all-purpose flour
- ½ teaspoon salt
- ½ cup shortening
- 4 to 5 tablespoons cold water
- ¾ cup sugar
- 3 tablespoons cornstarch
- 2 cans (14½ ounces each) pitted tart cherries
- 1 tablespoon butter
- ¼ teaspoon almond extract
- 4 to 5 drops red food coloring, optional

1. In a small bowl, combine flour and salt. Cut in shortening until mixture resembles coarse crumbs. Add enough water until dough forms a ball. Refrigerate for 30 minutes.

2. On a lightly floured surface, roll out dough to ⅛-in. thickness. Cut out eight 5-in. circles. Place each over an inverted custard cup on an ungreased 15-in. x 10-in. x 1-in. baking pan; flute edges.

3. Bake at 450° for 10-11 minutes or until golden brown. Cool for 5 minutes before removing tart shells from custard cups; cool completely on wire racks.

4. For filling, in a large saucepan, combine sugar and cornstarch. Drain cherries, reserving 1 cup juice. Set the cherries aside. Stir the reserved juice into sugar mixture until smooth. Bring to a boil; cook and stir for 2 minutes or until thickened. Remove from the heat; stir in the cherries, butter, extract and food coloring if desired. Cool to room temperature. Spoon about ¼ cup filling into each tart shell.

Peach Blueberry Pie

What a flavor! That's what I hear most often after folks try this pie I invented one day when I was short of peaches for a full crust.

—**SUE THUMMA** SHEPHERD, MI

PREP: 15 MIN. • **BAKE:** 40 MIN. + COOLING • **MAKES:** 6-8 SERVINGS

- 1 cup sugar
- ⅓ cup all-purpose flour
- ½ teaspoon ground cinnamon
- ⅛ teaspoon ground allspice
- 3 cups sliced peeled fresh peaches
- 1 cup fresh or frozen unsweetened blueberries
  Pastry for double-crust pie (9 inches)
- 1 tablespoon butter
  Milk
  Cinnamon-sugar

1. In a large bowl, combine sugar, flour, cinnamon and allspice. Add the peaches and blueberries; toss gently.

2. Line pie plate with bottom crust; add the filling. Dot with butter. Top with a lattice crust. Brush crust with milk; sprinkle with cinnamon-sugar.

3. Bake at 400° for 40-45 minutes or until crust is golden brown and filling is bubbly. Cool completely on a wire rack.

NOTE *Frozen fruit may be used if it is thawed and well drained.*

Caramel Peanut Fantasy

Packed with peanuts and gooey with caramel, this do-ahead treat is one sweet dream of a dessert to serve company. With an easy cookie crust and scrumptious candy bar layers, it goes together quickly and will disappear just as fast!

—TASTE OF HOME TEST KITCHEN

PREP: 30 MIN. + CHILLING • **MAKES:** 12 SERVINGS

- 2 **cups crushed vanilla wafers (about 60 wafers)**
- ⅓ **cup butter, melted**
- 20 **caramels**
- 15 **miniature Snickers candy bars**
- ½ **cup caramel ice cream topping**
- ½ **cup heavy whipping cream, divided**
- 2 **cups salted peanuts, chopped**
- ¾ **cup semisweet chocolate chips**

1. In a small bowl, combine wafer crumbs and butter. Press onto the bottom of a greased 9-in. springform pan. Place on a baking sheet. Bake at 350° for 8-10 minutes. Cool on a wire rack.

2. In a heavy saucepan, combine the caramels, candy bars, caramel topping and ¼ cup cream; cook and stir over low heat until smooth and blended. Remove from the heat; stir in peanuts. Spread over crust. Cover and refrigerate for 1 hour.

3. In a microwave, melt chocolate chips and remaining cream; stir until smooth. Spread over caramel layer. Cover and refrigerate for 1 hour or until serving.

Cherry-Berry Streusel Pie

I entered this delicious pie in the Oklahoma State Fair and won a ribbon. It's very pretty and tastes great, especially served with a scoop of vanilla ice cream.

—ROSALIE SEEBECK BETHANY, OK

PREP: 1 HOUR + CHILLING • **BAKE:** 55 MIN. + COOLING
MAKES: 8 SERVINGS

2½ cups all-purpose flour
1 tablespoon sugar
1 teaspoon salt
1 cup cold butter, cubed
7 to 8 tablespoons cold water

FILLING
2 cans (21 ounces each) cherry pie filling
1 cup fresh or frozen raspberries
¼ cup packed brown sugar
¼ teaspoon ground cinnamon

TOPPING
1 cup yellow cake mix
½ cup chopped pecans, toasted
½ cup flaked coconut
¼ cup butter, melted
2 tablespoons 2% milk
2 tablespoons sugar

1. Place the flour, sugar and salt in a food processor; cover and pulse until blended. Add butter; cover and pulse until mixture resembles coarse crumbs. While processing, gradually add water until dough forms a ball.

2. Divide dough in half so that one portion is slightly larger than the other; wrap each in plastic wrap. Refrigerate for 30 minutes or until easy to handle.

3. On a lightly floured surface, roll out larger portion of dough to fit a 9-in. deep-dish pie plate. Transfer pastry to pie plate; trim pastry to ½ in. beyond edge of plate. Combine the filling ingredients; spoon into crust. Sprinkle with dry cake mix, pecans and coconut. Drizzle with butter.

4. Roll out remaining pastry to a 13-inch circle; cut into strips for a lattice top. While creating the lattice top, twist the pastry strips for a decorative effect. Seal and flute edges of pie.

5. Brush lattice top with milk; sprinkle with sugar. Cover edges loosely with foil. Bake at 375° for 55-65 minutes or until crust is golden brown and filling is bubbly. Cool on a wire rack.

Bakeshop TIP

Pretty Flower Pie

Try a flower-topped pie instead of a lattice crust. To make, use a paring knife to cut the pie dough into strips of various size. Use a 2- or 3-in. round cookie cutter to make the center of the flower. Lay the strips on top of the pie, overlapping them at random. Top with the round center in the middle. Adhere strips together by dabbing with water as you go, or brush egg wash over the finished pie. Sprinkle with coarse sugar and bake.

Classic Cherry Pie

My dad loves all kinds of fruit pies, especially this one, so I make it for his birthday every year.

—JOHANNA GEROW RAYTOWN, MO

PREP: 40 MIN. • **BAKE:** 35 MIN. + COOLING • **MAKES:** 6-8 SERVINGS

    2 cans (14 ounces each) pitted tart cherries
    1 cup sugar
    ¼ cup cornstarch
    ⅛ teaspoon salt
    2 tablespoons butter
    ½ teaspoon almond extract
    ½ teaspoon vanilla extract
    ¼ teaspoon red food coloring, optional
       Pastry for double-crust pie (9 inches)
    1 egg yolk, lightly beaten
       Additional sugar

1. Drain cherries, reserving 1 cup juice. Set cherries aside. In a large saucepan, combine the sugar, cornstarch and salt; gradually stir in reserved cherry juice until smooth. Bring to a boil; cook and stir for 2 minutes or until thickened. Remove from the heat; stir in the butter, extracts and food coloring if desired. Fold in cherries. Cool slightly.
2. Line a 9-in. pie plate with bottom crust; trim pastry even with edge. Pour filling into crust. Roll out remaining pastry; make a lattice crust. Trim, seal and flute edges. Brush lattice top with egg yolk. Sprinkle with additional sugar.
3. Cover edges loosely with foil. Bake at 425° for 15 minutes. Remove foil. Bake 20-25 minutes longer or until crust is golden brown and filling is bubbly. Cool on wire rack.

Bakeshop HOW-TO

Creating a Lattice-Topped Pie

Make a pastry for a double-crust pie. Line a 9-in. pie plate with the bottom pastry and trim to 1 in. beyond the edge of plate. Roll out remaining pastry to a 12-in. circle. With a fluted pastry wheel, pizza cutter or a sharp knife, cut pastry into ½-in.- to 1-in.-wide strips. Lay strips in rows about ½ in. to ¾ in. apart. (Use longer strips for the center of the pie and shorter strips for the sides.)

Fold every other strip halfway back. Starting at the center, add strips at right angles, lifting every other strip as the cross strips are put down.

Continue to add strips, lifting and weaving until lattice top is complete.

Trim strips even with pastry edge. Fold bottom pastry up and over ends of strips and seal. Flute edges.

Pear Frangipane Tart

Pears and almonds make a pleasing match in this classic dessert. It looks lovely with the sliced fruit arranged on top. How can something so simple taste this wonderful?

—LILY JULOW GAINESVILLE, FL

PREP: 25 MIN. • **BAKE:** 40 MIN. • **MAKES:** 6-8 SERVINGS

- 1¼ cups blanched almonds
- ½ cup plus 4½ teaspoons sugar, divided
- ⅓ cup all-purpose flour
- ¼ teaspoon salt
- 5 tablespoons cold butter, divided
- 2 eggs
- ¼ cup milk
- 1 can (15¼ ounces) pear halves, drained and thinly sliced

1. In a food processor, combine almonds and ½ cup sugar. Cover and process until blended; transfer to a bowl. Stir in flour and salt. In a microwave-safe bowl, melt 4 tablespoons butter; whisk in eggs and milk. Stir into almond mixture.

2. Pour into a greased 9-in. fluted tart pan with a removable bottom. Arrange pear slices over batter. Sprinkle with remaining sugar; dot with remaining butter.

3. Place on a baking sheet. Bake at 350° for 40-45 minutes or until crust is golden brown. Serve warm or at room temperature. Refrigerate leftovers.

German Apple Pie

I first tasted this pie many years ago when my children's baby sitter made it. I asked for the recipe and have prepared it many times since.

—MRS. WOODROW TAYLOR ADAMS CENTER, NY

PREP: 20 MIN. • **BAKE:** 65 MIN. + COOLING • **MAKES:** 8 SERVINGS

- 1½ cups all-purpose flour
- ½ teaspoon salt
- ½ cup shortening
- 1 teaspoon vanilla extract
- 2 to 3 tablespoons ice water

FILLING
- 1 cup sugar
- ¼ cup all-purpose flour
- 2 teaspoons ground cinnamon
- 6 cups sliced peeled tart apples
- 1 cup heavy whipping cream
  Whipped cream, optional

1. In a small bowl, combine flour and salt; cut in the shortening until crumbly. Add vanilla. Gradually add water, tossing with a fork until dough forms a ball. Roll out pastry to fit a 9-in. pie plate. Transfer pastry to pie plate. Trim pastry to ½ in. beyond edge of pie plate; flute edges.
2. For filling, combine the sugar, flour and cinnamon; sprinkle 3 tablespoons into crust. Layer with half of the apples; sprinkle with half of the remaining sugar mixture. Repeat layers. Pour cream over all.
3. Bake at 450° for 10 minutes. Reduce heat to 350° bake for 55-60 minutes or until the apples are tender. Cool on a wire rack. Store in the refrigerator. Serve with whipped cream if desired.

Spiced Winter Fruit Pie

This flavorful pie makes any gathering a celebration. It's a delightful choice for Thanksgiving or Christmas.

—MARIAN PLATT SEQUIM, WA

PREP: 25 MIN. • **BAKE:** 55 MIN. + COOLING • **MAKES:** 6-8 SERVINGS

- Pastry for double-crust pie (9 inches)
- ¾ cup sugar
- 3 tablespoons cornstarch
- 1 teaspoon ground cinnamon
- ¼ teaspoon ground allspice
- 5 cups sliced peeled fresh pears
- 2 cups fresh or frozen cranberries, thawed
- 2 tablespoons butter
- 1 egg
- 1 tablespoon whole milk
  Additional sugar

1. Line a 9-in. pie plate with bottom pastry; set aside. In a large bowl, combine the sugar, cornstarch, cinnamon and allspice. Add pears and cranberries; toss to coat. Spoon into crust; dot with butter.
2. Roll out remaining pastry; make a lattice crust. Trim, seal and flute edges.
3. In a small bowl, whisk egg and milk; brush over pastry. Sprinkle with additional sugar. Cover pie loosely with foil to prevent overbrowning.
4. Bake at 450° for 15 minutes. Reduce heat to 350° and remove foil; bake for 40-45 minutes or until crust is golden brown and filling is bubbly. Cool on a wire rack.

1. In a large bowl, toss the apples with lime juice. Combine the sugar, flour, cinnamon and salt; add to the apples and toss lightly.

2. Line a 9-in. pie plate with bottom crust and trim even with edge; fill with apple mixture. Dot with butter. Roll out remaining pastry to fit top of pie. Place over filling. Trim, seal and flute edges; cut slits in pastry.

3. Bake at 400° for 40-45 minutes or until golden brown and apples are tender.

4. For topping, melt butter in a small saucepan. Stir in brown sugar and cream; bring to a boil, stirring constantly. Remove from the heat and stir in pecans.

5. Pour over top crust. Bake 3-4 minutes longer or until bubbly. Place on a wire rack. Serve warm.

White Chocolate Berry Pie

When strawberries are in season, I love to make this pretty pie. It's so easy and doesn't require any baking!

—**CONNIE LAUX** ENGLEWOOD, OH

PREP: 20 MIN. + CHILLING • **MAKES:** 8 SERVINGS

- 5 ounces white baking chocolate, chopped, divided
- 2 tablespoons milk
- 1 package (3 ounces) cream cheese, softened
- ⅓ cup confectioners' sugar
- 1 teaspoon grated orange peel
- 1 cup heavy whipping cream, whipped
- 1 graham cracker crust (9 inches)
- 2 cups sliced fresh strawberries

1. In a microwave, melt four ounces of white chocolate with milk; stir until smooth. Cool to room temperature.

2. Meanwhile, in a large bowl, beat cream cheese and sugar until smooth. Beat in orange peel and melted chocolate. Fold in whipped cream.

3. Spread into crust. Arrange strawberries on top. Melt remaining white chocolate; drizzle over berries. Refrigerate for at least 1 hour. Store in the refrigerator.

Candy Apple Pie

This is the only apple pie my husband will eat, but that's all right since he makes it as often as I do. Like a combination of apple and pecan pie, it's a sweet treat that usually tops off our holiday meals from New Year's all the way through to Christmas!

—**CINDY KLEWENO** BURLINGTON, CO

PREP: 20 MIN. • **BAKE:** 45 MIN. • **MAKES:** 8 SERVINGS

- 6 cups sliced peeled tart apples
- 2 tablespoons lime juice
- ¾ cup sugar
- ¼ cup all-purpose flour
- ½ teaspoon ground cinnamon
- ¼ teaspoon salt
  Pastry for double-crust pie (9 inches)
- 2 tablespoons butter

TOPPING

- 2 tablespoons butter
- ¼ cup packed brown sugar
- 1 tablespoon heavy whipping cream
- ¼ cup chopped pecans

Lemon Burst Tartlets

You'll love the taste of lemon and raspberry in these quick and easy bites. Their little size makes them perfect for a party.

—PAM JAVOR NORTH HUNTINGDON, PA

START TO FINISH: 20 MIN. • **MAKES:** 2½ DOZEN

- 1 **jar (10 ounces) lemon curd**
- 1 **carton (8 ounces) frozen whipped topping, thawed**
- 5 **to 6 drops yellow food coloring, optional**
- ⅔ **cup raspberry cake and pastry filling**
- 2 **packages (1.9 ounces each) frozen miniature phyllo tart shells**
- 30 **fresh raspberries**

1. In a large bowl, combine the lemon curd, whipped topping and food coloring if desired until smooth.

2. Spoon 1 teaspoon raspberry filling into each tart shell. Pipe or spoon lemon mixture over filling. Garnish each with a raspberry. Refrigerate leftovers.

NOTE *This recipe was tested with Solo brand cake and pastry filling. Look for it in the baking aisle.*

Creamy Peanut Butter Pie

Quartered peanut butter cups top this rich, smooth pie. It's always a hit at gatherings. It saves time, too, because it can be made in advance and frozen until needed.

—**RHONDA MCDANIEL** ROSSVILLE, GA

PREP: 15 MIN. + CHILLING • **YIELD:** 6-8 SERVINGS

- 2 **packages (8 ounces each) cream cheese, softened**
- 1 **cup sugar**
- ⅔ **cup creamy peanut butter**
- ⅔ **cup whipped topping**
- 14 **peanut butter cups, divided**
- 1 **chocolate crumb crust (9 inches)**

1. In a small bowl, beat the cream cheese, sugar and peanut butter until light and fluffy. Fold in whipped topping. Coarsely chop half of the peanut butter cups; stir into cream cheese mixture.

2. Spoon into crust. Quarter remaining peanut butter cups; arrange over the top. Refrigerate for at least 4 hours before serving.

Peach Streusel Pie

A delightful summertime pie, this dessert is overflowing with fresh peach flavor. Each slice is like a sweet trip down memory lane. The streusel topping makes this pie a little different than the ordinary and adds homemade flair.

—SALLY HOLBROOK PASADENA, CA

PREP: 15 MIN. • **BAKE:** 40 MIN. + COOLING • **MAKES:** 8 SERVINGS

- 1 **egg white, lightly beaten**
- 1 **unbaked pastry shell (9 inches)**
- ¾ **cup all-purpose flour**
- ½ **cup packed brown sugar**
- ⅓ **cup sugar**
- ¼ **cup cold butter, cubed**
- 6 **cups sliced peeled fresh peaches**

1. Brush egg white over pastry shell; set aside.

2. In a small bowl, combine flour and sugars; cut in butter until mixture resembles fine crumbs. Sprinkle two-thirds into pastry; top with peaches. Sprinkle with remaining crumb mixture.

3. Bake at 375° for 40-45 minutes or until filling is bubbly and peaches are tender.

Chocolate Chip Banana Cream Pie

This rich treat is a hit every time I serve it. The creamy filling, brimming with bananas, is refreshing, and the cookie crust provides a chocolaty crunch. Even a small sliver will satisfy the biggest sweet tooth.

—TAYLOR CARROLL PARKESBURG, PA

PREP: 35 MIN. + CHILLING • **MAKES:** 6-8 SERVINGS

- 1 **tube (16½ ounces) refrigerated chocolate chip cookie dough**
- ⅓ **cup sugar**
- ¼ **cup cornstarch**
- ⅛ **teaspoon salt**
- 2⅓ **cups 2% milk**
- 5 **egg yolks, lightly beaten**
- 2 **tablespoons butter**
- 2 **teaspoons vanilla extract, divided**
- 3 **medium firm bananas**
- 1½ **cups heavy whipping cream**
- 3 **tablespoons confectioners' sugar**

1. Cut cookie dough in half widthwise. Let one portion stand at room temperature for 5-10 minutes to soften (return the other half to the refrigerator for another use).

2. Press dough onto the bottom and up the sides of an ungreased 9-in. pie plate. Bake at 375° for 11-12 minutes or until lightly browned. Cool on a wire rack.

3. In a large saucepan, combine the sugar, cornstarch and salt. Stir in milk until smooth. Cook and stir over medium-high heat until thickened and bubbly. Reduce heat; cook and stir 2 minutes longer. Remove from the heat. Stir a small amount of hot filling into egg yolks; return all to the pan, stirring constantly. Bring to a gentle boil; cook and stir 2 minutes longer. Remove from the heat; stir in butter and 1 teaspoon vanilla.

4. Spread 1 cup filling into prepared crust. Slice bananas; arrange over filling. Pour remaining filling over bananas. Refrigerate for 2 hours or until set.

5. In a large bowl, beat cream until it begins to thicken. Add confectioners' sugar and remaining vanilla; beat until stiff peaks form. Spread over pie. Refrigerate for 1 hour or until chilled.

Maple Butter Tarts

These individual tarts are so scrumptious and syrupy that I often double the recipe so I have enough for guests to take home. They're a little slice of heaven alongside a cup of coffee.

—**LORRAINE CALAND** SHUNIAH, ON

PREP: 20 MIN. • **BAKE:** 20 MIN. + COOLING • **MAKES:** 8 TARTS

- 1 **package (15 ounces) refrigerated pie pastry**
- 1½ **cups raisins**
- 2 **cups boiling water**
- 1¾ **cups packed brown sugar**
- 3 **eggs**
- ½ **cup butter, melted**
- ¼ **cup maple syrup**
- 1 **teaspoon maple flavoring**
   Butter pecan or vanilla ice cream, optional

1. Cut each pastry sheet into quarters; roll each quarter into a 6-in. circle. Transfer pastry to eight ungreased 4-in. fluted tart pans with removable bottoms. Trim pastry even with edges. Place on baking sheets. Bake at 450° for 5-6 minutes or until golden brown. Cool on wire racks. Reduce heat to 350°.

2. Place raisins in a large bowl. Cover with boiling water; let stand for 5 minutes. Drain. In another bowl, beat the brown sugar, eggs, butter, syrup and flavoring; stir in raisins. Divide filling among tart shells.

3. Bake for 16-20 minutes or until centers are just set (mixture will jiggle). Cool on a wire rack. Serve with ice cream if desired.

Lemon Tart with Almond Crust

Arizona produces an abundance of lemons, and everyone is always looking for new ways to use them. This beautiful tart is my delicious solution to the excess-lemon problem!

—**LOIS KINNEBERG** PHOENIX, AZ

PREP: 40 MIN. • **BAKE:** 10 MIN. + COOLING • **MAKES:** 6-8 SERVINGS

- 1 **cup all-purpose flour**
- ½ **cup sliced almonds, toasted**
- ¼ **cup sugar**
- 6 **tablespoons cold butter**
- ½ **teaspoon almond extract**
- ¼ **teaspoon salt**
- 2 **to 3 tablespoons cold water**

FILLING

- 3 **eggs**
- 3 **egg yolks**
- 1 **cup sugar**
- ¾ **cup lemon juice**
- 2 **tablespoons grated lemon peel**
   Dash salt
- 6 **tablespoons butter, cubed**

1. Place the flour, almonds, sugar, butter, extract and salt in a food processor. Cover and pulse until blended. Gradually add water, 1 tablespoon at a time, pulsing until mixture forms a soft dough.

2. Press onto the bottom and up the sides of a greased 9-in. fluted tart pan with a removable bottom. Bake at 400° for 15-20 minutes or until golden brown. Cool on a wire rack. Reduce heat to 325°.

3. In a small heavy saucepan over medium heat, whisk the eggs, egg yolks, sugar, lemon juice, peel and salt until blended. Add butter; cook, whisking constantly, until mixture is thickened and coats the back of a spoon. Pour into crust. Bake for 8-10 minutes or until set. Cool on a wire rack. Refrigerate leftovers.

Rustic Caramel Apple Tart

Like an apple pie without the pan, this scrumptious tart has a crispy crust that cuts nicely under a yummy caramel topping.
—BETTY FULKS ONIA, AR

PREP: 20 MIN. + CHILLING • **BAKE:** 25 MIN. • **MAKES:** 4 SERVINGS

- ⅔ **cup all-purpose flour**
- 1 **tablespoon sugar**
- ⅛ **teaspoon salt**
- ¼ **cup cold butter, cubed**
- 6½ **teaspoons cold water**
- ⅛ **teaspoon vanilla extract**

FILLING

- 1½ **cups chopped peeled tart apples**
- 3 **tablespoons sugar**
- 1 **tablespoon all-purpose flour**

TOPPING

- 1 **teaspoon sugar**
- ¼ **teaspoon ground cinnamon**
- 2 **tablespoons caramel ice cream topping, warmed**

1. In a large bowl, combine the flour, sugar and salt; cut in butter until crumbly. Gradually add water and vanilla, tossing with a fork until dough forms a ball. Cover and refrigerate for at least 30 minutes.

2. On a lightly floured surface, roll dough into a 10-in. circle. Transfer to a parchment paper-lined baking sheet. Combine the filling ingredients; spoon over pastry to within 2 in. of edges. Fold up edges of pastry over filling, leaving center uncovered. Combine sugar and cinnamon; sprinkle over filling.

3. Bake at 400° for 25-30 minutes or until the crust is golden and filling is bubbly. Using parchment paper, slide the tart onto a wire rack. Drizzle with caramel topping. Serve warm.

Caramel Pecan Pie

This is hands down the best pecan pie—it's so good, it's scary! I make it for Thanksgiving because there will be others around to share it with me. Toss the bag of caramels to your kid or spouse and promise they can eat whatever is left after they unwrap your 36 caramels.

—DOROTHY REINHOLD MALIBU, CA

PREP: 25 MIN. • **BAKE:** 35 MIN. + COOLING • **MAKES:** 6-8 SERVINGS

- 36 caramels
- ¼ cup water
- ¼ cup butter, cubed
- 3 eggs
- ¾ cup sugar
- 1 teaspoon vanilla extract
- ⅛ teaspoon salt
- 1⅓ cups chopped pecans, toasted
- Frozen deep-dish pie shell
- Pecan halves, optional

1. In a small heavy saucepan, combine the caramels, water and butter. Cook and stir over low heat until caramels are melted. Remove from the heat and set aside.
2. In a small bowl, beat the eggs, sugar, vanilla and salt until smooth. Gradually add caramel mixture. Stir in chopped pecans. Pour into pie shell. If desired, arrange pecan halves over filling.
3. Bake at 350° for 35-40 minutes or until set. Cool on a wire rack. Refrigerate leftovers.

German Plum Tart

The buttery crust of this fruit-filled treat will simply melt in your mouth. You can substitute sliced apples or peaches for the plums with tasty results. I've also used fresh blueberries.

—HELGA SCHLAPE FLORHAM PARK, NJ

PREP: 10 MIN. • **BAKE:** 35 MIN. • **MAKES:** 6-8 SERVINGS

- ½ cup butter, softened
- 4 tablespoons sugar, divided
- 1 egg yolk
- ¾ to 1 cup all-purpose flour
- 2 pounds plums, quartered (about 4 cups)

1. In a small bowl, cream butter and 3 tablespoons sugar until light and fluffy. Beat in egg yolk. Gradually add flour, ¼ cup at a time, until mixture forms a soft dough. Press onto the bottom and up the sides of a 10-in. pie plate.
2. Arrange plums, skin side up with edges overlapping, in crust; sprinkle with remaining sugar. Bake at 350° for 35-45 minutes or until the crust is golden brown and fruit is tender.

Low-Fat Key Lime Pie

For a taste of paradise, try this light, fluffy and creamy confection. It's low in fat, sugar and fuss. Dessert doesn't get any better than that!

—FRANCES VANFOSSAN WARREN, MI

PREP: 20 MIN. + CHILLING • **MAKES:** 8 SERVINGS

- 1 package (.3 ounce) sugar-free lime gelatin
- ¼ cup boiling water
- 2 cartons (6 ounces each) key lime yogurt
- 1 carton (8 ounces) frozen fat-free whipped topping, thawed
- 1 reduced-fat graham cracker crust (8 inches)

In a large bowl, dissolve gelatin in boiling water. Whisk in yogurt. Fold in whipped topping. Pour into crust. Chill for at least 2 hours or until set.

Pastries

Almond Venetian Dessert

These beautiful bars feature three colorful cakelike layers, an apricot filling and a chocolate topping.

—REVA BECKER FARMINGTON HILLS, MI

PREP: 35 MIN. • **BAKE:** 15 MIN. + CHILLING
MAKES: ABOUT 2 DOZEN

- ½ cup almond paste
- ¾ cup butter, softened
- ½ cup sugar
- 2 eggs, separated
- ¼ teaspoon almond extract
- 1 cup all-purpose flour
- ⅛ teaspoon salt
- 5 drops green food coloring
- 4 drops red food coloring
- ⅔ cup apricot preserves
- 3 ounces semisweet chocolate, chopped

1. Grease the bottoms of three 8-in. square baking dishes. Line with waxed paper and grease the paper; set aside.
2. Place almond paste in a large bowl; break up with a fork. Add the butter, sugar, egg yolks and extract; beat until smooth and fluffy. Stir in flour and salt. In another bowl, beat egg whites until soft peaks form. Stir a fourth of the whites into the dough, then fold in the remaining whites (dough will be stiff).
3. Divide dough evenly into three portions, about ⅔ cup each. Tint one portion green and one portion pink; leave the remaining portion white. Spread each portion into a prepared pan. Bake at 350° for 13-15 minutes or until edges are golden brown. Immediately invert onto wire racks; remove waxed paper. Place another wire rack on top and turn over. Cool completely.
4. Place green layer on a large piece of plastic wrap. Spread evenly with ⅓ cup apricot preserves. Top with white layer and spread with remaining preserves. Top with pink layer. Bring the plastic over layers. Slide onto a baking sheet and set a cutting board on top to compress layers. Refrigerate overnight.
5. In a microwave-safe bowl, melt the chocolate. Remove the cutting board and unwrap dessert. Spread melted chocolate over top; let stand until set. With a sharp knife, trim the edges. Cut into 2-in. x ⅝-in. bars. Store in an airtight container.

Presto Peach Napoleons

When your family has a taste for pie but time is ticking away, make this fast and fruity dessert. For a tasty twist, use cherry pie filling instead.

—TASTE OF HOME TEST KITCHEN

PREP: 20 MIN. + COOLING • **MAKES:** 6 SERVINGS

- 1 sheet frozen puff pastry, thawed
- 1 egg white
- 1 tablespoon water
- 1½ teaspoons sugar
- 1 can (21 ounces) peach or cherry pie filling
- ¼ teaspoon almond extract
- 2 cups whipped topping

1. On a lightly floured surface, unfold the pastry and roll to ⅜-in. thickness. Cut along the fold lines into three pieces. Cut each piece in half widthwise; place on an ungreased baking sheet.
2. Beat egg white and water; brush over pastry. Sprinkle with sugar. Bake at 400° for 9-11 minutes or until golden brown. Cool on a wire rack.
3. Split each pastry in half horizontally. Combine pie filling and extract; spoon over bottom halves of pastries. Top with whipped topping and pastry tops.

Mini Cherry Tarts

I use refrigerated crescent dough to bake up these little tarts in no time flat. No one can resist the cherry cheesecake-like flavors tucked inside.

—FRANCES POSTE WALL, SD

PREP: 20 MIN. • **BAKE:** 15 MIN. + COOLING • **MAKES:** 2 DOZEN

- 1 **tube (8 ounces) refrigerated crescent rolls**
- 1 **package (3 ounces) cream cheese, softened**
- ¼ **cup confectioners' sugar**
- 1 **cup canned cherry pie filling**
- ¼ **teaspoon almond extract**

1. Place crescent dough on a lightly floured surface; seal seams and perforations. Cut into 24 pieces; press onto the bottoms and up the sides of greased miniature muffin cups. In a small bowl, beat cream cheese and confectioners' sugar until smooth. Place about ½ teaspoon in each cup. Combine pie filling and extract; place about 2 teaspoons in each cup.

2. Bake at 375° for 12-14 minutes or until the edges are lightly browned. Remove to wire racks to cool. Refrigerate until serving.

Apple Dumplings for Two

I watch a lot of cooking shows and like to dabble when I can. Sometimes it's nice to have a dessert without any leftovers.

—ROGER SLIVON GENESEE DEPOT, WI

PREP: 15 MIN. • **BAKE:** 40 MIN. • **MAKES:** 2 SERVINGS

- 1 **sheet frozen puff pastry**
- 2 **small tart apples, peeled and cored**
- 4 **teaspoons brown sugar**
- 1 **tablespoon chopped walnuts**
- ⅛ **teaspoon ground cinnamon**
- 4 **teaspoons butter, divided**

GLAZE
- 3 **tablespoons confectioners' sugar**
- ½ **teaspoon 2% milk**
- ½ **teaspoon lemon juice**
- ⅛ **teaspoon vanilla extract**

1. Using a sharp knife, cut pastry sheet in half. Return half to the freezer. Thaw remaining pastry. On a lightly floured surface, roll pastry into a 14-in. x 7-in. rectangle. Cut into two 7-in. squares.

2. Place an apple on each square. In a small bowl, combine the brown sugar, walnuts and cinnamon. Spoon into center of each apple; top each with 1 teaspoon butter. Gently bring up corners of pastry to center; pinch edges to seal. Place in a shallow 3-cup baking dish coated with cooking spray. Melt remaining butter; brush over pastry.

3. Bake at 375° for 40-45 minutes or until the apples are tender and pastry is golden brown. In a small bowl, combine the glaze ingredients. Drizzle over dumplings. Serve warm.

Bakeshop HOW-TO

Tart Tampers Make It Easy

Place a portion of dough in each mini muffin cup. Using firm pressure, push the dough down and up the sides of the cup. If the dough has not moved up the sides of the cup as far as you want, try rocking the tamper back and forth.

Banana Cream Eclairs

To surprise my banana-loving family, I made this dessert for a reunion, where it stood out among the usual fare. These special treats look and taste delicious.

—RUBY WILLIAMS BOGALUSA, LA

PREP: 40 MIN. • **BAKE:** 25 MIN. + COOLING • **MAKES:** 16 SERVINGS

- 1 **cup water**
- ½ **cup butter, cubed**
- ¼ **cup sugar**
- ½ **teaspoon salt**
- 1 **cup all-purpose flour**
- 4 **eggs**

FILLING

- 2½ **cups heavy whipping cream**
- 3 **tablespoons sugar**
- 1 **teaspoon vanilla extract**
- 3 **to 4 medium firm bananas**

GLAZE

- ½ **cup confectioners' sugar**
- 2 **tablespoons baking cocoa**
- 2 **tablespoons butter, melted**
- 1 **teaspoon vanilla extract**
- 1 **to 2 tablespoons boiling water**
- ½ **cup finely chopped pecans**

1. In a large saucepan, bring the water, butter, sugar and salt to a boil. Add flour all at once and stir until a smooth ball forms. Remove from the heat; let stand for 5 minutes. Add eggs, one at a time, beating well after each addition. Continue beating until dough is smooth and shiny.

2. Insert a ¾-in. round tip into a pastry bag; add dough. Pipe 3-in. strips about 3 in. apart on a greased baking sheet. Bake at 400° for 25-30 minutes or until golden brown. Remove to wire racks. Immediately split puffs open; remove tops and set aside. Discard soft dough from inside. Cool puffs.

3. In a large bowl, beat cream until it begins to thicken. Add sugar and vanilla; beat until stiff peaks form. In another bowl, mash bananas; gently fold in whipped cream. Spoon into eclairs; replace tops.

4. In a small bowl, combine the confectioners' sugar, cocoa, butter and vanilla. Add enough water to make a thin glaze. Spread over eclairs. Sprinkle with pecans. Refrigerate leftovers.

Strawberry Tuile Cannoli

My mom and I created this recipe by combining two different ones. The cute cookies are crispy on the outside yet light and fluffy inside. You could also bake them flat and serve the filling as a cookie dip.

—CRYSTAL BRIDDICK COLFAX, IL

PREP: 40 MIN. • **BAKE:** 5 MIN./BATCH • **MAKES:** ABOUT 2 DOZEN

- 4 **ounces cream cheese, softened**
- ¼ **cup sugar**
- 2 **tablespoons seedless strawberry jam**
- ¼ **cup heavy whipping cream, whipped**
- 1 **to 3 drops red food coloring, optional**

BATTER
- ½ **cup sugar**
- ⅓ **cup all-purpose flour**
- 2 **egg whites**
- ¼ **teaspoon vanilla extract**
- ⅛ **teaspoon salt**
- ¼ **cup butter, melted and cooled**
    Chopped fresh strawberries, optional

1. For filling, in a small bowl, beat the cream cheese, sugar and jam until blended. Fold in whipped cream and food coloring if desired. Chill.

2. In a small bowl, whisk the sugar, flour, egg whites, vanilla and salt until smooth. Whisk in butter until blended. Line baking sheets with parchment paper. Preparing four cookies at a time, drop the batter by 1½ teaspoonfuls 4 in. apart onto prepared pans. Bake at 400° for 5-8 minutes or until edges are lightly browned.

3. Loosen each cookie and curl around a wooden spoon handle. Press lightly to seal; hold until set, about 20 seconds. Remove and place on waxed paper to cool. Continue with remaining cookies. If cookies become too cool to shape, return to oven for 1 minute to soften.

4. Just before serving, pipe or spoon filling into cookie shells. Dip ends of cookies into chopped strawberries if desired. Refrigerate leftovers.

Funnel Cakes

These are much simpler to make than doughnuts but taste just as good. They have been a regular treat of ours since we came across them when we lived in the Ozarks.

—**MARY FAITH YODER** UNITY, WI

PREP: 15 MIN. • **COOK:** 5 MIN./BATCH • **MAKES:** 8 CAKES

- 2 eggs
- 1 cup milk
- 1 cup water
- ½ teaspoon vanilla extract
- 3 cups all-purpose flour
- ¼ cup sugar
- 1 tablespoon baking powder
- ¼ teaspoon salt
  Oil for deep-fat frying
  Confectioners' sugar

1. In a large bowl, beat eggs. Add milk, water and vanilla until well blended. Combine flour, sugar, baking powder and salt; beat into egg mixture until smooth. In an electric skillet or deep-fat fryer, heat oil to 375°.

2. Cover the bottom of a funnel spout with your finger; ladle ½ cup of batter into the funnel. Holding the funnel several inches above the oil, release your finger and move the funnel in a spiral motion until all the batter is released (scraping with a rubber spatula if needed).

3. Fry for 2 minutes on each side or until golden brown. Drain on paper towels. Dust with confectioners' sugar and serve warm.

NOTE *The batter can be poured from a liquid measuring cup instead of a funnel.*

Apple Pie Pastries

My co-worker Debbie treated the office to these spectacular mini apple pies. Everyone fell in love with the warm filling and flaky, buttery crust.

—**GINNY ALFANO** CANASTOTA, NY

PREP: 40 MIN. + CHILLING • **BAKE:** 30 MIN. • **MAKES:** 16 SERVINGS

- 2 cups all-purpose flour
- 1 teaspoon salt
- 1 cup cold butter, cubed
- 1 tablespoon cider vinegar
- ½ cup milk

FILLING

- ¾ cup packed brown sugar
- 1 tablespoon all-purpose flour
- 1 teaspoon ground cinnamon
- 5 tablespoons cold butter, divided
- 5-6 small tart apples, peeled and cored
- ¼ cup sugar

1. In a large bowl, combine flour and salt. Cut in butter until crumbly. Sprinkle with vinegar. Gradually add milk, tossing with a fork until dough forms a ball. Cover and refrigerate for 20 minutes or until easy to handle.

2. Meanwhile, in another bowl, combine the brown sugar, flour and cinnamon. Cut in 2 tablespoons butter until crumbly; set aside. Melt the remaining butter. Cut apples into ½-in.-thick rings.

3. Shape dough into sixteen 1½-in. balls; roll into 5-in. circles. Brush with 2 tablespoons melted butter.

4. Place one apple ring in center of each circle. Top each with 2 teaspoons brown sugar mixture. Fold edges of the dough over apple rings, leaving centers uncovered; crimp edges. Brush the dough with remaining melted butter; sprinkle with sugar.

5. Place 1 in. apart on ungreased baking sheets. Bake at 375° for 30-35 minutes or until golden brown and apples are tender. Serve warm.

Caramel Apple Dumplings

When our apples become ripe, it's not unusual for me to make as many as 30 of these fruity dumplings! I've relied on the recipe for more than 50 years.

—OMAHA PETERSON KINTA, OK

PREP: 30 MIN. • **BAKE:** 50 MIN. • **MAKES:** 7 SERVINGS

- 2¼ cups all-purpose flour
- 2 teaspoons plus ¼ cup sugar, divided
- 1 teaspoon salt
- 1 cup shortening
- 2 eggs
- ¼ cup water
- 2 teaspoons white vinegar
- 7 medium tart apples, peeled and cored
- 7 tablespoons butter
- ¼ teaspoon ground cinnamon

CARAMEL SAUCE
- 1 jar (12¼ ounces) caramel ice cream topping
- 1½ cups packed brown sugar
- 1 cup water
- ¼ cup butter, cubed

1. In a large bowl, combine the flour, 2 teaspoons sugar and salt; cut in shortening until crumbly. In a small bowl, combine 1 egg, water and vinegar; gradually add to crumb mixture, tossing with a fork until dough forms a ball. Divide into seven portions.

2. On a lightly floured surface, roll each portion into a 7-in. square. Place an apple on each pastry square; place 1 tablespoon butter in the center of each. Combine cinnamon and remaining sugar; sprinkle over apples.

3. Bring up corners of pastry to center; pinch edges to seal. Beat remaining egg; brush over pastry. Place in a greased 13-in. x 9-in. baking dish. Bake at 350° for 15 minutes.

4. Meanwhile, in a large saucepan, combine the sauce ingredients. Bring to a boil; cook and stir until smooth and blended. Pour over apples. Bake 35-40 minutes longer or until apples are tender and pastry is golden brown, basting occasionally with sauce. Serve warm.

Easy Cherry Strudels

The original recipe for these strudels called for phyllo dough sheets and was very time-consuming . Once, by mistake, I bought puff pastry sheets and found that they were much faster.

—SUSAN DANCY TALLAHASSEE, FL

PREP: 15 MIN. • **BAKE:** 20 MIN.
MAKES: 2 STRUDELS (5 SLICES EACH)

- 1 can (14½ ounces) pitted tart cherries
- 1 cup sugar
- ½ cup dried cranberries or raisins
- 1 tablespoon butter
- 3 tablespoons cornstarch
- 1½ cups chopped walnuts
- 1 package (17.3 ounces) frozen puff pastry, thawed
- 1 egg, lightly beaten

1. Drain the cherries, reserving ⅓ cup juice. In a large saucepan, combine the cherries, sugar, cranberries and butter. Cook and stir over medium heat until heated through. Combine cornstarch and reserved juice and add to the pan. Bring to a boil. Cook and stir 1-2 minutes longer or until thickened. Remove from the heat; stir in walnuts.

2. Unfold one pastry sheet and cut in half. Mound half of the cherry mixture on one pastry half to within ½ in. of edges. Top with remaining pastry half; pinch edges to seal. Repeat with remaining pastry and filling.

3. Place on a greased foil-lined baking sheet. With a sharp knife, cut diagonal slits into tops of strudels; brush with egg. Bake at 400° for 20-25 minutes or until golden brown.

Easy Elephant Ears

You'll love the classic cinnamon-sugar flavor of these crispy bite-size treats. Even more, you'll love that they call for just three ingredients and are so simple to assemble.

—BOB ROSE WAUKESHA, WI

PREP: 20 MIN. • **BAKE:** 15 MIN./BATCH • **MAKES:** ABOUT 2½ DOZEN

- **1 package (17.3 ounces) frozen puff pastry, thawed**
- **½ cup sugar**
- **2 teaspoons ground cinnamon**

1. On a lightly floured surface, roll one sheet of puff pastry into an 11-in. x 8-in. rectangle. Combine sugar and cinnamon; sprinkle half of mixture over pastry.

2. Working from the short sides, roll up dough jelly-roll style toward the center. With a sharp knife, cut roll into ½-in. slices. Place on parchment paper-lined baking sheets. Repeat with remaining pastry and sugar mixture.

3. Bake at 375° for 12-15 minutes or until crisp and golden brown. Remove from pans to wire racks.

Lemon Cream Puffs

The fluffy filling for these cream puffs has an unexpected citrus flavor. It's a refreshing change from other cream puffs.

—DOREEN MARTIN KITIMAT, BC

PREP: 20 MIN. + CHILLING • **BAKE:** 30 MIN. + COOLING
MAKES: 10 SERVINGS

- ½ cup water
- ¼ cup butter, cubed
- ½ cup all-purpose flour
- 2 eggs

LEMON FILLING
- 1 egg, beaten
- ⅓ cup sugar
- 3 tablespoons lemon juice
- 2 tablespoons butter, cubed
- 1 cup heavy whipping cream
- 2 teaspoons sugar
  Confectioners' sugar

1. In a large saucepan, bring water and butter to a boil. Add flour all at once, stirring until a smooth ball forms. Remove from the heat; let stand for 5 minutes. Add eggs, one at a time, beating well after each addition. Continue beating until mixture is smooth.

2. Drop by rounded tablespoonfuls 3 in. apart onto greased baking sheets.

3. Bake at 400° for 30-35 minutes or until golden brown. Remove to wire racks. Immediately split puffs and remove tops; discard soft dough from inside. Set puffs and tops aside to cool.

4. For filling, in a small heavy saucepan, combine the egg, sugar, lemon juice and butter. Cook and stir over medium heat until mixture is thick enough to coat the back of a spoon. Transfer the mixture to a small bowl; refrigerate until partially set.

5. In a large bowl, beat cream and sugar until stiff peaks form; fold into lemon mixture. Fill cream puffs; replace tops. Dust with confectioners' sugar.

Thelma's Chocolate Eclair

I love eclairs but making the actual pastry is difficult so I came up with this recipe as a substitute. It still satisfies my cravings with the same wonderful flavors.

—THELMA BEAM ESBON, KS

PREP: 20 MIN. + CHILLING • **MAKES:** 12-15 SERVINGS

- 18 whole graham crackers
- 3½ cups cold milk
- 2 packages (3.4 ounces each) instant vanilla pudding mix
- 1 carton (8 ounces) frozen whipped topping, thawed
- 2 ounces semisweet chocolate
- 2 tablespoons butter
- 1½ cups confectioners' sugar
- 3 tablespoons milk
- 1 teaspoon vanilla extract
- 1 teaspoon light corn syrup

1. Line a 13-in. x 9-in. dish with nine whole graham crackers; set aside.

2. In a large bowl, whisk milk and pudding mixes for 2 minutes. Let stand for 2 minutes or until soft-set; fold in whipped topping. Spread over graham crackers. Top with remaining crackers.

3. In a microwave-safe bowl, melt the chocolate and butter. Stir in the remaining ingredients. Spread over the graham cracker layer. Cover and refrigerate for 8 hours or overnight.

Java Cream Puffs

These fun and fancy goodies have chopped pecans in the puffs and mouthwatering mocha cream filling.

—IOLA EGLE BELLA VISTA, AR

PREP: 25 MIN. + CHILLING • **BAKE:** 30 MIN. + COOLING
MAKES: 8 SERVINGS

- ½ cup water
- ¼ cup butter, cubed
- ⅛ teaspoon salt
- ½ cup all-purpose flour
- 2 eggs
- ¼ cup finely chopped pecans

MOCHA CREAM FILLING
- ½ cup strong brewed coffee
- 24 large marshmallows
- 1½ cups heavy whipping cream
- ¼ cup hot fudge ice cream topping, warmed

1. In a large saucepan, bring water, butter and salt to a boil. Add flour all at once and stir until a smooth ball forms. Remove from the heat; let stand for 5 minutes. Add eggs, one at a time, beating well after each addition. Continue beating until mixture is smooth and shiny. Stir in pecans.
2. Drop by rounded tablespoonfuls 3 in. apart onto a greased baking sheet. Bake at 400° for 30-35 minutes or until golden brown. Remove to a wire rack. Immediately split puffs open; remove tops and set aside. Discard soft dough from inside. Cool puffs.
3. For filling, in a large saucepan, combine coffee and marshmallows. Cook over low heat until marshmallows are melted. Transfer to a large bowl; cover and chill just until thickened.
4. In a large bowl, beat cream until soft peaks form. Whisk chilled coffee mixture until light in color; fold in whipped cream. Just before serving, fill each puff with about ⅓ cup filling. Replace tops and drizzle with fudge topping.

Bakeshop HOW-TO

Making Cream Puffs

Bring water, butter and salt to a boil in a saucepan. Add the flour all at once; stir briskly until the mixture leaves the sides of the pan and forms a ball.

Remove from heat; let stand for 5 minutes to allow mixture to cool before adding the eggs. Beat well after adding each egg. Continue beating until mixture is smooth and shiny.

Drop dough 3 in. apart onto a greased baking sheet. Bake as directed.

Remove puffs from pan to a wire rack. Immediately split puffs and set tops aside; remove soft dough from inside with a fork and discard. Fill as directed.

Apple Strudels

This is one of my favorite recipes to make during autumn. The aroma of homemade strudel baking on a cool, crisp day is absolutely wonderful.

—HELEN LESH FORSYTH, MO

PREP: 20 MIN. + CHILLING • **BAKE:** 55 MIN. + COOLING
MAKES: 3 STRUDELS (12 SLICES EACH)

- 1 **cup cold butter, cubed**
- 2 **cups all-purpose flour**
- 1 **cup (8 ounces) sour cream**
- ¼ **teaspoon salt**

FILLING

- 2 **cups dry bread crumbs**
- ¼ **cup butter, melted**
- 4 **medium tart apples, peeled and chopped**
- 2 **cups sugar**
- 1 **cup golden raisins**
- ½ **cup chopped pecans**
- 2 **teaspoons ground cinnamon**
  Confectioners' sugar, optional

1. In a large bowl, cut butter into flour until mixture resembles coarse crumbs. Stir in the sour cream and salt. Shape the dough into a ball; cover and refrigerate overnight.

2. For filling, combine bread crumbs and butter. Add the apples, sugar, raisins, pecans and cinnamon, set aside. Divide dough into thirds; turn onto a floured surface. Roll each into a 15-in. x 12-in. rectangle. Spoon filling evenly onto dough; spread to within 1 in. of edges. Roll up from a long side; pinch seams and ends to seal.

3. Carefully place each loaf seam side down on an ungreased baking sheet. Bake at 350° for 55-60 minutes or until lightly browned. Cool completely on wire racks. Dust with confectioners' sugar if desired.

Baby Boston Cream Pies

A vanilla custard is sandwiched between cakelike cookies.

—**EVANGELINE BRADFORD** ERLANGER, KY

PREP: 70 MIN. + CHILLING • **BAKE:** 5 MIN./BATCH + COOLING
MAKES: 4 DOZEN

- 6 **tablespoons sugar**
- 3 **tablespoons cornstarch**
- ¼ **teaspoon salt**
- 1 **cup 2% milk**
- 6 **tablespoons heavy whipping cream**
- 1 **egg yolk, beaten**
- 2 **teaspoons vanilla extract**

COOKIES
- 9 **tablespoons butter, softened**
- 1 **cup sugar**
- 2 **egg yolks**
- 1 **egg**
- 2 **teaspoons vanilla extract**
- ½ **teaspoon grated lemon peel**
- 1 **cup plus 2 tablespoons cake flour**
- 1 **cup all-purpose flour**
- ¾ **teaspoon baking soda**
- ½ **teaspoon salt**
- ½ **cup plus 2 tablespoons buttermilk**

GLAZE
- 2 **ounces unsweetened chocolate, chopped**
- 4 **teaspoons butter**
- ½ **cup whipping cream**
- 1 **cup confectioners' sugar**

1. In a small heavy saucepan, combine sugar, cornstarch and salt. Stir in milk and cream until smooth. Cook and stir over medium-high heat until thickened and bubbly. Reduce heat to low; cook and stir 2 minutes longer.
2. Remove from heat. Stir a small amount of hot mixture into egg yolk; return all to the pan, stirring constantly. Bring to a gentle boil; cook and stir 2 minutes longer. Remove from the heat. Stir in vanilla. Cool for 15 minutes, stirring occasionally. Transfer to a small bowl. Press waxed paper onto surface of custard. Refrigerate for 2-3 hours.
3. In a large bowl, cream butter and sugar until light and fluffy. Beat in the egg yolks, egg, vanilla and lemon peel. Combine the cake flour, all-purpose flour, baking soda and salt; gradually add to creamed mixture alternately with buttermilk and mix well.

4. Drop by rounded teaspoonfuls 2 in. apart onto greased baking sheets. Bake at 400° for 5-7 minutes or until firm to the touch. Remove to wire racks to cool completely.
5. Spread custard over the bottoms of half of the cookies; top with remaining cookies.
6. For glaze, place the chocolate and butter in a small bowl. In a small saucepan, bring the cream just to a boil. Pour over the chocolate and butter; whisk until smooth. Stir in the confectioners' sugar. Spread over the cookies; let dry completely. Store in the refrigerator.

Baklava

Here's my recipe for the traditional sweet and nutty Greek pastry. It's a tasty end to any meal.

—**JOSIE BOCHEK** STURGEON BAY, WI

PREP: 1¼ HOURS • **BAKE:** 45 MIN. + COOLING • **MAKES:** 3 DOZEN

- 4 **cups finely chopped walnuts**
- ¼ **cup sugar**
- 1 **tablespoon ground cinnamon**
- 1 **cup butter, melted**
- 1 **package (16 ounces) frozen phyllo dough, thawed**

SYRUP
- 1 **cup sugar**
- ½ **cup water**
- ¼ **cup honey**
- 1 **teaspoon lemon juice**
- 1 **teaspoon vanilla extract**

1. In a small bowl, combine the walnuts, sugar and cinnamon; set aside. Grease a 13-in. x 9-in. baking dish with some of the melted butter. Unroll phyllo dough sheets (keep dough covered with plastic wrap while assembling).
2. Place one sheet of phyllo in baking dish; brush with butter. Top with a second sheet; brush with butter. Fold long ends under to fit the dish. Sprinkle with about ¼ cup nut mixture. Repeat 18 times, layering two sheets, brushing with butter and sprinkling with nut mixture. Top with remaining dough; brush with butter. Cut into 2-in. diamonds with a sharp knife.
3. Bake at 350° for 45-55 minutes or until golden brown. Meanwhile, in a saucepan, combine the syrup ingredients; bring to a boil. Reduce the heat; simmer, uncovered, for 10 minutes. Pour over warm baklava. Cool on a wire rack.

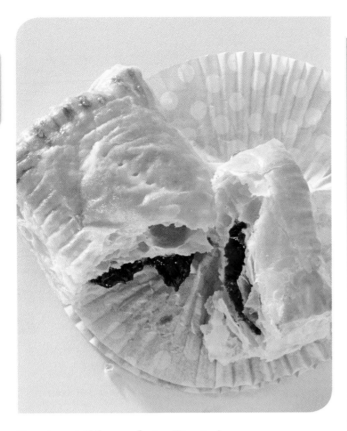

Pizzelle Cannoli

We made two Italian treats into one with beautiful pizzelle cookies wrapped around a rich, chocolaty cannoli filling. If you don't have a pizzelle iron, try the filling in the simple baked cannoli shells on page 374.

—TASTE OF HOME TEST KITCHEN

PREP: 45 MIN. + COOLING • **COOK:** 5 MIN./BATCH
MAKES: 12 FILLED PIZZELLE

- 1   **egg**
- ¼   **cup sugar**
- ¼   **cup butter, melted**
- ½   **teaspoon vanilla extract**
- ¼   **teaspoon grated lemon peel**
- ⅛   **teaspoon almond extract**
- ½   **cup all-purpose flour**
- ¼   **teaspoon baking powder**

FILLING
- ¾   **cup sugar**
- 3   **tablespoons cornstarch**
- 1   **cup milk**
- 1⅛ **teaspoons vanilla extract**
- 1   **drop cinnamon oil, optional**
- 1¾ **cups ricotta cheese**
- 1   **milk chocolate candy bar with almonds (4¼ ounces), chopped**
- ½   **cup chopped pistachios**

1. In a large bowl, beat the egg, sugar, butter, vanilla, lemon peel and almond extract until blended. Combine the flour and baking powder; stir into egg mixture and mix well.

2. Bake in a preheated pizzelle iron according to manufacturer's directions until golden brown. Remove cookies and immediately shape into tubes. Place on wire racks to cool.

3. In a small saucepan, combine sugar and cornstarch. Stir in milk until smooth. Bring to a boil; cook and stir for 2 minutes or until thickened. Stir in vanilla and cinnamon oil if desired. Cool completely.

4. In a large bowl, beat ricotta cheese until smooth. Gradually beat in custard mixture. Fold in chocolate. Spoon or pipe into shells. Dip each side in pistachios. Serve immediately. Refrigerate leftovers.

Instant Chocolate Pastries

My sister and I became addicted to Nutella while traveling in Europe. Now we're always thinking of ways to incorporate it into recipes. This one came about after making puff pastries with apple filling. We thought, "Why not try chocolate?"

—DEE WOLF SYRACUSE, UT

START TO FINISH: 20 MIN. • **MAKES:** 6 SERVINGS

- 1   **sheet frozen puff pastry, thawed**
- 6   **tablespoons Nutella**
- 1   **egg, beaten**
     Confectioners' sugar, optional

1. Unfold puff pastry; cut into six rectangles. Place on a greased baking sheet. Spread 1 tablespoon Nutella over half of a rectangle; fold dough over filling. Press edges with a fork to seal. Repeat for remaining pastries. Brush with egg; prick tops with a fork.

2. Bake at 400° for 10-14 minutes or until puffy and golden brown. Sprinkle with the confectioners' sugar if desired. Serve warm.

Crisscross Apple Crowns

Wake 'em up on chilly mornings with the tempting aroma of apples and cinnamon filling the house. I love making these for breakfast. They're different and so easy.

—TERESA MORRIS LAUREL, DE

PREP: 30 MIN. • **BAKE:** 20 MIN. • **MAKES:** 8 SERVINGS

- 1⅓ cups chopped peeled tart apples
- ⅓ cup chopped walnuts
- ⅓ cup raisins
- ½ cup sugar, divided
- 2 tablespoons all-purpose flour
- 2 teaspoons ground cinnamon, divided
  Dash salt
- 1 package (16.3 ounces) large refrigerated flaky biscuits
- 2 teaspoons butter, melted

1. In a large microwave-safe bowl, combine the apples, walnuts, raisins, 3 tablespoons sugar, flour, ¾ teaspoon cinnamon and salt. Microwave on high for 2-3 minutes or until almost tender.

2. Flatten each biscuit into a 5-in. circle. Combine remaining sugar and cinnamon; sprinkle a rounded teaspoonful of sugar mixture over each. Top each with ¼ cup apple mixture. Bring up edges to enclose mixture; pinch edges to seal.

3. Place seam side down in ungreased muffin cups. Brush tops with butter; sprinkle with remaining sugar mixture. With a sharp knife, cut an X in the top of each.

4. Bake at 350° for 18-22 minutes or until golden brown. Cool for 5 minutes; remove from pan to a wire rack.

Chocolate Eclairs

With creamy filling and fudgy frosting, homemade eclairs are extra special. Family and friends will love these.

—JESSICA CAMPBELL VIOLA, WI

PREP: 45 MIN. • **BAKE:** 35 MIN. + COOLING • **MAKES:** 9 SERVINGS

- 1 **cup water**
- ½ **cup butter, cubed**
- ¼ **teaspoon salt**
- 1 **cup all-purpose flour**
- 4 **eggs**

FILLING

- 2½ **cups cold milk**
- 1 **package (5.1 ounces) instant vanilla pudding mix**
- 1 **cup heavy whipping cream**
- ¼ **cup confectioners' sugar**
- 1 **teaspoon vanilla extract**

FROSTING

- 2 **ounces semisweet chocolate**
- 2 **tablespoons butter**
- 1¼ **cups confectioners' sugar**
- 2 **to 3 tablespoons hot water**

1. In a large saucepan, bring the water, butter and salt to a boil. Add flour all at once and stir until a smooth ball forms. Remove from the heat; let stand for 5 minutes. Add eggs, one at a time, beating well after each addition. Continue beating until mixture is smooth and shiny.

2. Using a tablespoon or a pastry tube with a No. 10 or larger tip, form dough into 4-in. x 1½-in. strips on a greased baking sheet. Bake at 400° for 35-40 minutes or until puffed and golden. Remove to a wire rack. Immediately split eclairs open; remove tops and set aside. Discard soft dough from inside. Cool eclairs.

3. In a large bowl, beat milk and pudding mix according to package directions. In another bowl, whip cream until soft peaks form. Beat in sugar and vanilla; fold into pudding. Fill eclairs (chill any remaining filling for another use).

4. For frosting, in a microwave, melt chocolate and butter; stir until smooth. Stir in sugar and enough hot water to achieve a smooth consistency. Cool slightly. Frost eclairs. Store in refrigerator.

Sugar Cookie Tarts

These little tarts are pretty enough for an elegant occasion, but are super easy to make. For a nice look, arrange the fruits in a circular pattern. Fresh fruit tastes the best, but you can substitute canned for a darling treat in a snap.

—**BARB WHITE** LIGONIER, PA

PREP: 20 MIN. + CHILLING • **MAKES:** 4 SERVINGS

- 5 **tablespoons sugar, divided**
- 1 **teaspoon cornstarch**
  Dash salt
- 3 **tablespoons water**
- 2 **tablespoons orange juice**
- 1 **tablespoon lemon juice**
- 1 **package (3 ounces) cream cheese, softened**
- 4 **large sugar cookies (3 inches)**
  Assorted fresh fruit

1. For glaze, in a small saucepan, combine 3 tablespoons sugar, cornstarch and salt. Gradually stir in the water, orange juice and lemon juice. Bring to a boil over medium heat; cook and stir for 2 minutes or until thickened. Remove from the heat; cool.

2. In a small bowl, beat cream cheese and remaining sugar until smooth. Spread over each cookie; arrange fruit on top. Drizzle with glaze. Refrigerate until chilled.

Cranberry-Pear Strudel

This stylish dessert is sure to please everyone. It's delicious served warm with a scoop of reduced-fat ice cream or whipped topping.

—**LEAH BEATTY** COBOURG, ON

PREP: 35 MIN. + COOLING • **BAKE:** 20 MIN. + COOLING
MAKES: 10 SERVINGS

- ½ **cup sugar**
- 1 **tablespoon cornstarch**
- 3 **large pears, peeled and finely chopped**
- ½ **cup fresh or frozen cranberries, thawed**
- 2 **tablespoons butter**
- ½ **cup dried cranberries**
- 1 **teaspoon ground ginger**
- 1 **teaspoon grated orange peel**
- ½ **teaspoon ground cinnamon**
- 6 **sheets phyllo dough (14 inches x 9 inches)**
  Cooking spray
- 1 **teaspoon confectioners' sugar**

1. In a large bowl, combine sugar and cornstarch. Add pears and cranberries; toss gently to coat. In a large nonstick skillet, melt butter over medium-high heat. Add fruit mixture; cook and stir for 7-8 minutes or until cranberries pop. Stir in the dried cranberries, ginger, orange peel and cinnamon. Cool.

2. Line a baking sheet with foil and coat the foil with cooking spray; set aside. Place one sheet of phyllo dough on a work surface; coat with cooking spray. Repeat layers five times. (Keep phyllo dough covered with plastic wrap and a damp towel until ready to use each sheet.)

3. Spread cranberry mixture over dough to within 1 in. of edges. Fold in sides. Roll up, starting at a long side. Place seam side down on prepared baking sheet.

4. Bake at 400° for 20-23 minutes or until golden brown. Remove from pan to a wire rack to cool. Dust with confectioners' sugar before serving.

Cheesecakes

Magnolia Dream Cheesecake

Your guests will be amazed when they learn that you made this gorgeous cheesecake at home! The Italian-style dessert is flavored with a delightful combination of hazelnut and peach.

—CHARLENE CHAMBERS ORMOND BEACH, FL

PREP: 50 MIN. • **BAKE:** 1½ HOURS + CHILLING
MAKES: 16 SERVINGS

- 1 cup hazelnuts, toasted, divided
- 12 whole graham crackers
- ¼ cup sugar
- 6 tablespoons unsalted butter, melted

FILLING
- 1½ pounds ricotta cheese
- 2 packages (8 ounces each) cream cheese, softened
- 2 cups (16 ounces) sour cream
- 1½ cups sugar
- 6 tablespoons all-purpose flour
- 4 tablespoons hazelnut liqueur, divided
- 6 eggs, lightly beaten
- 3 medium peaches, sliced

1. Place a greased 10-in. springform pan on a double thickness of heavy-duty foil (about 18 in. square). Securely wrap foil around pan.

2. Place hazelnuts in a food processor; cover and pulse until coarsely chopped. Set aside ¼ cup for garnish. Add graham crackers and sugar to food processor; cover and process until finely chopped. Add butter; process until blended. Press onto the bottom and 1 in. up the sides of prepared pan. Place pan on a baking sheet. Bake at 325° for 10 minutes. Cool on a wire rack.

3. In a large bowl, beat the ricotta, cream cheese, sour cream and sugar until well blended. Beat in flour and 2 tablespoons liqueur. Add eggs; beat on low speed just until combined. Pour into crust. Place springform pan in a large baking pan; add 1 in. of hot water to larger pan.

4. Bake at 325° for 1½ hours or until center is just set and top appears dull. Remove springform pan from water bath. Cool on a wire rack for 10 minutes. Carefully run a knife around edge of pan to loosen; cool 1 hour longer. Refrigerate overnight.

5. Toss peaches with remaining liqueur; arrange over top of cheesecake. Sprinkle reserved hazelnuts in the center. Remove sides of pan.

Raspberry Cheesecake Pie

This creamy cheesecake pie with a raspberry layer is refreshing and light. It's perfect after a heavy meal.

—STEVE JOSSERAND DECATUR, IL

PREP: 50 MIN. + CHILLING • **MAKES:** 6-8 SERVINGS

- 2 packages (8 ounces each) cream cheese, softened
- ½ cup sugar
- ½ teaspoon vanilla extract
- 2 eggs, lightly beaten
- 1 chocolate crumb crust (8 inches)
- 1½ teaspoons unflavored gelatin
- 2 tablespoons cold water
- ½ cup seedless raspberry jam
- 1 cup heavy whipping cream
- 2 tablespoons confectioners' sugar

1. In a large bowl, beat the cream cheese, sugar and vanilla until smooth. Add the eggs; beat on low speed just until combined. Pour into crust. Bake at 325° for 25-30 minutes or until the center is almost set. Cool on a wire rack for 1 hour. Refrigerate overnight.

2. In a small saucepan, sprinkle gelatin over cold water; let stand for 1 minute. Cook over low heat, stirring until gelatin is completely dissolved. Stir in jam. Refrigerate for 10 minutes.

3. In small bowl, beat cream until it begins to thicken. Gradually add confectioners' sugar; beat until stiff peaks form. Remove ½ cup for garnish; cover and refrigerate.

4. Gently stir ¾ cup whipped cream into the raspberry mixture just until blended. Fold in the remaining whipped cream; spread over cheesecake. Refrigerate for at least 1 hour. Garnish with reserved whipped cream.

Decadent Brownie Swirl Cheesecake

It may look picture perfect, but this cheesecake is so fast. The secret is the speedy crust—it's from a packaged brownie mix! You don't need to be an experienced cook to make the elegant chocolate swirls on top.

—TASTE OF HOME TEST KITCHEN

PREP: 30 MIN. • **BAKE:** 1½ HOURS + CHILLING
MAKES: 16 SERVINGS

- **1** package fudge brownie mix (13-inch x 9-inch pan size)
FILLING
- **4** packages (8 ounces each) cream cheese, softened
- **1** cup sugar
- **4** eggs, lightly beaten
- **3** teaspoons vanilla extract or 1 teaspoon almond extract and 2 teaspoons vanilla extract
Fresh raspberries and chocolate curls, optional

1. Prepare the brownie mix according to the package directions for chewy fudge brownies. Set aside ⅔ cup brownie batter; spread remaining batter into a greased 9-in. springform pan.

2. Place pan on a double thickness of heavy-duty foil (about 18 in. square). Securely wrap foil around pan. Bake at 350° for 25-28 minutes (brownies will barely test done). Cool for 10 minutes on a wire rack.

3. In a large bowl, beat cream cheese and sugar until smooth. Beat in eggs and vanilla on low speed just until combined. Stir ⅓ cup into reserved brownie batter; set aside. Spoon half of the cheesecake batter into crust; dollop with half of reserved chocolate cheesecake batter. Repeat layers. Cut through batter with a knife to swirl.

4. Place in a larger baking pan; add 1 in. of hot water to larger pan. Bake at 325° for 1½ hours or until surface is no longer shiny and center is almost set.

5. Remove pan from water bath and foil. Cool on a wire rack for 10 minutes. Carefully run a knife around the edge of pan to loosen; cool 1 hour longer. Refrigerate overnight. Remove sides of pan. Garnish with raspberries and chocolate curls if desired.

Bakeshop HOW-TO

Swirling Filling into a Cheesecake

Spoon small amounts of filling to be swirled in a random pattern onto cheesecake batter. Cut through cheesecake batter with a knife to swirl in the filling. Be careful not to draw the blade through the filling too often, or the filling will blend into the rest of the batter and you'll lose the pretty pattern.

Almond Apple Cheesecake

The flavorful apple-cinnamon-nut topping and the raspberry jam layer make this dessert outstanding.

—NORMA HARDER SASKATOON, SK

PREP: 20 MIN. • **BAKE:** 55 MIN. + CHILLING • **MAKES:** 12 SERVINGS

- 1 **cup all-purpose flour**
- ⅓ **cup sugar**
- ½ **cup cold butter, cubed**
- ⅓ **cup seedless raspberry jam**

FILLING

- 2 **packages (8 ounces each) cream cheese, softened**
- ½ **cup sugar**
- 2 **eggs, lightly beaten**
- 2 **teaspoons vanilla extract**

TOPPING

- ⅓ **cup sugar**
- ½ **teaspoon ground cinnamon**
- 3 **cups thinly sliced peeled tart apples**
- ½ **cup sliced almonds**

1. In a small bowl, combine the flour and sugar; cut in butter until crumbly. Press onto the bottom and 1½ in. up the sides of a greased 9-in. springform pan; prick with a fork. Place on a baking sheet. Bake at 350° for 10 minutes or until soft but set. Cool on a wire rack.

2. Carefully spread jam over crust. For filling, in a large bowl, beat cream cheese and sugar until smooth. Add eggs and vanilla; beat just until blended. Spread over jam. For topping, combine the sugar and cinnamon in a large bowl. Add apples and toss to coat. Spoon over filling. Sprinkle with almonds.

3. Bake at 350° for 55-60 minutes or until center is almost set. Cool on a wire rack for 10 minutes. Carefully run a knife around edge of pan to loosen; cool 1 hour longer. Refrigerate overnight. Remove sides of pan.

Lime Coconut Cheesecake

This refreshing cheesecake's delicate citrus flavor is complemented by a coconut crust.

—INGE SCHERMERHORN EAST KINGSTON, NH

PREP: 30 MIN. + CHILLING • **MAKES:** 12 SERVINGS

- 1½ cups flaked coconut
- 3 tablespoons ground macadamia nuts or almonds
- 3 tablespoons butter, melted
- 1 envelope unflavored gelatin
- ¼ cup cold water
- ¾ cup sugar
- 2 packages (8 ounces each) cream cheese, softened
- ¼ cup lime juice
- 1 tablespoon grated lime peel
  Green food coloring
- 1½ cups heavy whipping cream, whipped
  Toasted coconut and additional whipped cream, optional

1. In a bowl, combine coconut and nuts; stir in butter. Press onto the bottom of a greased 9-in. springform pan. Bake at 350° for 10-15 minutes or until crust is golden brown around the edges. Cool on a wire rack.

2. In a saucepan, sprinkle gelatin over cold water; let stand for 1 minute. Stir in sugar; cook over low heat until sugar and gelatin are dissolved. Remove from the heat. In a bowl, beat cream cheese until smooth. Gradually beat in gelatin mixture. Add lime juice and peel; beat until blended. Tint pale green with food coloring. Fold in whipped cream. Pour over crust. Refrigerate for 5 hours or overnight.

3. Carefully run a knife around the edge of pan to loosen. Remove sides of pan. Garnish with coconut and additional whipped cream if desired.

Cheesecake Squares

These tempting bites are sure to steal top billing at any summer meal or social. Let family and friends choose from a warm drizzle of caramel and almonds, a dollop of fresh fruit and jam or a chocolate-dipped strawberry to top off their cheesecake.

—TASTE OF HOME TEST KITCHEN

PREP: 30 MIN. • **BAKE:** 30 MIN. + CHILLING • **MAKES:** 9 SERVINGS

- 1¼ cups chocolate wafer crumbs
- ¼ cup butter, melted
- 2 packages (8 ounces each) cream cheese, softened
- ⅔ cup plus 2 tablespoons sugar, divided
- 2 eggs, lightly beaten
- 1½ teaspoons vanilla extract, divided
- ¼ teaspoon almond extract
- 1 cup (8 ounces) sour cream

CHOCOLATE STRAWBERRIES

- 2 ounces dark chocolate candy bar, chopped
- 3 fresh strawberries
- 1 ounce white baking chocolate, chopped

CARAMEL TOPPING

- 6 caramels
- 1 tablespoon heavy whipping cream
  Whipped cream
- 1 tablespoon sliced almonds, toasted

BERRY TOPPING

- ¼ cup seedless raspberry jam
- 6 fresh raspberries
- 6 fresh blackberries
- 6 fresh blueberries

1. In a small bowl, combine crumbs and butter. Press firmly onto the bottom of an 8-in. square baking dish.

2. In a small bowl, beat the cream cheese and ⅔ cup sugar until smooth. Add the eggs; beat on low speed just until combined. Stir in ½ teaspoon vanilla and the almond extract.

3. Pour over crust. Bake at 325° for 45-55 minutes or until set. Cool for 5 minutes.

4. Meanwhile, in a small bowl, combine sour cream with remaining sugar and vanilla. Spread over filling; bake 5 minutes longer. Cool on a wire rack for 1 hour. Refrigerate for at least 5 hours or overnight.

5. In a microwave, melt candy bar; stir until smooth. Dip strawberries in chocolate; allow excess to drip off. Place on a waxed paper-lined baking sheet; let stand until set. Melt white chocolate; stir until smooth. Drizzle over strawberries. Refrigerate until serving.

6. Just before serving, cut cheesecake into nine squares. Place chocolate strawberries on three cheesecake squares.

7. For caramel topping, in a small microwave-safe bowl, combine caramels and cream. Microwave, uncovered, on high for 45 seconds, stirring once. Spoon over three cheesecake squares. Top with a dollop of whipped cream; sprinkle with almonds.

8. For berry topping, in a small microwave-safe bowl, combine the jam and berries. Microwave, uncovered, on high for 45 seconds, stirring once. Spoon over remaining squares.

NOTE *This recipe was tested in a 1,100-watt microwave.*

Pistachio Cheesecake

Here's an appealing dessert with a pretty pistachio filling and chocolate drizzle. I created it one Christmas Eve and my family raved about it. I've never seen cheesecake disappear so quickly!

—**KAREN ANKERSON** MANISTEE, MI

PREP: 15 MIN. • **BAKE:** 65 MIN. + COOLING • **MAKES:** 12 SERVINGS

- 2 **cups all-purpose flour**
- ½ **cup ground almonds**
- ½ **cup cold butter**
- 6 **packages (8 ounces each) cream cheese, softened**
- 1 **can (14 ounces) sweetened condensed milk**
- 2 **packages (3.4 ounces each) instant pistachio pudding mix**
- 5 **eggs, lightly beaten**
  Chocolate syrup
  Whipped cream and chopped pistachios, optional

1. In a small bowl, combine the flour and almonds; cut in butter until crumbly. Press onto the bottom and 1¼ in. up the sides of a greased 10-in. springform pan. Bake at 400° for 10 minutes.

2. Meanwhile, in a large bowl, beat cream cheese, milk and pudding mixes until smooth. Add eggs; beat on low speed just until combined. Pour over crust.

3. Place the pan on a baking sheet. Reduce heat to 350°. Bake for 55-60 minutes or until the center is almost set. Cool on a wire rack for 10 minutes. Carefully run a knife around edge of the pan to loosen; cool 1 hour longer. Refrigerate overnight.

4. Slice cheesecake; drizzle slices with chocolate syrup. Garnish with whipped cream and pistachios if desired.

Coffee Toffee Cheesecake

My husband and I host both sides of our families on Thanksgiving every year. I came up with this candy-topped cheesecake a few years ago, and everybody went nuts over it.

—**TAMMY BAKER** BOWLING GREEN, KY

PREP: 45 MIN. • **BAKE:** 55 MIN. + CHILLING • **MAKES:** 12 SERVINGS

- 2½ **cups chocolate wafer crumbs**
- ½ **cup butter, melted**
- 2 **tablespoons sugar**
FILLING
- 1 **cup (6 ounces) semisweet chocolate chips**
- ¼ **cup heavy whipping cream**
- 4 **teaspoons instant coffee granules**
- 3 **packages (8 ounces each) cream cheese, softened**
- 1⅓ **cups sugar**
- 1½ **cups (12 ounces) sour cream**
- 1 **tablespoon vanilla extract**
- ⅛ **teaspoon salt**
- 3 **eggs, lightly beaten**
- 4 **Heath candy bars (1.4 ounces each), chopped**
- 1 **dark chocolate candy bar (1.45 ounces)**

1. Place a greased 9-in. springform pan on a double thickness of heavy-duty foil (about 18 in. square). Securely wrap foil around pan. In a small bowl, combine wafer crumbs, butter and sugar. Press onto the bottom and 1 in. up the sides of prepared pan. Place pan on a baking sheet. Bake at 350° for 10 minutes. Cool on a wire rack.

2. In a microwave-safe bowl, melt the chips and cream; stir until smooth. Stir in coffee granules until dissolved. Set aside.

3. In a large bowl, beat cream cheese and sugar until smooth. Beat in the sour cream, vanilla and salt; gradually beat in chocolate mixture. Add eggs; beat on low speed just until combined. Pour into crust. Place springform pan in a large baking pan; add 1½ in. of hot water to larger pan.

4. Bake at 350° for 55-65 minutes or until center is just set and top appears dull. Remove springform pan from water bath. Cool on a wire rack for 10 minutes. Sprinkle with Heath bars.

5. Carefully run a knife around edge of pan to loosen; cool 1 hour longer. Refrigerate overnight. Chop the dark chocolate candy bar; melt in a microwave and stir until smooth. Drizzle over top of cheesecake.

Cranberry Orange Cheesecake

I can't go to any Christmas gathering without this showstopping dessert in tow. The combination of cranberries, chocolate and orange is a winner.

—LAURIE LUFKIN ESSEX, MA

PREP: 45 MIN. • **BAKE:** 1 HOUR + CHILLING • **MAKES:** 12 SERVINGS

- 1 **cup finely chopped pecans**
- ⅔ **cup chocolate wafer crumbs**
- ¼ **cup butter, melted**
- 3 **tablespoons brown sugar**
- 2 **packages (8 ounces each) cream cheese, softened**
- 2 **cartons (8 ounces each) Mascarpone cheese**
- 1¼ **cups sugar**
- 2 **tablespoons cornstarch**
- 2 **teaspoons orange juice**
- 1 **teaspoon orange extract**
- 4 **eggs, lightly beaten**
- ¾ **cup whole-berry cranberry sauce**
- ¼ **cup dried cranberries**
- 1 **tablespoon water**
- ¼ **cup chocolate ice cream topping, warmed**

1. Place a greased 9-in. springform pan on a double thickness of heavy-duty foil (about 18 in. square). Securely wrap foil around pan.

2. Combine the pecans, wafer crumbs, butter and brown sugar. Press onto the bottom and 1 in. up the sides of prepared pan. Place on a baking sheet. Bake at 325° for 8-10 minutes or until lightly browned. Cool on a wire rack.

3. In a large bowl, beat the cheeses, sugar, cornstarch, orange juice and extract until smooth. Add the eggs; beat on low speed just until combined. Pour half of the batter over crust.

4. Place the cranberry sauce, cranberries and water in a food processor; cover and process until blended. Gently spread over batter in pan; top with remaining batter.

5. Place springform pan in a large baking pan; add 1 in. of hot water to larger pan. Bake at 325° for 60-70 minutes or until center is just set and top appears dull.

6. Remove pan from water bath. Cool on a wire rack for 10 minutes. Carefully run a knife around edge of pan to loosen; cool 1 hour longer. Refrigerate overnight. Just before serving, drizzle with chocolate topping.

Tropical Cheesecake

This recipe has been a favorite of mine for years because of its simple preparation. It makes a sweet and light dessert.

—**DELORES MASON** JACKSONVILLE, IL

PREP: 20 MIN. + CHILLING • **MAKES:** 8-10 SERVINGS

- 1 package (8 ounces) cream cheese, softened
- ½ cup confectioners' sugar
- 1 can (8 ounces) crushed pineapple, drained
- 2 envelopes whipped topping mix (Dream Whip)
- ½ cup cold milk
- ½ teaspoon vanilla extract
- 1 graham cracker crust (9 inches)

1. In a large bowl, beat cream cheese and confectioners' sugar until fluffy. Stir in pineapple.

2. In another bowl, combine dessert topping mix with milk and vanilla; beat until stiff. Fold into pineapple mixture. Spread evenly into crust. Chill.

Bakeshop HOW-TO

Making a Cheesecake Crumb Crust

Place cookies or crackers in a heavy-duty resealable plastic bag. Seal bag, pushing out as much air as possible. Press a rolling pin over the bag, crushing the cookies or crackers into fine crumbs. Or process cookies and crackers in a food processor.

Use a small glass or flat-bottomed measuring cup to firmly press the crumb mixture onto the bottom (and up the sides if directed in the recipe) of a springform pan.

Gingersnap Berry Torte

This cheesecake-like dessert is loaded with fresh fruit, making it perfect for a small summertime gathering.

—**SUSAN PETTY-BAILER** WEST HARTFORD, CT

PREP: 25 MIN. + CHILLING • **MAKES:** 4 SERVINGS

- ½ cup finely crushed gingersnap cookies (about 9 cookies)
- ⅓ cup finely crushed vanilla wafers (about 10 wafers)
- 2 tablespoons finely chopped walnuts
- 2 tablespoons butter, melted

FILLING
- 2 packages (3 ounces each) cream cheese, softened
- ¼ cup sugar
- 1 teaspoon vanilla extract
- 1½ cups fresh blueberries, divided
- ¾ cup sliced fresh strawberries

1. In a bowl, combine gingersnap crumbs, wafer crumbs, walnuts and butter. Press onto the bottom and 1½ in. up the sides of a greased 6-in. springform pan. Bake at 375° for 5-7 minutes or until crust is set. Cool on a wire rack.

2. In a small bowl, beat cream cheese and sugar until smooth. Beat in vanilla. Gently spread about ⅓ cup mixture over crust. Top with half of the blueberries. Layer with about ⅓ cup cream cheese mixture and the strawberries. Spread with remaining cream cheese mixture; top with remaining blueberries. Chill for at least 4 hours.

Mocha Chip Cheesecake

The chocolate crust and miniature chocolate chips are a great contrast to the creamy coffee filling in this cheesecake.

—RENEE GASTINEAU SEATTLE, WA

PREP: 20 MIN. • **BAKE:** 50 MIN. + CHILLING
MAKES: 12 SERVINGS

CRUST
- 2 cups chocolate wafer crumbs (about 32 wafers)
- ½ cup sugar
- ½ cup butter, melted

FILLING
- 3 packages (8 ounces each) cream cheese, softened
- 1 cup sugar
- 3 tablespoons all-purpose flour
- 4 eggs, lightly beaten
- ⅓ cup heavy whipping cream
- 1 tablespoon instant coffee granules
- 1 teaspoon vanilla extract
- 1 cup (6 ounces) miniature semisweet chocolate chips, divided

1. In a large bowl, combine crumbs and sugar; stir in butter. Press onto the bottom and 2 in. up the sides of a greased 9-in. springform pan; set aside.

2. In a large bowl, beat cream cheese and sugar until smooth. Add flour and beat well. Add eggs, beating on low speed just until combined.

3. In a small bowl, combine the cream and coffee granules; let stand for 1 minute. Add to cream cheese mixture with vanilla; beat just until combined. Stir in ¾ cup chocolate chips. Pour into the crust. Sprinkle with the remaining chocolate chips.

4. Bake at 325° for 50-55 minutes or until center is almost set. Cool on a wire rack for 10 minutes.

5. Carefully run a knife around edge of pan to loosen; cool 1 hour longer. Refrigerate overnight. Remove sides of pan.

Pumpkin Cheesecake

My wife and I think this is a perfect ending to a good meal. The cheesecake is smooth and creamy.

—DEWHITT SIZEMORE WOODLAWN, VA

PREP: 20 MIN. • **BAKE:** 1 HOUR + CHILLING • **MAKES:** 12 SERVINGS

- 1½ cups graham cracker crumbs
- 1 tablespoon sugar
- 5 tablespoons butter, melted

FILLING
- 3 packages (8 ounces each) cream cheese, softened
- 1 cup sugar
- 1 teaspoon vanilla extract
- 3 eggs, lightly beaten
- 1 cup canned pumpkin
- ½ teaspoon ground cinnamon
- ¼ teaspoon ground nutmeg
- ¼ teaspoon ground allspice
  Whipped cream

1. In a small bowl, combine cracker crumbs and sugar; stir in butter. Press onto the bottom and 2 in. up the sides of a greased 9-in. springform pan. Bake at 350° for 5 minutes. Cool on a wire rack.

2. In a large bowl, beat the cream cheese, sugar and vanilla until smooth. Beat in the eggs on low speed just until combined. Combine the pumpkin, cinnamon, nutmeg and allspice; fold into cheese mixture. Pour into crust.

3. Bake at 350° for 1 hour or until center is almost set. Cool on a wire rack for 10 minutes.

4. Carefully run a knife around edge of pan to loosen; cool 1 hour longer. Refrigerate overnight. Remove sides of pan. Garnish with whipped cream.

Chocolate-Covered Cheesecake Bites

Satisfy your cheesecake craving with these bite-size delights! They're party favorites and perfect for the holidays.

—ESTHER NEUSTAETER LA CRETE, AB

PREP: 1½ HOURS + FREEZING • **MAKES:** 49 SQUARES

- 1 **cup graham cracker crumbs**
- ¼ **cup finely chopped pecans**
- ¼ **cup butter, melted**

FILLING
- 2 **packages (8 ounces each) cream cheese, softened**
- ½ **cup sugar**
- ¼ **cup sour cream**
- 2 **eggs, lightly beaten**
- ½ **teaspoon vanilla extract**

COATING
- 24 **ounces semisweet chocolate, chopped**
- 3 **tablespoons shortening**

1. Line a 9-in. square baking pan with foil and grease the foil. In a small bowl, combine the graham cracker crumbs, pecans and butter. Press into prepared pan; set aside.

2. In a large bowl, beat the cream cheese, sugar and sour cream until smooth. Add eggs and vanilla; beat on low speed just until combined. Pour over crust.

3. Bake at 325° for 35-40 minutes or until center is almost set. Cool on a wire rack. Freeze overnight.

4. In a microwave, melt chocolate and shortening; stir until smooth. Cool slightly.

5. Using foil, lift cheesecake out of pan. Gently peel off foil; cut cheesecake into 1¼-in. squares. Work with a few pieces at a time; keep remaining squares refrigerated until ready to dip.

6. Using a toothpick, completely dip squares, one at a time, in melted chocolate; allow excess to drip off. Place on waxed paper-lined baking sheets. Spoon additional chocolate over the tops if necessary to coat. (Reheat chocolate if needed to finish dipping.) Let stand for 20 minutes or until set. Store in an airtight container in the refrigerator or freezer.

Lemon Dream Cheesecake

Light and lemony, this creamy dessert is just the thing for a spring or summer's day.

—**BONNIE JOST** MANITOWOC, WI

PREP: 30 MIN. • **BAKE:** 55 MIN. + CHILLING • **MAKES:** 16 SERVINGS

- 2 cups graham cracker crumbs
- 6 tablespoons butter, melted
- ¼ cup sugar

FILLING

- 4 packages (8 ounces each) cream cheese, softened
- 1 cup sugar
- ½ cup heavy whipping cream
- ¼ cup lemon juice
- 2 tablespoons all-purpose flour
- 1 tablespoon grated lemon peel
- 2½ teaspoons vanilla extract
- 1 teaspoon lemon extract
- 10 drops yellow food coloring, optional
- 5 eggs, lightly beaten

1. In a small bowl, combine the cracker crumbs, butter and sugar. Press onto the bottom and 2 in. up the sides of a greased 10-in. springform pan. Place pan on a baking sheet. Bake at 325° for 10 minutes. Cool on a wire rack.

2. In a large bowl, beat cream cheese and sugar until smooth. Beat in the cream, lemon juice, flour, lemon peel, extracts and food coloring if desired. Add eggs; beat on low speed just until combined. Pour into crust. Return pan to baking sheet.

3. Bake for 55-65 minutes or until center is almost set. Cool on a wire rack for 10 minutes. Carefully run a knife around edge of pan to loosen; cool 1 hour longer. Refrigerate overnight. Remove sides of pan.

Cheesecake Pops

These cute, lollipop-like bites will make any occasion memorable. The topping possibilities are endless.

—**EVELYN MOORE** ELK GROVE, CA

PREP: 2 HOURS + FREEZING • **MAKES:** 45 CHEESECAKE POPS

- 3 packages (8 ounces each) cream cheese, softened
- 1 cup sugar
- 1 cup (8 ounces) sour cream
- 1 teaspoon vanilla extract
- 3 eggs, lightly beaten
- 1 cup graham cracker crumbs
- 45 lollipop sticks (4 inches long)
- 3 packages (10 to 12 ounces each) white baking chips
- 3 tablespoons shortening
  Toppings: grated coconut, grated chocolate, assorted sprinkles and chopped nuts

1. Line bottom of a 9-in. springform pan with parchment paper; coat paper and sides of pan with cooking spray.

2. In a large bowl, beat cream cheese and sugar until smooth. Beat in sour cream and vanilla until blended. Add eggs; beat on low speed just until combined. Pour into prepared pan.

3. Place pan on a baking sheet. Bake at 350° for 45-50 minutes or until center is almost set. Cool on a wire rack for 10 minutes. Carefully run a knife around edge of pan to loosen; cool 1 hour longer. Cover and freeze overnight.

4. Remove from the freezer and let stand for 30 minutes. Place cracker crumbs in a shallow bowl. Working quickly, scoop out 1-in. balls of cheesecake; roll each in cracker crumbs and insert a lollipop stick. Place on waxed paper-lined baking sheets. Freeze for 1 hour or until firm.

5. In a microwave, melt white chips and shortening at 70% power; stir until smooth. Place toppings in shallow bowls. Dip cheesecake pops in white chip mixture; allow excess to drip off. Roll in toppings. Place on waxed paper; let stand until set. Store in the refrigerator.

Two-Tone Cheesecake

Looking to create an original for the Alaska State Fair contest, I came up with my eye-catching layered cheesecake. It won Grand Champion!

—**CINDI PAULSON** ANCHORAGE, AK

PREP: 25 MIN. • **BAKE:** 1 HOUR + COOLING • **MAKES:** 12 SERVINGS

  1½ cups chocolate graham cracker crumbs
   6 tablespoons sugar
   6 tablespoons butter, melted
FILLING
   4 packages (8 ounces each) cream cheese, softened
  1¾ cups sugar
   ¾ cup heavy whipping cream
   4 eggs, lightly beaten
   6 ounces semisweet chocolate, melted and cooled
TOPPING
   4 ounces semisweet chocolate, finely chopped
   ½ cup heavy whipping cream

1. In a large bowl, combine the cracker crumbs, sugar and butter. Press onto the bottom of a greased 10-in. springform pan. Place on a baking sheet. Bake at 325° for 10 minutes. Cool on a wire rack.

2. In a large bowl, beat cream cheese and sugar until smooth. Gradually beat in cream. Add eggs; beat on low speed just until combined.

3. Remove 3½ cups to a small bowl; gently stir in melted chocolate. Pour filling over crust. Gently pour remaining filling over chocolate layer. Bake at 325° for 1 to 1¼ hours or until center is almost set.

4. Cool on a wire rack for 10 minutes. Carefully run a knife around edge of the pan to loosen; cool 1 hour longer. Meanwhile, place chopped chocolate in a small bowl.

5. In a small saucepan, bring cream just to a boil. Pour over chocolate; whisk until smooth. Cool slightly; gently pour over cheesecake. Cover and chill overnight. Remove sides of pan.

Blueberry Swirl Cheesecake

My wife, Gail, and I host an annual cheesecake party. For the event's 10th anniversary, we prepared 10 family favorites, including this fruity creation.

—**SCOTT FOX** FERGUS FALLS, MN

PREP: 20 MIN. • **BAKE:** 40 MIN. + CHILLING • **MAKES:** 12 SERVINGS

   1 package (12 ounces) frozen blueberries, thawed
   1 tablespoon sugar
   1 tablespoon water
  1½ teaspoons cornstarch
CRUST
  1¼ cups graham cracker crumbs
   ¼ cup sugar
   ⅓ cup butter, melted
FILLING
   3 packages (8 ounces each) cream cheese, softened
   1 can (14 ounces) sweetened condensed milk
   ¼ cup lemon juice
   3 eggs, lightly beaten

1. In a food processor, process the blueberries, sugar, water and cornstarch until blended. Transfer to a heavy saucepan; bring to a boil. Reduce heat; cook and stir over medium heat for 2 minutes or until thickened. Set aside ⅓ cup for filling. Refrigerate remaining sauce for topping.

2. Combine crust ingredients. Press onto the bottom of a greased 9-in. springform pan; set aside. In a large bowl, beat cream cheese and milk until smooth; beat in lemon juice. Add eggs; beat on low speed just until combined. Pour half of the filling over crust; top with half of the reserved blueberry mixture. Repeat layers. Cut through filling with a knife to swirl. Place pan on a baking sheet.

3. Bake at 325° for 40-45 minutes or until center is almost set. Cool 10 minutes. Carefully run a knife around the edge of pan to loosen; cool 1 hour longer. Refrigerate overnight. Remove sides of pan. Serve with blueberry sauce.

Tiramisu Cheesecake Dessert

I wasn't a big fan of tiramisu until I tried this recipe with its distinctive cheesecake- and coffee-flavored layers. It's one of my favorite desserts to make during the fall.

—CHRISTIE NELSON TAYLORVILLE, IL

PREP: 20 MIN. • **BAKE:** 40 MIN. + CHILLING • **MAKES:** 12 SERVINGS

- 1 **package (12 ounces) vanilla wafers**
- 5 **teaspoons instant coffee granules, divided**
- 3 **tablespoons hot water, divided**
- 4 **packages (8 ounces each) cream cheese, softened**
- 1 **cup sugar**
- 1 **cup (8 ounces) sour cream**
- 4 **eggs, lightly beaten**
- 1 **cup whipped topping**
- 1 **tablespoon baking cocoa**

1. Layer half of wafers in a greased 13-in. x 9-in. baking dish. In a small bowl, dissolve 2 teaspoons coffee granules in 2 tablespoons hot water. Brush wafers with half of coffee; set remaining mixture aside.

2. In a large bowl, beat cream cheese and sugar until smooth. Beat in sour cream. Add eggs; beat on low speed just until combined. Divide batter in half. Dissolve remaining coffee granules in remaining hot water; stir into one portion of batter. Spread over wafers. Layer with remaining wafers; brush with reserved coffee. Top with remaining batter.

3. Bake at 325° for 40-45 minutes or until center is almost set. Cool on a wire rack for 10 minutes. Carefully run a knife around edge of dish to loosen; cool 1 hour longer. Refrigerate overnight.

4. Spread with the whipped topping; dust with cocoa. Refrigerate leftovers.

White Chocolate Pumpkin Cheesecake

You'll want to put this delectable cheesecake on a pedestal! The crunchy almond topping is a delightful finishing touch.

—PHYLLIS SCHMALZ KANSAS CITY, KS

PREP: 30 MIN. • **BAKE:** 55 MIN. + CHILLING • **MAKES:** 12 SERVINGS

- 1½ cups crushed gingersnap cookies (about 32 cookies)
- ¼ cup butter, melted
- 3 packages (8 ounces each) cream cheese, softened
- 1 cup sugar
- 3 eggs, lightly beaten
- 1 teaspoon vanilla extract
- 5 ounces white baking chocolate, melted and cooled
- ¾ cup canned pumpkin
- 1 teaspoon ground cinnamon
- ¼ teaspoon ground nutmeg

ALMOND TOPPING
- ½ cup chopped almonds
- 2 tablespoons butter, melted
- 1 teaspoon sugar

1. In a small bowl, combine gingersnap crumbs and butter. Press onto the bottom of a greased 9-in. springform pan; set aside.

2. In a large bowl, beat cream cheese and sugar until smooth. Add eggs and vanilla; beat on low speed just until combined. Stir in melted white chocolate.

3. Combine pumpkin and spices; gently fold into cream cheese mixture. Pour over the crust. Placet he pan on a baking sheet.

4. Bake at 350° for 55-60 minutes or until center is just set. Cool on a wire rack for 10 minutes. Meanwhile, combine the topping ingredients; spread in a shallow baking pan. Bake for 10 minutes or until golden brown, stirring twice. Cool.

5. Carefully run a knife around edge of springform pan to loosen cheesecake; cool 1 hour longer. Refrigerate overnight. Transfer topping to an airtight container; store in the refrigerator. Remove sides of pan. Just before serving, sprinkle topping over cheesecake.

No-Bake Cherry Cheesecakes

My husband and I both work full-time, and taxiing our two teenagers around town leaves me little time in the kitchen. Using ready-to-go crust and pie filling, I can extend a no-bake mix to make two light, fancy-looking pies in just 15 minutes!

—PAM NOFFKE TYLER, TX

PREP: 15 MIN. + CHILLING • **MAKES:** 2 PIES (6-8 SERVINGS EACH)

- 1 package (11.1 ounces) no-bake cheesecake mix
- ½ cup butter, melted
- 2 tablespoons sugar
- 1½ cups cold milk
- 1 package (8 ounces) cream cheese, softened
- 1 cup confectioners' sugar
- 2 cups whipped topping
- 1 graham cracker crust (9 inches)
- 2 cans (21 ounces each) cherry pie filling

1. In a large bowl, combine the cheesecake crust mix, butter and sugar. Press onto the bottom and up the sides of an ungreased 9-in. pie plate. Refrigerate.

2. In another large bowl, beat the cheesecake filling mix and milk on medium speed for 3 minutes. In a small bowl, beat cream cheese and confectioners' sugar until smooth. Add to the cheesecake mixture and beat well. Fold in the whipped topping.

3. Spoon half of cheesecake mixture into chilled crust; spoon the remaining half into the purchased crust. Refrigerate for at least 1 hour. Top each with pie filling.

Chocolate Almond Cheesecake

This cheesecake is easy to make but it's definitely not easy to wait until the next day to eat it! It's a spectacular make-ahead party dessert.

—DARLENE BRENDEN SALEM, OR

PREP: 25 MIN. + CHILLING • **BAKE:** 50 MIN. + CHILLING
MAKES: 16 SERVINGS

CRUST
- 1 package (9 ounces) chocolate wafer cookies, crushed (about 2 cups)
- ¼ cup sugar
- ¼ teaspoon ground cinnamon
- ¼ cup butter, melted

FILLING
- 2 packages (8 ounces each) cream cheese, softened
- 1 cup sugar
- 1 cup (8 ounces) sour cream
- 8 ounces semisweet chocolate, melted and cooled
- ½ teaspoon almond extract
- 2 eggs, lightly beaten

TOPPING
- 1 cup (8 ounces) sour cream
- ¼ teaspoon baking cocoa
- 2 tablespoons sugar
- ½ teaspoon almond extract

1. In a small bowl, combine crust ingredients; reserve 2 tablespoons for garnish. Press remaining crumbs evenly onto the bottom and 2 in. up the sides of a 9-in. springform pan. Chill.

2. For filling, in a large bowl, beat cream cheese and sugar until smooth. Beat in the sour cream, chocolate and extract. Add the eggs; beat on low speed just until combined. Pour into crust.

3. Place pan on a baking sheet. Bake at 350° for 40 minutes (filling will not be set). Remove from oven and let stand for 5 minutes.

4. Meanwhile, combine topping ingredients. Gently spread over filling. Sprinkle with reserved crumbs. Bake 10 minutes longer.

5. Cool on a wire rack for 10 minutes. Carefully run a knife around edge of pan to loosen; cool 1 hour longer. Refrigerate overnight.

1. In a large bowl, beat cream cheese and sugar until smooth. Beat in sour cream and vanilla. Fold in whipped topping. Spread half of the mixture evenly into crust. Fold cocoa and confectioners' sugar into remaining mixture; gently spread over cream cheese layer. Refrigerate for at least 4 hours.

2. Cut into slices; top each slice with cherry pie filling.

Peanut Butter Cheese Torte

This dessert has long been a favorite with my family. I especially like the fact that it requires no baking—and who doesn't melt for the combination of peanut butter and chocolate?

—RUTH BLAIR WAUKESHA, WI

PREP: 20 MIN. + CHILLING • **MAKES:** 16 SERVINGS

CRUST
- 1 cup graham cracker crumbs
- ¼ cup packed brown sugar
- ¼ cup butter, melted
- ½ cup finely chopped peanuts

FILLING
- 2 cups creamy peanut butter
- 2 packages (8 ounces each) cream cheese, softened
- 2 cups sugar
- 2 tablespoons butter, softened
- 2 teaspoons vanilla extract
- 1½ cups heavy whipping cream, whipped

CHOCOLATE TOPPING
- 4 ounces semisweet chocolate chips
- 3 tablespoons plus 2 teaspoons brewed coffee
  Chopped peanuts, optional

1. Combine all crust ingredients. Press onto the bottom and halfway up the sides of a 10-in. springform pan. Chill.

2. For filling, beat peanut butter, cream cheese, sugar, butter and vanilla in a large bowl on high until smooth, about 2 minutes. Fold in whipped cream. Gently spoon into crust; refrigerate 6 hours or overnight.

3. For topping, in a microwave, melt chocolate with coffee; stir until smooth. Spread over chilled torte. Refrigerate until firm, about 30 minutes. Garnish the top with chopped peanuts if desired.

Black Forest Cheesecake

I take this popular cheesecake to every gathering. I created the recipe about 15 years ago and my family has been asking for it ever since.

—CHRISTINE OOYEN WINNEBAGO, IL

PREP: 20 MIN. + CHILLING • **MAKES:** 6-8 SERVINGS

- 1 package (8 ounces) cream cheese, softened
- ⅓ cup sugar
- 1 cup (8 ounces) sour cream
- 2 teaspoons vanilla extract
- 1 carton (8 ounces) frozen whipped topping, thawed
- 1 chocolate crumb crust (8 inches)
- ¼ cup baking cocoa
- 1 tablespoon confectioners' sugar
- 1 can (21 ounces) cherry pie filling

Chocolate Mallow Pie

This rich and fudgy cream cheese pie should serve eight, but it never does because so many folks request a second slice! I've been cooking for more than 60 years and this is the best chocolate pie recipe I've found.

—LOUISE GENN COSMOPOLIS, WA

PREP: 25 MIN. + CHILLING • **MAKES:** 8 SERVINGS

- 1¼ cups Oreo cookie crumbs
- ¼ cup butter, melted
- 2 tablespoons sugar
- 2 packages (one 8 ounces, one 3 ounces) cream cheese, softened
- ½ cup chocolate syrup
- 1⅓ cups semisweet chocolate chips, melted
- 1 carton (8 ounces) frozen whipped topping, thawed
- 2 cups miniature marshmallows
  Chocolate curls, optional

1. In a large bowl, combine the cookie crumbs, butter and sugar. Press into a 9-in. pie plate. Bake at 375° for 8-10 minutes or until set; cool completely on a wire rack.

2. In a large bowl, beat cream cheese and chocolate syrup until blended. Beat in melted chips. Set aside ¼ cup of whipped topping. Fold marshmallows and remaining whipped topping into chocolate mixture.

3. Spoon filling into crust. Refrigerate for at least 8 hours or overnight. Top with reserved whipped topping. Garnish with chocolate curls if desired.

Frosted Raspberry Truffle Brownies

On the outside, these look like traditional brownies. But when people bite in, they are pleasantly surprised! It's almost like eating a filled chocolate candy.

—LESLIE KNICL MAHOMET, IL

PREP: 30 MIN. • **BAKE:** 30 MIN. + CHILLING
MAKES: ABOUT 2½ DOZEN

- ½ cup butter, cubed
- 1¼ cups semisweet chocolate chips
- 2 eggs
- ¾ cup packed brown sugar
- 1 teaspoon instant coffee granules
- 2 tablespoons hot water
- ¾ cup all-purpose flour
- ½ teaspoon baking powder

FILLING
- 1 cup (6 ounces) semisweet chocolate chips
- 1 package (8 ounces) cream cheese, softened
- ¼ cup confectioners' sugar
- ⅓ cup seedless red raspberry jam

GLAZE
- ¼ cup semisweet chocolate chips
- 1 teaspoon shortening

1. In a microwave, melt butter and chocolate chips; stir until smooth. Cool slightly. In a large bowl, beat eggs and brown sugar until blended. Dissolve coffee granules in water; add to egg mixture. Beat in chocolate until well blended. Combine flour and baking powder; stir into chocolate mixture just until blended.

2. Spread in a greased 9-in. square baking pan. Bake at 350° for 30-35 minutes or until brownies test done. Cool on a wire rack.

3. For filling, in a microwave, melt chocolate chips; stir until smooth. Cool. In a small bowl, beat cream cheese and confectioners' sugar until smooth. Beat in jam; stir in melted chocolate. Spread over cooled brownies.

4. For glaze, in a microwave, melt chocolate chips and shortening; stir until smooth. Drizzle over filling. Chill before cutting. Store in the refrigerator.

Raspberry Sachertorte

It may look like this torte took hours to make, but it has a surprisingly short list of ingredients. A small slice splendidly satisfies a sweet tooth.

—**ROSE HOCKETT** COLORADO SPRINGS, CO

PREP: 50 MIN. • **BAKE:** 25 MIN. + STANDING • **MAKES:** 12 SERVINGS

- 4 **eggs, separated**
- 5 **tablespoons butter**
- ⅔ **cup sugar**
- 9 **ounces bittersweet chocolate, melted**
- ¾ **cup ground almonds**
- ¼ **cup all-purpose flour**
- ¼ **cup seedless raspberry jam**

GLAZE

- 3 **ounces bittersweet chocolate, chopped**
- 2 **tablespoons butter**

1. Place the egg whites in a large bowl; let stand at room temperature for 30 minutes. In another bowl, beat butter and sugar until crumbly, about 2 minutes. Add egg yolks and melted chocolate; beat on low speed until combined. Combine almonds and flour; stir into butter mixture just until blended.

2. In another bowl with clean beaters, beat egg whites until stiff peaks form; fold into batter. Transfer to a greased 9-in. springform pan. Bake at 350° for 25-30 minutes or until a toothpick inserted near the center comes out clean. Cool on a wire rack for 10 minutes. Carefully run a knife around edge of the pan to loosen; remove sides of the pan. Cool completely.

3. Spread jam over top of cake. For glaze, in a small saucepan, melt chocolate and butter; spread over jam. Let stand at room temperature for 1 hour or until set.

Cream-Filled Chocolate Supreme Muffins

Because of her reputation for baking up yummy things, Mom used to sell muffins at my dad's workplace. Among my favorites were these cupcake-like treats.

—**SUSANNE SPICKER** NORTH OGDEN, UT

PREP: 30 MIN. • **BAKE:** 25 MIN. + COOLING • **MAKES:** 1 DOZEN

- 3 **cups all-purpose flour**
- 2 **cups sugar**
- ½ **cup baking cocoa**
- 2 **teaspoons baking soda**
- 1 **teaspoon salt**
- 2 **cups cold water**
- ¾ **cup canola oil**
- 1 **egg**
- 2 **tablespoons white vinegar**
- 2 **teaspoons vanilla extract**

FILLING

- 4 **ounces cream cheese, softened**
- ¼ **cup sugar**
- ⅛ **teaspoon salt**
- 2 **tablespoons beaten egg**
- ½ **teaspoon vanilla extract**
- ¾ **cup milk chocolate chips**
    Confectioners' sugar, optional

1. In a large bowl, combine the flour, sugar, cocoa, baking soda and salt. In another bowl, combine the water, oil, egg, vinegar and vanilla. Stir into tje dry ingredients just until moistened.

2. For filling, beat the cream cheese, sugar and salt until smooth. Beat in egg and vanilla. Fold in chips.

3. Fill 12 paper-lined jumbo muffin cups half full with batter. Drop a rounded tablespoonful of cream cheese mixture into center of each; cover with remaining batter.

4. Bake at 350° for 25-30 minutes or until a toothpick inserted in muffin comes out clean. Cool for 5 minutes before removing from the pans to wire racks to cool completely. Sprinkle with confectioners' sugar if desired.

Sour Cream Chocolate Cupcakes

My husband and I often enjoy these moist, chocolaty cupcakes. The sour cream is definitely the ingredient that gives them their distinctive flavor and texture.

—ALICSA MAYER ALTA VISTA, KS

PREP: 30 MIN. • **BAKE:** 20 MIN. + COOLING • **MAKES:** 2 DOZEN

- ¼ **cup butter, cubed**
- 4 **ounces unsweetened chocolate, chopped**
- 2 **eggs**
- 2 **cups sugar**
- 1 **cup water**
- ¾ **cup sour cream**
- 1 **teaspoon vanilla extract**
- 2 **cups all-purpose flour**
- 1 **teaspoon baking soda**

FROSTING
- ½ **cup butter, cubed**
- 4 **ounces unsweetened chocolate, chopped**
- 4 **cups confectioners' sugar**
- ½ **cup sour cream**
- 2 **teaspoons vanilla extract**

1. In a microwave, melt butter and chocolate; stir until smooth. Cool for 10 minutes. In a large bowl, beat the eggs, sugar, water, sour cream and vanilla. Combine flour and baking soda; add to the egg mixture and mix well. Add chocolate mixture; beat on high speed for 2-3 minutes.

2. Fill paper-lined muffin cups two-thirds full. Bake at 350° for 18-20 minutes or until a toothpick inserted near the center comes out clean. Cool for 10 minutes before removing from pans to wire racks to cool completely.

3. For frosting, in a large microwave-safe bowl, melt butter and chocolate; stir until smooth. Cool for 10 minutes. With a portable mixer, beat in the confectioners' sugar, sour cream and vanilla on low until smooth. Frost cupcakes. Store in the refrigerator.

Melty Microwave Brownies

These rich, fudgy brownies can't be beat for a quick dessert.

—SUE GRONHOLZ BEAVER DAM, WI

PREP: 10 MIN. • **COOK:** 5 MIN. + COOLING • **MAKES:** 1 DOZEN

- ½ cup butter, cubed
- 2 ounces unsweetened chocolate, chopped
- 2 eggs
- ¾ cup sugar
- ½ cup all-purpose flour
- 1 teaspoon baking powder
- 1 teaspoon vanilla extract
- ½ cup semisweet chocolate chips
  Confectioners' sugar

1. In a microwave, melt butter and chocolate; stir until smooth. Cool slightly. In a large bowl, beat the eggs for 2 minutes. Gradually add sugar, beating until thick and pale yellow. Combine flour and baking powder; add to the egg mixture. Stir in the melted chocolate mixture, vanilla and chips.

2. Pour into a greased 8-in. square microwave-safe dish. Cook on high for 3½ to 4 minutes or until a toothpick inserted near the center comes out clean. Place on a wire rack; cool for 10 minutes. Dust with confectioners' sugar.

NOTE *This recipe was tested in a 1,100-watt microwave.*

Chocolate Velvet Dessert

This extra-speical creation is the result of several attempts to duplicate a dessert I enjoyed on vacation. It looks so beautiful on a buffet table that many folks are tempted to forgo the main course in favor of it.

—MOLLY SEIDEL EDGEWOOD, NM

PREP: 20 MIN. • **BAKE:** 45 MIN. + CHILLING • **MAKES:** 16 SERVINGS

- 1½ cups chocolate wafer crumbs
- 2 tablespoons sugar
- ¼ cup butter, melted
- 2 cups (12 ounces) semisweet chocolate chips
- 6 egg yolks
- 1¾ cups heavy whipping cream
- 1 teaspoon vanilla extract

CHOCOLATE BUTTERCREAM FROSTING
- ½ cup butter, softened
- 3 cups confectioners' sugar
- 3 tablespoons baking cocoa
- 3 to 4 tablespoons 2% milk

1. In a small bowl, combine wafer crumbs and sugar; stir in butter. Press onto the bottom and 1½ in. up the sides of a greased 9-in. springform pan. Place on a baking sheet. Bake at 350° for 10 minutes. Cool on a wire rack.

2. In a large microwave-safe bowl, melt chocolate chips; stir until smooth. Cool. In a small bowl, combine the egg yolks, cream and vanilla. Gradually stir a small amount of mixture into melted chocolate until blended; gradually stir in remaining mixture. Pour into crust.

3. Place pan on a baking sheet. Bake at 350° for 45-50 minutes or until center is almost set. Cool on a wire rack for 10 minutes. Carefully run a knife around edge of pan to loosen; cool 1 hour longer. Refrigerate overnight.

4. In a large bowl, combine the butter, confectioners' sugar, cocoa and enough milk to achieve a piping consistency. Using a large star tip, pipe frosting on dessert.

Mud Pie

Having grown up in the South, we naturally fell in love with chocolate pie filled with pecans. It could take all day to put one together, but my version takes only 15 minutes. Oh, yeah!

—**DEBORAH WOOLARD** LAS VEGAS, NV

PREP: 15 MIN. + CHILLING • **MAKES:** 8 SERVINGS

- 3   ounces semisweet chocolate, chopped
- ¼   cup sweetened condensed milk
- 1   chocolate crumb crust (8 inches)
- ½   cup chopped pecans
- 2   cups cold 2% milk
- 2   packages (3.9 ounces each) instant chocolate pudding mix
- 1   carton (8 ounces) frozen whipped topping, thawed, divided

1.   In a microwave, melt chocolate; stir in condensed milk until smooth. Pour into crust; sprinkle with pecans.

2.   In a small bowl, whisk the milk and pudding mixes for 2 minutes (mixture will be thick). Carefully spread 1½ cups of pudding mixture over pecans.

3.   Fold ½ cup whipped topping into the remaining pudding mixture; spoon over pudding layer. Top with remaining whipped topping. Chill until set.

Cookie Dough Brownies

When I take these rich brownies to a get-together, I carry the recipe, too, because it always gets requested. Children of all ages love the tempting "cookie dough" filling. These brownies are typically the first to be gone from the buffet table—even before the entrees!

—**WENDY BAILEY** ELIDA, OH

PREP: 20 MIN. + CHILLING • **BAKE:** 30 MIN. + COOLING **MAKES:** 3 DOZEN

- 4   eggs
- 1   cup canola oil
- 2   cups sugar
- 2   teaspoons vanilla extract
- 1½   cups all-purpose flour
- ½   cup baking cocoa
- ½   teaspoon salt
- ½   cup chopped walnuts, optional

FILLING
- ½   cup butter, softened
- ½   cup packed brown sugar
- ¼   cup sugar
- 2   tablespoons 2% milk
- 1   teaspoon vanilla extract
- 1   cup all-purpose flour

GLAZE
- 1   cup (6 ounces) semisweet chocolate chips
- 1   tablespoon shortening
- ¾   cup chopped walnuts

1.   In a large bowl, beat the eggs, oil, sugar and vanilla until well blended. Combine the flour, cocoa and salt; gradually beat into egg mixture. Stir in walnuts if desired.

2.   Pour into a greased 13-in. x 9-in. baking pan. Bake at 350° for 30 minutes or until the brownies test done. Cool completely.

3.   For filling, in a large bowl, cream butter and sugars until light and fluffy. Beat in milk and vanilla. Gradually beat in flour. Spread over the brownies; chill until firm.

4.   For glaze, in a microwave, melt chocolate chips and shortening; stir until smooth. Spread over filling. Immediately sprinkle with nuts, pressing down slightly. Let stand until set.

Chocolate Silk Pie

This quick and creamy chocolate pie not only melts in your mouth, it also melts any and all resistance to dessert!

—MARY RELYEA CANASTOTA, NY

PREP: 30 MIN. + CHILLING • **MAKES:** 6-8 SERVINGS

- 1 **unbaked pastry shell (9 inches)**
- 1 **jar (7 ounces) marshmallow creme**
- 1 **cup (6 ounces) semisweet chocolate chips**
- ¼ **cup butter, cubed**
- 2 **ounces unsweetened chocolate**
- 2 **tablespoons strong brewed coffee**
- 1 **cup heavy whipping cream, whipped**

TOPPING

- 1 **cup heavy whipping cream**
- 2 **tablespoons confectioners' sugar**
   Chocolate curls, optional

1. Line unpricked pastry shell with a double thickness of heavy-duty foil. Bake at 450° for 8 minutes. Remove foil; bake 5 minutes longer. Cool on a wire rack.

2. Meanwhile, in a heavy saucepan, combine the marshmallow creme, chocolate chips, butter, unsweetened chocolate and coffee; cook and stir over low heat until chocolate is melted and mixture is smooth. Cool. Fold in whipped cream; pour into crust.

3. For topping, in a large bowl, beat cream until it begins to thicken. Add confectioners' sugar; beat until stiff peaks form. Spread over filling. Refrigerate for at least 3 hours before serving. Garnish with chocolate curls if desired.

Bakeshop **HOW-TO**

Making Chocolate Curls

For a pretty garnish to accent any dessert, use a vegetable peeler to "peel" curls from a solid block of chocolate. To keep the strips intact, allow them to fall gently onto a plate or a single layer of waxed paper.

If you get only shavings, your chocolate may be too hard. Allow it to warm slightly.

Chocolate Cheesecake

This luscious cheesecake has a hint of almond in the creamy chocolate filling. Just one slice and your sweet tooth will rejoice!

—**LORI COULTHARD** LARAMIE, WY

PREP: 20 MIN • **BAKE:** 45 MIN. + CHILLING • **MAKES:** 12 SERVINGS

- 1¼ cups graham cracker crumbs (about 20 squares)
- ½ cup sugar
- ¼ cup baking cocoa
- 6 tablespoons butter, melted

FILLING

- 3 packages (8 ounces each) cream cheese, softened
- ¾ cup sugar
- 3 eggs, lightly beaten
- 1 cup (6 ounces) semisweet chocolate chips, melted
- 1 teaspoon almond extract
- ½ teaspoon vanilla extract

TOPPING

- ¼ cup semisweet chocolate chips
- ⅓ cup heavy whipping cream
- 1 tablespoon honey

1. In a large bowl, combine the cracker crumbs, sugar and cocoa; stir in butter until crumbly. Press onto bottom and 1-in. up side of a greased 9-in. springform pan; set aside.

2. In a small bowl, beat cream cheese and sugar until smooth. Add eggs; beat on low speed just until combined. Stir in melted chocolate and extracts just until blended. Pour into crust.

3. Bake at 350° for 45-50 minutes or until center is almost set. Cool on a wire rack for 10 minutes. Carefully run knife around the edge of pan to loosen; cool 1 hour longer. Refrigerate until completely cooled.

4. In a small saucepan over low heat, melt the chocolate chips, cream and honey; stir until smooth. Remove from the heat; cool for 5 minutes. Pour topping over the cheesecake. Chill for at least 4 hours or until topping is set.

Chocolate Cinnamon Rolls

Here's a yummy departure from regular cinnamon rolls. When I take them to morning bowling league, they are quickly devoured!

—MYRNA SIPPEL THOMPSON, IL

PREP: 30 MIN. + RISING • **BAKE:** 25 MIN. • **MAKES:** 20 ROLLS

- 2 packages (¼ ounce each) active dry yeast
- 1½ cups warm water (110° to 115°), divided
- ½ cup butter, softened
- ½ cup sugar
- 1 teaspoon salt
- 4½ to 4¾ cups all-purpose flour
- ⅔ cup baking cocoa

FILLING
- 2 tablespoons butter, melted
- ⅓ cup sugar
- ½ teaspoon ground cinnamon
- 1 cup miniature semisweet chocolate chips
- ⅔ cup finely chopped nuts, optional

ICING
- 2 cups confectioners' sugar
- ½ teaspoon vanilla extract
- 2 to 3 tablespoons milk
  Additional miniature semisweet chocolate chips, optional

1. In a large bowl, dissolve yeast in ½ cup warm water. Add the butter, sugar, salt and remaining water. Stir in 2½ cups flour and cocoa. Beat on medium speed for 3 minutes or until smooth. Stir in enough remaining flour to form a soft dough.

2. Turn onto a lightly floured surface; knead until smooth and elastic, about 6-8 minutes. Place in a greased bowl, turning once to grease the top. Cover and let rise in a warm place until doubled, about 1 hour.

3. Turn onto a lightly floured surface; divide in half. Roll each portion into a 12-in. x 10-in. rectangle; brush with melted butter. Combine the sugar, cinnamon, chocolate chips and nuts if desired; sprinkle over dough to within ½ in. of edges.

4. Roll up each jelly-roll style, starting with a long side; pinch seams to seal. Cut each into 10 slices. Place cut side down in a greased 15-in. x 10-in. x 1-in. baking pan. Cover and let rise until doubled, about 45 minutes.

5. Bake at 375° for 25-30 minutes or until lightly browned. Meanwhile, in a small bowl, combine the confectioners' sugar, vanilla and enough milk to reach desired consistency. Spread over rolls while slightly warm; sprinkle with additional chocolate chips if desired.

Bakeshop TIP

Keep Cocoa on Hand

Cocoa is easy to mix into recipes with flour and other dry ingredients to create genuine chocolate flavor. But because cocoa doesn't contain the natural fats that are found in chocolate, it has a much longer shelf life. Cocoa stays fresh in the pantry for about two years!

Special Pleasure Chocolate Cheesecake

When we have time, we enjoy making cheesecakes. In fact, we've come up with a couple of our own recipes. We like this fail-proof dessert because it's so easy to prepare and has just the right mix of ingredients to make it a special pleasure for any palate.

—BENJAMIN & SUE ELLEN CLARK WARSAW, NY

PREP: 20 MIN. • **BAKE:** 40 MIN. + CHILLING • **MAKES:** 24 SERVINGS

- 1 **package (18 ounces) ready-to-bake refrigerated triple-chocolate cookie dough**
- 1 **package (8 ounces) milk chocolate toffee bits**
- 1 **package (9½ ounces) Dove dark chocolate candies**
- 3 **packages (8 ounces each) cream cheese, softened**
- 1 **can (14 ounces) sweetened condensed milk**
- ¾ **cup (6 ounces) vanilla yogurt**
- 4 **eggs, lightly beaten**
- 1 **teaspoon vanilla extract**
  Whipped cream

1. Let dough stand at room temperature for 5-10 minutes to soften. Press nine portions of dough into an ungreased 13-in. x 9-in. baking dish (save remaining dough for another use). Set aside 2 tablespoons toffee bits for garnish; sprinkle remaining toffee bits over dough.

2. In a microwave, melt chocolate candies; stir until smooth. In a large bowl, beat the cream cheese, milk and yogurt until smooth. Add eggs; beat on low speed just until combined. Stir in vanilla and melted chocolate. Pour over crust.

3. Bake at 350° for 40-45 minutes or until center is almost set. Cool on a wire rack. Refrigerate for 4 hours or overnight. Garnish with whipped cream and reserved toffee bits.

Brownie Truffle Torte

This over-the-top truffle cake tastes like it takes all day to make, but we managed to trim some steps to give you scrumptious results in less time.

—TASTE OF HOME TEST KITCHEN

PREP: 30 MIN. + COOLING • **BAKE:** 25 MIN. + CHILLING
MAKES: 16 SERVINGS

- 1 **box fudge brownie mix (8-inch square pan size)**
- 3 **cups (18 ounces) semisweet chocolate chips**
- 2 **cups heavy whipping cream, divided**
- 6 **tablespoons butter, cubed**
- 1 **tablespoon instant coffee granules**
- 3 **tablespoons vanilla extract**
- 14 **to 16 Pirouette cookies, cut into 1½-inch pieces**

1. Prepare brownie batter according to package directions. Spread into a greased 9-in. springform pan. Place on a baking sheet. Bake at 350° for 25-30 minutes or until a toothpick inserted near the center comes out clean. Cool on a wire rack.

2. Place chocolate chips in a food processor; cover and process until finely chopped. In a small microwave-safe bowl, combine 1 cup cream, butter and coffee granules. Microwave, uncovered, on high for 1 to 1½ minutes or until butter is melted; stir until smooth. With food processor running, add cream mixture to chocolate chips in a slow, steady stream. Add vanilla; cover and process until smooth.

3. Cut a small hole in the corner of a pastry or plastic bag. Fill with ¼ cup chocolate mixture; set aside for garnish. Transfer remaining chocolate mixture to a large bowl.

4. Remove sides of springform pan. Spread half of the remaining chocolate mixture over brownie layer, spreading evenly over top and sides. In a small bowl, beat remaining cream until soft peaks form; fold into remaining chocolate mixture. Spread over chocolate layer. Gently press cookies into sides of dessert.

5. Pipe reserved chocolate mixture on top. Refrigerate for at least 4 hours or overnight. Remove from the refrigerator 5 minutes before cutting.

NOTE *The amount of vanilla called for in the recipe is correct.*

Bakeshop HOW-TO

Brownie Truffle Torte

With a cookie crust and two layers of rich chocolate encasing a yummy brownie, this impressive dessert only looks difficult to make!

Prepare and bake brownie. For chocolate layer, slowly add hot cream mixture to the chocolate chips while the food processor is running.

Spread some of the chocolate mixture over the brownie layer, evenly covering the top and sides.

Fold whipped cream into remaining chocolate mixture to create the chocolate truffle layer. Spread over top and sides of torte.

Add cookies around the perimeter and garnish as desired.

Special-Occasion Chocolate Cake

This recipe won the top prize at my state fair, and with one bite, you'll see why! The decadent chocolate cake boasts a luscious ganache filling and fudge buttercream frosting.

—CINDI PAULSON ANCHORAGE, AK

PREP: 40 MIN. + CHILLING • **BAKE:** 25 MIN. + COOLING
MAKES: 12 SERVINGS

- 1 cup baking cocoa
- 2 cups boiling water
- 1 cup butter, softened
- 2¼ cups sugar
- 4 eggs
- 1½ teaspoons vanilla extract
- 2¾ cups all-purpose flour
- 2 teaspoons baking soda
- ½ teaspoon baking powder
- ½ teaspoon salt

GANACHE
- 10 ounces semisweet chocolate, chopped
- 1 cup heavy whipping cream
- 2 tablespoons sugar

FROSTING
- 1 cup butter, softened
- 4 cups confectioners' sugar
- ½ cup baking cocoa
- ¼ cup 2% milk
- 2 teaspoons vanilla extract

GARNISH
- ¾ cup sliced almonds, toasted

1. In a small bowl, combine cocoa and water; set aside. In a large bowl, cream butter and sugar until light and fluffy. Add eggs, one at a time, beating well after each addition. Beat in vanilla. Combine the flour, baking soda, baking powder and salt; add to creamed mixture alternately with cocoa mixture, beating well after each addition.

2. Pour into three greased and floured 9-in. round baking pans. Bake at 350° for 25-30 minutes or until a toothpick inserted near the center of the cake comes out clean. Cool for 10 minutes before removing from pans to wire racks to cool completely.

3. For ganache, place chocolate in a small bowl. In a small heavy saucepan over low heat, bring cream and sugar to a boil. Pour over chocolate; whisk gently until smooth. Refrigerate for 35-45 minutes or until ganache begins to thicken, stirring occasionally.

4. For frosting, in a large bowl, beat the butter until fluffy. Add the confectioners' sugar, cocoa, milk and vanilla; beat until smooth.

5. Place one cake layer on a serving plate; spread with 1 cup frosting. Top with second layer and 1 cup ganache; sprinkle with ½ cup almonds. Top with third layer; frost top and sides of cake. Warm ganache until pourable; pour over cake, allowing some to drape down the sides. Sprinkle with remaining almonds. Refrigerate until serving.

Special-Occasion Mocha Cake: Add 2 tablespoons instant coffee granules to the boiling water-cocoa mixture. In the frosting, substitute Kahlua for milk.

Low-Fat Chocolate Mini Chip Cupcakes

These tender little cupcakes are chock-full of sweet flavor, yet each has only 139 calories and 2 grams of fat.

—LINDA UTTER SIDNEY, MT

PREP: 20 MIN. • **BAKE:** 15 MIN. + COOLING • **MAKES:** 14 CUPCAKES

- 2 **tablespoons butter, softened**
- ¾ **cup sugar**
- 1 **egg**
- 1 **egg white**
- ½ **cup plus 2 tablespoons buttermilk**
- ⅓ **cup water**
- 1 **tablespoon white vinegar**
- 1 **teaspoon vanilla extract**
- 1½ **cups all-purpose flour**
- ¼ **cup baking cocoa**
- 1 **teaspoon baking soda**
- ½ **teaspoon salt**
- ⅓ **cup miniature semisweet chocolate chips**

1. In a large bowl, beat butter and sugar until crumbly, about 2 minutes. Add egg, then egg white, beating well after each addition. Beat on high speed until light and fluffy. Beat in the buttermilk, water, vinegar and vanilla. Combine the flour, cocoa, baking soda and salt; beat into batter just until moistened. Stir in chocolate chips.

2. Fill muffin cups coated with cooking spray three-fourths full. Bake at 375° for 15-18 minutes or until a toothpick inserted in the muffin comes out clean. Cool for 5 minutes before removing from pans to wire racks.

Flourless Chocolate Cake

One bite of this and you'll agree it's pure pleasure for confirmed chocoholics! A small slice of this rich, dense dessert goes a long way. Chocolate ganache on top takes it to the next level.

—TASTE OF HOME TEST KITCHEN

PREP: 30 MIN. • **BAKE:** 40 MIN. + COOLING • **MAKES:** 16 SERVINGS

- 4 eggs, separated
- 10 tablespoons butter, cubed
- ½ cup sugar, divided
- 6 ounces semisweet chocolate, chopped
- 3 ounces unsweetened chocolate, chopped
- 2 teaspoons vanilla extract
- ¼ cup finely ground pecans, toasted
  Chocolate Ganache (recipe at right), optional
  Sliced strawberries and fresh mint, optional

1. Let the egg whites stand at room temperature for 30 minutes. In a heavy saucepan, melt butter, ¼ cup sugar and chocolates over low heat, stirring constantly. Cool until the mixture is lukewarm.

2. In a large bowl, beat egg yolks until thick and lemon-colored, about 3 minutes. Beat in vanilla. Gradually beat in pecans and chocolate mixture.

3. In a small bowl and with clean beaters, beat egg whites on medium speed until soft peaks form. Gradually add remaining sugar, 1 tablespoon at a time, beating on high speed until stiff peaks form. Stir a small amount of whites into chocolate mixture. Fold in remaining whites.

4. Pour into a greased 9-in. springform pan. Place on a baking sheet. Bake at 350° for 40-50 minutes or until a toothpick inserted near the center comes out with a few moist crumbs. Cool on a wire rack for 20 minutes.

5. Carefully run a knife around edge of pan to loosen; remove sides of pan and cool completely. Frost with Chocolate Ganache if desired. Garnish with strawberries and mint if desired.

Chocolate Ganache

This satiny smooth chocolate treat will bring a touch of elegance to even the simplest dessert. It's so versatile!

—TASTE OF HOME TEST KITCHEN

PREP: 15 MIN. + CHILLING • **MAKES:** 1¼ CUPS

- 1 cup (6 ounces) semisweet chocolate chips
- ⅔ cup heavy whipping cream

1. Place chocolate chips in a small bowl. In a small saucepan, bring cream just to a boil. Pour over chocolate; whisk until smooth.

2. For a pourable ganache, cool, stirring occasionally, until mixture reaches 85°-90° and is slightly thickened, about 40 minutes. Pour over cake, allowing some to drape down the sides. Spread ganache with a spatula if necessary to evenly coat, working quickly before it thickens. Let stand until set.

3. For spreadable ganache, chill, stirring occasionally, until mixture reaches a spreading consistency. Spread over the cake.

White Chocolate Ganache: Substitute 6 ounces chopped white baking chocolate for the chocolate chips. Proceed as directed.

Sandy's Chocolate Cake

This velvety, rich cake won first prize at The Greatest Cocoa Cake Contest in my home state. It's so tall and pretty, it's guaranteed to impress.

—SANDY JOHNSON TIOGA, PA

PREP: 30 MIN. • **BAKE:** 35 MIN. + COOLING • **MAKES:** 12 SERVINGS

- 3 **cups packed brown sugar**
- 1 **cup butter, softened**
- 4 **eggs**
- 2 **teaspoons vanilla extract**
- 2⅔ **cups all-purpose flour**
- ¾ **cup baking cocoa**
- 1 **tablespoon baking soda**
- ½ **teaspoon salt**
- 1⅓ **cups sour cream**
- 1⅓ **cups boiling water**

FROSTING

- ½ **cup butter, cubed**
- 3 **ounces unsweetened chocolate, chopped**
- 3 **ounces semisweet chocolate, chopped**
- 5 **cups confectioners' sugar**
- 1 **cup (8 ounces) sour cream**
- 2 **teaspoons vanilla extract**
   Chocolate curls and decorations, optional

1. In a bowl, cream brown sugar and butter until light and fluffy. Add the eggs, one at a time, beating well after each addition. Beat in vanilla. Combine the flour, cocoa, baking soda and salt; add alternately with sour cream to creamed mixture. Mix on low just until combined. Stir in the water until blended.

2. Pour into three greased and floured 9-in. round baking pans. Bake at 350° for 35 minutes. Cool in pans 10 minutes; remove to wire racks to cool completely.

3. For frosting, in a small saucepan, melt butter and chocolates over low heat. Cool for several minutes.

4. In a bowl, combine the confectioners' sugar, sour cream and vanilla. Add chocolate mixture and beat until smooth. Spread frosting between layers and over top and sides of the cake. Top with chocolate garnishes if desired. Store in the refrigerator.

Chocolate Upside-Down Cake

Here's a dessert that's simply out of this world. All of your guests will agree that it's the best ever. I enjoy it with a scoop of vanilla ice cream.

—IOLA EGLE BELLA VISTA, AR

PREP: 15 MIN. • **BAKE:** 55 MIN. + COOLING
MAKES: 12-15 SERVINGS

1¼ cups water
¼ cup butter, cubed
1 cup packed brown sugar
1 cup flaked coconut
2 cups (12 ounces) semisweet chocolate chips
1 cup chopped pecans
2 cups miniature marshmallows
1 package (18¼ ounces) German chocolate cake mix

1. In a small saucepan, heat water and butter until butter is melted. Stir in brown sugar until blended. Pour into a greased 13-in. x 9-in. baking pan. Sprinkle with coconut, chocolate chips, pecans and marshmallows.
2. Prepare cake batter according to package directions; carefully pour over marshmallows. Bake at 325° for 55-60 minutes or until a toothpick inserted near the center comes out clean. Cool for 10 minutes before inverting cake onto a serving plate.

Chocolate Oreo Bars

A friend brought these fudgy bars over to my house to tempt me with yet another chocolate treat. They are simple to make, and cleanup is a breeze!

—**NANCY CLARK** ZEIGLER, IL

PREP: 15 MIN. • **BAKE:** 10 MIN. + COOLING
MAKES: ABOUT 4 DOZEN

- 1 **package (15½ ounces) Oreo cookies, crushed**
- ¾ **cup butter, melted**
- 1 **can (14 ounces) sweetened condensed milk**
- 2 **cups (12 ounces) miniature semisweet chocolate chips, divided**

1. Combine cookie crumbs and butter; pat onto the bottom of an ungreased 13-in. x 9-in. baking pan.
2. In a microwave, heat milk and 1 cup chocolate chips; stir until smooth. Pour over crust. Sprinkle with remaining chips.
3. Bake at 350° for 10-12 minutes or until chips begin to melt but do not lose their shape. Cool on a wire rack.

Chocolate Ganache Torte

Here's to that chocolate fix we all need. Cream makes this dessert extra rich.

—**KATHY KITTELL** LENEXA, KS

PREP: 40 MIN. • **BAKE:** 20 MIN. + COOLING • **MAKES:** 12 SERVINGS

- ¾ **cup butter, softened**
- 1½ **cups sugar**
- 1 **egg**
- 1 **teaspoon vanilla extract**
- 1 **cup buttermilk**
- ¾ **cup sour cream**
- 2 **cups all-purpose flour**
- ⅔ **cup baking cocoa**
- 1 **teaspoon baking soda**
- ¼ **teaspoon salt**

FILLING

- 4 **ounces semisweet chocolate, chopped**
- 1 **cup heavy whipping cream**
- ½ **teaspoon vanilla extract**

GANACHE

- ¾ **cup heavy whipping cream**
- 8 **ounces semisweet chocolate, chopped**
- ¼ **cup butter, cubed**

1. In a large bowl, cream butter and sugar until light and fluffy. Beat in egg and vanilla. Combine buttermilk and sour cream. Combine the flour, cocoa, baking soda and salt; add to creamed mixture alternately with buttermilk mixture, beating well after each addition.
2. Pour into two greased and waxed paper-lined 9-in. round baking pans. Bake at 350° for 20-25 minutes or until a toothpick comes out clean. Cool 10 minutes; remove from pans to wire racks to cool completely.
3. In a heavy saucepan, melt chocolate with cream over low heat. Remove from the heat; stir in vanilla. Transfer to a small mixing bowl; chill until slightly thickened, stirring occasionally. Beat on medium speed until light and fluffy. Chill until mixture achieves spreading consistency.
4. For ganache, in a heavy saucepan, bring the cream just to a boil. Remove from the heat; stir in the chocolate and butter until melted. Chill until slightly thickened. Place one cake layer on a serving plate; spread with the filling. Top with remaining cake layer. Slowly pour ganache over top of cake.

Chocolate Mini Loaves

Rich and moist, these special mini breads will remind you of pound cake. Slice them for snacking or to serve as dessert with a cup of coffee or tea.

—ELIZABETH DOWNEY EVART, MI

PREP: 15 MIN. • **BAKE:** 30 MIN. + COOLING
MAKES: 5 MINI LOAVES (6 SLICES EACH)

- ½ cup butter, softened
- ⅔ cup packed brown sugar
- 1 cup (6 ounces) semisweet chocolate chips, melted
- 2 eggs
- 2 teaspoons vanilla extract
- 2½ cups all-purpose flour
- 1 teaspoon baking powder
- 1 teaspoon baking soda
- 1½ cups applesauce
- ½ cup miniature semisweet chocolate chips

GLAZE
- ½ cup semisweet chocolate chips
- 1 tablespoon butter
- 5 teaspoons water
- ½ cup confectioners' sugar
- ¼ teaspoon vanilla extract
  Dash salt

1. In a large bowl, cream butter and brown sugar until light and fluffy. Beat in the melted chocolate chips, eggs and vanilla. Combine the flour, baking powder and baking soda; add to creamed mixture alternately with applesauce just until moistened. Fold in miniature chips.

2. Divide batter among five greased 5¾-in. x 3-in. x 2-in. loaf pans, about 1 cup in each. Bake at 350° for 30-40 minutes or until a toothpick inserted near the center comes out clean. Cool for 10 minutes before removing from pans to wire racks to cool completely.

3. For glaze, combine the chocolate chips, butter and water in a saucepan; cook and stir over low heat until chocolate is melted. Remove from the heat; stir in confectioners' sugar, vanilla and salt until smooth. Drizzle over loaves.

NOTE *Two 8-in. x 4-in. x 2-in. loaf pans may be used; bake for 50-55 minutes.*

Chocolate Truffle Cake

This luxurious cake is ideal for chocolate lovers. With a ganache glaze and a bittersweet filling, the indulgence is so worth it!

—JO ANN KOERKENMEIER DAMIANSVILLE, IL

PREP: 35 MIN. + CHILLING • **BAKE:** 25 MIN. + COOLING
MAKES: 16 SERVINGS

- 2½ cups 2% milk
- 1 cup butter, cubed
- 8 ounces semisweet chocolate, chopped
- 3 eggs
- 2 teaspoons vanilla extract
- 2⅔ cups all-purpose flour
- 2 cups sugar
- 1 teaspoon baking soda
- ½ teaspoon salt

FILLING
- 6 tablespoons butter, cubed
- 4 ounces bittersweet chocolate, chopped
- 2½ cups confectioners' sugar
- ½ cup heavy whipping cream

GANACHE
- ⅔ cup heavy whipping cream
- 10 ounces semisweet chocolate, chopped

1. In a large saucepan, cook the milk, butter and chocolate over low heat until melted. Remove from the heat; let stand for 10 minutes.

2. In a bowl, beat the eggs, vanilla and chocolate mixture until smooth. Combine flour, sugar, baking soda and salt; gradually beat into chocolate mixture (batter will be thin).

3. Transfer to three greased and floured 9-in. round baking pans. Bake at 325° for 25-30 minutes or until a toothpick inserted near the center comes out clean. Cool for 10 minutes before removing from pans to wire racks to cool completely.

4. For filling, in a small saucepan, melt butter and chocolate. Stir in confectioners' sugar and cream until smooth.

5. For ganache, in a saucepan, bring cream just to a boil. Add chocolate; whisk until smooth. Cool; stir occasionally, until ganache reaches a spreading consistency.

6. Place one cake layer on a serving plate; spread with half of the filling. Repeat layers. Top with the remaining cake layer. Spread ganache over top and sides of cake. Store in the refrigerator.

Candy Bar Cheesecake

With this recipe, you can easily create a cheesecake that tastes like a fancy store-bought treat. It's always requested when I'm asked to bring dessert to a function.

—JULIE CERVENKA ST. LOUIS, MO

PREP: 25 MIN. • **BAKE:** 1¼ HOURS + COOLING
MAKES: 12 SERVINGS

1¾ cups crushed chocolate wafers (about 28 wafers)
¼ cup sugar
⅓ cup butter, melted

FILLING
3 packages (8 ounces each) cream cheese, softened
1 can (14 ounces) sweetened condensed milk
1 cup chocolate syrup
2 teaspoons vanilla extract
3 eggs, lightly beaten
6 Snickers candy bars (2.07 ounces each), coarsely chopped, divided
Additional chocolate syrup

1. In a small bowl, combine wafer crumbs and sugar; stir in butter. Press onto the bottom and 1½ in. up the sides of a greased 9-in. springform pan.

2. Place pan on a double thickness of heavy-duty foil (about 18 in. square); securely wrap foil around pan. Place pan on a baking sheet. Bake at 325° for 12 minutes. Cool on a wire rack.

3. In a large bowl, beat the cream cheese, milk, chocolate syrup and vanilla until smooth. Add eggs; beat just until combined. Stir in 2½ cups chopped candy bars. Pour into crust. Place springform pan in a large baking pan; add 1 in. of hot water to larger pan.

4. Bake at 325° for 75-80 minutes or until center is just set and top appears dull. Remove springform pan from water bath. Cool on a wire rack for 10 minutes. Carefully run a knife around edge of pan to loosen; cool 1 hour longer. Refrigerate overnight.

5. Top with remaining chopped candy bars; drizzle with additional chocolate syrup.

Muffins & Scones

I Want S'more Muffins

These fun muffins feature a fluffy marshmallow creme in the center. The s'more flavors are sure to bring back fond childhood memories.

—SALLY SIBTHORPE SHELBY TOWNSHIP, MI

PREP: 20 MIN. • **BAKE:** 15 MIN. • **MAKES:** 6 MUFFINS

- 3 tablespoons butter, softened
- ¼ cup packed brown sugar
- 4 teaspoons sugar
- 1 egg
- ⅓ cup sour cream
- 3 tablespoons 2% milk
- ⅔ cup all-purpose flour
- ½ cup graham cracker crumbs
- ¼ teaspoon salt
- ¼ teaspoon baking powder
- ¼ teaspoon ground cinnamon
- ⅛ teaspoon baking soda
- ⅓ cup milk chocolate chips
- 6 tablespoons marshmallow creme

1. In a small bowl, cream butter and sugars until light and fluffy. Beat in the egg, then the sour cream and milk. Combine the flour, graham cracker crumbs, salt, baking powder, cinnamon and baking soda; beat into creamed mixture just until moistened. Fold in chocolate chips.
2. Coat six muffin cups with cooking spray; fill one-fourth full with batter. Spoon 1 tablespoon marshmallow creme into each muffin cup. Top with remaining batter.
3. Bake at 400° for 14-16 minutes or until a toothpick inserted near the center of the muffins comes out clean. Cool for 5 minutes before removing from pan to a wire rack. Serve warm.

Cream Cheese Cranberry Muffins

Moist and packed with colorful, nutritious berries, these marvelous muffins are a seasonal specialty. They are light and tasty, and they freeze very well.

—LEONARD KESZLER BISMARCK, ND

PREP: 15 MIN. • **BAKE:** 20 MIN. • **MAKES:** 2 DOZEN

- 1 cup butter, softened
- 1 package (8 ounces) cream cheese, softened
- 1½ cups sugar
- 4 eggs
- 1½ teaspoons vanilla extract
- 2 cups all-purpose flour
- 1½ teaspoons baking powder
- ½ teaspoon salt
- 2 cups fresh or frozen cranberries
- ½ cup chopped pecans

DRIZZLE
- 2 cups confectioners' sugar
- 3 tablespoons 2% milk

1. In a large bowl, cream the butter, cream cheese and sugar until light and fluffy. Add eggs, one at a time, beating well after each addition. Beat in vanilla. Combine the flour, baking powder and salt; stir into creamed mixture just until moistened. Fold in cranberries and pecans.
2. Fill greased or paper-lined muffin cups three-fourths full. Bake at 350° for 20-25 minutes or until a toothpick inserted near the center comes out clean. Cool for 5 minutes before removing from pans to wire racks.
3. Combine the confectioners' sugar and milk; drizzle over the muffins.

Iced Raspberry Cheesecake Muffins

These moist, cakelike muffins are flavored with raspberries and walnuts. The sweet drizzle of icing makes them pretty enough to serve guests.

—PHYLLIS EISMANN SCHMALZ KANSAS CITY, KS

PREP: 25 MIN. • **BAKE:** 25 MIN. + COOLING • **MAKES:** 8 MUFFINS

- 1 package (3 ounces) cream cheese, softened
- 2 tablespoons butter, softened
- ½ cup sugar
- 1 egg
- 1 egg white
- 3 tablespoons buttermilk
- ½ teaspoon vanilla extract
- ¾ cup all-purpose flour
- ½ teaspoon baking powder
- ⅛ teaspoon baking soda
- ⅛ teaspoon salt
- ¾ cup fresh raspberries
- 2 tablespoons chopped walnuts, toasted
- ¼ cup confectioners' sugar
- 1 teaspoon 2% milk

1. In a small bowl, cream the cream cheese, butter and sugar until smooth. Beat in egg and egg white. Beat in buttermilk and vanilla. Combine the flour, baking powder, baking soda and salt; add to creamed mixture just until moistened. Fold in raspberries and walnuts.

2. Fill paper-lined muffin cups three-fourths full. Bake at 350° for 25-28 minutes or until a toothpick inserted in muffin comes out clean. Cool for 5 minutes before removing from pan to a wire rack to cool completely.

3. Combine confectioners' sugar and milk; drizzle icing over the muffins.

Pecan Pie Mini Muffins

While these are delicious year-round, you could easily turn them into a Christmas gift. They look festive on a tray wrapped in red or green cellophane or tucked into a cookie plate. And don't forget to include the recipe so your recipient can enjoy this treat over and over again!

—PAT SCHRAND ENTERPRISE, AL

PREP: 10 MIN. • **BAKE:** 25 MIN. • **MAKES:** ABOUT 2½ DOZEN

- 1 **cup packed brown sugar**
- ½ **cup all-purpose flour**
- 1 **cup chopped pecans**
- ⅔ **cup butter, melted**
- 2 **eggs, lightly beaten**

1. In a large bowl, combine the brown sugar, flour and pecans; set aside. Combine butter and eggs. Stir into brown sugar mixture.

2. Fill greased and floured miniature muffin cups two-thirds full. Bake at 350° for 22-25 minutes or until a toothpick inserted near the center comes out clean. Immediately remove from pans to wire racks to cool.

NOTE *This recipe uses only ½ cup flour.*

Hazelnut Chip Scones

When I made a friend's scone recipe, I didn't have enough milk, so I substituted hazelnut-flavored coffee creamer and added chocolate chips. Everyone loved the results!

—ELISA LOCHRIDGE BEAVERTON, OR

PREP: 20 MIN. • **BAKE:** 15 MIN. • **MAKES:** 16 SCONES

- 4 **cups all-purpose flour**
- 3 **tablespoons sugar**
- 4 **teaspoons baking powder**
- ½ **teaspoon salt**
- ½ **teaspoon cream of tartar**
- ¾ **cup cold butter**
- 1 **egg, separated**
- 1½ **cups refrigerated hazelnut nondairy creamer or half-and-half cream**
- 1½ **cups semisweet chocolate chips**
  Additional sugar

SPICED BUTTER
- ½ **cup butter, softened**
- 3 **tablespoons brown sugar**
- ¼ **teaspoon ground cinnamon**
- ¼ **teaspoon ground allspice**
- ⅛ **teaspoon ground nutmeg**

1. In a large bowl, combine the first five ingredients; cut in butter until crumbly. In a small bowl, whisk egg yolk and creamer; add to dry ingredients just until moistened. Fold in chocolate chips.

2. Turn onto a floured surface; knead 10 times. Divide dough in half. Pat each portion into a 7-in. circle; cut into eight wedges. Separate wedges and place on greased baking sheets.

3. Beat egg white; brush over dough. Sprinkle with additional sugar. Bake at 425° for 15-18 minutes or until golden brown. Meanwhile, in a small bowl, combine the spiced butter ingredients; beat until smooth. Serve with warm scones.

Cranberry Gingerbread Muffins

This wonderful treat can be served as a breakfast or brunch bread. The spices and cranberries really put people in the holiday spirit!

—LISA VARNER EL PASO, TX

PREP: 20 MIN. • **BAKE:** 20 MIN. • **MAKES:** 1 DOZEN

- 2¼ cups all-purpose flour
- ½ cup packed brown sugar
- 2 teaspoons ground ginger
- 1 teaspoon baking powder
- 1 teaspoon ground cinnamon
- ¾ teaspoon salt
- ½ teaspoon baking soda
- 1 egg
- ¾ cup water
- ½ cup fat-free plain yogurt
- ⅓ cup molasses
- ¼ cup canola oil
- 1 cup fresh or frozen cranberries, coarsely chopped

1. In a large bowl, combine the first seven ingredients. In a small bowl, combine the egg, water, yogurt, molasses and oil. Stir into dry ingredients just until moistened. Fold in the cranberries.

2. Coat muffin cups with cooking spray or use paper liners; fill ¾ full with batter. Bake at 350° for 18-22 minutes or until a toothpick comes out clean. Cool for 5 minutes before removing from pan to a wire rack.

Pumpkin Cheesecake Muffins

My mother-in-law came up with these tender treats by combining a few of her favorite muffin recipes. Chock-full of pumpkin, they feature both a sweet cream cheese filling and crunchy praline topping.

—LISA POWELSON SCOTT CITY, KS

PREP: 25 MIN. • **BAKE:** 15 MIN. • **MAKES:** 2 DOZEN

- 3 cups all-purpose flour
- 2 cups sugar
- 2 teaspoons baking soda
- 2 teaspoons baking powder
- 1 teaspoon salt
- 1 teaspoon ground cinnamon
- 4 eggs
- 1 can (15 ounces) solid-pack pumpkin
- 1½ cups canola oil

CREAM CHEESE FILLING
- 1 package (8 ounces) cream cheese, softened
- ½ cup sugar
- 1 egg
- 1 tablespoon all-purpose flour

PRALINE TOPPING
- ⅔ cup chopped pecans
- ⅓ cup packed brown sugar
- 2 tablespoons sour cream

1. In a large bowl, combine the first six ingredients. In another bowl, whisk the eggs, pumpkin and oil. Stir into dry ingredients just until moistened. Fill greased or paper-lined muffin cups one-third full.

2. For filling, beat the cream cheese, sugar, egg and flour until smooth. Drop by tablespoonfuls into center of each muffin. Top with remaining batter.

3. For topping, in a small bowl, combine the pecans, brown sugar and sour cream; spoon over batter. Bake at 400° for 15-18 minutes or until a toothpick inserted in the muffin comes out clean. Cool for 5 minutes before removing from pans to wire racks. Serve warm. Refrigerate leftovers.

Mango Colada Scones

The mango adds a great tropical flavor to these scones. I love to serve these for tea or for breakfast.

—CHERYL PERRY HERTFORD, NC

PREP: 20 MIN. • **BAKE:** 15 MIN. • **MAKES:** 10 SCONES

2½ cups biscuit/baking mix
2 tablespoons brown sugar
3 tablespoons cold butter
½ cup thawed non-alcoholic pina colada mix
1 cup chopped peeled mango
3 tablespoons flaked coconut
¼ cup macadamia nuts, chopped

1. In a large bowl, combine biscuit mix and brown sugar. Cut in 2 tablespoons butter until mixture resembles coarse crumbs. Stir in pina colada mix just until moistened. Fold in mango.

2. Turn onto a floured surface; knead 10 times. Pat into a 9-in. x 7-in. rectangle. Cut into 10 rectangles; separate rectangles and place on a greased baking sheet. Melt remaining butter; brush over scones.

3. Bake at 400° for 12 minutes. Sprinkle with coconut and nuts; bake 2-4 minutes longer or until golden brown. Serve warm.

Banana Brickle Muffins

Toffee bits add great flavor to these delicious banana muffins. Serve them at breakfast, lunch, dinner or as a special snack.

—**ANDRA COGAN** GROSSE POINTE PARK, MI

PREP: 15 MIN. • **BAKE:** 20 MIN. • **MAKES:** 1 DOZEN

- 2 **cups all-purpose flour**
- ½ **cup packed brown sugar**
- 1 **tablespoon baking powder**
- 1 **cup mashed ripe bananas**
- ½ **cup milk**
- ⅓ **cup canola oil**
- 1 **egg**
- 1 **package (8 ounces) brickle toffee bits, divided**

1. In a large bowl, combine the flour, brown sugar and baking powder. In a small bowl, combine the bananas, milk, oil and egg. Stir into dry ingredients just until moistened. Fold in 1 cup toffee bits.

2. Fill greased muffin cups three-fourths full. Sprinkle with remaining toffee bits. Bake at 350° for 18-20 minutes or until a toothpick inserted near the center comes out clean. Cool for 5 minutes before removing from pan to a wire rack. Serve warm.

Cherry Almond Muffins

As a kid, I loved doughnuts filled with custard or jelly. So I decided to experiment with fillings in muffins. The result was this terrific recipe. These fancy muffins are almost like pastries with their sweet-tart, rich and creamy centers.

—**JOHN MONTGOMERY** FORTUNA, CA

PREP: 20 MIN. • **BAKE:** 30 MIN. • **MAKES:** 7 MUFFINS

- 1¾ **cups all-purpose flour**
- ½ **cup plus 1 tablespoon sugar**
- ½ **teaspoon baking powder**
- ½ **teaspoon baking soda**
- ¼ **teaspoon salt**
- ½ **cup cold butter, cubed**
- 1 **egg**
- ¾ **cup sour cream**
- 1 **teaspoon almond extract**

FILLING
- 1 **package (8 ounces) cream cheese, softened**
- 1 **egg**
- ¼ **cup sugar**
- ½ **teaspoon vanilla extract**
- ¾ **cup cherry preserves, warmed**

TOPPING
- ⅓ **cup all-purpose flour**
- 2 **tablespoons sugar**
- 2 **tablespoons cold butter**
- ⅓ **cup chopped sliced almonds**

1. In a large bowl, combine flour, sugar, baking powder, baking soda and salt. Cut in butter until the mixture resembles coarse crumbs. Beat the egg, sour cream and extract until smooth; stir into dry ingredients just until moistened (batter will be thick).

2. In a large bowl, beat cream cheese, egg, sugar and vanilla until smooth. In a saucepan over low heat, warm preserves. For topping, combine flour and sugar in a small bowl; cut in butter until crumbly. Stir in almonds.

3. Fill greased jumbo muffin cups half full with batter. Divide cream cheese filling and preserves evenly among muffin cups; swirl gently. Cover with remaining batter. Sprinkle with topping.

4. Bake at 350° for 30-35 minutes or until a toothpick inserted in muffin comes out clean. Cool for 5 minutes before removing from pans to wire racks. Serve warm.

NOTE *Recipe may be prepared in 14 regular-size muffin cups; bake muffins for 20-25 minutes.*

Walnut Orange Muffins

These glazed orange muffins are so moist, butter isn't needed. Serve them warm with mugs of coffee or hot apple cider.

—PAT HABIGER SPEARVILLE, KS

PREP: 20 MIN. • **BAKE:** 20 MIN. • **MAKES:** ABOUT 1 DOZEN

- 1 cup butter, softened
- 1 cup sugar
- 2 eggs
- 1 cup buttermilk
- 4 teaspoons grated orange peel
- 2 cups all-purpose flour
- 1 teaspoon baking soda
- ¼ cup chopped walnuts
- 1 cup orange juice
- ½ cup packed brown sugar

1. In a bowl, cream butter and sugar until light and fluffy. Beat in the eggs, buttermilk and orange peel. Combine flour and baking soda; add to creamed mixture just until blended. Stir in walnuts.

2. Fill greased or paper-lined muffin cups two-thirds full. Bake at 350° for 20 minutes or until a toothpick inserted in the muffin comes out clean.

3. In a bowl, combine the orange juice and brown sugar until dissolved. Spoon over warm muffins. Cool for 5 minutes before removing from pan to a wire rack.

Oatmeal Apricot Scones

Besides farming and raising cattle, our family has a home bakery that serves area restaurants and health food stores. We dry lots of local fruit for use in our recipes, like the apricots in these golden scones that are so popular with our customers.

—LINDA SWANSON RIVERSIDE WA

PREP: 25 MIN. • **BAKE:** 15 MIN. • **MAKES:** 6 SCONES

- 1½ cups all-purpose flour
- ½ cup quick-cooking oats
- ¼ cup sugar
- 2½ teaspoons baking powder
- ¼ teaspoon salt
- ⅓ cup cold butter, cubed
- 2 eggs
- ¼ cup sour cream
- 1 tablespoon milk

- ¾ cup finely chopped dried apricots

FILLING
- 3 tablespoons brown sugar
- 1 tablespoon quick-cooking oats
- 1 tablespoon butter, softened
   Additional sugar

1. In a bowl, combine the dry ingredients; cut in butter until mixture resembles fine crumbs. In a small bowl, beat eggs; set aside 1 tablespoon for glaze. In another bowl, combine the sour cream, milk and remaining beaten eggs; add apricots. Stir into crumb mixture until the dough clings together.

2. Turn onto a lightly floured surface; knead 12-15 times. Divide dough in half. Pat one portion into a 7-in. circle on a greased baking sheet. Combine the brown sugar, oats and butter; sprinkle over dough. Roll out remaining dough into a 7-in. circle; place over filling.

3. Brush with reserved egg; sprinkle with additional sugar. Cut into wedges but do not separate. Bake at 400° for 15-20 minutes or until scones are golden brown. Cool slightly; cut again if necessary. Serve warm.

Bakeshop HOW-TO

Making Scones

Most scone recipes suggest patting the dough into a circle. For proper baking, be sure the circle meets the dimensions noted in the recipe.

Cut the dough into wedges with a dough scraper or knife. It may be helpful to flour the utensil's edge between cuts to prevent the dough from sticking to it.

Whole Wheat Blueberry Muffins

Whole wheat flour gives a nutritious boost to these yummy muffins packed with juicy blueberries. Fresh from the oven, they'll warm you up on cold winter days.

—**SHEILA SIEM** CALUMET, MI

PREP: 15 MIN. • **BAKE:** 20 MIN. • **MAKES:** 1½ DOZEN

- 1½ cups all-purpose flour
- 1 cup whole wheat flour
- ½ cup sugar
- 2 teaspoons baking powder
- ½ teaspoon baking soda
- ½ teaspoon salt
- ⅛ teaspoon ground nutmeg
- 2 eggs
- 1 cup buttermilk
- ½ cup canola oil
- 2 cups fresh or frozen blueberries

1. In a large bowl, combine the flours, sugar, baking powder, baking soda, salt and nutmeg. In another bowl, beat the eggs, buttermilk and oil. Stir into dry ingredients just until moistened. Fold in blueberries.

2. Fill greased or paper-lined muffin cups three-fourths full. Bake at 375° for 18-20 minutes or until a toothpick inserted in muffin comes out clean. Cool for 5 minutes before removing from pans to wire racks. Serve warm.

NOTE *If using frozen blueberries, use without thawing to avoid discoloring the batter.*

Chocolate Chip Mini Muffins

I bake a lot of different muffins, but this is the recipe I use the most. Their small size makes them hard to resist!

—JOANNE SHEW CHUK ST. BENEDICT, SK

PREP: 15 MIN. • **BAKE:** 10 MIN. • **MAKES:** ABOUT 3 DOZEN

- ½ cup sugar
- ¼ cup shortening
- 1 egg
- ½ cup 2% milk
- ½ teaspoon vanilla extract
- 1 cup all-purpose flour
- ½ teaspoon baking soda
- ½ teaspoon baking powder
- ¼ teaspoon salt
- ⅔ cup miniature semisweet chocolate chips

1. In a large bowl, cream sugar and shortening until light and fluffy. Beat in egg, then milk and vanilla. Combine the flour, baking soda, baking powder and salt; add to butter mixture just until combined. Fold in chocolate chips.

2. Spoon about 1 tablespoon of batter into each greased or paper-lined mini-muffin cup. Bake at 375° for 10-13 minutes or until a toothpick inserted near the center comes out clean. Cool in pans for 5 minutes before removing to wire racks. Serve warm.

Apple Streusel Muffins

My husband and children enjoy these tender coffee cakelike muffins as a quick breakfast or snack on the run. Add the drizzle of glaze and they're pretty enough for company.

—DULCY GRACE ROARING SPRING, PA

PREP: 20 MIN. • **BAKE:** 15 MIN. + COOLING • **MAKES:** 1 DOZEN

- 2 cups all-purpose flour
- 1 cup sugar
- 1 teaspoon baking powder
- ½ teaspoon baking soda
- ½ teaspoon salt
- 2 eggs
- ½ cup butter, melted
- 1¼ teaspoons vanilla extract
- 1½ cups chopped peeled tart apples
- **STREUSEL TOPPING**
- ⅓ cup packed brown sugar
- 1 tablespoon all-purpose flour
- ⅛ teaspoon ground cinnamon
- 1 tablespoon cold butter
- **GLAZE**
- 1½ cups confectioners' sugar
- 1 to 2 tablespoons milk
- 1 teaspoon butter, melted
- ¼ teaspoon vanilla extract
- ⅛ teaspoon salt

1. In a large bowl, combine the flour, sugar, baking powder, baking soda and salt. In another bowl, combine the eggs, butter and vanilla; stir into dry ingredients just until moistened (batter will be stiff). Fold in apples.

2. Fill greased or paper-lined muffin cups three-fourths full. In a small bowl, combine the brown sugar, flour and cinnamon; cut in the butter until crumbly. Sprinkle over the batter.

3. Bake at 375° for 15-20 minutes or until a toothpick inserted near the center of the muffins comes out clean. Cool for 5 minutes before removing from pan to a wire rack to cool completely. Combine glaze ingredients; drizzle over muffins.

Sugar Plum Scones

Dried plums and a sprinkling of coarse sugar make these treats delightfully Christmasy. Spread them with butter, cream cheese or preserves and revel in their holiday flavor.

—JULIE MCQUISTON BRADENTON, FL

PREP: 20 MIN. • **BAKE:** 15 MIN. • **MAKES:** 1 DOZEN

- 3 **cups all-purpose flour**
- ½ **cup sugar**
- 3 **teaspoons baking powder**
- ½ **teaspoon salt**
- ½ **cup cold butter**
- 1 **egg**
- 1 **cup buttermilk**
- 1 **cup pitted dried plums, chopped**
- 1 **tablespoon grated orange peel**

TOPPING
- 1 **egg**
- 1 **tablespoon 2% milk**
- 2 **tablespoons coarse sugar**

1. In a large bowl, combine the flour, sugar, baking powder and salt. Cut in butter until mixture resembles coarse crumbs. Whisk egg and buttermilk; stir into crumb mixture just until moistened. Stir in plums and orange peel. Turn onto a floured surface; knead 10 times.
2. Divide dough in half; pat each into a 7-in. circle. Cut each into six wedges. Separate wedges and place on a greased baking sheet. Combine egg and milk; brush over scones. Sprinkle with coarse sugar. Bake at 375° for 15-20 minutes or until golden brown. Serve warm.

Raspberry Jam Muffins

I like to linger over a cup of coffee and a warm, sweet treat on weekend mornings. These muffins are perfect because making them ties up so little time in the kitchen. I sometimes serve them with holiday meals for something different.

—TERESA RAAB TUSTIN, MI

START TO FINISH: 30 MIN. • **MAKES:** 1 DOZEN

- 2 **cups biscuit/baking mix**
- 2 **tablespoons sugar**
- ¼ **cup cold butter, cubed**
- ⅔ **cup 2% milk**
- ¼ **cup raspberry jam**

GLAZE
- ½ **cup confectioners' sugar**
- 2 **teaspoons warm water**
- ¼ **teaspoon vanilla extract**

1. In a large bowl, combine biscuit mix and sugar. Cut in butter until the mixture resembles coarse crumbs. Stir in milk just until moistened (batter will be thick).
2. Spoon about 1 tablespoon of batter into 12 paper-lined muffin cups. Top with 1 teaspoon jam. Spoon the remaining batter (about 1 tablespoon each) over jam.
3. Bake at 425° for 12-14 minutes or until a toothpick inserted near the center of the muffin comes out clean. Cool in pans for 5 minutes.
4. Meanwhile, in a small bowl, combine glaze ingredients until smooth. Remove muffins to a wire rack. Drizzle glaze over warm muffins. Serve warm.

Bakeshop TIP

Tender Muffins & Scones

To ensure tender muffins and scones, mix all of the dry ingredients well before adding wet ingredients, including already-beaten eggs. Stir in the wet ingredients just until the batter or dough comes together. (Muffin batter may contain some lumps, which is normal.) By taking care to avoid overmixing, you'll ensure a finished product that's tender, not tough or chewy.

Lemon-Yogurt Tea Cakes

Light, soft and tangy, these little lemon cakes will be the belle of the brunch. They're also great for lunch, supper or snacking.

—RUTH BURRUS ZIONSVILLE, IN

PREP: 20 MIN. • **BAKE:** 20 MIN. + COOLING
MAKES: ABOUT 1 DOZEN

2¼ cups all-purpose flour
1 cup sugar
¾ teaspoon baking powder
½ teaspoon baking soda
½ teaspoon salt
½ cup cold butter
1 cup (8 ounces) fat-free plain yogurt
3 egg whites
2 tablespoons lemon juice
4 teaspoons grated lemon peel
1 teaspoon lemon extract

1. In a large bowl, combine the flour, sugar, baking powder, baking soda and salt; cut in butter until mixture resembles coarse crumbs. Whisk yogurt, egg whites, lemon juice, peel and extract; stir into crumb mixture just until moistened.
2. Fill greased or paper-lined muffin cups three-fourths full. Bake at 350° for 18-22 minutes or until a toothpick inserted near the center of the muffins comes out clean. Cool for 10 minutes before removing from pan to a wire rack to cool completely.

Coffee Cakes &
Sweet Rolls

Peach Cobbler Coffee Cake

My family took an immediate liking to this special coffee cake. I sometimes make it with apricots and apricot filling, and it's delicious, too.

—VIRGINIA KRITES CRIDERSVILLE, OH

PREP: 25 MIN. • **BAKE:** 70 MIN. + COOLING • **MAKES:** 12 SERVINGS

- 1 cup butter, softened
- 1 cup sugar
- 2 eggs
- 3 teaspoons vanilla extract
- 3 cups all-purpose flour
- 1 teaspoon baking powder
- 1 teaspoon baking soda
- ½ teaspoon salt
- 1¼ cups sour cream
- 1 can (21 ounces) peach pie filling
- 1 can (15¼ ounces) sliced peaches, drained

TOPPING

- 1 cup packed brown sugar
- 1 cup all-purpose flour
- ½ cup quick-cooking oats
- ¼ teaspoon ground cinnamon
- ½ cup cold butter, cubed

GLAZE

- 1 cup confectioners' sugar
- 1 to 2 tablespoons 2% milk

1. In a large bowl, cream butter and sugar until light and fluffy. Add eggs, one at a time, beating well after each addition. Beat in vanilla. Combine flour, baking powder, baking soda and salt; add to creamed mixture alternately with sour cream. Beat just until combined.

2. Pour half of the batter into a greased 13-in. x 9-in. baking dish. Combine the pie filling and peaches; spread over batter. Drop the remaining batter by tablespoonfuls over filling.

3. For topping, combine the brown sugar, flour, oats and cinnamon in a bowl. Cut in butter until mixture is crumbly. Sprinkle over batter.

4. Bake at 350° for 70-75 minutes or until a toothpick inserted near the center comes out clean. Cool on a wire rack. In a small bowl, combine confectioners' sugar and enough milk to achieve desired consistency; drizzle glaze over the coffee cake.

Mini Toffee Rolls

I found this delicious recipe in a magazine years ago and adapted the original to make it my own. The rich, bite-sized treats are full of cinnamon flavor!

—CAROL GILLESPIE CHAMBERSBURG, PA

PREP: 20 MIN. • **BAKE:** 15 MIN. • **MAKES:** 4 DOZEN

- 6 tablespoons butter, softened
- ½ cup packed brown sugar
- 1 teaspoon ground cinnamon
- ⅓ cup milk chocolate English toffee bits
- 2 tubes (8 ounces each) refrigerated crescent rolls
- 1 cup confectioners' sugar
- 4½ teaspoons 2% milk
- ¼ teaspoon vanilla extract

1. In a small bowl, cream the butter, brown sugar and cinnamon until light and fluffy. Stir in toffee bits.

2. Separate each tube of crescent dough into four rectangles; seal perforations. Spread evenly with butter mixture. Roll up each rectangle jelly-roll style, starting with a long side.

3. Cut each into six 1-in. slices; place cut side down into two greased 8-in. square baking dishes. Bake at 375° for 14-16 minutes or until golden brown.

4. In a small bowl, combine the confectioners' sugar, milk and vanilla until smooth. Drizzle over warm rolls.

Cappuccino Cinnamon Rolls

Rich coffee flavor emboldens the filling of these gooey rolls. The icing goes on while they're still warm—and they never last long!

—SHERRI COX LUCASVILLE, OH

PREP: 45 MIN. + RISING • **BAKE:** 25 MIN. • **MAKES:** 1 DOZEN

- 1 package (¼ ounce) active dry yeast
- 1 cup warm water (110° to 115°)
- ¾ cup warm milk (110° to 115°)
- ½ cup warm buttermilk (110° to 115°)
- 3 tablespoons sugar
- 2 tablespoons butter, softened
- 1¼ teaspoons salt
- 5½ to 6 cups all-purpose flour

FILLING
- ¼ cup butter, melted
- 1 cup packed brown sugar
- 4 teaspoons instant coffee granules
- 2 teaspoons ground cinnamon

ICING
- 1½ cups confectioners' sugar
- 2 tablespoons butter, softened
- 1 to 2 tablespoons milk
- 2 teaspoons cappuccino mix
- ½ teaspoon vanilla extract

1. In a large bowl, dissolve yeast in warm water. Add the milk, buttermilk, sugar, butter, salt and 4 cups flour. Beat on medium speed until smooth. Stir in enough remaining flour to form a soft dough (dough will be sticky).

2. Turn onto a floured surface; knead until smooth and elastic, about 6-8 minutes. Place in a greased bowl, turning once to grease the top. Cover and let rise in a warm place until doubled, about 1 hour.

3. Punch the dough down; turn onto a floured surface. Roll into an 18-in. x 12-in. rectangle; brush with butter. Combine the brown sugar, coffee granules and cinnamon; sprinkle over dough to within ½ in. of edges.

4. Roll up jelly-roll style, starting with a long side; pinch seam to seal. Cut into 12 slices. Place rolls, cut side down, in a greased 13-in. x 9-in. baking pan. Cover and let rise until doubled, about 30 minutes.

5. Bake at 350° for 22-28 minutes or until golden brown. Place pan on a wire rack. In a small bowl, beat the icing ingredients until smooth. Spread over rolls. Serve warm.

Pull-Apart Caramel Coffee Cake

The first time I made this delightful treat for a brunch party, it was a huge hit. Now I get requests every time family or friends do anything around the breakfast hour! I always keep the four simple ingredients on hand.

—JAIME KEELING KEIZER, OR

PREP: 10 MIN. • **BAKE:** 25 MIN. • **MAKES:** 12 SERVINGS

- 2 tubes (12 ounces each) refrigerated flaky buttermilk biscuits
- 1 cup packed brown sugar
- ½ cup heavy whipping cream
- 1 teaspoon ground cinnamon

1. Cut each biscuit into four pieces; arrange evenly in a 10-in. fluted tube pan coated with cooking spray. Combine the brown sugar, cream and cinnamon; pour over biscuits.

2. Bake at 350° for 25-30 minutes or until golden brown. Cool for 5 minutes before inverting onto a serving platter.

Maple Twist Coffee Cake

If you like maple, you will love this recipe. It is so pretty with all the twists and is always a hit when I take it to bake sales.

—DEANNA RICHTER ELMORE, MN

PREP: 45 MIN. + RISING • **BAKE:** 20 MIN.
MAKES: 16 SERVINGS

- 1 package (¼ ounce) active dry yeast
- ¾ cup warm milk (110° to 115°)
- ¼ cup butter, softened
- 3 tablespoons sugar
- 1 egg
- 1 teaspoon maple flavoring
- ½ teaspoon salt
- 2¾ to 3 cups all-purpose flour

FILLING
- ½ cup sugar
- ⅓ cup chopped walnuts
- 1 teaspoon ground cinnamon
- 1 teaspoon maple flavoring
- ¼ cup butter, melted

GLAZE
- 1 cup confectioners' sugar
- 2 tablespoons butter, melted
- 1 to 2 tablespoons milk
- ½ teaspoon maple flavoring

1. In a large bowl, dissolve yeast in warm milk. Add the butter, sugar, egg, maple flavoring, salt and 1½ cups flour. Beat until smooth. Stir in enough remaining flour to form a soft dough.

2. Turn onto a floured surface; knead until smooth and elastic, about 6-8 minutes. Place in a greased bowl, turning once to grease top. Cover and let rise in a warm place until doubled, about 1 hour. Meanwhile, in a small bowl, combine the sugar, walnuts, cinnamon and maple flavoring; set aside.

3. Punch dough down. Turn onto a lightly floured surface; divide into thirds. Roll each portion into a 12-in. circle; place one circle on a greased baking sheet or 12-in. pizza pan. Spread with a third of the butter; sprinkle with a third of the filling. Repeat layers twice. Pinch edges of the dough to seal.

4. Carefully place a glass in center of circle. With scissors, cut from outside edge just to the glass, forming 16 wedges. Remove glass; twist each wedge five to six times. Pinch ends to seal and tuck under. Cover and let rise until doubled, about 30 minutes.

5. Bake at 375° for 18-20 minutes or until golden brown. In a small bowl, combine glaze ingredients; set aside.

6. Carefully remove coffee cake from pan by running a metal spatula under it to loosen; transfer to a wire rack. Drizzle with the glaze.

Cranberry Almond Coffee Cake

Cranberries add delightful tartness to a coffee cake that has become a Christmas morning tradition for my family. I make my own almond paste to use when baking up this treat.

—ANNE KEENAN NEVADA CITY, CA

PREP: 20 MIN. • **BAKE:** 45 MIN. + COOLING • **MAKES:** 9 SERVINGS

- ½ cup almond paste (recipe on opposite page)
- 6 tablespoons butter, softened
- ½ cup plus 2 tablespoons sugar, divided
- 3 eggs
- 1⅓ cups all-purpose flour, divided
- 1 teaspoon baking powder
- 1 teaspoon almond extract
- ½ teaspoon vanilla extract
- 2¼ cups fresh or frozen cranberries

1. In a small bowl, cream almond paste, butter and ½ cup sugar until fluffy. Add two eggs, beating well after each addition. Combine 1 cup flour and baking powder; add to creamed mixture. Beat in the remaining egg and flour. Stir in extracts. Gently fold in cranberries.

2. Spread evenly into a greased 8-in. square baking dish; sprinkle with remaining sugar. Bake at 325° for 45-55 minutes or until a toothpick inserted near the center comes out clean. Cool on a wire rack.

Homemade Almond Paste

When a recipe I wanted to try called for almond paste, I decided to make my own. It saves the expense of a store-bought product and results in baked goods that are lighter in texture.

—ANNE KEENAN NEVADA CITY, CA

PREP: 10 MIN. + CHILLING • **MAKES:** 1½ CUPS

- 1½ cups blanched almonds
- 1½ cups confectioners' sugar
- 1 egg white
- 1½ teaspoons almond extract
- ¼ teaspoon salt

1. Place almonds in a food processor; cover and process until smooth. Add the confectioners' sugar, egg white, extract and salt; cover and process until smooth.

2. Divide almond paste into ½-cup portions; place in airtight containers. Refrigerate for up to 1 month or freeze for up to 3 months.

Classic Long Johns

I came across the recipe for these wonderful treats many years ago. You can frost them with maple or chocolate glaze, then top with nuts, jimmies, toasted coconut or sprinkles.

—ANN SORGENT FOND DU LAC, WI

PREP: 30 MIN. + RISING • **COOK:** 5 MIN./BATCH + COOLING
MAKES: 2 DOZEN

- 2 packages (¼ ounce each) active dry yeast
- ½ cup warm water (110° to 115°)
- ½ cup half-and-half cream
- ¼ cup sugar
- ¼ cup shortening
- 1 egg
- 1 teaspoon salt
- ½ teaspoon ground nutmeg
- 3 to 3½ cups all-purpose flour
  Oil for deep-fat frying

MAPLE FROSTING
- ¼ cup packed brown sugar
- 2 tablespoons butter
- 1 tablespoon half-and-half cream
- ⅛ teaspoon maple flavoring
- 1 cup confectioners' sugar

CHOCOLATE FROSTING
- 2 ounces semisweet chocolate, chopped
- 2 tablespoons butter
- 1 cup confectioners' sugar
- 2 tablespoons boiling water
- 1 teaspoon vanilla extract

1. In a large bowl, dissolve yeast in warm water. Add the cream, sugar, shortening, egg, salt, nutmeg and 3 cups flour. Beat until smooth. Stir in enough remaining flour to form a soft dough (dough will be sticky).

2. Turn onto a floured surface; knead until smooth and elastic, about 6-8 minutes. Place in a greased bowl, turning once to grease the top. Cover and let rise in a warm place until doubled, about 1 hour.

3. Punch dough down; divide in half. Turn onto a lightly floured surface; roll each half into a 12-in. x 6-in. rectangle. Cut into 3-in. x 2-in. rectangles. Place on greased baking sheets. Cover and let rise in a warm place until doubled, about 30 minutes.

4. In an electric skillet or deep fryer, heat oil to 375°. Fry long johns, a few at a time, until golden brown on both sides. Drain on paper towels.

5. For maple frosting, combine the brown sugar and butter in a small saucepan. Bring to a boil; cook and stir for 2 minutes or until sugar is dissolved. Remove from the heat; stir in the cream and maple flavoring. Add the confectioners' sugar; beat for 1 minute or until smooth. Frost cooled long johns.

6. For chocolate frosting, in a microwave, melt chocolate and butter; stir until smooth. Stir in remaining ingredients. Spread over cooled long johns; let stand until set.

Strawberry Cheesecake Turnovers

When I first served these turnovers, folks thought I bought them from a bakery. Everyone was surprised to hear they start with refrigerated crescent rolls and pie filling.

—JOLENE SPRAY VAN WERT, OH

START TO FINISH: 25 MIN. • **MAKES:** 8 SERVINGS

- 1 package (3 ounces) cream cheese, softened
- 2 tablespoons confectioners' sugar
- ¼ teaspoon almond extract
- 1 tube (8 ounces) refrigerated crescent rolls
- ⅓ cup strawberry pie filling
- ⅓ cup crushed pineapple, drained
- 2 to 3 tablespoons apricot spreadable fruit

1. In a small bowl, beat the cream cheese, sugar and extract until smooth. Unroll crescent dough and separate into eight triangles. Place 1 heaping teaspoonful of cream cheese mixture in the center of each triangle. Top with 1 teaspoon of pie filling and 1 teaspoon of pineapple.

2. With one long side of pastry facing you, fold right and left corners over filling to top corner, forming a square. Seal edges; tuck ends under. Place on an ungreased baking sheet. Bake at 375° for 15-17 minutes or until lightly browned. Brush with spreadable fruit.

Overnight Cherry Danish

With their cherry-filled centers, these rolls melt in your mouth and put a touch of color on your table. Best of all, they store well, unfrosted, in the freezer.

—LEANN SAUDER TREMONT, IL

PREP: 1½ HOURS + CHILLING • **BAKE:** 15 MIN. + COOLING
MAKES: 3 DOZEN

- 2 packages (¼ ounce each) active dry yeast
- ½ cup warm 2% milk (110° to 115°)
- 6 cups all-purpose flour
- ⅓ cup sugar
- 2 teaspoons salt
- 1 cup cold butter, cubed
- 1½ cups warm half-and-half cream (110° to 115°)
- 6 egg yolks, lightly beaten
- 1 can (21 ounces) cherry pie filling

ICING
- 2 tablespoons butter, softened
- 3 cups confectioners' sugar
- ¼ teaspoon vanilla extract
  Dash salt
- 4 to 5 tablespoons half-and-half cream

1. In a small bowl, dissolve yeast in warm milk. In a large bowl, combine the flour, sugar and salt. Cut in butter until crumbly. Add the yeast mixture, cream and egg yolks; stir until mixture forms a soft dough (dough will be sticky). Cover and refrigerate overnight.

2. Punch down the dough; divide into quarters. Roll each portion into an 18-in. x 4-in. rectangle and cut into 1-in. x 4-in. strips.

3. Place two strips side by side; twist together. Shape into a ring; pinch ends together. Repeat with remaining strips. Place 2 in. apart on greased baking sheets. Cover and let rise in a warm place until doubled, about 45 minutes.

4. Using the end of a wooden spoon handle, make a ½-in.-deep indentation in the center of each roll. Fill each with about 1 tablespoon pie filling.

5. Bake at 350° for 14-16 minutes or until lightly browned. Remove from pans to wire racks to cool.

6. For icing, in a large bowl, beat butter until fluffy. Gradually beat in the confectioners' sugar, vanilla, salt and enough cream to achieve a drizzling consistency. Drizzle over rolls.

Carrot Cake Doughnuts

I love carrot cake and wanted to carry its flavor over into a doughnut recipe. My experiments worked and these are now my family's favorite doughnuts. The recipe is easy to make, too.

—TAMERA DANFORTH THE DALLES, OR

PREP: 30 MIN. • **COOK:** 5 MIN./BATCH • **MAKES:** 1½ DOZEN

- 2 tablespoons butter, softened
- 1 cup sugar
- 2 eggs
- 1 teaspoon grated orange peel
- 3½ cups all-purpose flour
- 4 teaspoons baking powder
- 1½ teaspoons ground cinnamon
- 1 teaspoon baking soda
- ¾ teaspoon each salt, ground nutmeg and cloves
- ⅓ cup 2% milk
- 1 cup shredded carrots
   Oil for deep-fat frying

GLAZE
- 1 cup confectioners' sugar
- 2 tablespoons orange juice
- 1 tablespoon finely shredded carrot
- ½ teaspoon vanilla extract
- ¼ cup finely chopped walnuts

1. In a large bowl, cream the butter and sugar until light and fluffy. Add the eggs, one at a time, beating well after each addition. Stir in orange peel. Combine the flour, baking powder, cinnamon, baking soda, salt, nutmeg and cloves; add to creamed mixture alternately with milk. Fold in the carrots.

2. Turn dough onto a lightly floured surface; roll out to ½-in. thickness. Cut with a floured 2½-in. doughnut cutter.

3. In an electric skillet or deep-fat fryer, heat oil to 375°. Fry doughnuts, a few at a time, for 1½ to 2 minutes on each side or until golden brown. Drain on paper towels.

4. For glaze, combine the confectioners' sugar, orange juice, carrot and vanilla; drizzle over warm doughnuts. Sprinkle with walnuts.

Cinnamon Swirl Rolls

When you don't have time to make from-scratch cinnamon rolls, rely on this recipe that begins with refrigerated breadsticks. Little helpers will like shaping these sweet treats.

—TASTE OF HOME TEST KITCHEN

START TO FINISH: 30 MIN. • **MAKES:** 4 SERVINGS

- ⅓ cup packed brown sugar
- ¼ cup sugar
- 1 teaspoon ground cinnamon
- 1 tube (11 ounces) refrigerated breadsticks
- 3 tablespoons butter, melted
- ¾ cup confectioners' sugar
- 4 teaspoons milk
- ¼ teaspoon vanilla extract

1. In a shallow bowl, combine the brown sugar, sugar and cinnamon. Separate dough into 12 breadsticks; brush all sides with some of butter, then coat with sugar mixture.

2. On a greased baking sheet, form three breadsticks into a coil, overlapping ends slightly. Secure with a toothpick through the overlapped ends and at the end of the swirl. Repeat with the remaining breadsticks. Drizzle the remaining butter over rolls; sprinkle with any remaining sugar mixture.

3. Bake at 375° for 15-17 minutes or until golden brown. Remove to a wire rack. Discard toothpicks. Combine the confectioners' sugar, milk and vanilla; drizzle over rolls. Serve warm.

Nut Roll Coffee Cake

This walnut-swirled coffee cake is a great taste to wake up to. As a finishing touch, drizzle it with glaze or add a dusting of confectioners' sugar.

—PATRICIA MELE LOWER BURRELL, PA

PREP: 40 MIN. + CHILLING • **BAKE:** 40 MIN. + COOLING
MAKES: 16 SERVINGS

- 2 packages (¼ ounce each) active dry yeast
- ¼ cup warm water (110° to 115°)
- 1 cup butter, melted
- ½ cup warm 2% milk (110° to 115°)
- 4 egg yolks
- 2 tablespoons sugar
- ¾ teaspoon salt

- 2½ cups all-purpose flour
  FILLING
- 3 egg whites
- 1 cup plus 3 tablespoons sugar, divided
- 2 cups ground walnuts
- 2 tablespoons 2% milk
- 2 teaspoons ground cinnamon

1. In a large bowl, dissolve the yeast in warm water. Add the butter, milk, egg yolks, sugar, salt and flour. Beat until smooth (mixture will be sticky). Cover the dough and refrigerate overnight.

2. For filling, in a small bowl, beat egg whites on medium speed until soft peaks form. Gradually beat in 1 cup sugar, about 2 tablespoons at a time, on high until sugar is dissolved. In a large bowl, combine the walnuts, milk, cinnamon and remaining sugar; fold in egg whites.

3. Divide dough in half. On a well-floured surface, roll each portion into an 18-in. x 12-in. rectangle. Spread the filling evenly over rectangles to within ½ in. of edges. Roll each up jelly-roll style, starting with a long side; pinch the seam to seal.

4. Place one filled roll seam side up in a greased 10-in. tube pan. Top with second roll, seam side down. Bake at 350° for 40-45 minutes or until golden brown. Cool for 10 minutes before removing from pan to a wire rack.

Maple Sticky Buns

My family has a small sugaring operation in our backyard. This recipe makes good use of the maple syrup we make. It's a family tradition to serve these sticky buns on Thanksgiving every year.

—PRISCILLA ROSSI EAST BARRE, VT

PREP: 30 MIN. + CHILLING • **BAKE:** 25 MIN. • **MAKES:** 2½ DOZEN

> 2 packages (¼ ounce each) active dry yeast
> 2 cups warm water (110° to 115°)
> ¼ cup shortening
> ½ cup sugar
> 1 egg
> 2 teaspoons salt
> 6 to 6½ cups all-purpose flour
> 6 tablespoons butter, softened
> ¾ cup packed brown sugar
> 1 tablespoon ground cinnamon
> ¾ cup chopped walnuts
> 1½ cups maple syrup
>   Additional brown sugar

1. In a large bowl, dissolve yeast in water. Add shortening, sugar, egg, salt and 5 cups flour. Beat until smooth. Add enough remaining flour to form a soft dough. Cover and refrigerate or up to 24 hours.

2. Punch dough down. Turn onto a floured surface; knead until smooth and elastic, about 6-8 minutes, adding more flour if needed. Divide into thirds. Roll each portion into a 16-in. x 10-in. rectangle.

3. On each rectangle, spread 2 tablespoons butter; sprinkle each with ¼ cup brown sugar, 1 teaspoon cinnamon and ¼ cup walnuts. Pour syrup into three greased 9-in. round baking pans. Sprinkle with additional brown sugar.

4. Tightly roll up each rectangle, jelly-roll style, starting with a short side. Slice each roll into 10 pieces; place over syrup. Cover and let rise until doubled, about 30 minutes.

5. Bake at 350° for 25-30 minutes or until golden brown. Cool in pans for 5 minutes; invert onto serving plates.

NOTE *11-in. x 7-in. baking pans may be substituted for the 9-in. round pans.*

Bakeshop HOW-TO

Shaping Cinnamon Rolls and Sticky Buns

Roll dough into a rectangle. Spread or brush with butter; sprinkle with filling. Roll up, starting from a long end, and pinch seam to seal.

Slice into rolls. Place cut side down in a greased baking pan.

Cover and let rise until doubled. Rolls will begin to touch each other.

After baking, combine glaze ingredients if called for in the recipe; spoon over warm rolls.

Cherry Crescent Coffee Cake

A can of pie filling and a few tubes of crescent rolls help me assemble this sweet treat. It's the perfect addition to hot cups of coffee and good conversation.

—VALERIE BELLEY ST. LOUIS, MO

PREP: 25 MIN. • **BAKE:** 15 MIN. • **MAKES:** 12 SERVINGS

- **1 package (8 ounces) cream cheese, softened**
- **¾ cup confectioners' sugar, divided**
- **1 egg**
- **½ teaspoon vanilla extract**
- **2 tubes (8 ounces each) refrigerated crescent rolls**
- **1 can (21 ounces) cherry pie filling**
- **2 to 3 teaspoons milk**

1. In a small bowl, beat the cream cheese and ¼ cup confectioners' sugar until smooth. Beat in egg and vanilla just until combined; set aside.

2. Unroll crescent dough and separate into triangles. Set four triangles aside. Place remaining triangles on a greased 14-in. pizza pan, forming a ring with wide ends facing outer edge of pan and pointed ends toward the center; leave a 3-in. hole in the center. Lightly press seams together.

3. Spread cream cheese mixture over dough to within ½ in. of edges. Top with pie filling to within ½ in. of cream cheese edges. Cut reserved triangles into thirds, starting at the wide end and ending at the point. Arrange over pie filling with points facing outer edge of pan, forming spokes. Press ends at center and outer edges to seal.

4. Bake at 375° for 15-20 minutes or until golden brown. Cool on a wire rack. Combine remaining confectioners' sugar and enough milk to achieve drizzling consistency; drizzle over coffee cake.

Fresh Plum Kuchen

In summer when plums are in season, this tender fruit-topped cake is delectable! For variety, use fresh pears or apples instead.

—ANNA DALEY MONTAGUE, PE

PREP: 20 MIN. • **BAKE:** 40 MIN. + COOLING
MAKES: 10-12 SERVINGS

- ¼ cup butter, softened
- ¾ cup sugar
- 2 eggs
- 1 cup all-purpose flour
- 1 teaspoon baking powder
- ¼ cup milk
- 1 teaspoon grated lemon peel
- 2 cups sliced fresh plums (about 4 medium)
- ½ cup packed brown sugar
- 1 teaspoon ground cinnamon

1. In a small bowl, cream butter and sugar until light and fluffy. Beat in eggs. Combine flour and baking powder; add to the creamed mixture alternately with milk, beating well after each addition. Add lemon peel. Pour into a greased 10-in. springform pan. Arrange plums on top; gently press into batter. Sprinkle with brown sugar and cinnamon.

2. Place the pan on a baking sheet. Bake at 350° for 40-50 minutes or until top is golden and a toothpick inserted near the center comes out clean. Cool for 10 minutes. Run a knife around edge of pan; remove sides. Cool on a wire rack.

Maple-Glazed Long Johns

This is a very old recipe from my aunt that I revamped to use with my bread machine. The pastries are deep-fried, then glazed with a simple maple frosting. They're very good with coffee.

—PEGGY BURDICK BURLINGTON, MI

PREP: 30 MIN. • **COOK:** 5 MIN./BATCH • **MAKES:** ABOUT 2½ DOZEN

- 1 cup water (70° to 80°)
- 1 egg
- ½ teaspoon vanilla extract
- ½ cup sugar
- ¼ cup shortening
- ½ teaspoon salt
- 3 cups bread flour
- 2¼ teaspoons active dry yeast
- Oil for deep-fat frying

GLAZE

- 2 cups confectioners' sugar
- ¼ cup half-and-half cream
- 1 tablespoon maple flavoring

1. In bread machine pan, place the first eight ingredients in order suggested by manufacturer. Select dough setting (check dough after 5 minutes of mixing; add 1 to 2 tablespoons of water or flour if needed).

2. When cycle is completed, turn dough onto a lightly floured surface. Divide into four portions. Roll each into a 12-in. x 5-in. rectangle. Cut each rectangle widthwise into 1½-in. strips.

3. In an electric skillet or deep-fat fryer, heat oil to 375°. Drop dough strips, a few at a time, into hot oil. Turn with a slotted spoon and fry for 1 minute on each side or until golden brown. Drain on paper towels.

4. In a small bowl, combine the glaze ingredients. Place the long johns on a wire rack; drizzle with glaze.

NOTE *We recommend you do not use a bread machine's time-delay feature for this recipe.*

Orange-Hazelnut Spiral Rolls

By switching up a coffee cake recipe that was popular with my family, I came up with these scrumptious rolls. I make them for special occasions throughout the year.

—LORAINE MEYER BEND, OR

PREP: 30 MIN. + RISING • **BAKE:** 20 MIN. • **MAKES:** ABOUT 2 DOZEN

- 5 to 5½ cups all-purpose flour, divided
- 1 cup mashed potato flakes
- ¼ cup sugar
- 2 packages (¼ ounce each) quick-rise yeast
- 1 teaspoon salt
- 2 teaspoons grated orange peel
- 1 cup milk
- ½ cup butter, cubed
- ½ cup sour cream
- ¼ cup water
- 2 eggs

FILLING

- ⅓ cup butter, softened
- 1 cup confectioners' sugar
- 1 cup ground hazelnuts

GLAZE

- ½ cup sugar
- ¼ cup thawed orange juice concentrate
- ¼ cup sour cream
- 2 tablespoons butter

1. In a large bowl, combine 4 cups flour, potato flakes, sugar, yeast, salt and orange peel. In saucepan, heat the milk, butter, sour cream and water to 120°-130°. Add to dry ingredients; beat just until moistened. Add eggs; beat until smooth. Stir in enough remaining flour to form stiff dough.

2. Turn onto floured surface; knead until smooth and elastic, about 6-8 minutes. Place in greased bowl, turning once to grease top. Cover; let dough rest in a warm place for 20 minutes.

3. Punch dough down. Turn onto a floured surface; roll into a 22-in. x 14-in. rectangle. For filling, combine butter, confectioners' sugar and nuts. Spread lengthwise over half of the dough. Fold dough over filling, forming a 22-in. x 7-in. rectangle. Cut into 7-in. x ¾-in. strips.

4. Twist each strip 4 or 5 times and shape into a ring. Pinch ends together. Place on two greased 15-in. x 10-in. x 1-in. baking pans. Cover the rings and let rise for 30 minutes or until doubled.

5. Bake at 375° for 17-20 minutes or until golden brown. Remove to wire racks. Meanwhile, in a saucepan, combine glaze ingredients over medium heat. Bring to boil; cook and stir for 3 minutes or until thickened. Remove from the heat. Drizzle over warm rolls.

Bakeshop HOW-TO

Shaping a Tea Ring

Roll into a rectangle. Spread filling evenly over dough to within 1/2 in. of edges. Roll up jelly-roll style, starting with a long side; pinch seam to seal.

Place seam side down on a pan; pinch ends together to form a ring.

With scissors, cut from outside edge to two-thirds of the way toward center of ring at 1-in. intervals.

Separate the pieces slightly and twist each to allow the filling to show.

Swedish Tea Ring

This showstopper will add a special touch to any holiday spread. It's absolutely spectacular.

—**ELSIE EPP** NEWTON, KS

PREP: 30 MIN. + RISING • **BAKE:** 20 MIN. + COOLING
MAKES: 1 RING (24 SLICES)

- 1 tablespoon active dry yeast
- 1½ cups warm water (110° to 115°)
- ¼ cup sugar
- ¼ cup canola oil
- 2 egg whites, lightly beaten
- 1¼ teaspoons salt
- 5½ to 6 cups all-purpose flour
- ½ cup chopped walnuts
- ½ cup chopped maraschino cherries, patted dry
- ¼ cup packed brown sugar
- 1 teaspoon ground cinnamon
- 2 tablespoons butter, melted

ICING
- 1 cup confectioners' sugar
- 1 to 2 tablespoons fat-free milk

1. In a large bowl, dissolve yeast in warm water. Add the sugar, oil, egg whites, salt and 1 cup flour; beat until smooth. Stir in enough remaining flour to form a soft dough.

2. Turn onto a lightly floured surface; knead until smooth, about 6-8 minutes. Place in a bowl coated with cooking spray, turning once to coat the top. Cover and let rise until doubled, about 1 hour.

3. Combine the walnuts, cherries, brown sugar and cinnamon; set aside. Punch dough down; roll into an 18-in. x 12-in. rectangle. Brush with butter; sprinkle with nut mixture to within ½ in. of edges. Roll up jelly-roll style, starting with a long side; pinch seam to seal.

4. Place seam side down on a 14-in. pizza pan coated with cooking spray; pinch ends together to form a ring. With scissors, cut from outside edge two-thirds of the way toward center of ring at scant 1-in. intervals. Separate strips slightly; twist to allow filling to show. Cover and let rise until doubled, about 40 minutes.

5. Bake at 400° for 20-25 minutes or until golden brown. Remove from pan to a wire rack to cool.

6. In a small bowl, combine confectioners' sugar and enough milk to achieve desired consistency; drizzle icing over the tea ring.

Coffee-Klatch Kolaches

These crowd-pleasing Czech treats are the perfect partner for a cup of joe. They're easy to make with canned cherry pie filling, but the homemade prune filling is a delicious option, too.

—CAROL HOUDEK MINNEAPOLIS, MN

PREP: 45 MIN. + RISING • **BAKE:** 10 MIN. + COOLING
MAKES: 2 DOZEN

- 1 **package (¼ ounce) active dry yeast**
- ¼ **cup warm water (110° to 115°)**
- ¾ **cup warm 2% milk (110° to 115°)**
- ⅓ **cup sugar**
- ⅓ **cup shortening**
- 1 **teaspoon salt**
- ⅛ **teaspoon ground nutmeg**
- 2 **eggs**
- 4 **cups all-purpose flour**
- 1 **can (21 ounces) cherry pie filling**
- 3 **tablespoons butter, melted**

GLAZE
- 1 **cup confectioners' sugar**
- 1 **tablespoon butter, melted**
- 5 **teaspoons 2% milk**

1. In a large bowl, dissolve yeast in warm water. Add the milk, sugar, shortening, salt, nutmeg, eggs and 2 cups flour; beat until smooth. Add enough remaining flour to form a soft dough. Turn onto a floured surface; knead until smooth and elastic, about 6-8 minutes.

2. Place in a greased bowl, turning once to grease the top. Cover the dough and let rise in a warm place until doubled, about 1 hour.

3. Punch dough down. Divide in half; shape each half into 12 balls. Place 3 in. apart on greased baking sheets. Flatten each ball to a 3-in. circle. Cover and let rise in a warm place until doubled, about 30 minutes.

4. Make a depression in the center of each roll; add a rounded tablespoonful of filling. Bake at 350° for 10-15 minutes or until golden brown. Brush rolls with butter. Remove from pans to wire racks to cool. Combine glaze ingredients; drizzle over the tops.

Prune Kolaches: In a small saucepan, bring an 18-oz. package of pitted dried plums and 2 cups water to a boil. Reduce heat; simmer, uncovered, for 15 minutes or until plums are tender. Drain. Transfer to blender; add ¼ cup sugar and ½ teaspoon ground cinnamon. Cover and process until pureed; cool. Proceed as directed.

Peachy Cheese Danish

I've prepared these pretty sweet rolls for late-night snacks and for breakfast when we have guests.

—**CAROLYN KYZER** ALEXANDER, AK

PREP: 20 MIN. • **BAKE:** 15 MIN. • **MAKES:** 4 SERVINGS

- 1 tube (8 ounces) refrigerated crescent rolls
- 4 ounces cream cheese, softened
- ¼ cup sugar
- 2 tablespoons lemon juice
- 8 teaspoons peach preserves or flavor of your choice

GLAZE

- ¼ cup confectioners' sugar
- ½ teaspoon vanilla extract
- 1 to 2 teaspoons milk

1. Separate dough into four rectangles; seal perforations. On a lightly floured surface, roll each into a 7-in. x 3½-in. rectangle. In a small bowl, combine cream cheese, sugar and lemon juice until smooth; spread over rectangles. Roll up from a long side; pinch edges to seal. Holding one end, loosely coil each.

2. Place on an ungreased baking sheet. Top each coil with 2 teaspoons preserves. Bake at 350° for 15-20 minutes or until golden brown. Remove from pan to wire rack.

3. For glaze, in a small bowl, combine confectioners' sugar, vanilla and enough milk to achieve desired consistency. Drizzle over warm rolls.

Petite Sticky Buns

Start your morning on a sweet note with these tender maple sticky buns. They are fantastically light and airy. But be careful not to overbake, or they're difficult to get out of the pan!

—**LISA NAUGLE** FAYETTEVILLE, PA

PREP: 30 MIN. + RISING • **BAKE:** 15 MIN. • **MAKES:** 2 DOZEN

- 3 to 3¼ cups all-purpose flour
- ¼ cup sugar
- 1 package (¼ ounce) active dry yeast
- 1 teaspoon salt
- 1¼ cups milk
- ¼ cup butter, cubed
- 1 egg

TOPPING

- 1 cup packed brown sugar
- ¾ cup butter, cubed
- ¾ cup chopped pecans, toasted
- 2 tablespoons honey
- 1 teaspoon ground cinnamon
- ½ teaspoon maple flavoring

1. In a large bowl, combine 2 cups flour, sugar, yeast and salt. In a small saucepan, heat the milk and butter to 120°-130°. Add to dry ingredients; beat just until moistened. Add egg; beat until smooth. Stir in enough remaining flour to form a soft dough (dough will be sticky). Do not knead. Cover and let rise in a warm place until doubled, about an hour.

2. In a small saucepan over low heat, cook topping ingredients until butter is melted. Drop by rounded teaspoonfuls into 24 well-greased muffin cups.

3. Stir dough down. Fill greased muffin cups half full. Cover muffin pans and let rise in a warm place until doubled, about 30 minutes.

4. Place muffin cups on foil-lined baking sheets. Bake at 375° for 12-15 minutes or until golden brown. Cool for 2 minutes before inverting onto baking sheets. Transfer to serving platters. Serve warm.

Jumbo Cinnamon Rolls

I especially like recipes that make just enough for the two of us, and these yummy sweet rolls fit the bill. Because these treats begin with a ready-made dough, they couldn't be more convenient to whip up.

—EDNA HOFFMAN HEBRON, IN

PREP: 15 MIN. + RISING • **BAKE:** 15 MIN. • **MAKES:** 2 SERVINGS

- 4 frozen Texas-size dinner rolls
- 2 tablespoons butter, melted
- ¼ cup coarsely chopped pecans
- 2 tablespoons sugar
- ¾ teaspoon ground cinnamon

HONEY BUTTER
- 2 tablespoons butter, softened
- 2 teaspoons honey

1. Let rolls rise in a warm place until doubled, about 45 minutes. Punch down. Roll each into a 12-in. rope; brush with butter. In a shallow bowl, combine the pecans, sugar and cinnamon; roll ropes in nut mixture.

2. Twist two ropes together; pinch ends to seal. Place in a greased 10-oz. custard cup. Repeat with remaining ropes. Cover and let rise for 30 minutes or until doubled.

3. Bake at 375° for 15-20 minutes or until golden brown. Meanwhile, combine the honey butter ingredients. Serve with rolls.

Glazed Cinnamon Braids

This recipe has been a tradition in my family for many years. The Red Hot candies give it such a yummy zing.

—GEORGIA STULL HARRISONVILLE, MO

PREP: 40 MIN. + RISING • **BAKE:** 25 MIN.
MAKES: 2 LOAVES (12 SLICES EACH)

- 2 packages (¼ ounce each) active dry yeast
- ¼ cup warm water (110° to 115°)
- 1 cup warm 2% milk (110° to 115°)
- 2 eggs
- ½ cup sugar
- ¼ cup shortening
- 2 teaspoons salt
- 5 to 5½ cups all-purpose flour

FILLING
- 1 cup chopped pecans
- ½ cup Red Hot candies
- ¼ cup sugar
- 2 teaspoons ground cinnamon
- 2 tablespoons butter, softened

GLAZE
- 1 cup confectioners' sugar
- ½ teaspoon vanilla extract
- 1 to 2 tablespoons 2% milk

1. In a large bowl, dissolve yeast in warm water. Add the milk, eggs, sugar, shortening, salt and 3 cups flour. Beat until smooth. Stir in enough remaining flour to form a soft dough.

2. Turn onto a floured surface; knead until smooth and elastic, about 6-8 minutes. Place in a greased bowl, turning once to grease top. Cover and let rise in a warm place until doubled, about 1 hour. Meanwhile, in a small bowl, combine the pecans, Red Hots, sugar and cinnamon; set aside.

3. Punch dough down. Divide in half. On a greased baking sheet, roll out one portion into a 12-in. x 10-in. rectangle. Spread 1 tablespoon butter down the center; sprinkle with half of the pecan mixture.

4. On each long side, cut 1-in.-wide strips about 2½ in. into center. Starting at one end, fold alternating strips at an angle across filling. Pinch ends to seal. Repeat, making second loaf. Cover and let rise until doubled, about 45 minutes.

5. Bake at 350° for 25-30 minutes or until golden brown. Remove from pans to wire racks. Combine the glaze ingredients; drizzle over loaves. Serve warm.

Cranberry-White Chocolate Cinnamon Rolls

A basket of warm cinnamon rolls is a sure way to impress family and friends. Add cranberries and white chocolate to the ingredient mix, and these treats become incredibly memorable.

—MEG MARRIOTT TACOMA, WA

PREP: 45 MIN. + CHILLING • **BAKE:** 30 MIN. + COOLING
MAKES: 16 SERVINGS

- 2 packages (¼ ounce each) active dry yeast
- 2 cups warm water (110° to 115°)
- 1 cup butter, melted
- ½ cup sugar
- 2 teaspoons salt
- 5 to 6 cups all-purpose flour

FILLING
- 1 cup butter, softened
- ½ cup packed brown sugar
- 2 teaspoons ground cinnamon
- 1 package (10 to 12 ounces) white baking chips
- 1 cup dried cranberries
- ½ cup chopped pecans

GLAZE
- 2 cups confectioners' sugar
- 2 teaspoons vanilla extract
- 5 to 6 tablespoons heavy whipping cream

1. In a large bowl, dissolve yeast in warm water. Add the butter, sugar, salt and 4 cups flour; beat until smooth. Stir in enough remaining flour to form a soft dough.

2. Turn onto a floured surface; knead until smooth and elastic, about 6-8 minutes. Place in a greased bowl, turning once to grease the top. Cover and refrigerate overnight.

3. Punch dough down. On a lightly floured surface, roll into a 24-in. x 12-in. rectangle. For filling, combine the butter, brown sugar and cinnamon; spread over dough to within ½ in. of edges. Sprinkle with chips, cranberries and pecans. Roll up jelly-roll style, starting with a long side; pinch seam to seal.

4. Cut into 16 slices. Place cut side down in two greased 13-in. x 9-in. baking pans. Cover and let rise in a warm place until doubled, about 45 minutes.

5. Bake at 350° for 30-35 minutes or until golden brown. Meanwhile, in a small bowl, combine the confectioners' sugar, vanilla and enough cream to achieve desired consistency; drizzle over warm rolls. Cool on wire racks.

Upside-Down Apple Gingerbread

Don't expect any leftovers when you serve this moist and tender cake. People love its heartwarming seasonal flavor.

—**FLORENCE PALMER** MARSHALL, IL

PREP: 15 MIN. • **BAKE:** 45 MIN. + COOLING • **MAKES:** 9 SERVINGS

- ¼ **cup butter, melted**
- ⅓ **cup packed brown sugar**
- 2 **large apples, peeled and sliced**

GINGERBREAD

- ½ **cup butter, softened**
- ½ **cup sugar**
- ⅓ **cup packed brown sugar**
- 1 **egg**
- ½ **cup molasses**
- 2 **cups all-purpose flour**
- 1 **teaspoon baking soda**
- 1 **teaspoon ground cinnamon**
- 1 **teaspoon ground ginger**
- ½ **teaspoon ground cloves**
- ½ **teaspoon salt**
- ¼ **teaspoon ground nutmeg**
- ¾ **cup brewed tea**

1. Pour butter into a 9-in. square baking pan; sprinkle with brown sugar. Arrange apples over sugar; set aside.

2. For gingerbread, in a large bowl, cream butter and sugars until light and fluffy. Beat in egg, then molasses. Combine dry ingredients; add to sugar mixture alternately with tea, beating well after each addition. Pour over apples.

3. Bake at 350° for 45-50 minutes or until a toothpick comes out clean. Cool for 10 minutes before inverting onto a plate.

Swedish Doughnuts

One day, my father got a hankering for doughnuts and asked me to make him some. Dad—and everyone else—loved the results.

—**LISA BATES** DUNHAM, QC

PREP: 20 MIN. + CHILLING • **COOK:** 5 MIN./BATCH
MAKES: 2½ DOZEN

- 2 **eggs**
- 1 **cup sugar**
- 2 **cups cold mashed potatoes (mashed with milk and butter)**
- ¾ **cup buttermilk**
- 2 **tablespoons butter, melted**
- 1 **teaspoon vanilla or almond extract**
- 4½ **cups all-purpose flour**
- 4 **teaspoons baking powder**
- 1 **teaspoon baking soda**
- 1 **teaspoon salt**
- 2 **teaspoons ground nutmeg**
- ⅛ **teaspoon ground ginger**
  Oil for deep-fat frying
  Additional sugar, optional

1. In a large bowl, beat eggs and sugar. Add the potatoes, buttermilk, butter and vanilla. Combine the flour, baking powder, baking soda, salt, nutmeg and ginger; gradually add to egg mixture and mix well. Cover and refrigerate for 1-2 hours.

2. Turn onto a lightly floured surface; roll to ½-in. thickness. Cut with a floured 2½-in. doughnut cutter. In an electric skillet or deep-fat fryer, heat oil to 375°.

3. Fry doughnuts, a few at a time, until golden brown on both sides, about 2 minutes. Drain on paper towels. Roll warm doughnuts in additional sugar if desired.

Daily Breads

Cranberry Orange Bagels

These morning treats have a bright, sweet-tart taste. Switch up the flavor, if you'd like, by using raisins and cinnamon.

—**KRISTY REEVES** LEROY, KS

PREP: 30 MIN. + STANDING • **BAKE:** 20 MIN. + COOLING
MAKES: 9 BAGELS

- 1 cup plus 4 tablespoons water (70° to 80°), divided
- ½ cup dried cranberries
- ⅓ cup packed brown sugar
- 4½ teaspoons grated orange peel
- 1 teaspoon salt
- ¼ teaspoon ground cloves
- 3 cups bread flour
- 1 package (¼ ounce) active dry yeast
- 1 tablespoon sugar
- 1 egg white
- 1 tablespoon cornmeal

1. In bread machine, place 1 cup plus 2 tablespoons water and the next seven ingredients in order suggested by manufacturer. Select dough setting (check after 5 minutes of mixing; add 1 to 2 tablespoons of water or flour if needed).

2. When cycle is completed, turn dough onto a lightly floured surface. Shape into nine balls. Push thumb through centers to form a 1-in. hole. Stretch and shape dough to form an even ring. Cover and let rest for 10 minutes; flatten rings slightly.

3. Fill a Dutch oven two-thirds full with water; add sugar and bring to a boil. Drop bagels, two at a time, into boiling water. Cook 45 seconds; turn and cook 45 seconds longer. Remove with a slotted spoon; drain on paper towels.

4. Whisk egg white and remaining water; brush over bagels. Grease a baking sheet; sprinkle with cornmeal. Place bagels on pan 2 in. apart. Bake at 400° for 18-22 minutes or until golden brown.

Caramelized Onion Flatbread

I top pizza crust with sweet, buttery onions and grated cheese for easy homemade bread in one hour!

—**DEIRDRE DEE COX** MILWAUKEE, WI

PREP: 45 MIN. • **BAKE:** 15 MIN. • **MAKES:** 15 SERVINGS

- 3 large sweet onions, thinly sliced
- 2 tablespoons brown sugar
- 1 tablespoon Marsala wine or apple juice
- ¼ teaspoon salt
- ¼ teaspoon pepper
- 2 tablespoons butter
- 1 tube (13.8 ounces) refrigerated pizza crust
- 1 tablespoon olive oil
- ¼ cup shredded Parmesan cheese

1. In a large skillet, cook the onions, brown sugar, wine, salt and pepper in butter over medium-low heat for 30-40 minutes or until onions are caramelized, stirring frequently.

2. On a greased baking sheet, roll out pizza crust into a 13-in. x 10-in. rectangle. Brush the crust with oil. Top with onions and cheese.

3. Bake at 400° for 15-18 minutes or until lightly browned. Serve warm.

beat until well combined. Stir in enough remaining all-purpose flour to form a soft dough.

2. Turn onto a floured surface; knead until smooth and elastic, about 6-8 minutes. Place in a greased bowl, turning once to grease the top. Cover and let rise in a warm place until doubled, about 1 hour.

3. Punch dough down. Turn onto a lightly floured surface; divide into 24 pieces. Shape each into a ball. Place in a greased 13-in. x 9-in. baking pan. Cover and let rise until doubled, about 30 minutes.

4. Bake at 375° for 20-22 minutes or until golden brown. Melt remaining butter; brush over rolls. Remove from pan to a wire rack.

Pumpernickel Muffins

These savory muffins are a perfect accompaniment to a hearty entree. Molasses, chocolate and dried cherries add just the right hint of sweetness to a rich rye dough.

—NANCY MUELLER HIGHLANDS RANCH, CO

PREP: 20 MIN. • **BAKE:** 15 MIN. • **MAKES:** 6 MUFFINS

- ¾ **cup rye flour**
- ⅔ **cup all-purpose flour**
- 3 **tablespoons sugar**
- 1 **teaspoon baking powder**
- ½ **teaspoon ground cinnamon**
- ¼ **teaspoon baking soda**
- ¼ **teaspoon salt**
- 1 **egg**
- ⅔ **cup buttermilk**
- ¼ **cup canola oil**
- 1 **tablespoon molasses**
- ½ **ounce unsweetened chocolate, melted and cooled**
- ¼ **cup dried cherries**

1. In a large bowl, combine the flours, sugar, baking powder, cinnamon, baking soda and salt.

2. In another bowl, combine the egg, buttermilk, oil, molasses and chocolate. Stir into dry ingredients just until moistened. Fold in cherries.

3. Fill greased or paper-lined muffin cups three-fourths full. Bake at 400° for 15-20 minutes or until a toothpick inserted in the muffin comes out clean. Cool for 5 minutes before removing from pan to a wire rack. Serve warm.

Honey-Oat Pan Rolls

These tender rolls are a welcome addition to any meal. Whole wheat flour and oats make them nutritious, too.

—ARLENE BUTLER OGDEN, UT

PREP: 45 MIN. + RISING • **BAKE:** 20 MIN. • **MAKES:** 2 DOZEN

- 2½ to 2¾ **cups all-purpose flour**
- ¾ **cup whole wheat flour**
- ½ **cup old-fashioned oats**
- 2 **packages (¼ ounce each) active dry yeast**
- 1 **teaspoon salt**
- 1 **cup water**
- ¼ **cup honey**
- 5 **tablespoons butter, divided**
- 1 **egg**

1. In a large bowl, combine 1 cup all-purpose flour, whole wheat flour, oats, yeast and salt. In a small saucepan, heat the water, honey and 4 tablespoons butter to 120°-130°. Add to dry ingredients; beat just until moistened. Add egg;

Ezekiel Bread

This bread bakes up tender and chewy with a hint of sweetness. It's great to give as a gift or to accompany your Sunday dinner.
—**ROGER HAWLEY** VALLEY PARK, MO

PREP: 45 MIN. + RISING • **BAKE:** 30 MIN. + COOLING
MAKES: 4 LOAVES (16 SLICES EACH)

- 3 **packages (¼ ounce each) active dry yeast**
- 5 **cups warm water (110° to 115°), divided**
- 1 **tablespoon plus ⅔ cup honey, divided**
- ⅔ **cup canola oil**
- ½ **cup sugar**
- 2 **teaspoons salt**
- 4 **cups whole wheat flour**
- 1 **cup toasted wheat germ**
- 6 **to 8 cups bread flour**

1. In a large bowl, dissolve yeast in ¾ cup warm water and 1 tablespoon honey. Add the remaining water and honey, oil, sugar, salt, whole wheat flour, wheat germ and 3 cups bread flour. Beat until smooth. Stir in enough remaining bread flour to form a soft dough (dough will be sticky).

2. Turn onto a lightly floured surface; knead until smooth and elastic, about 6-8 minutes. Place in a bowl coated with cooking spray, turning once to coat the top. Cover and let rise in a warm place until doubled, about 1 hour.

3. Punch dough down. Shape into loaves. Place in four 9-in. x 5-in. loaf pans coated with cooking spray. Cover and let rise until nearly doubled, about 30 minutes.

4. Bake at 350° for 30-35 minutes or until golden brown. Remove from pans to wire racks to cool.

Honey White Loaves

When I was searching for a moist bread that wouldn't crumble when thinly sliced, a friend recommended her grandmother's cherished recipe. It slices perfectly.

—**LOIS KAMPS** HUDSONVILLE, MI

PREP: 20 MIN. + RISING • **BAKE:** 25 MIN. + COOLING
MAKES: 3 LOAVES (12 SLICES EACH)

 2   packages (¼ ounce each) active dry yeast
2½ cups warm water (110° to 115°)
 ½   cup butter, melted
 ½   cup honey
 2   eggs
 3   teaspoons salt
 8   to 9 cups all-purpose flour

1. In a large bowl, dissolve yeast in warm water. Add the butter, honey, eggs, salt and 4 cups flour. Beat on medium for 3 minutes. Stir in enough of the remaining flour to form a soft dough.

2. Turn onto a floured surface; knead until smooth and elastic, about 6-8 minutes. Place in a greased bowl, turning once to grease top. Cover and let rise in a warm place until doubled, about 1 hour.

3. Punch dough down; shape into loaves. Place in three greased 8-in. x 4-in. loaf pans. Cover and let rise until doubled, about 30 minutes.

4. Bake at 375° for 25-30 minutes or until golden brown. Remove from pans to wire racks to cool.

Rosemary Olive Focaccia

These are so delicious! For a thinner, crispier focaccia, try using three 10-inch rounds instead of two to bake up this recipe. Just remember to adjust the bake time accordingly.

—**TASTE OF HOME TEST KITCHEN**

PREP: 35 MIN. + RISING • **BAKE:** 25 MIN.
MAKES: 2 LOAVES (8 SLICES EACH)

 3   cups all-purpose flour
 1   package (¼ ounce) active dry yeast
 1   teaspoon sugar
 1   teaspoon dried rosemary, crushed, divided
 ¾   teaspoon salt
 ⅛   teaspoon coarsely ground pepper
 1   cup warm water (120° to 130°)
 4   tablespoons olive oil, divided
 ⅓   cup sliced ripe olives
 2   tablespoons yellow cornmeal
 2   tablespoons grated Parmesan cheese
     Additional coarsely ground black pepper and rosemary

1. In a large bowl, combine flour, yeast, sugar, ½ teaspoon rosemary, salt and pepper. Stir in warm water and 2 tablespoons oil. Turn out onto a lightly floured surface; knead 3 minutes. Add olives and remaining rosemary; knead 1 minute longer. Place in a greased bowl, turning once to grease the top. Cover and let rise until doubled, about 45 minutes.

2. Punch dough down and divide in half. Cover and let rest for 5 minutes. Sprinkle cornmeal on greased baking sheets. Roll each piece of dough into a 10-in. circle; place on baking sheets. Cover and let rise until doubled, about 30 minutes. With fingertips, make several dimples over top of dough.

3. Brush dough with remaining oil. Sprinkle with cheese and additional pepper and rosemary. Bake at 375° for 25-30 minutes or until golden brown. Serve warm.

Golden Oat Bread

This wholesome bread incorporates grains that my sons, Tim and Jon, wouldn't normally touch. But even they can't resist these beautiful loaves!

—KAY KRAUSE SIOUX FALLS, SD

PREP: 30 MIN. + RISING • **BAKE:** 20 MIN. + COOLING
MAKES: 2 LOAVES (16 SLICES EACH)

- 3 to 4 cups all-purpose flour
- 1 cup old-fashioned oats, divided
- ¼ cup sugar
- 3 tablespoons chopped walnuts
- 2 tablespoons sunflower kernels
- 2 teaspoons active dry yeast
- ¾ teaspoon salt
- ¾ cup water
- ⅓ cup canola oil
- ¼ cup buttermilk
- ¼ cup honey
- 2 eggs
- ¾ cup whole wheat flour
- 1 tablespoon cold water

1. In a large bowl, combine 2 cups all-purpose flour, ¾ cup oats, sugar, walnuts, sunflower kernels, yeast and salt. In a small saucepan, heat the water, oil, buttermilk and honey to 120°-130°. Add to dry ingredients; beat until well blended. Beat in 1 egg until smooth. Stir in whole wheat flour and enough remaining all-purpose flour to form a soft dough.
2. Turn onto a floured surface; knead until smooth and elastic, about 6-8 minutes. Place in a greased bowl, turning once to grease the top. Cover and let rise in a warm place until doubled, about 1 hour.

3. Punch the dough down; turn onto a lightly floured surface. Divide in half; shape into round loaves. Sprinkle 2 tablespoons oats on a greased baking sheet; place loaves over oats. Cover the dough and let rise until doubled, about 45 minutes.
4. Beat remaining egg and cold water; brush over loaves. Sprinkle with remaining oats. Bake at 350° for 20-25 minutes or until golden brown. Cool on wire racks.

Irish Soda Bread

I've been making bread since I was a young girl, and this is one of my favorites. It's moist with a wonderful texture and flavor. Golden raisins peek out of every slice.

—ANN LAUVER LITITZ, PA

PREP: 30 MIN. + RISING • **BAKE:** 30 MIN. + COOLING
MAKES: 1 LOAF (12 SLICES)

- 1 package (¼ ounce) active dry yeast
- ½ cup warm water (110° to 115°)
- 3 tablespoons sugar, divided
- 1 cup warm buttermilk (110° to 115°)
- 2 tablespoons butter, softened
- ½ teaspoon salt
- ½ teaspoon baking soda
- 3½ to 4 cups all-purpose flour
- ¾ cup golden raisins

1. In a large bowl, dissolve yeast in warm water. Add 1 tablespoon sugar; let stand for 5 minutes. Beat in the buttermilk, butter, salt, baking soda, 1 cup flour and remaining sugar until smooth. Stir in raisins and enough remaining flour to form a soft dough.
2. Turn onto a floured surface; knead until smooth and elastic, about 6-8 minutes. Place in a greased bowl, turning once to grease the top. Cover and let rise in a warm place until doubled, about 40 minutes.
3. Punch dough down. Turn onto a lightly floured surface; knead for 2 minutes. Shape into a round loaf. Place on a greased baking sheet. Cover and let rise until doubled, about 30 minutes. With a sharp knife, cut a ¼-in.-deep cross on top of loaf.
4. Bake at 350° for 30-35 minutes or until golden brown. Remove from pan to cool on a wire rack.
NOTE *Warmed buttermilk will appear curdled.*

Baker's Dozen Yeast Rolls

A yummy honey-garlic topping turns these easy dinner rolls into something extra special. Try 'em with soups and chili.

—TASTE OF HOME TEST KITCHEN

PREP: 25 MIN. + RISING • **BAKE:** 15 MIN. + COOLING
MAKES: 13 ROLLS

- 2 to 2½ cups all-purpose flour
- 2 tablespoons sugar
- 1 package (¼ ounce) quick-rise yeast
- ½ teaspoon salt
- ¾ cup warm water (120° to 130°)
- 2 tablespoons plus 4 teaspoons butter, melted, divided
- ¾ cup shredded sharp cheddar cheese
- 2 teaspoons honey
- ⅛ teaspoon garlic salt

1. In a large bowl, combine 1½ cups flour, sugar, yeast and salt. Add water and 2 tablespoons butter; beat on medium speed for 3 minutes or until smooth. Stir in cheese and enough remaining flour to form a soft dough.

2. Turn onto a lightly floured surface; knead until smooth and elastic, about 4-6 minutes. Cover and let rest for 10 minutes. Divide into 13 pieces. Shape each into a ball. Place in a greased 9-in. round baking pan. Cover and let rise in a warm place until doubled, about 30 minutes.

3. Bake at 375° for 11-14 minutes or until lightly browned. Combine the honey, garlic salt and remaining butter; brush over rolls. Cool on a wire rack.

Tomato-Herb Focaccia

With its medley of herbs and tomatoes, this rustic bread will liven up any occasion, from a family meal to a game-day get-together. And it won't stick around long.

—JANET MILLER INDIANAPOLIS, IN

PREP: 30 MIN. + RISING • **BAKE:** 20 MIN.
MAKES: 1 LOAF (12 PIECES)

- 1 **package (¼ ounce) active dry yeast**
- 1 **cup warm water (110° to 115°)**
- 2 **tablespoons olive oil, divided**
- 1½ **teaspoons salt**
- 1 **teaspoon sugar**
- 1 **teaspoon garlic powder**
- 1 **teaspoon each dried oregano, thyme and rosemary, crushed**
- ½ **teaspoon dried basil**
- **DASH PEPPER**
- 2 **to 2½ cups all-purpose flour**
- 2 **plum tomatoes, thinly sliced**
- ¼ **cup shredded part-skim mozzarella cheese**
- 1 **tablespoon grated Parmesan cheese**

1. In a large bowl, dissolve the yeast in warm water. Add 1 tablespoon oil, salt, sugar, garlic powder, herbs, pepper and 1½ cups flour. Beat until smooth. Stir in enough remaining flour to form a soft dough (dough will be sticky).
2. Turn onto a floured surface; knead until smooth and elastic, about 6-8 minutes. Place in a greased bowl, turning once to grease the top. Cover and let rise in a warm place until doubled, about 1 hour.
3. Punch dough down. Cover and let rest for 10 minutes. Shape into a 13-in. x 9-in. rectangle; place on a greased baking sheet. Cover and let rise until doubled, about 30 minutes. With fingertips, make several dimples over top of dough.
4. Brush dough with remaining oil; arrange tomatoes over the top. Sprinkle with cheeses. Bake at 400° for 20-25 minutes or until golden brown. Remove to a wire rack.

Buttery Whole Wheat Dinner Rolls

These whole grain rolls are tender and delicious just eaten plain; they don't even need butter. I adapted the recipe from one my mom made after she sampled a similar roll at a restaurant.

—ANGELA COFFMAN KANSAS CITY, MO

PREP: 30 MIN. + RISING • **BAKE:** 10 MIN. • **MAKES:** 16 ROLLS

- 1 tablespoon active dry yeast
- ¾ cup warm water (110° to 115°)
- ⅓ cup sugar
- ⅓ cup nonfat dry milk powder
- 4 tablespoons butter, softened, divided
- 1 egg
- 1 teaspoon salt
- 2 cups whole wheat flour
- ½ to 1 cup bread flour

1. In a small bowl, dissolve yeast in warm water. Add the sugar, milk powder, 2 tablespoons butter, egg, salt and whole wheat flour. Beat until smooth. Stir in enough bread flour to form a soft dough (dough will be sticky).

2. Turn onto a floured surface; knead until smooth and elastic, about 6-8 minutes. Place in a greased bowl, turning once to grease the top. Cover and let rise in a warm place until doubled, about 1 hour.

3. In a shallow microwave-safe bowl, melt remaining butter. Punch dough down. Turn onto a lightly floured surface; divide into 16 pieces. Shape each into a ball; roll in melted butter. Place 2 in. apart on greased baking sheets. Cover and let rise until doubled, about 30 minutes.

4. Bake at 375° for 8-10 minutes or until golden brown. Remove from pans to wire racks.

English Batter Buns

Since receiving this easy-to-prepare recipe from a dear friend, I've made these rolls often for the holidays.

—GERALDINE WEST OGDEN, UT

PREP: 15 MIN. + RISING • **BAKE:** 10 MIN. • **MAKES:** 1 DOZEN

- 2 packages (¼ ounces each) active dry yeast
- 1 cup warm milk (110° to 115°)
- ½ cup shortening
- 2 tablespoons sugar
- 1 teaspoon salt
- 2 eggs
- 3½ cups all-purpose flour
  Melted butter

1. In a large bowl, dissolve yeast in warm milk. Add the shortening, sugar, salt, eggs and 2 cups flour; beat on medium speed for 3 minutes. Stir in remaining flour until smooth. Cover and let rise in a warm place until doubled, about 30 minutes.

2. Stir batter vigorously for 25 strokes (dough will be slightly sticky). Spoon into greased muffin cups. Tap pans to settle the batter. Cover and let rise until batter reaches tops of cups, about 20 minutes.

3. Bake at 400° for 10-15 minutes or until golden brown. Brush with butter.

Bakeshop TIP

Batter Up!

Easy batter bread lets you enjoy homemade yeast bread without the work of kneading. It dirties fewer dishes and leaves your counter clean, as the dough stays in its mixing bowl for the first rise. Since beating the batter with a mixer takes the place of kneading, be sure to beat for the time specified in the recipe. Batter bread dough is more loose and sticky than traditional kneaded doughs.

Cheddar Herb Rings

These impressive cheese loaves are great sliced into thin wedges to go with soup, salads or casseroles. I've served this to large crowds. One year, I gave a loaf to our neighbor for Christmas.

—**EVELYN BEAR** KINGSTON, ID

PREP: 35 MIN. + CHILLING • **BAKE:** 20 MIN. + COOLING
MAKES: 2 LOAVES (12 SLICES EACH)

- 1   package (¼ ounce) active dry yeast
- ¼   cup warm water (110° to 115°)
- 1   cup warm milk (110° to 115°)
- ¼   cup canola oil
- 2   tablespoons honey
- 1   egg
- 1   teaspoon salt
- 1   cup whole wheat flour
- 2½ cups all-purpose flour
- 1   teaspoon each dried oregano, basil and rosemary, crushed

FILLING
- 1½ cups (6 ounces) shredded cheddar cheese
- ½   teaspoon dried parsley flakes
- ¼   teaspoon garlic powder
- ¼   teaspoon paprika

TOPPING
- 1   egg, lightly beaten
- 2   teaspoons sesame seeds
- 4   teaspoons grated Parmesan cheese

1. In a large bowl, dissolve yeast in warm water. Add milk, oil, honey, egg, salt, whole wheat flour, 1 cup all-purpose flour and herbs. Beat until blended. Stir in enough remaining all-purpose flour to form a soft dough. Cover and refrigerate overnight.

2. Punch dough down and turn onto a floured surface; divide in half. Roll one portion into a 15-in. x 10-in. rectangle. Combine filling ingredients; sprinkle half over dough. Roll up jelly-roll style, starting with a long side; pinch seams to seal.

3. Place seam side down on a greased baking sheet; pinch ends together to form a ring. With a sharp knife, cut ½-in. slashes at 2-in. intervals. Repeat with remaining dough and filling. Cover and let rise in a warm place until doubled, about 30 minutes.

4. Brush each ring with egg; sprinkle with sesame seeds and cheese. Bake at 350° for 20-25 minutes or until golden brown. Remove from pans to wire racks to cool.

Garlic Knots

Here's a handy bread that can be made in no time flat. Refrigerated biscuits make preparation simple. The Italian flavors complement a variety of meals.

—**JANE PASCHKE** UNIVERSITY PARK, FL

START TO FINISH: 30 MIN. • **MAKES:** 2½ DOZEN

- 1   tube (12 ounces) refrigerated buttermilk biscuits
- ¼   cup canola oil
- 3   tablespoons grated Parmesan cheese
- 1   teaspoon garlic powder
- 1   teaspoon dried oregano
- 1   teaspoon dried parsley flakes

1. Cut each biscuit into thirds. Roll each piece into a 3-in. rope and tie into a knot; tuck ends under. Place 2 in. apart on greased baking sheets. Bake at 400° for 8-10 minutes or until golden brown.

2. In a large bowl, combine the remaining ingredients; add the warm knots and gently toss to coat.

Bakeshop HOW-TO

Shaping Knot Rolls

Divide dough as directed; roll each portion into a rope. Tie into a knot. Tuck and pinch ends under.

Sunflower Seed & Honey Wheat Bread

I've tried other bread recipes, but this one is a staple in our home. I won $50 in a baking contest with a loaf that I had stored in the freezer.

—MICKEY TURNER GRANTS PASS, OR

PREP: 40 MIN. + RISING • **BAKE:** 35 MIN. + COOLING
MAKES: 3 LOAVES (12 SLICES EACH)

 2 packages (¼ ounce each) active dry yeast
 3¼ cups warm water (110° to 115°)
 ¼ cup bread flour
 ⅓ cup canola oil
 ⅓ cup honey
 3 teaspoons salt
 6½ to 7½ cups whole wheat flour
 ½ cup sunflower kernels
 3 tablespoons butter, melted

1. In a large bowl, dissolve yeast in warm water. Add the bread flour, oil, honey, salt and 4 cups whole wheat flour. Beat until smooth. Stir in sunflower kernels and enough remaining flour to form a firm dough.

2. Turn onto a floured surface; knead until smooth and elastic, about 6-8 minutes. Place in a greased bowl, turning once to grease the top. Cover and let rise in a warm place until doubled, about 1 hour.

3. Punch dough down; divide into three portions. Shape into loaves; place in three greased 8-in. x 4-in. loaf pans. Cover and let rise until doubled, about 30 minutes.

4. Bake at 350° for 35-40 minutes or until golden brown. Brush with melted butter. Remove from pans to wire racks to cool.

Mini White Breads

These small and tender loaves have wonderful flavor and texture. I've found them to be the perfect size when cooking for a smaller number or when preparing them for gifts around the holidays.

—NILA TOWLER BAIRD, TX

PREP: 20 MIN. + RISING • **BAKE:** 20 MIN. + COOLING
MAKES: 2 LOAVES (4 SLICES EACH)

- 1 **package (¼ ounce) active dry yeast**
- 1 **tablespoon sugar**
- ⅓ **cup warm water (110° to 115°)**
- 2¼ to 2½ **cups all-purpose flour**
- 1 **teaspoon salt**
- ½ **cup milk**
- 2 **teaspoons butter, melted**
  Additional melted butter

1. Combine yeast, sugar and water in a large bowl. Add 1½ cups of flour, salt, milk and butter. Mix for 3 minutes on medium speed. Stir in enough remaining flour to form a soft dough.

2. Turn onto a floured surface; knead until smooth and elastic, 6-8 minutes. Place in a greased bowl, turning once to grease the top. Cover and let rise in a warm place until doubled, about 45 minutes.

3. Punch dough down; shape into loaves. Place in two greased 5¾-in. x 3-in. x 2-in. pans. Cover and let rise until doubled, about 30 minutes.

4. Bake at 375° for 20-25 minutes or until golden brown. Remove from pans to wire racks to cool. Brush tops with melted butter.

From-Scratch Bagels

Instead of going to a baker, head to the kitchen and surprise your family with homemade bagels. For variation and flavor, sprinkle them with cinnamon-sugar instead of sesame and poppy seeds.

—REBECCA PHILLIPS BURLINGTON, CT

PREP: 30 MIN. + RISING • **BAKE:** 20 MIN. + COOLING
MAKES: 1 DOZEN

- 1 **teaspoon active dry yeast**
- 1¼ **cups warm milk (110° to 115°)**
- ½ **cup butter, softened**
- 2 **tablespoons sugar**
- 1 **teaspoon salt**
- 1 **egg yolk**
- 3¾ to 4¼ **cups all-purpose flour**
  Sesame or poppy seeds, optional

1. In a large bowl, dissolve yeast in warm milk. Add the butter, sugar, salt and egg yolk; mix well. Stir in enough flour to form a soft dough.

2. Turn onto a floured surface; knead until smooth and elastic, about 6-8 minutes. Place in a greased bowl, turning once to grease the top. Cover and let rise in a warm place until doubled, about 1 hour.

3. Punch dough down. Shape into 12 balls. Push thumb through centers to form a 1½-in. hole. Stretch and shape dough to form an even ring. Place on a floured surface. Cover and let rest for 10 minutes; flatten bagels slightly.

4. Fill a Dutch oven two-thirds full with water; bring to a boil. Drop bagels, two at a time, into boiling water. Cook for 45 seconds; turn and cook 45 seconds longer. Remove with a slotted spoon; drain well on paper towels.

5. Sprinkle with sesame or poppy seeds if desired. Place 2 in. apart on greased baking sheets. Bake at 400° for 20-25 minutes or until golden brown. Remove from pans to wire racks to cool.

Pizza Pan Bread

People are astounded to learn that I make this yummy bread from scratch in less than an hour. With this recipe from my brother-in-law, hot homemade bread is an easy alternative to garlic toast. I sometimes serve it as a snack or appetizer.

—SANDRA WINGERT STAR CITY, SK

PREP: 20 MIN. + RISING • **BAKE:** 15 MIN.
MAKES: 1 LOAF (16 PIECES)

- 2½ cups all-purpose flour
- 1 tablespoon quick-rise yeast
- 1 teaspoon sugar
- 1 teaspoon salt
- 1 cup warm water (120° to 130°)
- 1 tablespoon canola oil

TOPPING
- ¼ to ⅓ cup prepared Italian salad dressing
- ¼ teaspoon salt
- ¼ teaspoon garlic powder
- ¼ teaspoon dried oregano
- ¼ teaspoon dried thyme
  Dash pepper
- 1 tablespoon grated Parmesan cheese
- ½ cup shredded part-skim mozzarella cheese

1. In a large bowl, combine 2 cups flour, yeast, sugar and salt. Beat in water and oil until blended. Stir in enough remaining flour to form a soft dough.

2. Turn onto a floured surface; knead for 1-2 minutes or until smooth and elastic. Place in a greased bowl, turning once to grease the top. Cover and let rise in a warm place for 20 minutes.

3. Punch the dough down; place on a greased 12-in. pizza pan and pat into a 12-in. circle. Brush with salad dressing. Combine the seasonings; sprinkle over top. Sprinkle with the cheeses.

4. Bake at 450° for 15 minutes or until golden brown. Serve warm.

Swedish Rye

This recipe came from my mother, and it's long been a family favorite. You can make a meal of it with soup and a salad.

—MARY ANN ROSS CROWN POINT, IN

PREP: 25 MIN. + RISING • **BAKE:** 30 MIN.
MAKES: 4 LOAVES (10 SLICES EACH)

- 1 package (¼ ounce) active dry yeast
- 1¾ cups warm water (110° to 115°), divided
- ¼ cup packed brown sugar
- ¼ cup molasses
- 2 tablespoons shortening
- 2 teaspoons salt
- 2½ cups rye flour
- 3¾ to 4¼ cups all-purpose flour
- 2 tablespoons butter, melted

1. In a large bowl, dissolve yeast in ¼ cup water. Add sugar, molasses, shortening, salt and remaining water; stir well. Add rye flour; beat until smooth. Add enough all-purpose flour to form a soft dough.

2. Turn onto a floured surface; knead until smooth and elastic, about 6-8 minutes. Place in a greased bowl, turning once to grease the top. Cover and let rise in a warm place until doubled, about 1½ hours. Punch dough down.

3. Shape into four round loaves. Place on greased baking sheets. Cover and let rise until doubled, about 45-60 minutes. Bake at 350° for 30-35 minutes or until golden brown. Brush with butter.

Cloverleaf Bran Rolls

These tender and delicious rolls are great for a gathering. They're especially good served warm.

—**MARVEL HERRIMAN** HAYESVILLE, NC

PREP: 40 MIN. + RISING • **BAKE:** 15 MIN. • **MAKES:** 2 DOZEN

- 1 **cup All-Bran**
- 1 **cup boiling water**
- 2 **packages (¼ ounce each) active dry yeast**
- 1 **cup warm water (110° to 115°)**
- 1 **cup shortening**
- ¾ **cup sugar**
- 1 **teaspoon salt**
- 2 **eggs, beaten**
- 6 **cups all-purpose flour**

1. In a small bowl, combine bran and boiling water; set aside. In another bowl, dissolve yeast in warm water.

2. In a large bowl, cream shortening, sugar and salt. Add eggs and yeast mixture; mix well. Add bran mixture and 2 cups flour; beat well. Gradually add enough remaining flour to form a soft dough.

3. Turn onto a floured surface; knead until smooth, about 6-8 minutes. Place in a greased bowl, turning once to grease top. Cover and let rise until doubled, about 1 hour.

4. Punch dough down. Turn onto a lightly floured surface. Divide into six portions; divide each into 12 pieces. Shape each into a ball; place three balls in each greased muffin cup. Cover and let rise until doubled, about 1 hour.

5. Bake at 350° for 15-18 minutes or until lightly browned. Remove from pans to wire racks.

Bakeshop HOW-TO

Shaping Cloverleafs

Divide dough into balls. Make balls smooth by pulling the edges under. Place smooth side up in greased muffin cups.

Challah

This traditional Jewish bread uses more eggs than most, which give it a rich flavor and attractive golden color.

—TASTE OF HOME TEST KITCHEN

PREP: 30 MIN. + RISING • **BAKE:** 30 MIN. + COOLING
MAKES: 2 LOAVES (16 SLICES EACH)

- 2 packages (¼ ounce each) active dry yeast
- 1 cup warm water (110° to 115°)
- ½ cup canola oil
- ⅓ cup sugar
- 1 tablespoon salt
- 4 eggs
- 6 to 6½ cups all-purpose flour

EGG WASH

- 1 egg
- 1 teaspoon cold water

1. Dissolve yeast in warm water. Add oil, sugar, salt, eggs and 4 cups flour. Beat until smooth. Stir in enough of the remaining flour to form a firm dough. Turn onto a floured surface; knead until smooth, 6-8 minutes. Place in a greased bowl, turning once to grease the top. Cover and let rise until doubled, about 1 hour.

2. Punch the dough down. Turn onto a floured surface; divide in half. Divide each portion into thirds; shape each into a 15-in. rope.

3. Place three ropes on a greased baking sheet and braid; pinch ends and tuck under. Repeat. Cover and let rise until doubled, about 1 hour.

4. Beat the egg and cold water; brush over braids. Bake at 350° for 30-35 minutes or until golden brown. Cool on wire racks.

Rustic Rye Bread

This gorgeous rye bread has just a touch of sweetness and the perfect amount of caraway seeds. With a crusty top and firm texture, it holds up well to sandwiches...but a pat of butter will do the job, too.

—HOLLY WADE HARRISONBURG, VA

PREP: 20 MIN. + RISING • **BAKE:** 30 MIN. + COOLING
MAKES: 2 LOAVES (12 SLICES EACH)

- 1 package (¼ ounce) active dry yeast
- 1¾ cups warm water (110° to 115°), divided
- ¼ cup packed brown sugar
- ¼ cup light molasses
- 3 tablespoons caraway seeds
- 2 tablespoons canola oil
- 3 teaspoons salt
- 1¾ cups rye flour
- ¾ cup whole wheat flour
- 1¾ to 2¼ cups all-purpose flour

1. In a large bowl, dissolve yeast in ¼ cup warm water. Add the brown sugar, molasses, caraway seeds, oil, salt and remaining water; mix well. Add rye flour, whole wheat flour and 1¾ cups all-purpose flour. Beat until smooth. Stir in enough remaining all-purpose flour to form a firm dough.

2. Turn onto a lightly floured surface; knead until smooth and elastic, about 6-8 minutes. Place in a bowl coated with cooking spray, turning once to coat the top. Cover and let rise in a warm place until doubled, about 1 hour.

3. Punch dough down; shape into two round loaves. Place on a baking sheet coated with cooking spray. Cover and let rise until doubled, about 1 hour.

4. Bake at 350° for 30-35 minutes or until golden brown. Remove from pan to wire rack to cool.

Indexes

Frosted Banana Bars, 236

General Index

ALMOND PASTE

Almond-Butter Cookie Bouquet, 170
Almond Venetian Dessert, 371
Cranberry Almond Coffee Cake, 448
Nutty Chocolate Batons, 291

ALMONDS

Almond Apple Cheesecake, 391
Almond Coconut Bars, 225
Almond Kiss Cookies, 131
Almond Sandies, 57
Almond Sugar Cookies, 54
Almond Truffle Brownies, 216
Berry-Almond Sandwich Cookies, 177
Buttery Almond Cookies, 139
Cherry Almond Muffins, 437
Chewy Almond Cookies, 106
Chocolate Almond Cheesecake, 405
Cinnamon Almond Crescents, 136
Cranberry Almond Coffee Cake, 448
Lemon Tart with Almond Crust, 366
Macadamia Almond Delights, 81
Pear Frangipane Tart, 359
Pineapple Almond Bars, 251
Raspberry Almond Strips, 128
Simple Raspberry Almond Bars, 243
Toffee Almond Sandies, 11
White Chocolate Pumpkin
    Cheesecake, 404
Whole Wheat Toffee Sandies, 295

AMARETTO

Amaretto Butter Frosting, 311
Amaretto Dream Cupcakes, 311

ANISE

Anise Butter Cookies, 165
Anise Cutout Cookies, 169
Itty Bitty Peppernuts, 291

APPLES

Apple Butter Cookies, 77
Apple Dumplings for Two, 372
Apple Peanut Butter Cookies, 74
Apple Pie in a Goblet, 343
Apple Pie Pastries, 375
Apple Streusel Muffins, 441
Apple Strudels, 381
Apple Walnut Squares, 224
Applesauce Spice Cupcakes, 319
Candy Apple Pie, 362
Caramel Apple Cupcakes, 334
Caramel Apple Dumplings, 376
Crisscross Apple Crowns, 385
German Apple Pie, 361
Mini Apple Tarts, 353
Rustic Caramel Apple Tart, 368
Upside-Down Apple Gingerbread, 465
Vanilla-Glazed Apple Cookies, 59

APRICOTS

Apricot Angel Brownies, 208
Apricot Bars, 224
Apricot Cheese Crescents, 124
Apricot Coconut Treasures, 132
Apricot Cream Cheese Drops, 69
Apricot Date Squares, 223
Oatmeal Apricot Scones, 438
Pineapple Upside-Down Cake, 322
Pistachio Apricot Bars, 256
Sachertorte, 333

BAGELS

Cranberry Orange Bagels, 467
From-Scratch Bagels, 479

BANANAS

Banana Brickle Muffins, 437
Banana Chocolate Chip Cookies, 27
Banana Cream Eclairs, 373
Banana Nut Bars, 244
Banana Nut Brownies, 203
Black-Bottom Banana Bars, 256
Chocolate Chip Banana Cream Pie, 365
Frosted Banana Bars, 236
Hummingbird Cake, 329

BARS (also see Blondies; Brownies)

Almond Coconut Bars, 225
Apple Walnut Squares, 224
Apricot Bars, 224
Apricot Date Squares, 223
Banana Nut Bars, 244
Black-Bottom Banana Bars, 256
Blueberry Squares, 251
Butterscotch Peanut Bars, 258
Caramel-Cashew Cake Bars, 239
Caramel Cereal Treats, 243
Caramel Cranberry Bars, 281
Caramel Heavenlies, 273
Cherry Coconut Bars, 230
Chewy Pecan Bars, 228
Chocolate Oreo Bars, 427
Chocolate Peanut Squares, 253
Coconut Pecan Bars, 236
Cranberry Nut Bars, 227
Cranberry Shortbread Bars, 229
Crimson Crumble Bars, 248
Crunchy Peanut Bars, 232
Frosted Banana Bars, 236
Frosted Creams, 252

Chocolate-Covered Cheesecake Bites, 399

CHOCOLATE

COOKIES (continued)

Cupcakes

Dessert

Doughnuts

Muffins

Pastries

Pies

Quick Bread

Scones

Tarts

CINNAMON

(also see Cinnamon Rolls & Sticky Buns)

CINNAMON ROLLS & STICKY BUNS

COCONUT

Bars

COOKIES (continued)

Cheery Cherry Cookies, 79

tasteofhome.com

COOKIES (continued)

Honey Lemon Cookies, 91

Cranberry Pear Crisp Pie, 347

Irish Mint Brownies, 219

Whole Wheat Blueberry Muffins, 439

FOOD EQUIVALENTS

FOOD	EQUIVALENT
Apples	1 pound (3 medium) = 2¾ cups sliced
Apricots	1 pound (8 to 12 medium) = 2½ cups sliced
Bananas	1 pound (3 medium) = 1⅓ cups mashed or 1½ to 2 cups sliced
Berries	1 pint = 1½ to 2 cups
Bread	1 loaf = 16 to 20 slices
Bread Crumbs	1 slice = ½ cup soft crumbs or ¼ cup dry crumbs
Butter or Margarine	1 pound = 2 cups or 4 sticks 1 stick = 8 tablespoons
Cheese	
Cottage	1 pound = 2 cups
Shredded	4 ounces = 1 cup
Cherries	1 pound = 3 cups whole or 3½ cups halved
Cocoa, Baking	1 pound = 4 cups
Coconut, Flaked	14 ounces = 5½ cups
Corn Syrup	16 ounces = 2 cups
Cornmeal	1 pound = 3 cups uncooked
Cranberries	12 ounces = 3 cups whole or 2½ cups finely chopped
Cream Cheese	8 ounces = 16 tablespoons
Cream, Whipping	1 cup = 2 cups whipped
Dates, Dried	1 pound = 2¾ cups pitted and chopped
Dates, Dried and Chopped	10 ounces = 1¾ cups
Egg Whites	1 cup = 8 to 10 whites
Flour	
All-Purpose	1 pound = about 3½ cups
Cake	1 pound = about 4½ cups
Whole Wheat	1 pound = about 3¾ cups
Frozen Whipped Topping	8 ounces = 3½ cups
Gelatin, Unflavored	1 envelope = 1 tablespoon
Graham Crackers	16 crackers = 1 cup crumbs
Grapefruit	1 medium = ¾ cup juice or 1½ cups segments

FOOD	EQUIVALENT
Grapes	1 pound = 3 cups
Honey	1 pound = 1⅓ cups
Lemons	1 medium = 3 tablespoons juice or 2 teaspoons grated peel
Limes	1 medium = 2 tablespoons juice or 1½ teaspoons grated peel
Marshmallows	
Large	1 cup = 7 to 9 marshmallows
Miniature	1 cup = about 100 marshmallows
Nectarines	1 pound (3 medium) = 3 cups sliced
Nuts	
Almonds	1 pound = 3 cups halves or 4 cups slivered
Ground	3¾ ounces = 1 cup
Hazelnuts	1 pound = 3½ cups whole
Pecans	1 pound = 4½ cups chopped
Walnuts	1 pound = 3¾ cups chopped
Oats	
Old-Fashioned	1 pound = 5 cups
Quick-Cooking	1 pound = 5½ cups
Oranges	1 medium = ⅓ to ½ cup juice or 4 teaspoons grated peel
Peaches	1 pound (4 medium) = 2¾ cups sliced
Pears	1 pound (3 medium) = 3 cups sliced
Pineapples	1 medium = 3 cups chunks
Popcorn	⅓ to ½ cup unpopped = 8 cups popped
Raisins	15 ounces = 2½ cups
Rhubarb	1 pound = 3 cups chopped (raw) or 2 cups (cooked)
Semisweet Chocolate Chips	6 ounces = 1 cup
Shortening	1 pound = 2 cups
Strawberries	1 pint = 2 cups hulled and sliced
Sugar	
Brown Sugar	1 pound = 2¼ cups
Confectioners' Sugar	1 pound = 4 cups
Granulated	1 pound = 2¼ to 2½ cups
Yeast, Active Dry	1 envelope = 2¼ teaspoons

INGREDIENT SUBSTITUTIONS

INGREDIENT SUBSTITUTIONS

WHEN YOU NEED:	IN THIS AMOUNT:	SUBSTITUTE:
Allspice	1 teaspoon	½ teaspoon ground cinnamon plus ½ teaspoon ground cloves
Apple Pie Spice	1 teaspoon	½ teaspoon ground cinnamon plus ¼ teaspoon ground nutmeg, ⅛ teaspoon ground allspice and ⅛ teaspoon ground cardamom, ginger or cloves
Baking Powder	1 teaspoon	½ teaspoon cream of tartar plus ¼ teaspoon baking soda
Broth	1 cup	1 cup hot water plus 1 teaspoon bouillon granules or 1 bouillon cube
Buttermilk	1 cup	1 tablespoon lemon juice or white vinegar plus enough milk to measure 1 cup; let stand for 5 minutes. Or 1 cup plain yogurt
Chocolate	1 square (1 ounce)	3 tablespoons baking cocoa plus 1 tablespoon shortening or canola oil
Chocolate, Semisweet	1 square (1 ounce)	1 square (1 ounce) unsweetened chocolate plus 1 tablespoon sugar or 3 tablespoons semisweet chocolate chips
Corn Syrup, Dark	1 cup	¾ cup light corn syrup plus ¼ cup molasses
Corn Syrup, Light	1 cup	1 cup sugar plus ¼ cup water
Cornstarch (for thickening)	1 tablespoon	2 tablespoons all-purpose flour
Cracker Crumbs	1 cup	1 cup dry bread crumbs
Cream, Half-and-Half	1 cup	1 tablespoon melted butter plus enough whole milk to measure 1 cup
Egg	1 whole	2 egg whites or 2 egg yolks or ¼ cup egg substitute
Flour, Cake	1 cup	1 cup minus 2 tablespoons (⅞ cup) all-purpose flour
Flour, Self-Rising	1 cup	1½ teaspoons baking powder plus ½ teaspoon salt and enough all-purpose flour to measure 1 cup
Garlic, Fresh	1 clove	⅛ teaspoon garlic powder
Gingerroot, Fresh	1 teaspoon	¼ teaspoon ground ginger
Honey	1 cup	1¼ cups sugar plus ¼ cup water
Lemon Juice	1 teaspoon	¼ teaspoon cider vinegar
Lemon Peel, grated	1 teaspoon	½ teaspoon lemon extract
Mace	1 teaspoon	1 teaspoon ground allspice or nutmeg
Milk, Whole	1 cup	½ cup evaporated milk plus ½ cup water or 1 cup water plus ⅓ cup nonfat dry milk powder
Molasses	1 cup	1 cup honey
Onion	1 small (⅓ cup chopped)	1 teaspoon onion powder or 1 tablespoon dried minced onion
Pumpkin Pie Spice	1 teaspoon	½ teaspoon ground cinnamon plus ¼ teaspoon ground ginger, ⅛ teaspoon ground nutmeg and ⅛ teaspoon ground cloves
Sour Cream	1 cup	1 cup plain yogurt
Sugar	1 cup	1 cup packed brown sugar or 2 cups sifted confectioners' sugar
Sugar, Light Brown	1 cup	½ cup dark brown sugar plus ½ cup granulated sugar
Yeast	1 package (¼ ounce) active dry	1 cake (⅝-ounce) compressed yeast